HIS

OF

PIKE COUNTY

ILLINOIS;

TOGETHER WITH SKETCHES OF ITS CITIES, VILLAGES AND TOWNSHIPS, EDU-
CATIONAL, RELIGIOUS, CIVIL, MILITARY, AND POLITICAL HISTORY;
PORTRAITS OF PROMINENT PERSONS AND BIOGRAPHIES
OF REPRESENTATIVE CITIZENS.

HISTORY OF ILLINOIS,

EMBRACING ACCOUNTS OF THE PRE-HISTORIC RACES, ABORIGINES, FRENCH,
ENGLISH AND AMERICAN CONQUESTS, AND A GENERAL REVIEW
OF ITS CIVIL, POLITICAL AND MILITARY HISTORY.

DIGEST OF STATE LAWS.

ILLUSTRATED.

VOLUME 2

PELICAN PUBLISHING COMPANY
GRETNA 2006

Printed in the United States of America
Published by Pelican Publishing Company, Inc.
1000 Burmaster Street, Gretna, Louisiana 70053

PREFACE.

The history of Pike county possesses features of unusual interest in comparison with those of other neighboring counties, especially those in the Military Tract. Here the sturdy pioneer located and began to exert his civilizing influence long before other sections contained a settler; and this is not only the oldest settled county of all north of its south line, but it was the first county organized in the Military Tract. Another fact worthy of note is, that it originally embraced all the country lying between the great Father of Waters and the placid Illinois, extending east to the Indiana line, and north to the Wisconsin line. Peoria, Rock Island, Galena and Chicago were originally little settlements of this then vast county.

In matters of general public interest and progress, Pike county has ever taken a leading and prominent position. Here have lived men who have taken no unimportant part in the affairs of the State,—in moulding the political sentiments and destiny of the country. Pike county has been the scene of conflict between some of the most giant intellects of the nation. Here the shrewd and enterprising Easterner, the courtly Southerner and the sturdy, practical Westerner, have met and mingled, have inherited the better traits possessed by each other, and thus have formed a society, a people superior in many particulars to that of most localities. The original settlers, the earliest pilgrims, have nearly all passed away. Here and there we see the bended form and whitened head of some of these veterans, but they are not numerous. Most of them have gone to that country which is always new, yet where the trials, struggles and hardships of pioneer life are never known.

Accurate and reliable history is most difficult to write. Those who have never experienced the difficulties incident to such labor cannot realize how nearly impossible it is, or can appreciate the earnest, honest and faithful labor of the historian. After the most careful and painstaking searches and inquiry upon any particular subject or about any event, he will even then find many doubts arising in his mind as to its accuracy and entire truthfulness. Each individual of whom inquiry is made will give you a different account of any event. One of them may be as honest as the other and try to relate his story correctly, yet they will be so widely different that the most searching and logical mind will be unable to harmonize them. This fact is forcibly illustrated in an incident related of Sir Walter Raleigh. While in prison in a tower of England he engaged himself in writing the history of the world. One day a brawl occurred in the yard of the tower, of which he desired to learn the particulars. Two of the principal actors came before him, and each related the account of the trouble, yet so widely different were they that he found it utterly impossible to tell what the facts were. He then remarked, "Here I am engaged in writing the history of events that occurred 3,000 years ago, and yet I am unable to learn the facts of what happens at my window." This has been the channel of our experience, and that of all others who have attempted national or local history. As an example in Pike county, we noticed in a Pittsfield cemetery "Orvillee" on the headstone as the name of the person buried in a certain grave, and "Orval E." on the footstone.

Aside from mistakes occurring from the above causes, doubtless there are many others to be found within these pages. To suppose that a volume of this magnitude, and containing so many thousands of names and dates and brief statements would be wholly accurate, is a supposition we presume no sane man will make. While we do not claim for this work critical accuracy or completeness, yet we are quite certain that it will be found measurably and practically so. Let it rest as the foundation for the future historian to build upon.

As one of the most interesting features of this work, we present the portraits of numerous representative citizens. It has been our aim to have the prominent men of to-day, as well as the pioneers, represented in this department, and we flatter ourselves on the uniform high character of the gentlemen whose portraits we present. They are in the strictest sense representative men, and are selected from all the callings and professions worthy to be represented. There are others, it is true, who claim equal prominence with those presented, but as a matter of course it was impossible for us to represent all the leading men of the county.

As we quit our long, tedious, yet nevertheless pleasant task of writing and compiling the History of Pike County, we wish to return the thanks of grateful hearts to those who have so freely aided us in collecting material, etc. To the county officials and editors of the various newspapers we are particularly grateful for the many kindnesses and courtesies shown us while laboring in the county. To James Gallaher, editor of *The Old Flag*, we especially acknowledge our indebtedness for the excellent historical sketch of Pittsfield presented in this volume. Last and most of all we wish to thank those who so liberally and materially aided the work by becoming subscribers to it. We feel we have discharged our duties fully, have fulfilled all our promises, have earned the laborer's pay. Thus feeling, we present the volume to the critical, yet we hope and believe justly charitable citizens of Pike county—or more especially, our subscribers.

CHAS. C. CHAPMAN & Co.

Chicago, May, 1880.

CONTENTS.

HISTORY OF ILLINOIS.

HISTORY OF PIKE COUNTY.

CONTENTS.

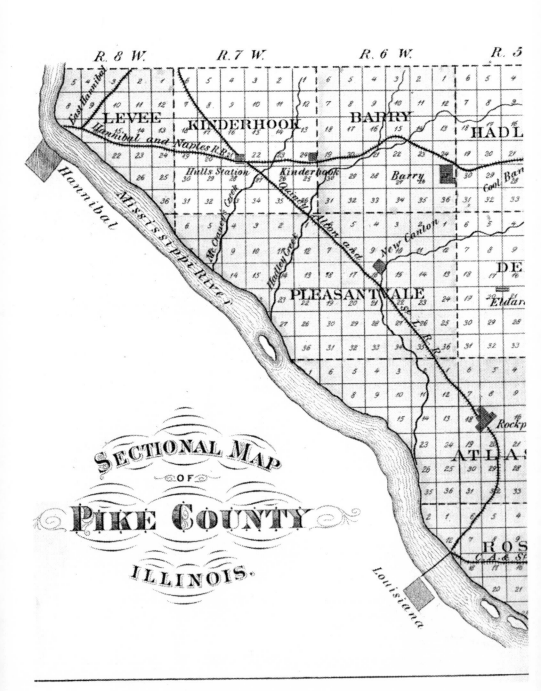

R. 8 W. R. 7 W. R. 6 W. R. 5

LEVEE KINDERHOOK BARRY HADL

Hannibal Mississippi River

Hulls Station Kinderhook Barry Coal Bank

New Canton DE

PLEASANTVALE Eldar

Rockp

ATLAS

Louisiana ROS

Sectional Map
OF
Pike County
Illinois.

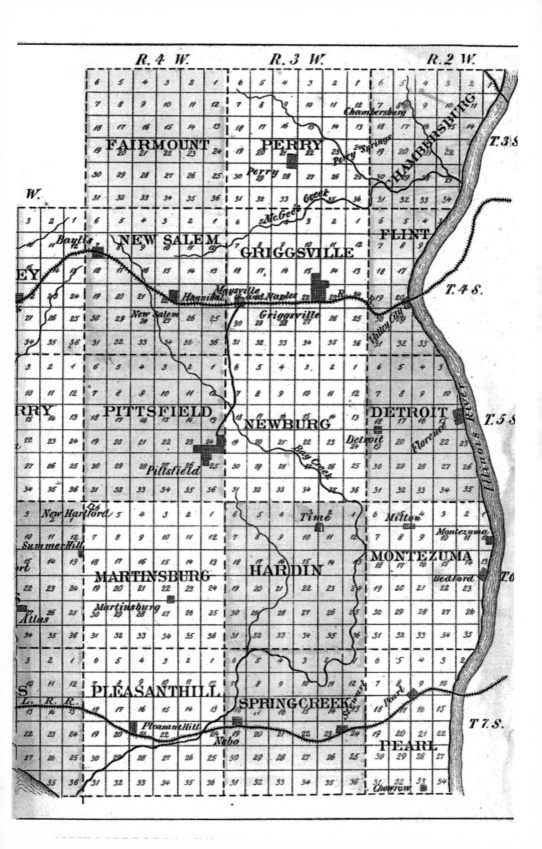

PEARL TOWNSHIP.

This is the most southeastern township of the county. It is mostly timbered land, with a small strip of prairie land near its center. It is bounded on the east by the Illinois river, and a greater part of the township is very rough, and is adapted principally to stock-raising. The first settlers to locate within its borders came about 1824 or 1825, and were A. Perkins, J. R. Ottwell, William Pruett and John Ottwell. The first improvements were made on sections 15 and 27. Among the more prominent early settlers of the township were Thomas S. Long, Thomas Lumley and William Camerer. The first child born in the township was John Ottwell, and the first person to die was Thomas Murray. The first parties married were William Ottwell and Miss Rachel Collins. They were united by Rev. Mr. Osborn, a Baptist minister, who also preached the first sermon in the township, in 1829, in the house of John Ottwell. The first school-house was erected in 1837 on section 28. The first church was built in 1867. The first Justice of the Peace was James McConnell.

VILLAGES.

Pearl.—The village of Pearl is quite an old town, and is situated on sections 16, 17 and 20, and contains about 50 inhabitants.

Bee Creek village is situated on Bee creek, section 33, and is about the size of Pearl. It contains a postoffice, a small store, a saw, a flouring mill, a blacksmith shop and a physician.

Bee Creek Mills.—This establishment was first built in 1856 as a horse-mill, and in 1857 it was propelled by steam. In 1867 it was torn down and rebuilt by George Schutz. Mr. Wm. Wheeler purchased it the same year and is still its owner. It is now operated by G. W. Roberts, and be it to his credit to say that Mr. Roberts makes the best quality of flour and has a large run of custom. A few years ago people came a distance of 25 miles to this mill. There is also a saw-mill attached to it.

Pearl Station.—This is the largest village in the township, containing about 150 inhabitants, and is situated upon the Louisiana branch of the Chicago, Alton & St. Louis railroad. It was surveyed by order of Thomas S. Long, guardian of the heirs of Samuel Fulcher, and is located on the southwest quarter of section 10. It was surveyed in September, 1872, by County Surveyor H. J. Harris. *Chowrow* is the name of a little settlement on section 33.

CHURCHES.

Trinity M. E. Church is located at Pearl Landing on the Illinois river. It was organized in 1856 by Rev. E. Elliott, with six members, at the house of T. H. Lincoln. It was known by the name of Pearl Landing M. E. Church, which name it continued to bear until 1871, when the present church structure was erected. The Society worshiped in Mr. Lincoln's house for two years, when they removed their place of worship to the Pearl Prairie school-house. While worshiping at this place the Society was more commonly known as the Pearl Prairie M. E. Church, but was really the same organization. In 1869 the Society moved to the new school-house at Pearl Landing, and in 1871 occupied the present church edifice. Rev. Charles McKown is Pastor.

Pearl Prairie Christian Church was organized several years ago, and in 1867 erected a neat house of worship in Pearl on section 20.

Below we give personal sketches of some of the more prominent citizens of the township.

James H. Dawson, physician, was born in Warren county, Ind., Aug. 3, 1836, and is a son of John W. and Effie A. Dawson; was educated in the common schools, and at the age of 24 enlisted in the late war, Co. D, 1st Mo. Inft., where he served for 2 years. He is a graduate of the Keokuk Medical College, in Keokuk, Iowa; began the practice of medicine in Pleasant Hill, this county, in 1874, remaining there one year. He then located in Chowrow, this county, where he still resides and has built up a good practice. In Feb., 1858, he married Miss Sarah Hamner, daughter of Jesse Hamner, deceased, an early settler of this county, and they have 3 children—Mollie, Anna and Flora.

Enoch W. Garrison was born in Posey county, Ind., Dec. 22, 1818. He is a son of Elijah Garrison, who landed his family in this county long before railroads were thought of and when the Indians and wild animals roamed at large, and the wolves made the night hideous by their constant howling. He located in Montezuma tp. Enoch W. hunted coons where Milton now stands, and on one occasion a panther chased their dogs from the hunting grounds. He was deprived of educational advantages, as there were no schools in the first settlement of this county. In a few years, however, came the days of subscription schools and teachers with ox gads in their hands; he attended school for a short time in a log cabin where Milton now stands. He has been married three times, and is the father of 8 children, of whom 4 are living; William, Lewis A., Hannah L. and Enoch W. Mr. G. is engaged in farming and stock-raising, and resides on sec. 2, this tp.; has been a hunter all his life; hunting and trapping in winter and farming during the summer.

Ransom Kessinger, a native of Scott county, Ill., was born Sept. 3, 1830, and is a son of Solomon Kessinger, deceased, well known in the pioneer days of Scott county. He was a native of Kentucky and came to Jacksonville in 1825, when there was but one house in that city; came to this county with his family in 1844 and settled in Pearl tp., where he resided until his death, which occurred Feb. 10, 1862. Our subject was raised on a farm and received a common-school education; served 3 years in the late war in Co. I, 99th Reg. I. V. I., and was in the following battles: Hartsville, Mo., siege of Vicksburg, Champion Hills, Black River Bridge, Matagorda, Fort Gaines, on Mobile Bay, and others; he was honorably discharged in 1865. June 11, 1863, he married Sarah J. Peacock, daughter of Henry Peacock, deceased, an early settler of Pike county; they have had 10 children, of whom 8 are living,— Henry, Nancy, Catharine, Jacob, Peter, Ransom, Martha and John. Mr. Kessinger is engaged in farming and stock-raising, and resides on sec. 20. He is Justice of the Peace.

Thomas S. Long was born in Bucks county, Pa., Oct. 3, 1807: parents first moved to New Jersey; he moved from that State with his family in an early day and located in this then wild country. They are the oldest married immigrants living in Pearl tp. Mr. Long is a son of Morgan and Rachel Long, deceased. Mrs. Long was born Nov. 7, 1810, and is a daughter of Barney and Margaret Deemer, deceased; they have had 9 children, of whom 5 are living —Thomas S., Morgan, Mary A., Elizabeth and Rachel. Mr. Long engaged in the mercantile business for 3 or 4 years after the close of the war, but now is retired from active business and resides in Pearl, on sec. 16. In early days he had to go a distance of 18 or 20 miles to mill; at one time he went in a wooden-wheeled wagon, was water bound while gone, and was unable to get to the mill; he stopped at a horse-mill and staid over Sunday, when they ground the corn the same day, and he returned on Monday.

Thomas S. Long, jr., was born June 21, 1833, in Bucks county, Pa., and is a son of Thomas S. Long, of Pearl Prairie; came to Illinois with his parents in 1835. Aug. 27, 1854, he married Mary C. Peacock, daughter of Henry Peacock, dec., an early settler of Calhoun county, Ill., and they have had 10 children, 8 of whom are living.—Henry T., Fannie L., Sarah M., Nancy A., Polly C., James W., Ettie C., and Ransom A. Mr. Long is a carpenter, and also a farmer, on sec. 16 this tp.

A. J. Ottwell is the oldest settler living in Pearl tp., and was born in Ross county, O., April 22, 1817; is a son of John and Zyporiah Otwell, dec., who were natives of Delaware. Mr. Ottwell was brought here by his parents in 1828, was raised on a farm, received but 4 months' schooling, and that in a subscription school. He is a self-made man, and has filled every office in the tp. except Justice of the Peace. The Black Hawk Indians camped on the same land Mr. Otwell now owns. At that time there were but 3 families in the tp., viz: ·Joshua and John Ottwell and Abraham Janes. He went 20 miles to mill. His father was the first blacksmith in the county and erected a shop near the mouth of Bee creek in Pearl tp., in Dec., 1828. The next shop was erected in Atlas by Benjamin Barney in 1830. When people came from Atlas and the surrounding country to Mr. Ottwell's shop, they would make a visit of several days, and fish and hunt while their work was being done in the shop. Feb. 29, 1844, he married Miss Mary A. Henry, daughter of Jacob Henry, dec., an early pioneer. They have had 12 children, 8 of whom are living, namely, Mary J., Charles, George A., Elizabeth, Alex. J , Louise, Sarah and Emalissa C. In early life Mr. Otwell engaged in boating 8 years, but is now a farmer and stock-raiser, residing on sec. 9.   •

Joshua R. Ottwell, a native of this county, was born Oct. 6, 1845, and is a son of William Ottwell; was raised on a farm, and educated in the common schools; was a soldier in the late war in Co. G, 137th Reg. I. V. I. In 1865 he married Miss Lucy Woods, daughter of James Woods, dec. They have had 6 children, of whom 4 are living, namely,—Thomas J., Frances L., Jesse E. and Walter J. Mr. O. is engaged in farming and stock-raising, and resides on the old homestead, sec. 28.

George W. Roberts was born in Kinderhook Dec. 25, 1841, and is a son of Ezekiel Roberts. In 1852, he, in company with his eldest sister, started for California; when about half way across the plains his sister sickened and died, leaving him, but a boy, alone in a dreary country. He returned and worked by the month in this county until he accumulated some capital, when he engaged in the mercantile business on Bee creek; he sold out to Mr. Smith in 1876, and has since been operating the Bee Creek Mills. He has served 8 terms as Supervisor, and has filled every other tp. office except Justice of the Peace. He married Lowena Albert, by whom he had 7 children, viz: Josephine, George E., Ezekiel, Mary, Wm. J., James W. and Florence.

William Wheeler was born in Clermont county, O., March 7, 1823, and is a son of Benjamin Wheeler, dec. He came to this county in 1834, and is a farmer and stock-raiser, on sec. 32. In 1843 he married Matilda Battershell, and they have had 12 children; 7 are living, viz : Washington W., Nancy, Matilda W., Amanda M., Dora E , Sarah E. and Lora M. Mr. W. went to California in 1849, and returned in 1852. He used to kill deer and turkeys ; helped raise a house in 1836 in a valley where sycamores have since grown 12 inches in diameter.

William T. Williams, physician, was born in Adams county, Ill., March 20, 1841, and is a son of G. W. Williams, of that county. He received a common-school education, and at the age of 16 years began to read medicine; he was graduated at the Iowa Medical College at Keokuk, and began practice in this tp. in April, 1869, where he still resides and has a large practice. July 16, 1863, he married Margaret A. Walker, daughter of Archibald Walker, dec., and they have had 5 children, 3 of whom are living, namely, George F., Hattie B. and Myra Grace. Few doctors have built up so large a practice in so short a time as has Dr. Williams. He was in the late war in Co. K., 53d Mo.

PERRY TOWNSHIP.

This township, which in many respects is second to none in the county, is in the northern part of the county, and is bounded upon the north by Brown county, on the east by Fairmount township, on the south by Griggsville, and on the west by Chambersburg township. When it was first settled there was but little prairie land within its borders; almost the entire surface was covered with timber; much of it, however, was of small growth. We now behold highly improved and cultivated farms throughout the township, the result of the well-directed labor of the pioneers, their descendants, and those who came here in later years. Among the early pilgrims who located here prior and up to 1835, we mention James H. Chenoweth, Robert Gregory, William Browning, James Ritchie, Matthew Dale, Gideon Bentley, Joseph King, David Johnson, B. L. Matthews, Nicholas James, David Callis, John Bond, Chas. Dorsey, Joseph Cavender, John Hume, Abel Shelley, John Matthews, Mr. Lovelady and John Gillaspie. The latter six gentlemen came to the county as early as or even before 1829. James Wells came in 1825, and his son, Stephen V. Wells, who was born the same year, was the first white child born in the township. George Bright, a veteran of the Revolutionary war, came in 1827. Only two or three of these pioneers are living in the township at the present time. Some have moved to other scenes of labor, but by far the greater number are dead. After 1835 settlers came in quite rapidly, and improvements were made throughout the township.

The following very interesting historical article was furnished us by Mr. A. Hinman, and is given in his own language:

"Go back with me 50 years and compare our condition then with what it is at present. Fifty years ago our inhabitants consisted of a few hundred hardy pioneers who settled along the river bluffs and around the edges of groves of timber, and were living in little log cabins and subsisting on corn bread, wild game and honey, with such vegetables as they could raise on their new improvements. We had very few roads then, only such as were naturally made by the settlers passing from one settlement to another. We had no bridges across streams, nor conveyance of any kind except by horseback or in an ox wagon; no railroads or steamboats in those days; what little transportation was done in those days was done with keel-boats. We had no schools nor free-school system, and when our little log school-houses began to spring up it was by the individual effort of the poor settlers. Although these schools were of a very poor character, they were a great benefit to the children of pioneers, who were able to attend one or two winters. We had no churches, stores, shops or manufacturing establishments; we had no railroads in the State, or telegraph lines; but many of us have lived to see the wonderful changes that have taken place in half a century. From a few hundred settlers we have multiplied to many thousands. The land that was bought by the early settler for $1.25 per acre has advanced in price until it is worth from $40 to $100 per acre. Public roads have been laid out, graded and bridged. The log school-house has given place to fine frame and brick structures, which are supplied with competent teachers, good books, etc. Instead of horseback and ox-wagon rides we have fine carriages, spring wagons, etc.; and instead of keel-boats we have magnificent steamers plying up and down our noble rivers. In the last few years over 100 miles of railroad have been built within our county, with two bridges spanning the Father of Waters, connecting us with our Western States and Territories. Fifty years ago our State had not a single rod of railroad: now she has 10,000 miles. The first of this grand system of railroads was commenced in 1837 or '38, at Naples, on the Illinois river, and was built to Jacksonville. A few days ago I was on this road at Naples and found still in use some of the old original ties upon which the road was first built. They are red cedar, and were brought from Tennessee.

"We have seen the time when our grand old county's credit was so poor that she could not borrow $200 to buy the 160 acres of land upon which to locate our county-seat. I have seen the credit of our State so poor that the interest-bearing bonds could not be sold for 25 cents on the dollar; but now these things are all changed; and I feel thankful to the Giver of all Good that I have been permitted to live out so nearly the time allotted for man's existence here. Among all those improvements for the good of our people none has given me more satisfaction than our free-school system, where every child in the land has an equal chance to gain an education. I pay no tax more cheerfully than my school-tax, although individually I never had the benefit of one cent of the public money for my education, for the reason that I lived a little too early in a new country to get an education at all."

The first school taught in the township was in 1830, in the southeastern corner; John Cavender was the teacher. He was one of the strict "old masters" who have lived their day of usefulness and have given place to the more modern teacher. Our free-school system was not inaugurated until many years after this school was taught. So much per quarter was charged for each pupil. Evidently Mr. Cavender carried on an excellent school,—at least in his own estimation, for his charges were high. Each pupil was required to pay $3.50 per term. Mr. Cavender was remarkably strict as to the deportment of his pupils. He would "blaze" the trees between the boys and girls, keeping them separate; and the one who dared overstep the bounds suffered for it. He made it a rule to "flog" at least one-half the scholars each day.

Perry Springs.—These springs are located in the east part of the township, and are greatly valued for their curative properties. We quote the following descriptive and historical article concerning these springs, published in 1872:

"Perry Springs have received a national celebrity, being the most noted resort in the West. They are situated most beautifully near a creek among the hills west of the Illinois river, and at the confluence of several deep ravines. The surrounding country is very broken, hills are steep, and covered with a beautiful forest growth. These springs have long been known by the Indians. What is now known as the Magnesia Spring gushes through a rock in great quantities, and was called by them "spring in the rock." Its medicinal qualities were well known to them, and they brought their sick to it from great distances to be healed. Little cabins were used by invalids until 1856, when Zack Wade, who was attracted there for his health, erected a very good hotel building. To B. A. Watson, Esq., of Springfield, Ill., is due the credit of developing not only this spring but also others in close proximity, erecting another very large hotel, with many extensive improvements; and to his indefatigable energy and determination through numerous unforeseen obstacles, is to be given the praise of furnishing the country the finest natural resort in America. The water is strongly impregnated with magnesia, lime, iron, potassa, soda, salt, etc., etc. There are three springs within a few steps of the hotel building, called respectively Magnesia, Iron and Sulphur springs. Each not only tastes differently, but operates differently; and what a wise provision of Providence is here illustrated,—three springs but a few rods apart, all strongly medicated and having each different medicinal properties; and of all the diseases that afflict the human family but very few of them but what one of these springs would relieve, if not wholly cure. It is a singular fact that these springs are not affected in their flow of water by dry or wet weather, or their temperature by either hot or cold weather. In the summer the water ranges at 50°, and in the winter at 48° Fahr."

The name of the township was derived from the town situated near its center, and the histories of the two are so closely identified that we pass from the history of the township to that of the town.

PERRY.

This beautiful little village is situated on sections 21 and 28 of Perry township. It was laid out by Joseph S. King, Feb. 16, 1836, and first christened " Booneville," in honor of the famous Kentucky hunter. It was settled largely by Kentuckians, and a great many of these people and their descendants still reside here; but a majority of the population are Eastern people: the German predominate above every other foreign class. There is not a negro in the town. When one occasionally "strikes" the place the boys all gather around him, anxious to see this curious colored man, which annoys this dark-skinned gentleman not a little, and he consequently makes his stay brief.

As above mentioned, the town was first named Booneville, but was subsequently changed to Perry, in honor of Com. Perry, of lake Erie fame. This name was given by David Callis, with whom the honor of naming the town was left. Mr. Callis was the father of Mrs. Reynolds, wife of Thos. Reynolds, now living near Perry.

Joseph S. King, who came to Perry in 1832, was its first merchant. Dr. Sutphin, who came in 1835, was its first physician. The town has enjoyed its season of prosperity as well as adversity, and is now quite a business point. It contains several good stores, three of which are quite large establishments. They carry a general line of merchandise, and a large and well selected assortment. Among the business men and the business houses are the following: Shastid & Cockill, A. S. Whittaker, and J. F. Metz, all general dealers; Dunn & Brengelman and Dana Ayers, druggists; three restaurants; one hotel, kept by H. J. Chenoweth; two barber shops; one livery stable; four blacksmith shops, and one mill. It also contains one school-house, six churches, and one newspaper.

The first school-house in the town was built in 1835. It was a log structure and school was taught here by Hannah French. The present school building was erected at a cost of $4,000. It contains four rooms. There are in attendance at present an average of 200 pupils. Prominent among the teachers who have taught here are Mr. Freeman, Richard Noyes and Allen. C. Mason. Mr. Luce is the present teacher.

The Perry Cornet Band was organized in 1876. They have fine instruments, and the band is one of the best in the county. Geo. W. Ham, B. Hume, C. Norris and Frank Bright are all that were members when it was organized. A. Gregory was the first leader, and A. A. Hinman is the present leader.

CHURCHES.

Methodist Church.—A nucleus of the present church at Perry was formed by a few people who met at the house of David Callis about the year 1832. At that time a class was formed consisting of David Callis and wife, Ira Andrews and wife, Mr. Gillaspie and wife, Margaret Matthews, G. W. Hinman and wife, Isaac Davis and wife, B. L. Matthews and wife, N. W. Reynolds and wife, and Susan Beard. From that time regular meetings were held at private houses, but principally at the residences of David Callis and J. B. Matthews. These meetings were held only once in four weeks.

Wilson Pitner was the first regular preacher employed by this Society, his circuit extending as far as Atlas and other points in the county . The first house of worship was built on sec. 28 in 1839. It was about 20 by 24 feet in size, made of hewn logs, and it had a seating capacity of about 100 persons. The first Trustees of this Church were Z. Wade, Isaac Davis, N. W. Reynolds, B. L. Matthews and John McFarland. The first Steward was Isaac Davis. The Society occupied this building for religious meetings until 1848, when a new house of worship was built. This structure was located in Chenoweth's addition, was 30 by 40 feet in size, and cost about $2,000. It has been remodeled at a cost of $1,000. Its present size is 30 by 50 feet, with sittings for 350 people. Among the early pastors were Revs. Wm. H. Taylor, Mr. Hunter, Mr. Piper, Isaac Kimber, James Matteson. Among others who served in that capacity in later years were Revs. W. F. Gilmer and J. C. H. Hobbs. The present Pastor is Wm. H. Wilson, and the present membership about 200. After the building was repaired the Society bought a good organ, which is still in use. The Trustees are, Dr. Harvey Dunn, Asahel Hinman, S. D. Fagin, Rufus Reynolds and Z. Wade. The Sunday-school has a regular attendance of about 100 scholars, and is superintended by Dr. R. F. Harris.

Christian Church.—The first meeting for the organization of this Church took place at the house of Nicholas Hobbs, on the southeast quarter of sec. 29, about the year 1837. Nicholas Hobbs and wife, Abraham Chenoweth and wife, Gideon Bentley and wife, Samuel Van Pelt, Wm. Van Pelt and wife, Wm. Chenoweth and wife and others, met at that time for the purpose of organizing a Church. Samuel Van Pelt, Wm. Van Pelt and Nicholas Hobbs were the officiating Elders on this occasion. Religious meetings were held at different private houses throughout the neighborhood until 1839, when the congregation erected a house of worship. This building was a frame 18 by 24 feet in size, and was located on the southeast quarter of sec. 28, which was in the village of Perry. The congregation was supplied with traveling preachers for a number of years, among whom were Elders Wm. Strong and John Keari. The first Elders elected at the organization were Nicholas Hobbs, Wm. Van Pelt and Wm. Chenoweth. The first Deacons were Abraham Chenoweth and Gideon Bentley. The principal preaching was done by the Elders for the first few years, when the congregation engaged Elder David Hobbs to officiate as Pastor.

In April, 1843, the great revivalist, Elder Wm. Brown, of Kentucky, held a protracted meeting in this church, lasting over two weeks. The religious fervor produced by his efforts was very satisfactory, and some 80 conversions were made. The old church building being too small to hold the immense crowds that were drawn to hear him, one side was removed and a large shed addition was built, which was capable of holding some 500 people. For the next few years meetings were held in the old building, at the school-house, and occasionally in the Baptist church. In 1851 a more

James H. Chenoweth

PERRY TP.

commodious house of worship was built on lot 4, block 1, Thompson's addition. It was 34 by 50 feet, with seats for 400 people, and was erected at a cost of about $2,000. The building committee were James H. Chenoweth, David Johnson and Charles Dorsey. Elder Alpheus Brown for a while previous to this had been regular Pastor. Being a carpenter, he in company with John Reed took the contract for and erected this church. Elder Brown continued his services with the congregation. This building was occupied until 1879, during which time the congregation employed the regular services, as pastors, of Elders Donan, Wm. McIntyre, Samuel Johnson, A. G. Lucas, H. R. Walling, Clark Braden and others. During the labors of these worthy and able men, there was much good done, and many accessions were made to the ranks of the Church.

In April, 1879, the congregation commenced agitating the question of the necessity for and propriety of building a more modern and commodious house of worship. A building committee was appointed with full power to examine and adopt plans for the erection of a suitable building. This committee consisted of Jon Shastid, Alex. Dorsey, John S. Dorsey, Bennett F. Dorsey, Matthias Gregory, Jasper M. Browning, Dr. W. D. C. Doane and James Walker. Jon Shastid was appointed Treasurer of the committee, and Alex. Dorsey and James Walker executive officers. Plans were accepted, contracts made, the work vigorously prosecuted, and the building completed by the first of January, 1880. It is built in the Gothic style, is 38 by 64 feet in size, with an auditorium finely frescoed and furnished, and with a seating capacity to accommodate 500 people. It cost about $4,000, and it is a credit to the society and an ornament to the town. The present membership of the congregation is about 330. The Pastor is Elder J. T. Smith, who took an active part in, and was one of the main workers in collecting money for, the erection of the new building. The Elders are Jasper M. Browning, Alex. Dorsey and Bennett F. Dorsey. The Deacons are Wm. Love, Wm. M. Browning, Henry Mays and Edward Wade. Clerk, J. E. Smith, and Treasurer D. S. Rickart. The Sunday-school is conducted by Superintendent J. B. Warton, and has an average attendance of over 100.

Zion Church is located on sec. 4, and was erected in 1852. It is a substantial structure, and meetings have been held in it since its erection every two weeks, with few exceptions. The society had held meetings years previous to the erection of this edifice. Rev. Smith was the first minister. The congregation numbered but 10 members when the house was built; at present the membership is 50. Since the erection of the building they have not missed a month without holding Sunday-school in it.

Lutheran Church.—This Church was organized in 1859, and was the first church of that denomination in Pike county. The congregation met for the first 10 years in the Christian church, but in

29

1869 built a new church, at a cost of $2,200. The present member-ship numbers 80. Rev. Recker is the present Pastor.

PERSONAL SKETCHES.

As a portion of the history of Perry and Perry township we give biographical sketches of pioneer and leading citizens, believing such personal mention forms the better part of local history. Those who have made and are making the history of Perry and the township deserve special mention in a work of this nature.

Dana Ayres was born in Massachusetts Dec. 7, 1809; is the son of Jason and Betsey (Holman) Ayres; was educated in the common schools of Massachusetts, and between the ages of 16 and 26 manufactured salt from sea water. In 1836 he came to this county, and in 1838 settled in the town of Perry, since which time he has followed the drug business. In 1838 he married Alice Cleland, and they have 2 children, a son and daughter. In politics Mr. Ayres is a Republican. He voted the Free-Soil ticket in 1840, and in 1842 was elected County Magistrate. He has been School Trustee, Collector, and Trustee for the Corporation.

George W. Baldwin was born in New York city in 1830; is the son of David and Ann (Desney) Baldwin. His early educational advantages were very limited. In 1858 he married Sarah Jane Mason, a native of New Hampshire. Of their 6 children 5 are living, 4 sons and one daughter. One son is studying dentistry, and one of his daughters is a teacher. By occupation Mr. Baldwin is a miller, but has at present retired from business.

Stephen Banning, son of Thomas and Keziah Banning, was born May 15, 1815. His father was from Virginia, and his mother from Maryland; both are of German descent. He was educated in a sub-scription school, and came from Ohio to Illinois in 1837, settling near Chambersburg. December 10, 1839, he was married to Eliza-beth Rigg. Of their 8 children, only 3 girls are living, and are married. Mr. B. has been School Director and Road-master. He owns 160 acres of good land on sec. 26. In politics he is a Democrat.

W. A. Beavers, deceased, son of Wm. Beavers, was born in Missouri Dec. 1, 1824; emigrated to Pike Co. in 1869, and followed merchandising for several years. In 1860 he married Mary Elizabeth Smith, who was born in Pike Co. Aug. 26, 1838. Her parents, Aberland and Lucy A., were natives of Kentucky. Mr. and Mrs. Beavers have 3 children: Herschel V., born Aug. 26, 1861; Averill, born in 1863, and L. F. (a girl), born Sept. 29, 1870. Mr. B. owned 160 acres of land, and followed farming several years previous to his death, which occurred Jan. 13, 1873.

Williamson Bond was born July 12, 1837, and is the son of John (a native of Virginia) and Frances Ann (*nee* Aikins, a native of Tennessee) Bond. Both parents are of German descent. In 1858 he was married to Jennie James. They have one daughter, Frances Ann, born in 1861. Mr. Bond has been School Director for 2 years; is a Democrat. He owns 130 acres of land on sec. 36.

Benj. F. Bradbury was born in Ohio in 1824, the son of Benjamin and Betsy (Davis) Bradbury, natives of Maine, and of English descent. He is by occupation a farmer; came to Pike county in 1853, where he now has 190 acres of land. Sept. 13, 1848, he married Elizabeth Carlisle. They have 3 sons and 4 daughters. He is a Baptist, and she a Presbyterian; he is also a Granger and a Democrat.

H. H. Brengelman, druggist, Perry, Ill.

Robert Brim, deceased, was a farmer on sec. 7; was born in South Carolina in 1832, and emigrated to Pike county in 1846; he ran a restaurant 2 years in Perry, and 2 in Chambersburg. In 1856 he married Catharine Taylor. Of their 6 children 2 are dead. Mrs. B. is a daughter of Simon H. Taylor, who came to Pike county 54 years ago. At one time he owned 520 acres of land in Pike county, and other lands in other counties, entering his choice land at $1.25 an acre. Mr. Taylor is still living, and Mrs. Taylor died in 1876. Mr. Brim was a Democrat.

Archibald Brooks, farmer, sec. 16; P. O. Chambersburg; was born in this county in 1850, and is the son of Archibald and Sophia (Sutliff) Brooks, the father a native of Tennessee, and the mother a native of Indiana; educated in the common school; owns 120 acres of land. In 1872 he married Emily Remington, daughter of Orson R., of Perry. Their 3 children, boys, are all living. Mrs. B. is a member of the Christian Church in Chambersburg. Mr. B. has been 3 years a School Director, and is a Democrat.

Jasper M. Browning; P. O. Perry; born in this township July 1, 1834, is the son of Caleb and Penelope (Power) B., both of English descent. His father is a farmer, who came to this county in 1833, but at the present time is living in Kansas. Jasper M. is also a farmer on sec. 15, where he owns 140 acres of land. In 1865 he married Rachel Allen, and they have 5 boys and 2 girls. Members of the Christian Church. Republican.

Lemuel Calhoun, farmer, sec. 11; P. O., Perry; was born in Tennessee May 30, 1829, the son of Hansel and Harriet (Carpenter) Calhoun; educated in the subscription school; emigrated to this county in 1835, and has lived on sec. 11 for 27 years. In 1852 he married Mary Elizabeth Thompson. Of their 6 children 4 are living, all girls. He has been School Director; is an Odd Fellow; owns 138 acres of land, and pays all his debts once a year; is a Democrat. Himself and wife are members of the Christian Church.

Wm. H. H. Callis was born in Brunswick Co., Va., Nov. 7, 1822, son to David and Sarah (Walpole) Callis, natives of Virginia, and of English descent; went to school but one year in his life, and that was in the old-fashioned log school-house in this county, having emigrated here in 1829. He has seen every man, woman and child within 10 miles of his father's house all there at one time, and fed on old-fashioned corn hominy; he has killed many panthers in Perry township. In 1844 he married Harriet Eliza Ingalls; of their 4 children 3 are living and married; one child died in 1845. Mr. C. has given his children a good education, at one time moving even into Iowa for the purpose of sending them to a good school. His son is a graduate of Simpson Centennial College. He is now living on his farm on sec. 25. He drilled with Abraham Lincoln in the Black Hawk war. Mr. and Mrs. Callis are members of the M. E. Church.

John Campbell, undertaker, carpenter and builder, and dealer in coffins, caskets, shrouds, etc., Perry, was born Dec. 21, 1845, the son of A. and K. C. (Coffee) Campbell, both of Kentucky; educated in the high school at Griggsville; commenced to learn his trade at 17 years of age, and has followed it ever since. In 1868 he married Emma Smith : Katie, born July 8, 1870, is their only child. Mr. C. is a Republican, an Odd Fellow, and belongs to the United Workmen; and he and his wife are Methodists.

Milton Cheek was born in Bedford Co., Va., Nov. 16, 1804; parents both natives of Virginia, and of English descent; went to school but two months in his life; is a farmer; came to Pike county in 1832, undergoing the usual hardships of pioneer life. He once walked 10 miles to Jeff Hume's mill, and offered to split 200 rails for a bushel of meal; but Jeff did not want rails; he wanted money. Mr. Cheek was compelled to go home that long distance after sundown without any meal and even without any supper; and his family had to subsist upon potatoes a while longer. At present he owns a farm of 79½ acres. In 1826 he married Martha Carroll, and they had 10 children. Mrs. Cheek died in 1860, and in 1863 he married Marinda Crystal, and they have had 3 children. He is School Director and Road Overseer : is a Democrat.

D. J. Chenoweth was born in this county Jan. 13, 1848, son of James H. and Artemisia C. (Burkhead) Chenoweth, natives of Kentucky, and of German descent. He owns a farm of 20 acres and runs a meat market in Perry. In 1867 he married Eleanor Dorsey, and they have 4 children living. Both he and wife are members of the Christian Church. He is a Republican.

H. J. Chenoweth was born in Kentucky Oct. 29, 1819; his parents, Abraham and Rachel, were natives of that State and of Welsh descent; emigrated to Pike county Nov. 16, 1836, settling one mile east of Perry, and in company with his father improved 160 acres of land. He followed farming until 1851, when he started a saw-mill 3 miles northeast of Perry, and after running it 18 months he sold it; then farmed for 3 years, then was in Missouri 4 years, and then (1861) came back to this place and continued farming and clearing land. In 1872 he started the first hotel in Perry. H. J. married in 1841, and is the father of 9 children, 6 of whom are living, 2 boys and 4 girls. Mr. C. has been School Director and member of the Town Board. Republican.

Jacob V. Chenoweth was born in this township June 27, 1850, son of James H. and Artemisia C. (Burkhead) Chenoweth ; is a farmer and dealer in live stock. May 13, 1875, he married Elizabeth Parke, and they have 2 little girls. Mr. and Mrs. C. are members of the Christian Church. Mr. C. owns a farm of 81 acres in Pike county, and 80 acres in Kansas.

James H. Chenoweth, one of Pike county's oldest and most respected citizens, was born in Nelson Co., Ky., July 9, 1801. His father, Wm. Chenoweth, went to that State from Virginia when a young man, and took part in many an Indian fight on " the dark and bloody ground." He married the widow of John Hinton, whose maiden name was Mary VanMeter; of this family were 10 children, all of whom lived to be grown: William, Jacob, Abraham, Isaac, Miles, James, Hardin, Letitia, Ruth and James H. Jacob, Abraham and James all came to Pike county and were among its more worthy and substantial pioneer citizens. James H., the subject of this sketch, first came to this State in 1832, stopping for a while in Scott Co., and came to Pike in the spring of 1833, locating on secs. 27 and 28, Perry tp., where he entered 240 acres of land. He at once erected a double log cabin, in which he lived for several years; he then built the frame house which still occupies the site ; 30 acres of this farm Mr. C. laid off in town lots as "Chenoweth's Addition to the Town of Perry." Mr. C. is one of the oldest residents of the county, and is a good example of what industry and economy will accomplish. He is now 78 years of age, and is the owner of between 500 and 600 acres of land in this county, as well as land in Missouri.

Mr. C. was married in 1831 to Artemisia Burkhead, of Nelson Co., Ky. One child, Abraham, was born to them in Kentucky; James H., jr., Mary, Joseph K., deceased, Joseph S., Robert A., Ruth, David J., Jacob V. and Susanna R., deceased, were all born in Pike county; the 8 children living are all married. Three, David, Jacob and Ruth (the latter the wife of Chas. O. Turner) are still living in this county. Mr. C.'s wife died Jan. 4, 1874, and Mr. C. is now living with his daughter, Mrs. Turner. Mr. C. was formerly a Whig, but since the organization of the Republican party he has voted with that party. One of his sons, Robert A., served two years during the Rebellion in the 33d Ill. Inft. Mr. C. is a member of the Christian Church, as also was Mrs. C.; and in the affairs of the Church he has always taken a prominent part. All of his children are also members of that Church.

Mr. C. is familiarly known as " Uncle Jim," and no man in the township is better known, and has fewer enemies. He was always full of fun, and liked to fish and hunt, and enjoy himself in such sport. His average weight is 212 pounds. One of his favorite games was tying men who boasted of their strength. He would take his rope and tell his man that he would tie him, giving him leave to fight or do anything but gouge and bite : that was all he asked of the strongest man, and he never yet failed in his object. He drank whisky with the " boys," and sometimes when alone, from the time he was 16 years old until he was 74. At present he only takes wine. He thinks he averaged a quart of liquor per day for 57 years ; and the other day he figured it up, counting only one pint per day, and it made over 72 barrels, of 44 gallons each! He is willing to throw off 2 barrels in the estimate, which would leave even 70 barrels, or 3,080 gallons. Now, if it cost $2 per gallon, it would amount to $6,160; and if the whisky he has drank were sold at 10 cents a drink, allowing 10 drinks to the pint, it would amount to $24,640; and he thinks he has drank twice that amount, or $49,-280 worth of whisky! Perhaps he has given away as much as he has drank, which would make a total expense of $98,560! And he is yet stout enough to round this number out to even $100,000, either by drinking the liquor or giving it away! Mr. Chenoweth's portrait appears in this volume.

Job Clark, farmer, sec. 29, was born in Hamilton Co., O., Jan. 6, 1825, and is the son of John and Christiana (Reed) Clark, the father a native of Greene Co., Pa., and his mother of Hamilton Co., O. He received his education in the common schools of Illinois; he came to Pike county in May, 1857; by occupation he was a millwright, but since he came here he has been farming, meeting with splendid success. His residence is as good as any in the township, if indeed not the best. He is engaged in raising Poland-China hogs and thorough-bred cattle. He was married in 1853 to Miss H. E. Gilham. Mr. C. has served his township in various offices, and politically is a Democrat.

W. O. Cobb was born in Perry, Pike Co., July 19, 1855, and is the son of Chauncey and Elizabeth (Parks) Cobb. Mr. C. at the present time is keeping a barber shop in the town of Perry ; formerly he was by occupation a carpenter. He is a natural genius, and capable of doing anything well that he undertakes. Politically he is a Republican.

F. M. Cooper was born in Morgan Co., Ill., Jan. 19, 1831, son of G. W. and Mahala (Clayton) Cooper, his father a native of N. C. and his mother of Georgia; is a farmer and plasterer. He was married in 1858 to Artemisia Hobbs, and they have 6 boys and 1 girl, and are members of the Christian Church. Mr. C. is a Democrat, in politics.

Job Dixon, son of Thomas and Mary (Barker) Dixon, was born in England in 1828, where he was educated ; he is a farmer and owns 280 acres of land, one of the best stock farms in Illinois. In 1858 he emigrated to Pike county, and Oct. 4 of the same year married Ann Stephenson, a native of England. They have had 6 boys and 3 girls. Mr. Dixon is a Democrat.

Luther Dodge was born in Vermont in 1815; was educated in a subscription school, and is at present a farmer. He has been twice married, the second time to Margaret Crawford, in 1861. She is a native of Tennessee, and was born in 1822. She was the fourth child of a family of 14 children, 11 of whom are living, all married but one, who has taught school 14 years. Her name is Rachel Crawford. Mrs. Dodge's stepmother, Mrs. Elizabeth Crawford, lives with her, and is 81 years of age. Mr. Dodge is a Republican.

Deacon Alexander Dorsey, the son of Charles Dorsey, was born in Rutherford county, Tenn., Nov. 29, 1824; his father was born in North Carolina in 1795, and was the son of Wm. Dorsey, who served for several years in the Revolutionary war. Oct. 16, 1823, Charles Dorsey married Miss Eleanor Broiles, of his native county. She was born June 25, 1805. Dec. 31, 1828, Mr. Dorsey landed in Pike county and wintered in a board tent. During the following spring he cleared a piece of land on which a portion of Detroit now stands. In the spring of 1831 he moved to Perry township and settled on sec. 24, and was one of the leading farmers and stock-raisers of the county. Alexander Dorsey received his education in Pike county; in the winter of 1845–'6 he made a visit to his old home in Tennessee, where he married Miss Jane Fox, who was born in Rutherford county, Nov. 29, 1829. Mr. and Mrs. Dorsey are both members of the Christian Church, and he has been Elder and Deacon for many years, and was a member of the executive committee that erected the new church building.

B. F. Dorsey was born near the celebrated Mineral Springs of Perry, Nov. 11, 1832; he is the fourth son of Charles and Eleanor Dorsey, the former a native of Raleigh, N. C. Our subject on arriving at the age of 18, was married to Miss Matilda, daughter of Elder David Hobbs, who, as well as his wife, were natives of Kentucky, and came to Illinois in 1829, settling in Scott county; and Mrs. Dorsey was born Oct. 8, 1832. They have a family of two children: Edgar, the elder, was born May 9, 1859, and Asa L., March 22, 1861. Edgar married Anna, daughter of M. B. Chenoweth, Dec. 31, 1877; reside at the old homestead and have a little daughter, Dottie D. Dorsey. Asa married Carrie Clark, May 15, 1879,: she was a daughter of Job Clark, a native of Ohio, and she was born in this county.

The sons are engaged with their father, under the firm name of B. F. Dorsey & Sons, in importing and breeding Berkshire and Poland hogs, and Spanish or American Merino sheep, sending stock of this kind to Colorado, Michigan, Mexico, Texas and Pennsylvania. They have a farm of 387 acres on sec. 22, known as the Wolf Grove stock farm. It is said that they have on this fine farm the champion herd of sheep in America. It consists of 500 thorough-bred Merino sheep, one buck in which herd cost Mr. Dorsey $600, and clipped the past season 28¼ pounds of wool; another cost $300. They also have a herd of 100 thorough-bred Berkshire and Poland-China hogs. One of these, "Knight of Gloucester, No. 201," was bought by the firm in England, and is worth $560.

They exhibited at the first fair ever held in Pike county, which was in the year 1851, since which time they have exhibited their stock at some of the leading fairs in Illinois and Missouri, and always successful as competitors. They have taken over 600 prizes within the last four years, never failing to carry off the sweepstakes at each and every fair. At the Illinois State Fair in 1879 they took on their herd nine first and four second prizes, including the breeders and sweepstakes in each class. The breeders on which the prize was given consisted of one boar and four sows. They took it on Berkshires and Polands, which was never done at the Illinois State Fair, or indeed at any other State fair, so far as is known to us.

Mr. D. is a member of the Christian Church, and has been for 32 years. He has served 12 or 15 years as Elder. As a representative citizen of Pike county we give Mr. Dorsey's portrait in this volume.

Charles Dorsey, son of Alexander and Jane (Fox) Dorsey, was born in Pike county in 1855; he had only the benefits of the common school, and has engaged in farming and clerking. In 1877 he was married to Ada Chenoweth, and they have one girl, Anna.

John S. Dorsey; residence Perry; was born in April, 1830, in this county; he is the son of Charles and Eleanor (Broiles) Dorsey, referred to above; by occupation he is a farmer and stock-raiser; he owns 370 acres of land near Perry, and is counted as one of the leading farmers of the county; he devotes considerable time and attention to breeding fine blooded stock, and makes the Poland-China hog and American Merino sheep a specialty; in this business he is connected with his brother, Alexander Dorsey. In 1857 Mr. D. was married to Mary Hardy, and they have four children—two boys and two girls. Mr. D. is a member of the Christian Church, and Mrs. D. of the Methodist Church. He is a member of the Town Board of Perry, and has been for three terms.

John W. Dorsey was born in Pike county, Ill., in 1853, and is the son of Alexander and Jane Dorsey, *nee* Fox. Mr. D. owns 110 acres of land on sec. 21, in this township, and is engaged in raising fine stock. Oct. 27, 1872, he was married to Sarah Jane Ham, who was born in Chambersburg township in 1856. Their children are: Izzie Jane, Mary L. and Minnie Bell. Mr. D. is a member of the Christian Church, of Lodge No. 76, I. O. O. F., and Secretary of Perry Grange. Mrs. D. is also a member of the Christian Church.

T. B. Dunn was born in the town of Chambersburg, Pike Co., in 1842, and is the son of Harvey and Phadima (Winegar) Dunn; the former was born in Feb. 2, 1806, and his mother, June 29, 1819. His father died Dec. 28, 1868, and his mother, June 11, 1848. Mr. Dunn received his education in the common schools of this county; from 1864 to 1868 was engaged in the dry-goods business in Chambersburg, since which time he has been engaged in farming. April 5, 1864, he was married to Nancy Jane Banning, daughter of Stephen Banning, one of the pioneers of the county. They have two boys and two girls. Both he and his wife are members of the Christian Church. Among the curiosities which he has in his possession is a mirror which came over in the Mayflower.

S. D. Fagin, farmer, P. O. Perry; was born in Ohio in 1843; his father, George Fagin, was a native of the Buckeye State; his mother was Julia Hahn. Mr. F. received a common-school education; was married in 1866 to Mary, daughter of Capt. B. L. Mat-

PERRY TP

thews, and they have 3 children, all boys, and living. They are members of the M. E. Church.

John P. Gardner, farmer, sec. 7; was born in England, Nov. 15, 1828, and is the son of John S. and Elizabeth (Powell) Gardner, both natives of England. John P. received his education in the high schools of England; he started to travel at an early age in life; when he was only 16 years old he went on a cruise to South Africa; when 21 he came to America. In 1852 he married Anna Parker. He is a successful farmer. P. O., Perry.

Alpheus Glines was born in Perry Jan. 26, 1853, the son of L. D. and Ellen (Cruthers) G.; his father was a native of New York, and mother, of Ohio; father came to Illinois in 1851. Alpheus received a common-school education and learned the trade of a stone mason, the occupation of his father. He and his brother have been engaged in bridge-building in this and adjoining counties. Alpheus is a member of the M. E. Church at Perry.

Joseph A. Gould was born in the town of Perry Dec. 28, 1853; his parents were Josiah P. and Lucy C. (Watson) Gould. He received his education in the common schools of this county, and by occupation is a plasterer. At the early age of 16 he began to learn his trade, at which he has worked ever since. In 1875 he was united in marriage with Lydia Burnett: they have 2 children, both girls. He and his wife are both members of the Christian Church in Perry. At present he resides in Griggsville.

Matthias Gregory, farmer, sec. 22. Mr. Gregory was brought to Pike county in 1829, and has seen the vast wilderness transformed into a garden, as it were. There was not a house in the town of Perry or Griggsville at that time. Mr. G. was born in Coffee county, Tenn., Feb. 12, 1822, and is the son of Robert and Nancy (Broiles) Gregory, both natives of South Carolina, and of English descent. He received his education in the log schoolhouses of Pike county. In 1843 he was married to Mary Chenoweth. They have 5 children, all boys, and 3 of them are married. Both he and his wife are members of the Christian Church at Perry. He is a Trustee of the Church, and a member of the building committee. He has served 15 years as School Director. In 1862 he enlisted in Co. B, 99th Ill. Inf., under Capt. Matthews.

Clayborn Ham. The subject of this sketch was born in March, 1827, in Bedford county, Tenn. He is the son of James and Mary (Broiles) Ham; his father a native of North Carolina and his mother of South Carolina, and both of German descent. By occupation Mr. H. is a farmer, which business he has followed for 31 years. He has been very successful, now owning 400 acres of land in this county. In 1836 he came to this county and settled on sec. 36, Perry township, where he still lives. He has been twice married. In 1848 he was united in marriage with Miss Margaret Smith, by whom he had 3 children; 2 are living. He married his second wife, America C. James, in 1857, and they have 8 children, 3 boys and 5 girls, all living. His wife is a member of the M. E.

Church. He served as School Director for 8 years, and as Road Commissioner 3 years. His father, though illiterate in respect to school education, not being able to write his own name, was a very successful business man. When he came to the county in 1829 he was not worth $100, but when he made a division of his property among his children he owned 1,700 acres of land, and personal property to the value of $14,000.

George W. Ham, farmer, sec. 21 ; P. O. Perry. Mr. Ham is a son of William and Elizabeth Ann (Elliott) Ham, natives of the Eastern States, and of English descent ; he was born Sept. 5, 1859; he attended the common schools and entered the Illinois College at Jacksonville, where he graduated in 1876 ; he then entered the dry-goods store of Metz & Wilson, where he clerked for two years. In 1878 he was united in marriage with May Reed. A son was born to them Dec. 3, 1879. Mr. Ham is a prominent member of the Perry Cornet Band.

James T. Ham is the son of Clayborn and Margaret C. (Smith) Ham, natives of Tennessee and Missouri, respectively. James T. was born on sec. 36, Perry tp., Aug. 8, 1851. He owns a farm on sec. 35, this tp., where he is engaged in agricultural pursuits. In 1871, March 31, he was united in the holy bonds of matrimony with Melissa C. James. Alma A., born Feb. 9, 1873, and Lola Estella, born Dec. 23, 1877, are their 2 children. His grandfather, James Ham, was one of the early pioneers of, and one of the wealthiest men in Pike county.

Elijah Hamilton, farmer, sec. 1; P. O. Chambersburg. Mr. H. is a native of Kentucky, where he was born in 1815 ; his parents were Allen and Salina Hamilton, who came to Illinois in 1820, settling in Sangamon county. In 1839 Elijah Hamilton came to Pike county, locating on sec. 1, where he has ever since resided, and owns 200 acres of land. In politics he is a Democrat, but has not voted for several years. He is a bachelor, and his widowed sister, Mrs. Jane Webb, lives with him. She was born July 26, 1805. Elijah is one of a family of 11 children, only 3 of whom are now living.

John Hardy was born in Ohio Feb. 8, 1839, the son of John and Maria Hardy, both natives of Ohio and of English descent. Mr. Hardy came to Illinois in 1840 and to Pike county in 1846, and lives on sec. 19, where he owns a farm of 213 acres, which is said to be the best farm between the two rivers. He has refused to accept $100 per acre for it. In 1858 he was united in marriage with Rebecca Walker, the daughter of Robert Walker, an early settler of Pike county. In 1872 Mr. Hardy took a trip to Europe for his health, benefiting him greatly. He has also traveled over the Western States considerably.

Martin Harrington was born in Worcester Co., Mass., Dec. 24, 1797. His father, Samuel Harrington, was a native of Grafton, Mass., and was born Aug. 3, 1769. On arriving at the age of twenty-six, he was married to Miss Abigail Putnam, who was born Sept. 15,

1775. She was a daughter of Zadock Putnam, who was closely related to the daring, brave and patriotic Gen. Israel Putnam, of Revolutionary fame. Mr. Putnam's father was Nathaniel Putnam, who built the first wagon set up in Worcester Co., Mass. It is related that over 200 came from long distances to see one pair of wheels following another.

The subject of this sketch is connected by a long line of ancestry as far back as the original Puritans who came over in the "May Flower." Among that highly honored and respected band who landed on the cold, bleak shores of Plymouth, is made honorable mention of the Harringtons, whose names yet stand engraved on that ever memorable rock, around which clusters the purest and brightest thoughts of all true lovers of American liberty. The Harringtons are also connected, on the paternal side, with the Brighams, of early Massachusetts history, and on the maternal side, with the as yet revered name of the Elliots. Major Elliot, great-grandfather of the subject of this sketch, served with distinction during the Revolutionary struggle.

Mr. Samuel Harrington had a family of 4 children, of whom Martin is the second. Three are yet living at quite an advanced age. Mr. Harrington died at his residence, October 5th, 1802. His wife survived him until April, 1871. After being a widow seven years, she was married to Capt. David Trask, of Leicester, Worcester county, Mass. They had a family of 5 children. The subject of our sketch was early thrown upon his own resources by the death of his father, but with that true Yankee pluck and stick-to-it-iveness, he overcame all obstacles in his way, and succeeded in acquiring a good English education; but that served only a nucleus, around which he has been constantly adding to his store of knowledge, until now we find him possessed with conversational powers seldom surpassed by the most cultured men of the country —not only being informed in local matters, but his range of intellect grasps the broadest questions. In his conversation one can not long be a listener without being richly compensated by his large fund of information. Previous to his marriage, his vocation was that of a scythe manufacturer.

On the 22d of June, 1822, he was married to Miss Myra, daughter of Josephus Willard, Esq., of Grafton, Mass. They had a family of 3 children, of whom two are yet living. In the year 1827 he moved with his family, to Amsterdam, New York, at which place he was the first manufacturer of turned carriage axle-trees, with pipe-boxes, which business he continued for a period of 9 years, with other machine business. Mrs. Harrington died at her residence, New York, in 1832, and the following year (1833) Mr. Harrington married his second wife, Miss Catharine, daughter of Evert Hagaman. She departed this life April 27, 1875: her remains rest in the new cemetery in Perry. A fine monument erected to her memory by her husband marks the spot. They have had born to them a family of five children. His son, F. M. Harrington, is now practicing law in Kirksville, Mo., where he has grown into a large and lucrative practice. In 1836 Mr. Harrington left New York and came to Illinois, locating in Pike county. He says he was in the county when settlements and improvements were scarce. He is, therefore, justly classed among the old settlers. By industry and perseverance Mr. Harrington has succeeded in getting together considerable wealth, so that his old days can be passed in reaping the reward of a well spent life. His son-in-law in Missouri has been twice elected to the legislature of that State, and all his children are getting wealthy. The family is one of the oldest and most respected in the county. Mr. Harrington's brother, Hon. Charles Harrington, who was for some time Judge of the County Court of Pike county, in its early organization, was also one of the pioneer preachers of this section of the country.

The subject of our sketch, now far past the meridian of life, enjoys excellent health, and his is another of the many instances of what can be accomplished by a well directed industry. By his generous and straightforward principles, he has won the confidence and esteem of his neighbors and fellow-citizens. During the war he was a strong supporter of the cause of the Union. He is a member of the Republican party. A few years since he retired from the active pursuits of life, and is now residing at his residence in Perry. We give the portrait of Mr. H. in this volume.

Asahel Hinman. The ancestor in a direct line of the subject of this sketch and the founder of the Hinman family in America, was Sergt. Edward Hinman, who emigrated from England, his native country, between 1650 and 1652, settling at Stratford, Conn. Soon afterward he was married to Hannah, daughter of Francis and Mary Stiles, of Windsor, Conn. Their first child was named Sarah, born at Stratford, in 1652. Sergt. Hinman was an extensive farmer, and was largely engaged in the buying and selling of land, owned and operated a mill, etc. He died at Stratford in 1681, leaving a family of 4 sons and 4 daughters. There has been a tradition in the family from the early settlement that Sergt. Hinman was Sergeant-at-Arms for King Charles I. He, like many others, became exiled to escape the vengeance of Oliver Cromwell, as it was well known that Cromwell was firm in condemning to death the supporters and defenders of Charles I. This proves him to have been a most trustworthy loyalist and honest man, for no other could have received the confidence of the crown at that critical period. It would also appear from the above that Sergt. Hinman was a respectable Englishman, and of a good family, as none other would have been selected to have constituted the body guard of the King.

Edward Hinman, jr., youngest son of Sergt. Hinman, was born at Stratford in 1672. He was married to Hannah Jennings, and they had 12 children. Jonas Hinman, the eldest son of Edward, jr., was born at Stratford in the year 1700. When a young man he went to live at Newark, N. J., where he married Elizabeth Crane. Ten children were born of this union. Mary Hinman, his youngest child, married Asahel Hinman, a son of James Hinman, and was a grandson of Sergt. Edward Hinman. After the close of the Revolution Asahel Hinman and family became pioneers in the wilds of Kentucky, locating in Bullitt county. Next to the youngest child in this family was George W. Hinman, who was the father of the subject of this sketch, and the first of the family to settle in Pike county.

George W. Hinman was born in Bullitt county, Ky., in April, 1791. When he was 8 years old his father and family removed to Ohio county, Ky. He was married in the year 1815 to Miss Nancy Stewart, of that county. Here 2 children were born to them,—Maria and Asahel, the latter the subject of this sketch. In 1819 he moved to Indiana, where 2 more children were born,—Eliza Ann, now deceased, and Phœbe. In 1829 he came to this county, locating on the S. W. ¼ of sec. 14, Griggsville tp. In his house on this land took place the first religious meeting in this part of the county. Geo. W. Hinman was a man of sterling worth and unblemished honor. He was a man of deep thought, strong religious convictions, undeviating honesty, a fit and honorable representative of his worthy ancestors. Such qualities, together with the experience in pioneer life in Kentucky and Indiana, fitted him to take a prominent part in the affairs of the county. In 1830 he was elected one of the three County Commissioners. He was appointed with two others, by the Legislature, to expend certain moneys accruing under the internal-improvement act on the roads of the county, and in many other ways serve the public. "Hinman's Chapel" (Methodist) was principally built by him. He and his wife are both buried in the ground attached to the Chapel. He died Dec. 8, 1854.

Asahel Hinman is the only child of Geo. W. Hinman, now living in Pike county. He was born in Ohio county, Ky., Jan. 19, 1817, and was brought to this county with his parents in 1829. On reaching his majority his father gave him $100, with which he entered 80 acres of land. Dec. 23, 1838, he was married to Sarah McLain, daughter of John and Mary McLain, of Adair county, Ky. In the spring of 1839 he built a hewed-log cabin 18 feet square on his land. It was a story-and-a-half house, and contained two rooms. Here he lived for 28 years. His farm now consists af 600 acres, and is one of the finest improved in the county. He is also the owner of the large flouring-mill at Perry, called "Hinman's Mill," and which is carried on by his sons, George W. and Asahel A., in company with himself. He was one of the original stock-holders in organizing the 5th National Bank of Chicago; also the Griggsville National Bank, of which he is a Director. He is also one of the organizers of the Farmers' Insurance Company of Griggsville, and was chosen its President.

Mr. and Mrs. H. are now residing in Perry, surrounded by their family, consisting of three children,—George W., Sarah F. and Mary. Asahel, the youngest, is married and living at Perry.

Catharine, the eldest child, married the Rev. Thomas Bonnel, and resides in Christian county, Ill. John W. and Nancy J. are deceased. We give Mr. Hinman's portrait in this volume.

A. A. Hinman was born in Pike county in 1859, and is the son of Asahel and Sarah (McLain) Hinman. He attended the common schools of Pike county and also the Wesleyan University at Bloomington, Ill. He was united in marriage in 1878 with Ella Oat, and they have one child, A. J. A. Hinman. Mr. Hinman is a miller, owning an interest in the Hinman Mills. Politically he is a Democrat.

George W. Hinman, son of Asahel Hinman, whose sketch is given above, was educated in the high schools of Perry and Griggsville, and also attended the Chicago law school, where he graduated in 1871. He began the practice of his profession the same year in Missouri. Subsequently he moved to Perry, where he practiced 8 years, meeting with remarkable success, seldom losing a case. At present he is turning his attention to milling, being a partner of the firm of Hinman & Sons. He is a member of the M. E. Church.

James Higgins, jeweler, Perry, was born in Clinton, N. J., Oct. 11, 1845; he is the son of Lewis and Anna Higgins; received his education in the common and select schools of New Jersey; he came to Perry in 1867, where he clerked for 5 or 6 years; then engaged in the hardware business, and in 1876 started a jewelry store, and thus far in his business has met with success. In 1871 he was married to Mary L. Cleveland, and they have 3 children, 2 girls and a boy. His wife is a member of the M. E. Church. In 1863 he enlisted in the 35th N. J. Zouaves and was in all the battles that the corps was in from Chattanooga to Savannah.

Henry Hippe, jr., farmer, sec. 8; P. O. Perry; Mr. Hippe was born in Germany in 1818, and is a son of Herman Hippe; was educated in the schools of Germany, and came to America in 1832, stopping at New Orleans, and the same year settling on sec. 8, this tp., where he owns 80 acres of land. His eldest son, Henry, is carrying on the farm at the present time.

Hinson S. Hobbs was born in Kentucky in 1814, and is the eldest of a family of 9 children; his parents were Solomon and Mary L. (Young) Hobbs; his father was born in the fort where Cincinnati now stands, and is of English descent; his mother was born in Kentucky and is of German descent. Solomon Hobbs and wife with 6 children, in company with Obadiah Mitchell and wife, 7 children and one negro, Benj. Morris and wife and 4 children, with one wagon and 8 pack-horses, came from Kentucky to Illinois. Our subject came to Pike county in 1834; since 1842 he has been farming, meeting with success; he is the owner of 600 acres of land, nearly 400 of which are in Perry tp. He was married in 1842 to Mary M. Taylor, daughter of one of the pioneers of Pike county. They have had 7 children, 4 boys and 3 girls: two of the former and one of the latter are married. His wife is a member of the M. E. Church, and he is a Republican in politics.

Isom L. Ingram was born in Smith county, Tenn., June 12, 1822, and is a son of Joshua P. and Susanna (Lenix) Ingram, natives of Tennessee, and of English descent. He engaged in the coopering business for 15 years, then followed the carpenter's trade, and.for several years has been engaged in farming, and owns 172 acres of land on sec. 2, this township. He came to Pike county in 1833, and Oct. 25, 1843, he was united in marriage with Perlina Rusk; 8 children have been born to them. His wife is a member of the Presbyterian Church. He has served as School Director for 15 years.

A. J. Johnson, farmer, sec. 36, was born in Indiana, and is a son of Enos and Sarah (Caw) Johnson, the former a native of Pennsylvania and of English descent, and the latter of Virginia and of Dutch descent; in 1846 he came to Pike county, where he is engaged in farming. In 1862 he enlisted in Co. F, 99th Ill. Inf., under Capt. Smith; he was discharged in 1865; he served in 13 hard-fought battles. In 1850 he was united in marriage with Amanda Bond; 7 children have been born to them. His wife is a Missionary Baptist, and he is a Methodist.

David Johnston, dec., one of the earliest and most respected citizens of this county, was born in Wythe county, Va., July 13, 1797, and was a son of Larkin and Mary (Davis) Johnston; he emigrated to Kentucky, where he married Miss Sarah Day, daughter of Joseph and Margaret Day, of Kentucky. In 1826 he came to Illinois, locating in Sangamon county; and in 1828 he located on a farm near Griggsville, Pike county, which he improved, and where he lived for two years; in 1830 he moved to Perry tp., where he resided until his death, which occurred in Sept., 1879, when he was at the advanced age of 82 years, 2 months and 8 days. In 1835 he was elected County Surveyor, and served in that capacity for about 13 years. He and his wife Sarah (Day) Johnston had a family of 9 children, whose names were: Mary, now Mrs. David Winslow, of DeWitt Co., Ill.; Margaret E., now Mrs. H. J. Chenoweth, of Perry; Sarah J., wife of Hinson Hobbs, of Kansas; Minerva A., wife of Wm. Taylor, Perry; Delilia, now Mrs. James Hughes, of Clay Co., Neb.; Harvey D., who married Maria Swakyer, and resides in Mo.; Thomas, who married Mary E. Chenoweth, and lives at Marysville, Mo.; Artemisia, now Mrs. James B. Chenoweth, of Clinton Co., Mo., and Ann Eliza, now Mrs. Thomas Seaborn, of McDonough Co., Ill., Sept. 9, 1865, Mrs. Sarah J. Johnston died, and Sept. 14, 1871. Mr. J. married Mrs. Sarah E. Lucas. For some years previous to his death Mr. Johnston was engaged in the mercantile business at Perry. Mrs. Lucas was the widow of J. B. Lucas, her maiden name being Adams. She was born in Harrison county, Kentucky, in 1831. By her last marriage she has one son, David L., born Mar. 15, 1874. Mrs. J. lives with her two sons, David L. and James P. Lucas, a son by a former marriage. Mr. J. was a member of the Christian Church for 28 or 30 years, and led an exemplary life. Mrs. J. is also a member of the Christian Church, and has been for 15 or 16 years.

Joseph Jones, farmer, sec. 16; P. O. Perry; is a native of Pennsylvania, where he was born Jan. 6, 1814; his parents, Joseph and Susanna Jones, were natives of the Keystone State, the former of Welsh and the latter of German ancestry; Mr. J. was united in marriage with Miss Elizabeth Cheek in 1841; five children have been born to them, two boys and three girls, all of whom are living. Mr. J. came to this county in 1835. He never was inside of a courtroom.

Joseph Kirgan; residence, Perry; was born in Clermont county, O., April 10, 1829; his father, Thomas Kirgan, was a native of Ireland; his mother, Mary (Fred) Kirgan, was a native of Ohio; parents were farmers, in good circumstances; by occupation Joseph is a farmer and has had some experience in milling; at present he is engaged in business in Perry, and owns a substantial residence in town. He was married Jan. 1, 1863, to Sarah Wilkins, who is a member of the Christian Church. He is a member of the order of Odd Fellows.

Fred Lipcaman, sr., is a native of Germany; came to America in 1836; lived one year in New York, and then came to Pike county, where he has ever since resided; he is a farmer, owning 160 acres of land on sec. 9. In 1840 he was united in marriage with Barbara Lutz, and to them have been born 10 children, 6 boys and 4 girls. Both he and his wife are members of the M. E. Church.

Fred Lipcaman, jr., farmer, sec. 16, was born in Pike county, Jan. 14, 1847, and is a son of Fred and Barbara (Lutz) Lipcaman, natives of Germany; he was married in 1872 to Kate Hose; three children, one boy and two girls, have been born to them, all of whom are living. He and his wife are members of the M. E. Church. He is a diligent, successful farmer.

George Lipcaman, sr., resides on sec. 9, P. O. Perry.

George Lipcaman, jr., farmer, sec. 5; P. O. Perry; the subject of this sketch is a native of Pike county, where he was born in 1841; he is the son of Fred and Barbara (Lutz) Lipcaman, spoken of above. He received his education in the common schools of this county. In 1862 he enlisted in the service to defend his country and served until 1865; took part in the siege of Vicksburg, and participated in many of the important engagements of the war. He was married in 1867 to Anna Bradbury.

Thomas J. Magee, miller, Perry, is a native of this county, and was born Aug. 2, 1851; his parents, Thomas M. and Mary (Crosier) Magee, are of Irish descent; his father is one of the prominent citizens of Perry. Thomas received his education in the common schools of Adams county. Recently in company with his father, he, has started a first-class mill in Perry. Oct. 8, 1874, he was united in marriage with Martha H. Burton. They have one child, a girl.

William Manton, farmer, sec. 26; P. O. Perry. The subject of this sketch was born in England in 1843; he is the son of James and Charlotte (Hammerton) Manton. He came to Illinois in 1854, and as a farmer has been quite successful. In 1866 he was married

PERRY

to Lucinda Jane Layton. Two boys and two girls have been born to them. Politically Mr. M. is a Democrat; has served as School Director 7 years, Assessor two years, and Road Commissioner 3 years. He is a member of the Odd Fellows Lodge, No. 76, and of Encampment No. 27. Both he and his wife are members of the M. E. Church.

Capt. B. L. Matthews, the son of John B. and Margaret (Leach) Matthews, was born Dec. 15, 1806, in Rouen county, N. C. His father was a native of Rockingham county, Va., his mother of North Carolina. She was a daughter of Benj. Leach, who was of Welsh descent. Her ancestors emigrated to North Carolina long before the Revolution, in which they took an active part on the side of the Colonies. Their direct paternity also took part in the war of 1812. The father of John B. Matthews was a native of the county of Tyrone, Ireland, and came to North Carolina in a very early day, where he died. John B. Matthews was among the very earliest settlers in Pike county, having located here in 1825. Crossing Phillips' ferry over the Illinois river, he settled on land in Flint tp., where he engaged in farming. When he arrived many remnants of once powerful Indian tribes yet remained on their favorite hunting-ground. He said that 500 Indians seen in one gang was not an uncommon sight.

They brought with them a family of 6 children : Benj. L., who was born in N. C.; Alvira and John, born in Ky.; James, Nancy and Robert, born in White county, Ill., where the elder Matthews emigrated about 1818; two more children, Austin and Albert, were born to them in this county. All of these are living except John and James. After one year's residence in Flint tp., Mr. M. moved to sec. 12, Griggsville tp., where he resided for several years; then to New Salem tp., where he lived two or three years; and then to Perry tp. His wife, Margaret (Leach) Matthews, died on sec. 32, Perry tp., in 1851 or '52. John B. went to Missouri in 1856 and resided with his daughter, Mrs. Alvira Tucker, where he died in 1857.

Capt. Matthews, the subject of this sketch, obtained his early education in the old-fashioned log school-houses of Kentucky and Illinois. Dec. 24, 1829, he was married to Minerva Carrington, a native of Kentucky, and a daughter of Asa Carrington. Mrs. M. died Oct. 15, 1841, leaving a family of 4 children, an infant some two years old dying 5 days previously. The names of the children were Martha, Asa C., Joseph H., Lucinda and Benjamin. Asa C., the well known Col. Matthews, of Pittsfield, and Martha, are the only two now living. Mr. Matthews was married a second time to Sarah Wattles, in 1842. She was a native of Connecticut, and died March 2, 1861, leaving 2 children, Harriet and Mary. He was married to his 3d and present wife, Mary Layton, in Dec., 1861. She is a native of Pennsylvania and a daughter of Joseph Layton. They have 1 child, Anna B.

30

At the age of 21 Capt. Matthews commenced active life with not so much as a dime, and with no expectation of anything being given to him. He first started for the Galena lead mines; for one year prospected, worked by the month, etc., not being very successful; the second year he took job work, running a smelting furnace and cutting wood. He laid up about $300 this year, when he went near Naples, Morgan Co., now Scott Co., and invested a part of this in 80 acres of land, upon which he erected a log house, and in this he commenced housekeeping after he was married. He then bought land on sec. 33, Perry tp., upon which he moved in 1833. Up to 1856 Mr. M. turned his entire attention to farming and stock-raising. That year, in company with Cephas Simmons, he built the first steam grist-mill that was built in Griggsville. This mill is now run by Mr. Frye. Mr. M. since that time has occupied his time in farming mostly, and resides with his family on sec. 28, this tp.

Capt. Matthews is a Republican in politics; was formerly a Whig. During the war of the Rebellion he took a prominent and active part in support of the administration of President Lincoln, and for the preservation of the Union. He raised Co. B of the 99th Ill. Inft., and was unanimously chosen its Captain. He served for about six months, when he was severely attacked with chronic rheumatism, on account of which he was obliged to resign his office and return home, and suffered severely for three years afterward. The Captain has been a member of the M. E. Church for the last 46 years. We give his portrait in this book, which was engraved from a photograph taken at the age of 69 years.

J. C. Meredith was born in Missouri Feb. 2, 1849; is a son of William and Amelia (Beatty) Meredith, the former a Welshman, his mother a native of Connecticut. J. C. attended the common schools of this county, where he received his education; he has followed farming, but at present is engaged in keeping a restaurant in Perry. In 1879 he was joined in the holy bonds of matrimony with Melissa Bradbury: both of them are members of the Baptist Church. Mr. M. is a member of the Odd Fellows order and also of the Ancient Order of the United Workmen.

Joseph F. Metz, merchant, was born in Harrison county, Va., Jan. 31, 1824, and is the son of Isaac and Lucy (Hoskinson) Metz. His father was born in Berks county, Penn., June 7, 1799, and his mother in Monongahela county, Va., June 19, 1800. His father was of German descent and his mother of Welsh. Has been engaged in the mercantile business for 20 years, since 1844 at Chambersburg. He came to Perry in November, 1875. He was united in marriage in 1852 with Elizabeth Akin. Three children, 2 girls and a boy, have been born to them. Mrs. M. died June 13, 1867. James A., the eldest son, is married and engaged in the store with his father. May 7, 1872, he was married to Elizabeth Elliott, who is a member of the M. E. Church at Perry. Mr. M. is a member of both the Masonic and Odd Fellows orders.

George S. Metz, farmer, sec. 13; P. O. Perry. Mr. Metz was born in Pike county in 1841; he is the son of Isaac and Lucy (Hoskinson) Metz, the former a native of Pennsylvania and the latter of Virginia. Geo. S. owns 220 acres of land in this county. Aug. 23, 1862, he enlisted in Co. B, 99th Ill. Inf., under Capt. J. W. Fee, and served until 1865. He was in the 40-day siege of Vicksburg under Gen. Grant, and was in every battle that the Regiment was in. He is a radical Republican, politically.

Thomas Morgan was born in county Warwick, England, Feb. 22, 1816. James and Letitia (Clark) Morgan, his parents, were natives of England. He was educated in the common and high schools of his native country. He came to America in 1842, and lived in St. Louis, then in Alton, Missouri, and Kansas, and then came to Pike county in 1862. By occupation he is a stone and brick mason, having learned his trade in England. He was married in 1839 to Anna Toltom, a native of England. They have 3 children, all girls. Mr. M. is a Democrat and a Free Mason.

A. J. Morris, farmer, sec. 35; P. O. Perry. Mr. Morris was born in Scott county, Ill., Nov. 29, 1840; he received his education in the common schools of Missouri; he formerly conducted a saw-mill, and is now the owner of a farm in Perry tp. His parents were James and Prudy (Barrett) Morris. In 1868 he was married to Mary Hewey. Three children were born to them: James Walter, dec., Melissa Ellen and Edward Nathaniel.

W. W. Morris was born in this county in 1837, and is the son of John and Emily (Henly) Morris, natives of Kentucky. He is a farmer, owning 190 acres of land in this township. In 1859 he married Mary F. Metz, and they have 7 sons and 2 daughters. He is a Democrat, has been School Director two terms, and he and his wife are Methodists.

John E. Morton was born in Kentucky Sept. 9, 1833, the son of Charles M. and Mary L. (Hawkins) Morton, natives of Orange county, Va., the former of Scottish descent, and the latter English; John E. obtained his school education in Adams county, Ill., whither the family had emigrated when he was an infant. In October, 1861, he came into Pike county. He followed farming until 1860, kept store in Adams county two years, then continued the mercantile business at Perry Springs, in partnership with his father-in-law, two years: went to Perry in 1865, where he kept store two years, and then commenced the business of packing pork and dealing in grain and lumber. In 1871 his building was burned down, and he lost nearly $4,500. He is now farming. In 1855 he married Emily J. Brown, and they have had 3 children. He is a Master in Lodge No. 95 of the Masonic Order; his wife is a Presbyterian.

Maj. W. K. Oat was born in Philadelphia, Pa., July 25, 1804, a son of Jesse and Charlotte (Happle) Oat, of German descent; for thirty years he followed farming in Hunterdon county, N. J., and in 1858 he emigrated West, settling in the town of Perry. Dec.

4, 1845, he married Mary M. (Bensted), widow of J. W. Calvert. The major has been married three times. He and his present wife are Presbyterians. He is a Republican, and has been School Director and member of the Town Board.

Jesse Pierce was born in Adams county, Ill., in 1844, and is the son of John and Nancy (Wilson) Pierce, natives of Kentucky. He is a farmer on sec. 7. In 1862 he enlisted in Company H., 129th regiment, under Capt. Case, and was discharged June 8, 1865. He went with Sherman on his Grand March to the Sea. In 1867 he married Martha Green, and their children are 4 boys and 3 girls. Mr. Pierce is a Republican.

Dr. J. G. Phillips was born in Lexington, Ky., in 1826. His parents, Joseph M. and Nancy (Miller) Phillips, were natives of Pennsylvania and Kentucky, respectively. He received his common-school education in Illinois. In 1855 he graduated in medicine at the Missouri University, and practiced in Iowa nine years; most of the time in Illinois he has been in Brown county. In 1878 he came to Perry, where he has a successful practice. In 1850 he married Mary Ann Thompson, and in 1869 he married a second wife, Minerva A. McClure. He has been a School Director and Town Trustee in Mount Sterling. He served two terms in the Legislature as a representative of Brown county. Politics, Democrat. In 1847 he was in the Mexican war, and discharged in 1848 at Santa Fe. In 1862 he enlisted in the war of the Rebellion; was Captain of 36th Ill., but so on resigned on account of ill health.

W. A. Reed, wagon and carriage manufacturer, Perry, was born in Hamilton county, O., May 11, 1838, the son of Joseph and Mary (Ward) Reed, the former a native of Kentucky, and of Irish ancestry. He received his education in the common and select schools of Ohio, and Perry, Ill.; he learned the blacksmith's trade, but at present is engaged in the manufacture of wagons, buggies, etc., at which he is very successful. In 1860 he was married to Lizzie Lynn, in Winchester, Ill., and they have 2 children, both girls. Both Mr. and Mrs. R. are members of the M. E. Church, of which he has been Recording Steward. He has served as Town Clerk and Police Magistrate.

O. Remington was born in Ohio in 1830; his father, Anthony, was a native of Massachusetts, and his mother, Wealthy Ann, *nee* Aldridge, was born in Ohio. Their ancestry was English. The subject of this sketch came to Pike county in 1835, and has lived in this county ever since. He followed farming until 1877; then he was in the hardware business a little over a year in Perry. In 1854 he was married, but his wife died, and he married again in 1872. He has had 3 children by each wife. He is a Democrat; has been Road Commissioner, School Trustee and Director. He was a partner in the Perry Woolen Mills two years.

Norman Reynolds was born in Scott county, Ill., in 1844, and is the son of Allen B. and Louisa (Bradbury) Reynolds. His father was born in Putnam county, N. Y., and his mother in Brown county, O., and both of Scotch-Irish ancestry. The subject of this sketch is a farmer by occupation. In 1861 he enlisted in the 33d Ill. Vol. Inf., and while serving as cook he lost his sight and became so blind that in 1863 he was discharged. He was in the battles of Cotton Plant and Boliver Bend, both in Arkansas. He is a man of more than ordinary energy. He says that he can do any kind of work now that he ever could do when he could see, and will walk all over and around the town of Perry, and even go into the country four or five miles. He superintends all his work. In 1877 he married Mattie A. Crawford. They are members of the Presbyterian Church. In politics he is a Republican.

N. W. Reynolds was born in North Salem, West Chester Co., N. Y., April 4, 1802; he is the son of Zadok M. and Polly Reynolds, natives of the Empire State, and of English descent; he emigrated West in an early day and Aug. 11, 1837, located in the town of Perry, where he has ever since lived. At the age of 16 our subject commenced to learn the trade of manufacturing saddles, harness and trunks, which business he followed until 1864. In 1844 he started the first hotel in the town of Perry, called the Perry House, and conducted it with success until 1860. In 1824 he married Eliza C. Crissey, who died Sept. 11, 1859. They had 4 children, all now married and doing well. In 1860 Mr. R. married again. His present wife is a Baptist, while he is a member of the Methodist Church and has been Class-Leader, Steward and Trustee; in politics he is a Republican. He is a charter member of the Masonic Lodge at Perry, No. 95, and also of the Chapter.

Thomas Reynolds, one of the early settlers and now one of the most prominent citizens of Perry tp., was born at Argyle, Washington county, N. Y., Aug. 8, 1816; his father, William, was a native of Ireland and his mother, Nancy (*nee* Martin) Reynolds, a native of New York and of Scottish ancestry. His father came to America when 20 years of age, locating at Argyle, N. Y., where he married. In 1826 he moved to the western part of New York State. He and his wife both died at Jamestown, N. Y., aged 64 and 60 respectively. Thomas first settled in Pike county in the summer of 1842, when he bought a grain thresher and separator, the first in the county, and followed threshing with some kind of machine in connection with farming for 23 years. Feb. 4, 1844, he married Lucy Jane Callis, daughter of David and Sarah (Walpole) Callis, of Virginia, and early settlers in this county. The ancestry of the Walpoles is traced in a direct line to Sir Edward Walpole, of England, a branch of the family having settled in Virginia previous to the Revolution. Mr. and Mrs. Reynolds have 6 children: Nancy Malvina, who married Robert Buckthorp; Sarah Jane, who married Henry Cocking: these reside at Jacksonville, Ill.; David M., who married Ada Burrows and resides in Spring Creek township, this county; William T., John W. and

Hugh Lee are with their parents. Mr. Reynolds and most of his family are Methodists.

Although Perry tp. is largely Republican and Mr. Reynolds is a Democrat, he has been elected to fill nearly every office in the gift of the township, besides having been County Treasurer two years. He was Supervisor for 9 or 10 years, School Director 20 years, Road Commissioner, etc., etc. He was elected County Treasurer in 1876, when he furnished security of $1,100, 035, which was far heavier than any ever before given in the county. He was expected to collect and pay off bonds for the Sny levee. During his term of office the county prosecuted a suit against the railroads to collect tax on their capital stock, and the decision was in favor of the county. Mr. R. took an active part in securing this result. While Treasurer he resided in Pittsfield. He is now on his farm, N. W. ½ sec. 26. In 1845 he bought 180 acres, but he now has 240 at his homestead, 216 on secs. 31 and 32, Chambersburg tp., and 240 on secs. 10 and 11, Spring creek tp. Mr. Reynolds' portrait will be found in this volume.

Joseph B. Rickart, carpenter and contractor, was born Aug. 5, 1847, and is a son of David S. Rickart, who is a native of Ohio and a merchant in Perry, where Joseph also resides. His mother is of German ancestry. By occupation Mr. R. is a carpenter, and is accounted one of the best mechanics in Perry. He began to learn his trade at the age of 20, and has continued to follow it with energy and success. He does considerable contracting, and is a man who loves the association of books.

Charles Schaffnit, insurance agent and dealer in musical instruments and sewing-machines, Perry, was born in Pike county, Oct. 24, 1848, and is a son of Martin and Mary (Lutz) Schaffnit, natives of Germany. He received his education partly in the common schools, and also attended the Central Wesleyan College of Missouri. He came to Perry in 1871, where he has met with eminent success in his business. He represents the German Insurance Company of Freeport, the Phœnix of Hartford, the American of Chicago, and the Home Life of New York. His father came to Illinois in 1847; in 1872 the subject of this sketch was married to Louisa Yockey; to them have been born 3 children,—2 boys and 1 girl, all living. He and his wife are members of the M. E. Church, of which he has been Steward. Mr. L. is Justice of the Peace of Perry, and handles the Whitney & Holmes organ and all kinds of sewing machines.

D. D. Schaub, carpenter, was born in Monroe, O., Feb. 23, 1838; his parents, David and Catharine B. (Bitz) Schaub, were both of German descent. He received his early education in the Baldwin University of Ohio. At the early age of 14 he began to learn the carpenter's trade, and most of his life since has been spent in this calling. He is a Trustee of the town of Perry, and a member of the Masonic order. In 1863 he was united in marriage with Caroline Feldner. Both of them are members of the M. E. Church.

FIRST JAIL AT PITTSFIELD

Jon Shastid was born in Tennessee, June 2, 1827, and is a son of John G. and Elizabeth (Edwards) Shastid, the former a native of Tennessee, and his mother of North Carolina. John came to Pike county in 1836, locating at Pittsfield. In 1862 he moved to Perry. He received his education in the common schools and the Illinois College at Jacksonville. He followed teaching from 1844 to 1868. He taught three terms in the country and has taught in Pittsfield, Griggsville, Perry, Barry, Mt. Sterling and Lewistown. In 1869 he embarked in the commercial business with his father-in-law, under the firm name of Kockill & Shastid, and they have transacted a successful business. In 1864 Mr. Shastid was united in marriage with Esther Anna Kockill, and both are members of the Christian Church.

Benjamin Taylor Shoemaker, deceased, was born in New Jersey, Feb. 12, 1812, and was the son of Daniel Shoemaker. He was reared on a farm and received his education in the common schools of his native State. He was a natural genius and a mechanic of superior ability. As a farmer he was very successful, and was considered one of the best farmers in the county where he lived in New Jersey. He came to Illinois in 1868, and died Oct. 26, 1872. His wife, whom he married in 1863, bought 120 acres of land near Perry. She was a widow lady at the time they were married, having been the wife of Mr. Felmley: her maiden name was Ellen Voorhees. Mr. Shoemaker had 5 children by a former wife, all of whom are living and married. Mrs. S. had 2 children by her former husband. The elder son, David, is teaching in Carrollton, Greene county. He has been attending college at Ann Arbor, Mich.

John C. Smith, dec., was born in Illinois in 1833, and was the son of Absalom and Sarah (Tunnel) Smith. He was engaged in farming during his life, at which business he was successful, and owned a farm at the time of his death in 1875. He was united in marriage in 1868 with Miss Elizabeth T. Shelton; two children, one boy and one girl, were born to them. Mrs. S. was born in Pike county, Ill., in 1845, and is the daughter of C. Shelton, one of the pioneers of Pike county. She is a member of the M. E. Church at Perry.

W. W. Smith was born in West Virginia in 1833, the son of Gabriel and Elizabeth (Nair) Smith, natives of Virginia; father of German, and mother of Irish descent; was educated in the common schools of W. Va.; is engaged in farming, owning 200 acres in this county. For 10 years he was engaged in threshing in Pike county. Aug. 16, 1860, he was joined in the holy bonds of matrimony with Frances A. Brown. Ella V., George M. and Harvey D. are their living children. Both Mr. and Mrs. S. are members of the M. E. Church. He is a member of the Masonic and Odd Fellows fraternities, Ancient Order of the United Workmen, and of the society for protection against horse-thieves. He came to this county in 1857, settling at Perry, at which place he has since resided.

John Jacob Snider, farmer, sec. 6 ; P. O. Perry. Henry and Catharine Snider are the parents of the subject of this sketch, and they emigrated to this county in 1850 ; John Jacob, who was born in Germany April 7, 1840, came to this county and located at Perry in 1853 ; he was educated in the common schools. He learned the trade of a tailor, at which business he was engaged 8 years. Sept. 21, 1865, he was united in marriage with Maria Herche ; 4 children, 2 boys and 2 girls, were born to them. Both Mr. and Mrs. S. are members of the M. E. Church.

George W. Steele, miller, Perry, was born in Pike Co., Ill., Jan. 29, 1840 ; his parents, L. J. and Sarah (Walker) Steele, were natives of Kentucky, his father of German, and his mother of English descent. Geo. W. received his education mostly in Adams Co., Ill. He has been engaged in Hinman Mills at Perry for the last 8 years. In 1859 he was united in marriage with Catharine Mull : of the 7 children born to them 6 are living,—5 boys and one girl. Both Mr. and Mrs. S. are members of the M. E. Church.

James Stewart, farmer, sec. 2 ; P. O. Perry. The subject of this biography was born in the State of Kentucky March 17, 1818; he is the son of Peter Stewart, of Delaware, and Tamar Stewart, *nee* Hancock, of Maryland, and both of Scottish descent. Mr. Stewart did not have the advantages of school, never having attended a day in his life. Until he was 18 years of age he did not live within 20 miles of a school-house. He came to Pike county in 1825. He is the owner of 300 acres of land, and as a farmer is successful. In 1839 he was united in marriage with Miss K. Arnott. His third wife was Martha Jane Newton, who was born in Brown Co., O., May 29, 1840. When Mr. Stewart first came to Morgan county his nearest neighbor was 6 miles distant, and there was only one house in Jacksonville.

Ransom Stowe, manufacturer, Perry, is a son of David and Sally (Palmer) Stowe, natives of Vermont ; he was born in 1815; received his education in the common schools of the Green Mountain State ; in 1850 came to Illinois, and in 1852 to Perry, where he has since resided. He had been engaged in farming, but since that date has been running a plow manufactory in Perry, and has been moderately successful. In 1835 he took unto himself a wife in the person of Ann Prindle ; by this union 2 children were born. Mrs. S. died in 1871, and in 1873 Mr. Stowe was united in marriage with Sarah Stewart. Israel F., born in 1874, is their only child. Mrs. S. is a member of the M. E. Church.

Richard Sweeting, farmer, sec. 33 ; P. O. Perry. Mr. S. is a native of England, and was born Sept. 10, 1819. His parents, Jonathan and Mary (Norfolk) Sweeting, were also natives of England. Richard came to America at the age of 19, and to Pike county in 1850, where he has since resided. He was united in marriage with Dorotha Marshall, and they have had 11 children, 7 of whom are living. Mr. S. learned the bakery and confectionery trade in England, but has been farming since he came to America. He arrived in his adopted country with $3.75. He now owns a good farm of 160 acres. His wife is a member of the Church of England.

Sutphin Taylor, farmer, sec. 18 ; P. O. Perry ; was born in Pike county in 1844, the son of Simon H. and Nancy Taylor, Kentuckians,—his father of Welsh and mother of German descent. Mr. T. is the youngest of a family of 13 children. For several years he engaged in blacksmithing. In 1870 he was united in marriage with Lucinda Barnett. Mr. T. is a member of the Masonic lodge at Perry. Politically he is a Democrat.

William Taylor, the son of Wm. and Charlotte (Philpot) Taylor, was born in Connecticut in 1838; his parents were natives of England. He received his education mostly in Pike county, where he came in 1850, and went to Ottawa, La Salle Co., where in 1861 he enlisted in Co. E, 26th Ill. Inf., and was discharged in 1863 on account of disability. He was in the battle of Corinth, Iuka, Parker's Cross Roads, Farmington, and several skirmishes while in Missouri. Has resided in Perry since his discharge from the army, where he has been elected township Collector for 7 years in succession. In 1865 he was married to Elmira Francis. They have two children, both girls. He is a member of the Christian Church at Perry.

William Thompson, farmer, sec. 15; P. O. Perry. Wm. Thompson was born in Boston, Mass., Oct. 31, 1828; his parents were Wm. and Hannah (Lowe) Thompson, the former of the Keystone, the latter of the Bay State. Mr. T. came to Pike county in 1835, and has resided on sec. 15, Perry tp., ever since, engaged in farming, at which business he has been very successful, owning three farms in this county. His father died Sept. 11, 1871, and his mother is living with him. In his father's family were 8 children, 2 boys and 6 girls, 5 of whom are living, and all in this county except one. His mother, Hannah (Lowe) Thompson, was born in 1802, and his father was born June 3, 1795, and served in the war of 1812.

Wm. M. Todd was born Oct. 12, 1840, in this county, and is the son of Wm. and Lucy (Morris) Todd, of Kentucky ; he received only a common-school education. He was united in marriage in 1875 to Mrs. Elizabeth Davis, *nee* Remington. They have two children. By occupation Mr. T. is a farmer, but also has followed the business of a plasterer. Mr. T. is a member of the M. E. Church. Politically he is a Democrat, and has served as Constable.

Charles Wade, farmer, sec. 7; P.O. Perry. On the 4th day of January, 1854, there was born to John and Vibiler (Taylor) Wade, a son, the subject of this sketch; he attended the common schools in this county. He was married April 8, 1877, to Fannie M. Hobbs. In politics he is a Republican.

John Wade, deceased, was born in Kentucky in 1829, and early became a resident of Pike county, and engaged in farming. He was married in 1850 to Vibiler Taylor, and of the 5 children born to them—3 boys and 2 girls—one son and one daughter are married. Mr. Wade died several years ago. Mrs. Wade is the daughter of Simon H. Taylor, who emigrated to Pike county in 1825, and has since resided here. Mrs. W. resides on sec. 8.

Z. Wade was born in Kentucky June 4, 1823, and is the son of Josiah and Frances Wade, the father of Virginia and of English descent, and the mother of Kentucky and of Welsh descent. Mr. Wade came to Pike county in 1830, and has seen a vast wilderness transformed into a fruitful field. He is the first man who discovered the medical properties of the famous Perry Springs; he conducted them very successfully for 6 years. As a farmer he has been quite successful : he now owns two farms. In politics he is a Republican; has served three terms as a Supervisor, and has been a School Trustee, Road Commissioner, etc. In 1849 he was married to Mary Morrison, and they have a family of one boy and two girls. Both Mr. and Mrs. W. are members of the M. E. Church, of which Mr. W. has ever been an active member.

Leonard Wagner, farmer sec. 4; P. O. Perry; was born in Pike county in 1841, and is the son of John and Catharine (Lutz) Wagner, both natives of Germany. Mr. W. is engaged in farming on sec. 4, where he owns 80 acres. In 1862 he enlisted in Co. B, 99th Ill. Inf., under Capt. B. L. Matthews; he was in almost all the battles in which his regiment was engaged; he was discharged in 1865. He was married in 1867 to Caroline Schwer. Both he and his wife are members of the M. E. Church.

William Wagner, farmer sec. 6; P. O. Perry. The parents of the subject of this sketch, John and Catharine Wagner, were natives of Germany; William was born in this county in 1842; attended the common schools and received a fair education; his father came to Pike county 43 years ago. William is engaged in farming, owning a farm of 135 acres. In 1867 he was united in marriage with Miss Louisa Jane Rider, and they have a family of 4 boys and 4 girls. Both Mr. and Mrs. W. are members of the Zion M. E. Church.

W. C. Walpole was born in Tennessee, and is the son of William and Rebecca (James) Walpole, the former a native of Virginia, and the latter of Tennessee; he came to Pike county in 1833 and has resided here ever since. In 1862 he enlisted in the 99th Ill. Inf., Co. B, under Capt. Matthews, and served until 1865; was in the battles of Port Gibson, Champion Hills, Black River, siege of Vicksburg, Matagorda, Tex., and Spanish Fort, but was never wounded or taken prisoner. In 1854 he was united in marriage with Marina Piper, and they have a family of one boy and one girl, at home. All are members of the M. E. Church. His wife's father, Abraham Piper, was one of the earliest settlers of Pike county.

Henry Warren was born in Ohio, Sept. 30, 1827, and is a son of John and Sarah (Brantlingter) Warren, both natives of Ohio, mother of German, and father of English ancestry. Henry began to learn his trade when a boy, and has worked at it ever since, and has conducted a shop in Perry for several years. In 1854 he was married, and his wife died May 16, 1869. He has a family of 2 boys and 2 girls. He has served as a member of the Board of Trustees of Perry.

B. A. Watson, proprietor of the Perry Mineral Springs, is a native of Tennessee. Here he was born in 1818. His parents, W. W. and Maria (Cape) Watson, were natives of New Jersey and Kentucky respectively. When our subject was 18 years of age he emigrated to Illinois, and from 1840 to 1865 he was engaged in the manufacture of confectioneries at Springfield, at which business he was quite successful. Thinking to better his condition he moved to the celebrated Perry Springs, where he expended the enormous sum of $100,000 in the erection of buildings and other improvements. These Springs are very largely attended by parties from all parts of the United States. We speak at length of them in our history of the township. Mr. W. was married to Miss Emma R. Planck, in 1845; by this union 7 children have been born. The eldest son and daughter are both married, the latter the wife of Dr. A. B. Carey, of Pittsfield. Mrs. W. died in 1870. Mr. W. has served as Postmaster in Perry Springs for the last 10 years.

Jacob Weber, born in Germany in 1829, is the son of John and Mary (Readiner) Weber, natives of Germany, where they both died. He received his education in the common schools, and emigrated to America in 1852; is a blacksmith, and commenced to learn his trade at the age of 14, and worked at it 8 years in Germany; also 8 years in Philadelphia; the last 18 years he has followed farming, with success. He owns 150 acres of land on sec. 17. In 1854 he married Mary Klos, a member of the M. E. Church. They have 2 sons and 5 daughters. Mr. Weber is a Democrat.

A. S. Whittaker was born Oct. 25, 1818, in Greene county, N. Y.; he is the son of William E. and Anna (Dubois) Whittaker, natives of New York, the former of English ancestry, and the latter of French. He commenced to learn the carpenter's trade at the age of 14 and worked at it until 1853, since which time he has kept a general store. He has had 2 partners since starting in business here, but for the last 5 years he has been alone. In 1840 he married Lucinda Smith, and they have 5 daughters and one son. Mr. and Mrs. W. are Universalists, and he is a member of Lodge No. 95, A. F. and A. M.

Smith Wilkins, wagon and carriage manufacturer, was born in Ross county, O., in 1851. His parents were Peter and Elizabeth (Bowen) Smith, natives of Ohio, and of German ancestry; he was educated in a common school. For several months he has been running the engine at Hinman's Mill. June 11, 1875, he married

Sarah Kelley, and they have 2 sons and one daughter. Politically, Mr. Wilkins is a Republican.

W. H. Wilson was born Sept. 16, 1845, in England, and is the son of Henry and Catharine S. (Stratton) Wilson, natives of England; received his school education in the common school in Brown county, Ill.; six months he attended Bryant & Stratton's Commercial College. He has lived in Pike county since 1855, except one year, 1864, he was in the army. He now lives half a mile from Perry, where he and his father own 400 acres of land and follow farming. In 1869 he married Miss C. E. Bradbury, and they have 2 daughters,—Grace, 9 years old, and Bessie, 5. Mr. and Mrs. W. are Presbyterians. As to politics Mr. W. votes for the best man. Mr. Wilson pays as he goes, never contracting debts.

Henry Winters was born in 1845, in Calhoun county, Ill.; when young his parents brought him into Pike county, but he was educated at the Warren Institute at Warrenton, Mo. By occupation he is a barber. During the war he enlisted in Co. B, 99th Reg. Ill. Vol., and was in the battle of Hartsville, Mo., and the siege of Vicksburg. Seven holes were shot through his coat, but he received no wound. He was in Gen. Grant's command.

Frank Wright, carriage blacksmith, was born in 1855, son of Robert and Harriet Wright, his father of Irish ancestry, and his mother a native of Pennsylvania. After traveling and working in several States he, in 1867, settled in Pike county. He has followed the trade of blacksmithing ever since he was 16 years of age. In 1878 he married Flora Schaub, and Charley, born in 1879, is their only child. He is a Democrat, and she a Methodist.

Fred Zimmerman, farmer, sec. 7; P. O. Perry; was born in this county Sept. 19, 1843; his parents were George and Anna Maria (Lutz) Z., natives of Germany. He owns 124 acres of good land, and is a successful farmer. In 1866 he married Catharine Bemer, and they have 3 boys and 2 girls. They are both Methodists, and he is a Democrat and an Odd Fellow.

George Zimmerman, farmer, sec. 4; P. O. Perry; was born Oct. 7, 1810, in Germany, and is an early settler of this county, having come to America in 1833, stopping 4 years in New York, and in 1837 settling in Pike county, on the place where he still resides. In 1836 he married Anna Maria Lutz, and their 8 children are all living, 5 of them married. He and his wife are both members of the M. E. Church. He is an independent Democrat; has served as a School Director. He owns 160 acres of land.

GRIGGSVILLE TOWNSHIP.

Among the beautiful, productive and well-improved lands in the Military Tract—and there is no fairer section in this great State—Griggsville township stands foremost. It possessed many of the charms that were likely to attract the attention and receive the favor of the pioneer seeking a home in a new country,—the fine points of timber, high rolling land, running water, and the absence of all those things which were popularly supposed to produce prevalent sickness in a new settlement. Accordingly, early in the history of Pike county we find the groves and " points " of this township settled; as early as 1825 came Henry Bateman, who located on sec. 14. He doubtless had traveled this region over, and had selected this spot because of the particular charms it possessed for him. He was not molested by the encroachment of new settlers for some years. From 1829 to 1831 came several pioneers, among whom were George W. Hinman, Abel Shelley, Uriah Elledge, Abraham Goldman, Nimrod Phillips and others. The first birth in the township was the son of Mr. Bateman, and the first person to die was his wife.

Ere many years had rolled by all the good points of timber had been taken. Many years, however, elapsed before any considerable number of the pioneers pushed out upon the beautiful prairie land. It was formerly believed that these wild prairies never would be inhabited. They might do for cattle to rove over, as they do over the vast pampas of South America. As late as 1850 the argument used by Stephen A. Douglas in securing the passage, through Congress, of the act granting to the State the alternate sections of land for six miles on either side of the railroad (the Illinois Central) to be built, was that in no other way could these vast prairies ever be settled. A wonderful revolution has been made in this respect, however, as in many others. Now the timbered land is forsaken for the poorest of prairie.

Elledge Canon.—This township is not without its natural features of interest as well as the works of nature's art. One is known as " The Canon," which the writer has christened "Elledge Canon." This narrow, deep hollow, is situated on sec. 6, on the south branch of McGee's creek, and upon the land of Thomas P. Elledge; hence its name. As we wended our way through this narrow pass, observing with deepest interest the mossy cliffs on either side, we determined to name it a canon. On mentioning our intentions, however, to Mr. Elledge, we learned that it had been known as "The Canon" for several years. We therefore prefixed the word "Elledge," which we deem but just and proper.

The Unfortunate Calf.—In the pioneer days of this county there occurred many laughable incidents. Among those which were related to us as happening in this township is the following, showing how great a trouble may arise from a little matter. On a certain occasion John Dix purchased a calf and tied it to his cart to lead home. On the way home his oxen took fright and ran away, dragging the poor calf over the rough roads by the neck. We imagine it an interesting scene to observe Mr. Dix running at the top of his speed, and keeping barely close enough to reach the caudal appendage of the calf as it dangled among the brush. He finally overtook the oxen and rescued the choking calf by lifting it up and throwing it into the cart. A neighbor's dog subsequently bit the calf, from the effects of which it died. Had this been the last of the calf it would have been better for all the parties concerned, but it still lives in the memories of many. Had it been forgotten, a vast amount of time, worry and expense would have been saved. Not being able to settle the case among themselves, Mr. Dix sued his neighbor. From the Justice's Court it was appealed to the Circuit Court, which then sat at Atlas. After a somewhat extended trial for so small a case, it was finally settled, as it was thought; but one day an officer of the Court came to Mr. Dix with a demand for the costs of the case, which surprised him not a little. The demand however was upon Levi Dix, another individual. Mr. Dix refused to pay it, and another lawsuit occurred, which was finally settled by Mr. Dix proving that Levi Dix never owned a calf.

EDUCATIONAL.

The settlers of Griggsville township, like all the setlers of 50 years ago, had many difficulties to overcome before any perceptible progress could be made in establishing educational institutions. The first efforts at instruction of any kind were very simple lessons in rudimentary knowledge, given at the residences of the early settlers. The first school was taught by John Cavender in a small log cabin on the Judge Harrington farm, where now resides George Harrington. The first school-house was built before there were any regular schools. It was erected on sec. 14 in 1833. Since, the schools have multiplied, and at present they stand second to none in the county, great care being taken in the selection of teachers and the use of proper text-books. This locality has a system of schools that the patrons may well be proud of. There are now seven school-houses in the township, besides the city schools of Griggsville.

ORGANIZATION.

The township of Griggsville was organized under the township organization law in 1850. The first election was held in April of that year. At that election Amos Hill was chosen Supervisor, James A. Kenney, Town Clerk; Porter Cotton, Assessor; Samuel Reynolds, Collector; Samuel Hill, Wm. Hinman and James Shinn, Commissioners of Highways; John Crow and B. F. Coffey, Justices of the Peace; S. B. Elledge and Frank Hatch, Constables.

GRIGGSVILLE.

This city is pleasantly located upon the Wabash Railway, about four miles from the Illinois river. It is situated upon a beautiful eminence. In its immediate vicinity the land is sufficiently rolling, requiring no drainage, and makes what is apparently a healthy location. It was laid out in 1833, by Joshua Stanford, Nathan W. Jones and Richard Griggs, and was named Griggsville by Mr. Jones in honor of Richard Griggs. It consisted of eight blocks on the north side and eight upon the south side of Quincy Avenue. Each block contained eight lots of one-quarter of an acre each. The original plat made provisions for a public square, containing two acres. It was subsequently re-platted, however, and instead of a public square two lots in block 3, two lots in block 14, two lots in block 2 and two lots in block 15, were given for Church and school purposes. There has since been added to the original plat Johnson's, Jones & Purkitt's, McConnell & Clark's, Parsons', Simmons' and Hatch's additions. The place was incorporated by a vote under an act of the General Assembly approved Sept. 10, 1849, on the 16th of November, 1852; and on the 23d of the same month, Reuben Hatch, Porter Cotton, Jesse G. Crawford, Charles Kenney and Marshal Ayers were elected Trustees. On the 26th of November, 1878, it was voted to organize as a city under an act of the General Assembly approved Sept. 10, 1872. At an election held April 15, 1879, the following officers were elected : Mayor, Daniel Dean; Aldermen—James B. Morrison, H. L. Hurt, Wm. A. Wise, James Oliver, David Borrowman, John W. Stead; Clerk, E. A. F. Allen; Attorney, Edward Doocy; Treasurer, James A. Farrand.

An Abolition Melee.—In the year 1838 there occurred an incident in Griggsville which, although not commendable in itself, would be well to record in the annals of Griggsville's history. In those early days, as in more modern times, there were the pro-slavery and the anti-slavery parties. At the annual election that autumn each party brought forth a strong man for Constable. Marshall Key was the Democratic candidate, and B. F. Coffey the Whig candidate. A very hot contest ensued, which resulted in the election of Coffey. Some of the opposition seemed to take offense at the proceedings. Whether Coffey was fairly elected or not we are not prepared to say. Be that as it may, however, a Key man assaulted a Coffey man immediately after the election, striking him in the back. A general *melee* then followed, but no one was seriously hurt.

In a few weeks after the above occurrence a gentleman visited Griggsville, holding anti-slavery meetings and circulating a petition to Congress asking that honorable body to abolish slavery in the District of Columbia, and the non-admission of Texas as a State. The petition was first presented for signers at a religious meeting at the Methodist Church. Previous to the close of the service the minister gave notice that the above petition was in the hands of a gentleman present, and that he would be pleased to have any one present who felt so disposed, sign it. Quite a number walked forward and signed their names. A few parties in the audience signified their disapproval of such proceedings, excitement running high among the more ignorant class. They met in a saloon, known then as a "grocery," where liquor was sold, and passed resolutions that the parties who had signed that obnoxious petition should be compelled to erase their signatures from it. To carry out this design, on the morning following the last anti-slavery meeting, they pursued the gentleman who held the petition, overtaking him on the farm of J. K. Moore, and compelled him to produce the document. They then returned and waited upon those parties whose names appeared upon the paper, and demanded of them that they should immediately erase them, under the penalty of violence if they should refuse. Some complied with this demand, but others did not. These disturbers of the peace then notified the obstinate ones that they must erase their names, and accordingly appointed an evening to "finish up the business." They again met in the same grocery to more fully complete their organization, and "fire up." The good people of the country being afraid of their man œuvers, came pouring into town about twilight, well armed and equipped, to act on the defensive. They met with the peaceable people of Griggsville in the hotel and organized, appointing Mr. Blood as their Captain. A committee was also appointed to confer with a committee of the other party, in which conference the committee from the citizens informed the disturbers that they must immediately disband, or else they would be dealt with harshly, and that the first man who dared to intimidate another petitioner would receive a "fresh supply of ammunition."

The disturbers then seeing the turn of affairs, decided to abide the decision of the citizens and immediately disbanded. Thus ended what might have assumed the form of a riot, had it not been for the timely aid and energy of the peaceful citizens of the neighborhood.

War Record.—It is no wonder that this township, whose political education has consisted largely in means of bringing discomfort to the slaveholders and their hired slave-catchers, should take a deep interest in a war which, though not primarily waged in the interest of the colored race, must nevertheless result in their liberation. To that end Griggsville made a large and precious sacri-

Robert Seabonn

GRIGGSVILLE

fice. The alarm of war had scarcely sounded before the able-bodied citizens of the township were seen marching toward the nearest recruiting stations in squads, as it were. It is difficult to give the number that went from the township, but suffice it to say that more enlistments are recorded from Griggsville than from any other point in the county.

Quite a number of those who went to defend their country from Griggsville were killed in actual conflict. Some died in rebel prisons from starvation, and others of wounds or disease contracted in the army. Their bones lie mingled with the soil of the country which they went out to rescue from the hands of those who sought to destroy it. The sacrifice was a costly one, but their country demanded it, and they gave it willingly.

RELIGIOUS.

The old pioneers, though they would not have hesitated much to engage in a rough-and-tumble fight, and did not hesitate to take a dram once in a while (though they say the whisky did not contain as much infernal fire as it does now), were yet almost universally pious people, and enjoyed themselves religiously quite as well as the more fastidious church-goers of to-day. The religious services were simple, the church buildings were simple, the methods of conveyance to and from the church were simple, and the manners, dress and intercourse of the people who attended church were primitive in the extreme. But some of the old pioneers assert that the natural organs of voice with which they praised God were to be preferred to the organ now pumped by a boy, and skillfully manipulated by a popular but not pious young lady or gentleman, dressed in silk or broad-cloth instead of the ancient linsey-woolsey or jeans. In a religious point of view, from the very earliest days this township has always taken a great interest in the establishment of Churches and missions.

Baptist Church.—The first regular Baptist church at Griggsville was organized Aug. 4, 1834, by Rev. Alvin Bailey, with seven members. Henry Carmer was chosen Deacon and Clerk, which position he held until 1861, when he removed from the place. The first members were Amos Blood, two ladies by the name of Susan Blood, Joseph B. Cooper, Sarah Bradstreet, Henry Carmer and Mary B. Carmer. This church struggled hard in its infancy, but by the earnest labors of its faithful members has grown to a large and prosperous organization. For some time the church held regular services in a house owned by Mr. Blood, and they had no pastor until in 1835, when Rev. Calvin Greenleaf took charge and held the position until 1838; then Thomas H. Ford to 1840; Chandler Curtis from 1840 to 1841; Ambler Edson from 1843 to 1844; B. B. Carpenter from 1845 to 1870. Since that time the following-named pastors have served: L. C. Carr, H. L. Stetson, R. F. Gray, B. W. Morgan, and C. R. Lathrop, the present Pastor.

In the year 1836 the congregation began the erection of a frame

31

building, 40 by 54 feet in size, which was finished in 1840. About
the year 1853 they built an addition to this structure. In 1873
the old building was torn down and a new brick edifice was
erected, at a cost of about $20,000. Services are held each Sunday
morning and evening by Rev. C. R. Lathrop, Pastor, and Sunday-
school at 12 o'clock. The present number of communicants is 213.
When Mr. Carmer removed in 1861, Mr. John Petrie was elected
his successor as Deacon, and Henry Lynde as Clerk, which
positions they both hold at present. This Church has enjoyed
various revival seasons, and over 650 different persons have at various times been members of the Church.

Griggsville M. E. Church.—This Church was organized in 1835
by Rev. William Hunter, with the following charter members:
Dr. James M. Higgins, Mrs. Margaret Higgins, Jesse G. Crawford, Peleg Gardner, Mrs. Caroline Gardner, James Hutchinson,
sr., and James Hutchinson, jr., and Samuel, Mary, Eliza and
Sarah Hutchinson. Dr. Higgins was the first Class-Leader.
Among the early pastors was the Rev. Wilson Pitner, a very earnest worker, and a preacher well fitted for conducting revivals and
camp-meetings. On one occasion during a camp-meeting here,
while discoursing upon the day of judgment and upon the appearance of Gabriel with his trumpet on that great and awful day, the
appearance of the saints robed in white, etc., the women became
very happy and set up a shout which completely drowned the sten-
torian voice of the enthusiastic minister. In order to quiet them
he reached back and took the horn, which was used for calling the
audience together, and began blowing it. This only intensified the
excitement of the almost fanatical persons who were engaged in
shouting. They thought, without looking to see from whence the
noise came, that Gabriel had indeed come, and was now in their
very midst, blowing his trumpet. It was some time before the
people could become quieted.

There was a "class" organized in the county about two miles
east of Griggsville, previous to 1831, but the members of this society united with the Griggsville Church immediately after the erection of a church edifice, which was in 1836 or 1837. In 1846 the
society erected another building, and so rapid was the growth of
the congregation that they soon found it necessary to erect another
structure, which was accomplished in 1852. This society now has
a membership of about 250. Services are held each Sunday morning and evening by Rev. H. Shaw, the Pastor. Sunday-school at
2:30 P. M.

Congregational Church.—On Feb. 1, 1837, 11 persons, residents
of Griggsville, but members of different Congregational and Presbyterian Churches elsewhere, met for the purpose of consulting
respecting the organization of a Church. Resolutions were passed
declaring that it was expedient to organize a Church, and the day
previous to the organization was to be set apart as one of fasting
and prayer. In accordance with the resolutions the 16th day of

February, 1837, was observed as a day of fasting and prayer ; on the following day the Church was duly organized, with Rev. A. G. Norton as Pastor. Geo. T. Purkett was regularly appointed Deacon Jan. 4, 1838. The Sunday school was organized May 12, 1837. Rev. A. G. Norton closed his labors with the Church in February, 1838, and has been succeeded by the following Pastors, given in their order : Revs. Wm. Whittlesey, A. L. Pennoyer, J. Ballard, J. T. Holmes, G. B. Hubbard, W. H. Starr, T. Lyman, Rollin Mears, W. Herrott, N. P. Coltrin, W. W. Whipple, G. H. McArthur, E. C. Barnard, G. H. Bailey and S. M. Wilcox, the present Pastor. The whole number of members, from the organization to the present time, has been 563 ; the present membership is 169.

Hinman Chapel M. E. Church.—The church edifice of this society is on sec. 6, this township. The class worshiped in private and schoolhouses for several years. About the year 1844 they erected a house of worship. Services are held each alternate Sabbath by Rev. A. P. Stover, Pastor. Sunday-school each Sunday.

Maysville United Brethren Church was organized in 1842, in the house of Lewis Dunham. Caleb Boyer, now of Fulton county, was among the first ministers. This society erected a small house of worship about the year 1857, and in the year 1870 they erectee a new edifice, at a cost of $1,000 besides the labor. Services ard held each Sunday, and preaching each alternate Sunday by the Pastor, Rev. Wm. Pease. The number of communicants at present is 65.

Griggsville Church of Christ was organized July 26, 1874, with the following 12 members : J. E. Alcorn, M. E. Alcorn, Jesse Fielding, Atlanta Fielding, Theodore Ball, Anna Crawford, Adelia Elledge, Phœbe Rickart, Rachel Mason, Eadie Jenkins, Amos Williams and Ellen Williams. This was at the beginning of, or soon before, a protracted effort which closed Aug. 25, 1874, with a membership of 141. The Trustees elected were J. E. Alcorn, I. L. Lewis and Peter Harshman. The congregation completed the erection of a house of worship in 1877, at a cost of $1,800. The present membership numbers 72.

MILLING.

Mill interests in the early history of the county were considered of much greater importance than at present. The easy communication between neighborhoods, towns and cities by means of the railroad has revolutionized almost everything, but nothing more than that of transforming the grain into flour or meal. To the early settler one of the most important items in his calculations was the grinding of his grain. There were no steam mills then, and a site for a water mill was an important thing. The pioneers were all poor, and though mill sites might have been plenty, they could not improve them. Therefore numerous devices were invented to convert wheat and corn into bread. A few were possessed of hand-mills, not greatly unlike those in use some 2,000 years ago, and to which allusion is made in the Bible, Matthew xxiv, 41: "Two women shall be grinding at the mill," etc. By and by some of the more forehanded farmers brought in a kind of horse-mill, which, though a very primitive affair, was considered a valuable accession to the industries of the neighborhood, and a wonderful convenience. These mills were mostly used for simply cracking corn, upon which the old pioneers lived. Corn was the staple feed for man and beast, and upon it they all thrived and grew healthy and strong.

The " *Pike Mills* " were erected in 1877, by the firm of McMahan & Co., composed of L. W. McMahan, D. P. Baldwin and G. P. Baldwin. The latter has sold out his interest. The machinery is all of the latest improved style, adapted to the new-process system, and this was the first mill of the kind in this section of the State. It has proven a success to the owners, giving a larger yield and better quality of flour than the old system. The building is four stories high, with four run of burrs and a capacity of 200 barrels in 24 hours. They have a large patronage in the New England States and in Chicago for their flour.

L. W. McMahan has been a resident of the county for 24 years. For a number of years previous to going into the present business he was in the grain trade. His acquaintance with the valuable milling qualities of the wheat raised in this section induced him to invest in this enterprise.

Frye's Flouring Mill.—This mill was erected about the year 1855, by Mr. C. Simmons. After passing through different hands, Mr. Frye, in 1877, purchased it, and in 1878 he sold a half interest to Mr. McWilliams, of Griggsville. The mill has been re-modeled by Mr. Frye, and is one of the best mills in the county. Its capacity is 80 barrels in 24 hours, and the flour is of excellent quality.

BIOGRAPHICAL DEPARTMENT.

In justice to the pioneers and prominent citizens of the city and township of Griggsville—those who have made and are now making the history of this section—we wish to speak personally, and short biographical sketches of them here follow:

Edward A. F. Allen was born in Beverly, Essex Co., Mass., July, 13, 1823; he came to Quincy, Ill., in 1838, and to Griggsville in 1841. He served three years in the late war in Co. I., 33d Ill. Inf., and one year of this time was 2d Lieutenant. He was subsequently in the Quartermaster's department for three years. He was married July 13, 1844, to Sarah A. Lyon. They had 9 children, of whom 6 are living: Henrietta, now Mrs. Gilbert Brooks, of Clinton, Ill.; John J., M. E. preacher, of Monroe City, Mo.; Martha E.

now Mrs. James Vannatta, of West Chicago; David E., Hattie M. and Ruth. David E. is a painter by profession.

Robert Allen, sr., was born in Cumberland Co., Ky., May 31, 1803. He was married to Miss Amanda Turk in 1824, and removed to Henry Co., Tenn., thence to Naples, Ill., 1834, where for three years he was extensively engaged in building flat-boats, trading in live stock, and freighting to New Orleans and other Southern points. He left Naples in 1837, and took up his residence in Griggsville, dealing in live stock and butchering. Mr. and Mrs. Allen were the parents of 7 children, of whom 3 are living: A. S. and R. P., prominent citizens of Griggsville, and Mrs. Wm. Jones. now of Chillicothe, Mo. Mrs. Allen died Jan. 16, 1841. In 1842 Mr. Allen again was married, this time to Sarah Stanford, who now survives him. Mr. Allen gave liberally to the support of Churches and missions, and held positions of honor and trust; one being that of Postmaster during President Buchanan's administration. He was a member of the M. E. Church, and died Jan. 1, 1880, from a stroke of paralysis received some years before. In the death of Mr. Allen his wife lost a loving husband, his children a kind father, and the community an honest and influential man.

Wm. F. Anderson, deceased, was born in Baltimore, Md., in 1801. He was the oldest of 4 brothers, whose father, Capt. Wm. Anderson, was lost at sea, in the year 1813. Mr. Anderson was one of the firm of Beecher & Anderson, of New York, for about 5 years. He came West during the financial crisis of 1836, and traveled in different parts of the country until 1841, when he married Laura E. Gilpin. They settled in Springfield, Ill., where he engaged in farming for 2 years. In 1849 he engaged in business in St. Louis. In 1851 he came to Griggsville and engaged in the mercantile business with J. D. Philbrick for a short time, when the latter retired and Mr. Anderson carried on the business alone until his death, which occurred May 21, 1857. Mr. and Mrs. Anderson had 7 children, whose names are Eloise L. (now widow of Henry Cotton), Wm. F., M. Louise, deceased, A. G., Alexander C., Charles H. and Geo. S.

Isaac Bailey was born in Cumberland Co., Me., in 1829; son of Josiah Bailey. He was raised on a farm, and at his majority began working on the railroad as a section hand, then as section boss; in 1854 he came to Illinois and was Roadmaster of the C., B. & Q. for some time; then section boss again for 3 years, then Roadmaster again on the H. & St. Joe R. R. 7 months; 2 years on the Mississippi Central, and is at present Roadmaster on the Hannibal branch of the Wabash R. R. Oct. 9, 1861, he married Miss Lizzie E. Pitney, and they have had 5 children, of whom Geo. W., Minnie and Frank are living.

David Baldwin, deceased, was born in Newark, N. J., in 1793. He was a large contractor in New York city for 25 or 30 years. He came to Pike county in 1835, located in Perry and purchased large tracts of land; also engaged in farming. In 1849 he erected the Perry Flouring Mill; was the father of 5 children, of whom 3 are living: Alex., David P. and Geo. W. Mr. Baldwin died in 1854.

T. K. Ball, son of G. O. and Delia (Kellogg) Ball, the father formerly of New York, was born in this county in 1848; was educated in the common schools; has followed farming until the last three years. In 1867 he married Anna Cadwell, and their 6 children are all living. He belongs to the Christian Church, and in politics is a Democrat.

Levi Bartlett is a native of New Hampshire and came to Illinois about the year 1867; is engaged in all kinds of mechanical jobbing in light machinery, making sewing-machines a speciality: he also re-plates spoons, etc. He was married in 1861 to Harriet G. Crane, and they have 2 children, Albert J. and Gracie G.

E. W. Baxter is a native of Hillsboro, N. H., and was born July 19, 1837; he is the son of M. E. Baxter, of Griggsville. Mr. Baxter came in September, 1857, to Griggsville, where he engaged in the meat business for 15 years, holding an interest in the same for four years afterward. In Jan., 1872, he associated himself with Allen & Bryant, grain and live-stock dealers. This firm dissolved in Sept., 1873, Messrs. Baxter and Bryant continuing in the business for 6 years, for the most part in connection with merchandising. In 1877 Mr. Baxter purchased the entire interest in the mercantile business, and is now conducting the same. He also has a stock of groceries, queensware, and is doing a large business. He was married in April, 1857, to Helen M. Harvey, sister of Dr. Harvey, of this place. They have 6 children: Mary E., Helen M., Emma F., Harvey E., Geo. E. and Arthur.

John Bickerdike was born in Yorkshire, England, Aug. 18, 1835, and is a son of John Bickerdike, deceased, who came to this county in 1842. He selected a location for his future home and returned to England, bringing his family here the following year. He was the father of 9 children, of whom our subject is the 5th. Mr. B. was reared on a farm and educated in the common schools of Pike county. His brother, George, was killed during the late war. Mr. Bickerdike has been married twice, and is the father of 7 children, of whom five are living: Wm. A., George F., Charles E., Mary R. and Nancy E. His first wife was Rebecca J. Pearcy, and the second was Elizabeth Perry. He resides on sec. 36, Griggs-ville tp., and is engaged in farming and stock-raising. P. O. Griggsville.

Ephraim Biggs. The subject of this sketch was born in Preble county, O., June 30, 1822. He was raised on a farm, came to Defiance county, O., about the year 1854, where he remained until 1867, when he removed to Pike county, Ill., where he still resides, and is engaged in farming and stock-raising. He was married to Mary A. Mendenhall, by whom he had 8 children, of whom 4 are living, namely, Sarah M., Martha E., Rachel A. and Melissa. Mrs. Biggs died in 1848. Mr. Biggs was again married in 1860, this time to Mrs. Phœbe Grimes. They had one child, Wm., deceased. This second wife died in 1862, and in 1864 Mr. Biggs married Mrs. Nancy Fribley. They had 2 children, Geo. W. and Fannie. The third Mrs. Biggs died in 1866, and in the year 1870 he married Mrs. Rosanna Moore. They had one child. Mr. Biggs' father served in the war of 1812.

M. Blake & Sons. These enterprising farmers reside on sec. 8, Griggsville tp. Mr. Blake was born in Adams Co., O., Oct. 22, 1822. He was married in 1849 to Melinda Thompson. They had 7 children, 6 of whom are living; John, Nicholas, and Henry, who are engaged in business with their father; Robert, Rebecca J. and Melinda A. Mr. Blake came West in 1851, and settled in Missouri, residing in Macon, Shelby and Marion counties, but in 1865 he removed with his family to Pike Co., Ill., where they still reside. He was a soldier in the late war, in Co. G, 30th Regiment, Mo. Vol. Inf. For some time he was disabled by sickness, yet he served his time out, and was honorably discharged in 1865.

John Blake was born in Adams Co., O., June 26, 1850; is a member of the Christian Church in Perry. He received a common-school education, and his vocation is farming and stock-raising.

Nicholas is a member of the M. E. Church at Hinman Chapel, Griggsville tp.; was educated in the common schools of Ohio, and is also a farmer. He is a native of Missouri, and was born May 2, 1852.

Henry was born in Missouri, and is also a farmer.

J. M. Bodine is chief miller in Pike Mills, Griggsville.

David Borrowman was born in Lanarkshire, Scotland, in 1825. He came to St. Louis with his parents in 1838; is a marble and stone-cutter, and has carried on this business in Griggsville for 15 years. He uses the celebrated Kinderhook limestone, which is a superior quality of stone. Mr. B. was married in 1854 to Jane Barker, of Nashville, Tenn. They had 5 children, of whom but two are living. Mr. B's father, John Borrowman, located in Calhoun Co., Ill., in 1841, where he engaged in farming and stock-raising until his death from cholera, which occurred in 1849, during the prevalence of that fearful scourge in this country.

Ellen Brakefield, a native of this county, was born Jan. 19, 1835, and is the daughter of Abraham Goldman, so well known in the early settlement of Pike county. Mr. Goldman helped to erect the first log house in Griggsville. Mrs. Brakefield was married June 28, 1849, to Samuel Brakefield; they had 4 children; two only are living,—Olive and Llewella. Mr. B. was born Nov. 27, 1824, in Pennsylvania, was taken to New York by his parents when very small. He came to Pike county about the year 1848, where he engaged in farming and stock-raising. He had previously been engaged in the manufacture of brooms. On the morning of the 13th of June, 1874, Mr. Brakefield was killed while in the act of crossing the railroad track with a team in front of a train of cars. His body was carried several yards by the cars, and mutilated in a most shocking manner. He was a prominent citizen and a member of the M. E. Church. Few men possessed so many virtues, and few as well respected as he. It is no wonder that the entire community was thrown into consternation at the intelligence of his untimely death.

James Brakefield was born in Kent, England, April 22, 1822, and when he was about one year old his parents, Charles and Mary Brakefield, brought him to America, settling in Clinton county, Pa., whence they soon removed to Schenectady, N. Y. At the age of 22 years James located at Griggsville, Ill., where he followed farming and broom manufacture. In 1845 he married Elizabeth Carmer, a native of Paterson, N. J., and daughter of Henry and Mary (Hunt) Carmer, who were early settlers in this county, coming here in 1831-'2. Henry Carmer was a native of New York city, and his wife of Philadelphia, neither of whom is now living. Mr. C. was reared in the mercantile business, but in an early day he came to Pike county, where he followed farming until his death in December, 1862, at the age of 70 years, his wife having died the previous August. In March, 1857, Mr. Brakefield went into mercantile business with J. M. Crandall, but after 3 years' partnership he returned to his former vocation. In 1866 he entered partnership with L. W. Dix. In 1871 his health commenced to fail, consumption setting in, and he died April 26, 1873. During his life Mr. Brakefield was prominently identified with the interests of the county.

Henry R. Brown, a pioneer of Pike Co., was born in Brown Co., O., July 15, 1821, and is a son of the late William Brown, so well known in the pioneer history of this county. He came here with his parents in 1834 and settled on sec. 29, Griggsville tp.; has dropped corn on Griggsville prairie after a large breaking plow, the rows being one mile in length. This was for Nathan W. Jones, who now resides in Griggsville. He also worked in a cotton gin in Morgan county for about 3 years. Like all other boys of those early days, Mr. Brown was deprived of educational advantages, and was compelled to undergo many hardships and privations. He saw the first steamboat that sailed on the Illinois river. He has seen over 20 deer in one drove, but never shot one. He was married Jan. 18, 1842, to Harriet Park, and had one son, Geo. W. Mrs. Brown died Jan. 18, 1844. Mr. Brown was again married Dec. 22, 1847, this time to Jane Chapman, daughter of E. W. Chapman, deceased, so well known in the early history of this county. Mr. and Mrs. Brown have had 8 children, 6 of whom are living: John Q., Mary J., Sarah F., Alice, Amos W. and Willy H. They are all married except the two youngest.

J. Q. Brown was born in Griggsville township, Oct. 13, 1848, and is a son of H. R. Brown. He was reared on a farm and

James Bickfield

GRIGGSVILLE

FOR BIOGRAPHICAL SKETCH SEE PAGE 526.

educated in the common and high schools of Griggsville. He was married Nov. 26, 1873, to Ella E. Eastman, daughter of Lycurgus Eastman, of Griggsville, whose biography also appears in this work. Mr. and Mrs. Brown have two children, Alice E. and Richard E. Mr. Brown is engaged in farming and resides on sec. 8, Griggsville township.

Eben F. Bryant was born in East Cambridge, Mass., Feb. 7, 1832, and was brought to this county by his parents in the year 1837 ; was raised on a farm until 18 years of age, when he went to Georgetown, Harrison Co., O., and there apprenticed himself to Heberling & Russell, machinists. He remained with them about 18 months, then returned to Illinois, where he engaged in farming until he reached his majority ; then went to sea. He sailed first from New Bedford, Mass., on a whaling vessel, and at New Zealand changed to a merchant vessel, bound for Salem, Mass. They rounded Cape Horn, stopped at Rio Janeiro, and arrived in Salem in October, 1854. This completed his voyage around the world, which was quite a rare thing for a Pike county boy. Mr. Bryant then returned to his old home in Pike county, following farming for 2 years, then in 1856 he again sailed, but this time on the Illinois river. He remained here until 1868, except one trip to the Hudson river, via New Orleans and Boston. He then again engaged in farming, which is his present occupation, and resides on sec. 25, Griggsville tp. Mr. Bryant is the son of Eben Bryant, who was born in South Reading (now Wakefield), Mass., in June, 1806. He was a shoemaker by trade, but on removing to Illinois he became a farmer. He was a member of the Baptist Church for several years, and died in 1869. Our subject was the oldest son, and was married in May, 1863, to Edith Dean, daughter of Jonathan Dean, a boot and shoe merchant of Prairie City, Ill. Mr. Dean spent several years of his life in Montana, where he engaged in mining and farming.

J. B. Bryant was born in Pike county in 1848 ; was educated in the common schools, and in the year 1871 engaged in the jewelry business in Griggsville. His father, Eben Bryant, was a native of Wakefield, Mass., and came to this county in 1838, settling in Griggsville tp., where he engaged in farming until his death, which occurred May 3, 1869.

Amos Butterfield, son of the late Leonard Butterfield, well known in this county, was born in Griggsville tp. May 17, 1849 ; was educated in the common schools of this township, and raised a farmer. He was married Aug. 16, 1872, to Mary Hensel, daughter of Robert Hensel, of Griggsville tp. They have one little girl, Minnie, born Aug. 17, 1873.

Leonard Butterfield, deceased, was born Dec. 14, 1805, in Nashua, N. H.; was married to Susan Lamson in the city of Boston Sept. 27, 1832. He spent the 5 following years in the State of North Carolina, as a missionary among the Cherokee Indians, and in 1837 came to Griggsville, where he resided until the death of his wife, which occurred Aug. 21, 1870 ; he then visited his brothers and sisters in the East. He returned to Griggsville in 1873, where he remained until May 27, 1874 ; June 2 of this year he was married to Rebecca Noyes, and resided in New Hampshire until his death, which took place July 29, 1877. He was for many years a member of the Baptist Church.

Henry Carmer, deceased, was a native of New York city, and was born July 25, 1793; was educated in New York, and was a hardware merchant for several years in Patterson, N. J. In 1831 he removed with his family to Richmond, Ind., where he remained till 1833, when he came to Griggsville township. There were but three houses in Griggsville at that time. He engaged in farming for about 17 years, and was bookkeeper for Reuben Hatch, of Griggsville, for a few years, and afterward for Brakefield & Crandall. In the year 1861 he removed to Hancock Co., where he died Dec. 19, 1862. He was the father of 3 children,—Elizabeth W., now Mrs. James Brakefield; Mary W., now widow of Henry Goldman; and Lydia, now Mrs. Thomas Brakefield. Elizabeth W. was married to James Brakefield, April 22, 1845. They had 7 children, of whom 3 are living,—Mary W., now Mrs. Simmons; Henry C., Lillie C. and Ettie J. Mr. B. was a prominent merchant of Griggsville for a number of years. He died April 26, 1873.

Rev. B. B. Carpenter was born in Vermont, Dec. 3, 1810, and was taken by his parents to Schoharie Co., N. Y., when but six months old, where he remained until he was sixteen years of age, when he went to Washington Co., N. Y. He was apprenticed to John Hughes, a tailor, of Cambridge, N. Y., with whom he remained for three years. He pursued this occupation for three and a half years, when he began preparing for the ministry. He attended the Brandon Academy two and a half years, and then entered the Hamilton University. He completed only the Sophomore year on account of ill health. He was married in 1841 to Mary Richards, and they had 4 children: 3 are now living,—James B., Chester L., and Charles D. The name of the deceased was Laura. Mr. Carpenter came to Illinois in 1839, and was ordained minister in the Baptist Church at Dixon in 1840, where he remained as Pastor of the Church until 1844, when he took charge of the Lamoille (Ill.) Baptist Church for one year; he then was Pastor of the Griggsville Baptist Church for twenty-five years, but is now retired on account of ill health.

David F. Coffey, deceased, one of the pioneers, was born in Simpson county, Ky., May 18, 1817, and was a son of Nathan Coffey, deceased, well known in this county, who brought his family here in 1829 and settled on sec. 3, Griggsville township, at the summit of the hill which was afterward christened "Coffey Hill," and is still called by that name. He was the father of 13 children, of whom David F. was the 6th. The latter was married in 1842 to Elizabeth Conner, daughter of Francis Conner, deceased, who came to Franklin Co., Ill., in 1832. Mr. and Mrs. Coffey had 10 children, of whom 9 are living,—Sarah E., Nathan F., J. Hardin, Delitha M., Daniel F., Burton B., Thomas M., Mary J. and Grace L. Mr. Coffey was Captain of Co. B, 68th Regt. Ill. Inf., in the Rebellion, but was detailed to hospital service during the second battle of Manassas. He died Sept. 22, 1867, at the age of 50 years; had been a member of the Baptist Church for about twenty-seven years.

John Craven, sr., a native of Yorkshire, Eng., was born Jan. 7, 1802; was married in 1831 to Esther Warton, and the same year came to America and settled in the wilds of Morgan Co., Ill., 6 miles west of Jacksonville, where he remained until 1850, engaged in farming. He then removed with his family to Pike county and settled on sec. 20, Griggsville tp., where he again engaged in farming and stock-raising. He is now retired from active life and resides on a little farm adjoining Griggsville on the west. Mr. and Mrs. Craven have 2 children: Sarah A., now Mrs. E. T. Williams, and John, who resides at the old homestead in this township.

John Craven was born in Morgan Co., Ill., Feb. 13, 1835, and is a son of John Craven, sr., of Griggsville tp. He was raised on a farm and educated in the common schools of Morgan Co. He came to this county with his parents in 1850, settling on sec. 20, Griggsville tp., where he still resides, and is engaged in farming and stock-raising. He was married May 12, 1864, to Henrietta George, daughter of Samuel George, deceased, who came to Griggsville in 1847. Mrs. Craven was born Oct. 17, 1837, in London, England. Mr. and Mrs. Craven have had 6 children, of whom 5 are living: Mary E., Anna, Maud and Jennie (twins) and John.

Jesse G. Crawford was born in Overton Co., Tenn., May 6, 1810. He received a common school education there and emigrated to Illinois in 1829, settling in Macoupin Co.; in 1830 he came to Jacksonville, where he remained three and a half years, then came to Griggsville in 1833. At that time there was no town there. A log house stood near where the center of Quincy Avenue now is. It still stands just back of the postoffice, but is weather-boarded, and is owned by J. R. Stanford's heirs. Mr. C. erected the first two-story frame house on the Griggsville prairie in 1833, for Amos Blood. He was married in the fall of 1833 to Jane Avery, daughter of Nicholas Avery, an early settler in Pike Co. They had 4 children, —only one living, James. Mrs. Crawford died in 1847. Mr. Crawford again married, this time Maria J. Houts. They have 3 children,—Abbie M., now Mrs. A. H. Butler; Clara E., now Mrs. Henry Hatch; and George B.

D. W. Cree was born in Griggsville tp. in 1844, and is the son of Walker Cree, of Griggsville. In the year 1863 Mr. Cree engaged in the sale of furniture, stoves, and tinware, wall paper, picture frames, etc., with a capital of $300. He now carries a stock of $4,000, and has a large trade.

James M. Cree was born in Maysville, this county, Jan. 15, 1842. He came to Griggsville when 14 years old, where he still resides, and is proprietor of the Cree House in this place, one of the best hotels in the county. He was married March 31, 1865, to Lida A. Pond.

Nathan H. Davis was born in Strafford Co., N. H., Aug. 4, 1812; was raised on a farm and educated in the public schools of Canada, his parents having moved there with their children in 1818. When he obtained his majority he went to Boston, Mass., where he learned the carpenter's trade. He worked on the bridges of the Boston & Lowell R. R. for three successive summers. In 1837 Mr. Davis started for the then far West and arrived in Quincy, Ill., Aug. 14 of the same year, and in a few days came to Barry, this county, where he pursued his profession for a number of years and then purchased a farm in Derry township, on sec. 1. He then engaged in farming, working at his trade at intervals. July 18, 1839, he was married to Sarah Lourimore, daughter of Robert S. and Mary Lourimore, deceased. Mrs. Davis was born in Butler Co., O., May 8, 1817, where she remained until 8 years of age, when her parents took her to Dark Co., O., and in 1837 they moved to Pike Co., Ill., where she still resides. Mr. and Mrs. Davis have had 7 children, of whom 4 are living,—Josephine, Frances, Louisa and David; all are married. Mr. Davis is a farmer, and has been extensively engaged in stock-raising. He is a son of Nathan Davis, who was born in N. H., Nov. 22, 1772. His mother was Sally Boynton, who was born in 1777 in Old Salem, Mass.

Aaron H. Dean was born in Litchfield, Conn., March 17, 1831, son of Hiram L., and nephew of Daniel Dean, Mayor of Griggville, but he came to Pike Co. in an early day (1836), with his parents; educated in the old-fashioned log school-house; learned the blacksmith's trade; settled on sec. 36, whence he walked 3 miles every day to his shop in Griggsville, working for $1.25 a day. Wolves sometimes followed him on his trips. On his way to a Thanksgiving dinner one day, in an ox cart, the oxen ran away with family and all, into the brush; but the family got to their dinner all right at last. With these oxen they did all their teaming for 5 or 6 years. Hiram L. Dean died Sept. 7, 1876, aged 68 years. He was a member of the M. E. Church. In 1830 he married Wealthy M. Saunders, by whom he had 2 children,—Harriet M., now Mrs. David Stover, and Aaron H. Mrs. Dean was born in Litchfield, Conn., March 17, 1811. She is now residing at the old homestead with her son. Jan. 1, 1852, our subject married Delilah Seniff, by whom he has had 2 children,—Martha E. and Mary E. Mrs. Dean died in June, 1856, and in November, 1858, Mr. Dean married Nancy C. Dunniway. Their only son, David F., is deceased.

Daniel Dean was born Sept. 2, 1815, in Litchfield, Conn., and is the son of Amos Dean, an early settler of Pike Co., who came here in 1836 and settled in Griggsville tp. Daniel was educated in the free schools of Litchfield, and in the year 1837 he followed his parents to this county, where he engaged in farming and stock-raising until 1867, when he retired, and is now residing in Griggsville and is the present Mayor of the city. He was married in 1836 to Lydia Scranton, by whom he had 3 children,—Jane, Mary A. and Wm. H. The latter has charge of the farm. Mrs. Dean died Nov. 19, 1877. She had been a member of the M. E. Church for over 40 years.

Henry E. Dean, deceased, was born in Litchfield, Conn., Oct. 5, 1809, where at the age of 22 he united with the Congregational Church. He removed with his parents to this county in the fall of 1836, and settled on sec. 34, Griggsville tp. Here he united with the M. E. Church. He died March 15, 1877, leaving a wife and 7 children. He was married Jan. 13, 1842, to Mary L. Cohenour, daughter of John Cohenour, deceased. Mr. and Mrs. Dean had 8 children, of whom 7 are living,—Annie E., Harriet A. (now Mrs. John Hedges, of Christian Co., Ill.,) John A., Geo. H., Mary J., Oliver R. and Charles D. Mrs. Dean was born in Huntingdon Co., Pa., Jan. 9, 1821, where she was raised until 15 years of age, when she came with her parents to this county, settling in Griggsville tp.

Lucy M. Dickerson, a native of England, was born Sept. 19, 1842, and is the daughter of Wm. Hobson, who came to Illinois about the year 1847, and settled in Flint tp. He was a stone mason and was killed while the Griggsville high school building was under the process of erecton, by a runaway team. Our subject was married in 1858 to James D. Dickerson. They have 5 children,— Orson J., Wm. I., Ella M., Stephen L. and Laura M.

Theodore Dickerson was born in Northfield, Mass., Dec. 24, 1796, and there received his education. In 1811 he was apprenticed to Gustus Lyman, a blacksmith, of Deerfield, Mass., where he served 6 years. In 1818 he went to Salem, Mass., worked at his trade one year, went to Boston in 1819, and in 1820 began business in that place for himself. In 1831 he came to Pike county, and settled on sec. 1, Griggsville tp. In 1833 he removed to Griggsville, which then contained but three or four houses; kept boarding house in 1833, when 3 families lodged in the same room. In 1822 Mr. D. was married in Boston, to Mary T. Beckford, a native of Salem, Mass. She was born Jan. 1, 1800. They have had 7 children, 4 of whom are living,—Theodore F., Elijah, Emma A. and Horace P.

J. E. Dix & Son, boot and shoe dealers. This enterprising firm embarked in the boot and shoe trade in Griggsville in 1859, in which they are still engaged, enjoying a large trade.

John Dix, while residing in his native place, Townsend, Mass., studied the books and reports concerning the West, from which he learned that " all the worthless land belonged to Uncle Sam, while the very best land belonged to the soldiers." He therefore purchased a soldier's claim in 1837, and started West to occupy the land, coming by water around Florida and up the Mississippi, meeting with many exciting experiences. On arriving at the promised land in this Great West, he found it rough and bluffy, and not worth two cents an acre. Having been brought up in a city, Mr. Dix said he was very "green•" when he came to the West; and after settling on his land he "started up the creek to hunt for a rock to make a grindstone, to grind his ax, to chop some logs, to build a cabin, to make some shingles in, to sell to buy pork with." He relates many other awkward experiences he had in his introduction to Western pioneer life. We give one more. Hearing of a mill at some distance he loaded some corn upon his ox-cart, and blazing the trees as he went to mark the way, he at last arrived at the mill, when lo! it was only a saw-mill! Night overtook him on his way home and he was obliged to get out of the cart and feel for the blazed trees in order to find his way home. In 1818 Mr. Dix married Mary Wilson, a native of Lynn, Mass. They had 7 children, of whom but 2 are living, Ellen M. and John E.

Levi W. Dix, deceased, was a native of Malden, Mass., and was born Feb. 15, 1821; was the son of John Dix, now of Griggsville. He came to Illinois with his father in 1837, and was married in 1841 to Ruth E. Kiddle, a native of Yarmouth, Nova Scotia, and daughter of Arthur Kiddle, deceased. They had 5 children, 3 living,—Sarah F., Rollin M., and Margaret E. Mr. Dix engaged in merchandising with James Brakefield in Griggsville, and died April 30, 1874.

John W. Doan was born Nov. 12, 1834, in Clermont Co., O., and is a son of Wm. and Susanna Doan, deceased. The former was a native of Connecticut and the latter of Massachusetts. Our subject was educated in the common schools of Ohio, and was raised on a farm. He came to Pike county with his mother and family in 1859, where he has since resided. His father was the Hon. Wm. Doan, an ex-Member of Congress from Ohio, and also a surgeon of the 1st Reg't, 3d Brigade, and 8th Division in the Ohio State Militia. Our subject resides on sec. 15, Griggsville tp., and is engaged in farming and stock-raising.

Edward Doocy was born Oct. 24, 1851, in Griggsville, and is a graduate of Illinois College at Jacksonville, Ill., of the class of 1871. He read law about 3 years, was admitted to the bar in 1874, and is now practicing in Griggsville. He is now a successful practitioner, and bids fair to become one of Pike county's foremost attorneys. He is President of the Pike County Christian Temperance Union.

Abel Dunham, a native of Harrison Co., O., was born July 16, 1819, and is a son of Wm. and Mary (Chaney) Dunham, deceased; was raised on a farm and received a limited education in a subscription school. He was married Aug. 13, 1839, to Rachel Hardin, by whom he had 10 children, and of these 6 are living, Amanda, Isabelle, Mary E., Frances A., Joshua L. and Joseph M. His father was a soldier of the Revolution and was among the number who cut their shoes into pieces, broiling them in the fire and making coffee of them. Our subject came to Illinois in 1845, arriving at Griggsville Landing Nov. 26, 1845, at 8 P. M. He followed farming and stock-raising until within a few years ; is now retired and resides in the village of Maysville. Mr. and Mrs. Dunham are both members of the United Brethren Church.

Nathaniel Dunham is a native of Maryland; was a son of Lewis Dunham, who brought his family to this county in 1844, and was born Sept. 12, 1802 ; was a cooper by trade, but for the most part followed farming after moving West. He died Sept. 14, 1866. Our subject was born in Warren Co., O., Feb. 14, 1834, and came with his parents to this county in 1844, where he has since resided. He was married Oct. 26, 1854, to Mary A. Kiser, daughter of Daniel Kiser, deceased, who also settled in Pike county in 1844. Mr. and Mrs. Dunham have had 7 children, of whom 5 are living,—Daniel, Wm. H., Lewis O., Charles E. and Orpha J. Mrs. Dunham was born in Warren Co., Ind., May 3, 1838. Mr. D. resides on sec. 18, engaged in farming and stock-raising.

Wm. Dunham was born in Harrison Co., O., April 17, 1829, son of Lewis and Sarah A. D., who with the family emigrated to this county in 1844. Lewis died in Sept., 1865, and Sarah A. is now Mrs. Leander Filson, of Maysville, this Co. In 1850 Mr. D. went to California and followed mining and trading in stock ; on his return he was shipwrecked Nov. 15, 1853, off the coast of the island Anicapa, 350 miles from San Francisco, and was not rescued for 5 days. The crew and passengers also had another narrow escape from death by explosion of a boiler, which was discovered red hot. He returned to this county Jan. 12, 1854, and for a time followed breaking prairie. Aug. 9, 1855, he married Miss Nancy, daughter of Thos. Carnes, now of Schuyler Co., Ill. They have had 11 children, of whom 6 are living : Thomas, Elizabeth A., Julia B., William H., Nathaniel W. and Jason. Mrs. Dunham died May 28, 1877, and Mr. D. married the widow of Wm. Ervin, Oct. 4 following. Mrs. Dunham had 5 children by her first husband, of whom 4 are living,—George H., Sarah J., Martha D. S. and Harriet R. E. Mr. D. is a farmer on sec. 7. Mr. D. helped to construct the first railroad in Illinois, that from Naples to Jacksonville.

Lycurgus Eastman. Roger Eastman, an ancestor of our subject, was born in Wales in 1611, and came to Massachusetts in 1640, locating at Salisbury ; his wife's name was Sarah, who died Dec. 16, 1694, aged 83 ; had 10 children. Philip, the 3d child, moved to Haverhill, where his house was burned by the Indians and some of the family taken prisoners. Ebenezer, a son of his, was born Jan. 10, 1689, and died July 28, 1748 ; his 3d child, Capt. Joseph, was born June 10, 1715, married Abigail Mellen, who died in March, 1801 ; of their 6 children the 3d was Moses, who was born March 3, 1743, and who married Lucretia Tyler in Pembroke, N. H.; he died in 1796, and his eldest son, Charles, was born Dec. 11, 1774, and married Sally Bradley Nov. 29, 1798, at Concord, N. H.; she died Dec. 9, 1809, and he Sept. 26, 1847 ; but by his second marriage he had 6 children, of whom Lycurgus, the subject of this sketch, was the youngest ; he was born in Concord, N. H., July 4, 1807, where he resided until 17 years old, when he was apprenticed to learn the wheelwright's trade at Quincy, Mass.   In 1834 he emigrated West, locating on sec. 8, this tp., where he remained 33 years, and then sold his farm and moved to Griggs-ville, where he now lives.   In 1832 he married Elouisa B. Sim-mons, and their 4 children are :   Maria B., now Mrs. E. O. Hills, of Chicago ;   Susan B., wife of Peter Northrop, of Turner, Ill.; Harriet N., a missionary teacher in Toungoo, Burmah; and Charles L., of Whiting, Kansas.   Mrs. Eastman died Aug. 12, 1844, and Mr. E. again married, in May, 1845, this time Rebecca L. Hum-phris, by whom he had 7 children ; 4 are living, namely, Emeline H., now the wife of Dr. J. L. Love, of Whiting, Kan.; Lucy J., teacher of grade 4 in Griggsville Union School ; Ella E., now Mrs. John Q. Brown, a farmer in this tp.; and George E., of Whiting, Kan.   The names of the deceased were Elouisa R., Lucretia G. (Mrs. Henry C. Love) and Etta Adelaide.

Thomas P. Elledge is a son of Boone Elledge, and great-grandson of Neddie Boone, a brother of Daniel Boone, the hero of pioneer days of Kentucky.   The Elledges still keep up the name of Boone in the family.   Thomas P. was born in Harrison Co., Ind., April 27, 1825; was educated in the common schools of Indiana and Illinois, and came with his parents to this county in 1836, settling on sec. 6, Griggsville tp., where he still resides, and is engaged in farming and stock-raising.   He was married Feb. 11, 1847, to Margaret J. Simpson, daughter of the late Matthew Simpson, and they have had 6 children, Rebecca J., James A., Hattie A., Matthew B., Mary C. and an infant.   The three latter are deceased.

Uriah Elledge, son of Boone Elledge, deceased, was born in Clark Co., Ky., Nov. 22, 1802.   He came to Scott Co., Ill., in 1823; had to go to Upper Alton on Wood river, a distance of 125 miles, to mill.   In 1826 a Mr. John Pearson erected a horse-mill within about 2 miles of Mr. Elledge's house.   While in Scott county Mr. E. worked for Alex. Bell 18 months.   He was married March 26, 1825, to Catharine Scott, daughter of John Scott, for whom the county was named.   They had 8 children, of whom 5 are living,— Rebecca E., Mary M., John H., Emily J. and Uriah D.   Mr. and Mrs. Elledge removed to where Griggsville now stands, in 1825, but on account of sickness returned to Scott county, the following autumn.   In 1830 he came back to Griggsville tp., where he resides on sec. 13.   Mrs. Elledge died Jan. 9, 1855, and Dec. 12, 1858, Mr. Elledge married Mrs. Delia Ball, by whom he has had 4 children,— Anna B., Florence M., Charles H. and Frederick O.   In the year 1849 Mr. Elledge, accompanied by his son, Daniel B., went over-land to California, with the first emigrant train that went in search of gold.   Daniel died there, and Mr. Elledge returned in December, 1851.   He served in the Winnebago war, and 3 of his sons, William, John and Uriah, were in the late war.   William died while in the

L. Eastman

GRIGGSVILLE

service. His daughter Rebecca was the first female child born in Griggsville tp., which occurred Oct. 26, 1831.

Moses Elliott was born in Wheeling, Va., March 18, 1819, and is the son of John and Esther Elliott, deceased; was raised on a farm in Ross county, O.; received a common-school education, and was the eldest of 10 children. He was married Oct. 2, 1853, to Jane Perry, daughter of Joseph Perry, deceased, and now resides on sec. 35, Griggsville tp., engaged in farming and stock-raising. Mrs. Elliott was born in Ireland Aug. 24, 1815, and came with her parents to Canada in 1834, and to Pike county in 1849. Mr. and Mrs. Elliott have had 2 sons,—Geo. P. and Richard W.

E. G. Farrand was born in Bridgeport, Vt., Nov. 13, 1814; left his native State at the age of 18 and went to Michigan, where he remained until 1845, then removed to Morgan county, Ill., and in 1849 went to California, where he remained until 1852. He then returned to Illinois and settled in Griggsville. Since 1861 he has been successfully engaged in the lumber trade, and dealing in doors, sash, blinds, etc., carrying a stock of $12,000 to $15,000. In 1852 he married Elizabeth J. McWilliams, of Griggsville, and they have 4 boys,—James A., M. K., Harvey L. and Frederick H.

Joseph A. Ferguson, son of David and Margaret Ferguson, was born in Franklin Co., Pa., May 2, 1822; was raised a farmer; came to this county in 1847; bought a farm on sec. 16, Griggsville tp., where he still resides, and is engaged in farming and stock-raising. He was married Dec. 17, 1845, to Jennie N., daughter of James and Martha Stark, of Franklin Co., Pa. Mr. and Mrs. Ferguson have 5 children,—Wm. J., Margaret J., David A., Albert P. and Edward C. Wm. J. is married to Ella Hitch and resides in Griggsville; Margaret J. is married to Wm. S. Murray, and resides in Murrayville, Morgan Co., Ill.

David Fielding, deceased, was born in Miami Co., O., May 11, 1807. He was raised on a farm and educated in New Carlisle, O. He was married Dec. 1, 1835, to Mary (Moore) Smalley, widow of Jesse Smalley, and daughter of Samuel Moore. She was born in Dayton, O., Oct 18, 1805, when there were but 6 buildings in that place. She had 3 children by her first husband,—Ellen, Abigail, deceased, and Prudence R. Mr. and Mrs. Fielding had 6 children, —Charlotte, Mary, Jesse, Fannie, Clara and Albert. The two latter are deceased. Mr. Fielding was a worthy member of the Baptist Church for 31 years. He died March 9, 1867, loved and respected by all. His last words were, "I never thought it would be so easy when I came to die." He left messages for absent children, requesting them to meet him in Heaven. He partook of the Lord's Supper just before his death. Mr. Fielding had been married once before, to Charlotte Miller, by whom he had 4 children, —Maria, Jeremiah, Daniel and Henrietta.

Nathan French was born in Merrimac Co., N. H., in 1804, and was raised on a farm until 18 years old; then went to sea and remained 8 years. During this time he crossed the Atlantic 14 times and

32

visited the cities of Rochelle, St. Petersburg, Amsterdam, Stockholm and others.   He sailed around Cape Horn on his way to Japan during his whaling voyage, wherein 72 whales were caught, from which 2,500 barrels of oil were obtained.   In 1831 he removed to New Orleans, where he resided for three years and followed carpentering.   In 1835 he located at Alton, and came to Griggsville one year afterward.   At that time Griggsville contained 150 inhabitants. In 1840 Mr. F. was married to Harriet, daughter of the late David Hoyt, of pioneer history.   They had 4 children, of whom 3 are living,—Wm. H., Lizzie E. (now Mrs. Barnhart) her husband being of the firm of Barnhart Bros. & Co., Chicago) and Mary W., teacher in the high school at Decatur, Ill.   Wm. H. is agent for the Western Associated Press, Chicago.

Francis Frye was born in Detroit tp., Pike Co., in 1843, and is the son of the noted Jonathan Frye, the great pioneer miller of Big Blue river.   Our subject was married in Aug., 1867, to Mary L., daughter of J. M. Griffin, of Kansas.   They have 5 children, —Alta, Wm. E., Eva Lee, John W. and Lora E.   Mr. Frye is one of the proprietors of Frye's Mill in Griggsville.

Peleg Gardner was born in Hancock Co., Me., April 20, 1803, and is the son of Peleg Gardner, deceased.   He went to Boston, Mass., in 1824, where he remained for 11 years, working at the carpenter's trade.   He was married in Boston July 16, 1826, to Caroline Hutchinson, by whom he had 4 children, all of whom are dead.   He came to Griggsville in 1835, where he pursued his profession for several years.   Mrs. Gardner died in 1850 and the year following Mr. Gardner married Maria J. Fielding, who died May 14, 1853.   Sept. 4th of the same year he was married to Elizabeth C. Bazin.   After toiling many years in improving the town of Griggsville Mr. Gardner had a stroke of paralysis which has rendered him a permanent invalid.

Jacob Goldman is a native of Clark county, Ky., where he was born Oct. 15, 1816.   When but 13 years of age he came to Pike county with his parents, who settled on sec. 23, Griggsville tp., where he has resided since that time.   He has enjoyed many a deer and wolf hunt.   Once he saw 36 deer in one herd, and at one time killed 9 wolves.   He saw the first steam-boat that plied the Illinois river and knows all about grubbing and picking brush, rolling logs, etc.; and after working hard all day he would grind corn in a hand-mill until 9 or 10 o'clock at night, to procure bread for the following day.   They used harness and single and double trees of their own manufacture, which were made of hickory bark, corn " shucks " and poles.   Mr. Goldman helped to raise the first house in Pittsfield and hewed the first timber that was used for building purposes in Griggsville.   He has been chased by wolves when bringing home his game on old " Blaze," but his faithful dog " Tiger " was ever on the alert, and would invariably drive them away.   He has been married twice, the first time to Bethlehem Wade, and the second time to Otelia Jaritzs, who crossed the ocean in 1834.   Mr.

Goldman is the father of 12 children, of whom 8 are living,—Josiah, Newton B., Ellen H., Hardin H., Emma J., Melvin, Elizabeth and Victoria. He is engaged in farming on sec. 34, Griggsville tp.

Alfred Gordon, a pioneer of Pike county, was born in Hillsboro Co., N. H., Nov. 4, 1794; was raised on a farm and educated in the common schools. He came to this county in 1836 and settled in Griggsville tp. In 1843 he purchased a farm on sec. 16 of this tp., where he still resides. He was married in March, 1824, to Mary D. Jones, by whom he had 5 children,—Alfred A., Nathaniel H., Moses, Mary A. and Geo. Washington, all of whom are dead except George, who resides with his father and attends to the farm. In 1857 George was married to Ellen Smith, daughter of John Smith, deceased, an early settler of Pike county. They have had 4 children, 3 of whom are living,—Charley, Willie and Nellie. The two latter are twins. Mrs. Alfred Gordon died April 24, 1867. Our subject was a soldier in the war of 1812, under Gen. Dearborn, and endured unusual hardships and privations. He has been a member of the Baptist Church for over 47 years and has held many offices of trust. In N. H. he was Overseer of the Poor and was a member of the State Legislature of that State for 4 successive terms. He has been Justice of the Peace and Treasurer of the school fund in Pike Co.; is also a surveyor, which business he has pursued more or less. In the year 1842 he taught school in Griggsville.

Daniel B. Griffin was born in Pike Co., Oct. 17, 1839, and is the son of Lorenzo D. Griffin, deceased. He was married in 1860 to Mary E. Baker, and they had one child. Mrs. Griffin and child both died in 1862, of the small-pox, as also did Mr. G.'s father. In 1864 he again married, this time Sarah A. Fowler, and they had 6 children, of whom 3 are living,—Lizzie, Riley and Noley. Mr. Griffin is an engineer by profession, but is now engaged in packing and shipping flour with McMahan & Co.

M. Hainsfurther, merchant, Griggsville, is a native of Germany; came to America in 1853 and located in Winchester, Scott Co., Ill., and engaged in the dry goods business; also clothing, boots and shoes. He located in Griggsville in 1860, where he followed the same business. He carries a stock of about $18,000, and has a large trade. He commenced business by peddling over the country, carrying his goods on his back. He was married in 1863 to Rebecca Cohn, and they have had 6 children, 5 of whom are living,— Millie, Nathan, Bessie, Harry and Lusettie.

Abel Harrington was born in Albany county, N. Y., Feb. 20, 1824, and is a son of the late Judge Harrington, so well known in the pioneer history of this county. Our subject came to this county with his parents in 1835, where he has since resided. He was married Feb. 7, 1847, to Eliza J. Sheeley, daughter of Abel and Mary A. Sheeley, well known in the history of this and Morgan counties. She was born in Naples, Scott Co., in 1825. Mr. H.'s mother-in-law, Mrs. Mary A. (Kenney) Sheeley, was born in Lancaster, Pa.,

May 16, 1801; she came to what is now Scott county in 1821, and to this county in 1829. She was married in Feb., 1819, to John Hollins. They had two children. Mr. Hollins died in 1822, and in 1824 his widow married Abel Shelley. They had 9 children, 4 of whom are living. Mr. Harrington resides on sec. 2; P. O., Griggsville.

Charles Harrington, deceased. Judge Charles Harrington was born in that part of Grafton, Mass., known as New England village, in 1795; in 1811 he went to Rodman, N. Y., where he remained three years, engaging in the woolen business; his factory, with two others, was burned, it is supposed, by a jealous Canadian; he then taught school for a time and located in Guilderland, N. Y., where he formed a partnership with Charles Mason in the manufacture of woolen goods; he remained there until 1835, when he came to Griggsville and continued his residence in Pike county until his death, which occurred Aug. 15, 1873. He was a worthy member of the Baptist Church for 47 years, and an ordained minister for 29 years. He was called to the pastoral charge of the Perry Baptist Church, where he remained for several years. Upon the organization of the Quincy Baptist Association in 1843, he was elected Moderator, and held the position for 11 years. In 1850 he was elected County Judge for Pike county. He was ever a bold, fearless champion of the cause of temperance, truth and morality. His efforts in the cause of temperance when a young man, as well as his activity and zeal in religious meetings after he made a profession of religion, led the Church in Schenectady, of which he was first a member, to see his aptness to teach, and they granted him license to preach. He was a very forcible, convincing speaker, but never depended upon preaching for a support. He supplied many weak and destitute churches at different times.

Charles W. Harrington was born in Griggsville tp. Dec. 14, 1852, and is the son of the late Samuel Harrington, an early pioneer. He was raised on a farm and educated in the common schools; was married in Aug., 1875, to Anna, daughter of Christian Hoss, of Griggsville tp. They have had 3 children.—Mattie, Ellis and Freddie. Mr. H. is engaged in farming and owns 80 acres of valuable land on secs. 11 and 12, Griggsville tp. In 1874 he took a tour through Kansas and Missouri, and returned the same year.

Geo. P. Harrington, son of Judge Harrington, was born in Griggsville tp., sec. 1., on the farm where he now resides, July 17, 1839. Judge Harrington, a native of Grafton, Mass., was born Nov. 17, 1795; was married Jan. 9, 1823, to Hannah Scranton, by whom he had 6 children,—Abel, Samuel, Daniel, James, Abbie and George P., who is the youngest. Mrs. Harrington was born in Stephentown, Rensellaer Co., N. Y., Oct., 1801, and died Oct. 25, 1878. Our subject was married Jan. 26, 1867, to Louisa, daughter of Ebenezer C. Maddux, deceased. They had 6 children, of whom 4 are living,—Bertha, Jennie, Hannah and Louisa. Mrs. Harrington died Dec. 18, 1879, loved and respected by all. She was born in Hamilton Co., O., June 20, 1848. In 1868 the family removed to Kansas, where Mrs. H. was attacked with chills, from which she never recovered. The following year they returned to Pike county. The *Independent Press*, of Griggsville, contained the following obituary notice Dec. 25, 1879:

"Loving hearts are doomed to sorrow,
Trusting souls to pine and die;
Beauteous flowers bloom and perish
'Neath the hot and burning sky.

"Then, if all in life is fleeting,
If on earth no joy is given,
Let us seek for rest unchanging,
In the Christian's home in heaven."

Samuel M. Harrington was born in Albany Co., N. Y., April 19, 1827, and is a son of the late Judge Harrington. He came to this county with his parents in 1835. He was married in 1848 to Charity Elledge, daughter of William and Tabitha Elledge; they have had 4 children, of whom 3 are living,—Sarah A., Charles W. and Ada Belle. Mr. H. spent one year in Colorado during the gold excitement. His grandfather, Samuel Harrington, was born in Grafton, Mass., Aug. 13, 1769, and his grandmother was Abigail Putnam, a relative of Gen. Israel Putnam, renowned in the war of the Revolution. Mr. H. was a member of the U. B. Church. He died June 24, 1875. If we should attempt to enumerate his many virtues we should fill pages of history.

Perry Harshman was born in Preble Co., O., Oct. 13, 1842, and is the son of Peter Harshman, now of Griggsville tp. He came with his parents to this county in 1852, where he has since resided. He now lives near Griggsville, and is engaged in general farming and owns about 320 acres of land.

Peter Harshman, son of Peter Harshman, sr., deceased, was born in Preble Co., O., in 1813. He was raised on a farm and received a limited education in a subscription school. He was married in 1836 to Susannah Sherer, daughter of Daniel and Catharine Sherer, deceased, and a sister of Dr. D. J. Sherer, of Grandview, Edgar Co., Ill. Mr. and Mrs. Harshman have had 10 children, of whom 5 are living,—Noah L., Perry, Eli, Rachel Ann and Daniel. They removed to this county in 1852 and settled in Pittsfield tp., where they resided until the spring of 1869, when they removed to Griggsville tp. and settled on sec. 11. Mr. H. and his son Noah are now traveling in Washington Territory and the West. He has always been engaged in farming. Mrs. Harshman's father was in the war of 1812, and was one of the soldiers of Hull's army that surrendered at the siege of Detroit.

Dr. L. J. Harvey was born in Warner, N. H., Oct. 6, 1851; had an academical education; came to Griggsville in 1872 and read medicine under the late Dr. Wilson; attended Bellevue Hospital

Medical College, of New York city, and also the St. Louis Medical College, where he graduated in 1875; after spending a few months in the city hospital there he located in Griggsville, where he has a large practice. In May, 1876, he married Bella Kenney, daughter of Charles Kenney, of Griggsville, and they have one little boy, Ira K.

Frank Hatch was born in Hillsboro Co., N. H., March 21, 1825, and is a son of Reuben Hatch (deceased), who was also a native of New Hampshire. He was reared and educated for the most part, in Griggsville, having come to this place with his parents in 1836. He was married Nov. 30, 1852, to Rebecca Bennett, daughter of Simeon Bennett (deceased). They have 3 children,—Charles P., Celia J. and Marshall P. Mr. Hatch has seen the rough places made smooth, and the vacant prairies of Pike county made into valuable farms. He resides on sec. 16, Griggsville tp., where he is engaged in farming and stock-raising, making the latter a specialty.

Isaac A. Hatch, banker, was born in Hillsboro, N. H., Sept. 13, 1812; came to Griggsville in 1835, where he still resides; has followed farming, milling, collecting revenue, merchandising and banking in this county; is now in the last named business. October, 1840, he married Lydia B., sister of Moses E. Baxter, of Griggsville. Their 2 children are Abbie A. and John Franklin.

Mason Hatch was born in this township April 26, 1846, son of Sylvanus Hatch, deceased; the latter was born in Hillsboro, N. H., in 1816; was a farmer by occupation, and died March 17, 1868. Mason was educated in the State University at Bloomington, Ill., and has taught school most of the time for 8 years, but is now farming on the old home place, sec. 9.

Jacob Hendricks was born in Harrison Co., O., March 22, 1831, and is a son of Andrew Hendricks, of Adams Co., Ill. He was raised on a farm, and received a common-school education; was married Aug. 28, 1855, to Nancy M. Robison, daughter of William Robison, deceased, who brought his family to this county in 1847. Mr. and Mrs. Hendricks have had 10 children, of whom 7 are living,—Leah J., William R., Mary E., Andrew G., Laura O., Estella E., and Charles R. Mr. Hendricks is a farmer, but is now engaged in the grain and stock business at Maysville.

George D. Hensell was born in Wheeling, W. Va., March 23, 1854, son of Robert Hensell, now of Griggsville; when our subject was one year old the family emigrated to Griggsville, where he was educated. For 3 years he has been teaching, and is now teaching his second term in Middle Flint district, Flint tp., where the growing prosperity of his school sufficiently attests his qualifications. June 12, 1878, he married Nellie Cover, daughter of Daniel Cover, sr., of Griggsville.

John W. Hensell was born in Portland, Jefferson Co., O., Aug. 8, 1848, son of Robert L., of Griggsville; he has lived on a farm since 10 years old, and now resides on sec. 26, Griggsville tp.; the emigration of his people to this county was in 1855. He was married Oct. 28, 1869, to Mary J. Warton, daughter of Wm. Warton, deceased, so well known in the early settlement of Pike county; and they have 4 children,—Fred, Della M., George O. and Estella.

Dr. James Montgomery Higgins, youngest son of John and Elizabeth Higgins, was born in Montgomery Co., Md., July 30, 1808; educated chiefly in Rockville, Md.; studied medicine in Washington, D. C.; graduated in the medical department of Columbia College in that city March 11, 1829, and has followed the practice of his profession ever since,—over half a century now. Jan. 25, 1831, he married Margaret Davis in Bourbon Co., Ky., niece of Gov. Edward Tiffin, first Governor of Ohio; in the following spring he emigrated to Jacksonville, Ill., and in Nov., 1834, he removed with his wife and infant child to Griggsville, this county, where physicians were scarcer than in Jacksonville; in 1846 he was elected Representative to the State Legislature; in 1848 he was elected Medical Superintendent of the Illinois State Hospital for the Insane at Jacksonville, where he superintended the building of the original hospital, at a cost surprisingly low, as attested by a Legislative commission; he opened the institution in the fall of 1851, and conducted it with great acceptability until the summer of 1854, when he returned to Griggsville, where he has practiced ever since except in 1862–3, when he was Surgeon of the 114th Reg. Ill. Vol.

Besides an infant son that died in Jacksonville in 1832, the Doctor and his wife have had 6 children, as follows: Isaac Newton, James M., Edward Tiffin, Mary E., Drusilla C. and Lizzie M.,—all living except the eldest daughter, Mrs. Mary E. Jones. Isaac N. studied and graduated in medicine, but has followed journalism up to the present time. In company with his brother James M., he published the *Pike County Union*, the first newspaper in Griggsville, and which was afterward transferred to Pittsfield; subsequently he became editor-in-chief of the *Illinois State Register* at Springfield, and after several years he became managing editor of the Chicago *Republican*, and for 10 years past has occupied that relation to the San Francisco *Morning Call*, a daily paper of 45,000 circulation. James M., jr., a practical printer, has been connected with the *Illinois State Register* in various relations, a part of the time one of its editors. Edward T. holds an important position in the W. U. Telegraph office at Chicago. Mary E. married J. Howard Jones in 1861, and died Aug. 9, 1874, in Chicago, leaving 2 sons and an infant daughter. Drusilla C. became the second wife of Mr. Jones on the Christmas of 1878, and they reside in Chicago. Lizzie M. is a teacher in the public schools of Griggsville.

Edwin Hitch, deceased, was born Sept. 25, 1843, in Adams county, Ill.; was educated in the schools of Perry, this county, and was raised on a farm. He engaged in buying and shipping stock for several years; was married Jan. 22, 1867, to Mary Simpkin, daughter of Thomas Simpkin, deceased. They had 4 boys—Edwin L., Thomas S., Rufus and Roy M. Mr. Hitch was a worthy citizen and highly esteemed. He died Jan. 29, 1877, in Griggsville.

Prof. R. M. Hitch is Principal of the High School at Griggsville. This department is in excellent running order; everything moves on with the system and regularity of clock-work, and the best of order prevails. Save one or two exceptions, the best series of text books is used. Miss Abbie Hatch, Assistant, Miss L. E. Campbell, Teacher of Grammar School.

Capt. B. B. Hopkins was born in London, England, Jan. 2, 1838, and is a son of Robert Hopkins, deceased; came to America when but 14 years old, arriving at Griggsville Landing, Dec. 9, 1852; spent a year crossing and re-crossing the Western plains as assistant wagon-master in the service of the Government; enlisted Sept. 5, 1861, as a private in the late war in Co. G, 5th Ill. Cav., under Capt. John A. Harvey, now of St. Louis, and brother of ex-Governor Harvey, of Kansas. Mr. Hopkins was promoted to the Captaincy of his Company in December, 1862; he resigned his commission in the army in July, 1864, on account of disability. He has been engaged in raising short-horned thorough-bred cattle and Cotswold sheep since 1865. He was married Nov. 15, 1864, to Ann, second daughter of Thomas Simpkin, deceased, known as the "land king" of Pike county. Mr. and Mrs. Hopkins have 5 children.

John Houston was born in 1817, in Hillsboro, N. H., and is the son of John Houston, deceased. He came to Illinois in 1837, and settled in Griggsville tp.: his brother William preceded him 2 years. Mr. Houston returned to N. H. in 1840, and remained there until 1843, when he returned to Illinois. In 1847 he again went to N. H., and was married to Mary Lane. They had 8 children, of whom 4 are living—Lavica, Samuel, Frederick and Alice. Mr. H. has been a successful brick and stone mason, and is also an excellent plasterer, but does not follow this as a business. In 1858, he was elected Sheriff of Pike county, in which capacity he served for 2 years.

Edward S. Hoyt; P. O., Griggsville; was born in this town Feb. 22, 1846; received a common-school education in Griggsville, and is also a graduate of the Jones Commercial College, of St. Louis, Mo. He followed boating on the Illinois river for seven years, and now has charge of the warehouse at Griggsville Landing. In the winter season he engages with his father in the packing of pork in Griggsville. He was married in November, 1869, to Emily, daughter of the popular Capt. Samuel Rider, of this county. They have 3 children—Herbert, Clara and Mary A.

Arnold Hughes, son of Elliott and Jane S. Hughes, was born in Danville, Montgomery Co., Mo. He is a grandson of Col. Thos. Hughes, of Paris, Ky.; his mother was the eldest daughter of John R. McConnell, of Lexington, Ky. In 1838 his parents removed to Montgomery county, Mo., within a few miles of where Daniel

GRIGGSVILLE T.P.

Boone lived and died. Our subject served an apprenticeship at the printer's trade in Milwaukee, Wis., and from there went on a "tour," working at St. Paul, Omaha, St. Joe, Kansas City, St. Louis, Jackson, etc. In Shelby county, Ill., he edited one of the best country papers in the State. He is editor of the "*Independent Press,*" published weekly at Griggsville, by Hughes & Nelson. These enterprising young men wield an influence that will make their paper a success. Mr. Hughes was married Sept. 26, 1878, to Miss E. D. Hudson.

Henry L. Hurt was born in Madison Co., Va., Aug. 21, 1825. His ancestry settled in King and Queen Co., Va., about two centuries ago. Mr. H. came to Pike county in the fall of 1856, and settled in Griggsville, where he now resides, S. E. corner of Cory and Washington sts. He is a miller by occupation, but he retired from that business some years ago. In politics he has always been independent, but since the formation of the Republican party he has generally voted with that party. In religion he is a Baptist, and has advocated the cause of temperance from boyhood, claiming to have had strictly temperance parents that set an example he has tried to follow. His first marriage was in Culpepper Co., Va., Jan. 5, 1854, with Elmira Smith, who died of consumption Jan. 9, 1870. She was a member of the Baptist Church. His second marriage was in Griggsville, Feb. 15, 1871, with Elizabeth, daughter of the late John C. Shaw, who came to Pike county when there were only about 3 houses between Griggsville and the Illinois river. Mr. and Mrs. Hurt have no children, but have adopted 2 nieces, Amy and Emma Copson, whom they are trying to educate. Mrs. H. is a member of the Baptist Church. John C. Shaw was born in Attleboro, near Nun Eaton, Warwickshire, England, March 12, 1796. His father, Josiah Shaw, acquired considerable wealth and was for many years engaged in ribbon manufacture. His mother's maiden name was Ann Clark. In 1819 he was married to Elizabeth Towe, and after carrying on the brick-making and building business for a number of years in his native place, he emigrated to America in 1829, and settled in Washington Co., N. Y., following farming. After remaining there about 3 years he removed to Illinois, and settled on sec. 13, Griggsville tp., Sept., 1833, where he resided until his death. In 1840 he built a flouring-mill, also a saw-mill, on Flint creek. A few years later he removed the mills to Griggsville Landing, on the Illinois river. After a few years he again commenced farming, which he followed until the infirmities of age caused him to retire from active life. He and his wife both united with the Baptist Church in Griggsville. They raised 9 children, 3 sons and 6 daughters.

Samuel Hutchinson, inventor and manufacturer of Hutchinson's adjustable harrow, was born in Boston, Mass., in 1813; came to Pike Co. in 1834, landing here with less than $5.00 in his pocket. He is a mechanic, and has helped to erect a great many houses in Griggsville. He was married in 1838 to Laura Bachelor, and they had 5 children, 3 of whom are living. He was again married in 1855, this time to Jane A. Edwards. He was married a third time to Sarah E. Jones, and they had 4 children, 2 of whom are living.

A. J. Ives was born in Canada, July 19, 1850; came to Illinois in 1869; was educated in the Wesleyan University at Bloomington; began teaching in 1873. His father was a farmer. Mr. Ives came to Pike Co. in 1876; was married to Rosella Kenedy, July 19, 1873. They have one child, Elmer K.

David Jenkins, a native of Clermont Co., O., was born Dec. 15, 1841; was educated in the common schools of Ohio, and came to Illinois with his parents in 1855, remaining in Altona, Knox Co., until the spring of 1857, when they removed to Pike Co., where they still reside. He was married July 26, 1872, to Ede A. Elder, daughter of William and Phœbe Elder, deceased. They have had 1 little girl, Anna. Mr. Jenkins is engaged in farming, and resides on sec. 25, Griggsville township. He served in Co. I, 33d Reg't. Ill. Vol., in the Rebellion for 4 years and 3 months, participating in several battles. His father, Joseph W. Jenkins, was born in Gloucester Co., N. J., March 9, 1800, and was raised on a farm; was brought to Clermont Co., O., by his parents in 1806; was married in 1841 to Susannah Fisher, by whom he had 3 children,— Catharine, Mary A. and David. He is a saddler and harness-maker by trade, at which he has worked most of the time during his life. Mr. and Mrs. Jenkins now reside with their son David.

Nathan W. Jones, one of the founders of Griggsville, was born in Worcester Co., Mass., April 27, 1803; emigrated in 1830 to Jacksonville, Ill., where he served as Steward of the Illinois College for one year; in the winter of 1831 he returned East, by way of New Orleans and New York, on account of high water, and in the spring he brought his family to Jacksonville; and in 1833 he came to this point, where he bought a piece of land and helped to lay out the town of Griggsville, and suggested the name of the town. He built the first frame house in Griggsville, which still stands. At first he was a farmer for a number of years, and since has followed merchandising, etc. In company with Joshua R. Stanford he kept the first store in Griggsville, taking in trade the first year (1833) 9 bear-skins, from bears killed within 10 miles of town. He owned the warehouses at Griggsville Landing for a number of years, and was an extensive grain merchant, being the first who paid cash for grain in this township. He and Mr. Winn cut the first harvest in this township without liquor. Mr. Jones' ancestry are of New England stock, and of English origin. They are referred to in Bancroft's History of the United States. In 1823 Mr. Jones married Hannah P. Glazier, and their 8 children are: Sarah, now widow of James H. Chase, Buffalo, N. Y.; George W., Clerk of Appellate Court at Springfield, and formerly Circuit Clerk of Pike Co.; John W., deceased; William H., who died in California in 1851, in his 20th year; John H., Confidential Clerk of the Grain Inspector of Chicago, formerly Assistant

Treasurer of Illinois; Lucy T. and Henrietta H., deceased; and Charles W., bookkeeper in Griggsville. Mr. Jones' portrait is given in this volume.

S. M. Kennedy was born in Clermont Co., O., Sept. 12, 1845; moved to Pike county in 1858, where he has since resided; is chief engineer in the Pike Mills, of Griggsville. He was married in 1870 to Harriet Baldwin, by whom he has had 3 children,—Willy, Nellie and Mervyn Rhea. He served 4 months in Co. H, 137th I. V. I., in the late war, and assisted in opposing Forest's raid on Memphis.

Kenney & Clark, the largest firm in Griggsville, established themselves in general merchandising in 1864, succeeding Mr. Charles Kenney. They carry a general stock of dry goods, clothing, boots and shoes, groceries, queensware, hats and caps, carpets, etc., etc., amounting to a stock of over $20,000. Mr. Clark's father, John Clark, was an early settler in Ogle Co., Ill., having located there about the year 1830, and came to this county in 1857, where he died in 1872. He was a farmer on sec. 15, Griggsville tp.

W. E. Kneeland is a native of Griggsville, and was educated in the union schools of this place. He engaged in the mercantile business in March, 1879, and has a general stock of dry goods, groceries, boots and shoes. His trade is increasing, and he carries a stock of $3,500.

John Lasbury was born in Kensington, near London, Eng., Nov. 11, 1830, and was educated in the same place. He learned the butcher's trade when quite young, and came to America in 1852 in a sail-ship : was 10 weeks coming from Liverpool to New Orleans, and 3 weeks from New Orleans to St. Louis. From St. Louis he walked to Griggsville in a deep snow, a distance of about 110 miles; this he accomplished in 3 days' time. He worked for the late Robert Allen, of Griggsville, for about 2 years ; was the first butcher in Griggsville: supplied Griggsville and Pittsfield both with meat from one beef, and sometimes would have some left, which he would take to Perry. He was married March 20, 1858, to Sarah Simpkin, daughter of Thos. Simpkin, deceased. Mr. and Mrs. Lasbury have 5 children,—Mary, Ann, Elizabeth, John and Vincent. Mr. L. resides on sec. 28, Griggsville tp., and is engaged in farming and stock-raising. He has some fine cattle, and he brought the first long-wooled sheep to this part of the country. These sheep were brought from Canada.

James B. Lewis is a native of Kentucky, and was born Nov. 10, 1835. His parents brought him to Woodford Co., Ill., in 1837, and to Adams Co. in 1842. He was educated in Quincy, and at the age of 15 was apprenticed to J. C. Bernard, a harness-maker of that place, with whom he remained 5½ years. He located in Griggsville in 1865, and remained here 17 months, and then removed to Alton, where he resided in 1858, when he returned to Griggsville. He was married in Alton, Ill., June 18, 1862, to C. F. Ferguson, and they have 3 children,—Mary H., Louise E. and Maud W.

Robert M. Love was born in Trenton, N. J., June 14, 1818, and is a son of Samuel and Lydia (Morgan) Love. The former is deceased, the latter resides in Pittsfield, and is 83 years old. Mr. Love has cut, split and hauled wood 7 miles for 6 " bits " a cord, and paid $1.50 a yard for Kentucky jeans to make himself a pair of pants. He was married Oct. 3, 1841, to Mary A., daughter of Charles Troy, deceased. She was born Jan. 5, 1824, in Morgan Co., Ill. The Troy family were burned out by the Indians and they suffered untold privations. Mr. and Mrs. Love had 10 children,— Henry C., deceased, Charles E., Lydia J., Jerome G., Georgia Ann, Eleanor, Julia, John E., Sarah E. and Robert F. Mr. Love first settled in Perry tp., but for 30 years has resided on sec. 17, Griggsville tp., where he is engaged in farming and stock-raising, and he owns 160 acres of land, 120 of which is well improved. He is a member of the M. E. Church, as also are Mrs. Love and 4 daughters.

Wm. E. Ludlow was born in Griggsville in 1858, and is the son of Robert McK. Ludlow, deceased. Mr. L. is a partner with Mr. Frye in Frye's flouring-mill. He was educated in the schools of Griggsville. His father was accidentally shot and killed while hunting in Dec., 1859.

Henry Lynde, Esq., was born in West Brookfield, Mass., Nov. 11, 1815; was educated in Munson Academy, Hampden Co., Mass.; came to Alton, Ill., Dec. 1, 1836, and the following spring engaged in the mercantile business in Griggsville, which he continued for 4 years, when he engaged in farming, which occupation he followed for 25 years within 2 miles of East Griggsville. In 1868 he rented his farm and retired to Griggsville, where he still resides, and is engaged in insurance and real estate business. He has filled the office of Justice of the Peace since 1873, and is also a Notary Public; has been Township Trustee of Schools for 21 consecutive years and has filled other offices of trust. He was married Sept. 13, 1838, to Ann C. Shaw, daughter of John C. Shaw, deceased. They had 10 children, of whom 6 are living,—Mary A. (now Mrs. Samuel Thackwray), Sarah J. (now Mrs. H. T. Frits), Burton C., H. Lovell (Mrs. Samuel L. Fiester); the two latter reside at Whiting, Kansas; Nellie W. (now Mrs. T. A. Hill, of Griggsville), and Minnie L. Their eldest son was killed during the Rebellion; their eldest daughter, Elizabeth, was married in Sept, 1863, to Dr. Wm. H. D. Noyes, and died in July, 1873, while on a visit to her friends in Griggsville. Mr. and Mrs. Lynde are members of the Baptist Church, and he has been Vice President of the S. S. County Convention for several years.

Wm. Marden, son of Frank Marden, of Chambersburg, was born in Perry, Pike Co., Nov. 19, 1855; was educated here and at the age of 21 engaged in the livery business in Perry, and is still proprietor of the Perry Livery Stable; is also proprietor of the Griggsville Livery Stable, doing a successful business in both places. His stock in Griggsville is about $2,300, and in Perry $2,000. He was married Oct. 17, 1878, to Venie, daughter of John E. Morton, of Perry.

Robert Marshall was born in Cadiz, Harrison Co., O., May 1, 1848, and is the son of Wm. Marshall, of Griggsville, who came here in 1851, where he still resides, and is a blacksmith. He is a first-class mechanic, and has built up a large trade. Mr. Marshall is the father of 9 children, of which our subject is the eldest. His son, Wm. Marshall, jr., is also a mechanic, and is working in the Griggsville Plow Manufactory.

Wm. Marshall was born near Greenburg, Westmoreland Co., Pa., March 1, 1822; is the father of 8 children, 4 of whom are now living. His eldest son, Robert, resides with his father; his second son, William, follows blacksmithing and is a promising young man. Mr. Marshall came to Pike county in the spring of 1851 and settled in Griggsville, where he has ever since carried on blacksmithing successfully.

Thomas Manton, a native of Lincolnshire, England, was born April 16, 1844, and is a son of James Manton, near Pittsfield, who brought his family to America in 1854, locating in Detroit tp., where he remained until 1857, and then came to Griggsville tp. Mr. Manton is at present a bachelor and resides on sec. 5, Griggsville tp., where he is engaged in farming and stock-raising. His sisters, Mary and Lizzie, preside over his house.

Wm. McBratney was born in Ireland in 1834, and is the son of John McBratney, deceased; was brought to America by his parents in 1836; remained in Pennsylvania one year; came to Adams Co., Ill., where John McBratney resided until his death, which occurred in 1871. Old Mrs. McBratney still resides in Adams Co., with her daughter, and is 87 years old. Our subject came to Griggsville in 1856, where he engaged in blacksmithing, which he still carries on. He worked 4 years as a journeyman after arriving in this town. He was married Oct. 5, 1865, to Lucinda McDonald, and they have 4 children,—Charles F., Frank, Jennie E. and Wm. Emmet. The latter was named for the noted Emmet, the first Representative in the British Parliament from Ireland, after the rebellion in that country. Mr. McBratney also manufactures plows and wagons, and deals in agricultural implements.

John McClain was born in Adair Co., Ky., in 1807; was educated there in a subscription school; came to Pike Co. in 1830 and settled in Griggsville tp. At that time there was not a fence between his farm and Atlas. In 1839 he married Abigail Shores. They had 6 children, of whom 3 are living,—Thomas S., Ann Eliza and Angeline, all married. He has been a successful farmer all his life, until within the past 9 years, during which time he has resided in Griggsville.

Levi W. McMahan was born in Marion Co., Ind., near Indianapolis, March 31, 1841; parents were Wm. and Maria (Thomas) McMahan. The former, a native of Clermont Co., O., was a farmer in Indiana, and came to Illinois in 1856 with his family, Levi W.

being then 14 years of age; has ever since been in the cabinet business in Griggsville; his wife was a native of Maine. At the age of 19 Levi opened a confectionery establishment in Griggsville for about one year, then followed farming 4 years, and then commenced general mercantile business at Griggsville; in 2 years he returned to farming again, and dealing in grain and stock; he now carries on milling. Mr. McMahan is one of the most active, enterprising and public-spirited men of the county, and has done much toward the improvement of the town where he lives. The business enterprise—the Pike Flouring Mills—of which he is at the head, is one of the most extensive in the county. April 28, 1861, he married Hattie, daughter of Cephas and Lucy Simmons; of their 3 children, Nellie and Alice are living. Mrs. McM. died May 6, 1876.

The "Pike Mills," owned by Mr. McM and D. P. Baldwin, were built on modern principles, with the new process for grinding flour; also an elevator with a storage capacity of 20,000 bushels of grain. The mill is 33 by 80 feet, three stories and basement, the eaves 36 feet from the ground, and the whole structure, built of brick, cost over $20,000. The mill and cooper-shop furnish a home market for 200,000 bushels of grain per annum. It has 4 run of stone, having a capacity of grinding 200 barrels of flour a day. The mill was planned by Mr. McMahan, and soon after work commenced on the building he took for partners two brothers, D. P. and George Baldwin, the former being his present partner. They give employment the year round to about 20 men on an average, at times to nearly double that number, including the cooper shop. The mill stands near the railroad track, is a very fine structure, and an ornament to the city. It is calculated to give the travelers who pass through a good impression of the enterprise and energy of the town of Griggsville. We give Mr. McMahan's portrait in this book.

Hon. James Mc Williams. The first of this gentleman's ancestry in America were Alexander McWilliams and wife, Highland Scotch, who emigrated to America in 1776. On board the vessel for this country Alexander McWilliams, the father of the subject of this sketch, was born. On arriving in America they settled at Brownsville, Pa.; they afterward moved to Ohio, Belmont county, where he died in 1824, aged 84 years. He and his wife were both members of the Union Presbyterian Church. Alex. McWilliams, jr., received his early education at Brownsville, where at the age of 22 he married Miss Jane Paxton, daughter of John Paxton, of Protestant Irish descent. In this family were born 3 children, the youngest of whom is James, the subject of this sketch. Mrs. McW. died about 1803. Her husband married a second wife a short time afterward, by whom he had 11 children. He died at the age of 65, at his residence in Union county, O. He always followed farming as an occupation.

James received the most of his education in the schools of Ohio, and until 22 his time was largely employed on his father's farm. He then (1824) married, in Belmont county, Miss Margaret, daughter of Alexander Latimer, formerly of Scotland. They had a family of 8 children, only one of whom is living. Mr. McW. first came to Illinois in the fall of 1834, landing at Naples, where he spent the winter. The spring following he bought 320 acres of land on sec. 20, Griggsville tp., on which he immediately settled with his family. After having lived here about four years his wife died (Dec. 28, 1838). In June, 1839, he married Miss Lucretia Prescott, a native of Groton, Mass.

Since first settling in this county Mr. McW. has taken an active and prominent part in its affairs, socially, financially and politically. As early as 1838 he was elected on the Democratic ticket a Representative in the State Legislature, where he served a term of two years, the first session being held at Vandalia, and the second at Springfield. Since then he has been County Commissioner, Supervisor of Griggsville Township, etc., etc., and has been continually in office of some kind. Up to 1848 he followed farming; he then engaged in the lumber trade at Griggsville, which he conducted successfully until 4 or 5 years ago. He was one of the original stockholders and organizers of the Griggsville National Bank, which was put in motion principally through his exertions. The bank opened for business Aug. 1, 1873, with a capital of $50,000, and has done a profitable business since that date. On its first organization Mr. McW. was elected its president, and he has acted in that capacity up to the present time. It was probably through his exertions more than any other man, that Griggsville enjoys its present railroad facilities, he having taken an active and prominent part in securing the road. Credit is also due him for the fact that the town is free from railroad debt, in the shape of bonds, he having taken a foremost part in the financial plans for liquidating the debt.

During the late war Mr. McWilliams was a firm supporter of President Lincoln's administration, using his means and exerting his influence at all times to encourage a bold and energetic prosecution of the war. His son, Capt. John McWilliams, served for 90 days in the 8th Ill. Inf., and immediately after returning home from service in that regiment he re-enlisted and participated in many an engagement during Gen. Sherman's campaign on his famous march to the sea.

Mr. McWilliams has a family of four children living, all of whom are married. He is now living at Griggsville, and is 78 years of age, enjoying good health, prepared to live in comfort. He is one of three of the oldest residents in the township now living. He and his wife are both members of the Congregational Church. We give his portrait in this volume. It is from a picture taken at the age of 63.

Jacob K. Moore was born in Merrimac Co., N. H., Jan. 27, 1808, son of Stephen and Phœbe (Kimball) Moore, deceased; reared on a farm and educated in the town of Canterbury, N. H.; was an itinerant seller of books at auction, and clocks and other articles for 7 years, then engaged in merchandising in Sanbornton, N. H., until

1837, when he lost all by fire. In 1835 he married Cynthia A. Gerrish, and they have had 5 children,—Frances A. (Russell, dec.) Joseph D., Phœbe K., Geo. H. and Albert. Mr. Moore came to Brown Co., Ill., by wagon in 1838, and purchased 40 acres of land, and next year he brought his family in a wagon to his new home in the West, a distance of 1,600 miles; they were 40 days on the road. They removed to Griggsville April 16, 1849. Mr. M. is an auctioneer, and has also followed farming. He now resides on sec. 22. Although zealous in the late war he has never aspired to any office. He is liberal toward all the Churches, although not a member of any particular one. When he first came West he had but $10 and a span of old horses, but he now owns 243 acres of valuable land, besides giving 800 acres to his children. He has also given his children a good education and interested himself in the establishment of good schools.

James B. Morrison, of the firm of Morrison & Kenney, grocery and hardware merchants in Griggsville, came here in 1854. This firm, established in 1865, carry a stock of about $5,000, and do the largest business in their line in Griggsville.

George A. Mure was born in Fayette Co., Ky., in 1833; was educated in Winchester, Scott Co., Ill., having come to that place in 1840 in emigration with his mother; learned the trade of saddle and harness-maker under Hale & Strawn, in Winchester; in 1855 he began business for himself in Griggsville, where he still remains, with a large trade. He has taken premiums constantly at the Pike Co. fair on all of his work, and has earned a first-class reputation. In 1864 he married Julia, daughter of Cephas Simmons, and they have had 4 children, of whom 3 are living, viz: Geo. W., Bertha and Helen.

Wm. Newhouse was born in Delaware Co., O., in 1830, and was reared on a farm; at 23 he engaged in the cooper business; he came to Pike county in 1852 and returned to Ohio the same year; in 1857 he came to LaHarpe, Hancock Co., Ill., where he remained 22 years; he then located in Griggsville, where he now carries on the coopering business; 30 years' practice has made him a fine workman. In 1856 he married Eliza J. Findley, and of their 3 children, 2 are living, Samuel and Freddie, the former being now in partnership with his father, and the firm is known as Newhouse & Son.

Samuel A. Oliver is a native of Maine; emigrated to Missouri in 1859, and in 1865 he became a merchant in Hannibal; in Nov., 1878, he came to Griggsville and opened a general stock of groceries, queensware, glassware, lime, salt and oil, keeping on hand about $3,500 worth. He has had much to contend with here, but by integrity and enterprise has won the confidence of the community. In 1861 he married Frances M. Davis, and their only child is Willie.

T. W. Parker is a native of Indiana, and a son of James Parker, now of Griggsville. He engaged in the drug business here in 1867

L. W. M°Mahan

GRIGGSVILLE

and now carries a stock of $4,500, in drugs, medicines, stationery, fancy goods, books, etc.; keeping on hand a well selected variety of articles in all these branches of the trade, prosperity attends him.

Otis Parsons was born in Gloucester, Mass., in 1812, the second of 9 children; was a merchant in Griggsville for several years, and farmer for a time. He came to Alton, Ill., in 1835, and to Griggsville the next year. His parents were also natives of Gloucester, Mass. His mother is still living (December, 1879) at the age of 97 years. She remembers that at the time of George Washington's death, she saw the messenger proclaiming the sad news that "Washington, the Great, is dead!" But 4 of her 9 children are living,— Solomon, Superintendent of Tremont Temple, Boston; Otis, Jacob and Samuel. Grandmother Parsons is the only child of Capt. Robert Tomlinson, who was a voyager and was lost at sea; says she has always been a Democrat from birth, and a strong advocate of temperance; has been a member of the Baptist Church a great many years. This good old mother has always been kind and affectionate to her children, but very firm. Our subject, Otis, is the father of 7 children, of whom 6 are living.

Giles Penstone is a native of England, and came to America in 1849, settling in Pike Co., Ill., where he has since resided. He was married in 1837 and has had 7 children, of whom 5 are living. His 2 sons, Giles H. and Edward, served 3 years in the late war in Co. H, 73d I. V. I.

Flavius J. Phillips, son of Andrew Phillips, deceased, was born in Pike Co., Ill., Aug. 21, 1831. He was educated mostly in Griggsville, and in the early part of his life he ran the ferry at Valley City, known as Phillips' Ferry. His grandfather, Nimrod Phillips, purchased the ferry in 1822, which has since borne his name. Our subject was married Jan. 13, 1856, to Elizabeth, daughter of Nathan Jester, deceased, an early settler in Western Illinois. They have had 9 children, of whom 7 are living,—James R., John C., Ellen, George L., Salina, Howard M. and Mary A. Mr. Phillips is engaged in farming and stock-raising. His father was born in North Carolina in 1801, and came with his parents to Illinois in the year 1822 and located in Scott Co., where he remained until 1826, when he came to Pike county.

James M. Phillips, son of Andrew Phillips, deceased, was born in Scott Co., Ill., Nov. 27, 1826, and like other pioneers has suffered many privations and hardships. He resided where Griggsville now stands before there was any town there, and was there during the deep snow of 1830–1; was educated in Griggsville, and in 1855 was married to Sarah J., daughter of Nathan Jester, deceased. They had 5 children, of whom 3 are living, — Stephen A. D., Emily J. and David M. Mr. Phillips is engaged in farming and resides on sec. 35, Griggsville tp. He had many interesting experiences with wolves and Indians. At one time, when they had been committing depredations, such as killing stock, etc., he assisted in driving them away. One Indian seemed deter-

33

mined to load his gun and fight, but was caught by one of the whites and severely whipped with a brush.

George Pratt, a native of Massachusetts, was born Aug. 5, 1812; spent 6 years of the early part of his life on the sea ; was superintendent of the Valentine & Chamberlain packing-house at Cambridgeport, Mass., for 2 years previous to coming West ; he came to Griggsville in 1837, where he has since resided ; was a cooper and pork packer for 25 years in this place, and then became broken down in health, and has since lived rather a retired life except to loan money on real estate. He is now serving his 4th term as Supervisor for Griggsville tp. Has been married 3 times and has had 6 children, of whom 4 are living,—George E., with Kenney & Clark in Griggsville ; Albert J., in dry-goods business, and of the firm of Atwater & Pratt, Jacksonville, Ill.; Franklin, farmer ; and Elizabeth, now Mrs. Edwin Plummer, of McPherson, Kan.

Samuel Ramsey was born in Gallia Co., O., Aug. 4, 1852, where he was raised and educated ; learned the blacksmith trade (which was his father's trade also); came to Pike county in 1875, and to Maysville in 1878, where he established a wagon and blacksmith shop, and is a first-class workman. He has pursued his occupation ever since grown, except for about 4 years, during which time he operated as engineer on the Ohio river. He was married Aug. 6, 1878, to Julia M., daughter of Wm. Hill, deceased.

James T. Reynolds, son of R. D. Reynolds, of New Salem, was born in Clermont Co., O., Dec. 9, 1839, and came to Pike county with his parents in 1851. He was married March 2, 1862, to Eliza J., daughter of James Rankin, of Antrim county, Ireland ; they have 4 children,—John J., James W., Thomas M. and Isaac N. Mr. R. enlisted in the late war in Co. E, 10th I. V. I., where he served for one year, and was then promoted to the position of Captain of Co. I, 18th I. V. I. He participated in the battles of New Madrid and Shiloh, and was wounded in the latter engagement, on account of which he was discharged. He is now engaged in farming, and resides on sec. 10, Griggsville tp.

A. Rollins, a native of Maine, was born March 5, 1812. His father, John Rollins, was a musician in the Revolutionary war. He removed with his family to Clermont Co., O., in 1815, when the subject of this sketch was but three years old. They settled in the timber with wild animals for neighbors; had no guns, hence the animals were unmolested, but they caught many turkeys in a kind of trap or pen made for that purpose. Mr. Rollins' early educational advantages were very limited, not having enjoyed the free schools, as do the boys of the present day. He is well versed in rolling logs, raising cabins, pulling dog-wood and other hard work. He was married March 17, 1835, to Hannah Tedrow, daughter of David Tedrow, deceased. They have had eight children, of whom 4 are living, Augustus W., Melissa, Amelia and Lecter. Mr. Rollins removed to Pike Co. in 1839, having been here in the fall of 1838 and bought a farm near the Pine Settlement. He however did not take possession of the farm, as he lost over $500 in cash while *en route* for his new home. He went to work with a will, after losing the $200 he had paid on the farm, so that in a few years he laid up enough to start again. He bought a farm near New Salem, where he resided about 15 years. He has been very successful, and now resides on sec. 4, Griggsville tp., engaged in farming and stock raising.

Lemuel Rounds was born June 7, 1806, in Brown Co., O., and is the son of Lemuel Rounds, deceased, a native of Maine. The latter emigrated to Ohio in 1800, settling in Brown Co. The subject of this biography came to Pike Co. in 1842, locating on sec. 15, Fairmount tp., where he followed farming and stock-raising until 1875; he then sold his farm and removed to Griggsville, where he now resides. He was married in 1825 to Elizabeth Jackson, by whom he had 6 children. Of these only John and Richard are living. Mrs. R. died Oct. 5, 1869; and Mr. R. Oct. 25, 1879, married Mrs. Martha Hagar, daughter of Charles F. Frye, a well-known early settler. Mr. Rounds' only daughter, Mrs. Amanda Martin, died Nov. 22, 1879. His son, Cephas S., was killed on the railroad at East St. Louis March 2, 1879.

Robert Seaborn, being an early pioneer of Pike county, should have more than a passing notice in the pages of this history. He was born in Frankfort, now part of the city of Philadelphia, Pa., Oct. 11, 1814, and is the son of Robert and Elizabeth (Rodgers) Seaborn. The former was a native of England and came to America during the latter part of the last century. He was then a single man, but soon after married. He was a merchant tailor at that place for several years, and died March 4, 1805, leaving a widow and 3 children, of whom our subject was the youngest. Robert passed his early years in the city of Philadelphia, where his mother went to live, and where he received his education. There, at the age of 15 or 16, he was apprenticed to Jacob Young to learn the carriage-smith's trade; at the age of 21, at the expiration of his term of apprenticeship, he went to New York city, and after a year or two went to New Haven, Conn., then to Boston, where he found employment with Theodore Dickinson, at present an old settler in this county; he remained there some three years, during which time he was married to Caroline Beckford, a sister of Mrs. Dickinson; he was married in the Hanover Street Congregational church, of which he was a member, by Rev. Lyman Beecher, father of Henry Ward Beecher. He then went to the British territories, looking for a location; but not finding a suitable place, returned to Boston; he then moved to Preble county, O., where he bought a small farm. In the summer of 1831 he came to Pike county for the first time, to look up a location, and bought 160 acres of land on sec. 11, Griggsville tp., and 160 acres in the creek bottom, both of which places were slightly improved. He made the return to Ohio for his family, which then consisted of a wife and two sons,—Robert, who was born in Boston, and George, who was born in Ohio. While living on sec. 11 he had the misfortune to have his house and every-thing in it destroyed by fire. Mr. S. met with another accident by fire previous to this, losing all earthly possessions. When he made his trip from Boston to Ohio he sent his household goods, books, etc., around by sea to New Orleans, then via the Mississippi and Illinois rivers; the boat on which they were sent, however, was destroyed by fire. When the last fire occurred they were obliged to live in a smoke-house for the season. This structure was an old log house, without any floor, and but poorly chinked and daubed. Dur-ing the year his friends and neighbors assisted him to build a frame dwelling. This was made of one and a half-inch plank stood on end, and two stories high; in this he lived several years. During this time every misfortune seemed to attend him, when he sold his farm and moved to Griggsville. There he lived for a year, when he bought a farm on sec. 9, of Jacob Bradbury; since that time he has prospered financially in all his business undertakings.

Mr. Seaborn's wife died on the 25th of March, 1842, leaving a family of 5 children,—Robert, George, Henry C., Elizabeth, who resided in McLean county, Ill., but is now deceased, and Ann Car-oline. April 20, 1842, Mr. S. was married to Mrs. Mary Ann Bryant, formerly Mary Ann Hovey, daughter of John and Mary G. Hovey, who were natives of Massachusetts, and lived for many years in this county. There were 4 children born of this union: David R., William H., Charles C. and Howard M. The two lat-ter died at the age of 18 and 21, respectively. David R. and Wil-liam H. are both living in New Salem township. William and Charles both enlisted in the Union army during the Rebellion, and served until the close of the war. Mr. and Mrs. Seaborn are both firm believers in the Christian religion, and have done their part in supporting and building churches, promoting educational inter-ests, etc. They are now living at their home about one mile west of Griggsville. Mr. Seaborn's portrait will be found in this volume.

A. P. Sharpe came to Pike Co. in 1834, when he was 25 years of age, and entered 200 acres of land on secs. 19 and 20, Griggs-ville tp., where he still resides. He also entered 80 acres on sec. 30, this tp., and 80 acres of timber land on sec. 24, Salem tp. To enter this land he went to Quincy alone on horseback, a distance of 50 miles, when there were but 2 cabins on the route, and Mr. S. shared all the hardships of pioneer life. He had to go to Mor-gan (now Scott) county to mill, and if successful in getting his grist ground immediately, he could make the trip in 3 days. He has actually sold wheat in Griggsville for two "bits" a bushel, taking his pay in trade, not being allowed to have any groceries at that. At one time he took 30 bushels of wheat to that town and gave half of it for a pair of cow-hide boots, and the other half for a small roll of cotton cloth. At another time he sold his crop of beans for 30 cents a bushel, taking his pay in sacks and a few little trinkets. Mr. Sharpe was born in Pomfret, Windham Co., Conn.,

Jan. 15, 1809; the first 2 years upon his lonely farm in Pike Co. he kept "bach," and Sept. 1, '37, in Connecticut, he married Miss F. L. Hutchins, who was born in the town of Thompson, Windham Co., Conn., Dec. 9, 1816. Mr. S. has been a very successful farmer and stock-raiser, owning now 283 acres of land. Mr. S. paid promptly for all his land by selling beef at $1.25 per cwt., pork at $1.50, and corn from 8 to 10 cents, and other things in proportion. Mr. and Mrs. S. are the parents of 11 children, of whom 8 are living, namely, Edwin H., Ellen (now Mrs. Fisher), Joseph K., Frederick L., Mary H., Anna T., Charles F. Mary H. and Mrs. Fisher are very fine artists. Many of their pictures decorate the State institutions of this State.

William Shaw, son of John Shaw, deceased, was born in Warwickshire, Eng., in 1826, and was brought to America by his parents in 1827, stopping in New York 4 years; then came to Pike Co. He has pursued various occupations, and now owns 200 acres of land, and is engaged in general farming on sec. 13, Griggsville tp. He was married in 1860 to Mary Alexander, daughter of Geo. Alexander, deceased. The building now used by Mr. Shaw as a barn was erected by his father in an early day on Flint creek, as a flouring mill.

James Shinn, sr., was born July 10, 1806, in Salem Co., N. J.; moved to Hamilton Co., O., in 1824, where he engaged in farming on the ground where a portion of Cincinnati now stands; came to Pike county in 1831, settling in Derry tp.; and after one year he removed to Griggsville tp., where he still resides. In 1827 he married Mary Smith, of Clermont Co., O.: they have had 10 children, of whom 6 are living, namely, Horace B., John B., Hannah A., Charles W., Kate and Victoria P. Hannah (now Mrs. Elder), lives in Washington Territory, and Kate (now Mrs. Stephens, is in Santa Rosa, Cal. Charles W. is an architect in Springfield, Ill.

James Shinn, son of S. L. Shinn, was born in Griggsville, Aug. 31, 1841; his father was born in Camden, N. J., in 1811. James served two years in the late war in Co. G, 8th I. V. I., participated in the battles of Fort Donelson, Shiloh, siege of Corinth, and the campaigns of Vicksburg and Red River, the latter including the defeat of Gen. Banks at Pleasant Hill; he was then transferred to the Signal Service under Gen. Meyer, where he served one year. In 1864 he married Kate Glenn, daughter of Wm. Glenn, and they have 3 children,—Herbert S., Della M. and Augusta.

John B. Shinn, son of James Shinn, of Griggsville, was born in Hamilton Co., O., Oct. 28, 1830, where Cincinnati now stands; came to this county with his parents in 1831 and settled near Atlas, where they remained one year; then removed to Griggsville tp., locating on sec. 24, where John was brought up; he attended McKendree College, at Lebanon, Ill., one year, and then married Charlotte E. Fielding, Sept. 6, 1853. Of their 8 children 7 are living, namely, Charles B., Grace L., Edwin F., John F., Annie M.,

Mary B. and an infant. Mr. S. is a farmer, and has taught school several years.

Parvin Shinn, son of John S. Shinn, of Griggsville, was born Oct. 10, 1838, in this tp.; married Oct. 20, 1863, Louise, daughter of Wm. Thackwray, deceased. Mrs. Shinn's mother, Hannah (Sweeting) Thackwray, is living in Flint tp., at the age of 80 years; and her grandfather, Richard Sweeting, came to Pike county in 1834. Mr. and Mrs. S. have four children, viz: Louise R., Eugenie, Eva L. and Ross. Mr. S. is a farmer on sec. 22, and has been prosperous.

Samuel L. Shinn was born in Salem Co., N. J., in 1811; came to Pike county in 1831, settling in Griggsville tp. His father, John Shinn, also came the same year and procured land for all his sons. So numerous were the Shinns that the locality was called "Shinntown." The subject of this sketch in 1834 married Sarah Evans, and they had 16 children, of whom only 7 are living: Clement, Joseph, James, John, Jane, Mary and Ellen. Mr. S. has been a Local Preacher in the M. E. Church for 25 years. He went with his father when he went to pray for the man who was frightened at the falling stars in 1833. Until 1879 he was a farmer; he then retired from farming, and went to Griggsville.

Wm. M. Shinn, deceased, was born in Hamilton Co., O., Dec. 1, 1830, and was a son of the Rev. John Shinn, so well known in the pioneer days of Pike county. At the age of two years he emigrated to this county with his parents, and was reared on a farm. He was educated in the common schools of Pike county, and at the age of 21, in company with others, went the overland route to California, with a train of wagons drawn by ox teams. He remained there for 8 years, traveling through Oregon and Washington Territory a portion of the time. He then returned to Pike county to live with his father, who was then very infirm. He was married Feb. 5, 1861, to Mary A. Jenkins, daughter of Joseph Jenkins, of Griggsville tp. Mr. and Mrs. Shinn had 4 children, of whom but one, Eva, is living, a bright little girl of 10 years. Mr. Shinn died Jan. 11, 1879, a worthy member of the Bethel M. E. Church, of Newburg tp.

Cephas Simmons was born in Bullitt Co., Ky., Sept. 3, 1809, the eldest son and 3d child of Richard and Sophia Simmons, early pioneers in that State. The country being new, they had to undergo untold suffering. The State at that early period of its history was sparsely settled, and they had none of the conveniences of modern times, while the native savages and ferocious animals were numerous. They could raise but little produce, and even then could find but poor markets. A patch of corn and a little patch of wheat comprised almost the sum total of their farming. When Cephas was only 3 years old his father died. He was therefore thrown upon his own resources at a very tender age, with no capital but his hands and will to begin with. He came to Illinois in 1827 and resided with his uncle, Enos Simmons, in Morgan Co., for 2 years, and there he married Lucy, daughter of Jacob and Patience Bradbury, who was born in Clermont Co., O., in 1810.

When first married Mr. Simmons' wealth consisted of a colt and two calves, but by energy and perseverance he has brought to himself better days. He now has a family of 7 children, all married. He sent two of his sons into the late war. D. C. volunteered for 3 years, and was wounded at the battle of Perryville, Ky., and still carries the ball in his body. Mr. and Mrs. Simmons are both prominent members of the Baptist Church, as also are most of their children. Among our portraits of prominent citizens of Pike Co., appears Mr. Simmons.'

Matthew Simpson, deceased, was born in Harrison Co., O., Nov. 13, 1807; settled here in 1837, enduring many of the hardships of pioneer life. He was a Methodist, and died Jan. 4, 1877, loved and respected by all. He was first married April 19, 1827, to Susannah Orr, by whom he had 7 children,—Margaret J., Mary, Isabella, Thomas, John, James and Alexander, twins, and deceased. He married afterward Mrs. Susan Pryor, and they had 2 children, —Edward, deceased, and Llewella M. Mrs. Simpson was born in Knox Co., O., April 22, 1828, daughter of Samuel Ward, deceased, who came to Pike Co. in 1844. She now resides on sec. 17, Griggsville tp. She was first married in 1854 to Nathaniel P. Pryor, who died the same year.

John G. Sleight, jr., a native of Lincolnshire, Eng., was born June 12, 1840, the son of John G. Sleight, sr., afterward of Flint tp. He came to America in October, 1857, settling in Flint tp. In 1866 he was married to Ruth Reynolds, and they have 2 children, Charles W. and Mary Leah. In 1869 he purchased 314 acres of land in Griggsville tp., secs. 2 and 3. This is one of the best farms in P ke Co. Mr. and Mrs. S. are Baptists.

Edward L. Staats was born in Warren Co., O., July 27, 1836; was raised mostly on a farm, and emigrated to Illinois with his parents in 1843, locating in Quincy; in 1844 they removed to this county, where he is engaged in farming. His father, Wm. Staats, is a native of Penn., and is now at Hot Springs, Ark. Edward's mother was born in N. C. May 6, 1810; of her 6 children our subject is the eldest. They have a farm of 160 acres on sec. 14, this tp. Edward in 1862 married Anna King, daughter of Joseph King, dec., of Perry. Mrs. S. died in Jan., 1864.

Peter T. Staats; P. O. Griggsville; born in Adams Co., Ill., June 30, 1843, the son of Wm. Staats; received a common-school education in Griggsville, and finished his education in Quincy. He is now engaged in the practice of law in Griggsville, in which he succeeds well; he also teaches school some. Dec. 23, 1867, he married Maria, daughter of Magruder Edmonson, of Versailles, Ill., formerly of Quincy. Their 3 children are Eugene A., Olin C. and Inez G.

Dr. E. R. Stoner was born in Clermont Co., O., and came with his parents to Schuyler (now Brown) Co., Ill., in 1836, where he remained until 1849, when he came to this county. He graduated in the Missouri Medical College of St. Louis in 1854, and began practicing the same year in Perry, this Co.; in 1861 he located in Griggsville, where he has built up a large practice. In 1856 he married Miss A. E. Whitaker, daughter of B. D. Whitaker, and their 3 children are Emma W., Stanley and Alice.

Charles Thrasher, deceased, was born in New Haven, Conn., Feb. 13, 1795. He was a shoemaker in his younger days, but subsequently engaged in farming. In 1853 he emigrated to Pike Co. and settled on sec. 11, Griggsville tp. Sept. 13, 1840, he married Mrs. Rigney, daughter of John Meagley, deceased, and they had 4 children, 3 of whom are living,—Matilda, Amaziah and Benjamin. Matilda is married to Samuel Layman and resides near Woodburn, Oregon; Amaziah is married to Mary Hope and resides in Tama, Iowa, and Benjamin is married to Belle Bright, and they also reside in Tama, Iowa. Mr. Thrasher has been married 3 times and is the father of 18 children. In 1853 he went overland to Oregon and California, but his health failed and he returned after 9 months. Mr. Thrasher died July 1, 1863, greatly lamented by all who knew him.

Wm. Turnbull, deceased, was born in the county of York, Eng., Oct. 16, 1805; was the 3d son of John and Elizabeth Turnbull, who were also natives of England. He received a good English and mechanical education in the best of schools in the town in which he resided. After finishing his education, his business while in England was that of general superintendent of the manufacturing establishment of his father. He came to the United States in the spring of 1830, landing in New York, thence proceeded to Maryland, locating near Baltimore, in which place he lived 4 years, still following the same vocation. In 1835 he traveled for Messrs. Garside & Co., of Manayunk, selling flax thread and traveling among the farmers, endeavoring to encourage them to grow the staple necessary to feed their manufactories. In 1836 he was married in Philadelphia to Grace Wade, daughter of Francis and Elizabeth Wade, who were also natives of England. Mr. and Mrs. T. have had one son and two daughters. In the fall of 1839 he came to Illinois, locating in Flint tp., where he followed farming. He has also traveled considerably in this country. He died Sept. 10, 1878.

Benjamin F. Wade, deceased, was born in Alton, Ill., in July, 1827; reared on a farm, experiencing in early days all the hardships of pioneer life; was a soldier in the Mexican war under Col. E. W. B. Newberry and Gen. Taylor, and participated in the battles of Palo Alto, Resaca De La Palma, Monterey and Buena Vista. In 1852 he went to California, where he followed mining four years; returned to Pike Co.; was married Sept. 10, 1850, to Jane Elliott, and they had 4 children, 3 of whom are living, Martha E., John K. and Dorcas H. Mrs. Wade was born in Ross Co., O., Oct. 14, 1823, and is a sister of Moses Elliott, of Griggsville tp. Mr. Wade was a member of the M. E. Church, and died Dec. 23, 1859.

Josias Wade was born in Franklin Co., N. Y., May 22, 1804; his father, Josias Wade, sr., was a soldier in the Indian war and

Geo. Yates

GRIGGSVILLE TP.

participated in the battle of Tippecanoe, under Gen. Harrison. In 1825 our subject was married to Cynthia Owens, and they had 8 children. In 1827 he removed to Missouri, and in 1830 he came to Pike Co., settling on sec. 7, Flint tp. Mrs. Wade died in July, 1863, and Dec. 20, 1870, he married Hannah C. Lyon. He resides in Griggsville, retired from active labor. He is the father of Austin and Coleman Wade, two prominent citizens of Flint tp.

Mrs. Margaret E. Wade was born in Jefferson Co., O., and is a daughter of Robert Spence, deceased, and widow of the late Brunce Wade. Mr. Wade was born in 1820, in Kentucky, and was married Aug. 22, 1860, to Miss Spence, and they had one daughter, Mary, now Mrs. Sylvester Vandament, who resides with her mother in Griggsville. Mrs. Vandament has 3 children,—Minnie, Myrtle and Ellen.

Robert J. Walker, farmer, sec. 12; was born near Boston, Lincolnshire, Eng., Dec. 28, 1819, and crossed the ocean in 1836. He apprenticed himself to Jesse G. Crawford, a carpenter of Griggsville, serving 3 years; after which he worked at his trade for 14 years, when he cut his knee with a broad-ax; he then began farming and the culture of fruit-trees, making the latter a specialty. Aug. 1, 1847, he married Amanda Evans, and of their 11 children 8 are living,—M. Jane, Ann L., Geo. J., Mary, Elizabeth, Emma C., Willard S. and Fannie.

Frank Warton, known throughout the country as "Banty," owing to his small stature, was born March 22, 1858, son of Wm. Warton, deceased, an early settler in Pike county. Mr. Warton is a farmer, owning a nice little farm on sec. 27, this tp.

John Warton was born in Yorkshire, Eng., June 24, 1815. In 1833 he was brought over the sea with his parents and stopped in Morgan Co., Ill., while he and his father erected a house on their land in Griggsville tp., sec. 27, where John still resides, engaged in farming and stock-raising. His parents were also natives of Yorkshire, Eng., and had 5 children, of whom John was the 4th. In Oct., 1841, he married Mary, daughter of George Haxbey, of Scott Co., Ill. Their 6 children are, Ann, Thomas, Rachel, John, Sarah J. and George. All married, except John and George.

Wm. Warton, a native of Yorkshire, England, was born in Dec., 1817. He came to America with his parents in 1833, remaining in Morgan Co., Ill., about five months, when they removed to Pike Co. He was married June 27, 1848, to Elizabeth Haxbey, daughter of George Haxbey, deceased. Mr. Haxbey came to Scott county in 1830, and suffered with others during the big snow. Mr. and Mrs. Haxbey had 4 children,—Mary J., now Mrs. John Hensell, William, Elizabeth and Frank. Mr. Warton was a farmer and resided on sec. 27, Griggsville tp., until his death, which occurred Oct. 30, 1859. Mr. Haxbey came first to New York, and then to Illinois, by way of the Great Lakes, in a sailing vessel. The journey occupied 10 weeks. When they arrived at Chicago they found a few French and Indians there, wading through the swamps. Mr. Haxbey and Richard Waugh employed some Frenchmen at Chicago to bring their families to Jacksonville, which at that time was a village of 4 or 5 houses. The Indians would approach them at night and sit around the camp-fire and converse with the Frenchmen, which frightened the families of the new arrivals very much. Mrs. Warton has vivid recollections of the pioneer days in Illinois, when wolves made the nights hideous by their constant howling. Great credit is due these pioneers for their untiring efforts in settling this wild country, and for the hardships and privations they endured in preparing the way for the prosperity of future generations.

William Warton, jr., was born July 20, 1852, in this tp., where he still resides on sec. 27, engaged in farming. When he was 8 years old his father, William W., sr., died, leaving a wife and 4 small children, of whom William, jr., is the 2d. After working by the month for different farmers for 6 years, he began agriculture for himself. In 1874 he went to Fort Scott in " grass-hopperdom," but the desolation which had just been wrought by that pestiferous insect so discouraged him, that he returned to old Pike. Sept. 3, 1878, he married Fannie McPherson, daughter of Stephen McP., dec., of Missouri. They have one child, Elsie May.

Dr. T. M. Watson, a native of Pike Co., was born Nov. 25, 1851, the son of John Watson, of Barry. He is a graduate of the Eclectic Medical Institute of Cincinnati, O., and began practice in Griggsville in 1874. He now practices the Homeopathic system of medicine exclusively, and is enjoying an extensive practice, having the patronage of a large portion of the wealthy and intelligent citizens. In May, 1874, he married Helena, daughter of J. L. Terry, of Barry. During a service of two terms upon the Municipal Board he has been prominently identified with every measure for public improvement, and for the best interests of the community.

John Weiler is a native of Hamilton Co., O., and came to Illinois in 1864, and to Pike county in Jan., 1879, where he engaged in the manufacture of carriages and spring wagons. He has a large business, employing 10 to 14 hands constantly. He also pursued the same occupation in Quincy for 12 years.

August Wellenreiter was born in Baden, Ger., Feb. 17, 1836, the son of Wesley W., deceased, who brought his family to America in June, 1856. Mr. W. married Nov. 24, 1863, Malinda Turner, and they have had 9 children, of whom 4 are living,—Lizzie, Johnnie, Charlotte and Wesley Leander. He is a prominent farmer of this tp., residing on the Thrasher farm.

B. D. Whitaker was born Jan. 23, 1809, in Greene Co., N. Y., in sight of the Catskill Mountains, and has not had a school education. In 1830 he went to New York city, where he remained until 1839. After prospecting West a year or two he settled in Perry, this Co., where he followed merchandising and pork-packing for 14 years; he then engaged in the wholesale grocery and commission business in St. Louis 25 years. While there he was a member of the "Old Guards," who were called into service twice during the late war, and who donated their wages to the Soldiers' Orphan Home near St. Louis. Mr. W. now resides in Griggsville, the possessor of a family Bible 155 years old, which contains the family record dating back to the birth of our subject's great-grand-father, Edward Whitaker, March 10, 1705, who was one of three brothers that came from Leeds, Eng., in a very early day. Mr. W. married Nov. 10, 1832, in New York city, Delia D. Wood, and they have had 6 children, of whom 4 are living : James K., of San Francisco, Cal.; Ann Eliza, now Mrs. Dr. Stoner, of Griggsville; Helena A., now Mrs. B. A. Dozier, of St. Louis, Mo.; and Emma F., now Mrs. Benj. Lacy, of Baltimore, Md.

M. W. White was born in Caledonia Co., Vt., Aug. 1, 1803, and is a son of Nicholas White, deceased. Our subject on his mother's side is the 17th generation from John Rogers, who was burned at the stake. His mother's maiden name was Baron, and his grand-mother was a Rogers. He was married May 9, 1837, to Susan M. Whitelaw, daughter of Robert and Mehetabel Whitelaw, of Rye-gate, Vt., and granddaughter of Gen. James Whitelaw, a native of Scotland, and the first surveyor of all the New England States. Mr. and Mrs. White have had 5 children, of whom 3 are living,—James H., Horace A. and Madeline, now Mrs. Thurlow Wilson, of Griggs-ville. Mr. White emigrated to Morgan Co. Ill., in 1837, when there was no railroad in the State, and deer and wolves roamed at will through the forests, and across the prairies. , He made keys for securing the rails by cross ties for the first railroad that was built in Illinois, viz.: that from Naples to Jacksonville. He re-moved with his family to Griggsville in 1855, having resided for , 17 years previous to this in Scott Co., and about 6 months in St. · Louis. He has engaged in various occupations, and now resides in Griggsville.

David Wilson, a native of Lincolnshire, Eng., was born in Nov., 1828, the son of Joseph Wilson, an early settler of Pike county. His parents came with him across the ocean in 1829, and to this county in 1831; he was raised a farmer, and is still engaged in this business. Dec. 21, 1856, he married Susan M., daughter of John Bell, deceased, who was an early settler of this county. They have one son, Wm. Joseph, who was born Nov. 19, 1856. Mr. Wilson still remains on the farm on sec. 12, Griggsville tp. He has re-sided in Pike county 48 years, and 42 years of that time in this tp.

Joseph Wilson was born in Lincolnshire, Eng., in March, 1793, the son of Isaac Wilson. He came to America in 1829, stopping in New York State 2 years, then coming to this county, settling on sec. 12, this tp., where he still resides. His many experiences in pioneer life are such as those related in our chapter on that gen-eral subject. In 1826 he married Elizabeth Walker, and they have had 10 children, of whom 6 are living,—Louisa, now Mrs. Levi Butler ; Martha, now Mrs. John Scott ; Elizabeth, now the wife of Geo. Wilson ; David, Joseph and George. David and Joseph are married.   Mrs. Wilson died Sept. 20, 1876, having been a member of the M. E. Church over 50 years.   The youngest son, George, remains at home attending the farm.   Mr. W. has never been out of the State but once since he first located here, and that was a two weeks' visit in Indiana.   He is unusually active, still attending to business.   He owns 280 acres of land.

James Winn, deceased, was born in West Cambridge, Mass., Jan. 31, 1808, where he was reared and educated ; he was a farmer and horticulturist, and was in the Quincy vegetable market in Boston for several years ; in 1834 he came to Pike county, entering land in this tp.; he also purchased the undivided one-half of the north half of sec. 28, and the south half of sec. 21, in this tp. May 12, 1836, he married Hannah Converse, daughter of Joseph Converse, dec., and they had 9 children, of whom 7 are living,— Hannah J., Sarah L., James, Harriet, Charles, Abba and Julia E. For 5 or 6 years after arriving in this county he engaged in pork-packing, and for 2 years was a partner of Nathan W. Jones in farming.   Mr. Winn was a Congregationalist, and died Jan. 10, 1860, a great loss to all who knew him.

NEWBURG TOWNSHIP.

The history of Newburg township is so closely interwoven with the associations and early settlement of Pittsfield that to separate the intricate facts is almost impossible, and would involve discussions as to the correctness of its record regarding dates, etc. Besides, in order to secure a thorough history of a township an undivided interest must be manifested, and the assistance of those settlers whose knowledge dates back to its primitive days secured. Therefore the history of Newburg bears the expression and interest of its people.

The wealth and magnificence of this county grew from its beautiful groves as much as from any other one thing. These goodly forests in their primeval beauty drew the pioneer as surely as the magnet does the needle. No other considerations overbore the generous shelter which these islands of shade and cool streams gave,—about the only comforts which these early settlers found in their new home; all others were surroundings of discomfort. The cramped cabins, the absence of schools and markets, sickness,—always the attendant of new locations,—severe storms, depredations of wild beasts, fires, snakes, poorly paid toil and the uncertainties of the future,—all gave way to the supporting shelter of a grove of timber. Thus, when Daniel Husong, the first white settler in Newburg township, located here, he selected one of these beautiful groves. He built a log cabin on section 23, the site now occupied by the residence of David Kiser, in the year 1832. This was the first house erected in the township. Nicholas Criss, Hiram Reed and Hawkins Judd made improvements upon this section the same year. John Durand, Jacob Heavener and A. B. Quimby followed soon after, and the settlement became more extended. Peter K. Stringham, a native of Newburg, N. Y., came in 1833 and settled on section 33, where a town was laid out and a postoffice established. Stringham was followed by "Aunty" and John Dunham, who succeeded in retaining the establishment four or five years, but its neighbor, Detroit, was springing into existence, and hither the postoffice was removed under the appointment of B. Johnson. E. W. Hickerson came in 1833 and settled near Pittsfield. To him and Squire Hayden belongs the honor of being the oldest living settlers of the township.

The first sermon was preached by Rev. E. L. Allen, of the Baptist denomination, in 1830, in a log-school-house long since decayed. The first school-house was erected on section 15, in 1835, and school was taught here by Daniel Foster. The first church building was erected the same year, and was known as the Bethel Church, and was built by the Methodists. Robert Kerr, Emery Scott and the two Misses Criss, sisters, and daughters of Nicholas Criss, were the first parties married. The ceremony was performed by M. E. Rattan, Esq., of Pittsfield. The first death was that of George Westlake, father of Hon. Benj. F. Westlake. L. E. Hayden was the first Justice of the Peace.

When the township was organized, a committee of three was appointed to select a name. After some discussion it was named in honor of the birth-place of Peter K. Stringham and Capt. Benj. F. Westlake, both early pilgrims in this county and township. Newburg in its early days contained many acres of brush and timber, much of which has been swept away, and the works of the busy husbandman in well cultivated and productive fields are visible on every hand.

BIOGRAPHICAL DEPARTMENT.

In continuance of the local history of the township we will give personal sketches of many of the old settlers and prominent men of the same.

John Barney, retired farmer, sec. 18; was born in Berkshire Co., Mass., in 1809, came to this county in 1830, settling in Atlas tp., where he resided 4½ years, when he moved to Barry tp.; in 1855 he settled upon his present estate, at that time consisting of 200 acres, the most of which he has since sold, and is living in retirement. He was appointed County Treasurer by the County Commissioners in 1831 and re-appointed for 7 consecutive years. He was married in Pittsfield, in 1837, to Miss Clarissa Shaw, a native of Massachusetts, by whom he has 2 children,—Eliza J. and Orville H. Mr. B. numbers among the few who are left of the early pioneers of Pike Co.

Charles W. Bickerdike, farmer, sec. 5; P. O. Griggsville; is a son of John and Anna (Griggs) Bickerdike, natives of England, where the subject of this sketch was born in 1842; the family emigrated the following year to this country, settling in Griggsville tp., where his parents both died. Mr. B. was married to Miss N. E. Shrigley, a native of Ohio. They have one daughter, Anna J. Mr. B. has a farm of 160 acres, valued at $40 an acre. He and his wife are members of the M. E. Church.

Francis Casteel, farmer, sec. 14; P. O. Detroit; Mr. C. was born in Knox Co., Tenn., in 1822, the son of Daniel Casteel, who settled in Bond Co., Ill., where he died July, 1834. The same year Francis came to this county and settled north of Detroit, where he resided 8 years. He moved upon his present estate in 1848, consisting of 200 acres of highly improved and well cultivated land, the soil of which then held the grim grasp of mighty monarchs, the growth of centuries. Mr. C. was married to Miss Lucinda Cooper, a native of Kentucky, and is the father of 4 children. Is School Director. Belongs to the Methodist Church, and is identified with the Republican party.

Stephen Casteel, farmer, sec. 9; P. O. Pittsfield; owns 160 acres of land, valued at $50 per acre. He is the son of Daniel and Rhoda (Hensley) Casteel, both natives of Tennessee; he was born in Knox Co., Tenn., Oct. 15, 1824; he was married in this county March 8, 1849, to Elizabeth Bush, who was born in Indiana in 1819; they are the parents of 5 children, and have as members of their family two grandchildren. Mr. C. has held local offices, and is a member of the Masonic fraternity.

C. P. Chapman, miller, is a native of Tolland county, Conn., where he was born in 1825; he came to this county in 1847; he first engaged as a clerk for Ross & Gay; in 1854 a partnership was formed to carry on the milling business under the name of Gay, Chapman & Co. Mr. Gay retired from the firm two years afterward, and in 1869 the old mill was supplanted by the erection of the present structure, it being the largest mill in this section of the State. Mr. A. Dow was admitted to the firm in 1872, and they now command a large trade. Mr. Chapman organized the 1st National Bank in 1869, of which he is Vice President and Director, and was also principal mover in the Woolen Mills company for three years, and has otherwise interested himself in the business welfare of Pittsfield.

Lafayette Crane, farmer, sec. 4; P. O. Griggsville. The subject of this sketch is a native of Kentucky, and ranks among the more prominent farmers of the county. He was married in Ohio in 1839, to Lydia Harns, who was a native of the Buckeye State, and was born in 1815, and died in 1840; he was again married in the same State, this time to Sarah Leeds, in 1842; she was also a native of Ohio; by this union 2 children were born, and in 1846 Mrs. C. died; in 1847 he was married to Susan Leeds, who was born in the same State in 1828; six of the 8 children born to them are still living.

John C. Cunningham, retired farmer, sec. 30; P. O. Pittsfield. Mr. C. is a native of Pike Co., Mo., where he was born in 1819, the son of Thomas and Hannah (Watson) Cunningham, early pioneers of Pike Co., Mo., and where his father died in 1845. Mr. C. was married in 1840 to Mrs. Elizabeth Morris; five children have been born to them, 3 of whom are living,—Elizabeth L., Mary E. and John T. Our subject came to this county in 1849, and located in Hardin tp., on sec. 19, where he resided 21 years; then he moved to his present estate, where he lives in retirement, and the enjoyment of a well-directed industry. Mr. C. has served 3 terms as Assessor, and has always taken an active interest in the welfare of the county.

I. R. Davidson, retired farmer, sec. 30, P. O. Pittsfield; is the son of John and Mary (Roberts) Davidson, natives of Ohio, and his father a soldier of the war of 1812, who died in 1840. His estimable wife is still living, in the 82d year of her age. The subject of this sketch was born in Highland Co., O., in 1826; was united in marriage to Miss Lucinda, daughter of Moses Hicks, a native of Brown Co., O. Five children have been born to them, only one of whom, Cornelia, is still living. The eldest and only son, Ira W., was killed by a horse in 1878. Adaline, wife of Geo. Hardin, died in 1879; the other two died in infancy. Mr. D. came to this county in 1867 and settled upon his present estate, consisting of 142 acres, valued now at $100 per acre. The family are members of the Christian Church. Mr. D. is a Republican.

John Dunham, youngest son of Hezekiah Dunham (a native of Saratoga Co., N. Y., a Baptist Deacon and soldier in the Revolutionary war, and who died in 1810), was born in Saratoga Co., N. Y., Jan. 1, 1793; he came to this county in 1838 and settled in this tp. near his present home; his marriage occurred in February, 1816, his partner in life's journey being Ann C. Pettis, a native of Grand Isle, Vt., where they were married. They have 5 children living. Mr. D. owns a small and valuable farm on sec. 14, is one of the earliest pioneers of this county, and earnest in the cause of Republican principles and religious teaching. P. O. Detroit.

Isaac Durand, who resides in Newburg tp., sec. 5, is the owner of 132 acres of well improved land, and is one of the substantial and enterprising farmers of the township. He was born in this county in 1838, and is the son of John and Rhoda (Riggs) Durand, who were early settlers here. John Durand is a native of Maine, and his wife of New York. Our subject's P. O. address is Pittsfield.

Moses Durand, farmer, sec. 6; P. O. Pittsfield. Mr. D. was born in Pittsfield tp. in 1833, and is the son of John Durand, an early settler of this county, and a resident of Pittsfield. He was married in 1861 to Miss Mary J. Rayburn, a native of McLean Co., Ill., by whom he has 5 children living,—William D., Edwin S., Rosa O., Francis E. and Hattie A. Mr. D. moved upon his present estate in 1877; it consists of 200 acres of very valuable land, valued at $60 per acre. He is a Republican, and he and his wife are members of the Baptist Church.

George Elliott, farmer, sec. 3, where he owns 135 acres of land; P. O. Griggsville. Mr. E. is the son of John and Esther Elliott, both natives of Ireland; he was born in Ross Co., O., March 9, 1829, and came to this county in 1847; Sept. 18, 1857, in this county, he was married to Sarah J. Lightle, a native of Ross Co., O., where she was born Sept. 29, 1831; they have 8 children by this union, 7 of whom are living,—Maria C., Lewis B., Hester A., Rebecca A., James F., Eunice J. and Warren; John W. is deceased.

George D. Foot, farmer, sec. 32; P. O. Pittsfield; was born in Albany Co., N. Y., in 1810; moved to Illinois in 1832, settling in St. Clair Co., where he was married in 1835 to Miss Abbie J. St. John, a native of Albany Co., N. Y., where she was born in

B. F. Westlake

NEWBURGH TP.

1816. They came to this county in the fall of 1836 and settled in Pittsfield, where he with others contracted for and built the present court-house; he then moved to Columbia, Boone Co., Mo., where he erected the State University; 4 years afterward he returned and settled upon his present estate of 200 acres, valued at $70 per acre. Fourteen children have been born to this highly respected couple, 12 of whom are living: Talmadge O., Edward N., Amelia M., John, James P., Lydia S., Josiah C., Jane, Henry, Almira C., Ida M. and May A. Mr. F. is a School Director, and numbers among the early settlers of the county.

Nicholas Foreman, farmer, sec. 26; P. O. Detroit. Mr. F. was born in Highland Co., O., in 1830, and is the son of David Foreman, who settled in Pittsfield in 1840, where he resided until his death in 1857. The subject of this sketch was married in 1859 to Miss Nancy Williams, a native of this county. They settled upon their present valuable farm of 320 acres in 1864. They have a family of 5 children.

G. L. Geisendorfer, farmer, sec. 33; P. O. Pittsfield. This gentleman was born in Bavaria, Ger., in 1818, and emigrated to America in 1840, locating on his present estate of 320 acres. In 1847 he married Miss Margaret Miller, a native of Germany, who died after raising a family of 3 children: Dorothy, Mary and John. His second wife, Henrietta Hooker, is a native of Prussia. By this union 7 children have been born: George, William, Siegel, Leonard, Edward, Emma and Frederick. Mr. G. is a School Director, and is well known throughout the town and county.

William Hildebrand, farmer, sec. 7; P. O. Pittsfield; is a native of Germany, where he was born in 1822; he emigrated to America in 1858 and settled upon his present estate the same year; it consists of 230 acres, valued at $50 per acre. He chose for his wife a daughter of his own native land, by whom he has 5 children: Mary, Lizzie, William, jr., Henry and Emma. Mr. H. is a Republican, and the family are members of the M. E. Church.

Asa L. Hill, retired farmer, sec. 20; P. O. Pittsfield. Mr. H. was born in Vermont in 1808; came to this county in 1833 and returned to his native State, but again settled here permanently in 1835. He was united in marriage in Putnam Co., Ill., to Miss Charlotte C. Pratt, who was born in Massachusetts in 1830. Of his several children 4 are living. His present farm consists of 160 acres valued at $80 per acre. Mr. H. has attained his present position in life by frugality, untiring energy and indomitable will. He numbers among the earlier pioneers of the county.

Isabel Hogsett, sec. 24; P. O. Detroit. Mrs. H. is the widow of James Hogsett, who was born in Greenbrier Co., Va., in 1817; he was married in 1843 to Miss Isabel, daughter of John and Isabel Hays, natives of Ohio, and where Mr. H. died at an early day. Mrs. Hays then came to this county with her children, and is at this writing residing with her daughter in the 87th year of her age. Mrs. Isabel Hogsett was born in Highland Co., O., in 1825, and

34

emigrated to the West in 1848.   Mr. H. settled on the estate now owned by his widow and children, of 130 acres, valued at $60 an acre.   After a life of activity and usefulness, and just when he began to enjoy the fruits of his industry, he was called from earth. He died in 1868, respected by all who knew him.

S. C. Howland, farmer, sec. 23; P. O. Detroit; is a son of Lucius and Mary (Childs) Howland, natives of Massachusetts, who settled in this tp. in 1839, and from which both were called to a better home in 1842.   The subject of this sketch was born in Geauga Co., O., in 1822; in 1844 he was married to Miss Amy, daughter of Samuel Parker.   After his marriage he purchased 50 acres of land in this section, and by his indomitable energy and perseverance has secured a handsome property, his present productive estate covering 240 acres of valuable land.   His wife died in 1850, and in 1857 he was married again to Miss Sarah E., daughter of E. W. Hickerson, an early pioneer of Pike county.   She was the first child born in Pittsfield.   Mr. H. has served as Supervisor and Town Collector, and numbers among the early pilgrims of Pike county.

Robert Hunter, farmer, sec. 28; P. O. Pittsfield.   Mr. H. was born in Donegal, Ireland, in 1843.   His mother with 4 children emigrated to America in 1854, settling in this county, Aug. 23, 1861. He enlisted in Co. B, 28th Ill. Inf., and served until Aug., 1864; he again enlisted in Co. G, 62d Ill. Inf., Feb. 8, 1865; he participated in the battles of Little Bethel, Pittsburg Landing, where he was wounded, Hatchie, Tenn., and Vicksburg.   He was united in marriage in 1872 with Miss Rebecca Kelley, a native of this county, by whom he has 4 children,—Sarah J., Alexander, James W. and Margaret.   Mr. H. is a School Director.

David F. Kiser, farmer, sec. 23; P. O. Pittsfield.   Mr. K. is a native of Indiana, where he was born in 1841; he was brought to this county by his parents, Jacob and Martha Kiser, when two years of age.   He was married to Janetta, daughter of Richmond Williams, an early pioneer of Pike who settled on this section, where he died.   The fruit of this union has been 3 children, 2 of whom are living,—Lydia and Essie.   Mr. K. and wife are both children of the pioneer generation.   Their fine farm and improvements attest the industry of its occupants.

Harvey Kiser is a son of Jacob Kiser, an early settler of Pike county, where the subject of this sketch was born in 1841.   He married Mary A. Casteel, daughter of Stephen Casteel, by whom he has one child, William C.   They have an adopted child, Loural.   Mr. K. has a farm of 80 acres, and politically he is a Republican.   He is engaged in farming on sec. 11, P. O. Griggsville.

Jacob L. Kiser, farmer, sec. 14; P. O. Detroit.   Mr. K. was born in Virginia in 1809; came to the county in 1841, and settled on sec. 29, where he resided until 1857, when he moved upon his present estate of 80 acres, valued at $100 per acre.   In 1839 he was united in matrimony to Miss Martha, daughter of David Foreman, by whom he has 7 living children. Mr. K. is a "stalwart" Republican, and numbers among those of the early settlers of Pike Co.

Mrs. Wm. Landers, sec. 17, P. O. Pittsfield; widow of William Landers, who was born in Highland Co., O., in 1825. Her maiden name was Elizabeth Sanderson, and she married Mr. Landers in 1846; ten years afterward they moved to this county, settling on the present estate, where he passed the remainder of his life. Four of their 6 children are living,—Perry, Mary, William and Leslie ; the last two reside on the homestead, as also the mother of Mrs. L., in the 83d year of her age.

Perry S. Landers, farmer, sec. 22, P. O. Pittsfield; was born in Highland Co., O., in 1852, son of William Landers, who settled in this tp. in 1856, where he died in 1879. In 1874 Perry S. married Dora, daughter of Dr. Boyd, by whom he has one child, Alice. He resides on the homestead, which consists of 177 acres of land, valued at $50 per acre.

Y. McAllister, farmer, sec. 11, P. O. Griggsville. The subject of this personal sketch is a native of New Jersey, where he was born March 31, 1818; he came to this county in 1839, and settled in Griggsville; the same year he was married in Delaware to Sarah A. Taylor. She was a native of Pennsylvania, where she was born in 1820; she died in 1844. By this union 4 children were born,—Edwin, John, Sarah and Caroline. He was again married in 1849 to Rachel Jones, also a native of the Keystone State, and born in 1820. Seven children were born to them, 6 of whom are living : Rebecca, Lucretia, Cyrus, Mary A., Naomi and Huldah; James, deceased. Mr. McAllister was licensed to preach in the M. E. Church in 1855, and has labored faithfully ever since in the propagation of the gospel, frequently preaching two or three times a day after laboring hard during the week on the farm.

E. M. Norton, farmer, sec. 13; P. O. Detroit; was born near Cincinnati, O., in 1822; is the son of John and Zerua (Chadwick) Norton, natives of Massachusetts, who settled in Hardin tp. in 1842, where they both died. The subject of this sketch crossed the plains to California in 1850, and returned 3 years afterward. In 1855 he was married to Miss Louisa Dinsmore, a native of this county, and located in Hardin tp.; 3 years afterwards he moved to Detroit, and in 1868 removed to California with his family, where he remained three years, when he returned and settled upon his present estate. He is the father of 8 living children: Emily, Mary, Margaret, Harry, John, Noel, Cora and Nora. Politically he is a Republican.

Giles H. Penstone, farmer, sec. 9; P. O. Griggsville. Mr. P. is the son of Giles and Sarah Penstone, natives of England, who came to America in 1849, and settled in this county. The subject of this sketch was born in London, Feb. 22, 1838. In Pike county, Aug. 1, 1867, he was married to Elizabeth J. Edom, who was born in the Buckeye State in 1844. They are the parents of 5 children.

Charles H., Mary E., Sarah J., Ellen E. and Edward J. Mr. P. has held several township offices, and owns a fine farm of 240 acres.

Francis A. Phillips, farmer, sec. 3; P. O. Griggsville; son of Nathan and Nancy Phillips, both natives of North Carolina; they emigrated to this State in an early day, settling in this county. The subject of this sketch is a native of Kentucky, where he was born in 1824; he was married to Mary Elliott, who was born in Ohio in 1827, and they are the parents of 5 children, 4 of whom are living: Maria, Martha, Benjamin and Newton; August, deceased. Mr. P. has held the office of constable 4 years and School Director several years. His father was in the war of 1812.

Job Pringle, retired, was born in England in 1844, and in emigration came with his parents to America when he was 8 years of age, and came to this county in 1856, settling in Pittsfield. He engaged in farming until 1861, when he enlisted in Co. B, 28th Ill. Inf. Vol., and served until the close of the war, participating in the battles of Shiloh, Jackson, Miss., Vicksburg, Hatchie, Miss.; was promoted to the position of Corporal, Sergeant and 2d Lieutenant; returned to Pittsfield, and for 11 years clerked in a dry-goods store. Nov. 11, 1879, he married Mahala Miller.

E. D. Rose, farmer, sec. 20; P. O. Pittsfield; born in Rensellaer Co., N. Y., in 1805; married in 1825 Roxana Allen, and they have 6 children. He came to this county in March, 1839, settling on his present estate of 160 acres of valuable land. Mr. Rose has served as Town Assessor and Constable. His son Henry enlisted in the 39th Regiment I. V. I., was taken prisoner at Sweetwater, Va., and confined in Andersonville prison, where he died from the effects of prison life and starvation.

Mrs. Sarah Ruby, sec. 7; P. O. Pittsfield. She is the widow of A. R. McKibbon, who was born in Highland Co., O. Her maiden name was Sarah Clark, a native of the same county, where she was born in 1832. She married Mr. McKibbon in 1849. He came to this county in 1850, and in the following year settled on the present estate of 180 acres, where he lived until his death in 1871. Their 7 children are all living: Eliza, Caroline, Margaret, Hester, Louy, Emma and Lewis. Mrs. McK. was again married in 1877, this time to J. M. Ruby, and the family reside on the homestead. Members of the Christian Church.

Marcellus Ross is the son of Col. Wm. Ross, deceased, who is so often referred to in the pages of this volume. The subject of this sketch was born at Atlas, Nov. 11, 1824, the first white male child born within the present limits of Pike county; at the age of 11 years he was brought to Pittsfield (one mile east of town in Newburg tp.) by his parents, where he has ever since resided. Aug. 10, 1848, he married Miss Martha Kellogg, from Pittsfield, Mass., and their children now living are Henry J., Charles K., Frank C. and Mattie H. Charles and Frank are in Washington Territory. Mr. Marcellus Ross remembers a visit of Abraham Lincoln to their home in Atlas, when he, a little boy, was picked up and pleasantly talked to by that eminent statesman. Mr. Ross has in his house the first Masonic chest used in the lodge in this county, described on pages 241–2 of this book.

William Schemel, farmer, sec. 32; P. O. Pittsfield; was born in Germany in 1835, emigrated to America in 1854, settling in Pittsfield. In 1868 he married Mary, daughter of George Zimmerman, an early settler of this county; in 1868 he moved upon his present farm, consisting of 166 acres, valued at $65 per acre. George D., William A., Joseph A., Emma M., Anna J. and Ida E. are their living children.

Cicero Scobey, farmer, sec. 9; P. O. Pittsfield; son of James and Rhoda Scobey, natives of New York and Kentucky respectively, who first settled in Clark Co., Ill., and came to this county in 1839, settling on Griggsville Prairie. His father died in 1841, and his mother died in 1877. The subject of this sketch was born in Indiana in 1831, in which State he married Mary Duff, a native of Illinois, and their 2 children are William W. and Anna M. Mr. S. has a farm of 260 acres, valued at $40 an acre. He has been Assessor one year. He numbers among the early settlers of Pike county.

John Webb, farmer, was born near Jersey City in 1814, and was brought to this county by Daniel Shinn in 1820, the family settling near Atlas. Some years afterward Mr. W. clerked for Mr. Gay in Pleasant Vale tp., and 3 years afterward engaged in the wood business at Florence, until 1839, when he went into merchandising and farming at New Canton; in 1851 he came to Pittsfield and became interested in pork-packing and general merchandising, where he remained 23 years; in 1875 he settled on his present farm in Newburg, where he has since made it his home. In 1840 he married Cornelia Dunham, a native of Warren Co., N. Y. Mr. W. is the oldest living settler in Pike county at the present time, by four years.

John A. Weeks, farmer, sec. 5; P. O. Pittsfield; son of Ezekiel and Elizabeth (McFadden) Weeks, who settled in Harrison Co., O., in early day, where in 1826 John A. was born. The family emigrated to this county in 1848, settling upon their present place, where they have since made it their home. In 1841 Mr. W. was married to Angeline Stagg, who died in 1857, leaving 4 children. His present wife, Martha L. Wacaser, is a native of North Carolina, and they have 7 children. Mr. W. has a farm of 80 acres, valued at $40 per acre.

W. T. Weeks. The subject of this sketch is a native of Ohio, where he was born Aug. 2, 1838; 10 years later he was brought to this county, where he is now engaged in farming in this township. He was married in Kansas in 1861, to Rosanna Pennocks, who was born in New York in 1842. In 1863 Mr. W. enlisted in Co. L, 2d Nebraska Cavalry, and served for one year, and served as scout along the Missouri and Kansas line for 2 years. He is a member of the M. E. Church, and politically a Republican.

Capt. Benj. F. Westlake, whose portrait is given in the pages of this volume, resides on sec. 29, this tp.; his grandparents emigrated from England, their native country, prior to the Revolution, and his grandfather and three of his brothers served in the continental army under Washington. George Westlake, the father of the subject of this sketch, was a native of Orange county, N. Y., and for many years a minister of the Methodist Church; he came to this county with his son, Capt. Benj. F., where at his residence in 1842 he died, his being the first death that occurred in this township; his wife, Hester (Wilson) Westlake, a native of New Jersey, died here July 9, 1852. Capt. Westlake was born in Newburg, Orange Co., N. Y., March 8, 1810. He visited Illinois in 1836, meeting Stephen A. Douglas, of Springfield, with whom he traveled through many counties, mostly by stage; in 1837 he settled in Pittsfield, and served as jailor one year, when he moved on his present estate, at that time consisting of 1,120 acres; he purchased two yokes of oxen, built a brick kiln and made the brick of which his commodious residence is composed. He gave the name to Newburg township, christening it after his native town in New York.

Capt. Westlake commenced the study of medicine at the age of 18 with Dr. Gidney, of Newburg, N. Y., but owing to the feeble health of his father he returned home and devoted his attention to farming, which he has followed from that time, and at present has about 2,000 acres of good farm land, besides having given to his children about 1,000 acres. The Captain's early life was passed on his father's farm near Newburg, and his first experience in business was selling vegetables in that town, furnishing and hauling rock, which he did for the foundation of nearly every building in that town up to the time he left.

Capt. Westlake was president of the commission appointed by the County Court to construct the Sny levee. Under this commission the work was vigorously prosecuted and successfully completed, reclaiming about 100,000 acres of rich farming land. He represented his township in the Board of Supervisors from its organization until 1863; in 1862 he was appointed by President Lincoln Provost Marshal of the 9th District of Illinois, which position he filled with honor to himself and credit to the country, obtaining the enviable reputation of being one of the best officers in the State. He was one of the original stockholders in organizing the Peninsula Loan and Trust company, now the Pike County Bank, of which he is president.

He was married March 24, 1842, by Rev. Wm. Carter, in this tp., to Miss Charlotte Goodwin, who was born March 22, 1822. The names of the 11 children born to them are as follows: George, Fannie S., Hardin J., Susan, Ann, Catharine, Wm. Henry, Benj. F., jr., Charlotte, Charles F. and Thomas.

George W. Westlake, farmer, sec. 29; P. O. Pittsfield; was born in this tp., in 1843, and is the eldest son of B. F. Westlake. In

1875 he married Miss Mary E. Brown. He now owns a farm of 250 acres, valued at $90 per acre.

Luther Wheeler, blacksmith, was born in Fairfield in 1827; served his time at Bridgeport, coach ironing; emigrated to this county in 1858, and established himself in business in Pittsfield; also conducted a livery stable one year, and in 1861 he went to Montgomery county, and four years afterward returned and settled in Milton, where he remained until 1877, in which year he occupied his present place of business. In 1859 he married Annetta Yelliott, a native of this county; they have had 4 children, 2 of whom are living. Mr. W. has a fair trade, and is a thorough Republican.

HARDIN TOWNSHIP.

Two of the largest streams of the county traverse this township from the northern boundary, making their exit almost due south of where they enter; these are Bay and Honey creeks, and the timber bordering their banks and those of their numerous small tributaries, must have been picturesque and romantic in their original condition. Then doubtless the points of timber and the valleys were frequent resorts for the red man. Even now, when dotted over with fields, houses and barns, and lowing herds, one cannot help but admire the beauty of the scenery presented by these groves.

Embracing a good deal of timber land, as this township did, it soon attracted a liberal share of immigration, as it is a fact that all the pioneers sought the timber districts in which to locate their claims, believing that it would be easier to make farms by grubbing andclearing the lands than it would be to reduce prairie land to farm tillage and remunerative returns ; but as time advanced and later settlers were forced out upon the prairies and began to experiment upon them, the first settlers were made to realize that they had made some costly mistakes by selecting timbered claims. They had been pitching brawn and muscle against nature; for all that the prairies needed was to be tickled with the plow to make them yield living crops the first year, and heavy remunerative returns the second.

The first pilgrims in Hardin were Benjamin Barney, Nathaniel Bagby, Solomon Main, Jacob Henry, Joseph Halford, Jesse Mason and Aaron Thornton. The first couple united in marriage in the township were Nathaniel Thornton and Lucinda Bagby; the ceremony was performed by Rev. Lewis Allen. The first school taught by Jesse Garrison, in 1833, upon sec. 2.

TIME.

The pleasant little village of Time is located where the four corners of secs. 2, 3, 10 and 11 meet. It is a small place, perhaps of 120 inhabitants, and contains four stores, two wagon and blacksmith shops and a flouring mill. It is also the residence of two physicians and one lawyer. There was at one time a woolen factory in Time, but times grew hard and the time came when Time must abandon the manufacture of cloth, we presume for all time to come. At present the old Time Woolen Mills is converted into a wagon shop and plow manufactory, which gives Time somewhat the appearance of old times.

James H Conroy

HARDIN TP

Star Mills.—This enterprise was inaugurated by Smith & Sonner. The building was erected in 1877, and is now owned and operated by Mr. Sonner. The capacity of the mill is about 50 barrels a day, besides being capable of grinding about the same amount of corn. Mr. Sonner makes a choice article of flour, and enjoys a good run of custom.

The Time Public Schools.—The system of education in Hardin township is well up to the standard in point of excellence. The Time public school has for its Principal Miss Ellen Cromwell, a lady of much ability and experience as an instructor.

Independence Christian Church was organized May 8, 1858, in the log school-house at Independence, by Elders James Burbridge, Robert Nicholson and Andrew Main, with the following 26 members: Robert Nicholson and wife, Andrew Main, Ephraim Nott and wife, Geo. W. Williams and wife, Barnett Collins and wife, James Collins, John Nicholson and wife, Cornelius Nicholson and wife, Mary Burbridge, Thomas Burbridge, Permelia Williams, Francis Scott and wife, George Ward, David Collins, Lydia Collins, Cynthia Burbridge, Emily Gunn, Joseph Troutner and Polly Burbridge. The first Elders were Robert Nicholson, Andrew Main and Joseph Troutner. Elder James Burbridge was the first Pastor. The congregation erected a house of worship in 1867 in Independence, and services are held each alternate Sunday by Elder J. W. Miller, Pastor. Present number of communicants is 50.

There are two other churches located in the township, one of the M. E. and the other of the Christian denomination, both of which are located at Time. After some considerable searching, however, we failed to find the records from which to glean any historical items.

PERSONAL SKETCHES.

We will now make personal mention of the leading citizens and old settlers of this township.

Benjamin Barney was born in Pike county, where Montezuma now stands, Feb. 1, 1825. His parents emigrated to this county from Ohio, in 1824. Being a pioneer, he knows all the hardships of pioneer life; as soon as he was large enough to ride on horseback he went to Frye's Mill on Big Blue, a distance of 12 miles, and nearly always had to remain all night to get his grinding done, and no place to sleep, except on the corn-sack; he has had many exciting scenes in the chase, having killed deer, wolves and wild-cats. Dec. 21, 1845, he married Miss Caroline Harvey, and they had 3 children,—William A., James B. and Alfred F. In 1852 Mr. Barney removed to Oregon with his family, where Mrs. Barney died the same year; in 1857 he returned to Pike county, where he married Cynthia H. Mays, and their 8 children are Andrew J., dec., John W., Henry L., Laura E., Marion, Robert A., Artilla D. and Minnie. Mr. B. is engaged in farming and stock-raising on sec. 26, this tp.

Francis M. Barney, a native of Pike county, was born May 12, 1837, and is a son of Joseph W. Barney, dec., who came to this county in 1824. His grandfather, Benjamin B. Barney, was one of the first pioneers of this county, and erected the first horse-mill in the county for grinding corn. This aged gentleman crossed the plains to California in 1849, being then in his 91st year, and arrived there in apparently good health, but died on ship-board while returning, in 1854. Our subject was raised on a farm and received a common-school education; in 1866 he married Miss S. A. Furry, daughter of Christopher Furry, dec. They have had 5 children, 3 of whom are living, viz:—Cora B., William R. and Edgar F. He has held the office of Town Clerk, and is at present the Police Magistrate for the village of Time. He served 3 years in Co. A, 20th Reg. I. V. I., as a private in the late war, and was in the battles of Fort Donelson, Shiloh, Siege of Vicksburg, Britton's Lane, Kenesaw Mountain, Champion Hills, Raymond and others; he also participated in the Meridian raid, in which he came well-nigh being captured. He is a harness-maker by trade, but failing health required him to seek another vocation, and he now keeps a grocery store in Time.

Henry Benn, son of William and Sarah Benn, was born Sept. 18, 1833, in this tp. His father, dec., came to this county in 1826, being one of the first settlers of Hardin tp., and was Captain of the Home Guards in the early days of the county's history. He was a native of Kentucky, and a farmer by occupation. He first settled on sec. 7, where he died in 1859. Mrs. Benn resides with her son David, in this tp., at the age of 74 years. Our subject was raised on a farm and is now engaged in farming and stock-raising on the old home place. April 17, 1858, he married Matilda J. Mc Clintock, daughter of Robert McClintock, dec., who came to this county in an early day. Mr. and Mrs. Benn have 9 children,—Charles F., Hettie M., Ida J., Evalina, William R., Lillie and Lulu (twins), Lora and John H. In the year 1857, while chopping wood with a neighbor, Mr. Benn received a blow, by accident, upon his left hand, from the ax of the neighbor, crippling him for life.

Thomas B. Burbridge, farmer and stock-raiser, sec. 29; son of Robert Burbridge, dec., a native of Kentucky, was born in Bath county, Ky., Feb. 28, 1818; came with his parents to Pike county, Mo., in 1825, where he remained until the Spring of 1840, when he removed to this county. His father followed farming until his death, which occurred in the spring of 1842. Our subject, being a pioneer, has seen many Indians, and has ridden on horseback to mill, a distance of 6 miles, where he sometimes had to wait all day and all night for his grinding, with nothing to eat but parched corn; he went 3 miles to school, which was taught by subscription, about 3 months in the year, in a log building, with split logs for seats, a log taken out of one side of the house for a window, a huge fire-place in one end of the room for heating; the writing desk consisted of a puncheon supported by pins in the wall. Mr B.

came to this county in 1839, where he has since resided. In 1842 he married Mary McNary, daughter of John McNary, dec., and they had 7 children,—Cynthia, Jaly, Robert, John, James, Thomas and Harriet. Mrs. B. died in 1862, and April 12, 1866, he married Emily Hodge, who died Oct. 9, 1875. Mr. B. is surrounded by his children, who take good care of him in his old age.

James H. Conboy is a native of Ireland, and was born in 1833; his parents died when he was quite young, leaving him penniless; about the year 1837 he was brought to America; is a shoemaker by trade, at which he has been very successful. He now resides at Time, owning 400 acres of valuable land, and is engaged in farming and stock-raising. In 1860 he married Lucy Bagley, and their children are John, William, Philip, Ella, Alvina and Raymond. We give Mr. C's portrait in this volume.

John Couch was born in Highland county, Ohio, April 4, 1833, and is a son of John and Elizabeth Couch; he was raised on a farm and came to this county in 1854; was married in 1855 to Margaret Colvin and they have 9 children, namely, Alfred M., Samantha A., Winfield S., Elizabeth J., John W., Benton, Charles, Wesley and Mary A. Mr. C. is engaged in farming and resides on sec. 27. P. O., Time.

Miss Ellen Cromwell, Principal of the Public Schools, Time, Pike county, Ill.

Benjamin C. Culver, sec. 20, was born in Chittenden county, Vt.; was raised on a farm and educated in the common schools at home. He came to this county in 1858, settling on sec. 20. He has been married 3 times and is the father of 9 children, viz: Lucina, Jackson, Clarissa, Giles, Judson, Jay L., Mary, Adell and Willy E., dec.

Jackson C. Culver, son of the preceding, was born in Erie county, Pa., April 20, 1834; came with his parents to Pike county in 1859; served 4 years and 7 months in the late war in Co. L, 12th Reg. Penn. Ca.v; was in the second battle of Bull Run, Antietam, Gettysburg, Winchester and others; was taken prisoner at Gettysburg and confined in Libby prison 6 weeks; was then removed to Bell island in James river, where he was held 3 months and exchanged. He was wounded near Harper's Ferry, in his right ankle, which rendered him a cripple for life. He is engaged in the mercantile business in Independence, this county, and carries a stock of about $3,000, consisting of dry-goods, groceries, boots and shoes, hardware, queensware,—in fact, everything kept in a first-class general store. He has won the confidence of the people and is doing a good business. Feb. 11, 1872, he married Martha, daughter of Samuel Smart, of Detroit tp.

James Dinsmore, an early pioneer, was born in Fleming county, Ky., Sept. 25, 1808; came to Scott county in 1825, where he saw plenty of Indians, and in 1831 he went into the Black Hawk war; was present or near by at the evacuation by the Indians of an Indian town at Rock Island, Ill. In May, 1819, he was married to

Sarah Mars, and they have had 14 children, 5 of whom are living, —Eldridge, Marshall, David, George and Jane, now Mrs. Dr. Scott, of Time. Mr. D. removed to this county in 1838, and has endured the hardships of the early pioneers; has ground corn in a hand-mill for bread.

Marshall Dinsmore, son of the preceding, was born March 4, 1827, in Scott county, Ill.; came with his parents to this county in 1838; went with the first emigration across the plains to California in 1849, and returned with the first company that returned by way of the Nicaragua route. When he visited Sacramento City, there was but one house there, and San Francisco was about the present size of Montezuma in this county. He helped to erect the first house in Georgetown, California. Dec. 31, 1854, he married Martha January, who was born in Greene county, Ill., April 16, 1834, and they have 4 children,—Susan J., William H., Mary E. and Noah E. Mr. D. is engaged in farming and stock-raising, and resides on sec. 27, this tp.; has held various offices of trust. Four of his brothers were in the late war.

I. J. Dyer, lawyer, was born in Rutledge, Granger Co., Tenn., July 8, 1839, and is a son of W. M. Dyer, dec., who came to Jacksonville with his family in 1841, where our subject was raised; but he educated himself after his marriage. He attended a common school, in company with his children, in this tp., and all the expenses of his education were defrayed by his own hand, by hard labor on the farm. He was in the late war and wounded in the left arm, disabling it for life. He has been married twice, and is the father of 3 children, namely, Lyman E. and Simon L., twins, and Effie B. He studied law in the Washington University Law School at St. Louis, and was admitted to the bar by the Supreme Court of Illinois, Sept. 13, 1873.

G. E. Fletcher, a native of Littleton, Massachusetts, was born Nov. 10, 1832; came with his parents to Pike county in 1838, where they remained until 1846, when they removed to Clarksville, Mo. He is a cooper and miller by trade; also operated a steam-engine. In 1855 he came to Pike county; here he engaged in farming for 2 seasons; has been married twice and is the father of 3 children,—John H., Mary E. and Sarah O., dec. In the fall of 1867 he engaged in the mercantile business in Time, and is doing a large business; carries a stock of $2,500, consisting of dry-goods, groceries, boots and shoes, queensware, etc.

Aaron Fuller was born in Jefferson county, Pa., Jan. 26, 1833; came to Greene county, Ill., in 1844; has resided in the States of Missouri, Kansas and Arkansas since he had a family. In Feb., 1854, he married Elizabeth Oaks, and they have had 7 children, of whom 4 are living, namely, Mary E., Ida H., Clara M. and Lillie B. Mr. Fuller is engaged in blacksmithing and wood work in Time, and does a good business; he manufactures a very good plow, which has an increasing demand.

R. H. Griffin, physician; was born in Georgetown, Brown Co., O., March 29, 1833, and is a son of William Griffin, dec., who emigrated with his family to this county in 1852. He graduated at the Eclectic Medical Institute at Cincinnati, O., receiving his diploma in 1879. He began the practice of medicine in this tp. in 1871; had been a medical student for 3 years previous to entering upon the duties of physician; during this time he taught school; he served in the late war in Co. E, 99th Reg. I. V. I., as First Lieutenant, and was in the battles of Magnolia Hills, Raymond, Jackson, Miss., Champion Hills, Black River Bridge, siege of Vicksburg, and others. In December, 1858, he married Louisa Hooper, daughter of William Hooper, dec., once County Treasurer of Pike county. They have had 9 children, of whom 7 are living, viz.: William W., Jessie G., Maggie, Nannie, Fannie, John and Hattie.

Otis A. Haskins, P. O. Time; was born in Bristol county, Mass., Nov. 21, 1816; came to this county in 1844, where he worked at the carpenter's trade for one year; then began farming as a renter. He now owns over 1,000 acres of valuable land, and is engaged in farming and stock-raising. March 12, 1844, he married Nancy Thomas, daughter of Samuel Thomas, of Greene county, Ill., and they have 4 children,—William H., Idelia, Mary J. and Samuel.

J. G. Haydon, Teacher of Pleasant Grove School, was born in Hendricks county, Ind., Oct. 13, 1842, and is a son of Abner Haydon, dec., who brought his family to Sangamon county, Ill., in 1844. He labored under great disadvantages in obtaining his education; at the age of 16 he was unable to write his name, but by industry and perseverance he has educated himself, and is now teaching. The pupils of his school are advancing rapidly in their respective studies. Oct. 29, 1869, he married Lovena J. Kent, daughter of Henry Kent, well known in the early settlement of this county. Their 4 children are,—Henry, J. G., Charley and Nellie.

George A. Henry, son of Jacob Henry, who came from Warren county, Ky., was an early pioneer, and has seen many hardships; he did the milling for 2 families; carried corn on a horse, and so thronged was the business at the old horse-mill at Milton that he would be compelled to arise at midnight and go to mill in order to get his grinding done in time to get home the next night; would frequently have to remain all night at the mill for his grinding, with no place to sleep, and nothing to eat but parched corn. On one occasion, he and another boy were there all night, and toward morning, becoming tired of parched corn, they concluded to have a change of diet. The proprietor retired, leaving them in charge of the mill. There was an old rooster on top of the mill, which, after chasing for some time, they succeeded in catching, and which they picked and roasted, and ate with a relish. Notwithstanding the hard times, there was plenty of wild game and honey to be obtained. July 24, 1850, Mr. Henry was married to Nancy J.

French, and they had 14 children; of these, 10 are living, and all at home but the eldest; their names are as follows: Franklin P., James M., Emeline, William, Austin, Mary, Flora, Ella, George and Minnie. Mr. Henry resides on sec. 2, this tp., on the old home place, and is engaged in farming and stock-raising. The house where he attended school was 12 by 14 feet, and had a mud-and-stick chimney and a clapboard door; the seats were sawed from a log with a whip-saw; they had no stove, but a large fire-place; the window consisted of a log cut out of one side of the house, with cloth pasted over the crack. On windy days the fire-place smoked so badly that the school would retire to the house of Mr. Henry. The ceiling consisted of poles covered with boards.

Chas. V. Johnson, farmer, sec. 21, was born in St. Lawrence Co., N. Y., May 15, 1815, and is a son of Charles and Rachel Johnson, dec.; he was raised on a farm and came to this county in 1837. In 1838 he married Emily Span; 4 of their 8 children are living, viz: Mary, Rebecca, Phila and Emma, all married. Mr. J.'s father was a soldier in the war of 1812, and his son was lost in the late war.

Henry Kent was born in Fayette Co., Ky., in 1801, and is a son of Henry and Mary Kent, dec.; he was educated in a log cabin, with round poles for seats, a log cut out of one side of the house, with a greased paper pasted over the crack for a window, and a huge fire-place in one end for warming the room. Coming in 1836 to this wild West, Mr. Kent has killed many a deer in this county, and witnessed the scenes of pioneer times. He is a black-smith by trade, but has engaged in farming and stock-raising and speculating in land since coming to Illinois. He has been married twice, and is the father of 15 children, of whom 8 are living,— George W., Martha, Mary, Eliza J., Fannie, Lovina, Charlotte and Henrietta. Two sons, Walter D. and Newton P., were soldiers in the late war.

David Lacy, farmer and stock-raiser, sec. 12, was born in Davidson Co., N. C., June 25, 1818, and is a son of Daniel and Elizabeth Lacy, dec., who brought their family to Pike county in 1839. Our subject came to this county in 1842, where he engaged in the masonry business until 1851; he was married in 1855 to Mrs. Catharine M. Devol, and they have 6 children,—Margaret A., Julia F., Lincoln S., Sarah E., Lucretia B. and Amanda J. Mr. Lacy went overland to California in 1852, and returned by ship in 1853.

Alvin Main, son of Andrew Main, was born Jan. 17, 1844, in this tp. He was raised on a farm, and when in his 18th year he enlisted in the late war, in Co. B, 28th Reg. I. V. I., and served 3 years; he was in the battles of Shiloh, Hatchie River, siege of Vicksburg and others. Sept. 7, 1865, he married Miss Lydia Foot, daughter of George D. Foot, of Newburg tp.; they have 6 children,—Clara M., Rufus H., Josiah S., Blanche M., R. I. and Georgiana. Mr. M. resides on sec. 8, this tp., and is engaged in general farming.

Andrew Main, farmer and stock-raiser, sec. 5, was born in Jackson Co., O., Aug. 6, 1817, and is a son of Solomon and Susan Main, so well known in the early settlement of this county, who came here in 1828. He loaned his gun to a friend to use in the Black Hawk war, which, at the close of the war, was returned, and he was also a soldier in that war. Andrew Main was educated in a log house with slab seats, greased paper for windows, and a large fire-place in one end. Mr. M. used to go to a horse-mill on horseback, and in the earlier part of their pioneer life he ground corn in a hand-mill; he hunted with the Indians and killed deer with them. Sept. 28, 1838, he married Lutilia Johnson, and they have had 15 children, 9 of whom are living; their names are Alvin, Andrew P., Colonel, Philip, George, William, Thomas, Jane and Minerva.

George Main was born in Beaver, now Lawrence, county, Pa., Dec. 17, 1838, and is a son of Daniel Main, dec., who brought his family to this county in 1859, settling in this tp., where he resided until his death, which occurred in 1873. Our subject was married in 1866 to Miss Myra Williams, and their children are Fred, George, Owen, Myrtle and Ralph. Mr. Main is a blacksmith, wagon and plow maker, in company with Mr. Philip, in Time; they do a good business, and give general satisfaction. Mr. Main has held various offices of trust in this tp.; served over 3 years in the late war in Co. K, 2d Reg. Ill. Cav., and was in 54 engagements, among which were the following: Middleburg, Lamare, Holly Springs, siege of Vicksburg, Sabine Cross Roads, Pleasant Hills, Yellow Bayou, etc. He was captured at Middleburg and held prisoner at Vicksburg for 6 weeks, when he was exchanged.

Jacob Main was born in Beaver Co., Pa., Sept. 14, 1848, and is a son of Daniel Main, deceased, who first came to this county about the year 1850, and moved his family here in 1852. Our subject was married Sept. 7, 1868, to Mary Mortion, daughter of Matthew Mortion, deceased. They have had 4 children, of whom 3 are living, viz: Effie, Ottie and Almira. Mr. Main is a farmer, and resides on sec. 19. P. O., Pittsfield.

Philip J. Main, brother of the preceding, was born in Beaver Co., Pa., Jan. 12, 1845; he is a brother and partner of George Main, of Time. He came to Illinois with his parents in 1859, and in 1871 was married to Josephine Horton, by whom he has had 2 children; only one, Vinnie, is living. He served 100 days in the late war, in Co. H, 137th Reg. I. V. I., and was in the battle of Memphis, Tenn.

Cyrus McFaddin was born in Brown Co., O., Jan. 16, 1840, and is a son of Jacob and Elizabeth McFaddin. He came to Illinois in 1852, remaining one year, when he returned to Ohio; came back to this county in 1855; he served 3 years in the late war in Co. G, 99th Reg. I. V. I., and was in the battles of Magnolia Hills, Champion Hills, Black River Bridge, siege of Vicksburg, Jackson, Miss., and others. Feb. 11, 1869, he married Miss Rebecca J.

Mitchell, and they have had 6 children; of these 4 are living, namely, Mary N., Frank W., Charles L. and George A. Mr. Mc-Faddin resides on sec. 22, and is engaged in farming and the raising of stock.

James B. Miller, deceased, was born in Fayette Co., Pa., April 25, 1818, and was a son of Samuel and Lydia Miller, deceased. He came to this county in the fall of 1853, and settled in Montezuma tp. 2 years, then removed to this tp., where he engaged in farming on sec. 16 until his death, which occurred Feb. 11, 1874. He was a worthy member of the New-School Presbyterian Church for many years; was also an Elder for 30 years. He was a generous, kind-hearted man. In 1841 he married Miss Mary Griffin, daughter of Wm. Griffin, deceased, who brought his family to this county in 1852 ; she is also a sister of Dr. Griffin, of Time ; Mr. and Mrs. Miller had 11 children; of these 8 are living, to-wit: Samuel W., Sarah F., William F., Elizabeth G., Lydia, Anna, Robert B. and James A. Mrs. Miller resides on the old home place. We give Mr. Miller's portrait in this volume.

James V. Moore, a veteran of the Mexican war, was born March 4, 1818, and is a son of James and Mary Moore, deceased, who moved with their family from Russellville, Ky., to Charleston, Coles Co., Ill., in 1836. Our subject was a school-mate of the noted desperadoes, the James boys, near Russellville, Logan Co., Ky. He served one year as 2d Lieutenant in Co. C, 5th Reg. I. V. I., when he became diseased, from the effects of which he has never recovered. He draws a small pension. In 1849 he married Mary A. Norton, and their children are Laura Tyler, of Fort Scott, Kansas, Charley, telegraph operator at Tallula, Ill., and Dora Smith, of St. Louis. Mr. and Mrs. Moore reside in Time.

William R. Moore, teacher of Union school, district No. 4, Hardin tp., is a native of Kentucky, and was born April 18, 1848. He was educated at North Missouri Normal School, at Kirksville, Mo. Dec. 24, 1872, he married Miss Jennie, daughter of William H. Bennett, of Pittsfield. Mr. Moore conducts his school on the latest normal plans, and is a successful teacher.

Alvin Petty was born in Pike county, Mo., Oct. 15, 1826. His father, Fisher Petty, came to this county in 1828, having emigrated from Columbus, Ohio, to Pike county, Mo., when a young man. When the Petty family located here, the land was nearly all vacant between their residence and where Pittsfield now stands. Atlas was then the county-seat. Deer, turkey, wolves, etc., were plenty at that time, deer being nearly or quite as tame as modern sheep; they would frequently come within a few rods of the house, and turkeys would pass through the yard. Feb. 7, 1849, Mr. Alvin Petty married Julia A. Duffield, daughter of James Duffield, of Martinsburg tp., who was a soldier in the war of 1812, and is 82 years old. Mr. and Mrs. Petty have had 8 children, of whom 7 are living,—Marion M., Catharine, Isaac N., James F., Ella, William and Frederick. Mr. Petty is a natural genius, and has worked at

James B. Miller

HARDIN TP

nearly all kinds of mechanical labor; but his general occupation is farming and stock-raising. He resides on sec. 5; owns 293 acres of valuable land.

J. H. Rainwater, teacher of Honey Creek school, this tp., was born Dec. 11, 1858, and is a son of John Rainwater, deceased, who died in Nashville, Tenn., during the Rebellion. Mr. R. was educated in Pittsfield, and has chosen teaching as his vocation. His school is well conducted, and he has won the confidence of parents and pupils.

Joseph M. Russell, a native of this county, was born in Martinsburg tp., May 7, 1837, and is a son of John and Mary Russell, deceased, so well known in the early history of this county; his father helped survey the present town plat of Pittsfield. The Indians were their nearest neighbors, and the wolves made the night hideous with their howling. Our subject was raised on a farm, and now resides on sec. 19. Aug. 26, 1859, he married Martha Kiser, daughter of Samuel Kiser, deceased. They have 6 children,—Eliza, John, Mary, George, David and Elmer. Mrs. Russell was born in Warren county, Ind., March 5, 1843, and was brought by her parents in the fall of 1844, to this county, where she has since resided.

Anthony Sonner was born Oct. 17, 1830, in Highland county, Ohio, and is a son of Jacob Sonner, deceased. He came to Pike county in 1860, where he has since resided; he is a miller by trade, but has been engaged in farming since coming to Illinois, until the last 3 years. In Oct., 1855, he married Miss Sarah Hicks, and they had 6 children; of these, 3 are living,—Charley, Ora and Brady.

Evans Scott, physician, was born in Somerset county, Pa., Feb. 7, 1835. He was educated partly in Ohio and partly in Pennsylvania. He graduated at the Medical College at Keokuk, Iowa, in 1864; he served over 3 years in the late war in the 3d Ill. Cav.; the greater part of the time he had charge of a ward in a hospital at Keokuk. He began practice at Time, in 1865. He now has a large practice.

Richard Thornton was born in this tp., May 18, 1840, and is a son of Nathan and Lucinda Thornton. He was raised on a farm and is now engaged in farming and stock-raising, and resides on sec. 17. He was married March 16, 1864, to Margaret Watson and their 4 children are James A., Benjamin F., Flora H. and Nella J. Mrs. Thornton died Jan 20, 1875, and March 10, 1876, Mr. T. married Phila V. Johnson, daughter of Charles V. Johnson: they have one child, Richard S.

John L. Troutner was born in this tp. May 11, 1847, and is a son of the late Rev. Joseph Troutner, who came to this county from Ohio, in 1838, settling near Pittsfield, and was a farmer and stock-raiser, and was also Deputy Sheriff of the county about as early as 1841; he was Justice of the Peace 24 years in succession, and was School Treasurer 12 years; also filled other offices of trust; he clerked in the first store at Pittsfield; he died at his residence in

35

this tp. Oct. 22, 1878, highly esteemed by all. John L. is the eldest of 12 children, all living; was married in July, 1849, to Isabella Elder, who was born in Florence, Pike Co. He resides on sec. 19, and is engaged in farming.

Harry White, son of Silas and Louisa (Jones) White, was born May 19, 1845, and raised as a wool-carder; he operated the woolen mills in Time from 1865 to 1870; he served 3 years in the late war in Co. D, 1st Reg. M. V. I.; was for awhile in Benton Barracks at St. Louis; has worked in a mill all summer and traveled in the winter; has gone from Buffalo to Denver; owns a farm in Franklin county, Kan.; was a farmer and stock-raiser in Kansas 4 years. In 1876 he married Mattie Bagby, daughter of E. D. Bagby, dec.; they have one child, Trula. He is a farmer and stock-raiser on sec. 9. While in the service he was in the battles of Pilot Knob, Round Pond, Mill Creek and others.

Samuel Willard, a native of this county, was born Aug. 25, 1843; was educated in a common school and raised on a farm. At the age of 19 he enlisted in the war and served 3 years in Co. E, 99th I. V. I., and was in the battles of Fort Gibson, Black River Bridge, siege of Vicksburg, Fort Blakely, Spanish Fort and others; was also detailed musician; was honorably discharged July 31, 1865. He was married in 1867 to Miss Frances Miller, daughter of James B. Miller, dec. Mr. W. owns 120 acres of land in Martinsburg tp., but now resides in Time.

Henry J. Williams was born in Scott county, Ky., Sept. 25, 1826, and is a son of Thompson Williams, who removed with his family to Jacksonville, Ill., in 1832, and in 1833 came to this county, locating in Montezuma tp., on what was known as Franklin Prairie, on sec. 9. Our subject was raised a farmer, and received his education in an old log school-house with a stick chimney, slab benches, and a fireplace in one end, between 7 and 8 feet wide. Mr. Williams was in Pittsfield when there was but one house there; the prairie grass was as high as a horse's back. He moved to Pittsfield in 1856, remaining there about 6 months, when he removed to sec. 22, this tp., where he still resides, and is engaged in farming and stock-raising; he has had a fine two-story brick residence, which was burned in 1861. He now owns 1,100 acres of valuable land. June 6, 1850, he married Ruth A. Chenoweth, who was born in Macomb, McDonough county, Ill. They have 11 children, viz: Abbie, Laura, Amanda, Henry, Mary E., Robert, Nola, Rose, John, Charley and Stella. The eldest is about 29 years old. It is a remarkable fact that there has never occurred a death or a wedding in this family. Mr. Williams' father and Jacob Hodgen founded the first Christian Church in Montezuma tp., which was the first Church of that denomination in the eastern part of Pike county. They had to grind their corn in a horse mill or an ox mill. Mr. W. has actually gone to mill every day in the week and returned with no meal on Saturday night, so thronged was the mill. He has ridden 10 miles on horseback many times to mill, and arrived there before daylight.

Andrew Yaeger, a native of Germany, was born Oct. 24, 1828; came to America in 1853, settling in Newburg tp., where he resided until 1867, and then removed to this tp., locating on sec. 14, where he still resides, engaged in farming and stock-raising. In 1853 he married Barbara, daughter of Adam Kern, dec. Not having money enough to marry according to the laws of Germany, Mr. Yaeger brought his intended wife to America and married her here. They have had 8 children, of whom 7 are living, namely, Lucy J., Mary A., John G., Barbara M., William F., Henry C., and Anna C.

SPRING CREEK TOWNSHIP.

This is one of the southern tier of townships, and is bounded · upon the north by Hardin, the east by Pearl, south by Calhoun county, and upon the west by Pleasant Hill township. It is a full Congressional township and received its name from the principal stream which runs through it. The surface is very broken and principally covered with timber, with small necks of prairie. Many springs of sparkling water are found gushing from the hillsides in this township.

Silas Wilson came to the township in 1832, and erected a log cabin and made other improvements, on sec. 8, where he remained for many years. Benj. Allison, David Scranton, Barnard Collins, J. P. Stark and Mr. Hollis came in soon after. These early pilgrims did not find all the conveniences which makes life pleasant. The hunting was better than now, but all those things which are now thought to be necessaries, were then wanting. Money was so scarce that it was hardly talked of as a commodity. In place of the Short-horn cattle and Berkshire hogs, which can be seen in every pasture and feed-yard in this magnificent county, were the black, brindle, pie-bald, polled, streaked and speckled cattle which, for the want of a name were usually called natives. They were as uneven in quality as variegated in color, and lacked all the beef qualities for which their successors, the Short-horns, are so famous. They answered the purpose for which they were wanted, however, perhaps full as well if not better than the present popular breed would have done. The working cattle were lively and endured fatigue and heat well, and even after they were fatted they stood the long drives which the then system of marketing demanded, much better than the cattle of the present day would. They could hardly have been called handsome, but they were in all ways the chief help and profit of the farmer. As much can hardly be said of the wind-splitting prairie rooters that were the only hogs then known in these parts; but they were hogs, and did not like to be trifled with. They lived on roots and nuts and could outrun a horse. When the farmer went to feed them he put the corn where he was sure the contrary fellows would find it. If he had tried to call them with that long, sonorous half shout and half groan now in use to bring hogs to their feed, the chances are decidedly that he would have scared them out of the timber and might never have seen them; but they were handy to drive, as men then had to drive hogs to market.

Rachel Collins was the first white child born in the township, her birth occurring in 1833. Joseph Collins, who died the same year, was the first person to die in the township. Joel Meacham and Sarah Adkins were the first couple united in marriage. The ceremony was performed by Rev. Levi Hinman, who also preached the first sermon in the township in 1833. He was a minister of the Baptist denomination. F. A. Collins was the first Justice of the Peace, and John P. Stark the first Supervisor. All of the earliest adventurers are now gone, most of them to that country which is always new, but where the hardships and privations of pioneer life are never known.

VILLAGES.

Nebo.—This little village is situated on the Louisiana branch of the Chicago & Alton Railroad, and is a lively business point. The gentlemen who represent the leading business interests of the town, —Wm. E. Davis, David Hollis, Mr. Moore, the miller, and Dr. Pollock,—are spoken of personally below.

Stewart.—This is a station on the Chicago, Alton & St. Louis Railway; is situated on the northeast quarter of section 23, and the northwest quarter of section 24, of this township, and was laid out by County Surveyor H. J. Harris, in 1872, for D. W. Knight, Daniel Allison and John McCormick.

CHURCHES.

The Nebo Baptist Church was organized on the first Saturday in April, 1863, by Rev. J. J. W. Place, with a membership of 37. The congregation erected a house of worship in 1864 and now has services once each month, and sustains a Sunday-school during the summer season. The present membership numbers 67. Rev. F. H. Lewis is Pastor.

The Regular Predestinarian Baptist Church at Spring Creek, was constituted in August, 1862, by Elder Samuel Applegate, with 16 members. The society worshiped for about five years in the Spring Creek school-house, which stood where Nebo now stands. They erected a house of worship in 1857 or 1858, which was burned in February, 1879. The following autumn they erected another and a more commodious and substantial church building. The present Pastor is S. R. Williams.

PERSONAL SKETCHES.

The personal mention of any community forms the most interesting feature of its history. As part of the history of Spring Creek township we make mention of the following early settlers and prominent citizens.

Nathan Allison. Being an old settler of Pike county, Mr. A. is identified with its history, and therefore, should have more than

passing notice in a work of this nature. He was born in Pike
county, O., March 8, 1817, and is the son of Benjamin Allison, one
of the pioneers of Pike county, and who removed from Ohio to
Indiana in 1824, and to this county in 1834; in 1836 he purchased
the farm of Silas Wilson on sec. 8, Spring Creek township, upon
which was the only house in the township, and the Allison family
was the only one residing in the township, until a few months later,
when the Scranton family moved in. Our subject located in Calhoun county in the fall of 1836, and there constructed quite a novel
mill, there being a stream in the hillside near his house. He made
a trough, which worked on a pivot. To one end of the trough was
attached a large maul or pounder, which set in a box or trough
beneath; the other end of the trough was placed under the falling
water on the hillside; as soon as the trough was filled with water
one   end   would   be   overbalanced,   and   at   the   same   time
the water would pour out of it, when immediately the pounder
would fall down with a thud, and smash the few grains of corn
that were in the mortar. Occasionally an unfortunate, coon would
step in to partake of some of the meal and would remain there
until some one came to his rescue, and he would come out all
mangled and bleeding, never more to return to the forest. Mr. A.
was married in 1836 to Elizabeth Wilson, daughter of Silas Wilson;
and they had four children, of whom two are living,—Mahala and
Felix. Mrs. Allison died in 1849. Mr. Allison is now living with
his fourth wife. He erected the first house in Nebo, and is now
engaged in farming and the raising of stock on sec. 30.

Wm. H. Bacus, teacher of Nebraska schools, Spring Creek township, was born in this county Oct. 19, 1843, and is a son of John S.
Bacus, deceased. He was married in 1873 to Martha J. Mays. To
them have been born three children,—Minnie D., James H. M.
and an infant, deceased. Mr. B. has a very large and interesting
school,—indeed, so large that one with the most unflagging energy
and dispatch can scarcely do justice to it. He hears 30 recitations
daily and keeps exceptionally good order, although many of the
pupils are very small.

William S. Buchanan, farmer and stock-raiser, sec. 36, was born
March 8, 1833, in Calhoun county, Ill., and is a son of the late
Henry P. Buchanan; he was reared on a farm in a wild section of
the country where deer, wolves, etc., were numerous, and has killed
many deer and other wild animals. There was no free-school system here in those early days, and money being a scarce article in
pioneer days, Mr. B.'s educational advantages were like those
of other pioneer boys, very meager. He was married in 1855
to Miss Catharine McConnell, daughter of Robert McConnell,
deceased, a pioneer of Pike county, Mo. They have had 12 children, only 4 of whom are living,—Robert H., Mary O., Thomas
A. and James A. Besides a farmer, Mr. B. is also a blacksmith and
wagonmaker,—in fact, he can do almost any kind of work he turns
his hand to.

John A. Bunn was born in Pike county, Mo., March 4, 1845, and is a son of George Bunn, deceased. Mr. B. went into Calhoun county, Ill., with his mother in 1851, where he remained until 1865, when he went to Missouri and remained five years; he came to this county in the spring of 1871 and resides on sec. 36, where he is engaged in farming. He was married in 1871 to Mary E. Borrowman, by whom he has four children,—Minnie O., Edgar R., deceased, Cora A. and Hattie A.

E. B. Collard was born Oct. 16, 1841, in Pleasant Hill township, this county, and is a son of John J. and Mary E. Collard, deceased, so well-known in the early settlement of Pike county. His father filled the office of County Clerk of Pike county for two terms and filled every county office as deputy, except that of Surveyor. Our subject was raised for the most part on a farm and educated in the common schools; he was married Nov. 25, 1877, to Miss Emily M. Harpole, daughter of L. C. Harpole, of this township. They have one child, Arthur B. Mr. Collard is engaged in the mercantile business at Strout Station, on the Chicago, Alton & St. Louis R. R., and carries a stock of about $1,500, consisting of dry-goods, groceries, boots and shoes, and the general variety usually kept in a first-class store. He is also Agent for the Railroad Company, express agent and Postmaster.

John Collyer was born in Owen county, Ind., June 30, 1838, and is a son of William Collyer, deceased; Mr. C. was reared on a farm, and is now engaged in farming and stock-raising on secs. 7 and 8; he came to this county in 1851, and was married Aug. 15, 1857, to Miss Ellen Baker; to them have been born five children, four of whom are living, namely, William E., Llewella, Nora A. and John M.

Leonard G. Hamner, agriculturist and stock-raiser, sec. 8, was born May 31, 1832, and is a son of Jesse Hamner, deceased; he was brought up on the farm and educated in the common school; Aug. 23, 1854, he married Miss Pearcy Wilson, by whom he has had six children: of these 3 are living, namely, Eliza J., Minerva A. and John Henry. P. O., Nebo.

Bruce Harpole, farmer, stock-raiser and dealer in stock, sec. 27. Was born in Pleasant Hill township, this county, Nov. 12, 1835, and is a son of Adam and Lucinda (McMullen) Harpole, so well known in the early settlement of this county. Mr. H. was raised a farmer's boy and knows all about grubbing and picking brush, rolling logs, driving oxen, etc. He has plowed with the wooden mold-board plow, used wooden-wheeled wagons and hickory-bark lines in driving horses. He was married Nov. 13, 1859, to Miss Rebecca E. Stark, daughter of John P. Stark. Four of their eight children are living,—Adam, Lucinda, Robert B. and Charlie A.

Charles E. Harpole was born in Calhoun county, March 22, 1846, and is a son of Adam and Lucinda Harpole; the former is deceased, and the latter is residing near her son in this county. Mr. H. was reared on a farm and received a common-school education.

He was married April 6, 1866, to Miss Martha A., daughter of Willis and Hannah (Mc Neely), of Calhoun county. They have had 5 children, 4 of whom are living,—Henry A., Mary O., Hattie J. and John B. Mr. H. resides on sec. 33 and is engaged in farming.

L. C. Harpole, farmer and stock-raiser, sec. 26, was born in Pleasant Hill township Dec. 11, 1830. His parents, Joel and Hannah Harpole, were well known to the pioneer days of Pike county. His father served in the Black Hawk war. Our subject was reared on a farm and knows all about the privations that pioneer boys are heir to. His educational advantages were very limited, there being no free schools in those days. His mother wove cloth to pay for his education. He has plowed many a day with a wooden mold-board plow, and has reaped grain with a hand sickle, trampled out wheat with horses, went to church in an ox wagon, and ground corn on a hand-mill and was compelled to do a good many other things which seem odd to the boys of this day. In 1853 he was united in marriage with Sarah Martin, daughter of Willis Martin, an early settler of Illinois. Of the 9 children born to them 7 are living,—James R., William H., Emily V., John D., Martha, and Albert and Alice, twins.

A. Hatch. This enterprising young man was born in Ontario county, N. Y., May 6, 1852. He came to Pike county with his parents in 1862. He received a good common-school education and a musical education, and is now teacher of cornet-band music, and has met with excellent success thus far. In Prairieville, Pike county, Mo., in 1879, he began with a class of new and inexperienced men, and in six months time it was demonstrated that that was the best band in the county. The parents of our subject are A. G. and Alvira Hatch, and he is the youngest of 3 children,—A. W., Ellen J. and himself. He resides with his mother on the farm, sec. 24, and during the summer season is engaged in farming.

David Hollis, Nebo, was born in Gibson county, Tenn., April 6, 1824, and is a son of A. L. and Sarah (Payne) Hollis, who brought their family to Illinois in 1830, and to Pike county in 1845. Mrs. Hollis is a second, or grand niece of Thomas Paine, the noted deist of revolutionary fame. Our subject was raised on a farm and received a limited education in the subscription schools, paying his own tuition with money he earned by hard work. He began active life with nothing but his hands and a determined will. He now owns 400 acres of land and a third interest in a large store at Nebo. This firm carries a stock of about $4,500, consisting of general merchandise, and is doing a large business, employing 3 to 4 clerks. Mr. Hollis held the office of County Treasurer for 2 years, and Justice of the Peace for Spring Creek township for 20 years. He was married in 1846 to Mary C. Leggett, and by this union 5 children were born: Sarah M., Lewis Y., Elizabeth J., Barbara E. and Mary, deceased. Mrs. H. died in 1868, and in 1878 Mr. H. married Sarah M. Mason, by whom he has 3 children,—Anna L., David P. and Nellie M.

Dennis Leary, deceased. The subject of this sketch was born in Ireland, June 24, 1812, and came to America when a young man. He was a painter by trade, and did a good deal of work in New Orleans, Mobile, and throughout the Southern cities generally. He owned land in Pike county for many years, and in 1872 purchased a farm on sec. 25 of this township. He was united in marriage Feb. 17, 1851, with Mrs. Eliza French, daughter of Wm. Morton, of the vicinity of Milton, this county. She was born Aug. 21, 1825, in East Tennessee. They had six children,—John, Leander, Thomas, Albert, deceased, Alfred and Elia. Mrs. Leary had two children by her former husband,—Martha and William French. Mr. Leary died May 7, 1876. His son Thomas, who is a subscriber for this book, is a prominent school-teacher, and is now (March 4, 1880) teaching at Pearl Prairie.

S. T. Moore, proprietor of Nebo Mills. This enterprising gentleman took charge of the Nebo flouring mills in 1877, and has operated them with the very best of success. Others have tried at different times to build up a trade here, but in vain. The secret of Mr. M.'s success is that he makes the very best of flour, and has won the confidence of the farmers of the surrounding country. He also has a corn-sheller attached to his mill, which enables him to pay the highest market price for that cereal. He was born in Monroe county, Ill., Jan. 12, 1836, and is a son of James B. Moore, of Brighton, Ill. He was married May 4, 1860, to Harriet F. Randolph, of Jersey county, Ill. They have had 7 children, of whom 5 are living,—Josephine C., Eddie, Frank T., Nellie R. and James L. Mr. Moore was raised on a farm and educated in the common schools, and also attended the McKendree College, of Lebanon, Ill.

Dr. R. R. Pollock, Nebo. The subject of this sketch was born in Union county, O., Feb. 28, 1843, and is a son of John D. and Rachel G. Pollock, who brought their family to Edgar county, Ill., in 1844, where they remained until 1856, when they removed to Polk county, Iowa. Our subject remained there until the breaking out of the rebellion, when he enlisted in Company A, 10th Iowa Inf., and served three years and two months. He participated in many of the leading battles of the war, such as Corinth, Black River Bridge, or Champion Hills, siege of Vicksburg, Chattanooga, Dalton, etc. The Doctor afterward attended Abingdon College, Knox Co., Ill., for two years, where he became acquainted with Miss Anna E. Ferguson, whom he married Aug. 8, 1866. The union has been blessed with two children, Robert Cleon and John Roy. The Doctor attended lectures at the Jefferson Medical College at Philadelphia, Pa., in 1870 and 1871, and began practice in Nebo in the latter year, where he enjoys a good patronage.

John W. Scranton was born in this township Jan. 19, 1847, and is a son of David Scranton, also of this township; he was reared on a farm and educated in the common schools of this county; before settling in life he took two trips through the West. March 3, 1872, he married Miss Mary E. Bowman, daughter of Robert and Mary

E. Bowman. They have two children, Cora Belle and William Otis. Mr. Scranton is engaged in farming and resides on sec. 7; P. O. Nebo.

John N. Smith, book-keeper, was born May 22, 1845, in this township, and is a son of Wm. E. Smith, of Nebo, and of whom we make further mention below. Mr. Smith was reared for the most part upon the farm, but worked in a flouring-mill prior to reaching his majority. He is now engaged as book-keeper in the Nebo flouring-mills. He was joined in matrimony Oct. 1, 1865, with Miss Sarah E. Creigmiles. Three children have blessed this union, namely, Laura M., Thomas T. and Ellen F. Mr. Smith served six months in the late war, in Company I, 70th Ill. Inf.

William E. Smith. Being an early settler of Pike county, Mr. Smith is entitled to personal mention in a work of this nature. He came with his parents from Oswego Co., N. Y., to this county in 1836. He was born in Columbus Co., N. Y., Dec. 14, 1819. His parents were Amasa and Sarah (Sikes) Smith. William was reared upon a farm, and received a common-school education, and has suffered many of the privations incident to pioneer life. Jan. 3, 1841, he was united in marriage with Miss Polly Allison, daughter of Benj. Allison, deceased, one of Pike county's pioneers. To them have been born 11 children, 4 of whom are deceased. The names of the children are, William, John, Mercy A., Mary J., Samuel H., Daniel W. and Charles W. Mr. Smith is engaged in the lumber trade at Nebo, carrying a stock of $2,500. He is also an undertaker.

John D. Wilson. The subject of this sketch was born in Lincoln county, Mo., March 21, 1834. His father, David Wilson, brought his family to this county in the autumn of 1834, and located in Pleasant Hill township, where he remained the rest of his life, save the last 3 years which he spent in Nebo. Our subject was raised upon the farm, and being a pioneer boy knows all about the privations of frontier life. He was married in 1856 to Miss Nancy, daughter of George Turnbaugh, so well known in the pioneer days of Pike county. Mr. W. is a farmer by occupation and resides in Nebo.

W. R. Wilson was born and raised on sec. 13, Pleasant Hill township, this county, and is a son of David and Isophena Wilson, deceased. His birth dates Aug. 17, 1844. May 13, 1870, he was united in marriage with Miss Ellen J., daughter of Harrison and Matilda Frye, of Pike county, Mo. Only 1 of the 3 children born to Mr. and Mrs. W. is living, whose name is Claudie. Mr. W. has been engaged in the mercantile business in Nebo for the last 12 years, but has recently sold to Fowler & Son, near Pittsfield.

Jacob Windmiller, proprietor of the Nebo Hotel, is a native of this county, and was born Jan. 3, 1849, the son of Peter and Sevelia Windmiller. Peter W. was one of the pioneers of Pike county, and, like other settlers, endured many privations and hardships in preparing the way for the prosperity of future generations.

For some time after he first settled here there was only one wheeled vehicle in this entire neighborhood, and that was a wooden-wheeled ox-cart. He often gathered his corn in a one-horse sled. Our subject was reared on a farm, and Nov. 27, 1873, was married to Mary Stone, and they have one child, Laren O.

FAIRMOUNT TOWNSHIP.

This is certainly one of the finest townships in this favored county, and for general agricultural purposes, is unrivaled by any. Where, less than half a century ago the deer, wolf and bear roamed at will, the native red man their only enemy, are now handsome residences, with fine grounds and convenient out-houses, churches, school-houses and well cultivated fields. The native prairies have been conquered from their virgin state by the energy and skill of the sturdy pioneer. Instead of rank growths of prairie grass, which blossomed in its beauty over these fertile prairies, we now behold the waving fields of corn, broad acres of undulating wheat, numerous herds of thorough-bred stock grazing in green pastures,—indeed, every evidence of wealth and prosperity.

To those who opened up and developed the wonderful resources of Fairmount, the present and coming generations will owe eternal gratitude. They suffered untold privations and inconveniences, labored with unflagging energy and will, receiving only meager compensation for their toil, were far away from their friends and their old homes, and with scarcely any means of communication with them. The pioneers were encouraged and kept up with the hope of soon establishing comfortable homes for themselves and their families and with a noble ambition of conferring on posterity blessings which shall ever be a monument to their memories.

The northern part of Pike county was not settled for over a decade after the southern portion was. It is a matter of no little surprise to know that for so many years this beautiful section was left without the pioneer. Many doubtless passed to and fro through it on their way northward and westward and return, and perhaps marveled at the beauty of its groves and prairies; but it was so far from civilization that the most sturdy and daring did not feel disposed to pitch their tents and make their home here. Over 11 years elapsed from the time that Ebenezer Franklin, Daniel Shinn and the Rosses came to the county, before Barker Crane, the first settler of Fairmount, came to live in this then wild country. Mr. Crane made improvements on sec. 3 in 1831, but even he remained for only a short period. We do not know whether it was his remoteness from other settlements that drove him away, or that he found a more desirable location, as none are left to inform us.

At the close of the Black Hawk war, and when the people of the older settled East and South were assured that no further apprehensions need be felt relative to Indian troubles, settlers came pouring into this fair State by the thousands, and the beautiful groves and prairies of Fairmount did not fail to receive her portion. Prior to 1841 we find the following settlers, besides others, living in this township: H. Lake, who located on section 10; John Wilson, on section 3; Thomas Kirgan, on section 2; John Brown, on section 14; Ebenezer Franklin, on section 12; Asa Lake, on section 10; Tandy Hume, on section 16; and Henry Benson, on section 19.

The children of these early settlers were not long without the instructions and discipline of the schoolmaster, for we find as early as 1840, Henry Benson taught school in a log school-house on sec. 16. This rude structure, which was erected by the contribution of the labor of the pioneers, would not compare favorably with the more modern, neat and tasteful frame and brick structures that adorn many of the knolls through this section. Jesse Elledge, a Baptist minister, was one of the earliest teachers of the township. Soon, too, the minister of the gospel found his way here among these pioneers. The first preaching was done by Elder Michael Hobbs, of the Christian denomination, in 1841. He was not a regular preacher, being engaged in farming, but desiring to see his friends and neighbors following the meek and lowly, yet truly divinely great Nazarene, would have them assemble in cabins and school-houses, and tell them of his love and earthly mission. His brother, the well known Elder David Hobbs, was also a preacher. For a time the Mormons, who were numerous in Adams county, which lies just north of this township, preached their peculiar faith to this people, and won many converts. A few years afterward, however, this community joined in the excitement incident to the expulsion of the Mormons from Illinois.

During the late war Fairmount proved loyal to the core, and furnished many of her brave sons as a sacrifice to retain an undivided Union. Many of those who went to the front, after enduring years of untold hardships and danger, were permitted to return to their homes, where they are now living, to enjoy the liberties they so nobly fought for. Many of them, however, went to return no more. They were pierced by the shot and shell from Southern musket and cannon, or died from the cruelties inflicted upon them in the prison pens to which they were consigned,—all for defending the best government ever established by man.

CHURCHES.

There are no villages in this township, yet the people enjoy almost equal religious privileges with the citizens of towns. There are in the township five church organizations, with three church buildings. The United Brethren church stands on sec. 29, near the school-house, and cost about $1,600. This is known as the Woodland Church, and was dedicated in 1867, and was the first church building erected in the township. It was dedicated by N. A. Walker. The Society was organized in 1866, by Rev. D. C. Martin, and meetings were held in the Woodland school-house until their church edifice was completed. The present membership is 140. Rev. W. P. Pease is Pastor. The attendance at the Sunday-school is about 80.

The Presbyterian church, which is located on sec. 10, cost about $1,500. The house of worship of the Baptist congregation is on sec. 7, and cost $400.

The Society of the Methodist denomination worship in the Presbyterian Church, while the Christian congregation hold their meetings in the South Prairie school-house, on sec. 11. The first Methodist preacher in the township was Rev. Mr. Cleveland. He preached his first sermon in this township at the residence of Wm. Morrison in 1840.

PERSONAL SKETCH HISTORY.

Following we give personal sketches of the early settlers and prominent citizens of the township, which forms an important factor in its history.

A. B. Allen was born in Ohio county, Ky., Sept. 14, 1825; his father, Asa Allen, was born in Tennessee and of German descent, his mother, Abigail (Campbell) Allen, a native of Kentucky and of English descent. Mr. Allen came to Pike county in 1844, and in 1846 was married to Emily Askew and they have had 11 children, 8 of whom are living. Mr. Allen was very poor in early life, and worked out for $8 per month. He now owns 320 acres of land, raises stock, and is considered a very good farmer. He belongs to the United Brethren Church, and is a Democrat.

Lewis H. Baldwin was born in Connecticut in 1812; is the son of John and Sarah Ann (Hawkins) Baldwin, the former a native of Connecticut, and of English descent. In early life Mr. B. worked at blacksmithing, but is now a farmer. He came to this county in 1835, and in 1836 married Maria Jane Elledge. After his marriage he worked out for $8 per month, but he now owns 500 acres of good land in Pike county, and he and his son own about the same amount in Missouri, and one acre within the corporation of Perry. He used to be an old-line Whig, but is now a Republican; has been School Director 25 years, and School Trustee. These are the only offices that he would accept. Mr. and Mrs. Baldwin have 4 children. Mrs. B. is a Baptist.

Philip S. Brower, farmer, sec. 14; P. O. Perry; was born in Madison county, N. Y., April 27, 1832; came to this county with his parents in 1842; his father, John Brower, was a native of New York, and his mother, Delight (Smith) Brower, also a native of New York. June 3, 1854, Mr. B. married Amanda Carolines, and they have had 5 children, 3 of whom are living, Malcolm C., Elmwood and Alpheus. In 1852 he took a trip to California and was absent 2 years. He owns 306 acres of land. His wife is a Methodist.

William Cory, farmer, was born in the State of New York, Feb. 20, 1820; he is the son of William and Rachel (Tombs) Cory, natives of New Jersey, the former of Irish, and the latter of Scotch descent; at the age of 18 he commenced to learn the carpenter's trade, at which he worked 10 years, since which time he has followed farming. In the fall of 1837 he visited Illinois to see the country, and in 1841 he settled in this tp., on sec. 10, where he has lived ever since. March 31, 1844, he married Nancy Jane Wilson, a native of New Hampshire, and of their 10 children, 9 are living,— 5 boys and 4 girls; one girl deceased. Mr. Cory and his wife are members of the M. E. Church; he is a Democrat, and has been Assessor, Township Treasurer, Justice of the Peace, Supervisor, Township Clerk, School Director, and Secretary of his Church. P. O., Fish Hook.

Joseph E. Coss, farmer, brother of Theodore S. Coss, was born in Ross county, O., in 1846; besides the common school he attended also the commercial College at Quincy. In 1870 he married Sarah Allen, and of their 4 children 2 are living,—Effie Ammarana and Orien Forest. Both himself and wife are members of the United Brethren Church. He is a Democrat, and has been Town Clerk. Six months he kept store at Fish Hook. October 22, 1864, he enlisted in Co. F, 28th Ill. Inf., under Capt. H. D. Hadsell, and was discharged Oct. 21, 1865. He was in the battles at Spanish Fort, and fort Blakely, where he was under fire 18 days, and other battles, skirmishes, etc. Was shipwrecked on the "George Peabody" when there was a storm for 36 hours; 120 horses were thrown overboard and 10 men were lost. Resides on sec. 28. P. O. Fish Hook.

Taylor M. Coss, farmer, sec. 29; P. O. Baylis; son of Edward and Annie Coss, natives of Ohio, was born in Ross county, O., in 1836; came to this county in 1854, and in 1869 was married to Miss Emma Phillips, born in this county in 1840; they have had 6 children, 4 of whom are living,—Florence B., William T., Ida M. and Ada E. Mr. C. has held the office of Supervisor, Collector, School Trustee, and School Director for many years. He owns 420 acres of excellent land, has been engaged in buying hogs for other parties, and raises considerable stock on his own farm. He had 1,500 bushels of wheat to market this season. Mr. and Mrs. C. and their eldest daughter are members of the United Brethren Church at Woodland.

Theodore S. Coss was born in 1840 in Ross county, O., and is the son of Edward and Anna (Moore) Coss, natives of the same State, the father of German, and the mother of English descent; in 1871 he married Belle Manns, a native of Kentucky, and they have one child, Cora May, born in February, 1872. During the war Mr. Coss enlisted in Co. G, 3d. Ill. Cav., under Capt. J. B. Moore, Aug. 6, 1861; was discharged April 10, 1863; was in the battle of Pea Ridge; was under Gen. Curtis when he drove Price from Springfield to the Boston Mountains, and was in several other engagements. Residence, sec. 20; P. O. Fish Hook.

George I. K. Crawford was born in this county in 1859, and is the son of J. G. and Rhoda (Mclear) Crawford; his father, who still owns land here, has been a resident of this township for 30 years. The subject of this sketch was educated in the common schools here. In 1879 he married Lillie Cory, and they have a child, born Nov. 21, 1879, whose name is Clarence Cory. By occupation Mr. Crawford is a farmer. In religion he is a Presbyterian, and in politics a Republican. His wife is a Methodist.

Samuel M. Crawford was born in this county July 29, 1856, educated in the common school, and Illinois College at Jacksonville, and at the Gem City Commercial College at Quincy; by occupation Mr. C. is a teacher; lived on the farm with his father until of age; he is not a member of any Church, and is a Republican.

W. D. C. Doan, M. D., was born in Ohio April 16, 1828, being the son of William and Susanna (Bennett) Doan, from the Eastern States, his father a physician. The subject of this paragraph began the study of medicine at the age of 18, with his father, who died two years afterward; he then finished reading with his uncle, Dr. Elijah Bennett, in Clermont county, O.; at 22 he commenced practice in this tp. He first came to Pike county in 1848, in 1850 to this tp., where he has since lived. In 1851 he married Rachel Hobbs, and of their 4 children but one is living, Rachel Effie, and they have one grandchild living with them, Mary E. Doan Crawford. The Doctor owns 215 acres of land. Resides on sec. 10. He is one of the oldest practitioners of the county. In politics he is a Democrat, and both himself and wife are members of the Christian Church. His postoffice is Perry.

Levi Gardner was born in Adams county, Pa., Dec. 17, 1810, and is the son of George and Elizabeth (Seybold), of German descent, who were in good circumstances and followed farm life. Levi obtained a fair education in the subscription schools of his native State. Came to Illinois in 1836, and has resided here most of the time since; he could ride all over this county when he first came, he tells us, without seeing scarcely any improvements; his father-in-law, who was one of the pioneers of this county, killed 7 bears in Fairmount tp., in one day. In 1837 he married Matilda Neal, by whom he had 8 children, 5 of whom are living,—one son and four daughters. By occupation Mr. Gardner is a tanner and currier; he had a tannery in this county 5 or 6 years, but since 1850 he has been farming. Lives now on sec. 5. In politics Mr. G. is a Republican, and both himself and wife are members of the United Brethren Church. In 1862 Mr. Gardner enlisted in the 99th regiment as a musician (a fifer); was in the battle at Magnolia, Miss., Champion Hills and Black River; he was discharged before the close of the year, that is, at the close of the siege of Vicksburg, where he was present.

John Henthorn, farmer, sec. 17; was born in England, April 20, 1820, of English parents; learned weaving by the hand-loom;

ATLAS TP.

emigrated to America in 1844, stopping in New York State, and in 1850 came to Adams county, Ill., and in 1852 to Pike county; for two years while in New York State he superintended a factory, where 62 looms were run. He now owns 360 acres of land, in good cultivation, and well stocked. In 1842 he married Bettie Holt, and of their 8 children 7 are living. Mr. Henthorn has been School Director several terms, and is a Democrat.

John D. Henthorn was born in this county, July 21, 1857, and is the son of John and Betsey (Holt) Henthorn, natives of England; received his education in the common schools of this county; by occupation he is a farmer, and his residence is on sec. 9. He has four brothers and two sisters living, and one sister dead.

Thomas Hull, residence sec. 29; P. O. Fish-Hook; is the son of Samuel and Sophia Hull, and was born in Ohio in 1830; received his education mostly in the common schools of his native State. In 1850 he married Elizabeth Bowman, who was born in 1830 in this county, and they have 8 children living. Mr. Hull is a farmer, and has been a resident of this county since 1845. In politics he is a Democrat, and both himself and wife are members of the United Brethren Church. He has been Justice of the Peace 10 or 11 years, Road Commissioner, Collector, School Director, Class-Leader and Sunday-school Superintendent. He is an industrious man, and has earned all he ever possessed.

Israel Kirgan. This gentleman's father, Thomas Kirgan, was a native of County Antrim, Ireland, and when a babe he was brought by his parents, Daniel and Mary Kirgan, to America, nearly 100 years ago. He was a tanner by trade, but followed farming and milling after his arrival in this county. He died March 30, 1877, in his 90th year, in Perry, this county, where he had lived many years. His 5 children still own the home farm, which consists of 280 acres, 2½ miles southwest of Perry. Mrs. Mary (Fred) Kirgan, his mother, was a native of Virginia. Israel, the subject of this biography, was born Aug. 12, 1815, in Clermont county, O. He first learned the tanner's trade, but when his father broke up he emigrated to this county, in 1835, settling on Fish-Hook creek, N. W. ¼ sec. 2, at which time he had only six "bits" in his pocket, one horse and a yoke of cattle, and was $40 in debt. From this start Mr. K. has become one of the most substantial and leading farmers in Fairmount township, now being the owner of 240 acres of land. About the first work he did was to split 9,600 rails, at six "bits" a hundred. Coming to this county as early as 1835, he has seen this country in its primitive state, with the wild animals roving over it in large numbers. One day he saw 65 deer in one grove. There were but five houses then on the south prairie, namely, Alfred Bissell, sec. 2; Mr. O'Neil, sec. 16; Mr. Mc-Gee, sec. 16; James Seybold, sec. 16; and Ebenezer Franklin, sec. 12;—all of whom resided in log houses. Israel's father's family used the first cooking-stove brought to this prairie.

The subject of this notice, in 1834, married for his first wife
36

Miss Margaret Jane Kennedy, a native of Ohio, who died in 1845, leaving a family of 5 children, namely, William, Benjamin, Mary, John and an infant: of these, William and John are all that are living now. March 3, 1855, Mr. K. married Sarah Jane Houston, and by her he had 9 children, of whom 8 are living: David L., Clinton D., Eben, Chapman, George B., Ira, Israel F. and Harvey D. In politics Mr. Kirgan is a Democrat, and in religion is still a believer in Christianity; used to be a member of the M. E. Church.

David Kurfman, farmer, sec. 7; P. O. Fish Hook; was born in Pennsylvania Jan. 29, 1815, and is a son of Daniel and Susannah (Barnett) Kurfman, natives of Maryland, and of German descent. David received his education in the schools of his native State; when he first started to school he could scarcely speak English. He was married the first time in 1837 to Hannah Deeter, and they were the parents of two girls, both of whom are married. His second marriage was with Nancy Bagby, in 1851; of this union 6 children were born,—4 boys and 2 girls. Both Mr. and Mrs. K. are connected with the Baptist Church. Mr. K. came from Pennsylvania to Pike county in 1850, and settled in Pittsfield township; in 7 years thereafter removed to Fairmount.

George Lake, farmer, sec. 10; P. O. Fish Hook. Mr. Lake was born in Fairmount, Pike Co., Ill., July 12, 1854, and is a son of Harvey and Elizabeth (Lee) Lake, the former a native of New York, and his mother of one of the Eastern States. He attended the common schools of this county, and received a fair education. In 1874 he was united in marriage with Nancy Groves. Jesse, their only child, was born in 1876.

John Lake was born in this township in 1853, and is the son of Harvey and Elizabeth Lake. He attended the common schools of this county, receiving a good common-school education. He is now engaged in farming on sec. 10. His postoffice address is Perry. Jan. 19, 1871, he was joined in the holy bonds of matrimony with Mary Olive Seybold, a native of Minnesota. She is a member of the Christian Church. Harvey Lake, the father of our subject, was one of the early settlers of Pike county.

Wm. H. Love was born Jan. 15, 1821, in New Jersey, the son of Samuel and Lydia (Morgan) Love; his father was a native of Ireland, and his mother of New York State. He was brought to Illinois in 1828 and to Pike county in 1833, and the family settled one mile west of Perry, on the farm at present owned by Esquire Morton. In April, 1846, he moved upon the farm where he now lives, owning 287 acres. He was married March 30, 1843, to Miss Harriet E. Bentley. To them have been born 9 children, 7 of whom are living,—6 boys and 1 girl. Mrs. Love is the daughter of Gideon Bentley, an early and prominent settler of Pike county. Both Mr. and Mrs. L. are members of the Christian Church, of which he is a Deacon. Mr. L. has been a farmer all his life, in which business he has been successful, although in the early days he suffered many hardships. His family started from New York in a skiff, which they would run over all the dams that were on their route, and they encountered eight or ten of them, and the women would get out of the boat and walk down past the dam. The first morning after their arrival in Fairmount tp. their nearest neighbor sent over after two ears of corn, the boy, who was bare-foot (and there was snow on the ground) stating that "they wanted it for breakfast!" Mr. L. also states that he called upon one of the neighbors one morning and found them partaking of their break-fast on parched corn and "sycamore tea!" All the table furniture they had was one plate, one knife and one fork. Mr. Love, when he first came, used oxen to plow with (using a wooden mold-board plow), and used a harrow with wooden teeth.

Lemuel Martin, farmer, sec. 11; P. O. Perry. The subject of this personal sketch was born Jan. 21, 1854; his parents are Samuel and Amanda (Rounds) Martin; he was the eldest son of a family of 10 children. There were two daughters, however, older than he. Mr. M. was united in marriage with Mary G. Glines, and they have two children, one boy and one girl. Both Mr. and Mrs. M. are members of the Christian Church in Perry. Politically he is a Democrat.

S. F. Martin was born in Kentucky, March 4, 1822; he is the son of Nehemiah and Drusilla (Cottrell) Martin, natives of Virginia and of German ancestry. His mother died when he was only two years old. In 1849 he came to this county and settled in Fairmount tp. In 1850 he was united in marriage with Amanda Rounds, and the union has been blessed with 10 children,—6 boys and 4 girls, 8 of whom are living. His wife died Nov. 22, 1879. She was a mem-ber of the Christian Church. Mr. M. is a Democrat in politics, and has served as School Director, School Trustee, Road Commis-sioner and Overseer of the Poor. He owns a farm of 160 acres on sec. 8.

A. G. Mason, farmer, sec. 15; P. O. Fish-Hook; is a native of Vermont, where he was born Aug. 19, 1811; he was the son of Carlo and Lydia Mason. His father was a carpenter. They came to Pike county from Kentucky in 1862. A. G. was married to Betsy C. Mason in 1834; this union has been blessed with a family of three children, all sons, and two of whom are married. Their names are A. H., Wm. and R. H. The latter enlisted in Co. F, 51st Wisconsin Infantry, and served for three months. Mrs. Mason died May 2, 1879.

R. B. McLaughlin, farmer, sec. 22; P. O. Perry; was born in Ohio, June 15, 1827, and is a son of William and Anna (Boggess) McLaughlin, the former a native of Virginia and of Irish descent, and the mother a native of Ohio and of English-German ancestry. His only opportunity for an education was in the common schools of Pike county in early day, where he was brought in 1837. In 1848 he was married to Sarah Flannagan. Three of their 7 chil-dren are living. He has held all the township offices, with the exception of that of Assessor. He and his wife are members of the

M. E. Church, of which he has been Steward. He has been engaged in farming all his life, in which he has great success. At present he buys and feeds considerable stock.

William McLaughlin is a native of the old Dominion State, and was born Dec. 2, 1802. His father, James McLaughlin, was a native of Ireland, and his mother, Sarah McLaughlin, *nee* Cole, was born in New Jersey. William was married in 1823 to Anna Boggess, a native of Ohio, where she was born in 1806, who bore him 12 children, 6 of whom are living. Four of the sons are married, and living in Fairmount township. His wife and all his children, except one, are members of the M. E. Church. Farming has been his life occupation, and he at present owns 575 acres of land in Pike county. When he arrived at Griggsville Landing, in this county, in 1836, he owned but one horse, $25 in money, and a very limited amount of household furniture, and had a family of wife and 5 children. From this meager position he has become one of the wealthiest men in the county, accumulating by close attention to business, hard labor and perseverance. He has seen the country change from its wild state to a fertile field of plenty. When he first settled here he thought he would always have plenty of outside range. He has held about all the township offices, and has been Steward, Class-Leader and Trustee of his church, and has been licensed as an Exhorter.

A. A. Ogle, farmer, sec. 6; P. O. Fish-Hook; is a son of James and Martha Ogle, both natives of St. Clair county, Ill., and was born in Adams county in 1855. He attended the common schools of that county, where he received a fair education. In 1874 he took unto himself a wife in the person of Sarah Elizabeth Bowman, who has borne him two children, both girls.

John M. Parker was born in this county in 1846, the son of John and Lydia Parker, natives of New England; married Sarah J. Whitten in 1862, who was born in Ohio in 1845, and they have had 7 children, one dec. Mr. P. has followed threshing and farming, and has been moderately successful. His residence is on sec. 27, Fairmount tp. P. O., Perry.

James A. Phillips was born in the State of Kentucky, Jan. 10, 1828, and is a son of Joseph and Sarah (Jackson) Phillips, the latter a native of Kentucky, and of Irish ancestry, the former of Scottish descent, and a native of Maryland. He was married in 1850 to Mary Wheeler, and the union has been blessed with 6 children, all of whom are living. James A. learned the trade of shoemaking, but never followed the business a great deal. For the 7 years subsequent to his marriage he worked out by the month; then bought a farm in this county, whither he had come in 1858, locating in this township, where he has since resided. He is a member of the United Brethren Church, and has served as Steward, Class-Leader, Trustee, and Sunday-school Superintendent.

Richard Razy was born in Tennessee, Sept 12, 1815; his father's name was Rufus Razy, who was born in New York; his mother was Mary Bigelow, also a native of the Empire State. Mr. R. emigrated to Pike county in 1852, locating in Perry. He never attended school but five days in his life, yet he is able to read. His mother died when he was but three days old. At present he is engaged in farming. He was married in 1836 in Watertown, Washington Co., O., to Harriet Mason. Eight children were born of this union, 4 boys and 4 girls. Two of the former are deceased. Mrs. R. was born in Castleton, N. Y., July 10, 1815; she was the daughter of Carlo Mason, who died in the town of Perry in 1855. They had two sons in the Rebellion, both in the 99th Illinois Infantry; Nathan, who was in Co. F, was killed in the first charge of Vicksburg; and James B., who was in Co. B., died of sickness. Among other Pike county boys of Co. F of this regiment who were killed in the first charge at Vicksburg, were Capt. Smith, Albert Orr, Andrew Scranton, John Elder and R. Lee.

Charles Read is a native of England, and was born in 1831; in 1836 he was brought to America by his parents, Robert and Susan (Callow) Read. He received his education in the common schools of this county, whither he was brought in 1837. He was married in 1857, to Mary Brown, a native of Ohio. The result of this union has been 9 children, 5 boys and 4 girls. Mr. M. is engaged in farming, and owns 280 acres of good land. He is a member of the Christian Church.

Silas Reed, farmer, sec. 25; P. O. Perry; was born in Ohio, Oct. 1, 1831, and is the son of William Reed, who had married a Miss Clark, of Pennsylvania. He received a good education, besides having attended the common schools. He entered an academy, now called Clermont College, and also attended the graded schools of Clermont county. He was married in 1861 to Rebecca, daughter of Lewis Baldwin, who was born Jan. 26, 1842, in Pike county. They have a family of 5 children. Mr. R. came to Pike county with his parents in 1859, and was engaged as school-teacher and book-keeper for some time, but is now engaged in farming.

Henry Robinson, farmer, sec. 22; P. O. Perry; is a son of James N. and Mary Allen (Cohenour) Robinson, and was born in Brown county, Ill., May 5, 1850; his father lived in this county 35 years ago, but at present he is living in Brown county, and has been very successful financially. Henry received his education in the common schools of Brown county, and since 1876 has been engaged in farming in this township. In 1877 he was married to Olive Poe. Their only son is James Herbert, who was born Aug. 5, 1878. Mrs. R. is a member of the M. E. Church.

Jerome W. Rush, farmer and stock-dealer, sec. 22; P. O. Perry. Mr. R. was born in Ross county, O., in 1827, and is a son of John W. and Sarah (Brown) Rush, the former a native of Virginia, and of German descent, the latter of Maryland, and of English descent. He attended schools in the log school-houses of this county, and the Mt. Sterling high school for two terms. In 1852, Oct. 12, he was married to Nancy C. Yates, and of the 5 children which have blessed their union, all are living. Both he and his wife are members of the M. E. Church. He came to Pike county in 1837, and located on sec. 36. He is now engaged as stock-raiser and stock dealer, and owns 400 acres of land, all but 80 acres of which is prairie. He keeps a deer park, in which he at times has as many as 20 deer.

Jasper Seybold. By occupation Mr. S. is a farmer, and owns 255 acres of land in this county. In 1866 he was united in marriage with Mary E. Stauffer, who has borne him 9 children, 4 boys and 5 girls, all of whom are living. Jasper Seybold was born in Madison county, Ill., June 26, 1833, and is a son of James and Olive (Gaskill) Seybold. His father was born in Illinois, and his mother in New York. He received his education mostly in log school-houses. He was brought from Madison county to Pike county in 1836, and has ever since resided in the county. He has served as Township Collector and as School Director for 20 years.

Ira W. Stevenson was born in Pike county Oct. 9, 1853, and is a son of John and Mary Ann (Wilson) Stevenson; the former was a well-known pioneer of this county, and died Feb. 1, 1880. He was a successful farmer, and owned 580 acres of land when he died. Ira W. received his education in the common schools, and, besides farming, he deals in stock. In March, 1874, he was united in marriage with Jennie Glines; only one of the two children born to them are living, Nellie May, who was born in 1877.

August Strauss, farmer, sec. 1; P. O., Perry. This gentleman was born in Germany, Aug. 11, 1840; he was landed in New York in 1857, and came to Pike county in 1858, where he has since resided, with the exception of three years spent in the army. He learned the trade of blacksmith in the old country, but since 1858 has been engaged in farming. Aug. 9, 1862, he enlisted in Co. B, 99th Ill. Inft., and remained in the service until the close of the war; he was in every battle that his regiment was in, and in all the marches, always being willing and ready for duty. He never received a wound. He was in the charge on Vicksburg and aided in carrying the Colonel off the field when he was wounded. Mr. S. was married Jan. 2, 1868, to Sarah Harter, and both of them are members of the Lutheran Church, of Perry, of which he is a Trustee. He is engaged in farming, and owns 80 acres of land.

Frederick Strauss was born Oct. 1, 1841, in Germany, and is a son of Henry D. and Wilhelmina (Baul) Strauss. Mr. S. came to Pike county in 1857, where he has since resided. He has a good German and a good English education. He is engaged in farming on sec. 12, and owns 80 acres of land. His is the oldest settled place in the township, part of his land having been under cultivation for over 50 years. In 1862 he enlisted in Co. B, 99th Ill. Inf., under Capt. Matthews; in 1863 was transferred to the 4th Reg. Vet. Res. Corps, in which he was a non-commissioned officer. He served three years, lacking 11 days. He was in many of the important battles of the war; was at the siege of Vicksburg, and says that the day after the rebels surrendered was the most lonesome day of his life. He had become so accustomed to the firing of the artillery that he was lost and lonesome without its constant roar. In 1869 he was married to Denia Hake, and they have a family of 6 children, 4 of whom are living. Both Mr. and Mrs. S. are members of the Perry Lutheran Church.

Merriman Tucker, farmer, sec. 5 ; P. O. Fish-Hook , was born in Virginia in 1819, and is the son of C. and Julia (Warren) Tucker, the former a native of North Carolina and the latter of Virginia, and both of Irish ancestry. His opportunities for an early education were very limited, and most of his education was obtained after he was 21 years of age. In 1842 he was married to Miss A. Reeves; 6 children have been born to bless their union. Mr. T. is a member of the M. E. Church, while she is a member of the Christian Church. Their son, Coalston Tucker, during the dark days of the rebellion went to defend his country, enlisting in the 14th Reg. Ill. Inf., and served till 1865. Mr. T. is engaged in farming and has made it a business to improve a farm and then sell it, He has followed this mode until he has improved 12 farms in Pike and Brown counties. When he first came here, he tells us, he could see wolves more frequently than he can hogs at large at the present day.

John Vail, farmer, owning over 200 acres of land, was born Sept. 24, 1815, in Ohio, son of Solomon and Jane Vail; the former was born in Washington Co., Pa., and of German descent, and his mother, in Westmoreland Co., of the same State, and of Irish ancestry. Mr. V. came to Illinois in 1842, landing at Quincy Oct. 10; he had then only $300. He embarked in farming and owns 200 acres of land and an interest in 160 more,—all in Pike county. In 1846 he was married to Helena A. Reed. Three boys and four girls were born to them. His wife, who was a member of the Christian Church, died May 4, 1868. Mr. Vail politically is a Democrat; has served as Town Clerk 3 years, and also as Supervisor, Assessor and Road Commissioner.

Leander Vail, farmer, sec. 23; P. O., Perry. Leander Vail was born in Pike county, Ill., Oct. 20, 1848; he is the son of John and Helena (Reed) Vail, early pilgrims to this county. He received his education in the common schools of Pike county. He was united in marriage Jan. 23, 1879, to Mary Elledge, daughter of A. A. Elledge, and was born in this county Oct. 25, 1848. Her father was one of the early settlers of this county. Mr. Vail has served the township as Collector, and is Clerk at the present time. As a farmer he has been successful. He deals in cattle and hogs, which he buys and sells to shippers.

J. W. Walker, farmer, sec. 24; P. O., Perry; is a native of this county and the son of Robert and Hannah (Scott) Walker, well known in the early history of Pike county. J. W. was born Nov. 27, 1850; received his education in the common schools of this county, and began life as a farmer, now owning 160 acres of good land.   In July, 1871, he was united in marriage with Ellen Batley, and to them have been born 3 children, one son and two daughters. Both Mr. and Mrs. W. are members of the Christian Church.

Richard T. Walmsley was born in Rhode Island in 1851; his parents are Richard and Mary (Carpenter) Walmsley, his father a native of England and his mother of Rhode Island. Richard T. attended the common schools of his native State, where he received a fair education; for a time he worked in the cotton factories of Rhode Island, Massachusetts and Kentucky, and in 1868 came to Illinois with his father, with whom, in connection with another brother, he owns 180 acres of land, and they are engaged in farming. His mother died Jan. 26, 1866.

Ira J. Wilson was born in New Hampshire, Jan. 7, 1831, and is a son of James and Mary Wilson, both natives of Vermont and of Irish descent.   Sept. 10, 1857, he was united in marriage with Marietta Corey, a native of this county.   Both he and his wife received a good common-school education.   Mr. W. went to Oregon in 1852, in 1854 to California, two years later returned to Illinois, and in the following year was married, as stated above, and is now engaged in farming in this township.   He came to Illinois in 1836 with his father, who settled in Griggsville, and in 1837 located on sec. 3, this tp.   Mrs. Wilson is a member of the M. E. Church.

James Woods, farmer, sec. 16; P. O., Fish Hook; is a native of Brown county, O., and was born in 1808, and is a son of Samuel and Elsie (Ritchie) Woods, the former of Irish descent and the latter a native of Ireland.   Mr. W. has a limited education which he received in the common schools of Ohio; he came to Pike county in March, 1845, and engaged in farming, now owning 160 acres of land on sec. 16.   He was married in 1829, to Rachel Jackson, and 6 of the 8 children born to them are living, all of whom are married.   In 1879 Mr. W. had been married for half a century, and both he and his wife have been members of the M. E. Church for 50 years.   She is 3 years and 4 months younger than he is.

Elijah Jeffers

NEW SALEM TP.

NEW SALEM TOWNSHIP.

This is a full Congressional township, and is officially known as township four south, range four west of the fourth principal meridian. New Salem is a prairie township, and in an agricultural point of view is an especially fine section of country. It was not settled as early as some of the more southern townships of the county were, but at present ranks with any in regard to improvements. It is settled with an enterprising class of people who never lag in such matters.

Although it is what we may term a prairie township it is well watered and drained. Strange to say, even in this peninsula, formed by the Mississippi and Illinois rivers, there is no well-defined water-shed. However, we find so many streams having their origin in this township and flowing in different directions, we conclude it to be one of the highest tracts of land in the county. Bay creek, and one of its main branches, have their origin in New Salem. Also the south Fork of McGee's creek, a branch of the Middle Fork of the same creek, and another small stream which runs off into Adams county, the name of which we do not know.

The first pioneer who ventured to locate in this township was Mr. Joab Shinn, who came in 1830 and located on sec. 14 in the edge of the beautiful grove there.

The next settlement was made in the southern part of the township, sec. 24, in 1831, by Isaac Conkright and his two sons. About the same time came William Scholl; also Nathan Swiggart and Samuel Griffith, who located on sec. 14, in company with Mr. Shinn. Then came William Crump, Henry Brown and others.

In 1832 the Black Hawk war occurred, and although the battle grounds were many miles distant, yet it was the cause of much excitement and apprehension in this county. The immediate result of this was to check immigration to this State, and for a few years few new settlers made their appearance in this section. However, after the lapse of a few seasons, when it began to be definitely understood in the East and South that no further molestations were likely to occur, a new tide of immigration set toward this county never before or since equaled. This began in 1834 and continued for about five years. A system of advertising and speculation similar to that now prevailing in the country several hundreds of miles further West, brought thousands upon thousands.

Not unlike the excitement which prevailed at later periods in regard to the Western gold, silver and lead mines, was that which swept through the Eastern and Southern States in regard to Illinois lands and town lots. During the years 1835–7, more than 500 towns were laid out in Illinois, many of these in Pike county. Railroads were projected through nearly all of them, and these, with the town sites, were platted, showing depot grounds, parks and drives, and were sent with the most exaggerated descriptions to all parts of the country. The State Government caught the epidemic, and bills for railroads, canals, and other internal improvements were passed, corresponding in magnitude with the universal expectancy of the people. In 1837 a financial crisis came and found this State but ill-prepared for the shock. As a consequence, the numerous railroads, canals and paper cities vanished in thin air. For a number of years after this, improvements and immigration was at a standstill. Of course this part of the country, having no extra inducements to offer, partook of the general stagnation, and for a score of years no remarkable advance was made either in population or improvement. Occasionally a new arrival was announced. A relation or friend writing to the old home in the East or South, would induce some one to come out to see the country, and perhaps work a year, and once here, he would likely stay. As in other parts of the State, the first settlers located in or near the timber, and there we find the first improvements. Ere many years, however, some of the more enterprising pushed out upon the fertile prairies. They discovered that farms much more profitable could be made, much easier and quicker than in the timber.

The first person who met death in this township was Mr. Carrington, who died in 1834. The first sermon preached was by Rev. Samuel Oglesby, a Methodist minister. This sermon was delivered at the funeral of Sarah Tedrow.

The first school-house in New Salem was built in 1834. The building stood on sec. 15 and for several years was used for religious purposes. The first church was built in the village of New Salem in 1844, by the Methodist brethren. The first steam-mill was built in 1856–7, by Cooper Temple, near the village of New Salem.

The Wabash Railroad passes through the township, entering from the east about the middle of sec. 24, running on a direct westerly line until the town of New Salem is reached, when it strikes a west northwest course to Pineville.

There are two pleasant little country villages in this township, both of which are on the line of the Wabash Railroad, and in the midst of a fine farming community. The older, New Salem, was laid out Dec. 22, 1847, by William F. Hooper and Jacob Shinn. It is located on secs. 22 and 15. The original town was further north than the main portion of the present village is. Pineville, which is located on the southwest quarter of sec. 7, was laid out by William Pine, jr., Oct. 26, 1869. The name has since been changed to Baylis, that being the name of the postoffice.

NEW SALEM UNIVERSALIST CHURCH.

The Universalist Church in New Salem owes its existence principally to the earnest efforts of Daniel Fisher and David Preble (two laymen whose wives were sisters), and a few zealous friends who aided their efforts.

They were among the early settlers of the town, and are gratefully remembered for what they were, and what they did to benefit society, for they have both gone to their final rest.

Their dwelling-houses were open for religious worship in the early days when church accommodations were wanting, and the ministers of other forms of faith besides their own held services in them.

Among the early advocates of Universalism who preached in New Salem and vicinity, were Revs. Abel Chandler, William Gamage, E. Manford and Father Wolf. The last mentioned was a Dunkard or German Baptist, who believed in the final salvation of all souls. The first seeds of the Universalist faith were sown principally by these men. Mr. Gamage was the first Universalist minister who had continuous appointments in the vicinity of New Salem. He probably preached in Mr. Fisher's house in 1849, and held services once a month for some two or three years. He resided a part of the time in Naples, and a part of the time in Barry, and depended principally upon school-teaching for his support.

The soil here was favorable to the growth of the Universalist faith, as is shown by the eagerness of the people to obtain that kind of religious reading. For when the Universalist State Missionary, Rev. W. E. Reily, visited New Salem, in the month of August, 1851, to preach on Sunday, but was prevented from holding religious services by a heavy rain storm that prevailed at the time, he sold twelve dollars worth of Universalist books.

When school-houses were built, and religious services were held in them, the appointment for a Universalist meeting sometimes created bitter opposition, and to avoid this, Messrs. Fisher and Preble concluded to make the attempt to build a church edifice, though the friends were neither numerous nor wealthy. They said we will get what help we can, and what is lacking we will pay ourselves. Mr. Fisher bought the land on which the church stands, and afterward deeded to the society, and the present church building, valued at $2,500, was completed and dedicated the 17th of December, 1854.

Rev. D. R. Biddlecome had been engaged to preach every other Sabbath, a short time before the dedication of the church, and he preached the dedication sermon. He continued his labors for two years and a half, and organized a Church August 5, 1855. A part of this time he occupied three-fourths of his time in New Salem, though he resided at Griggsville.

In the spring of 1857, Rev. A. M. Worden was engaged as Pastor, and continued his pastorate for six years, preaching one-half of the time in New Salem, and the other half in Barry; except the last year, when he preached all the time in New Salem. He resided all the time, except the last year, in Barry. The Sunday School was commenced during his pastorate in the summer of 1862.

Rev. William Gamage was engaged to teach the village school, in the fall of 1866, and was employed to preach every other Sunday in New Salem for two years.

During the years 1872–3and, 75, Rev. John Hughes preached one Sabbath a month here. The Church was re-organized during his ministry. He never resided in the parish, but usually came on Saturday and left on Monday, and of course had not much opportunity to do parish work, though he had large congregations. The strength of the parish at that time was 20 families, 30 church members, and a Sunday-school of 81 scholars and teachers.

Rev. T. H. Tabor supplied for the parish one Sunday in a month for six months during the summer of 1876. In the month of December, 1878, he returned to New Salem, held services every evening for a week, and the Sabbath previous and the Sabbath after these week meetings. During these meetings 27 new members united with the Church.

Mr. Tabor was engaged to preach for the parish one-half of the time in March, 1879, and is now the resident Pastor. The reported strength of the parish at the commencement of the year 1880 was 58

BIOGRAPHIES.

We give in connection with the above sketch brief biographies of the old settlers and prominent persons of the township. They will be found to form an interesting feature of this volume.

J. R. Allen; P. O., Baylis; was born in this county in 1850; his parents, J. M. and Mary Allen, were natives of Kentucky, and came here in an early day and settled on the farm where J. R. now resides. In 1867 he married Mahala A. Houston, who was born in Adams county, this State, in 1848, and they had 7 children, namely, William D., Charles T., Andy M., Leva (deceased), J. L., Jeff. R. and Mary M. Mr. Allen has followed carpentering and farming; owns 90 acres of land. He had one brother, who lost his life in the late war; was first wounded near Helena, Ark., and died at Cape Girardeau.

John Andrews, dealer in general merchandise, New Salem, is a native of England, where he was born Feb. 6, 1840; he came to the United States in 1854, and two years later came to this county, and in 1861 embarked in the mercantile business at New Salem. In 1863 he was united in marriage with Miss M. A. Temple; she was born in St. Louis in 1842, and died in 1865. In 1868 Mr. A. was married to Miss H. L. Fisher, a native of Ohio. To them have been born 5 children: Charles, Harry, Maud, Alice and John. Mr. A. has held the office of Postmaster, at New Salem, since 1867. He is a prominent member of the Universalist Church.

John Carnes, deceased, son of Thomas and Elizabeth Carnes, natives of Maryland, was born in 1812; at the age of 14 he moved to Ohio, and in 1858 married Michel Hardin, who was born in Harrison county, O., in 1814, and they had one child. He came to this State about 35 years ago, and located in this tp., where he lived until his death, which occurred in 1867. Mrs. Carnes carried on the farm until her son John was old enough to attend to it. Both Mr. and Mrs. Carnes were members of the United Brethren Church. P. O., New Salem.

Solomon G. Chaney, farmer, sec. 16; P. O., New Salem; was born in 1843, son of Elijah and Mary Chaney, the former a native of Maryland and the latter of England, who came to this county in 1835, and remained until their death. Solomon was married in 1866 to Emma Eddingfield, who was born in 1843 in Lancaster, O., and they had 7 children,—Emma E., Hiram E., Maude E., Alcyone A., Hermon G., Rosa C. and Mary L.; Maude is dead. Mr. C. enlisted in the late war in 1861, in Co. I, 33d Reg. Ill. Inf.; was in the battle at Fredericktown, Mo., campaign in Arkansas, then through Missouri, was in the siege of Vicksburg, at New Orleans, then on the Texas coast, then Mobile, Ala. He was mustered out Dec. 10, 1865, at Camp Butler, this State, and has since followed farming; owns 40 acres of land. Mr. and Mrs. Chaney are members of the Universalist Church. Mr. C. is also a Free Mason.

Joseph E. Chaney, farmer, was born in 1833, in Washington, D. C., and is a son of Elijah and Mary C. Chaney, the former a native of Maryland and the latter of England, who came to America in 1820. At the age of 1½ years Joseph E. went to England, and returned in 18 months, and has since been a resident of New Salem. He is a farmer and resides on sec. 20; owns 160 acres of land, and it is well improved. Mr. and Mrs. C. are members of the Universalist Church.

A. B. Cobb, physician; P. O., New Salem; was born in Steuben Co., N. Y., in 1830, and is a son of Philanthropy and Harriet Cobb, of English descent, his father a native of New York and mother of Massachusetts. At the age of 13 he came with his parents to this county and located in Perry, where he learned the harness and saddler's trade, which he followed for 6 years; then read medicine under Dr. Carey 3 years, and in 1856-7 attended the Missouri Medical College; then commenced practice in Hadley tp., and remained there 12 years. Was Postmaster 4 years, and also School Director. In 1853 he married Miss Emma J. Shields, who was born in 1836, in Fulton county, Ill., and died Feb. 8, 1868, in Hadley tp. They had 5 children, 4 of whom are living. In 1870 Dr. Cobb married Laura Huntley, born in 1835, and a native of Pennsylvania. They have one child, and are members of the Presbyterian Church.

A. W. Cochran, sec. 4; P. O., New Salem; was born in Belmont county, Ohio, in 1815; his father, James, a native of Ireland, was in the war of the Revolution, and present at St. Clair's defeat. His mother, Elizabeth, was a native of Germany. Our subject

came to this county in 1865. In 1851 he married Miss Rebecca
Cornwell, born in 1825, and they had 10 children; only 5 of these
are living. Mr. C. has followed butchering, and of late, farming
and trading on the Mississippi river. He has held the office of
School Director for the remarkably long period of 44 years, and
in Ohio was School Treasurer. During the war he supported 13
families while the husbands and fathers served in the field. Mr.
Cochran had an exciting experience in Ohio during the war, which
we relate. While he was electioneering for McClellan, a man who
was both preacher and doctor, accompanied by 8 soldiers, came to
Mr. C. and threatened to hang him; but when the soldiers learned
that Mr. C. was supporting 13 soldiers' families they released him
and were about to hang the reverend doctor, when they were dis-
suaded by the kindly feeling of Mr. Cochran.

John D. Combs was born in 1792 in France, and was the son of
John D. and Mary A. Combs, who were also natives of France;
the family emigrated to New Castile in Portugal, when he was
young; at the time of Bonaparte's defeat at this place, John D. fled
to seek shelter from the shot and shell of the British army; he got
lost from his mother and, supposing she had been killed, wandered
around in search of his father, he being on Bonaparte's staff, but
found him dead. Our subject was now left without parents,
brother or sister, and he knew not what to do; a Jewish peddler
proved to be a good Samaritan to him, taking him in charge,
feeding him and conveying him to Lisbon; here the orphan wandered about the city, sleeping out of doors and in abandoned re-
treats for 3 or 4 weeks, and getting nothing to eat except what he
could pick up from the back doors of hotels and boarding-houses.
Here again a good Samaritan appeared in the person of an American sea captain, and took him aboard of his ship and cared for him
until his (the captain's) death. The captain's wife then became
his guardian and bound him out to the boot and shoemaker's trade;
after 4½ years' stay he ran away from his master and enlisted in the
U. S. service for 5 years under Scott's command at Baltimore,
thence to New Orleans and up the Mississippi river, stopping at
Baton Rouge, St. Louis and Council Bluffs. This expedition was
for the purpose of making treaties with the Indians in Nebraska
and as far north as the Yellowstone. After 5 years' service he was
mustered out at Omaha, Neb., and went to New Orleans for his pay;
then returned to this State, then a territory, and located at Alton,
where he was first married. After working at his trade for several
years, he commenced selling goods on the Illinois river, at Perry,
and also at New Salem. He is at present living a retired life at
the age of 88 years. He has been 3 times married, but is now a
widower; is unusually spry and active for one of his age, and
challenges any man in the county for a half-mile race. P. O.,
New Salem.

J. S. Conkright, sec. 26; P. O., New Salem; was born in this
county in 1836; his parents, Isaac and Elizabeth Conkright, were

natives of Kentucky. He owns 160 acres of good land. In 1863 he was married to Harriet L. Bean, of this county, who was born in 1847; they have 2 children, John W. and Harris. They are members of the Universalist Church.

William Crump, farmer, sec. 24; P. O., New Salem; was born in Washington county, Penn., in 1815; his parents, Stephen and Nancy Crump, were natives of Virginia. From 1828 to 1835 the family lived in Virginia. Our subject came to this State in the spring of 1835 and settled in Quincy; while there he manufactured wagons. In 1837 he moved to this county, and in 1838 he married Miss Margaret Hooper, who was born in Clermont county, Ohio, in 1821, and they had 8 children,—Joseph, John, George W., Nathan, Mary E., Thomas H., Harriet E. and Jennie A.; the second and fifth are dead. Mr. Crump has followed farming, principally, since settling in this county. When he came here the settlement was very thin, there being but one family between his farm and Griggsville; the nearest mill was 8 miles away. Mr. and Mrs. C. are Methodists.

M. S. Darrah, sec. 15; P. O., New Salem; was born in this county in 1839, and is the son of John and Elizabeth Darrah; his father was a native of Ohio, and his mother of Pennsylvania. Except 10 years in Champaign County, this State, the subject of this sketch has always resided in this county. His occupation is that of a farmer, and he owns 120 acres, his residence being on sec. 15. Oct. 25, 1865, he married Maggie M. Hooper, who is also a native of this county, and they have 5 children,—Gertie, deceased; Gracie, deceased; Franklin, Freddie, Mary G. Mr. and Mrs. D. are members of the M. E. Church. Mr. D. served 3 months in the war, in the regimental band, and was discharged on account of bleeding at the lungs.

H. L. Davidson, son of Joshua and Susanna Davidson, natives of Pennsylvania, was born in 1818 in Ohio, where he was brought up; in 1856 he emigrated to this county, settling on a farm 1½ miles north-west of Baylis, where he followed both farming and black-smithing. In 1841 he married Miss Hannah Tipton, who was born in 1819 in Jefferson county, Ohio, and of their 8 children 3 are living, to wit: John H., Susan and Mary L. Mrs. D. died in 1878. In 1877 Mr. D. moved into Baylis, where he erected a wagon and blacksmith shop, and he does all kinds of work in his line. He was a local preacher in the M. E. Church 25 years, and for the last 6 years he has held the same position in the United Brethren Church.

W. H. Deeder was born in 1838 in Huntingdon county, Pennsylvania; when 10 years of age he came with his parents, Isaac and Sophia Deeder to this county, settling at Pittsfield; in 1859 he married Sarah J. Mountain, a native of Adams county, Ill., and they had one child. Mrs. D. died in 1863, and the next year Mr. D. married Sophronia Osborne, who was born in 1857 in Tennessee, and they have had 7 children, 5 now living. Mr. D. has been School

Director, and is now an ordained minister of the Baptist Church at Fairmount. He served 3 years and 8 months in the late war, in the 2d Regiment, Battery A, since which time he has followed farming and blacksmithing. Residence, sec. 4; P. O., Baylis.

Theodore Doyle, physician, was born in Marion county, Ohio, in 1846. His father, Nicholas Doyle, was a native of Ireland; his mother, Maria, was a native of Bedford county, Penn. At the age of 10 years he moved to Crawfordsville, Indiana, lived there 2 years, then moved to Champaign county, this State. In 1867 he came to this county, where he has since resided. He commenced the study of medicine while in the eastern part of the State. He graduated at the American Eclectic Medical College at St. Louis, and commenced practice in Kinderhook, this county. Sept. 4, 1870, Dr. Doyle married Delight S. Winsor, who was born Dec. 15, 1844, in this county, and they had 2 children. Mrs. D.'s parents were Alonzo and Margaret Winsor, natives of New York. The Dr. has an extensive practice. P. O., New Salem.

John W. Ellsberry, son of Wesley and Sarah Ellsberry, natives of Kentucky, was born in Clermont county, Ohio, in 1825. When he was 2 years old he moved with his parents to Brown county, O., where he was raised and educated. In 1848 he came to Pike county and located in this tp., where he has since resided. Oct. 23, 1852, he married Mary J. Mace, who was born in Somerset (now Piscataquis) county, Maine, in 1823, and came to this county in 1836, and they have had 4 children, namely: Henry B., John M., Ella D. and Harmon P.; the latter died in November, 1867. Our subject has held the office of Commissioner of Highways, School Director, Justice of the Peace, and Assessor. His principal occupation has been farming, though formerly he was a blacksmith; also carried on a saw-mill, and kept a lumber yard. He now owns 80 acres of land with good house on it, and well fenced. Mr. and Mrs. E. are members of the Universalist Church. P. O., New Salem.

G. W. English, farmer, sec. 9; P. O., New Salem; was born in Clermont county, O., in 1827. His parents, Robert and Martha English, were natives of New York, and came to this county when G. W. was 8 years old; at that time there was no house between them and Quincy, a distance of 25 miles; and here our subject has lived ever since, except 3 years spent in California, prospecting for gold. He went in 1852 and made $1,000; he went across the isthmus and returned the same way to New York. In 1850 Mr. English married Sarah E. Bryant, who was born in Vermont in September, 1832, and their 5 children are,—Nathan, George, Luella, Emma E. and Mary F. His eldest son is studying for the ministry, in Lincoln, Nebraska. Mary is a teacher in the public schools at Baylis, Ill. All the family, except Mary, are Methodists. Mr. E. is a zealous Sunday-school worker. Mr. English being also a worker in his country's cause, organized the Union League in many places in

Harrison Brown

PLEASANTVALE TP

this county, and was President of County League. He is a farmer and stock-raiser, and makes a specialty of Poland-China hogs.

John Ewing, farmer, sec. 6; P. O., Baylis; was born in Jefferson county, O., in 1817. His parents, Alexander and Susan Ewing, were natives of Pennsylvania. They came to Ohio in an early day, and in 1851 came to Illinois and died in this county. In 1841 our subject married Keziah Tipton, born in 1825, in Jefferson county, Ohio; and they have had 4 children, to wit: Alexander, Susan C. and Nancy A. Susan died 4 years ago. Mr. E. has been School Director. In early life he was in limited circumstances, but by industry and economy he has acquired 160 acres of land. His wife is a Baptist.

Charles B. Fisk, sec. 15; P. O., New Salem; son of Eleazer and Lucy Fisk; was born in New Hampshire in 1829; he was taken to Massachusetts with his parents when he was one year old, and in 1840 came to Griggsville, this county. In 1860 he married Betsey E. Cobbs, who was born in 1837 or 1838, in New York, and they have 2 living children. Mr. F. has been Overseer of Highways, School Trustee, and is now President of the Town Board of New Salem. Mrs. F. is a Methodist. When he commenced in life for himself Mr. Fisk was in very limited circumstances, but he now has 80 acres of nice land. On his arrival here his nearest neighbors were Amos Blood, A. P. Sharpe and Thos. Bates.

William H. Fish, physician; P. O., Baylis; was born in Milbury, Mass., in 1848. His parents, Robert and Susan Fish, were natives of England, and came to America in 1842, and located in Milbury, and then emigrated to Hadley, this county, in 1854, where our subject was raised and educated, and also taught common school. He graduated at the College of Physicians and Surgeons in Keokuk, Iowa, Feb. 14, 1878; had commenced practice at Benville, Brown county, in 1873. After remaining there 2 years, he came to this place, where he has since remained. Dr. F. is a member of the M. E. Church, and has a good, growing practice.

James M. Furry was born in Highland county, O., in 1828; his father, Christopher Furry, was a native of Pennsylvania, and his mother, Mary (*nee* Edward), was of Irish descent, and born in Ohio. Mr. Furry spent 8 or 9 years in Ross county, and in 1849 he married Elizabeth Ann Patton, born in Kentucky in 1828. They have had 11 children. Our subject came to this county in 1856, and is now a merchant. He deals in dry-goods, groceries, hats and caps, boots and shoes, crockery, etc. He was Justice of the Peace in Ohio, and Supervisor in Pittsfield. His oldest child died at the age of 5 years, and more recently his second son died, aged 28, who was traveling salesman for a St. Louis firm. Residence, New Salem.

J. P. Gibbons, son of Lile and Mary Gibbons, natives of Ohio, was born in Belmont county, Ohio, in 1847; at the age of 18 years he came to this county, and in 1871 married Catharine Ewing, a native of Wayne county, Ohio, born in 1847; and their 3 children are, M. H. G., Mettie C. and Joseph O. Mrs. G. is a Presbyterian. Mr. G. has been a farmer all his life; owns 92 acres of good land, and resides on sec. 9. P. O., New Salem.

John Gray, farmer and blacksmith, sec. 5; P. O., New Salem; was born in Harrison county, Ohio, in 1814; his parents, Thomas (a native of Vermont) and Hannah, came to Ohio in a very early day. At the age of 17 our subject went to Clermont county, O., and came to this county in 1838, and has lived here ever since. In 1840 he was married to Nancy Bradbury, a native of Clermont county, Ohio, and had 5 children. He afterward married Mrs. Stag Barnard, and they had 2 children. Mr. G. has held the office of Commissioner of Highways for the last 6 years. He owns 80 acres of land near New Salem.

Frederick Halbauer, farmer, sec. 33; P. O., New Salem; was born in 1824, in Saxony, Germany; his parents were Partaloms and Rosena Halbauer. Frederick came to America and located in Philadelphia, Pa., in 1848; then lived 7 years in Burlington county, same State, and came to this county in 1856. The same year he married Miss Rosena Enos, who was born in 1831 in Bavaria, and they have had 8 children, one of whom is dead. Mr. H. owns 90 acres of good land, well improved.

Dr. H. Hatch is a prominent physician in New Salem.

John Hooper, farmer, sec. 27; P. O., New Salem; son of John and Hannah Cooper, natives of New Jersey; was born in Clermont county, Ohio, in 1823. At the age of 12 he came with his brother Thomas to this State, and lived 2 years in Coles county; came to Pike county in 1837, where he has since resided. In 1844 he married Mary Ann Shinn, who was born in Indiana in 1825, and came to this county in 1835; they had 11 children, 7 of whom are living,—Hannah, Peter F., J. C., Asa, Newton N., Louisa and Minnie M. Mr. H. owns 200 acres of land, all acquired by his own industry; he has held the office of School Trustee for the last 20 years; been School Director several terms; has lived on his present farm 24 years, and is well known throughout this and adjoining townships as an efficient school officer. Mr. and Mrs. H. are Methodists. Mr. Hooper is also a Free Mason.

William R. Hooper, farmer, sec. 15; P. O., New Salem; was born in Clermont county, Ohio, in 1842. His father, Peter Hooper, was a native of New Jersey, and his mother, Lida Hooper, a native of Kentucky. He came to this county in 1848, locating in Griggsville tp., then lived in Champaign county, this State, 18 months; in 1866 he married Miss L. B. Dillon, who was born in 1844 in Clermont county, Ohio, and they have had 2 children, a boy and a girl. He enlisted in the army in 1862, in Co. K, 99th Reg. He was in several battles, and was discharged in 1865; since that time he has followed farming, and owns 154 acres of land. Mr. and Mrs. H. are members of the Universalist Church of New Salem.

Alonzo Hubbard, farmer, sec. 16; P. O., New Salem; was born in Portsmouth, Rockingham county, N. H., in 1816. His father, Joshua Hubbard, was a native of Maine, and his mother, Eliza H. C. Hubbard, a native of Pennsylvania. He had good educational advantages, having attended the Academy at Portsmouth, and also at Lowell, Mass. In 1837 he came to Mason county, Kentucky, followed farming and tobacco raising, then took a trip to New Orleans, thence to this county; after remaining one year he returned to Kentucky to settle business there, then came back and settled permanently in this tp. March 20, 1845, he married Charlotte Brown, who was born in Ireland in 1825, and came to America when 8 years old. Mr. and Mrs. Hubbard have 6 children, namely, Henry, William, Amos, Eliza H. C., Louise F. and Hilton. Two of the sons were in the army; Henry belonged to Co. K, 99th Ill. Vol., was with Sherman in his march to the sea. William belonged to Co. I, 18th Reg. I. V. I. Mr. and Mrs. Hubbard are members of the Universalist Church, at New Salem.

Elijah Jeffers, retired farmer, was born in Clermont county, O., Jan. 1, 1803; he is the son of William and Sarah (Rollins) Jeffers, the former a native of England, and the latter of Ireland. Our subject was reared upon a farm, and has successfully followed agricultural pursuits thus far through life. He came to this county Oct. 17, 1837; hence is one of the oldest pioneers who have helped to convert the native wilds of this county into fruitful fields. He had but a limited education and possessed only $300 when he came to the county. His first purchase was 80 acres of wild land, which he improved and to which he added from time to time, until one time he owned between 500 and 600 acres, most of which he has divided among his children. He has held local township offices and been class-leader in the M. E. Church over 20 years, of which Church he has been an active and prominent member for 53 years, as also has his wife. In 1826 or 1827, in Ohio, he was married to Hannah Pine, daughter of William and Hannah Pine, natives of England and New Jersey, respectively. Of this union 11 children have been born, 10 of whom are living: John C., William P., Mary A., Samuel, Isaac E., Rachel, James, Lucinda, Francis L. and Martha F. We give Mr. Jeffers' portrait.

George Johnston, blacksmith and wagon-maker; P. O., New Salem; was born in Westmoreland county, Penn., Dec. 4, 1834. His father, Robert Johnston, was a native of Ireland, and his mother, Nancy Johnston, a native of Pennsylvania; when 2 years old he moved with his parents to Harrison county, Ohio, where he was raised. In 1857 he came to Brown county, this State, where he followed blacksmithing, and in 1858 came to Pike county. In 1859 he married Sarah A. Reed, who was born in Brown county, this State, Feb. 12, 1836, and they have had 6 children. Mr. J. has followed blacksmithing 22 years. He is a member of the Masonic order.

Nathan Kinman, farmer, sec. 35; P. O., Pittsfield; is a son of Levi and Susannah Kinman, natives of North Carolina ; he was brought to this county with his parents in 1831. In 1843 he was united in marriage with Eliza Cadwell; she was born in the State of Kentucky in 1821, and died in 1868. To them were born 9 children, 7 of whom are living : Robert H., Joseph M., William F., John C., Lewis F., Mary C., Nathan J., Charles A. and Arthur L. After the demise of his former wife he was married to Eliza J. Conkright, who was born in the State of Ohio in 1839. Mr. K. has held the office of County Commissioner, and is a member of the Baptist Church.

James F. Lemmon, painter and carpenter; P. O., Baylis; was born in Adams county, Ill., in 1850. His parents were Wm. and Cornelia Lemmon, the former a native of Indiana and the latter of North Carolina. At the age of 13 he left his parents, and at 16 he began to learn the carpenter's trade; at 17 he went into the U. S. army and served three years and two hours. At first he was in Co. D, 37th Reg; then he was in Co. C, 5th U. S. Inf. In 1871 he was married to America Fox in Kansas City, Mo., who was born in 1846 in Chariton, Mo., and they have had 2 children, one of which has died. Since his return from the army he has been engaged in painting of all kinds. He is now Constable in New Salem tp. Mr. and Mrs. L. are Methodists.

John McCarter, farmer, sec. 20; P. O., New Salem; was born in Philadelphia, Penn., in 1833. His parents, James and Margaret McCarter, were natives of Ireland, and came to this country in 1832, locating where our subject was born ; then came to Illinois, settling in Adams county; in 1837 they came to this county, where John grew to manhood, receiving a common-school education. In 1870 he married Eliza M. Little, who was born in Tyrone county, Ireland, in 1841, and came with her parents to America in 1858. They had 3 children, namely, Emma, John William and Maud L. Mr. McC. followed carpentering 15 years, but is now a farmer and owns 380 acres of land, well improved ; he makes a specialty of raising short-horned cattle; also raises large crops of wheat. Mr. and Mrs. McC. are Presbyterians.

Archibald B. McDonald, farmer, sec. 4; P. O., Baylis; was born in Sumner county, Tenn., in 1814. His father, A. B. McDonald, was born in Scotland, and his mother, Elizabeth McDonald, was born in North Carolina. He came to this State in 1832 and located in Morgan county, and moved to this county in the spring of 1840. May 16, 1841, he married Rhoda E. Askew, who was born in Green county, Ky., in 1824, and they have had 12 children, 6 of whom are living. Mrs. McDonald died in 1875, and in 1878 Mr. McDonald married Mrs. Sarah J. Hull, a mother of 4 children; she was born in 1825 in Washington county, Ky., and is a member of the United Brethren Church.

John D. McIntire was born in Chester county, Pa., in 1819, son of Robert and Elizabeth McIntire, the former a native of Ireland.

Our subject grew to manhood in his native State, and in 1849 moved to Ohio; two years later he came to Illinois, locating in La-Salle county, where he remained 13 years, and in 1864 came to this county. He first learned the tailor's trade, which business he followed for 13 years, and then engaged in agricultural pursuits, and now owns 122 acres of land on sec. 6, this tp. He has held the offices of Collector, School Director, etc. He was married in 1846 to Miss Adeline Hutton, a native of Lancaster county, Pa., and daughter of Benjamin and Susan Hutton. Eight of their 11 children are living, namely: Anna L. (now Mrs. Jeffers), Clara, Nettie, Jesse, Herbert J., Frank N., Merritt L. and Nora E.

David Miller, farmer, sec. 19; P. O., Baylis; son of Thomas and Nancy Miller, natives of Pennsylvania, was born in this county in 1839. In 1863 he married Elizabeth Carnes, born in 1846, and they have 2 children living,—Mary A. and Francis. Mr. M. owns 69 acres of good land. He is a member of the M. E. Church, and has license to preach. Mrs. M. is a member of the United Brethren Church.

Hiram Moore was born in this county in 1845, the son of John and Sarah Moore, natives of Maryland, who came to this county 40 years ago; the former died in this tp., in 1876, the latter is still living with her children. Our subject married Miss Mary Dunham in 1865; she is a native of this county and was born in 1849; their children are Cora, Laura, Minnie, George E., Amos E. and Freddie. Mr. M. was reared upon a farm, and for the last 14 years has been engaged in farming for himself. When he first began in life he had only $100, but by close application and business tact he has accumulated considerable property. He and his wife are members of the United Brethren Church.

James Morgan, harness-maker, New Salem; is a native of England, and born in 1826; his parents were James and Letitia Morgan, also natives of England. He came to America with his parents when he was 14 years old and settled in Illinois. In 1866 he married Mary Ann Young, who was born in Illinois in 1835, and they have one living child. He has worked at his present employment for 35 years, and thoroughly understands his business.

Ashton Pilling, son of Samuel O. and Mary Pilling, was born in England in 1803. In early life he followed hand-weaving, and worked in the manufactory until he came to this country, which was in 1842. He landed in New York, then went to Rhode Island and remained 4 years, then came to Adams county, this State; thence in 1874 to this county. In 1825 he married Nancy Wild, who was born in England in 1809; they have 4 living children,—John, Mary, Jane and Cordelia. Mrs. Pilling died in 1854, and the same year Mr. P. married Sarah Blake, who was born in 1807, in Rhode Island; she is a member of the M. E. Church. During the past 5 years Mr. P. has lived a retired life. P. O., Baylis.

David F. Pine, farmer, sec. 7; P. O., Baylis; was born in this county in 1850. His father, William, was a native of New York, and his mother, Nancy, a native of Vermont. In 1871 he married Mary F. McKinney, who was born in this county in 1853. They have had 4 children; only 1 is living,—Frederick. Mr. P. has followed farming during his entire life, owning 40 acres of good land. His father laid out the town of Baylis. Mrs. Pine is a member of the M. E. Church.

John W. Pine, a brother of the preceding, is a farmer and resides on sec. 6, owning 105 acres of well-improved land. He came to Pike county with his parents in 1838, and in 1854 he married Mary McCleeny, who was born in Pennsylvania, in 1835, and they have 8 living children,—Lucinda, George M., Sarah E., Jennie, Lucetta, Mary E., Lucy and Irene. Mr. P. has always been a farmer. P. O., Baylis.

John G. Reynolds is a promising young man of 23 or 24 years of age, and is a teacher of vocal music, but now proposes to become a florist and fruit-grower; has studied 12 years, and has been instructed by F. K. Phœnix, of Bloomington, and J. R. Hull, of Hancock county; has visited the best florists of the State and of St. Louis, Mo. He has a nice hot-house well filled with flowers and bulbs. One of his flower stands brought $86 at the temperance supper in Valley City, Dec. 9, 1879.

R. D. Reynolds was born in Botetourt county, Virginia, in 1817. His parents, Thomas and Priscilla Reynolds, were also natives of Virginia. In 1838 he married Delilah Slade, who was born in Lexington, Ky., in 1815, and they have had 8 children,—James T., Cynthia M., Sarah E., Bell, John G. and Annie A. Mr. Reynolds came from Ohio to this county in 1851 and located on sec. 16, this tp., where he has resided ever since, following brick masonry and farming; he owns 82 acres of land. He has held the offices of School Director and Road Overseer. He and his wife are members of the M. E. Church. He is also a Freemason. P. O., New Salem.

Ernest Sannebeck was born in Prussia in 1834. His parents, Frank and Sophia Sannebeck, were natives of Prussia. Our subject came to this country and located in Baltimore, Md. While there he followed butchering; in 1856 he came to Louisville, Ky. He served in the late war in Co. A, 1st Reg. K. V. He was in Indiana 4 years, then in St. Louis, and in 1877 came to this place. In 1869 he married Miss M. Bolender, who was born in Hesse in 1845. Mr. S. carries on a butcher shop in Baylis, and also keeps the Pineville Hotel.

Meinhart Sannebeck, brother of the preceding, was born in Prussia in 1828; he came to America in 1854 and located at Baltimore. In 1858 he went to Louisville, Ky., and in 1859 and '60, was in Texas. In 1861 he went back to Louisville, and in 1873 went to Chicago, Ill.; in 1877 he moved to Barry, this county, thence to Baylis, where he is engaged in butchering; is also interested in the Pineville Hotel; he served 3 years in the Prussian army. In 1860 he married Catharine Bolender, who was born in 1834 in Germany. They have 3 children,—Frank, 19 years old,

Henry, 15 years old, and Conrad, aged 13 years,—all born in Louisville, Ky.

W. H. Seaborn, farmer, sec. 6; P. O., Baylis; son of Robert and Mary A. Seaborn, was born in this county in 1845. He entered the U. S. service in Co. B, 68th Reg. Ill. Inf.; served 3 months guarding posts; was mustered out; again enlisted as a teamster in the West; served 1 year, then returned home and engaged in buying and shipping stock. In 1872 he married Sallie Reed, who was born in 1849. They have had 2 children; one is dead, and they have adopted a child. Mr. S. now follows farming, owning 130 acres of land.

Henry Shaffner was born in Highland county, Ohio, in 1826, and is the son of Jacob and Elizabeth Shaffner, natives of Dauphin county, Penn. At the age of 16 he moved with his parents to Edgar county, Ill.; in 1844 moved to Brown county, and in 1851 he came to this county, at first locating one mile south of Salem, but in 1870 he settled on sec. 14, where he now resides. He used to be a cooper, but is now a farmer, owning 84 acres of land. In 1850 he married Martha Dunham, who was born in 1832 in Harrison county, Ohio. Their children are Mary J., John W., Louis, Sarah A. and Eliza. The first 2 are dead. United Brethren. P. O., New Salem.

W. O. Shaffner was born in 1848 in Brown county, Ill., and is a son of John and Susannah Shaffner, father a native of Pennsylvania, mother of Ohio. His father died in 1874, a worthy member of the U. B. Church, and a good citizen every way. W. O. still lives with his mother; up to 1868 he followed farming, and then he learned the wagon-maker's trade under C. C. Shaffner; for the last 5 years has conducted the business for himself in New Salem.

John Sigsworth was born in Yorkshire, Eng., Jan. 26, 1825; his parents, Joseph and Ann, were both natives of England, and emigrated to America in 1830, settling in Ohio, and in 1836 settled in this county. At the age of 25 John went to California where he followed herding cattle and farming; returned to this county in 1853; in 1854 went to California again, but since 1858 has followed shipping stock and farming in this county. In 1846 he married Sarah M. Brawley, who was born in 1826 in Ohio. Children,— Dennis B., Lida A., Mary E., Elizabeth J., Alice A., John A., deceased, and Joseph W. Mr. S. has been Assessor, Collector and School Director. P. O., New Salem.

David Starkey is a native of Pike county, a son of Jonathan and Jane Starkey, natives of Virginia. He was born in 1854, and has lived here all his life; is now on sec. 9, and owns 120 acres of nice land. He has never been as far as 75 miles from home but 3 times in his life. In 1876 he married Annie Gray and they had one child, who is not now living.

Henry A. Starkey was born in 1849 in Huron county, Ohio; his parents, James and Elizabeth, were born in Wheeling, Virginia; in 1874 he emigrated to Missouri and married Annie Stodgress, Dec. 20 of that year; she was a native of Ohio. In 1877 they emigrated to this county and now reside on sec. 4; P. O., New Salem. James Anderson is their only child. Mrs. S. is a member of the Christian Church.

Jonathan Starkey, farmer and stock-dealer, sec. 4, P. O., New Salem, and whose portrait appears in this volume, was born in Culpepper county, Va., in 1813. His parents were John and Mary (Groves) Starkey, also natives of the Old Dominion; they emigrated to Ohio when our subject was 7 years of age, where he remained until he was 23 years of age, when he came to Pike county, locating in New Salem tp., being one of the early pilgrims to this locality, and where he has since remained. When he first came he had but $40 in money, but through the kindness of a friend, from whom he borrowed $50, he was enabled to purchase 50 acres of land, which he did on sec. 9. Upon this land, which was then in its native condition, he erected a log cabin 14 by 16 feet in size, in which he lived for 5 years. Being a man of great energy, industrious, and of economical habits, he was enabled to add to his small means, until he has become one of the most extensive farmers and stock dealers in Pike county, owning at one time over 1,200 acres of fine farming land, and feeding from 100 to 150 head of cattle, and from 200 to 300 head of hogs annually, besides a large number of horses and sheep. He has provided liberally for his children, giving them nice farms, until now he has only a little over 200 acres left in the home farm, which is on sec. 4, and one of the finest farms in the county. Mr. Starkey has been a hard-working man, and has done as much perhaps as any one man in developing the wonderful resources of this fair county. Although a member of no church, he has never been behind any of his most enterprising neighbors in favoring any and all enterprises which he has been called upon to help push forward, having paid considerable to help erect school-houses and churches, and to pay the ministry. In fact, Mr. S. is one of Pike county's old, useful and honored citizens, and as such we present to our readers his portrait.

Mr. Starkey has been twice married,—the first time in Pennsylvania in 1834, to Jane L. Laughtery, who was born in the Keystone State in 1815. She died Sept. 28, 1876. To them were born 9 children, of whom 8 are living: Charles, Rachel, James, Nicholas, William, Mary, Maria and David. John was the name of the deceased. July 30, 1879, Mr. S. was again married, this time to Sarah, daughter of Thomas J. and Margaret Carothers.

William Starkey, farmer and stock-raiser, Baylis; was born in this county in 1846, the son of Jonathan and Jane Starkey, spoken of above. In 1873 he married Emeline Seybold, who was born in this county in 1850. Their children are Olive, Cora and Harry. Mr. S. is a prominent farmer, owning 215 acres of nice land. He is a member of the Masonic fraternity, and liberal in all public enterprises.

Jonathan Starkey

NEW SALEM TP.

William H. Stauffer was born in this county, Jan. 23, 1847. His parents were John and Sarah Stauffer, the former a native of Pennsylvania, and the latter of Virginia; his father came to this State in 1836, and settled in Fairmount tp., where he still resides. Our subject was raised on a farm, and follows that occupation. In 1871 he was married to Rachel E. Wood, who was born in 1851 in this county. They have 2 children,—George E. and Nelia A. Mr. S. owns 80 acres of well-improved land, with good buildings. P. O. Baylis. Residence, sec. 8.

Rev. T. H. Tabor was born in Rutland county, Vermont, in 1824. His parents were Arden and Phœbe Tabor, and moved to New York when our subject was 9 years of age. Mr. Tabor studied for the ministry, and by his own effort accomplished his work. In 1843 he married Eliza Leonard, who was born in 1824 in Hampshire county, Mass., and died in June, 1850, leaving 2 children. In 1856 he married Miss B. A. Morris, who was born in 1831 in Steuben county, N. Y. His 2 sons are also ministers, preaching the Universalist doctrine. Mr. Tabor's first work was in South Dansville, New York; thence in Oct., 1854, to Earlville, LaSalle county, this State ; next to Woodstock in 1856, then Briggsville, Wisconsin, in 1857; then went to Markesan, Wisconsin, remaining 6 years; next, in 1864, to Blue Island, and remained there until September, 1867. He there erected a church. In 1867 he went to Macomb and remained until the spring of 1872, then to Kirkwood, till 1874, next to Yates City, then for 2 years divided his time between Bradford and LaFayette, and occasionally visited New Salem; then in the fall of 1876 went to Bloomfield, Iowa, remaining one year ; then came back to Monmouth and remained until March, 1879, then came to New Salem, where he added 27 members to the society. He has been an ardent worker in the Master's cause. Residence, New Salem.

Capt. Isaac H. Walling, son of Isaac and Mary H. Walling, natives of New Jersey, was born in 1836 on sea, off Cape Hatteras, on his father's ship " Chingaoria;"at the age of 12 years he went to sea as cabin-boy, then as able seaman 2 years, then as mate for 4 or 5 years. In 1855 or 1856 he shipped on schooner "Kenosha" in Buffalo, N. Y., to run from there to Chicago; served 1 year, then went back to New York and shipped on a cruise to Liverpool, Isle of Man, and to Sligo, then back to New York; then shipped on schooner "T. A. Ward," Capt. Hoff, commander, and went to Cadiz, Malaga, Salona, Genoa, Barbary States, Rio Janeiro, S. A., and back to Baltimore; then shipped on a wrecking vessel, where a fortunate circumstance occurred to our subject, but fatal to a cousin of his named Bainbridge. He exchanged places with him to accommodate him, so that he might go to port and purchase supplies; while on the way the ship and all its crew were lost. He was first at the wreck of the " New Era " and " Powhattan," the latter of which, laden with human freight, sunk in sight, and all on board perished.   After this Capt. W. took many voyages; was shipwrecked several times; was taken prisoner at Charleston, S. C., by a man-of-war, during the Rebellion when he was at sea.   On the schooner "Harriet Harker," which was owned by our subject, he was cast away 35 miles north of Cape Hatteras, where he lay three days and nights in the water without anything to eat or drink, but at last landed safely.   At another time he escaped a watery grave by not taking a schooner when going to rescue another vessel, as it was taken by another party and was lost with all on board. Then went to launch a brig " Kedstow," 50 miles south of Cape Henry.   In 1876 he was again wrecked near Cape Charles, at the mouth of Chesapeake Bay.   This was his last trip at sea.   By the persuasion of his family, and being tired of sea life, he came West and located at Baylis, where he embarked in the mercantile trade, in which the wrecks are not so dangerous to life.

John White, farmer, sec. 31; P. O. New Salem; was born in Ireland in 1809.   His parents, John and Margaret White, were also natives of Ireland.   He came to America at the age of 22 and located at Philadelphia, where he remained 6 years, and most of the time followed weaving; then came to Quincy, this State, and followed teaming; came to this county in 1839 and located at New Philadelphia, then bought land where he is at present living.   In 1845 he married Margaret White, who was born in Scotland, and they had one child, now dead.   Mrs. W. died in 1846, and in 1856 he married Mary E. Cunningham, who was born in 1834 in Ireland, and came to America in 1856.   Their children are: William, Margaret, Anna B., Mary J., Joseph, Robert, Emmet, Emily and Frank.   The deceased are Thomas J. and an infant.   Mr. W. owns 640 acres of land at the home place and 80 acres in Pleasant Vale tp., all of which he has accumulated himself.   He and his wife are Presbyterians.

William H. Winterbotham, physician, was born in Massachusetts, in 1847; his parents, Jonathan and Margaret, are natives of England, who came to America about the year 1842 and located in Bristol, Rhode Island, then moved to where our subject was born. At the age of 2 years he came with his parents to this county, where he was raised on a farm, and attended the common schools; at the age of 19 he commenced the study of medicine under Dr. J. Sykes, of Beverly, Adams county, studied 2 years, then attended the College of Physicians and Surgeons at Keokuk, Iowa, graduated Feb. 22, 1872, and the March following began his practice in Baylis.   Feb. 24, 1870, he was married to Martha E. Harvey, who was born in June, 1846, and they had 4 children.   The Doctor is a Trustee of Schools, a member of the State Medical Association, and of the Masonic Order.

PITTSFIELD TOWNSHIP.

This township is situated more nearly in the geographical center of the county than any other. It is a full Congressional township and is officially known as township 5 south, and range 4 west of the 4th principal meridian. In an agricultural point the township ranks among the finest in this favored county. It contains a wealthy and intelligent class of agriculturists, who have made the very best of improvements throughout the township.

We shall not dwell at length upon the history of the township, as we give an extended sketch of the town of Pittsfield, which largely embraces the history of the township; and we also speak at some length in the personal sketches of the leading farmers of this community.

The pioneer who first located here was Joel Moore. He erected a little cabin on the northeast quarter of sec. 12; then came Ephraim Cannon and Moses Riggs, all of whom became prominent in the early history of the county, and located on secs. 20 and 23 respectively. In 1833 a site was chosen in this township by a special commission of the Legislature for the location of the county seat, principally because of its being more nearly in the center of the county, and a desirable and healthy location. At this place the principal scenes in the history of the township have been enacted, which we will now begin to chronicle.

PITTSFIELD.

Although but 47 years have passed since the town of Pittsfield was founded, it is difficult to realize the changes that have been made in its appearance and surroundings since then, or that so much has been accomplished in so brief a period. Where now stand stately public buildings, school-houses and churches, spacious stores and business houses, busy mills and workshops, elegant residences, surrounded with evidences of refinement and culture, tasteful cottages, the homes of a thrifty and contented people, miles of well-graded streets and sidewalks, filled with all the busy life of an energetic and prosperous town, but a little over a generation ago was an unpeopled waste, the beauty of its site unknown save to an occasional hunter or the Indian nomads. Many are still living in the town in the enjoyment of a hale old age, who aided in the foundation of the new town and erected some of its first rude buildings. They have lived to see the log cabins replaced by large and substantial buildings of frame or brick, have seen the little town spread out from the nucleus around "the Square," until its well-built streets extend in all directions, and the little village has become an important business mart, the center of a. thickly settled and wealthy community.

ORIGIN OF PITTSFIELD.

Having decided to locate the county-seat in the center of the county, George W. Hinman, Hawkins Judd and Benjamin Barney were selected as commissioners, who in March, 1833, laid out the site of the town, purchasing the quarter section of land from the United States Government at a cost of $200. The first sale of lots took place May 15, 1833, 11 lots being disposed of on that day. Several lots were reserved for public purposes, and the block in the northeast corner of the town, immediately north of the present residence of Jas. H. Wheeling, was set apart as a burying-ground, and a number of interments were made therein, until the South Cemetery was opened, and later the West and Episcopal Cemeteries, in the western limits of the town, when the old ground was no longer used for its original purpose.

EDUCATIONAL.

The location of the county-seat, and the natural beauty of the site, gave the young town a good start, and from the first its growth has been steady. It was named "Pittsfield," after the city of the same name in Massachusetts, whence many of its earliest and best citizens had come; and that infusion of New England enterprise, thrift, morals and culture has helped to give tone to its people, and aided in its subsequent career. From the earliest days, when no regular system of schools was yet established, it is an evidence of the public-spirited liberality of the young men of the town, that they voluntarily contributed for the support of the schools first opened for the education of the children; and the place has always been noted for the fostering care bestowed on this important branch.

The first school building was of wood, located on the west end of the lot now owned by Geo. W. Sanderson. It was a small affair, and painted the regulation color, red; and many a man who has since won distinction at the bar, the forum, or in letters, learned the first rudiments within its noisy portal. As the town grew, extended accommodations were needed, and several other small schools were started. Later the lower portion of the Christian Church was rented for a public school. In 1861–3 the public spirit found full expression in the erection of the present spacious and beautiful building, one of the largest and best in the Military Tract. Here, with a graded system and a large and efficient corps of teachers, pupils are instructed in all the ordinary branches, the High School department fitting students for college. A large clock with a fine

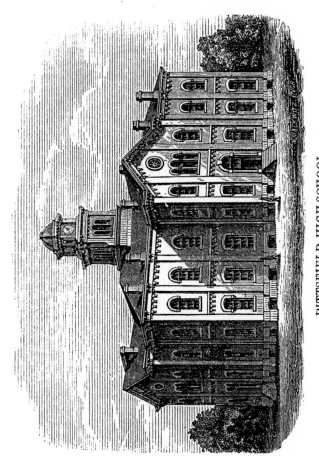

PITTSFIELD HIGH-SCHOOL.

bell attached, was placed in the dome shortly after the completion of the building.

The town also has a Library and Free Reading Room, organized by the ladies, and heretofore supported by the subscriptions of the members. There are about one thousand volumes, many of them of a standard character, besides a number of papers and periodicals. At the election last year the citizens voted to levy a small tax to support the institution, and extend its field of usefulness.

NEWSPAPERS.

In 1842 the first newspaper was started by Michael J. Noyes, and was called *The Sucker*. This was succeeded by the *Free Press*, started by Garbutt & Abbott. Later it was edited by John G. Nicolay, now Marshal of the United States Supreme Court at Washington, and at one time Private Secretary to President Lincoln, and afterward Consul at Paris. The *Free Press* was followed by *The Journal*, and it by *The Old Flag*, which is now published and is in a prosperous condition. These papers were Free-Soil, Whig and Republican, in natural succession.

The Sentinel was the first Democratic paper, and was started in 1845 by Turnbull & Smith. It was followed by the *Union*, in 1849, and it by the *Pike County Democrat*, in 1857, which still flourishes as the organ of the Democrats of the county. Several other newspaper ventures were made, but they existed only for a brief period. The mail facilities now enable the people to secure promptly the daily papers from the larger cities, and a large number are circulated.

STREETS.

Those who now admire the fine condition of the streets of the town, the easy grades, the long reaches of macadamized and graveled roads, and the miles of broad sidewalks, can hardly realize the primitive character of the thoroughfares that preceded them. The roads and streets were almost impassable in rainy weather, and the best efforts at sidewalks were eighteen-inch logs split in two and laid side by side, the round side down, and these only in the most favored localities. Elsewhere pedestrians did the best they could, and on dark nights they had a hard road to travel. During the past two years the corporation has spent about $10,000 in the improvement of the streets alone. And now, with public lamps in all the streets, over a district about a mile and a half square, travel is safe and comfortable.

THE PUBLIC SQUARE AND BUILDINGS AROUND IT.

A description of the Public Square and the short streets immediately around it, in the early days, should prove interesting. Nearly all the old buildings have been pulled down or removed, and the few landmarks that still remain must soon meet the same fate. On the north side of the Square there were but four buildings. A grocery or saloon occupied the corner where Shadel's meat market now stands; next west was Thomas Dickson's small frame store which long occupied the place of the present two-story brick edifice, and is still standing in the rear of its old site; next was the Court-House, now Joseph Heck's store, and next a one-story frame, which was afterward enlarged, and is now occupied by Field's jewelry store. In the lower portion of the lot, where the Pittsfield House now stands, was the house of Michael McGuire. The first store on the west side was that of Green & Barber, the building now occupied by Clayton's hardware store; next was the store of Jacob Hodgen, who afterward built the first brick store in town; and next, near the south corner, the harness shop of Hamilton Wills. On the south side was the log store of Jonas Clark, which stood where Seeley, Lloyd & Co.'s big store now stands; then the store of Talcott & Co., and then the Mansion House, which was then but two stories high and having about half its present frontage. East of this was Mrs. Mary M. Heath's house. (This venerable lady, who is said to have been the first white child born in Cincinnati, O., is still living in the town, and is looked upon and respected as one of the few living links connecting the present with the past generation.) East of Mrs. Heath's was Frank Spencer's blacksmith shop. On the east side of the Square, and occupying the site of Winans & Platner's furniture store, was the residence of Miss Bush, and north of that J. U. Grimshaw's store.

The Square itself was an unfenced playground, ornamented with a dense growth of hazel-brush.

OTHER BUILDINGS.

Scattered at some distance on the streets running from the Square were the dwellings of the citizens, none of them presenting much architectural beauty. The large two-story frame residence now occupied by Thos. Burt, was built by Col. Wm. Ross, when he first moved to the town. It was probably at that time the finest private dwelling in all the surrounding country, and its large rooms, wide halls and lofty ceilings were the admiration of all. In 1847 Col. Ross built the large brick residence just east of town, where he resided up to the time of his death. Mr. Oran Green, a hale and active veteran, still lives to boast that he carried all the mortar used in the erection of that fine building.

Near where Hicks' stable now stands was Turnbaugh's Row, a block of four stores, "all on the ground," all occupied by the same firm, and filled with a miscellaneous stock.

The building now occupied as a residence by Dr. Worthington, situated on one of the handsomest sites in the town, and surrounded by beautiful grounds, was intended for a seminary for young ladies, but for some reason the attempt to establish such an institution here was abandoned.

Jas. Ward and Samuel Smith built and kept a livery stable north of the present postoffice. Between that and the corner of the Square was a deep hollow, overgrown with hazel brush.

Fletcher & Huckaborn had a blacksmith and gun-shop back of Hunter's present shoe shop. Dorus Bates also had a blacksmith shop near his wagon manufactory.

Where Shibley's carriage factory now stands, was erected the first carding-machine. It was run by horse power, and was a ponderous concern, with broad wooden cog-wheels and beams. Here a child, who afterward lived to assume a noted manhood, had a miraculous escape from a horrible death. While the machinery was under full headway, he climbed upon the horse power, but slipped and fell. His head was caught between one of the broad spokes of the wheel and the timber of the frame. It was crushed nearly flat, but stopped the machine!

The child recovered and grew up to serve his country gallantly and well. That was one of the many escapes of Major D. E. Bates.

The first steam flouring-mill, now known as the "Old Mill," was built by Jonathan Frye and Stephen Gay in 1849, and for years was the largest in this section. The new mill was built in 1870 by Shaw, Rupert, Adams & Chapman, and is a fine large brick building, filled with the best machinery. Both mills are doing a heavy business, and Pittsfield brands of flour command a high price in the markets of New York and Boston.

The oldest building in the town was erected by William Watson. It is a small log store, and is now standing in the lot in the rear of the Mansion House. Mr. Watson was soon followed by Messrs. R. R. Greene and Austin Barber, who built and occupied the store owned by W. H. Clayton.

Mr. John U. Grimshaw had the first regular dry-goods store in town, near where L. Klemme's building now stands, but also carried a stock of miscellaneous goods. He was an Irishman by birth, well educated, and with a high sense of business integrity. He has been dead for some years.

PROMINENT CITIZENS.

The name of Col. William Ross is intimately associated with the early history of Pittsfield, and with its advancement and prosperity, up to the time of his death. He was its most prominent citizen, and aided nearly every enterprise. He was born in Massachusetts in 1792, emigrated to this county in 1820, subsequently removing to the new town of Pittsfield. A good sketch of his life is given in the biographical department of the history of this township.

Col. D. B. Bush, also a native of Massachusetts, born in 1790, settled in Pittsfield a year after the town was laid out, and has been a prominent and active citizen ever since. He practiced at the Bar, and has held several offices. He is still remarkably healthy for

PITTSFIELD

his years, and can be seen almost daily greeting his many friends with genial humor.

Hon. William R. Archer, the veteran member of the Bar, is still in active practice. He was born in New York in 1817, and emigrated to Pittsfield in 1838. He has repeatedly represented this district in the State Senate, and is known and honored throughout the State. He has a numerous family of sons and daughters, and the whole community call him friend.

Mr. Samuel Crane, who conducted the Union House for many years, is another surviving veteran, who can be seen any morning in the week, basket on arm, doing his own marketing. He has a neat place in the west part of town, and is a noted gardener.

Mr. Frank Keys, another of the early settlers, is about to remove to Logan county. He first engaged in store-keeping in Pittsfield, but later devoted his attention to farming and stock-raising, amassing a large property. He is of Scotch-Irish birth, and has all the energy and perseverance of that canny race.

Squire Hickerson, who lives some distance east of town, was probably the first settler in that vicinity. He is still a very active man, and is now serving as Collector of Newburg township. He has a remarkable memory, and is a veritable chronicle of the early history of the town and county.

James Ross is probably the oldest living resident of the town. He is a native of Ireland, and settled at Atlas in 1826. When Pittsfield was located he moved here, where he has since resided.

Thomas Dickson, who is a native of the island of Orkney, removed from New York to Pittsfield in 1839. He acted as clerk in William Watson's store for some years, and then engaged in business for himself. He is still an active business man, and gives promise to continue so for many years.

Capt. W. N. Shibley, another Mexican veteran, who is still carrying on his old business of carriage-making, was among the early settlers; and although he has had a career of considerable adventure, is as active as he was 30 years ago. He served through the Mexican war, and later spent many years fighting Indians on the Texas plains. He still has in his possession some of the scalps taken in his adventurous days, hideous trophies of border warfare.

Hon. Henry Mudd, now a prominent citizen of Missouri, was among the earliest merchants of Pittsfield, where he conducted a successful business for many years.

H. Atkinson, now the respected Vice President of the Pike County Bank, was an early comer. He came from Philadelphia and opened a tailor shop near the southwest corner of the Square. Afterward he engaged in the drug business, and later had a furniture and hardware store.

Col. D. D. Hicks, the veteran Cashier of the First National Bank, has long been a resident of the town, and has been a successful business man and popular public officer.

Dr. Campbell and Dr. Worthington were the first physicians

38

who settled here. Both were skillful practitioners and energetic men. Dr. Campbell has been dead for some years, but Dr. Worthington is still living. Having acquired a large property, he has devoted his later years to the study of geology and kindred subjects, and has been visiting the Rocky Mountains for some time in pursuit of his favorite studies. Dr. Norris and Dr. Comstock came some time later, and both practiced successfully. They have been called from their duties for many years. The widow of Dr. Norris still survives him, and is enjoying a genial and graceful old age. Young in heart and joyful in feeling, she is respected by all, and is especially loved by the young people, whose friend and confidant she is.

Among the local celebrities whose subsequent career has been a subject of pride with this people, is Col. John Hay, now Assistant Secretary of State at Washington. He spent his boyhood here, with his uncle, Hon. Milton Hay, now of Springfield. His " Pike County Ballads " have associated his name with his old home, although he exercised more than a poet's license in some of the pictures he drew. The hero of " Banty Tim," the most forcible of the ballads, is still a resident of this town, but his name is *not* Tilman Joy.

But probably the best known local character is Capt. Abe Butz, proprietor of the Oregon House. A native of Pennsylvania, he came West in early manhood, and has gone through a long life with philosophical cheerfulness. Noted for his patriotism, he observes with religious regularity all the National holidays, anniversaries of battles, etc., and is an especial admirer of Gen. Jackson, for whom he played; and also assisted at the reception of Gen. Lafayette at Philadelphia on his last visit to this country. Mr. Butz is also noted for his kindliness of heart, the poor always finding in him a charitable friend.

Mr. Metcalf opened the first tin shop in the town, and for a long time had a monopoly of that trade. L. Bennett had one of the first shoe shops, and Samuel Barber a tailor shop.

Robert R. Greene and Austin Barber came from Marietta, Ohio, and settled in Pittsfield when it was laid out. They were connected in business for many years, the store of Greene & Barber being known throughout the whole tract. Both partners still survive. Mr. Greene has been an invalid for some years, but Mr. Barber is as vigorous and active as many younger men.

BRICK KILN, ETC.

In 1843 the first kiln of brick was burned, by a man named Butler, his yard being located west of the fair grounds. Later a brick yard was started on North Monroe street, where the Haskell property now stands. Since then the business has grown steadily, until this day, when brick, tile, pottery, etc., form an important item in the industries of the town.

HOTELS.

The location of the Court-House here, with the consequent influx of strangers during term time, made hotels a necessity at an early day. The Union House, kept by Samuel Crane, and the Mansion House, met the demand at first. Then the Kentucky House, now known as the Mansion House, was built. In 1870 the spacious and handsome Pittsfield House was built by a stock company. The three last named houses are still open. These, with Shibley's establishment and the Oregon House, amply supply the town with hotel accommodations. The Union House was a frame building on the north side of the Square. The lower portion of the building is now occupied by the stores of M. R. Peckenpaugh and Dober & Blades.

MAIL FACILITIES.

The first postoffice was in a small log building which stood opposite the Episcopal Church, and was kept by Merrill E. Rattan. Mails arrived and departed only once a week, by horseback; and although communication with the outside world was limited, it was ample enough to meet the wants of the people. About 1845 a tri-weekly stage was run to Jacksonville by Hill & Watson, carrying the mails, and later, tri-weekly mails were extended to Winchester, Beardstown and Quincy, J. Shastid and Jesse French being the contractors. They were afterward bought out by Thomas Burt, who continued the lines for some time. In July, 1853, the first daily mail was established between Naples and Hannibal, via Pittsfield, Uncle Davie Stanton and S. P. Duffield being the contractors. Subsequently connection was made with the young and growing towns throughout the county, until now Pittsfield is in direct communication by mail and telegraph with all the outside world.

SHIPPING.

When the old Jacksonville & Naples Railroad was extended to Hannibal, and as the new line was located some six miles north of Pittsfield, it was feared it would retard the growth of the town. To prevent this possible result, in 1870 a branch line was built from Pittsfield to Maysville, connecting with the Hannibal & Naples line, and is now familiarly called the "Bob-Tail." The road is operated by the Wabash Railroad Company, and it is an evidence of the prosperous trade and importance of Pittsfield, that the Company's returns show the "Bob-Tail" to be one of the best paying sections operated by that important corporation.

For years after the settlement of the town, Florence, on the Illinois river, some twelve miles east, was the regular shipping point for Pittsfield, nearly all the goods being received and shipped by wagon to the steamboat's landing at that town. In 1851 a private corporation constructed a plank road, connecting Pittsfield and

Florence. It was kept in good repair for some years, and proved a great convenience, but the extension of lines in other directions diverted a portion of the traffic, and it was afterward thrown open to the public. In the early days, the settlers had not learned the economy of a division of business, or lacked the means and facilities. Then nearly every man who raised stock did his own slaughtering, the product being sold to storekeepers, who shipped it to St. Louis. Large quantities of grain and live stock were also shipped in the same way, and in a few years this trade became so important that a large amount of capital was invested in the business, and the warehouses of Pittsfield and Florence were filled with the products of the surrounding country. Now the facilities of transportation by rail and river have given a different feature to the trade. Much of the wheat finds its way to the far Eastern markets in the form of flour, while the shipment of grain, live stock and provisions is managed as separate lines of business.

PROTECTION AGAINST FIRES.

Although the town has never had a regularly organized fire company, an engine or apparatus, it has been remarkably exempt from destructive fires. But few buildings have been destroyed by fire, and in each instance the citizens turned out and worked with such determination that the fire was subdued before extending beyond the building where it originated. Although the town has been so fortunate heretofore, the danger of fires is a subject of solicitude among thoughtful citizens, and it is probable that a company will be organized and properly equipped, in anticipation of future contingencies.

TEMPERANCE.

For years there has been a strong temperance sentiment in this community, and the friends of the cause have repeatedly succeeded in electing an anti-license Board of Town Trustees. At the last two elections, however, they were defeated by a small majority, and four saloons have been licensed at a tax of $1,500 each per annum. During the temperance crusade some years ago, the ladies succeeded in arousing public sentiment, and license was abolished. Later, when the Murphy revival was inaugurated, it met with remarkable success here, several hundred persons having enrolled themselves in the blue ribbon organization. Within the past few months the temperance people have organized a new society, and already accomplished much good. The present movement is more quiet in its character than the crusade or Murphy revival, but it gives promise of accomplishing the end aimed at,—suppression of legalized traffic in liquors within the town.

MILITARY.

After the passage of the militia law by the State Legislature three years ago, two militia companies were organized in Pittsfield, one, the Pittsfield Guards, and the other, the Pike County Guards. After a few months the Adjutant General ordered the consolidation of the two companies, which was done, the organization taking the name of the Pittsfield Guards. The officers are J. W. Johnson, Captain; W. Steinhauer, 1st Lieut.; and Geo. Barber, 2d Lieut. The company is uniformed and well armed, having a well appointed armory in Dickson's Hall.

A notable day in the military annals of the town, and one long to be remembered, was the Annual Reunion of Army Veterans held here in August, 1878. Preparations for the event had been in progress for many days, all classes of citizens vieing with each other in efforts to make the celebration worthy of the occasion and of the town, and the result more than realized their highest expectations.

Daybreak of the eventful day was ushered in with a grand salute, and at an early hour the streets were thronged with an eager multitude, gathered from all the surrounding country. The buildings around the Public Square and on the principal streets were decorated with flags and patriotic emblems, while the Square itself presented a novel and most attractive appearance. On either corner decorated platforms were erected, on which were living groups of young girls and boys representing Liberty, the Army, the Navy, Justice, Industry, Commerce, Agriculture, etc., each figure in appropriate costume, and surrounded by implements and emblems illustrating the tableaux. Near the southwest corner of the Square a large platform was also erected for speakers and distinguished guests, and literally covered with flags, evergreens, wreaths, flowers, pictures and statuary. But the most attractive quarter was the north and east sides of the Square, where were spread long lines of tables loaded with all the substantials and luxuries a bountiful land afforded, while snowy covers, and glittering silver, china and glass, and a profusion of bouquets, festoons of flowers, etc., beautified the scene. These tables were in charge of the ladies, and as each tried to excel her neighbor in the luxury and elegance of her table, the result was such a banquet as was probably never before spread on a similar occasion.

The Pittsfield Guards and the Pike County Guards, the two local companies, were under arms at an early hour, and acted as escort to the veterans and their families arriving from abroad. At 10 o'clock the train from Springfield arrived, bringing Governor Cullom, Gen. Reese, ex-Governor Palmer and other distinguished visitors, with the Governor's Guard of Springfield as honorary escort, the Winchester Guards, and a long line of veterans in detached squads from Griggsville, Barry and other points. A procession was then formed, and after parading through the principal streets, mustered in the Square in front of the grand stand, where they were welcomed in an eloquent address by Rev. H. D. Clark, Pastor of the Christian Church, and himself a gallant soldier. Governor Cullom responded in an appropriate speech, paying a fitting

. tribute to the patriotism and gallantry of the citizen soldiery.   On
the platform were a number of distinguished veterans of the Rebellion and the Mexican war, and a small group of honored heroes
of the war of 1812.   After appropriate music by the glee clubs and
the bands, an adjournment was had for dinner.   The immense
crowd were billeted at the several tables, and were entertained with
profusion, all being satisfied,—men, women and children,—and
enough left over to feed a brigade.   After dinner there was a general interchange of greetings among old army comrades, and many
an experience of the march, the battle-field and the bivouac renewed and recounted.   Speaking was then resumed, when Col. A.
C. Matthews introduced Gen. Palmer in a neat address.   The latter was greeted with cheers and spoke for over an hour, giving
many amusing anecdotes of army life, all of which were thoroughly
enjoyed by the "boys."   Short addresses were made by other
speakers, followed by a parade and drill by the Governor's Guard,
under command of Maj. E. S. Johnson.   The remainder of the day
was taken up in a general jollification, in imitation of camp life,
and other amusements.   As the evening shadows fell, the strangers
from abroad departed amid the cheers of the people; the citizens
returned to their homes, and so ended one of the most memorable
days in the history of Pittsfield.

PUBLIC HALLS AND SOCIAL MATTERS.

The first public hall was in the Mansion House block.   Before
its erection the fun-loving folk held their dances and social gatherings in the Court-House, and the halls supposed to be sacred to
the disciples of Blackstone echoed to the sounds of merry-making,
while an occasional Church fair threw the mantle of charity over
all.   The whole community was noted for its sociability, and
pleasant gatherings were of frequent occurrence.   The young men
were also famous for their skill in athletic sports, foot-racing especially being very popular, and many a youth who has since
grown old and staid, has competed in contests of speed, on the
"track," along the south side of the Square.   The prizes usually
awarded would not be sanctioned by the friends of temperance.
Horse-racing also was very popular, and is still a favorite pastime
with many.

In 1845 a number of the young men organized a full brass band,
and thereafter furnished the music on the Fourth-of-July and other
public occasions.   Debating and literary clubs were also formed,
and a taste for literature of a high order was developed and fostered.

In the summer of 1846 an event occurred which marked a new
epoch in the annals of the young town.   This was the arrival of
Van Amburgh's circus and menagerie.   It was the first regular
"show" that had penetrated so far among the outlying settlements,
and its advent was hailed with wonder and delight by young and
old, the people flocking in from all the surrounding country to see
it.   Many a veteran who has lived to see scores of such exhibitions

still remembers with pleasure that first introduction to the delights and glories of the saw-dust ring. This was soon followed by others, and shortly afterward regular dramatic companies visited the town, and were well received. Now there is no dearth of public entertainments, a good company rarely failing to draw well.

THE MEXICAN WAR.

From the close of the Indian troubles until the declaration of war with Mexico, the people of Pittsfield had no military experiences, but the promptness with which troops were raised on the latter occasion shows their military and patriotic ardor. Special messengers who had been sent to Springfield hastened back with the news that volunteers were called for. A full company was organized in a few hours, most of the members being from Pittsfield and the immediate vicinity. They started at once for Springfield, arrived there the same night, and, reporting at headquarters, were mustered in as company K of the 5th Regiment, Illinois Volunteer Infantry. Nor had they any time to spare. Next day, Springfield was thronged with volunteers from the surrounding counties, who had to be rejected. Company K had completed the quota. When organized the officers of the company were : I. B. Donaldson, Captain; — Bostwick, 1st Lieut.; Emmet Hicks, 2d Lieut.; and Wm. Kinman, 3d Lieut. On the organization of the Regiment, Capt. Donaldson was promoted a field officer, and Lieut. Kinman was made Captain. The achievements of the gallant 5th are a part of the history of the nation, and company K won its full share of the laurels. All the old officers have answered the final muster save only Lieut. Hicks, who is still living in Pittsfield hale and hearty, and who with some of his old comrades in arms, fights over his old battles, and

> " Shoulders his cane,
> And shows how fields were won."

The same military and patriotic spirit was manifested by the people in the breaking out of the Rebellion.. Pittsfield promptly sent a large number of volunteers, who were on almost every battle-field of the South. No soldiers ever acquitted themselves more nobly than those who went from Pittsfield.

COURT-HOUSE.

Immediately after the town was laid out the first Court-House was erected, the order therefor being issued by the County Commissioners in June, 1833. It was a frame building, located on the north side of the Square, and was not remarkable for size or style. It is still standing, and is now occupied by Joseph Heck as a store. The coming season a new brick building is to take its place, and the old landmark will be removed. The present Court-House was erected in 1838-9, and was in that early day considered a spacious and commodious building. The offices of the Circuit and County Clerks are in a fire-proof building west of the Court-House. The handsome grounds which now surround it were then an uninclosed plat covered with hazel-brush. The stately trees that now adorn the grounds were planted by some of the young men of the town, the young members of the Bar being prominent in the good work. Their tall stems and wide-spreading branches stand as monuments of their enterprise and public spirit, and those who now enjoy the grateful shade should remember with gratitude the thoughtful planters.

PROMINENT MEMBERS OF THE BAR.

From the first organization of the county Courts the Bar has been noted for the distinguished men who have ornamented it. Within its walls some who have won national fame earned their earlier forensic laurels. Among its graduates were Col. E. D. Baker, the brilliant orator, the cultivated gentleman, the statesman and the hero, whose brilliant life was untimely ended at the fatal battle of Ball's Bluff; and Col. Daniel H. Gilmer, the genial friend and able lawyer, who fell a sacrifice to his patriotism at Stone River; and Col. Jackson Grimshaw, a keen and able lawyer, irresistible in debate, now gone to his rest; and Maj. Sam Hayes, an able lawyer, a free-hearted and jovial companion; and Archie Williams, and Dick Richardson, and Isaac N. Morris, and James Ward, and J. W. Whitney, are among the members of the Bar who have passed away.

Here in the early day such lawyers as Lincoln, and Douglas, and Browning came to plead. Of the living representatives who have won distinction may be mentioned Hon. Milton Hay, now of Springfield; C. L. Higbee, Judge of the Appellate Court; Wm. A. Grimshaw, member of the State Board of Charities, and who has filled many positions of honor in the State; Wm. R. Archer, State Senator for many years; Col. A. C. Matthews, Member of the Legislature; Scott Wike, late Member of Congress; Jas. S. Irwin, one of the ablest lawyers in the State; Richard B. Atkinson, ex-County Judge, and the veteran D. B. Bush. There are younger members of the Bar who bid fair to emulate the example of their seniors. Jefferson Orr, the District Attorney, is now filling his second term, and has proved an efficient and industrious officer. Hon. Strother Grigsby, the County Judge, has long been identified with the Bar. In his present position he has accomplished good work, and is the friendly adviser of all who appear in his Court.

JAIL.

The first jail was built near the site of the present town cala boose. It was not a pretentious building, but was sufficient for the wants of the county for many years. It was afterward sold, and was occupied as a tobacco factory, when it was destroyed by fire. The

James G. Willsey

PITTSFIELD T.P.

present handsome jail, on the northeast corner of the Public Square, was erected in 1861. It is a substantial brick building with a double tier of cells, necessary offices, and residence for the Sheriff.

But one execution has taken place in the Pittsfield jail, Bart. Barnes having been hanged December 29, 1871, for the murder of Mr. Gresham near Pleasant Hill. The execution was private, within the walls of the prison, but so great was the public curiosity over the event that hundreds of persons from the surrounding country crowded the streets around the jail.

In 1878 an attack upon the jail was threatened, and at one time it appeared as if it would result in serious loss of life. A Dr. Brown, of Milton, was found dead in his door-yard, with a gunshot wound in his head; and it was supposed he had been murdered. Some days before that he had been reported drugged and robbed, and a man named McDonald, a supposed tramp, had been arrested and lodged in jail, being suspected as one of the robbers. His trial was to come off in a few days, and just before that event Dr. Brown was found dead, as stated, and it was thought that some friend or chum of McDonald had murdered him to prevent his appearing against the latter. The friends and neighbors were intensely excited over the occurrence, and as the public had naturally become alarmed over the reiterated reports of outrages committed by tramps in other parts of the country, the excitement spread rapidly. A rigid search was instituted for the supposed murderer and kept up for days, but no one being discovered, the friends determined to wreak summary vengeance upon the prisoner, McDonald. A number of them mustered a short distance from town, with the avowed determination to march in after nightfall, break open the jail, and seize and lynch the prisoner. It was impossible for the sheriff to remove him to another place of confinement, as the roads were watched; whereupon the authorities communicated with Governor Cullom, and by his authority the militia companies were called out, and a strong force placed to protect the jail. For the first few nights the alarm was kept up, but fortunately the prompt action of the authorities had the desired effect. No attack was made, and the excitement quieted down. The result of the trial, which took place a short time afterward, proved the man McDonald entirely innocent of the charge of robbing, and consequently he had no motive for the killing of Dr. Brown, and he was discharged. This was the first serious attempt of the people to take the law into their own hands, and the result of the trial will go far toward preventing a similar occurrence in the future. Had the attempt proved successful it is certain that an innocent man would have been sacrificed. The citizens are proverbially law-abiding, and the McDonald emeute was as unexpected as it was unusual. The conduct of the militia during the trying occasion elicited the praise of the community.

Several attempts have been made by prisoners to escape, at different times, and although some of them have succeeded in cutting their way out, they have been recaptured after a short pursuit.

CHURCHES.

The history of the *Congregational Church* is intimately associ-.ated with that of the early days of the town. It was organized with a membership of twelve, and first worshiped in the Court-House. Rev. William Carter was the first minister in charge, and devoted long years of faithful and earnest work. The first church building was erected in 1838, but in a few years it proved too small for the congregation. The Pastor, aided by Col. Ross and other members, decided to erect a larger edifice, and the present structure was built and dedicated in 1846. They were assisted in the good work by Eastern friends. A project is now on foot for the erection of a large new building, and it is probable that the work will be accomplished at an early day. Rev. W. W. Rose is the present Pastor, and is an earnest worker.

The *Christian Church*, now one of the largest and most prosperous in the city, was organized in 1839 with twelve members, the first Pastor being Elder W. H. Strong. At first they worshiped in a small frame building which was afterward used as a school-house, and long occupied the lot in the rear of Judge Higbee's residence. It was afterward removed to the lot opposite Wm. Henry Harder's, and having been refitted nicely, it is now occupied by the German Lutheran congregation. The present Christian church was built in 1856, and has one of the largest audience rooms in the city, with Sunday-school rooms, etc., in the lower story. The Church has no Pastor, Rev. H. D. Clark, the late Pastor, having accepted a call to a Church in Baltimore, Md.

The *Methodist Episcopal Church* was organized at about the same date as the above Church. The first building was of brick, small and unpretending, and occupied the site of the present handsome edifice. The progress of the Church was slow, but a few faithful ones worked on hopefully. The present building was erected in 1876, at a cost of about $12,000, Miss Lucy Williams and Mrs. William Wills, two earnest Christian women, contributing most of that sum. The success of the undertaking, however, was largely due to the energy and perseverance of the Pastor, Rev. W. F. Gillmore, who commenced the work with small beginnings, but remained to see it completed and dedicated. The Church now has a large membership, is in a prosperous condition, and is, blessed with an efficient minister, Rev. M. Auer.

The *Baptist Church* was organized in 1839, and the house of worship was built of brick, and still stands upon its original site. For many years it was among the leading Church organizations in the town, but of late years it has not been so prosperous. It is now without a regular Pastor, but meetings are regularly held, and a call has been extended to a new minister.

St. Stephen's Episcopal Church was built in 1852, Hon. Wm. A. Grimshaw being the principal patron. Rev. Mr. Little is the Rector of the Parish, and is a cultivated gentleman and minister.

The first *Roman Catholic* Church was built in 1850, Rev. Mr. Dempsey being the first Priest in charge. It was a wooden building, which was subsequently removed to make room for the new church, and is now on a lot on the opposite side of the street, and used as J. H. Wheeling's auction room. The present brick building was erected in 1869, and was remodeled during the past year, and the steeple erected. The Church being the only one of that faith in the county, has a large membership, and is well attended. The present Pastor is Rev. Father Hoven, a man of ability and energy. It is probable the church building will be enlarged at an early day, to accommodate the growing congregation.

The *Presbyterian Church*, which had been closed for some years, was recently re-opened, with Rev. J. P. Dawson as Pastor. The congregation still worships in the building first erected, and now gives promise of new life and usefulness.

The *German Methodist Church* was not organized until 1869, when the society was drawn together, and the present brick structure erected. It is now in a very prosperous condition, being out of debt and with a united membership. Rev. M. Thalenhorst is the Pastor, who is proving a very acceptable minister.

A Church of *Latter-Day Saints* was organized in 1862 by Elder Lytle. Meetings have since been held at the houses of the members, but now the society is erecting a church building which will be completed and dedicated early in the spring.

The *Hebrews* number several families, but as yet have no regular place of worship. On the 11th of May, 1879, they organized a Sabbath-school, of which Mr. Albert Fishell is Superintendent, and L. D. Hirsheimer, Secretary. There are some 13 children on the rolls, and meetings are held in a room in the Odd Fellows building.

SECRET SOCIETIES.

In 1848 Pittsfield Lodge, No. 56, A. F. & A. M., was organized, the first Master being Michael J. Noyes, for many years a prominent and respected citizen. Union Chapter No. 10, R. A. M., was organized in 1859. Ascalon Commandery K. T. was organized in 1876, F. M. Casal, E. C. The Masonic bodies are in a very prosperous condition, the Lodge and Chapter owning a fine hall, and the Commandery another adjoining. The officers of the Lodge now are W. B. Grimes, W. M.; Thos. Worthington, jr., S. W.; G. W. Shaw, J. W.; C. R. Lame, Sec.; of the Chapter, W. B. Grimes is H. P.; Wm. Steers, E. K.; J. A. Rider, E. S. Secretary; of the Commandery, F. M. Casal is E. C. and V. A. Grimes, Rec.

The Odd Fellows have always been a popular order in this city. Pittsfield Lodge, No. 95, was organized in 1851 with a small membership. The first officers were Samuel Smith, N. G.; R. L. Howard, V. G.; John Hawkins, Sec. and N. Kelley, Treasurer. It has since grown steadily, and now has a large number of members. Some years ago a German Lodge was consolidated with the present body. The officers are J. L. Dobbin, N. G.; J. H. McClintock, V. G.; B. F. Fisk, Sec., and F. L. Shriver, Treas. The Encampment, which was organized Oct., 1865, is also in a good condition, but the increase in membership has been slow. The Odd Fellows own their hall, which is the handsomest in the town, being beautifully decorated and furnished.

The A. O. U. W. also have a very flourishing Lodge. It was organized in April, 1878, with a membership of twenty-five. Dr. C. H. Doss, M. W. It has grown steadily since then, the endowment feature proving a very popular one. The present officers are B. Hirsheimer, M. W.; C. W. Rayburn, Rec.

The I. O. M. A., a beneficial society also, was chartered about a year and a half ago. Its progress has been slow but steady, and it has good material among its membership.

The Knights of Honor organized a Lodge in 1879, and have a good membership, mostly young men. These three last named societies meet in Odd Fellows Hall.

BIOGRAPHICAL DEPARTMENT.

As a part of the history of the town and township, we give personal sketches of the old settlers and leading citizens.

Isaiah Adams, farmer, sec. 26; owns 80 acres of land, worth $75 per acre; is a native of New York and was born Jan. 5, 1806; came to this State in 1842, and settled where he now resides. Feb. 14, 1833, he married Anna Lester, who was born in 1809, in Connecticut; they are the parents of 7 children, 5 living, namely, Anna A., John P., Martha L., Buell R. and Orilla S.; Nancy and Isaiah, dec. Mr. A. has been Road Commissioner. Is a member of the Congregational Church, and a Republican.

Christopher Appleton, farmer and stock-dealer, sec. 11; P. O., Pittsfield; is the owner of 175 acres of fine land, worth $75 per acre. Mr. A. is the son of Christopher and Elizabeth Appleton, natives of England, and was born Dec. 12, 1818; came with his parents to America in 1819 and settled in Pennsylvania, remaining 17 years. They then moved to Missouri, and in 1872 to this county. Mr. Appleton handles about 100 head of cattle per year, and raises hogs and other stock. He was married in Missouri in 1845 to Charlotta Stennett, born in Virginia in 1827, and they have had 2 children, only 1 living,—Anna E., now wife of J. S. Sellsbery. Mr. A. is a Baptist, and an Odd Fellow.

Hon. William R. Archer, Attorney at Law and State Senator, was born in New York city April 13, 1817; his parents were Richard P., a merchant, and Jane (Alcock) Archer, a native of Ireland. His preliminary education was obtained at Flushing, L. I., whence he removed to New York city, where he studied law under John

L. Lawrence, and was admitted to the New York Bar Feb. 23, 1838. May 10 of the same year he settled in Pittsfield, where in August following he was admitted to the Illinois Bar and soon had an extensive practice; in 1847 he was a member of the State Constitutional Convention from Pike county, in which capacity he evinced sterling qualities; that was a trying time, as the question of township organization was then beginning to agitate the people. Mr. Archer was Circuit Clerk and Recorder from 1856 to 1860. He was then elected Representative in the State Legislature on the Democratic ticket with Benj. F. DeWitt, and represented the counties of Pike and Brown; in 1869 he was again elected to the State Constitutional Convention, which met the following year, and in 1872 was elected to the State Senate from the 38th District, comprising the counties of Pike, Scott and Calhoun; in 1876 he was re-elected to the same position, his present term expiring next November. He was a member of the Joint Commission appointed by the Legislature of 1877 to ascertain the damages arising to private property in lands by the construction of dams on the Wabash and Illinois rivers; this Commission consisted of 2 Senators and 3 Representatives, and they held sessions from July 9, 1877, to December 10 of the same year, at Springfield. Out of $185,000 damages claimed, the Commission awarded about $30,000, to pay which an appropriation was made by the last session of the Legislature. Subsequently Mr. Archer discovered a law passed in 1847, affecting claims entirely disconnected with the work of this Commission, which law had been obsolete for 10 years, and not brought forward in the revisions. It was a statute of limitations which had the effect to bar over $2,000,000 of claims presented to the Court of Claims. (This court consists of the Chief Justice of the Supreme Court and two Circuit Judges.) This statute, with a written argument in brief, Mr. A. presented to the Attorney General, and at his request he argued the case before the Court, which sustained the statute, and thus barred over $2,000,000 of the claims. For all this service Mr. A. did not receive a single dollar. Mr. Archer has recently been nominated for Governor of the State by several influential newspapers, and the *Old Flag*, an opposition paper in politics, says that Mr. A. is too good a man to be set up by a minority party, simply to be knocked over.

Feb. 1, 1838, Mr. Archer married Miss Anna Maria Smith, daughter of Jonas Smith, a former resident of Long Island, N.Y.; she died Sept. 26, 1859, leaving 7 children, 5 of whom are living; he was again married Dec. 15, 1860, to Henrietta E. Sergeant, daughter of Col. Aaron Sergeant, of New York city, and they have had one child.

Samuel Atwood, farmer, sec. 25, owns 240 acres of land worth $60 per acre; was born in Virginia in 1821; came to Pike county 1854, and settled near where he now resides. In 1851 he was married to Eliza J. Chaffy, who was born in Ohio in 1831; they are the parents of 10 children, of whom 6 are living,—William T., James

A., Charles E., Alla A., Nannie M. and Samuel F.   Mr. A. is a Democrat; his father was in the war of 1812.

Austin Barber, retired farmer, residence, Pittsfield; was born in Ohio in Oct., 1809; his first occupation was that of clerk in a dry-goods store; came to Illinois in 1833 and settled in Pittsfield; he established one of the first dry-goods houses here, which business he continued until 1841, then went to Florence for 5 years, then returned to Pittsfield again and purchased a farm, comprising 150 acres of fine farm land one mile from Pittsfield; he carried on farming until 1870.   In 1838 he married Caroline Johnson, who was born in Missouri in 1819; they are the parents of 6 children, 3 boys and 3 girls; the 3 girls are deceased.   The sons all served in the late war.   Mr. A. is a member of the Christian Church, and a Republican.

Edward F. Binns, County Clerk, is a son of Randolph and Elizabeth (McGlosson) Binns, both natives of Virginia.   They were among the pioneers of this county, having emigrated here as early as 1835.   Edward F. was born in this county, Jan. 23, 1841; he passed his boyhood days upon the farm and attended the common schools; at the age of 23 he embarked in business for himself, beginning at that time to buy and ship stock, cattle, hogs, sheep and horses.   These he shipped mostly to the Chicago market.   He then engaged in the mercantile business for a period of a year and a half.   He has held the offices of township Collector and Assessor, and in 1877 was elected to the responsible position which he now holds.   In 1868 he was united in marriage with Orpha Norton, who was born in Indiana in April, 1840.   To them were born 3 children,—Louisa, William S. and Bertha.   Mr. B. is a member of the Masonic fraternity, and an active and prominent member of the Christian Church.

E. W. Blades, of the firm of Dober & Blades, grocers, established by E. W. Blades ; the co-partnership was formed in 1879 and is one of the most reliable and successful firms in Pittsfield.   Mr. B. is a native of Delaware and was born in 1834.   He came to this county in 1856 and located at Barry, where he remained until 1876, during which time he was engaged in the dry-goods business.   His present location is on the north side of the Public Square, Pittsfield.   He was elected Sheriff in 1876 and served with credit until Mr. Kellogg, the present Sheriff, was chosen.   He was married July 24, 1856, to Phœbe A. Hammond.

James P. Blake, farmer, sec. 14; P. O., Pittsfield; was born in this county in 1844; was married in 1865 to Miss Melinda Richards, a native of this county, who died in 1876, leaving one child, Elnore. His present wife, Caroline Rookerd, is also a native of this county and was born in 1854; they have one child, Edward; they are members of the Christian Church, and Mr. Blake is well known throughout the county as one of Pike's enterprising farmers.

Henry Blei, farmer, sec. 25; is a native of Ireland, born in 1826; came to America in 1845 and settled in Calhoun county, Ill., the same year, and remained 16 years; came to this county in 1864; owns 140 acres of land worth $50 per acre. In 1852 he married in Calhoun county; his wife died in July, 1877, leaving a family of 8 children, of whom 6 are living. Their names are, Fred, Henry J., Katie E., Emma J., Frank L. and Charles E. Mr. B. is a Democrat. P. O., Pittsfield.

Rev. Wm. Carter, for many years Pastor of the Congregational Church of Pittsfield, was an eminent man. He was born at New Canaan, Conn., Dec. 31, 1803. His parents were Ebenezer and Rhoda (Weed) Carter. He graduated at Yale College in 1828 and subsequently at the theological school of the same institution. He and several fellow students soon became the founders of the Illinois College at Jacksonville, Ill., and Mr. Carter himself took charge of the Congregational Church at Jacksonville, the first church of this denomination west of Ohio (1833). This church prospered greatly under his pastoral care, but in 1838 he resigned the charge and soon afterward became pastor of the Congregational Church of Pittsfield, Ill., where he continued until 1868, laboring acceptably, not only at this place but also at Summer Hill and Rockport. He died Feb. 2, 1871, at Pittsfield, and his death was mourned by the whole community. During his life he was also a member of the Board of Directors of the Chicago Theological Seminary, was one of the organizers of the General Association of Illinois, and held many other responsible positions. He is regarded as the father of the Congregational Church at Pittsfield. His widow is still living in Pittsfield.

Dr. F. M. Casal, physician and surgeon, was born in Baltimore, Md., Sept. 20, 1842; emigrated in 1848 to Palmyra, Mo.; educated in the public high school in St. Louis, Mo., and Washington University; graduated at Rush Medical College, Chicago, in 1864; also attended Bellevue Hospital Medical College, and the College of Physicians and Surgeons of New York city; and, after spending three and a half years on the Pacific ocean, he located in Pittsfield in the summer of 1868, where he has since remained in medical practice. He is a member of the Adams County Medical Society, and of the Illinois State Medical Society. The Doctor has also been a member of the Town Board for three years, and President of the Board two years. In the Masonic order, he is Past Master of the Lodge of Pittsfield, No. 56, High Priest of Union Chapter No. 10, R. A. M., and Eminent Commander of Ascalon Commandery, K. T. Aug. 9, 1870, Dr. Casal married Amelia, daughter of B. H. Atkinson, of Pittsfield, and his children are: Mary, born Nov. 28, 1871; Annie, Jan. 27, 1874; and Isabel, August 24, 1877.

Isaac A. Clare, County Surveyor, son of Moses F. and Mary (Brown) Clare, natives of Kentucky, was born in this county Sept. 5, 1835. At the age of 16 he devoted his time and attention to civil engineering, for which profession he had received a thorough education. In 1875 he was elected County Surveyor of Pike county, and subsequently re-elected, and holds the position at the present time. He was married in this county in 1870, to Rebecca Welch, a native of Waterdale county, Ala., who was born in 1847. They have had a family of three children, two of whom are living. Their names are Moses N. and Alma. Allen is deceased. Mr. C. is a member of the Masonic and Odd Fellows fraternities, a Universalist in religion, and politically a Democrat.

Moses F. Clare, blacksmith, Pittsfield, is a native of Kentucky, where he was born Oct. 28, 1811; came to this county and settled at Atlas as early as 1832, where he remained until 1835, when he moved to Pittsfield, being one of the first settlers here. He attended the first sale of town lots, May 1, 1833. He learned the blacksmith's trade in St. Louis. In June, 1833, in this county, he was united in marriage with Maria Brown, a native of Kentucky. They are the parents of 4 children, 2 living,—Isaac A. and Moses H. Those deceased were Francis O. and Henry T. Mr. C. is a member of the Masonic order, and Mr. and Mrs. C. are members of the M. E. Church.

Thomas Clarkson, farmer and stock-raiser, sec. 29, owning 180 acres of land, was born in England May 28, 1820; raised on a farm; married in England in 1844, to Fanny Rodgers, born in England in 1818; they are the parents of 4 children. Mr. Clarkson came to the United States in 1851, settling in this county ; P. O., Pittsfield. Mr. C. is a Republican.

O. G. Cline is a farmer by occupation, though at present he is Superintendent of the County Poor, this being the second term he he has held the office. He owns 100 acres of land in Martinsburg tp., sec. 3, valued at $40 per acre. He was born in Scott county, Ill., March 26, 1843; married in Pike county in 1849, Lucretia Melton, who was born in Virginia. They have 4 children—Leon Lester, Glenn M., Alverdia and Fred K. P. O., Pittsfield.

Howard Cohenour, farmer, sec. 1; P. O., Pittsfield; was born in 1851, in this county, and is a son of Jacob and Jane Cohenour, natives of Pennsylvania, who emigrated to Pike county in 1836, where they remained until their death. April 2, 1872, Mr. C. married Mary A. Cop, who was born in Iowa Dec. 29, 1852. They are the parents of 4 children, viz.: Jacob, Gertrude E., William and Ira S. His grandfather on his father's side, was in the war of 1812. Mr. C. belongs to the M. E. Church, and is a Democrat.

Albert Coley, blacksmith, is a native of Kentucky, born in 1829, and is a son of Wm. B. and Elizabeth (McClane) Coley, the former a native of Virginia, and the latter of Kentucky. He came to this county in 1853, first settling in Atlas tp., and in 1867 moved to Wisconsin, where he remained 4 years, then came back to Pittsfield, where he has since resided. He learned his trade at the age of 27 years, which he has always followed. In 1857 he married Mary A. Sanders, a native of New York, born in 1832, and they have had 6 children; 2 are living, Minnie J. and Charles A. The names of the deceased are Lucy, Ella, George and Abigail.

W. R. Wills

PITTSFIELD TP.

Mr. C.'s father was in the war of 1812, for which he received a pension through life. Mr. C. owns 3 lots in Pittsfield, one with shop, and 2 with dwelling houses.

James Cosgrove, farmer, sec. 4; P. O., Pittsfield; was born in Ireland in 1812, and came to America in 1849, settling in Hartford, Conn., until 1865, when he moved to Pennsylvania, where he followed teaming. Two years afterward he settled in this county, and followed farming 3 years. By frugality and energy he was enabled to purchase his present farm in this tp., where he has since made his home. In 1836 he married Miss Margaret McDermott, a native of Ireland, and they have 7 children,—Ellen, Joseph, Christopher, Dora, James, Bridget and Thomas. Mr. C. is a member of the Catholic Church, and a staunch Democrat.

James Coulter, farmer, sec. 19; was born in Ireland March 6, 1829, brought by his parents to the United States in 1831, and at the age of 21 he came to this county. Aug. 5, 1859, he married Mary Jane White. His father, John Coulter, resides on the farm now owned and occupied by his son James. Mr. C. owns 101 acres of land, worth $50 per acre. He has been School Director for 9 years, and is a successful farmer; is a Democrat. P. O., Pittsfield.

William Coulter, farmer, sec. 19; was born in Tuscarawas county, O., and came to Pike county, Ill., in the spring of 1853. Jan. 9, 1868, he married Miss Lydia Hoskin, and they have 6 children, namely: Laura, Anna, Eliza, Minnie M., Letitia and Charles Sherman. Mr. C. owns 160 acres of land worth $50 per acre. Mr. C. takes great pride in raising good stock; also raises considerable wheat and corn, which he disposes of at home market. In politics he is a Democrat. P. O., Pittsfield.

A. G. Crawford, attorney, is the second son of J. G. Crawford, who settled in this county in 1830, where the subject of this sketch was born in 1854. He was educated in the Blackburn University at Carlinville, and began the study of law in the office of the State's Attorney at Pittsfield. In 1875 he entered the law school at Chicago, at which institution he was graduated the following year. In 1876 he married Mary E., daughter of Dr. W. C. Doan, who died in Oct., 1877. Mr. C. is yet young in years, and in the practice of his profession, but his native ability and energy will insure him success.

Elder W. H. Crow, County Superintendent of Schools, was born March 12, 1848, in Wheeling, W. Va., son of Charles and Margaret (Hughes) Crow, the former a native of Pennsylvania and the latter of Virginia, who settled in Wheeling in 1845, but emigrated to Huron county, Ohio, when the subject of this sketch was very young; in 1857 they removed to Clark county, Mo., and in 1859 to Macon county, Ill. Mr. Crow's mother died two years ago, and his father resides in Sullivan, Ill. At the age of 17 W. H. left the parental domicile to take care of himself, and graduated in 1872 at Eureka College, Woodford Co., Ill., and was ordained a minister of the

39

Gospel in the Christian Church, shortly after which he became Pastor of the Christian Church at Barry, this county. He commenced preaching, however, in Macon county, in 1866. Since 1878 Mr. Crow is by election, County Superintendent of Schools. In 1869 Mr. C. married Miss N. Clark, a native of Illinois. Residence, Pittsfield.

John Curless, sr., farmer, sec. 9; P. O., Pittsfield; is a native of Ohio, and was born in 1825; came to this State in 1851; was married in Ohio in 1845, to Elizabeth Girton, who was born in Ohio in 1828. They have 7 children, viz.: George, Timothy, Sarah A., John, Stephen, Thomas and Jesse. Mr. C. is a Methodist, and a Democrat. His parents were natives of New Jersey.

John Curless, jr., farmer, owning 3 acres of land with a nice dwelling; he is a son of Abiah and Anna (Hill) Curless. He is a native of Ohio, and was born in 1854; came to this State in 1860; was married in 1878 to Emily F. Dell, a native of this State, born in 1860; they have one child, Ina Pearl, born Oct., 1879. Mr. C. is a Republican.

Osborn Davis, farmer, sec. 12; P. O., Pittsfield; owns 160 acres of land, worth $35 per acre; was born in Pennsylvania in 1821; came to Illinois in 1845, located the same year in Pittsfield, where he has since resided; was married in this county about the year 1847, to Susan Troutlett, who was born in Ohio in 1825. She is deceased. He was married a second time, namely, to Miss Louisa Troutlett, also a native of Ohio. They have 10 children, only 4 of whom are living.

Thomas Dickson & Son, dealers in dry-goods and clothing; the senior member of this firm came to this county in 1837, and for 14 years worked at the tailor's trade. In 1850 he visited the Rocky Mountains; after returning, he clerked for Ross & Gay, and Watson & Abbott. Subsequently he formed a partnership with W. Abbott. Three years afterward Watson retired, and Gay was admitted to the firm. In 1860 the firm dissolved, and he opened his present place. His son was a participant in the late war, and was admitted as partner in business with his father in 1872. Mr. D. is a native of Scotland, where he was born in 1815, and is the oldest living merchant in Pittsfield.

Thomas Dilworth, farmer, sec. 32; P. O., Pittsfield; owns an interest in 160 acres of land, worth $60 per acre; his brother George, and sister Faith, are equal partners in this property. They are all unmarried, and live on the place together. They have raised a girl named Mary E. Carroll; they emigrated to this county with their mother in 1850, where they have since resided. All are Democrats.

J. L. Dobbin, attorney at law, office over Harder's drug store, west side of the Square. Will practice in any of the courts of the Eleventh Judicial Circuit, and attend properly to all legal business entrusted to his care.

C. H. Doss, physician, was born in Franklin, Simpson Co., Ky., Feb. 19, 1834, and began the study of medicine with his father, a resident physician at Hopkinsville, Ky. Two years afterward he came to Illinois, and completed his studies in the office of Dr. A. Bowman, at Carrollton, Ill. He first began practice at Fayetteville, Greene Co., Ill., where he was successfully engaged for 5½ years, when he moved to Manchester, Scott Co., and followed his profession until he came to this county in 1876, where he has since made his home. In September, 1856, he married Margaret A. Thrasher, a native of Griggsville, and they have 9 children, the eldest a graduate of Bennett Medical College, Chicago. The Doctor was made a charter member of the Illinois State Eclectic Association in 1868; also served as Treasurer in 1871 and 1872, and filled the office of President in 1873; was also a charter member of the Eclectic Medical Association, organized in Chicago in 1870, and 3 times represented this State to the National Eclectic Association. He has given much attention to farming and stock-raising, and owns 180 acres of land 3½ miles from Pittsfield, where he has established a breeding farm for horses; he has some fine blooded stock. Prominent among them are 2 Hambletonian colts (stallions), "Richard" and "Radiator;" the former a chestnut sorrel, white hind feet, 16 hands high, and weighs 1,200 pounds; foaled June 24, 1874; bred by S. W. Wheelock, Moline, Ill. "Radiator"—color, bright bay, 16 hands high, star in forehead, weighs 1,300 pounds, foaled May 31, 1874, and bred by same person. The pedigree of the above named stallions descends from the great trotting families of Kentucky. They have a natural gait, and show a flattering record of speed, etc.; are high-mettled and full of life, yet kind and safe to handle.

Augustus Dow, miller, was born Oct. 9, 1841. He began active life as clerk in a dry-goods store, which business he continued to follow until 1863, when he enlisted in the army, serving in the Paymaster's Department 3 years. In 1872 he came to Pittsfield and embarked in the milling business in company with C. P. Chapman, and they now conduct one of the largest mills in the State. Mr. D. was married in this county in 1865 to Jennie S. Weinand. She was born in New Jersey in 1841 and died in 1870. Mr. D. was then married, in 1872, in St. Louis, to Judith W. Morton, who was born in Massachusetts in 1840. Harry A., born in April, 1877, is their only child.

E. P. Dow, dealer in coal, wood and lime, is a native of Tolland county, Conn., where he was born in 1848; came to this county in 1865, and engaged in the mercantile business: was married in 1874 to Miss Florine Hicks, and is the father of 2 children. In 1878 he established himself in his present business, where he is enjoying a fair trade.

John Duran, a retired farmer, was born in Hamilton county, Maine, Jan. 16, 1800. His parents were John and Jane (Davis) Duran. He came to this county Nov. 18, 1831, and settled in

Newburg tp.; was married in 1825 to Miss Rhoda Ann Riggs, of Cincinnati, Ohio, and they have had 12 children, 6 boys and 6 girls, 10 of whom are living. Mr. D. was Road Commissioner for 25 years in Newburg tp.: is a member of the M. E. church, also of the Masonic Lodge. P. O., Pittsfield.

G. T. Edwards, proprietor of the Pittsfield House, was born in Tennessee, March 25, 1814; he emigrated with his parents to Illinois in 1828, and settled in Sangamon county, where he resided until 1835, when he came to this county and settled in Pittsfield, where he engaged in teaming. Two years afterward he was elected Constable, and appointed Deputy Sheriff under Col. Seeley, in which capacity he served for several years. In July, 1839, he married Miss Eliza M. Allred, a native of Tennessee, where she was born Oct. 29, 1822. They had 1 son and 1 daughter. Mrs. E. died July 30, 1842. The following year he married Miss Angeline Davis, a native of Kentucky, where she was born in 1821, and they had 3 children. She died Sept. 28, 1853. His present wife, Delilah (Goodwin) is a native of this State. Mr. E. was elected Sheriff of Pike county in 1854 and served 2 years, when he purchased a farm in Newburg tp., and followed farming a short time, then engaged in hotel-keeping in Pittsfield, and was proprietor of stages and mail contractor. In 1862 he organized Co. A, 99th Ill. Inf., and participated in many of the principal battles of the war. After a year of service he was compelled to resign on account of poor health, and he was honorably discharged. Returning to his family he became proprietor of a hotel at Naples, Scott Co., and at Griggsville, Pike Co. In 1869 he, with other enterprising citizens, formed a stock company and erected the Pittsfield House, which has since been under his supervision. It is one of the largest and best kept hotels in the West.

Charles A. Elliott, of the firm of Gano, Shriver & Elliott, dry-goods dealers, Pittsfield, is a son of Abner and Ruth (Wells) Elliott, the former a native of Virginia and the latter of Kentucky. Charles A. is a native of the Buckeye State, where he was born in 1854; he came to this county in 1872, and embarked in the mercantile business in Pittsfield in 1879.

George Ellis, farmer, sec. 32; P. O., New Hartford; owns 80 acres of land worth $50 per acre; he was born in this county, April 5, 1850, and was married in this county in 1871, to Amanda Mc-Clintock, also a native of this county, born in 1852; they have 2 children, Orville and Ethel. Mr. E. has been School Director, and is a Republican.

Aaron Enderby, farmer, sec. 3; P. O., Pittsfield; was born in Pike county in 1855, is a son of Conrad and Jane (Moore) Enderby, natives of North Carolina and early settlers of this county, and grandson of Joel Moore, the first settler in Pittsfield tp., where he passed a life of usefulness. Mr. Enderby resides on the homestead with his parents, and owns a farm of 120 acres worth $35 per acre. The family are members of the Christian Church. Mr. E. is unmarried and lends his industry to the care of the homestead and his aged parents.

Gano, Shriver & Elliott, dealers in dry-goods and clothing. This is the largest house of the kind in Pittsfield, and is a consolidation of the firms of Gano and Shriver Brothers. The firm has had an experience of 26 years in New York city, and Felicity, Ohio, and at present carries a stock of $40,000, with an average sale of $85,-000 per year. The store is 100 feet in length by 25 in width, and two stories high, all occupied. A custom tailoring department is connected with it on the upper floor, well stocked with goods. This firm has been identified with the mercantile interests of the city for many years, and possesses the energy, enterprise and reliability of business men.

D. H. Gilmer, deceased, was born in Kentucky, Sept. 10, 1814; came to this county at an early day, and was the partner of Milton Hay in the practice of law at Pittsfield. In 1861 he enlisted as private in the 38th Reg. I. V. I., and received promotion to the position of Colonel of that Regiment. He was killed at the battle of Chicamauga, Sept. 10, 1863. He was at one time Prosecuting Attorney in this county. In 1844 he married Miss Louisa M. Quinby. Six years after his death she was appointed Postmistress of this city, and executed the important duties of the office until her death, in 1869. She was succeeded by her daughter, Lizzie Gilmer, the present incumbent, who fills the position satisfactorily.

George Gooud, farmer, sec. 33, owns 80 acres of land, worth $50 per acre. He is a native of England, came to America in 1836, settling in New York, and came to Pike county in 1862; was married in this county in 1864 to Charlotte Cressnol, also a native of England, and born about the year 1843, and died in 1875; they had 2 children,—one living, Philip R. He then married Amanda E. Pringle, born in New York city in 1854; they have one child, named Elizabeth. Mr. G. is a Democrat.

John Gooud, farmer, sec. 33, owns 80 acres of land, worth $50 per acre; is a native of England, and was born in 1830; came to America in 1836, and settled in New York, where he was married in 1856 to Alice Pringle, also a native of England, where she was born about the year 1843. They have had 6 children,—one living, namely, Susanna. Mrs. Gooud had 2 children by a former husband; their names are Mary A. and Sarah J. Mr. G. is a Democrat.

Strother Grigsby, County Judge, born in Page county, Va., in 1819, came to Illinois in 1838, and settled in Adams county, where he engaged in teaching school for 4 years, then came to this county and followed the same calling for 10 years in Pleasant Vale tp. He subsequently settled in Pittsfield and soon after was called by the people to fill the office of County Treasurer. He also served 4 years as County Clerk, and is serving his present position the second term. He has also given time and attention to various other offices with which he has been identified. In 1845 he married Miss Amanda

Parkis, a native of Missouri, who died, leaving 4 children. His present wife, Missouri E. Reel, is a native of Jacksonville.

Wm. B. Grimes, Deputy County Clerk, was born in White Co., Ill., Nov. 25, 1828; in 1834 his parents moved with him to this county; in 1850 he went to California and remained two years, meeting with good success; on his return to this county he located at Milton and built the first saw-mill in that place; was in the lumber business about one year and then followed the tinware trade until 1869, when he was elected County Clerk. Mr. G. is now Deputy County Clerk, has been Supervisor of Pittsfield tp., and Chairman of the Board one term. The past four years he has also been Grand Lecturer in the Masonic order, and is now Grand Examiner and *ex-officio* Grand Lecturer. Mr. Grimes has had a good education, fine musical talent, and has held about all the local offices in his township. In 1853 he married Amanda A. Shock, who died in 1861, leaving three children ; in 1862 Mr. G. married Nancy J. Greathouse, and they have 3 children now living. The children are, Della, born in 1857, now the wife of Mark Hanes ; Ira A., born in May, 1859, is clerk in Lindsey & Co.'s grocery; both the latter are in Pittsfield; Henry W., born, 1861, died at the age of about 5 months; Ida, born in 1863, Alice in 1865, and Laura in 1875.

Hon. Wm. A. Grimshaw, attorney at law, is the son of William Grimshaw, who was an early and distinguished historian, having written and published the first History of the United States, a History of South America, of England, of France, a Life of Napoleon and other works, besides compiling histories of Greece, Rome, etc. It is said that at one time he had an income from his works of about $4,000 a year. He died in 1851. Wm. A.'s mother was Harriet, a native of Charleston, S. C., and daughter of James Milligan, a Captain in the Pennsylvania line in the American Revolution. Mr. Grimshaw was admitted to the bar at 19 years of age, in Philadelphia, and in May, 1833, he arrived in Pike county, Ill., and in November following he received license from the Supreme Court to practice law. This year he was also appointed Adjutant of the 17th Illinois Militia, and he often held with his Colonel, Benj. Barney, regimental and battalion trainings in this county. Mr. G. has probably held more commissions from State Governors than any other citizen of Pike county,—from Govs. Reynolds, Yates, Oglesby, Palmer and Cullom. Although a Whig in early day and Republican since, he has generally as a candidate for office run ahead of his ticket and sometimes been elected, even in a Democratic district. In 1847 he was elected delegate to the Constitutional Convention, the only Whig along with the three Democrats, Messrs. Archer, Montgomery Blair and Harvey Dunn, and was the author of that provision in the Constitution against dueling. He also favored such measures in that body as caused an advance in the State credit, the Illinois and Michigan canal bonds, for example, going up from 18 to 65 during the session of the Convention. Mr.

G. was also a delegate to both conventions which nominated Lincoln for President, and to other conventions; was also a personal friend of Douglas, praising him for his support of the Union cause. As an attorney Mr. Grimshaw has been eminent, defending suits for the Sny Levee Commissioners, the T., W. & W. and C. & A. R. R. Cos., and the Mississippi Bridge Company at Louisiana, Mo. For 14 years, ending in 1857, he was in partnership with his brother, the late Jackson Grimshaw. He owns fine farms, takes great interest in the welfare of the county, has been President of the Agricultural Society, the Antiquarian Society, etc., etc.; has been Trustee of the State Institution for the Blind, and is at present a member of the State Board of Charities.

We noticed some interesting old books in Mr. Grimshaw's library, as, *Les Reports de Sr. Creswell Levinz,* in three parts, printed in London in 1702; Law Commentaries or Reports of Edmund Plowden, printed at London in 1779; *Les Reports des Divers Special Cases argue & adjuge en le Court del Bank Leroy et Auxy en le Co. Ba. & l' Exchequer,* etc., printed in London in 1714,—all these in the Norman or Law French language; also a copy of the *Jurisconsult Exercitationes* in which is contained that noted sentiment, "The air of England is too pure for slavery to breathe."

William S. Grimshaw, druggist, original house of J. U. Grimshaw, grandfather of the present proprietor, who established himself here in 1835, his drug-store being the first in the city. He died in this city in 1848 and was succeeded by his son, T. C. Grimshaw, who conducted the business until 1868, when he sold out to Thomas Williamson and removed to the homestead. Subsequently the store fell into the hands of Adolph Fisher, who disposed of the stock to Wm. S. Grimshaw in 1876. The house carries a stock of $5,000, with average sales of $15,000 per year. It controls a large trade, and is one of the prosperous firms of the city.

Patrick Hulpin, proprietor of marble yard, Pittsfield, came to this county in 1850, established his present business in 1856, where he has a fair trade.

C. H. Harder, druggist, succeeded J. H. Crane in 1871. At present he carries a stock of $5,000. He came to this county in 1851, and here he has since made it his home. He was married in 1872 to Miss Susan Lorgby, by whom he has one child, Frank.

Henry Harder, carriage and wagon manufacturer, is a native of Columbia county, New York, where he was born in 1822. When of age, he settled in Berkshire county, Mass., where he married Miss Mary E. Griffin, a native of Rensellaer county, New York. He came to this county in 1851 and supervised the wood department of the Batesman factory until he erected his present building in 1869. The building is 2 stories high, with blacksmith and paint shops and store-room connected. He at present employs 6 men; has a large stock on hand, and contracts a fair trade. Mr. H. has 5 children.

Adam Harshman, farmer, sec. 8; P. O., Pittsfield; owns 20 acres, worth $60 per acre; is a native of Ohio, born in 1832; came to this State in 1840; was married in 1857, in this county, to Lucy J. McCune, who was born in this State in 1836 and died in 1858, leaving 1 child, Hamer; was again married in 1860, to Esther Aarbaw, who was born in this State in 1840. They have 4 children, Chandler, Lawrence, Leonora and Eliza. Mr. H. has been Clerk of the School Board 15 years, and is a Republican.

Joseph Heck, grocer, baker and confectioner, was born in Durmersheim, Grossherzogthum Baden, Oberamt Rastadt, in 1822; emigrated in 1846 and settled in Quincy after a residence in Philadelphia 2 years. His first home in this county was in Perry tp., where he resided until 1855, when he came to this city and opened his present establishment. He carries a stock of $15,000 to $18,000, and is one of the oldest houses in the city, occupying the old courthouse.

John Helme was born in Barnacre, Lancashire, England, Dec. 13, 1822. His grandfather, John Helme, was a native of the same place, where he died; his father, Wm. Helme, came to America in 1842, via New Orleans and landed at St. Louis in 1843, accompanied by our subject, then 20 years of age. They arrived in Pike county in April of the same year; both were carpenters and builders by trade, and the first work they did in this county was to make rails, a work they were wholly unaccustomed to. After being in the county about 3 years, John Helme married Amelia Wassell, a native of England. The next year he settled on 40 acres of land, given to him by his father-in-law, located on the N. E. of sec. 24, Derry tp., built a frame house 18x24 feet, cultivated 25 acres, and fenced the whole piece. Since that time he has been extensively engaged in farming. He has held the plow and driven the team for breaking over 1,000 acres of new land, 600 acres of which he himself put under cultivation. He now owns 447 acres, having sold several hundred acres. His residence is on N. W. $\frac{1}{4}$ of sec. 30, Pittsfield tp., the home farm consisting of 420 acres in one body. He raises on an average 100 to 140 acres of wheat, and about the same of corn, and feeds from 100 to 200 head of cattle per year, also 150 sheep. Mr. Helme is the largest buyer and dealer in cattle and hogs for shipment there is in the county, shipping to the Chicago and Buffalo markets, on an average, 150 car loads per year, 40 of these being cattle, and 110, hogs.

He was formerly a Whig, but is now a Republican; has been School Director over 20 years. He and wife are both members of the Christian Church of New Hartford. He is also a Mason. Mrs. H. died Dec. 24, 1857, leaving 5 children,—William, Elizabeth, John A., Amelia and Susan. The latter died at the age of 20 years. Mr. H. married his present wife, Hannah Ann Shinn, daughter of James Shinn, of Salem county, N. J., March 10, 1859, and they have 6 children,—Charles E., Matthew E., Sarah E., James, Mary and Lena May.

John Helme

PITTSFIELD T.P

Mr. Helme has made all the improvements on his home farm; has built a commodious frame house, 32 by 54, and a fine barn with a rock basement 8 feet high. The barn is 45 by 60 feet with 20 feet posts, and is one of the most convenient barns in the county. His father followed farming in this county many years, and died in 1865, in Derry tp.

In 1850 Mr. H. made a trip to California, worked in the mines 3 months, and returned with $2,500, which he invested in 200 acres of land. He was 4 months making his overland trip, and the same time returning by the Pacific via Nicaragua, Central America and New Orleans, being 10 weeks on the ocean. We give Mr. Helme's portrait in this book.

Col. D. D. Hicks, cashier of the First National Bank at Pittsfield, was born in Bennington Co., Vt., Aug. 12, 1812; while very young the family removed with him to New York State, where they remained till his mother died; they then resided in Vermont until 1830, then in New York State again until 1838, when they emigrated to Pittsfield, Ill., near which place the subject of this sketch taught school two years; after spending a few months in the East, he clerked in a store in Pittsfield till 1842, when he was appointed Deputy Sheriff by Ephraim Cannon; after serving four years in this capacity he was Sheriff for four years; subsequently he served four years as County Treasurer, and from 1850 to 1852 he followed merchandising; in 1865 he went into the First National Bank as clerk and teller, and in 1867 was elected cashier of the institution. His father, Truman V., was a celebrated physician, a member of the New York Legislature two terms, and for a time was Judge of Warren county, N. Y. His mother's maiden name was Barbara Hayes, a native of Vermont. Oct., 1842, he married Mary Jane Burbridge, of Pike Co.; Helen M. was their only child, who died at the age of 18; Mrs. H. died in March, 1844; in May, 1845, he married Julia Ann Burbridge, cousin of his first wife; of their 7 children all are living in Pittsfield, namely, Frances, now the wife of George Barber; Barbara E., wife of Henry R. Mills; Robert Truman, assistant cashier in the First National Bank; Florine E., wife of E. P. Dow; Emma, wife of Harry Higbee, Esq., Laura M. and James W.

Patrick Higgins, farmer, sec. 17; P. O., Pittsfield; born in County Down, Ireland, in 1827; came to America in 1848, and settled on his present estate the same year, which was then an unbroken wilderness. Here he erected a rude hut composed of poles and grass, in which he lived 6 months; he has a farm of 160 acres, well cultivated, and valued at $75 per acre. He was married in this tp. to Miss Margaret Reed, a native of Ireland, and who died in 1877, leaving 7 children, all now living. Mr. H. is one of the early settlers of this town and county, and well known and respected by all. He is a Democrat.

Henry Hoskins, farmer and stock-dealer, owns 140 acres of land worth $50 per acre. He is a son of John and Elizabeth (Brown) Hoskins, natives of Ireland, and was born in this State, Dec. 18,

1842. In Oct., 1866, he married Bridget Carney, a native of Ireland, born April 6, 1844. They are the parents of 6 children, viz.: John, Charley, Catharine, Elizabeth, Henry and Isaac. Mr. H. has been School Director 5 years, and belongs to the M. E. Church. His father's father was in the war of 1812. Mr. H. deals extensively in cattle, hogs and sheep.

John Hughes, farmer, sec. 27; P. O. Pittsfield; owns 120 acres of land, worth $60 per acre; he is a native of Ireland, born in 1820, and came to America in 1840; settled in Pennsylvania, where he remained 3 years; then was in Missouri 2 years, then came to this county in 1845, where he has since resided. In 1850 he married Jane Donnelly, a native of Ireland, born in 1820. They are the parents of one child, born in 1855. They are both Catholics, and Mr. H. is a Democrat.

Joseph Hunter, boot and shoe maker; born in Edinburgh, Scotland, in 1833, and emigrated to America in 1852. Same year was married to Miss Martha Hunter, by whom he has 9 children. Opened his first place of business in 1869, where he is conducting a good trade. Is a member of the School Board and City Council, taking an active interest in all that pertains to the welfare of the county.

F. W. Hurseman, boots and shoes. Associated himself in the business circles of this city in 1871, soon after his voyage from the fatherland, Germany, where he was born in 1855. Carries a stock of $3,000, with average sales of $5,000 per year. He is one of the active young merchants of the city, and made happy by a lucrative trade.

James S. Irwin, attorney, Pittsfield. The subject of this notice was born in Woodford county, Ky., March 23, 1820. He graduated at Center College, Ky., with the class of 1838, and in the winter of 1839 attended one course of medical lectures at Lexington. In March of the following year he moved to Jacksonville, Ill., where he commenced the study of law in the office of Brown & McClure, and Jan. 1, 1842, he received license to practice law. He immediately removed to Mount Sterling, where he remained 17 years, with the exception of a short period, in the practice of his profession. In the year 1849, like many others, he caught the California gold fever, went to the golden shore and remained till the spring of 1852, when he returned to Mount Sterling, a wiser if not a richer man, and resumed the practice of his profession. In the year 1844 he was married to Miss M. P. Giberson, formerly of Pennsylvania, and to whom four children have been born, two boys and two girls. By a sad and unfortunate accident one of his sons was killed by a gunshot wound while hunting, and the other died while in the prime of life, and giving promise of a brilliant career. Mr. Irwin has confined himself steadily to his profession, taking no very active part in politics, and has no desire for office. In 1856 he was one of the Fillmore Electors, and was in the Electoral College in 1872, where he cast his vote for Grant and Wilson.

Jan. 1, 1861, Mr. I. moved his family to Pittsfield, where he has since resided. By close attention to business, by trying to do his duty to his friends and patrons, he has acquired a fair and reputable practice, and a sufficiency of this world's goods to place him in comfortable circumstances. He was one of a family of 16 children, all of whom are dead except one sister and five brothers. Of the survivors, the sister is the wife of Col. G. M. Chambers, of Jacksonville. The eldest brother, William, is a farmer in Brown county, Ill.; the next older, Stephenson, is a farmer of Kansas; and two brothers are physicians.

D. E. James & Co., dry-goods dealers, Pittsfield; began business in the spring of 1878; the firm are active members of the business fraternity of Pittsfield, and control a large and reliable trade.

Henry James, farmer, sec. 7; P. O., Pittsfield; was born in England in 1817; came to America in 1851 and stopped in Cincinnati one year, then came to this county, where he has since resided; he has bought, sold and improved 5 different farms, and now owns 80 acres worth $50 per acre. He was married in England in 1850, to Jennette Francis, a native of Scotland, born in 1818, and they are the parents of 3 children, only one living, Thomas F., Alice M. and Wm. G., deceased. Mr. James has been Road Commissioner 6 years, and served several years as School Director. He is a member of the I. O. of O. F., an Episcopalian and a Democrat.

T. F. James, farmer, was born in Louisiana Nov. 24, 1851; came to this State with his father in 1852 and settled in this county, where he still resides; was married to Margaret Wilson, a native of this county, and who was born Dec. 21, 1854. They are the parents of 2 children, Jennette, born Dec. 24, 1875, and Elizabeth, Dec. 1, 1877. Mr. James owns 60 acres of land worth $50 per acre.

Benjamin Jellison, farmer, owns 60 acres of land worth $60 per acre; is a native of Maine, born Jan. 24, 1804; came to this county in 1844; was married in Maine May 7, 1827, to Mary Wyman, who was also born in Maine, and they are the parents of 5 children, only 3 of whom are living: Hiram, Charles H. and Mary. Delilah and Henry are deceased. Mr. S. is a member of the Baptist Church, and a Democrat.

J. W. Johnson, attorney at law, was born in Lewis Co., Mo., Nov. 24, 1845; was brought up at Palmyra, Mo., where he received a good education, studied law, and was admitted to the bar in 1869; came to Pike county, Ill., in 1870; taught school at Eldara and New Canton for two years; came to Pittsfield in Sept., 1873, where he has since remained, most of the time in the practice of law; is now in partnership with J. S. Irwin; from 1873 to 1877 he was acting Superintendent of Schools of this county. Dec. 18, 1867, at Palmyra, he married Miss M. V. Nicol, daughter of Henry and Catharine Nicol. The subject of our sketch is a son of Don Q. and Elizabeth A. (Rogers), the latter of Norfolk, Va., whose parents emigrated West with her in her infancy. Mr. Johnson's children are Nina E., born July 25, 1869; Leta J., born Aug. 16, 1871; Eliza-

beth A., Dec. 9, 1874; Albert Sidney, Feb. 21, 1878, and James
Irwin, Oct. 2, 1879.

J. W. Jones, farmer, secs. 8 and 9; P. O., Pittsfield; is a native
of Hamilton Co., O., born in 1818, and is a son of Jonathan and
Ann (Wilmington) Jones, natives of Virginia and Pennsylvania,
respectively. Mr. Jones is a gunsmith by trade, which occupation
he followed in Mount Sterling, Morgan county. In 1843 he settled
in Pike county near his present home, which at that time was but
a wilderness; he was married in this county to Miss Martha A.
Preble, a native of Ohio, and who was born in 1827. They have
had 7 children, all of whom are living: Mary, Eliza, Ann, Celestia,
Harvey P., Clara and John J. Mr. Jones is one of Pike's enterprising farmers; has served as Supervisor one term, and Road Commissioner 7 years. He had the first horse-plow used in the State,
and relates many interesting incidents of early life. Politically he
is a Greenbacker.

Timothy Kane was born in Ireland June 1, 1840, son of Cornelius and Catherine (Quinlan) Kane. He came to America July 4,
1857, and to this county the following summer ; has resided in
this tp. ever since. March 1, 1864, he married Miss Ellen
McElroy, of this county. She was born in 1842. They have had
8 children, 6 boys and 2 girls; 3 boys are dead; the children living are Patrick, John, Joseph, Mary and Jane. Mr. Kane owns
110 acres of land, most of which is under cultivation, and worth
$40 per acre. Both are Catholics, and Mr. Kane is a Democrat
and Greenbacker. P. O., Pittsfield.

Nathaniel Kellogg, farmer, secs. 21 and 22, is a native of Massachusetts, born in 1824; remained there until 1854, when he
married Miss Sarah M. Brown, daughter of Oliver and Lucy
Brown, born in the same State in 1826. Mr. and Mrs. Kellogg
came to Pittsfield in 1854, where they now reside. Mr. K. is the
son of Charles and Mrs. P. (Foot) Kellogg, the former a native of
Massachusetts, born in 1782, and died in the same State in 1853,
the latter also a native of Massachusetts, born in 1787; she came
to Illinois with her son, D. F. Kellogg, and died at his house in
1868, at the age of 81 years. Our subject is a well-to-do farmer.
P. O., Pittsfield.

Theodore Kellogg, Sheriff, son of Ira and Lydia Kellogg, who
settled in Naples, Scott county, in 1833. His father was the first
pilot on the Illinois river; came to this county in 1835, and
selected a home near Perry, where he died in 1856. The subject
of this biography was born in Genesee county, N. Y., in 1825.
He carried the mails between Quincy and Perry for 5 years, and
was proprietor of the hotel at the latter place. In 1860 he married Miss Sarah J. Cockill. He moved to Pittsfield and assumed
the proprietorship of the Pittsfield House, and the following year
was elected to his present office, which he ably fills. He is highly
respected by all.

Dr. J. H. Ledlie, physician and surgeon, was born in Dublin, Ireland, Feb. 14, 1833; graduated at the Royal College of Physicians and Surgeons in that city in 1854, when he emigrated to Pittsfield, Ill., where he has remained ever since in the practice of his profession, except the 4 years he was surgeon in the 99th regiment of Illinois volunteers in the last war; during his service in the army he was promoted to the position of Staff Surgeon and Medical Director of the 13th Army Corps, and finally Surgeon in Charge of the General Hospital at Jefferson City, Mo.; he was mustered out as Lieut. Col. in November, 1865, when he returned to Pittsfield. He is a member of the Adams County Medical Society, and of the American Medical Association. Dr. Ledlie has a very large practice, and one of the largest and best arranged offices in the country. April 4, 1856, in Brooklyn, N. Y., he married Elizabeth Betterton, a native of England, and their children are Elizabeth B., born April, 1857, Ann F., born in 1859, and died when about 6 weeks old, James C., born in 1861, and died Nov., 1878, and Mary H., born in 1863.

J. C. Lewis, druggist. This house was opened in 1877, being a copartnership of Lewis & Hyde, who carried on a lucrative trade for 15 months, when the firm dissolved. Under its present management it carries a stock of $4,000, with average sales of $30,000 per year, and is the finest and largest drug store in the county; it is located on the north side of the Public Square, Pittsfield. The subject of this sketch was born in Scott county, Ill., in 1849, and was married in Jan., 1878, to Miss Fannie Ray, a native of this county, and daughter of John and Margaret (Huber) Ray. They have one child, whom they have christened Ray, born April 13, 1879. Mr. L. is a member of the Christian Church.

J. C. Lindsay, of the firm of Lindsay & Silvernail, grocers, Pittsfield. The business here was originally carried on by H. H. Thomas, passing into the hands of his successor, J. C. Lindsay, in 1876. In 1879 Alfred Silvernail was admitted to the firm, and the concern is doing a thriving business. Mr. L. is a native of Highland county, O., where he was born in 1842.

William Lorett, farmer, sec. 22; P. O., Pittsfield; is a native of Vermont, born May 6, 1808; was married in Connecticut in 1829 to Sarah Graham, and they are the parents of 14 children, 10 girls and 4 boys; the latter were all in the late war. Mr. L. owns 195 acres of land worth $40 per acre; his father was in the war of the Revolution. He belongs to the Baptist Church, and is a Democrat.

James Manton, farmer, sec. 12; P. O., Pittsfield; is a son of John and Elizabeth Manton, both natives of England, where the subject of this sketch was born Jan. 2, 1815. He came to America in 1854, and settled in this county. Fourteen years prior to his coming to America he was united in marriage with Miss Charlotte Hamerton Shets, who is also a native of England. To them have been born 14 children, 10 of whom are living,—William, Thomas, George, Maria, Lucy A., James, Nancy, Anna, Lizzie and Fannie. The deceased are Rachel, Mary A., Emma and Charles. Mr. Manton is one of the largest farmers and land-holders in this county, owning 825 acres of land, valued at $55 per acre. When he came to America he was the possessor of but $15, and by energy, application and business tact he is able to rank among the solid men of Pike county, and as one of the leading and prominent citizens of the county we give his portrait in the pages of this volume.

Hon. A. C. Matthews, attorney at law and Representative from the 38th District, was born in Pike county, Ill., in 1833; brought up on a farm; graduated at Illinois College, Jacksonville, Ill., in 1855; was admitted to the bar in 1858; was the last commanding officer (Colonel) of the 99th Ill. Vol. Inf. in the late war; from 1869 to 1875 was Collector of Internal Revenue in the 9th District of Illinois, but, resigning this position, he was appointed Supervisor of Internal Revenue, which place he also resigned July 1, 1876, when he returned to the practice of law; but in November following he was elected as a Representative in the State Legislature, receiving 12,-600 votes, and in 1878 was re-elected by 5,563½ votes.

Azariah Mays, farmer, sec. 32; P. O., New Hartford; is a native of Ohio, born in 1827, and was married there in 1848, to Miss Rebecca J. Davis, who was born in Aug., 1828. They are the parents of 3 children,—Marcellus, Ellie, now wife of Edward Dunning, of this county, and William. Mr. M. came to this county in 1864; owns 100 acres of land, worth $60 per acre. He was in the late war, in Co. C, 49th Reg. O. I., and served 2 months, and was discharged in consequence of disability. He is a Republican.

J. H. McClintock, farmer, sec. 25; P. O., Pittsfield; is a native of this county, born April 28, 1839; is a son of William and Barbara (Ribble) McClintock, natives of Tennessee and Indiana, respectively. Aug. 28, 1874, he married Catharine Duffield, who was born in Indiana, March 7, 1845, and they are the parents of 6 children, 5 living; their names are Alice, Wm. F., Lucinda A., James L., Barbara C. and Paul. Mr. M. holds the office of Collector at the present time, and is a member of the Christian Church, and an Odd Fellow.

Edward McCoughey, farmer, sec. 11; owns 120 acres of land, worth $50 per acre; is a native of Ireland, born in 1819; came to America in 1844, and settled in Rhode Island; was married in New York in 1850, to Anna McCormick, also a native of Ireland, and was born in June, 1830. They have had 2 children, one living,—Patrick P. The name of the deceased was Sarah. Both Mr. and Mrs. McC. are members of the Catholic Church.

Jordan McSpawn, carpenter, is a native of Kentucky, where he was born in 1816; he came to this State in 1838; the same year he was united in marriage with Mary Badgely, a native of Pennsylvania, where she was born in 1819. To them have been born 7 children, 6 of whom are living. Mr. McSpawn has served as Constable four years, and Deputy Sheriff two terms. He is a member of the Christian Church, and politically a Republican.

H. R. Mills, dealer in books and stationery, Pittsfield, is a native of Ohio, where he was born in 1853; in 1869 he was united in marriage in this county with Miss Barbara, daughter of D. D. and Julia (Burbridge) Hicks. Their two children are Arthur H. and Frank W.. Both he and his wife belong to the Church of the Latter-Day Saints. Mr. M. has held the office of Town Clerk two terms. Politically he is a Republican.

James Mirrielees & Co., grocers, Pittsfield. The copartnership of this house was formed in 1867, and the firm carry a stock of $3,000, with annual average sales of $20,000, and enjoy increasing trade. Mr. M. is a native of Scotland, and was born in 1840; crossed the ocean to America in 1863, and settled in St. Louis, where he resided until he came to this county in 1867.

Rufus M. Murray, County Treasurer; was born in Kinderhook, Pike county, in 1837; is a son of Eleazer Murray, who settled in that tp. in 1832, and died in 1852. Jan. 1, 1868, Mr. Murray married Elizabeth, daughter of Squire Wilson, of Kinderhook. He has filled many local offices in his native tp., where he resided until called to fulfill the duties of his present position. He is one of the reliable men of the county, and has many warm friends.

C. L. Obst, photographer, was born in Saxony, Germany, in 1832; emigrated to this country in 1849 and settled in Baltimore, Md., where he engaged in decorative painting. Subsequently he removed to York, Pa., and to this county in 1857; the same year was married to Miss Elizabeth Wildin, and they have one child. He established himself in his present business in 1859 and is enjoying a fair trade.

Jeff Orr, State's Attorney, located in Pittsfield Feb. 26, 1873, and entered upon his profession the same year. Nov. 7, 1879, he married Ella M. Yates. He is a hard student of the law and wedded to his profession; is permanently located in Pittsfield, where he expects to devote the remainder of his life to his vocation. Ella M. is reading, and will take a thorough law course, to assist her husband in his profession. Mr. Orr is a native of Harrison county, Ohio.

C. W. Patterson is a native of Berkshire county, Mass., and was born Jan. 9, 1829; was married Sept. 10, 1848, to Mary V. Carpenter, a native of the same county, by whom he has 2 children. He is a blacksmith by trade and followed this occupation for 10 years after settling in Pittsfield; he subsequently officiated as Deputy Postmaster $2\frac{1}{2}$ years, and assisted as clerk in the store of J. B. Walmouth until elected Justice of the Peace, in which capacity he has served for 10 successive years, the duties of which he has always discharged to the satisfaction of the public.

Marcellus Peckinpaw, grocer; inaugurated himself in business on the west side of the Square in 1873, in company with John Boyd, in the sale of tobacco, etc. Eighteen months afterward the firm dissolved, and Mr. P. carried on a successful trade under his own name; subsequently he formed a partnership with J. C. Lindsay, to whom he afterward sold, and in 1878 he purchased a new stock and opened his present place; has a stock of $2,000.

William Pence, farmer, sec. 1 ; P. O., Pittsfield ; was born in Preble county, O., in 1839 ; was married in 1866 to Miss Sarah Little, and they have 2 children, Thomas A. and Ida M. Mr. P. came to this county in 1856 and settled in this tp., where he has since made it his home and owns 70 acres of land valued at $60 per acre. In politics he is a Democrat.

G. S. Pennington, ticket and station agent, Pittsfield; born in Greene county, Ill., in 1841, where his father, Joel, settled in 1839. Ten years afterward the family came to this city where Mr. P. engaged as clerk in the Circuit Clerk's office, where he remained for some years. Subsequently he entered the Illinois College, at Jacksonville, for the study of law, and at the breaking out of the Rebellion received an appointment as clerk in the disbursing office at Springfield, and was promoted to Chief Clerk, serving until the close of the war; returning home he was appointed to his present position in 1869, and the same year married Miss Annette Stout, who died, leaving one child, Frank. His present wife is Maggie, daughter of James Sutton, of Springfield.

George B. Purkitt is one of the early and prominent citizens of Pike county. He is the son of Henry and Mary W. (Tucker) Purkitt, the latter of whom is still living at the advanced age of 91 years. His father lived to the age of 92. George B. is a native of Massachusetts, where he was born in 1809. He came to Illinois in 1831 and settled in Jacksonville, where he attended college as a companion of Gov. Yates. The following year he came to Pike county. In 1836, in Morgan county, he was united in marriage to Harriet Provost, a native of New York, where she was born in 1819; she died in 1860; by this union two children were born, one of whom, a son, is living. He was again married in 1865, this time to Mrs. Phimelia Garbutt, also a native of the Empire State, and was born in 1816. Mr. P. is a member of the Congregational Church, and is one of the early and honored citizens of Pike county.

William H. Raftery, farmer, sec. 21; P. O., Pittsfield; owns 160 acres of land worth $40 per acre ; he is a native of this county, born Jan. 27, 1844; was raised on a farm, and had but limited means to commence active life with, but by industry and economy has obtained a good property. He has been Deputy Sheriff, discharging his duties acceptably. Was married in this county in 1868 to Nancy E. Mottley, who was born in this county, Dec. 2, 1843. They are the parents of 5 children, viz: John, William, Thomas, Robert E. and Clarence. Mr. R. is of Irish descent.

Jason A. Rider, Circuit Clerk and Recorder, was born in Barnstable county, Mass., in 1834; came West with his parents in 1852, locating at Griggsville, Pike Co. During most of the years from 1852 to 1864 he was engaged in steam-boating, as clerk, with his brother, Capt. Rider. In 1858 he married Miss Jennie E. Cree,

Wm Shinn

PITTSFIELD TP.

whose family were early settlers in the county. From 1864 to 1873, was engaged in the mercantile business at Griggsville; in 1874 was elected Justice of the Peace in that town, which office he held until elected to his present position in 1876, which position he fills with entire acceptability to the public. He has 5 children, the oldest of whom, Samuel W., is Deputy Clerk.

J. Willis Roberts, Justice of the Peace, was born in Martinsburg tp., this county, Oct. 13, 1854, son of J. S. Roberts, editor of *The Union*, and Justice of the Peace in Pittsfield; Aug. 10, 1868, he came to Pittsfield; 1873, etc., he taught school two terms in this county; from June, 1875, to May, 1877, he spent most of the time in Jersey county, and since then has been again a resident of Pittsfield. Mr. Roberts has a good education, is Clerk of Pittsfield Town Board of Trustees, and Sept. 19, 1878, he was elected Justice of the Peace, which position he now holds, his place of business being on the north side of the Public Square. He was married Oct. 30, 1879.

Charles Rogers, farmer, sec. 31; P. O., New Hartford; owns 102½ acres of land worth $50 per acre ; is a son of David and Elizabeth (Sargent) Rogers, the former a native of North Carolina and the latter of South Carolina. He was born in Pike county in 1841; in 1862 he enlisted in the war in Co. A, 99th Reg. I. V. I.; served 8 months and was mustered out in Missouri; was married in Pike county in 1867, to Harriet West, a native of England, who was born in 1842. Their children are David R. and Anna M. Those deceased are Ellen and William. Mr. R. belongs to the Masonic order, and is a Republican.

Col. Wm. Ross, deceased, was born April 24, 1792, in the town of Monson, Hampden county, Mass. His father, Micah Ross, in 1805, moved to Pittsfield, Mass. Upon the declaration of war in 1812, William Ross obtained a commission as Ensign in the 21st regiment United States Infantry, commanded by Col. E. W. Ripley, and was soon after ordered on recruiting service. In the spring of 1813, he was directed to unite his men with those of his brother, Capt. Leonard Ross, of the same regiment, at Greenbush, N. Y., and was subsequently dispatched to join the command of Major Aspinwall, about five hundred infantry of the 9th Regiment, who had been ordered to take up a forced march for Buffalo, then threatened by the enemy's forces. Arrived at Utica, the troops were met by an express, informing them of the capture and destruction of Buffalo, and directed their immediate march to Sackett's Harbor. Accordingly, proceeding to Oswego, on Lake Ontario, they embarked in fifty open row-boats, and set out for the harbor; but hardly had they made Stony Island than they heard the roar of cannon, and discovered the British fleet, with gun-boats and Indian canoes in the rear. They at once attempted to run the gauntlet of the enemy's armed vessels, and, rushing amid the fire of the gun-boats, twenty-five of their own frail craft succeeded in reaching the harbor, the remainder being captured by the British. Captain Ross

40

and the young Ensign were among the successful ones.   The next day took place the memorable battle of Sackett's Harbor, in which the brothers led about one hundred men, and in which 500 Americans drove back 1,300 British.   Of the detachment commanded by the Rosses, one-third was either killed or wounded in the conflict.

Soon after this battle, the Rosses were transferred to the 40th Regiment, infantry, and ordered to the seaboard, where the Captain took command of Fort Warren, in Boston Harbor, and William Ross was detached to Marblehead, to drill the troops of that post, and subsequently removed to the Gurnet fort, near Plymouth, Mass., where he remained till the close of the war.   He then returned to Pittsfield, and set up the business of a blacksmith, hiring workmen, however, as he possessed no knowledge of the trade himself.

In the summer of 1820, as spoken of elsewhere in this book, in company with four brothers, and a few other families, he started for what was then known as the Far West—the State of Illinois.

For awhile the prospects of these settlers were very flattering, but afterward sickness and death entered their ranks.   Col. Ross lost his first wife, one brother, and several of the company, the first year.   Subsequently, the Colonel visited New York, and married a Miss Adams, of that State, after which he returned to Illinois, laid out a town embracing his first location, and named it Atlas, which afterward became the county-seat of the county.   There had previously been established a postoffice, called Ross Settlement, but this designation soon gave way to the one now adopted by the Colonel, who soon commenced improving a farm, and built a mill, which was much needed at the time.   His efforts were now followed by the blessings of a kind Providence; and though he arrived in Illinois a poor man, he speedily, through economy and untiring energy, began to realize an increase of property and popularity. He became Judge of Probate for the county of Pike, which office he held for many years, enjoying the unbounded confidence of the people.   He also served as clerk of the Circuit and County Courts, and filled with credit many minor offices, among which were Colonel of Militia and Justice of the Peace, in all of which he won the esteem of his fellow-citizens.

In April, 1832, at the commencement of the Black Hawk war, Col. Ross was ordered by the Governor to raise a company out of his regiment forthwith, and join the forces at Beardstown.   He received the order on Friday, and on the following Tuesday presented himself at the rendezvous, in Beardstown, with double the number of men designated in the requisition.   He was selected as aide to the commanding general, served with much popularity throughout the campaign, and then returned once more to private life, devoting himself to building operations and the improvement of the county where he resided.   Prosperity still smiled on his every effort.   In 1835 he was elected to the Legislature of Illinois, and while a member of this body procured the passage of a law peculiarly adapted to the Military Tract, which afterward proved of great importance to that section of country. Col. Ross was subsequently chosen to the Senate several terms, serving five or six sessions in that body.

In private life the Colonel was a warm friend, and willing, moreover, to forgive his enemies. Punctual in his business relations, governed by strict integrity, and zealous in all his labors, he won the respect and esteem of his fellow-citizens in every walk.

As early as 1833, it became evident to the people of Atlas that the county-seat would at no distant day be removed to some point nearer the center of the county. Col. Ross joined heartily in this movement, and advanced to the county authorities the money with which to enter the land upon which Pittsfield is now located. The County Commissioners—Col. Barney, George Hinman, and Hawkins Judd—did the Colonel the honor to ask him to name the new county-seat, which he accordingly did, calling it Pittsfield, in honor of his old home in Massachusetts. In this beautiful place he erected a dwelling-house, 1835. It is safe to say that no public enterprise in the county ever escaped his observation, or was completed without his aid.

During the dark days of our late civil war, though incapacitated for the field by an almost total loss of sight, he used his influence and his purse to raise men to defend the flag. He assisted largely in getting up the 99th Illinois regiment, and other organizations of troops raised in Pike county. We give Col. Ross' portrait in the pages of this volume.

R. C. Scanland, Pittsfield, was born in Gallatin, now Carroll, county, near the mouth of the Kentucky river; came to this county in 1847 and settled in this city. During the Rebellion he was appointed to the important position of master of transportation at Cairo, which office he so well filled that upon his resignation he was presented with a beautiful and valuable solid silver service inscribed "Capt. R. C. Scanland, by his many friends." Leaving Cairo he returned to Pittsfield and engaged in merchandising until 1870, when he accepted the agency of the Continental and other insurance companies, and has since made that line a specialty, and the large business done attests his devotion to it. He has paid in losses over $25,000 in Pike county. Mr. S. was married to Miss S. A., sister of Hon. H. T. Mudd, of St. Louis, who lived but a short time after marriage. He was then married to Miss S. J., daughter of William Watson, who died, leaving a son and a daughter. His present wife was Miss C. S. Wicks, a native of Syracuse, New York.

R. S. Sellee, farmer, sec. 34; P. O., Pittsfield; owns 47 acres of land worth $50 per acre; was born in Missouri April 11, 1858; married in this county in 1877, to Emily C. Willsey, and they have 1 child, Mary E., born Jan. 13, 1878. Mr. S. is a Democrat.

Benjamin Sellon, farmer, sec. 27, owns 80 acres worth $50 per acre; was born in England July 28, 1818; came to America with his father in 1821, and to this county in 1836; in 1861 he enlisted in Co. D, 3d Reg. Mo. Inf. and served 2 years; was in the battle of

Arkansas Post, siege of Vicksburg, and several others. He was first promoted to Orderly Sergeant and then to 1st Lieutenant; served 2 years and was honorably discharged. He then organized a Reg. of colored troops, and was appointed 1st Lieut. He was married in this county in 1848 to Miss Harriet—who was born in Ireland in 1816, and they have 4 living children,—John, Harriet, William G. and Charlotte Maria. Mr. S. has held the offices of Assessor and Collector, etc. He is an Episcopalian. P. O., Pittsfield.

Dr. T. W. Shastid, physician and surgeon, was born in Sangamon county, Ill., near Petersburg (near where Abraham Lincoln once kept a grocery), Aug. 26, 1831, son of John G. and Elizabeth B. (Edwards), the former a native of Kentucky and a farmer, and the latter of North Carolina. When T. W. was $4\frac{1}{2}$ years of age the family moved to Pittsfield, where Mrs. S. died Dec. 8, 1863, and Mr. S. Feb. 5, 1874. The subject of this brief biography was educated in his boyhood in Pittsfield, and subsequently received his medical education with Prof. John T. Hodgen of Pittsfield, and at McDowell's College, which was the medical department of the University of the State of Missouri at St. Louis. After graduating he first settled at Pleasant Hill, practicing there for $5\frac{1}{2}$ years, in partnership with Dr. John A. Thomas for about 3 years; since then he has practiced at Pittsfield, where he is now Examining Surgeon for U. S. pensioners. Aug. 2, 1860, he married Mary F. Edwards, by whom he had one son, Wm. Edwards, March 12, 1863. Oct. 1 1865, he married a second time, taking Louise M. Hall, and their children are, Thomas Hall, born July 19, 1866, Jon Shepherd, Jan. 20, 1870; and Joseph Calvin, April 13, 1877.

William Shinn. The founders of the Shinn family in America were 3 brothers, who emigrated from England, their native country, about 150 years ago, 2 of them locating in New Jersey near Philadelphia and 1 in Virginia, where they reared families; they were prominent, respectable people, many of them being in the ministry, principally Methodists. The subject of this sketch descended from the New Jersey branch of the family. His father, Daniel Shinn, is the first of the family that located in Pike county, and is counted as one of the earliest and most respected of Pike county's pioneers. On his arrival here in 1820, he located near the present town of Atlas. He brought into the county at that time the first wagon that ever came within its boundaries; about 2 years afterwards he bought a farm of 160 acres on the N. W. $\frac{1}{4}$ of sec. 12, Atlas tp., on which he immediately erected a small log house, into which he moved with his wife and 6 children. He was married in the State of New Jersey to Mary Haskett, who was of Scotch descent, and the 6 children born to them before they came to this county, were all born near Cincinnati, Ohio; their names were Benjamin, John, Eliza, Mary, Hannah and Phœbe. The first, third and last, are the only ones now living.

The farm above mentioned was wholly in a wild state, in the

midst of heavy timber, no improvements of any kind, and consequently he had more to contend with than many in a new country, but he was endowed with that indomitable energy and perseverance so necessary to the pioneer, and went bravely to work; his means were limited, and with a large family to support, it was no small merit to obtain success. He was a man of strong religious convictions, generous and affable to all. He was the first to open the house for religious worship, Methodist meetings being held there for 10 years. He was prosperous, and gave his sons between 700 and 800 acres of land; he died in March, 1852, and his wife in Sept., 1849; they had a family of 13 children, 7 of whom were born in this county,—Nancy, Lydia, Henry, William, Daniel, Asa, and an infant, deceased. Of these 7, only Nancy, Lydia and William are living.

Wm. Shinn, the subject of this sketch, was born in this county Jan 7, 1827; his early education was obtained in the old-fashioned log school-house, with split logs or puncheons for seats and desks. He was principally employed on his father's farm during his boyhood, where he acquired habits of industry and application necessary to success.

June 27, 1846, he married Mary Jane Lytle, at the residence of her father, Andrew Lytle. Mr. and Mrs. S. had 5 children, 4 of whom are living,—Elizabeth, now married to Wm. Gay, of Atlas tp., Albion, married to Lucy Woolfolk, also living in Atlas tp., Wm. D. and Mary, who live with their parents, and Daniel, who died at the age of 6 years. Mr. Shinn followed farming until 1850, when he went to California, it being the height of the gold excitement. After an absence of nearly a year he returned, having met with fair success. He went the overland route, and remembers well talking with companions of the impossibility of the railroad ever going through that vast country. He again resumed farming, and has followed it ever since. He has been prominently identified with the business interests of Pike county, as an extensive buyer and shipper of cattle, hogs and sheep, for the Chicago and St. Louis markets. He has been engaged in this business for 30 consecutive years, is now one of the largest farmers in Pike county, having some 1,200 acres of farm land, raising, on an average, 200 acres of corn, 150 acres of wheat, and handles 150 head of cattle, and from 400 to 500 head of sheep, turning off each year from 125 to 140 fat sheep. About the year 1860 he bought his present residence and farm on sec. 32, Pittsfield tp., then consisting of 110 acres. To it has since been added so that there are now 530 acres.

Mrs. Shinn's father, Andrew Lytle, and his wife, Elizabeth (Wagoner) Lytle, were early settlers in this county, dating back to 1837. He was a native of Ross county, O., and his wife of Maryland.

Augustus Simpkins was born in Marion county, Ind., in 1833; came to this county in 1856, and settled on a farm in Martinsburg tp. Three years afterward he went to Rockport and engaged in merchandising, where he remained until 1870, when he was appointed Deputy Sheriff, and two years afterward was elected Sheriff. Before the close of his term he leased the Mansion House, which he kept for 14 months, then sold out, opening his present place of business. He was twice elected constable in this city, and Supervisor in Martinsburg tp. and Atlas, also a member of the Town Board for 3 years, and has always taken an active interest in county affairs. In 1854 he married Nancy J. Francis, and they have 5 living children.

J. A. Smith, stock-dealer, is a native of Ohio, where he was born in 1833; was reared upon a farm and adopted that as his profession, which he followed until 1861; he then embarked in the mercantile business. He erected a large mill at Time, this county, in 1867, which he conducted for 4 years. He now owns 3 houses in that town and 160 acres of land in Hardin tp., an interest in a warehouse at Montezuma, etc. He buys and ships cattle, horses, hogs and sheep, and is a large and liberal purchaser. He came to this county in 1853, and 2 years later was married to Mary Dinsmore, a native of this State. She was born in 1838, and died in 1871. To them were born 4 children. He was married in 1873 to L. H. Allen, who was born in Kentucky in 1838. Leslie is their only child.

Jeremiah Pence, farmer, sec. 6; P. O., Pittsfield; was born in Rockingham county, Va., in 1807; is a son of William and Christina (Sellers) Pence, of that State. He was married in Ohio in 1832, to Margaret A. Brawly, a native of North Carolina; he came to this county in 1837, and the following year he selected the site of his present home, which, from an unbroken wilderness, has been transformed to a well cultivated farm, comprising 185 acres, valued at $40 per acre. Mr. P. is one of the oldest settlers of the county, and a staunch Democrat. Of his several children 3 are living.

Dr. Abner F. Spencer, farmer, sec. 7 ; P. O., Pittsfield; son of Isaac and Rhoda (Beadsley) Spencer, the former a native of New York, and the latter of Connecticut. Abner F. is a native of Connecticut, and was born July 11, 1823; emigrated to this county in 1852, and settled in this tp. Dec. 12, 1850, he married Mary E. Sanders, a native of Kentucky, and who was born in 1833, and they have had 9 children, 7 living, namely: James S., Mary E., now wife of Miles Cox, of Kentucky, Elizabeth P., Lewis L., Martha B., Abner F. and Abgora. Those deceased are Frank and Isaac. The Doctor commenced his medical studies in 1846, graduating at the Sterling Medical College at Columbus, Ohio, in 1849, and commenced practice the same year and continued it until 1862. He now owns 160 acres of land worth $50 per acre. In religious faith he is a Swedenborgian, and in politics is a Republican.

F. Strubinger, Pittsfield, was born in Abbotstown, Pa., in 1832; came to this county in 1863 and settled 9 miles west of this city, where he engaged in farming, and working at his trade, plastering. Subsequently he visited his native State and returned to this city in 1866, and the following year opened the market now occupied by Mr. Simpkins. The next year he established himself in his present business.

Jacob Strauss, of the firm of Strauss Brothers, merchants, west side of the Square, Pittsfield, where they carry a large stock of dry-goods, clothing, etc. Jacob was born in February, 1843, and came to America in 1853 and settled in New York, where he remained 4 years, during which time he clerked in a dry-goods store; in 1863 he came to this county and embarked in business, where he has an extensive and increasing trade, carrying a large stock, and employing four salesmen. In 1873 he was united in marriage at Cincinnati with Minnie Herman, who was born in 1853, in his native country in Europe. They have two children, Emanuel and Samuel.

William M. Thompson, teacher, was born Oct. 19, 1846, in Carroll county, Va., and is a son of Raleigh Thompson, of Livingston county, Mo. He was a soldier in the Confederate army, and since that time worked by the month to obtain money to defray his expenses while attending school in Pittsfield. He taught 3 years at Fairview school-house near Pittsfield, and is now teacher of Independence School, Hardin tp., and is very successful as a teacher, and one of the most prominent teachers of the county.

Augustus Trombold, blacksmith, Pittsfield, is a native of Germany, born Nov. 22, 1847; came to America in 1849, remaining 7 years in New York, thence to Iowa, and in 1869 to Pittsfield, where he has since resided. He was married in Brown county in 1873 to Miss L. C. Ritter, a native of Ohio, born in 1854, and they have 3 children: Anna, George J. and Charles A. Mr. T. is a member of the Lutheran Church, and is a Democrat. In 1863 he enlisted in an Iowa Cavalry Reg't, serving one year.

William Watson, born in Chester Co., Pa., Feb. 26, 1798, son of Archibald Watson of that State, who emigrated to Missouri in 1818, and settled in Louisiana. Ten years after, he moved to St. Charles, where he passed the remainder of his days. The subject of this sketch was married at Galena in 1828, to Miss Diadema McQuigg, a native of Oswego, N. Y., where she was born in 1802. After marriage he returned to St. Charles, and in 1833 came to this city, and settled temporarily in a small hut or shanty, then located on the present site of the city Square, being the first settler of Pittsfield. Same year he erected a dwelling south of the Mansion House, where he opened a small stock of goods. Two pilgrims named Greene and Barber were boarders in the family at that time. This edifice still stands the test of time and as a living monument to his decaying memory and declining years. Five years later he built the Mansion House, which he conducted successfully for 14 years. His mercantile pursuit of 21 years was crowned with prosperity, and he retired from the active field of life with considerable wealth, so that his old age can be spent in reaping the reward of a well directed industry. He was at one time Judge of the Probate Court, and served as County Treasurer 4 years. He is residing with his only living child, Ellen, wife of Rev. Dr. Barrett, deceased, as of the pioneers of Pike county, a worthy and venerable citizen. We give the portrait of Mr. Watson in the pages of this book.

James Wassell, farmer, sec. 31; is a son of William and Susannah (Gray) Wassell, natives of England; who came to America in 1830, where the subject of our sketch was born in 1835. His parents brought him to this county in 1837. In 1857 he married Sarah E. Mather, who was born in Morgan county, this State, and after becoming the mother of 6 children, died. The names of the children are Mary, William, Elmer, Grant, Georgia and Arthur. In 1879 Mr. W. married Emma Bentley, a native of this county, who was born in 1850. He is a member of the Christian Church, and a Republican in politics.

Hon. Scott Wike, attorney at law, was born April 6, 1834, near Meadville, Pa., son of George and Ann (Grubb) Wike, natives of Pennsylvania, who came to Quincy in 1838, and to Pike Co. in the spring of 1844. Mr. George Wike still resides near Barry, where he formerly was a woolen manufacturer at the " Barry Woolen Mills." The subject of this sketch studied law one year at Harvard University, was admitted to the bar in 1858, and Oct. 8, 1859, he located in Pittsfield and commenced the practice of law; in 1862 and 1864 he was elected Representative in the State Legislature from Pike and Scott counties; and in 1874 he was elected to Congress. He commenced the practice of law alone, but afterward formed a partnership with Milton Hay and A. C. Matthews, then with C. L. Higbee until 1861 and then was alone again until February, 1879, when he entered into partnership with Mr. Matthews and Harry Higbee.

George Wilder, farmer, sec. 18; P. O., Pittsfield; born in York Co., Pa., in 1827; married Caroline Keener, a native of the same State, by whom he has 4 children; came to this Co. in 1857, and settled on his present estate, consisting of 160 acres well cultivated land, valued at $100 per acre. This farm and improvements may be considered the finest in this tp. The house is a two-story frame building, with all modern improvements. and occupies a sightly eminence above the road, commanding a fine view of the surrounding country. This farm is now open for purchase, and a bargain for a first-class farmer.

John H. Wildin, artist, Pittsfield, was born Feb. 14, 1844, and is a native of Pennsylvania, and a son of John and Magdalene (Stubinger) Wildin. Until 19 years of age he followed farming; came to Illinois in 1853, and settled in this county, and for the last 8 years has been practicing his profession. In 1876 he married Hester McFadden, who was born in Missouri in 1850. Politically he is a Democrat.

William Elza Williams was born in Detroit township near the town of Detroit, this county, May 5, 1857. He is the second child of David Anderson and Emily Adeline Williams, both of whom were reared in Pike county, and the offspring of hardy pioneer settlers. His great-grandfather *paterna*, ——Williams, came to this country from England previous to the Revolution, and fought for his adopted country throughout that war, and was at the surrender of Yorktown, and also was a soldier in the war of 1812 from North Carolina. The grandfather, John Anderson Williams, was born in Maryland in 1799, and removed with his father to North Carolina when but a small boy, whence he came to Illinois with a large family in 1834. He settled on sec. 32, Detroit township, where the subject of this sketch was afterward born. With the assistance of a large family he opened up an extensive farm and became a wealthy and influential citizen. He was a devoted member of the Baptist Church, a firm supporter of Jackson and Douglas, and died in 1876 at a ripe old age, in Sedalia, Missouri. David Anderson Williams, the father, was born in North Carolina in July, 1832. He was first married to Miss Martesia Scanland, of Pittsfield, who died the following year without offspring. On the 10th of May, 1854, he was married to Miss Emily Adeline Hayden, of Newburg, his present wife, and the mother of the subject of this sketch. He is now living on the old home place, a good and respectable citizen and neighbor. He proudly follows in the footsteps of his ancestors, a firm and unswerving Democrat. The mother is a daughter of Louis Elza Hayden, a resident of Newburg township, and was born in November, 1837, in Pike county. Her father, who came to Illinois from Missouri in 1834, was born in Kentucky in 1809, and is still living, a spry, active old man 71 years of age. His grandfather, Elisha Hayden, was the son of English parents and was born in Virginia in 1755. He was a Revolutionary hero from his native State, where his body now lies. His son, Elisha Hayden, the great grandfather of the subject of this sketch, was born in Virginia, removed to North Carolina and afterward to Kentucky, where he entered the military service and fought gallantly through the war of 1812.

W. E. Williams is now a practicing attorney in Pittsfield. He was reared on a farm with the privileges of a district school four months in the year, from which he entered Illinois College at Jacksonville, at the age of 19. He immediately became a member of a college society, and from the first exhibited great powers as a debater, and was among the first scholars in school. During his last collegiate year he commenced the study of law, and Aug. 12, 1878, entered the law office of J. W. Johnson at Pittsfield, and became a close student. After the formation of the firm of Irwin & Johnson with James S. Irwin the following year, he remained under the instructions of both until March 5, 1880, when he passed a successful examination before the Appellate Court, 1st District, at Chicago. On the 24th of August, 1879, he was married to Miss Maggie Gallaher, of Pittsfield, daughter of James Gallaher, editor of the *Old Flag*, and was born in N. Y. City June 11, 1857.

Abner V. Wills, whose portrait may be found in this volume, was born Feb. 14, 1849, at Summer Hill, this county, and is a son of the well known Wm. R. Wills, sr. Mr. Wills is at present one of the largest farmers in Pike county, having about 1,100 acres of land. He raises annually on an average 200 acres of wheat, 300 acres of corn, and turns off about 300 sheep, of which he keeps high grades, and thorough-bred stock of all kinds, and in which he is quite extensively engaged. He is also an extensive dealer and trader in land, etc. His own residence is on the southwest quarter of sec. 21.

March 22, 1868, he was married to Miss Elizabeth Helme, daughter of John Helme, and they have a family of 6 children, namely, John, William, Emily, Mille, Melinda and Emmet.

Charles Wills, barber, Pittsfield; born in Germany in 1840; came to America in 1854, stopping in St. Louis, Mo., where he remained until he came to this city in 1868, when he established himself in business. In 1863 he married Elizabeth Stueck, a native of Germany, and they have 5 children. Mr. W. is an enterprising man, and has a fair trade.

William R. Wills, sr., whose portrait we give in this volume, was born in New York in 1810; at the age of 8 his parents moved to the Buckeye State, where they remained 11 years; when 19 years of age he started South in company with a younger brother, A. V. Wills, and arrived in New Orleans, where they remained for several months; W. R. then returned North, locating in Pike county, where he worked as a laborer for six years. He was united in marriage with Miss Sarah M. Coles in 1836. She was born in New Hampshire in 1810; after his marriage he commenced farming on a rented farm in Atlas tp. His wife died in July of the same year. Being thus left alone in the world, he sold out what effects he had, and went East. Here he remained about 8 months; he then returned to Pike county and engaged in trading in various ways until 1838; in that year he married Miss L. D. Scott, who was born in the Empire State in 1812, and was brought to Illinois in 1818. Three years thereafter he purchased a farm near Summer Hill, sec. 12, Atlas tp. He remained there for six years, and then sold his farm and bought a valuable tract of land on secs. 20 and 21, Pittsfield tp. He owned at one time at least 4,000 acres of land in this county, and had at his decease about 2,000 acres; and he died Aug. 6, 1872, leaving a widow and three children, the former of whom resides in Pittsfield. The children are,—William R., jr., Abner Vine and Lucy, who married Jerome D. Chamberlain, and now resides in Franklin county, Kan.

Mr. W. held a commission as Lieutenant in the Black Hawk war. This commission, as well as the sword he used, is in the possession of his son, Wm. R. Wills, jr. He filled the office of Justice of the Peace in this county, and always took a prominent part in its politics. Perhaps few men had more influence in moulding the political sentiment of the public than he. He was formerly a Whig, but after the organization of the Republican party he voted with it. During the war he took an active part in furnishing means, encouraging enlistments, etc., for its prosecution. Owing to the prominent and firm position he took in these matters he gained many enemies among the opposition—so bitter indeed at times as to draw out threats against his life; but he at all times fearlessly followed the path of duty and patriotism. He was for many years a member of the Odd Fellows' order, and that society made the arrangements for, and attended his funeral.

Mr. W. was one of the most prominent traders in stock and lands, and one of the largest farmers that ever lived in Pike county. It is stated upon good authority that $25 was about the extent of his capital when he was 30 years of age. At his death, aged 62, he was estimated to be worth $140,000.

Mrs. Wills is a devoted member of the Methodist Church, superintending the Sunday-school for 15 years previous to her husband's death. She gave $3,000 toward the erection of their church.

William R. Wills, jr., was born Oct. 27, 1844, at Summer Hill, Pike Co., Ill., and is a son of Wm. R. Wills, sr., whose sketch is given above. He obtained his education principally in the common schools, but graduated at the Bryant & Stratton Commercial College at St. Louis. July 23, 1868, he married Elizabeth J. Wells, daughter of Robert and Mary Wells, of Pittsfield. She was born in this county Aug. 27, 1850. Five children have been born to them, one of whom is deceased. The names of those living are, Lucy E., Charles H., Orion R. and Isidora I. Ida was the name of the deceased.

Mr. Wills now resides on sec. 20, this tp., where he is extensively engaged in farming, owning about 820 acres of land. He has turned his attention, especially for the past 6 years, to the raising and breeding of fine stock, such as Short-horn cattle, Cotswold sheep, Berkshire hogs and fancy fowls, selling and shipping them throughout the Western States. At present he has a herd of about 60 Short-horn cattle, all of which are thorough-bred, and some of them imported.

Mr. W. is a Director in the Pike County Agricultural Society, and one of its most active and enterprising members. He is also Director and Treasurer of the Pike County Mutual Fire Insurance Company. It has been in active operation during the past few years, meeting with a fair degree of success, not having cost the policy-holders over 15 cents on the $100 for a period of four years. He is also a Director in the First National Bank of Pittsfield, and in every public enterprise he takes a leading part. He is a member of the Odd Fellows' society of Pittsfield, and politically a Republican. As one of the leading citizens of Pike county, we present to our readers the portrait of Mr. Wills.

Barnett J. Willsey, farmer, sec. 29; P. O., Pittsfield; was born in the State of New York in 1835; and is the son of Barnett Willsey. In 1840 he was brought by his parents to this county, who settled on the present estate, now consisting of 240 acres, valued at $50 per acre. Here he has lived ever since, except that from 1854 to 1857 he was in California, in the mining business, in which he was successful. At his home his vocation has always been farming, and in this occupation has been prosperous, being now one of the most enterprising and substantial farmers in the community. He also deals in stock to some extent. The past year he erected a fine two-story frame house, with L; also a large frame barn, etc. The improvements on this place are excelled by few, and the farm itself is in a most fertile district. In 1858 Mr. Willsey married Eliza Jane McClintock, a native of Indiana, and they have 3 children living,— Emily Alice, Charles L. and James O.; one child, Mary E., is deceased. We give Mr. Willsey's portrait in this volume.

James G. Willsey. The first of the Willsey family who came to this county was a parent of the subject of this sketch. They were natives of New York and emigrated to Ohio in 1837, where they remained until 1840, when they joined the tide of emigration westward and found a location on sec. 34, Pittsfield tp. Their names were Barnett and Cornelia (Kizer) Willsey. Upon this section they established themselves, where Mr. Willsey lived until his death, which occurred in 1858. He was buried on the old home farm. His widow still resides at the old homestead. James G. was born in the State of New York, Feb. 28, 1830, and was therefore about 10 years of age when his parents came to this county, with whom he remained until about 1851, when he married Miss Melinda Rogers; she was born in Greene Co., Ill., in 1830, and was the daughter of David and Fannie Rogers, early settlers in Martinsburg tp. The former died in 1871; his wife two years afterward.

Immediately after James G. Willsey's marriage he settled on 40 acres of land which his father gave him, where he remained until 1854, when he selected and purchased the northwest quarter of sec. 34, Pittsfield tp., which is one of the most fertile sections in this county. At that time this land was in a perfectly wild state; not an improvement of any kind had been placed upon it by the hand of man. It was a fine, rolling prairie, interspersed here and there with patches of scrub oak and hazel-brush. The first land cultivated on this farm was in the summer of 1854, when Mr. W. employed a man to break 40 acres, which he did with oxen. This he sowed in wheat that fall. The next season he planted this piece in corn, and broke another 40 acres for wheat. This land, as fast as broken, was surrounded with an eight-rail fence, Mr. W. hauling the rails for the same from the south part of Martinsburg tp., a distance of eight miles. In 1857 he erected a log cabin, on the north part of his farm, 16 feet square. It contained two rooms, one above and one below. Into this cabin he moved his family, and although rather tight quarters during the busiest seasons, found room and accommodations for as many as nine hired hands besides his own family. During the years 1868–9 the balance of the 160 acres was fenced and put under cultivation, with the exception of 50 acres which he has never plowed, but which he set aside for pasture for stock, there being several never-failing springs of pure water on this. Mr. W. ascribes much of his success in the raising of stock, especially hogs, to this pasture, and the fact of their always being able to procure pure spring water. He states that during the worst seasons of cholera, when hogs all around him were dying, he lost very few.

In 1860 Mr. W. built his present residence. It is a frame stru c ture, two stories in height, the main part 18 by 32, L 14 by 28; it is one of the finest farm residences in the county. The out-buildings are all of the modern construction and first-class in every way. Mr. W. has devoted much attention to floriculture, and has a fine greenhouse in addition to his residence, in which he has hundreds of choice plants, including exotics, etc. Take it all in all, the surroundings and improvements of this home farm render it one of the finest and most pleasant in the county.

Seventeen years ago he purchased the southwest quarter of sec. 27. It was partly improved, and he has brought it into a high state of cultivation. The winter of 1879–'80 he erected on this place a very fine residence, which in point of construction and modern conveniences is equaled by few. From the observatory on this dwelling one of the finest views of the surrounding country can be obtained, extending to the west, to Louisiana and Hannibal, a distance of 20 miles, and southeast to a distance of about 24 miles. Mr. W.'s only child and son, William Riley Willsey, who was born in July, 1853, now resides at this place.

As a relaxation from active business, to which he had applied himself with scarcely an intermission since he was a boy, in 1875 Mr. Willsey decided on making a visit to the Pacific slope to see the country and visit numerous relatives, also with some idea of locating there, if the golden shore should prove preferable to his old home. With the above objects in view, in company with his wife and son, he started on this trip, via the Union Pacific R. R. to San Francisco, where several days were agreeably spent in viewing the metropolis of California, when he departed by the steamer "J. L. Stephens" for Portland, Oregon, and from there to Oregon City, where he remained some ten days, and also visited the State Fair at Salem; then took passage up the Columbia river to Wallula, Washington Territory. This river he describes as furnishing the most beautiful scenery he ever beheld. From Wallula they took the cars to Walla Walla, where his sister, Mrs. Richard Wells, resided. At this place the party remained some four weeks, visiting and viewing different parts of the country, when they started on their journey homeward, via the Columbia to Portland, where they took the cars to Harrisburg; they then traveled by rail to Roseburg, then to the northern terminus of the Oregon and California Railroad; from this place they were obliged to travel 270 miles to Reading. During this stage trip, which lasted six days and six nights, it rained continuously. On several occasions the coach was mired down, taking much time and all hands to release it. The fatigue of this journey was so severe that a passenger, an old man, became temporarily insane. Our party, however, arrived safely at Reading, where they took the railroad for San Francisco ; then took the U. P. R. R. for home, where they arrived about four months after they had left. They were thoroughly satisfied with the trip, and also satisfied that they found no better place than at the old homestead in Pike. They traveled between 5,000 and 6,000 miles, 1,000 of which were on the Pacific Ocean.

Mr. Willsey's portrait will be found in this volume.

William B. Willsey, farmer, sec. 34; P. O., Pittsfield; is the owner of 50 acres of land worth $50 per acre; is a native of this county and was born Aug. 24, 1851; was married in this county Aug. 9, 1870, to Miss Loese W. Hoyt, a native of Vermont, and who was born June 11, 1847. They are the parents of 3 children, namely,—Charles H., born May 26, 1871, Ora C., Jan. 2, 1873, and Eva M., Jan. 1, 1876.

William W. Willsey, farmer, sec. 34; P. O., Pittsfield; is a son of Barnett and Caroline (Kizer) Willsey, natives of New York; is a native of this county, and was born in 1848. In 1868 he married Frances J. Robinson, also a native of Missouri, and was born in 1848. They have 3 children,—Perry A., Almira M. and Nancy C.; both Mr. and Mrs. W. belong to the Christian Church. Mr. W. owns 80 acres of land worth $60 per acre, and is a Democrat.

Conrad Winand, blacksmith; born in Germany in 1838; came to America in 1854 and settled in New York, where he remained 4 years; came to Pittsfield in 1859; married in this county in 1863 to Hannah Purset, a native of Pike county, born in 1848, and their 3 children are Lewis H., Franklin C. and Bertie E. In 1861 Mr. W. enlisted in Co. K, 2d Reg. Ill. Cav., and served 3 years; was in several hard-fought battles; had a horse shot from under him by a musket ball without injury to himself. He owns one lot with good dwelling and shop; is a member of the M. E. Church, and a Republican.

Isaac Winans, farmer, sec. 17; P. O., Pittsfield; was born in Essex, now Union Co., N. J., in 1829. Is a son of Jonas and Sarah (Stiles) Winans, of that State. The family came to this county in 1846, and settled south of Pittsfield, where his mother died in 1858. His respected father lived until 1878. The subject of this sketch was married in 1851 to Miss Sarah Webster, a native of Massachusetts, by whom he has 8 children: Norman W., William M., John S., Isaac, jr.; Jonas L., Elmer R., Emma P. and Horace G. Mr. W. has a farm of 400 acres valued at $40 per acre, and is one of the enterprising men of Pike county, and a Republican.

Thomas Worthington, M. D., was born near Knoxville, Tenn., June 10, 1808, and is a lineal descendant of the Worthington and Calvert (or Baltimore) families of England and Maryland. His father having died soon after his return from service in the war of 1812, Dr. Worthington removed to Illinois at an early day, and soon afterward saw service in the Black Hawk war. He graduated at the Medical College of Cincinnati, O., and settled in Pittsfield for the practice of his profession, in 1835. His success as a phy-

sician was very great.   In the year 1837 he was married to Amelia
J., youngest daughter of Col. Andrew K. Long, of Baltimore, Md.
In addition to his professional duties, he has taken an active interest in politics, when questions of great public interest were involved,
and twice represented his district in the State Senate.   In this
body he was an earnest advocate of the " two-mill tax," and his exertions largely contributed to save the State from repudiation.
From being a " Free-Soil Whig," he became one of the first and
most earnest members of the Republican party in Illinois.   To the
support of its principles, and other causes in which he was interested, he brought powers of eloquence and a breadth of information
which have rarely been equaled in the State.   Having by great
industry accumulated a considerable property, he is enabled to
spend the greater part of his time in the invigorating climate of
the Rocky Mountains, and in the pursuit of the favorite study of
his later years—geology.   His investigations upon this subject
have been conducted principally in the field, in almost all parts of
the United States, and have been of especial value in reference to
the " Glacial Period."   He contemplates publishing their results in
book form.   Dr. Worthington has long ranked as one of the most
intelligent, upright and respected citizens of his county and State.

   Thomas Worthington, jr., a son of the above, was born in Spencer, Tenn., June 8, 1850; graduated with distinction at Cornell
University, Ithaca, N. Y., in 1873, and at the Union College of
Law, Chicago, in 1877.   He was admitted to the bar in September
of the latter year, and is now practicing his profession in Pittsfield.

   Edward Yates, attorney, Pittsfield, was born in Pike county,
Sept. 21, 1846.   He is a son of George and Maria (Hinman) Yates,
the former a native of Kentucky, and born Jan. 17, 1807; he was
the second son of Samuel Yates, a native of Virginia, who emigrated in a very early day to Kentucky.   George Yates, who was
born in Barren Co., Ky., in 1807, came to Illinois as early
as 1823, and spent one year in Washington Co.   From there he
moved to Morgan Co., settling near Naples, which is now in
Scott Co.   In the spring of 1833 he crossed the Illinois river into
Pike Co. and settled on sec. 6, Griggsville tp., where he resided
until his death, which occurred at Griggsville, Aug. 13, 1878.
When at the age of 18 he started out in life to do for himself.
He hired to a gentleman by the name of Thomas Smith for $8
per month, one-half in trade.   He worked for 3 months, when he
was taken sick.   The elder Yates was one of those persons who made
of life a success.   He was charitable and liberal, yet accumulated
considerable property, owning at one time about 1,300 acres of
land under a high state of cultivation.   His family of children,
all of whom are respected for their enterprise, genial and social
qualities, were a great comfort when in his declining years.   He
was a man of Christian integrity, high moral principle, beloved
and esteemed by all who knew him.   He was plain and unostenta-

tious in his manners, a kind neighbor, a loving father and a faithful friend. He was greatly missed and deeply mourned, not only by his family, but by a large circle of friends and neighbors. Especially was he missed by the little Church (Hinman's Chapel) of which he was a member and pillar. His funeral, which took place at this church, was largely attended. The sermon was delivered by Elder J. P. Dimmitt, and his remains were laid at rest by the side of his wife, who preceded him to the spirit world about ten years.

The children of the elder Yates are, Nancy Catharine, now the wife of Jerome W. Rush, of Fairmount tp.; Wm. H. lives in Griggsville, and in company with his brother Monroe, owns the old homestead. Wm. H. is a Director in the Griggsville Bank; Emeline, the wife of J. W. Fisher, President of the Chillicothe Savings Bank, and resides at Chillicothe, Mo.; Ellen M., now the wife of Jefferson Orr, Pittsfield. Martha F., who lives at the old homestead, and Edward, the subject of this sketch.

Edward Yates, whose name heads this sketch, attended the McKendree, Jacksonville and Quincy Colleges, receiving a collegiate education. He chose the legal profession for his life labor, and was admitted to the bar Dec. 29, 1869. He began practice with the late Hon. Jackson Grimshaw, at Quincy. In 1871 he moved to Trenton, Mo., where he practiced until January, 1875, when he returned to his native county and located at Pittsfield. He associated himself in his profession with Jefferson Orr, present State's attorney. As a criminal pleader and prosecutor Mr. Y., although a young man, has few superiors in Illinois. He is energetic, and possesses the happy faculty of making friends wherever he meets his fellow men.

Barnett J. Willsey

PITTSFIELD TP.

MARTINSBURG TOWNSHIP.

The surface of this township is generally rolling, and beautifully timbered. From the eminence of some of the knolls in the northern part a grand and magnificent view meets the eye from every quarter. For miles either way during the growing season the eye beholds verdant fields dotted over with fine farm residences, schoolhouses, etc. Before the hand of man had subdued these lands, and when the prairies and woodlands were in their virgin state, the scenery from these eminences must have been supremely charming. With its green, flowery carpet, its undulating surface, skirted by beautiful and refreshing groves that more definitely mark the boundaries, it must have presented to the eye of the lone traveler or new settler a scene most beautiful and sublimely grand. No doubt Fisher Petty, the first settler of the township, was attracted by the beauty of its scenery, the fine timber, and the high, rolling land and running water. These were important things to be considered by the pioneer in making a selection for a home. When Messrs. Petty and Nicholson came here to look up a location, this land had not yet been offered for sale by Government. They were the very advance of the on-coming westward flight of civilization. Mr. Petty came in 1825 and located on sec. 15. As years passed, the groves received the in-coming settlers until about 1850, when all the timbered farms were being worked. About that time some of the more enterprising pushed out upon the prairies. It is not now remembered who was the first to be so adventurous.

Others of the early pilgrims to this locality were Joseph and Robert Goodin, Wm. Binns, Isaac Hoskins, Wm. Butler and Robert Richardson, most of whom were well-known in the early history of the county. Among the older settlers now living are Ira Briscoe, Moses Conner, Mr. McClintock and others.

The first children born in the township were Wm. Ward and Nancy Shinn. The former went to Texas, where he met his death by hanging, in 1862. He was a loyal Union man, and because he would not join the rebel army, was hanged by a band of outlaws. The first marriage was that of George Williams to Miss Nancy Nicholson, Rev. David Hubbard officiating. The first preaching was done by elder John Garrison, of the Christian denomination, and the first sermon was at the house of Robert Goodin.

41

The preachers of the gospel soon sought out and found the pioneers in their new homes, as above mentioned. Nor were they long without the school-house and "master." The former was a rude log cabin, and the latter fully as rude, the refractory pupils thought, and not well versed in our more modern studies. Both school-house and master, however, were well adapted to the times and the then existing surroundings. The first school-building was erected on sec. 7, in 1827, and the first school taught by Mr. Morrow.

The first church structure was erected by the Presbyterians on sec. 18, in 1839. It was known as the Bethel Church.

The township contains two towns, five churches and eight school-houses. The system of education adopted by a majority of the schools of this township is up to the high standard of any part of the county. Of some of the leading teachers we speak in the department of personal sketches given in connection with the history of the township.

Six-Mile creek, with its small and numerous branches, traverses the western part of the township from north to south. There are several small creeks which water the eastern portion. The soil is underlaid with a heavy bed of limestone, and is better adapted to raising wheat and fruit than general farming.

VILLAGES.

Martinsburg.—During the speculative period, when towns sprung up all over the State, this village was ushered into existence among the thousands of others. It was laid out by William Freeman and John Kingsbury, Aug. 24, 1836. It is located on secs. 22 and 27, and at present has a population of about 200. It contains one general store, a blacksmith shop, two churches, a school-house, etc. The churches are of the Christian and Baptist denominations, both of which have been founded for several years, and are in a prosperous condition.

New Hartford.—As a rival to Martinsburg, and at about the same time that that place was founded, this little village was laid out. It is in the extreme northwestern corner of the township, and in the midst of a fertile and well-improved part of the county. It was founded by Isaac Hoskins, Abner Clark, John Shinn and Nathan Brown. The latter kept the first store, and Mr. Rathburn was the first blacksmith. The first postmaster was Wm. Grimes. It now has two stores, two cooper shops, a blacksmith shop, a school-house, and two churches. There is one resident physician. The place contains now about 100 inhabitants.

The *Methodist Episcopal Church* at New Hartford was organized about 1840, by Rev. Mr. Troy, who was afterward thrown from a horse and killed. There were at first about 15 members. They erected a house of worship in 1850, which is still used by the Society. Services each alternate Sunday, by Rev. Mr. Drake, Pastor. Present number of communicants about 75.

The *Christian Church* at this place was first organized March 19, 1851, with the same number of souls that went into Noah's ark, by Elders James Burbridge and David Roberts. The society built a church in 1856. Since the organization there have been added to the congregation 116 males and 172 females. Present number of communicants, 100. Services each Sunday.

BIOGRAPHIES.

In justice to the pioneers, to those who have opened up and developed this township, and those who have taken a prominent part in the history of this community, we give a department of personal sketches as a portion of the history of the township.

Willard Andrews, deceased, was born in Massachusetts in 1813, the son of Alanson and Phœbe Andrews, natives of the Bay State; received a common-school education; in 1846 he married Cornelia Brockway, who was born in 1825 in New York State. Mr. Andrews came to this county in 1839, settling in Atlas tp., and came into this tp. in 1850. By trade he was a carpenter, but he also carried on farming, on sec. 6. He died Dec. 6, 1872, leaving a widow and children. The youngest son carries on the farm. Mrs. H. is a member of the M. E. Church. P. O., New Hartford.

A. F. Barnd, nurseryman, sec. 27; P. O., Martinsburg; was born in Perry county, O., in 1815, and is a son of Christian and Mary Barnd; was educated in the common schools, and in the spring of 1847 emigrated to this State, locating in McLean county, where he resided until 1861; he then came to Pike county, settling in this township, where he practiced medicine a number of years; he has now been in the nursery business for about 10 years. He has a fine nursery, comprising all varieties of fruit trees and plants. The Doctor also still attends to professional calls to some extent.

A. M. Bradburn, farmer, was born in Ohio, Nov. 1, 1827, and is a son of Mark and Mary (Keatley) Bradburn, natives of Ohio; was educated in the common schools of Ohio; in 1853 he married Emily Jameson, and all their eight children are living; one daughter is married. David N. is a teacher. Mr. Bradburn came to Pike county in 1864. In Missouri he was in the " Shirt-tail " militia, and he lost money while in that State. He has made all he has by hard work since he married, now owning 132 acres of land. In politics he is a Democrat. P. O., Pittsfield.

Ira Briscoe, farmer, sec. 28, where he owns 240 acres of land; P. O., Martinsburg; was born in Washington county, Ky., in 1798, the son of Edward and Peggy Briscoe; his father was born in Virginia, and his mother in Ireland; he received his education in the subscription schools which were kept in log school-houses in pioneer times in Kentucky, with greased-paper windows, mud-and-stick chimneys, etc. In 1818 he married Miss Polly Crump, who was born in Virginia in 1799; in 1834 he came to Pike county, settling on the place where he now lives; he has been a farmer all his life, but is now living in retirement. P. O., Martinsburg.

Jasper Brokaw, agriculturist, sec. 17; was born in Somerset county, N. J., Aug. 12, 1828, and is a son of Abraham and Sarah Brokaw, deceased; he worked with his father in the wood-yard until 18 years of age; came to Eastern Illinois with his parents in 1844, and in 1851 located in Pike county, and this year also he married Miss Martha Maroon, daughter of Wm. Maroon, deceased, and they had 6 children, namely, William, George, John, Sarah, Martha and Charley. Mrs. B. died in March, 1863, and Mr. B. the next year married Mrs. Amelia Toothaker, and they have had 6 children: Liona, Priscilla, Albert, Elmer, Cora A. and Eva V. Mr. B. is a farmer, making wheat-raising a specialty. His brother, Uriah, served over a year in the late war, where he lost his life.

John L. Cannon, deceased, was born in Pittsfield tp., this county, March 31, 1834, and was the son of Ephraim and Dorothy Cannon, dec.; was reared on a farm and received a common-school education. Nov. 9, 1854, he married Margaret A. Goodin, daughter of Hardin Goodin, of Martinsburg tp., and their 4 children were Charles E., Sarah E., William H. and Henry O. Mr. C. was a respected member of the Christian Church for 18 years previous to his death, which occurred at Hot Springs, Ark., Nov. 5, 1877. He was a valuable member of society and a kind husband and father; he was a good-natured man, and patient; during his last illness he suffered untold misery and pain, yet he bore it all with Christian fortitude and patience.

James Duffield was born in Chester District, S. C., Dec. 12, 1796; educated in a subscription school; brought to Indiana by his parents when a boy, where he resided until a man grown; came to this county several years ago and engaged in farming and raising stock. He now resides on sec. 3, at the advanced age of 84 years. Of his 6 children 5 are living. He was a soldier in the war of 1812, and fought under Gen. Jackson.

Lucinda A. Dyer, *nee* Thompson, New Hartford, is the wife of Eli Dyer, and they were married in 1840. Of their 9 children 5 are living,—Thomas W., Franklin W., Mary E., William H. and John K. Mr. Dyer was a farmer prior to the late war, in which he served 4 years; his son Franklin was also in the war, and was wounded at the battle of Pilot Knob. The Dyer family, while residing in Missouri, were Union people, and suffered many wrongs at the hands of rebels and black-legs. Mr. and Mrs. Dyer are both natives of Fairfax county, Va., and he was slave overseer in Maryland for four years; in 1854 they came to Pike county, Mo., and in 1864 to this county. Mrs. Dyer is proprietor of the best store in New Hartford, which is conducted under the firm name of T. W. Dyer & Bro. They carry a stock of $1,500, consisting of dry-goods, hats and caps, boots and shoes, groceries, hardware, glass and queensware, and in fact, everything usually kept in a first-class general store. Prices the very lowest.

David Goodin, farmer, sec. 4; P. O., Pittsfield; was born in this county in 1846, the son of Hardin and Rebecca Goodin, the former a native of Tennessee and the latter of Indiana; he was married in 1870 to Miss Jeames, who was born in Missouri in 1847; their two children are Benjamin F. and Wllliam H. Mr. Goodin commenced life in very limited circumstances, but he has been very successful as a farmer, now having 180 acres of land. He and his wife are members of the Christian Church.

J. W. Grabael, farmer, sec. 19, was born Dec. 14, 1840, in Monroe county, Ind., and is a son of Samuel and Margaret Grabael, the former a native of Virginia and the latter of North Carolina. At the age of 20 our subject came to this county and for a time lived near Summer Hill. In 1865 he was united in marriage with Miss Maria Stebbins, a native of this tp. and whose father was among the first settlers of the county. The following year Mr. G. located in this township. Mr. and Mrs. G. are the parents of 4 children,—Mary E., Herbert, Frank and Laura. Both he and his wife are members of the Congregational Church at Summer Hill. During the last winter Mr. G. unfortunately met with two men from whom he purchased the right of territory of this county to sell the " Practical Grubber and Stump-Puller,'' giving his note for the payment of over $3,000, with the understanding, however, that they would keep the note until he could make the money by selling the machine; but they disregarded this understanding, and immediately disposed of the note, causing Mr. G. great financial embarrassment.

I. M. Holloway. The subject of this sketch was born in Highland county, O., Dec. 9, 1850, and is a son of Isaac and Ellen Holloway, deceased, who came to this county in 1857; our subject was reared on a farm and received a common-school education. He was married Feb. 22, 1872, to Miss Kittie Petty, daughter of Alvin Petty, of Hardin tp. They have 4 children,—Nora, Adda, Emma and Athel. Mr. H. resides on sec. 18, this tp., and is engaged in farming and the raising of stock.

Horace Hoskins was born in Atlas tp., this county, July 3, 1832, and is a son of Isaac Hoskins, so well known in the pioneer days of Pike county, and who is now deceased. Mr. H. was reared on a farm and is now engaged in agricultural pursuits. March 6, 1851, he was united in marriage with Miss Lucinda Loutzenhiser, by whom he has had 13 children, 9 of whom are living: William, Marshall, John M., Mary J., Isaac, Emily, Orlando, Alice B. and George B. McClellan. Mr. H. served 3 years in the late war, in Co. G, 99th Ill. Inf., and participated in the battles of Hartsville, Mo., where he was wounded, siege of Vicksburg, etc. He was present at the surrender of Mobile, and was honorably discharged Aug. 12, 1865.

George James was born in Lincolnshire, England, Aug. 12, 1836, and is a son of George and Elizabeth James, deceased. He was educated in England, and came to this county in 1851; he went to Nebraska in 1865, where he remained two years, as salesman for

Rolfe & Terry, wholesale merchants in Nebraska City. He was engaged in Government freighting for some time; he went from Nebraska City to the Black Hills, where he worked on the Northern Pacific Railroad during its construction; he returned to Illinois in January, 1869, since which time he has followed farming, on sec. 3, this tp. June 14, 1861, he married Miss Mary J. Andrews, daughter of Willard G. Andrews, and of their 8 children the following 5 are living: Salome, Alicia, Willard G., Fred and Gracie Lee.

John W. Lynch, teacher of Highway school, was born in Putnam county, Ind., Feb. 19, 1843, the son of Caselton and Miriam Lynch, the latter deceased. He was educated mostly in Pittsfield, and began teaching in 1869; is now teaching the second year at Highland. In 1878 he married Louisa Brown, by whom he has one child, Jennie. As a teacher Mr. Lynch is particularly successful. His pupils keep excellent order and are full of the spirit of learning. He teaches on the latest normal methods, and his schoolroom is a pleasant place for both teacher and pupils.

James H. McCory is a native of Indiana, his parents being John and Betsey (Warman) McCory; he was educated in the common schools of Indiana, and by occupation is a farmer; has lived with his father all his life, who also is a farmer. He has run a threshing-machine for 16 seasons. He came to Pike county in 1875; is a member of the Christian Church, and in politics is a Democrat.

Joseph McDade, farmer, sec. 17; P. O., Summer Hill; was born in this county in 1846, and is a son of William and Sarah McDade, the former a native of Butler county, Ky., and the latter of Indiana; when 7 years old he went to Indiana, returning at the age of 9, then settled in Western Missouri, in 1866, then in Scott county in 1868, and then back to this county in 1878. In 1871 he married Betsey Ann McDade, who was born in 1835, in this county, and they have two children—Laura A., dec., and Sarah E. Mrs. McDade was the mother of 5 children when she married the subject of this sketch. Their names are John R., Franklin, Charles, Mary and Nancy. Mr. McDade is a successful farmer, owning 120 acres of land, all fenced.

Peter McGuire, farmer, sec. 8; P. O., Summer Hill; was born in Ireland in 1823, the son of John and Catharine (Hughes) McGuire, natives of Ireland. In the common schools of that country our subject was educated; in 1851 he married Alice Carrabry, and they have two sons and three daughters. They came to the United States in 1849, landing in New York, and came to Pike county in 1854. When he first came here he was worth about $18, but has now 172 acres of land. In politics he is a Greenbacker.

Michael McKanna, farmer, sec. 27; P. O., Martinsburg; was born in 1855 in county Tyrone, Ireland, son of Patrick and Ann McKanna. At the age of 15 our subject emigrated to the United States with a friend, locating first in Rhode Island; thence to New Orleans, where he remained 12 years, and 1849 to this county. In

1834 he married Miss Catharine Mediau, also a native of Ireland, and they had 6 children. Mrs. McK. died in 1844; Mr. McK. again married in New Orleans, in 1845, Miss Bridget Sheridan, also a native of Ireland, and they have had 8 children. Mr. McK. was formerly a bleacher in print works, but for the past 30 years has followed farming. He and his wife are members of the Catholic Church.

S. G. Miller, farmer, sec. 16: P. O., Summer Hill; was born in 1817 in Athens county, O., and is a son of Jacob S. and Sally Miller, natives of Maryland; educated in the subscription school. In 1847 he married Martha Bemiss, a native of Massachusetts, and she died in 1851. In 1853 he married Asenath McCord, who was born in 1824, in Massachusetts, and they have had 2 children, George B. and Cora E. Mr. Miller followed tailoring for 24 years, but since 1852 has followed farming, with good success; has now 132 acres of good land, well improved. He came to this county in 1845. He is a member of the Masonic Order, and Mrs. M. is a member of the Congregational Church.

J. C. Moore, farmer, sec. 18; P. O., Summer Hill; was born in Maine, the son of William and Margaret Moore, natives also of the same State; came to Pike county in 1856, settling in this tp. In 1848 he married Rachel Randolph, who also was born in Maine, in 1824, and they have had 3 children,—Marcellus, Josephine and Theodosia. Mr. M. has traveled a great deal; transacted business for a period of 25 years in British America and in Bangor, Me. Since he came here he has followed farming with good success, now owning nearly 300 acres of good land, well improved, but when he first set out in life he had but very little. He is a member of the Congregational Church.

James Posten, farmer, sec. 6; P. O., New Hartford; was born in Morgan county, O., May 16, 1821, and is a son of Joseph and Mary (Johnson) Posten, who were natives of Virginia, and of English ancestry; educated in the common schools of Ohio, and came to Pike county in 1843; in 1849 he married Rachel Lyton, and they have had 2 children. Mrs. P. is a member of the M. E. Church, and he is a Democrat.

W. M. Shanton, farmer, sec. 6; P. O., Summer Hill; was born in Ohio in 1841, the son of William and Elizabeth (Twiford) Shanton, natives of Ohio and of German descent. He came to Pike county in 1842. In 1865 he married Anna Thompson, and they have one son and three daughters. Mrs. S. is a member of the M. E. Church, and Mr. S. is a Democrat.

Conrad Shornhart, farmer, sec. 14; P. O., Martinsburg; was born in 1813 in Germany; emigrated to the United States in 1836, settling in Indiana; in 1849 he married Mary Fisher, and they have 6 children, viz: Harry, Mary, Margaret J., John, Sarah and Willie. He settled in this county in 1852, where he still resides, engaged in farming and the raising of stock.

J. N. Slade, teacher of the New Hartford school, is a son of Dr. Slade, of New Hartford, and has been teaching most of the time for 10 years. He was educated in the common schools, and in the State Normal University at Normal, Ill. He has recently had to encounter a vexatious variety of text-books, but now has the process for overcoming the obstacle under good headway. At the Jackson school he taught four terms in succession, and is desired to return. He was born July 7, 1850, in Crittenden county, Ky., and was brought by his mother to this county in 1852, his father having preceded them about six months. April 17, 1879, he married Miss Anna Moore, daughter of Robert Moore, of Louisiana, Mo., and born in Pittsfield, Aug., 1855.

Humphrey D. Harlow, deceased, was born in Albemarle county, Va., Jan. 20, 1800, and was the son of Daniel Harlow. He was raised on a farm but early learned the use of tools, and for several years after he settled in life he worked in wood work of various kinds, in connection with farming. In religion he was a prominent member of the Baptist Church, and was always respected for his consistency and zeal in the Master's cause. He died Feb. 7, 1880, at 6 P. M. He was married twice during life, and his second wife was Mrs. Amilda (McKinney) McCoy, by whom he has one child, Elizabeth, now Mrs. Nathan Zumwalt. Mrs. Harlow has 2 children living, and Mrs. Zumwalt has had 12 children, of whom 10 are living. She has also 14 grandchildren. Mr. and Mrs. H. emigrated to this county in 1836, and suffered the privations of pioneer life.

J. W. Varney was born in Clermont county, O., May 25, 1842, and is a son of J. N. and Matilda Varney, of Hannibal, Mo. He came to this county in 1859, and in 1861 he married Rebecca Conner, daughter of Moses Conner, who now resides with Mr. Varney, in his 81st year. Mr. Conner is a well known pioneer. Mr. and Mrs. Varney have had 7 children, of whom 5 are living, namely, William, Moses, Charles, John and Luetta. Mr. Varney has carried on coopering in New Hartford for 20 years, and is now doing a good business, employing from 6 to 9 hands.

PLEASANT HILL TOWNSHIP.

This township consists for the most part of broken land. The bluffs bordering the Mississippi valley extend northwest and southeast through the township, dividing it into two triangles; one of these is known as the Hill Triangle, the other the Bottom Triangle.

The township was first settled in March, 1821, by Belus and Egbert Jones, brothers. They located on sec. 25, where they erected a log cabin and made other improvements. Here they kept the first tavern of Pike county, and here, too, the first liquor was sold in the county. At the very first meeting of the County Commissioners' Court, and the very first business which it transacted, was to grant these brothers license to sell liquor. They also engaged in stock-raising, but were very much annoyed by wolves and other wild animals. Egbert Jones lived and died on the old homestead, and Belus died at Hamburg, Calhoun county.

The next settlement in the county was made by James W. Whitney and Thomas Proctor, both prominent characters in the early history of Pike county, and of whom we speak in former chapters in this work. They located on the northeast quarter of sec. 27, early in the month of March, 1825; in May of the same year Paul Harpole, of Ramsay Creek, Mo., came over and rented ground of the Joneses, raised a crop, and the following autumn brought his family over and settled on the southeast quarter of sec. 35, where he resided until his death. In the fall of 1825 Samuel Brewster began a settlement on the southeast quarter of sec. 7. The next settlement was made by Thomas Barton and Uriah Holland, in the spring of 1826. They first rented land of the Joneses, and the following fall settled on sec. 22, near the ford on Bay creek. These settlers came from Pike county, Mo., and the settlements that immediately followed the above were made principally by people from Pike and Lincoln counties, Mo.

These early pioneers of this township had other annoyances besides those given by the wild animals. These were by the treacherous and troublesome Indians, who were here in large numbers. The farms here were first opened by ox teams, and the first wagons consisted of wooden wheels, sawed from logs. They had their hard times in other ways. They had to grind corn in a hominy block and in hand-mills at first; a horse-mill was afterward erected on a stump near Pittsfield. The first mill of any note was operated by water power, and was erected by Elisha Harrington in the fall and winter of 1827, on the S. W. ¼ of sec. 8. The power was obtained through a race cut across from a bend in Six-Mile creek. This mill superseded in a great degree the hominy block and spring-pole, the hand and horse-mill.

Regardless of these hardships and inconveniences, the pioneers of this township were noted for their benevolence and hospitality.

The first school was taught in the spring of 1828 by Wm. Howell in a private house, and the next two terms of school were taught by Mr. Bailey. The first school-house was erected in 1832, on sec. 23.

The first sermon was preached in the house of Thomas Barton, by Rev. Stephen Ruddle, a Christian minister, in 1826. Every man, woman and child in the settlement went to hear this sermon. Elder Ruddle and his brother were carried away by the Indians when the former was 14 years of age, and kept until he was 30. The people of the Baptist faith erected the first Church in the village of Pleasant Hill in 1855. The first Justice of the Peace was Felix Collard, and the first Supervisor was Thomas Collard.

PLEASANT HILL.

The village of Pleasant Hill is very pleasantly located on secs. 16 and 21, and is on the line of the Chicago & Alton R. R. It was laid out by Eli and Charles Hubbard and John McMullen, in 1836, and was incorporated in 1869, Dr. John A. Thomas being its first president. It contains a postoffice, stores, blacksmith shop, etc.

Pleasant Hill Baptist Church.—The Martinsburg Church, from which the Pleasant Hill Baptist Church emanated, was organized pursuant to previous agreement on Saturday, Feb. 15, 1845, at the school-house in Martinsburg. After an appropriate sermon by Elder David Hubbard, the members proceeded to organize by choosing Joseph Baker Moderator, and Jacob Capps, Clerk, *pro tem.* The number of members that constituted the Church at that time was only 16. Jacob Capps was invited to assist Rev. Hubbard in constituting them a Church. They then unanimously adopted a series of Articles of Faith and Rules of Decorum, which the Pleasant Hill Church has since adopted, with some modifications.

After the above Church was organized it prospered under the pastoral care of Elder David Hubbard until Feb. 22, 1851, when Jacob Capps and the Pastor held a series of meetings at Martinsburg, and were abundantly blessed. Fifteen members were added to the Church. The meeting was then removed to Pleasant Hill and continued there for several days and nights, during which time 21 more joined the Church. The Church then continued under the pastoral care of Elder Hubbard until Thursday, week before the 4th Saturday in April, 1852, when a protracted meeting commenced at Pleasant Hill. The meeting was conducted by Elder J. F. Smith, of Missouri, and Elder Hubbard, and 25 more were added to the Church, which made a majority of the Church who resided at and near Pleasant Hill. In consequence of this there was a call meeting at the school-house at Pleasant Hill to devise a plan for establishing a branch of the Martinsburg Church at Pleasant Hill. A petition was sent to the Martinsburg Church, signed by 37 members. In response to the petition it was decided best for the members to remain together as one Church, but meet twice per month instead of once, at Martinsburg on the 4th Saturday in each month, and at Pleasant Hill on the 2d Saturday, the Church when in session at Pleasant Hill to have the same power to transact any business, as at Martinsburg.

The Church flourished under the above arrangements, and under the pastoral care of Elder Hubbard until the spring of 1853, when the much esteemed Pastor left, with several other prominent members, and removed to Oregon Territory. However, destitute as the Church was, it had another protracted meeting at Pleasant Hill, in August, 1853, conducted by Elder Ingmire, from Pittsfield, and Smith and Music from Missouri, and another glorious revival was experienced, during which 23 more were converted.

The Church now continued under the pastoral care of Elders Ingmire, Music and Landrum, until the spring of 1857.

The members near Pleasant Hill wishing to be constituted an independent Church at Pleasant Hill sent a petition to the mother Church at Martinsburg, which was granted May 4, 1857; whereupon the following persons received letters of dismissal for that purpose:

NAMES.

*G. W. Gregory.	Sarah Simpson.	Susannah Lewis.
*Wm. Mitchell.	Eliza J. Venable.	S. H. Lewis.
*Susan Mitchell.	Redman Crews.	David Wilson.
Joseph D. Brooks.	*Winny Crews.	Isaphena Wilson.
Mary J. Brooks.	Ann E. Crews.	Keziah Lewis.
*Lawson Turner.	*G. W. Bybee.	Lauretta Smith.
*Susan Turner.	Rhoda C. Bybee.	Daniel Crossman.
*John Lapp.	*Jacob Windmiller.	Nathan Allison.
*Frances Lapp.	Sarah Windmiller.	Mary Ann Taylor.
*Jacob Emmert.	*Wm. Jackson.	Abigail Turnbaugh.
Eliza Emmert.	Frances Triplett.	Margaret Craigmiles.
Mary Collard.	Jacob Turnbaugh.	John N. Collard.
*John Sapp.	*Smith W. Leek.	Mary A. Collard.
John A. Thomas.	Wm. E. Smith.	G. W. Branson.
*Sarah E. Thomas.	Mary Smith.	*Lydia Sinklear.
E. T. Gresham.	Elijah Antery.	*Wm. Cannon.
*Elenor Gresham.	L. C. Lewis.	Joseph S. Davis.
	Elizabeth Davis.	*John Sinklear.

Those marked * are dead.

At the April meeting, after letters to the above persons were granted, John A. Thomas was appointed to prepare the Articles of Faith and Rules of Decorum, and advised to copy from the Church book of the Martinsburg Church. Arrangements were also made for constituting at the next meeting in May (1857), and M. M. Modisett and Albert Mitchell from Missouri were invited to attend and assist in organizing and constituting the Church.

The following are the Articles of Faith upon which this Church was organized and constituted at Pleasant Hill, the 2d Saturday in May, 1857:

ARTICLES OF FAITH.

Art. 1. That the Scriptures of the Old and New Testaments are the infallible word of God.

Art. 2. That there is but one only true God, and in the Godhead or divine essence, there are Father, Son, and Holy-Ghost.

Art. 3. That by nature we are fallen, depraved creatures.

Art. 4. That salvation, regeneration, sanctification and justification are by the life, death, resurrection and ascension of Jesus Christ, and the operation of the Holy Spirit.

Art. 5. That the saints will finally persevere through grace to glory.

Art. 6. That believers' baptism by immersion is necessary to the receiving of the Lord's Supper.

Art. 7. That the salvation of the righteous and punishment of the wicked will be eternal.

RULES OF DECORUM.

Rule 1.—The business of the Church to be done the 2d Saturday in each month (unless otherwise determined by the Church), beginning at 10 o'clock. Every male member failing to attend shall be accountable to the Church for such neglect.

Rule 2.—A Moderator and Clerk to be chosen by a majority of the voices present until others are chosen. The Moderator is to preside in the Church while at business; he is to keep order, but always under the control of the Church; he is to withhold his own opinion until all other members who wish to speak have spoken (except by request of the Church). He shall take the voice of the Church when called on for that purpose.

Rule 3.—When the Church has met, after prayer, members of sister Churches to be invited to seats in council, who may give their light or advice on any subject, but shall not vote in decision of the case.

Rule 4.—The door of the Church to be opened for the reception of members.

Rule 5.—The Moderator to inquire whether all are in peace and fellowship, or any one has any matter of complaint to bring forward that has been treated in gospel order.

Rule 6.—The unfinished business of the Church, if any, to be now attended to.

Rule 7.—Any brother having a motion to make in the Church shall rise to his feet and address the Moderator with brotherly respect; a motion thus made not to be attended to without a second.

Rule 8.—No brother to be interrupted while speaking, except he depart from the subject, on which the Moderator or any other brother may call to order, of which point of order the Church may judge when applied to for that purpose.

Rule 9.—No brother shall speak more than twice to any subject without permission from the Church.

Rule 10.—There shall be no laughing, talking or whispering in time of public service. Nor shall there be any ungenerous reflections on any brother that has spoken before.

Rule 11.—All the business of the Church to be done by a majority of the members present, except receiving and excluding members; the former must be unanimous; two-thirds may exclude.

Rule 12.—That brotherly l ve may continue, the 18th of Matthew is to be attended to in all cases so far as practicable in treating with our brethren, and in all uncommon cases the Church to be the judge, and in all public transgressions acknowledgments are to be made to the Church.

Rule 13.—We consider it the duty of members in removing their residence to distant bounds to apply to the Church for a letter of dismission and join some other Church with speed, or as soon as duty and prudence will dictate.

Rule 14.—We consider it our duty to be tender and affectionate to each other and study the happiness of the children of God in general, and to be engaged singly to promote the honor of God.

Rule 15.—We consider it disorderly to attend frolics, plays, horse-racing, grog-ops, and charivaries.

By order of the Church.

JOHN A. THOMAS, Church Clerk.

The last rule was introduced by Dr. Thomas, the Clerk.

BIOGRAPHICAL.

The further details of the history of Pleasant Hill township are best given in short biographical sketches of its pioneers and prominent citizens.

William Barton is engaged in farming on sec. 21; P. O., Pleasant Hill.

Edward Bybee, farmer and trader, sec. 17; P. O., Pleasant Hill; was born in Monroe county, Ky., in 1851, and is a son of George W. and Rhoda C. Bybee, natives also of Kentucky; when he was very young his parents emigrated with him to this county, where he grew to manhood, receiving a common-school education. In 1874 he married Fannie V. Hubbard, who was born in St. Louis, Mo., in 1852, and their children are Minnie E., Edna F. and Lenois D. Mr. Bybee has been prosperous in his business, and now owns 160 acres of land, mostly in the Mississippi Bottom, and all fenced. He and his wife are members of the Baptist Church.

Peter Craigmiles, salesman and clerk in a general store at Pleasant Hill, was born in 1838, in this county, and is the son of James and Margaret Craigmiles; in 1863 he married Sarah Emert, who was born in Pike county, Mo., and they have had 6 children, 5 of whom are living. Mr. C. is well known in the vicinity of Pleasant Hill, as he has been clerking in one store for 17 years, although the establishment has changed hands two or three times; he has also been Town Clerk, Collector and Township Treasurer.

Ingham Doman, deceased, was born May 31, 1813, in Hampshire county, Va., where he was reared on a farm and educated in a subscription school; in 1839 he married Miss Eve Kurtz, daughter of Martin and Mary Kurtz; she was born Aug. 24, 1823; of their 10 children these 8 are living,—Mary J., Sarah C., Jeremiah, Thomas B., Margaret C., Rachel M., Benjamin F. and Delilah A. A son named John W. lost his life from a wound received while fighting for the stars and stripes in the war. Mr. Doman emigrated with his family to Illinois in 1845, settling in Madison county, and in 1857 he came to this county, where he died Nov. 17, 1872, his death being a great loss to his family and to the community. He was a farmer during life. His father also was a patriot, being a soldier in the war of 1812.

Thomas O. Eddins, farmer, sec. 5; P. O., Pleasant Hill; was born in Albemarle county, Va., in 1838, and is a son of B. R. and Eliza Eddins, also natives of Virginia; receiving a common-school education and growing to manhood, he emigrated, in 1860, to this tp.; in 1865 he married Elizabeth Furguson, who was born in this county in 1845, the daughter of Edward and Catharine Furguson, and they have had 6 children. Mr. Eddins served 3 years in Co. A, 8th Mo. Inf., and fought in the battles of Forts Henry and Donelson, Shiloh, Haines' Bluff, Arkansas Post, siege of Vicksburg, Champion Hills, Corinth, Miss., and Kenesaw Mountain, in all of which he did not receive a scratch. He now owns 120 acres of land, worth $50 per acre, having been successful as a farmer. He is a member of the K. of H. Society, and his wife is a member of the M. E. Church.

Mrs. Patience W. McElfresh, sec. 18; P. O., Pleasant Hill; was born in 1821 in Pike county, Mo., and is a daughter of Richard and Ruth Keer, both natives of Kentucky. She came to this county when 14 years of age, and was married first in 1837 to Mr. James Wells, the second time in 1846 to Job Smith, and the third and last time to Aquila B. McElfresh. Altogether she has had 8 children. Her first and second husbands were farmers, and the last a Methodist preacher. She is a member of the Baptist Church. She has now been conducting the farm for 17 years, with a family of 3 children. Her only son is still living with her.

Dr. H. D. Fortune was born in 1841 in Pike county, Mo., and is a son of R. C. and Mary Fortune, natives of Virginia; he received a common-school education; at the age of 19 began the study of medicine under Dr. C. R. Bankhead, at Painesville, Mo.; attended the St. Louis Medical College, where he graduated March 1, 1865; practiced his profession at Painesville 18 months; then went to Prairieville, Pike Co., Mo., where he practiced 7½ years, and in 1874 came to Pleasant Hill, where he has been enjoying a growing practice. In September, 1865, he married Miss E. I. Dougherty, who was born in Pike county, Mo., about 1842, and they have had 4 children. The Doctor is a member of the M. E. Church, and his wife of the Baptist Church. He is also a Free Mason, and a member of the Town Board.

William S. Freeman was born in Pulaski county, Ky., in 1851, and is a son of Stephen F. Freeman, now of Martinsburg, where he was reared from the age of 4 years; April 8, 1874, he married Harriet A. Barton, daughter of Uriah Barton, and their two children are Ida A. and Flora M. Mr. Freeman has taught school during the winter season mostly for 12 years, with great success. He now follows farming during the summer seasons.

Joseph B. Galloway, farmer and stock-raiser, sec. 10; was born in Lincoln county, Mo., April 28, 1826, and is a son of James Galloway, deceased, so well known in the early settlement of this county. Joseph B. was brought up on a farm and educated in a subscription school. The family removed to this county in 1832,

and have therefore experienced the scenes of pioneer life in this
wild West. One day Mr. Galloway witnessed the capture of a fox
by the school boys and their dogs. So many dogs caught the animal at once that they held him stretched out at full length above
the ground for some time, which was a rather comical situation,—
that is, to the boys, not to the fox. Mr. G. remembers when the
only wagons used here were of the old Virginia style, and there
were but few of them. The plows consisted of a piece of iron for
a point, and a wooden moldboard. Mr. Galloway has pounded corn
in a "masher mill," which consisted of a wooden mortar and a
pounder attached to a spring-pole. He once went to where Eldara
now stands, a distance of 15 or 16 miles, to a horse-mill there to
get some corn ground. In a few years after this Mr. Zumwalt
erected a water mill on Bay creek. James Galloway was a very
strong man. Even at the age of 60 years he could in a wrestle
throw men of 24 years of age, and at the age of 72 he made a full
hand in the harvest field. He was an industrious farmer, and also
worked more or less in wood work. He was a soldier in the Black
Hawk war, as also were his two elder brothers, William and Samuel. He died Nov. 17, 1872, at the age of 76 years. He leaves
one brother, Zorobabel, and many other friends to mourn his loss.
He was a public-spirited man, and did much for the improvement
of this county. Joseph B. was married Sept. 30, 1847, to Miss
Sarah Jennings, and their 12 children are: Mary E., Tabitha E.,
dec., Thomas S., James D., Lydia A., S. Margaret, Bales H., William H., Sarah A., Ida E., Joseph F. and Nellie Grant.

J. B. Harl, miller, merchant, grain-dealer, etc.; was born in
Mason county, Ky., in 1841, the son of John and Mary Harl, natives also of the same State, who emigrated to Saline county, Mo.,
when their son was 12 years old; in 1863 he came to this county,
where in 1865 he married Miss Nancy C. Grimes, who was born in
1845 in this county. They have had three children. Soon after
Mr. Harl settled here he erected a mill 36 by 68 feet, and 4 stories
high, with a capacity of 50 barrels of flour per day; the machinery
is driven by a 40-horse power engine, and he is able to make the
highest grade of flour. His miller, Mr. T. J. Mitchell, has been
superintending the mill ever since it was erected. Mr. H. is also
engaged in the mercantile business, carrying a larger assortment
than any other house in town, selling goods at the lowest cash price.
He also buys and ships large quantities of grain; in fact, he is the
most enterprising business man in the place. He is a noble-hearted
man, and well liked by all who know him.

Alexander Hemphill, farmer, sec. 27; P. O., Pleasant Hill.
This man was born in Calhoun county, Ill., in 1847, and is a son
of A. F. and Jennie A. Hemphill; when he was quite young his
parents came with him into this county, where he received a common-school education and grew to manhood ; in 1877 he married
Eliza J. Turnbaugh, who was born in this county in 1852. They
have one child. Mr. H. has had ordinary success as a farmer,

owning now 40 acres of land, worth $40 an acre. He is a member of the I. O. O. F.

S. W. Hemphill, deceased, was born in Pike county, Oct. 9, 1826, and was a son of Alex. and Margaret Hemphill, deceased; brought up at farming, he has pursued the occupation through life. He went overland to California when a young man, and returned the following year. Oct. 26, 1854, he married Sarah Sapp, daughter of Jacob and Nancy Sapp, deceased; she was born Oct. 3, 1833, in this county. Mr. and Mrs. H. have had 8 children, of whom 4 are living, namely, Nancy M., Robert M., Louisa C. and Austin E. The deceased were John F., Jacob A., Mary L. and Sarah L. Mr. H. died Jan. 13, 1871, a great loss to his family and the community in which he had lived. Mrs. H. resides on the homestead, sec. 16.

Mrs. Cynthia Huber, daughter of George and Rose Ann Sitton, was born in this county in 1844; she received a common-school education, and in 1860 married Jacob Huber, who was born in this county in 1838, and they had 7 children, 3 of whom are living. Mr. Huber during his life followed the cattle trade, and died in 1876, a member of the Masonic order. Mrs. Huber's father was born in 1811 in Virginia, and her mother was a native of Ohio. P. O., Pleasant Hill.

Roswell Ladow, carpenter, is the son of Charles F. and Mary Ladow, father a native of New Jersey and mother of East Virginia; he was born in 1831 in Athens county, O., where he received his education, and in 1852 married Maria Green, a native of Meigs county, O. They had two children. Mrs. L. died May 18, 1877. Mr. Ladow tried milling a while, but not with signal success; he does much better at carpentering. He owns a farm of 45 acres of good land near Rockport. While he lived in Atlas tp. he was for a time Constable. He now resides on sec. 17, this tp. P. O., Pleasant Hill.

T. J. Mitchell was born in 1835 in this county, and is the son of William and Susan (Craigmiles) Mitchell, natives of Tennessee; he was reared on a farm, and at the age of 21 he learned the milling business, in which capacity he worked a while for Brown, Harl & Co. Mr. Mitchell married Miss A. Huber, who was born in this county in 1836. They had 3 children. She died in 1870, and in 1875 Mr. M. married Miss M. E. Waugh, who was born in 1845 in this county, and they have one child. Mr. Mitchell has held the office of Township Clerk, Assessor, Constable and Trustee. He is a Freemason. P. O., Pleasant Hill.

George W. Moore, teacher, was born in Lincoln county, Mo., April 5, 1840, and is a son of Wm. Moore, whose sketch is next given and who now lives in Pleasant Hill. Geo. W. has taught school ever since he was 16 years of age, except four years during the war. He was a member of the Missouri State militia for 9 months. Has also been Riding Constable 9 or 10 years in this township, and was Town Clerk here also for 3 years. Aug. 29, 1860, he

married Miss Sarah J. Allen, daughter of Cary Allen, deceased, and they have had 3 children, of whom 2 are living,—Charles H. and Noble. Mr. Moore resides in Pleasant Hill, and is teaching his third term at Jacobsville school-house, and has taught 8 terms in the Dodge district, near Pleasant Hill.

William Moore, the son of Benjamin and Frances Moore, was born in Madison county, Ky., Feb. 10, 1814. In 1828 Mr. Moore emigrated to Missouri, and in Lincoln county, that State, Sept. 1, 1833, he married Miss Margaret Gilliland, who was born in Simpson county, Ky., July 12, 1815, and was taken to Missouri when a babe; in 1861 they came to this tp. Their 11 children are, John, De Francis, Geo. W., Wm. R., James W., Benjamin F., Margaret A., Henry Clay, Amy June, Mary Louisa and Stephen A. Douglas. Mrs. M. is a member of the Baptist Church, and Mr. M. is a member of the Masonic order. He has been Justice of the Peace: was also Orderly Sergeant in the Black Hawk War. He is a blacksmith by trade, and is doing a good business. His father was at Yorktown, Va., at the surrender of Lord Cornwallis.

W. R. Moore, wagon and buggy manufacturer and undertaker, Pleasant Hill, is the son of William and Margaret Moore, natives of Kentucky, and was born in Lincoln county, Mo., in 1841; at the age of 20 he emigrated to this county, where in 1863 he married Miss Nancy M. Mitchell, who was born in Tennessee in 1846; of their 5 children 4 are living. Mr. Moore has followed his present business in Pleasant Hill since 1862. He served 6 months in Co. G, 5th Mo.; has been a member of the Town Board four times, and at present is a School Trustee. His wife died in 1872, and in 1875 he married Miss Olivia Carver, who was born in 1844 in this county, and of their 4 children 2 are living. Mr. and Mrs. M. are members of the Church.

N. L. Page, Principal of the Pleasant Hill school, was born in Menard county, Ill., Jan. 23, 1848, and is the son of E. L. Page; he was reared on the farm, received a good education, began teaching at the age of 21, and has taught school 11 years—4 years in Missouri, and 7 in this county. In Shelby county, Mo., June 19, 1869, he married Anna E. Confry, and their 4 children are Frederick L., Esther A., Carrie V. and Arthur I. Mr. Page is now teaching his second year in Pleasant Hill, and well exemplifies the principles of the eminent professor of the same name, the author of the "Theory and Practice of Teaching."

Albert Pearson, farmer, sec. 22; P. O., Pleasant Hill; was born in Brunswick county, Va., in 1821, and is the son of John and Mida Pearson, natives also of the Old Dominion; when he was 12 years of age his parents moved with him to Ohio, and at the age of 25 he moved to Missouri; after living there 14 years he came to this county. In 1852 he married Elizabeth Ralston, a native of Kentucky, and they had 3 children; she died, and he subsequently married Elizabeth Murray, who was born in Kentucky in 1824.

42

and of their 8 children 4 are living. Mr. P. has been reasonably successful as a farmer, and now owns 74 acres of good land.

Ira Roberts, farmer, sec. 5; son of David and Lovina Roberts, was born in Ohio in 1837; his father was a native of Vermont and his mother of New York State, and they moved with him to this county when he was 2 years old; here he grew to manhood, receiving a common-school education; in 1867 he married Elizabeth Jeans, who was born in 1844 in this county, and they have had 4 children. Mr. R. spent one year in California, to examine the country. He has good success in farming here, now owning 122½ acres of good land, mostly under cultivation, and he has good farm buildings. He and Mrs. R. are members of the Christian Church. Mr. R.'s father was a prominent preacher from 1839 to his death in 1855.

Isaac Shelby, deceased, son of Samuel Shelby, was born in East Tennessee Feb. 12, 1826; was reared on a farm and educated in the common school; Feb. 17, 1846, he married Miss Leah Capps, daughter of John and Elizabeth Capps, dec., who was also born in East Tennessee, Jan. 11, 1830; in the spring of 1847 they emigrated to this tp., where 10 children were born to them, namely, Sarah E., James, Samuel O., Orlando C., Isaac M., Martin H., William M., Walter S., Cynthia L. and Frank L., all of whom are living,—a rare incident indeed. Mr. Shelby was a hard-working man, following farming and stock-raising, in which he was successful. He was a merchant in Martinsburg 3 years. He was a worthy member of the Baptist Church for 30 years prior to his death, which occurred Oct. 25, 1874. In his death the community lost a valuable citizen and the family a kind father. Mrs. S. resides on sec. 11.

Solomon Shultz, deceased, was born Sept. 1, 1808, in Pennsylvania; reared on a farm and received a common-school education; Jan. 16, 1830, he married Lovina Taylor, who was born in Franklin county, O., Oct. 29, 1809, and they had 9 children, 5 of whom are living, to wit: Sarah J., Margaret, Eliza, Thomas J. and Nathan R. Mr. S. was a member of the Presbyterian Church, a generous man, aiding all charitable institutions and the prosperity of schools.

James A. Sitton, farmer, sec. 11; P. O., Pleasant Hill; was born in 1837 in this tp., and is a son of J. G. and Mary A. Sitton, his father a native of Tennessee, and his mother of Kentucky; he was educated in the common schools; in 1859 he married Christina Huber, who was born in 1839 in this county, and of their 8 children the following 6 are living: Anna L., W. R., Frankie G., Minnie S., John F. and Jesse P. Mr. Sitton's father came to this county in 1836, and is the oldest settler in this tp. now living here. James A. is a successful farmer, now owning 212 acres of land, well improved. He is a Freemason, and both he and Mrs. S. are members of the Baptist Church.

Thaddeus Smith, farmer, sec. 13; P. O., Pleasant Hill; was born in 1850 in Jefferson county, Ind., and is a son of Barton and Elizabeth Smith, the former a native of Indiana, and the latter of Ohio; in 1874 the family settled near New Salem, this county. In 1877 the subject of this notice married Mary E. Dodge, a native of this county, and they have one child. Mr. Smith has followed farming most of his life, though he has clerked in a dry-goods and grocery store and followed the agency business to some extent.

S. F. Sutton, farmer, sec. 9; P. O., Pleasant Hill; was born in 1834 in Barren county, Ky., and is a son of James and Elizabeth A. Sutton, the former a native of Kentucky, and the latter of Vermont; parents moved to Boone county, Mo., when our subject was 3 years old, and when he was 17 they returned to Kentucky, and in 1853 they emigrated to Pike county, Ill., locating in this tp. In 1856 Mr. S. F. Sutton married Martha J. Cruise, who was born in 1834 in Kentucky, and of their 9 children 8 are living. Mr. S. has followed agriculture through life, and by hard work has obtained a comfortable home of 100 acres of land, with the stock and buildings.

John A. Thomas, M. D. The ancestors of Dr. Thomas were natives of Wales who emigrated to the United States about 40 years previous to the Revolution, settling in Buckingham county, Va. Charles Thomas, a grandfather of the subject of this sketch, served under Gen. Washington during the war, and was one of the army which secured the surrender of Lord Cornwallis at Yorktown; after the close of the war he returned to his farm in Virginia, and a short time afterward he removed with his family to Patrick county in that State, where he followed farming; he also acted as Justice for many years, and was high Sheriff of the county two terms; he died about 1836, at the advanced age of 93 years. During his life he killed 300 deer, 65 bears and 44 panthers—in Patrick county. He left a family of 8 children, the next oldest being Cornelius Thomas, the father of John A.; he was born Oct. 16, 1778; followed farming in his native county until 1831, when he moved to Pike county, Mo., with his wife (whose maiden name was Elizabeth Slaughter) and 8 children,—Anna, Susannah, Joab, John A., Martin, Constantine, Smith S. and Francis Marion, the latter two being twins. In 1840 he moved into Lincoln county, and in 1860 came into Pike county, Ill., and lived with his son, Dr. John A., where he died in 1860, aged about 83. His wife died in Lincoln county, Mo., in 1857.

Dr. John A. Thomas was born in Patrick county, Va., April 8. 1818; his early years were employed on his father's farm, attending subscription school during the winter. The school-house was a common log building daubed with mud, having a dirt floor, greased paper for windows, benches made of split logs, and desks of the same material. At the age of 15 years he commenced the study of medicine, and not being with any regular physician he borrowed all the works he could; at the age of 17 he commenced teaching school in the winter, and taught four successive winters, in the meantime continuing his medical studies, and taking lectures from Dr. Ballard, of Louisiana, Mo. In 1843 he married Sarah Griffith near Louisiana, who was a native of Bourbon county, Ky., born in 1824; he then moved to the spot where Pleasant Hill now stands, where only three families were then living, and from that time, and in this place, the Doctor has continued the practice of medicine. He is a self-educated man, but the Missouri Medical College at St. Louis granted him a diploma on examination in 1859, and he has also been granted a certificate by the Illinois State Board of Health. He has one of the finest medical libraries in the county, and has done as much riding and gratuitous practice as any physician in Pike county. He spent several years in lecturing on the physiology of the brain, moral philosophy, etc. He has also been an ardent and zealous advocate of the temperance cause, and a devout Sunday-school man, often lecturing on both topics. He had the honor in 1879 of being President of the Pike County Sunday-School Convention. The Doctor owns 840 acres of land under cultivation, and 200 acres of timber, and is largely interested in the farming interests of the county. His residence cost $6,000. His first wife died in 1860, who had 6 children, 4 now living. The Doctor's second wife was Sophia Blair, who was born May 3, 1836, in this county, and they have had 5 children, 4 of whom are living. His present wife is a graduate of the Methodist Female College, Jacksonville, and was at the time they were married filling the Chair of Mathematics in that institution, although she was then a member of the Baptist church, and the only Baptist connected with the college. The names of his children by his former marriage are Joel Smith, who graduated at the Ohio Medical College in 1872, and married Mollie Wells; Melissa Margaret, married T. J. Shultz; Mary Jane C. married H. C. Moore, and Cornelius John A., who married Miss Dille Bower. The names of his children by his present wife are Albert Joab, William Sherman, and Clarence Crittenden. Dr. Thomas is a Freemason, and both himself and wife are members of the Baptist Church. The Doctor's portrait will be found in this book.

Edward B. Venable, deceased, was born in Pike county, Mo., in 1827, and was the son of John and Rachel Venable, natives of South Carolina; when he was 16 years of age his parents moved with him to this county; in 1848 he married Eliza Gresham, who was born in 1828 in Christian county, Ky.; and of their 8 children only Louisa is living. Mr. Venable followed farming the most of his life; was in other occupations some. He died Dec. 19, 1879, a member of the Masonic order. During life he was a Constable and Justice of the Peace, two terms each. Mrs. V. has a very nice residence in Pleasant Hill, and she and her daughter are members of the Baptist Church.

Harmon Weaver, farmer, sec. 1; P. O., Martinsburg; was born in 1816 in Franklin county, O., and is a son of Asa and Lucretia Weaver, father a native of Connecticut, and mother of Pennsylvania; when Harmon was 16 years of age his parents moved with him to Delaware county, O., and in 1839 they came to this county; they settled in this township in 1851 or 1852. In 1838 Mr. Weaver married Sarah Roberts, who was born in 1820 in Delaware county, O., and 9 of their 10 children are living. Mr. Weaver has been School Director, and has followed farming with good success, now owning 280 acres of valuable land. He and his wife are members of the Christian Church.

Z. T. Webster, farmer, sec. 19; P. O., Pleasant Hill; was born in 1827 in Washington county, Ky., the son of James and Ada Webster, also natives of Kentucky; when he was 8 years old his parents moved with him to Mc Donough county, Ill., and in 1842 to this county, locating on the present homestead. In 1851 he married Margaret Briscoe, who was born in 1826 in Kentucky, and they had one child, who is now dead. Mrs. B. died in 1852, and Mr. W. married again, in 1854, Margaret J. Davis, who was born in this county in 1830, and they have had 4 children, all now living. Mr. Webster commenced in life without anything, and by honest industry he has now a comfortable home with 575 acres of good land, 455 of which are on the Mississippi bottom.

G. W. Wells, farmer, sec. 18; P. O., Pleasant Hill; was born in 1855 in this county, and is a son of Perry and Elizabeth Wells, father a native of Kentucky and mother of Missouri. G. W. received a common-school education, and in 1876 he married Miss Miriam Webster, daughter of Henry and Ellen Webster, who was born in 1858 in this county. Of their 5 children 2 are deceased. As a farmer Mr. Wells has had fair success, now owning 93 acres of bottom land.

Perry Wells, farmer, sec. 7; P. O., Pleasant Hill. This gentleman was born in 1814 in Madison county, Ky., the son of Richard and Mary Wells, the former a native of Pennsylvania and the latter of Kentucky. When Perry was young his parents moved with him to Missouri; in 1837 he came into this county. In 1840 he married his first wife, Miss Elizabeth J. Kerr, a native of Missouri. They had 6 children. Mrs. W. died in 1862, and he was again married in 1863 (May 5) to Miss Kate Tisler, who was born in 1836 in this county, and they have had 2 children. Mr. Wells commenced in life in very limited circumstances, but he now has 1,200 acres of land. The family are all members of the M. E. church at Stockland.

F. L. Zerenberg, farmer, sec. 14; P. O., Pleasant Hill. This man was born in 1837 in this county, and is the son of Charles and Christina Zerenberg, natives of Germany, who came to the United States in 1832, first settling in Pennsylvania, afterward (1834) in Pike county, Ill. The subject of this notice obtained a common-school education, and in 1858 he was married to Eliza Venable, who was born in 1838 in Pike county, Mo. They have had two children, but one has died. Mr. Z. has lived on the present farm since 1862; has followed farming all his life; he now owns 225 acres of good high land. In respect to public office Mr. Z. has been School Director, Road Commissioner, Supervisor, Collector and Assessor. He is a member of the Masonic order.

William Zerenberg, farmer and stock-raiser, sec. 14; was born in this county Feb. 27, 1843, and is a son of Charles Zerenberg, deceased, who was well known as an early settler in Pike county. Wm. was reared on a farm. At the age of 18 he enlisted in Co. C, 10th Mo. Inf., and took part in the battles of Champion Hills, siege of Vicksburg, Mission Ridge, siege of Corinth, etc. He was honorably discharged Aug. 31, 1864. In 1866 he married Mary E. Galloway, daughter of J. B. Galloway, of Pleasant Hill tp. Their two children are Laura A. and Francis B.

HADLEY TOWNSHIP.

This is a magnificent township, and for agricultural purposes is surpassed by few in the Military Tract. It is what may be properly termed a prairie township. The sight presented to the early settler must have been pleasant as he viewed this beautiful nature's lawn, now thickly studded with houses, orchards, hedges and all the insignia of healthy cultivation, before a furrow was struck or anything to disturb the eye nearer than the curling smoke of three or four cabins along the edges of the timber.

The first settler in this township after the Indians had been driven Westward, was not a white man, but a colored one. He was known as " Free Frank," and came with his wife and three children to this township, and located on sec. 22, in 1829. He was from Kentucky, and had spent the preceding winter in Greene county, Ill. He had purchased his freedom and that of his family. To conform to the custom of the age the Legislature gave Free Frank a surname, viz: McWorter, and he was always afterward known as Frank McWorter.

After Mr. McWorter had been recognized by the Legislature, in order to conform to the law he must be re-married. Accordingly he and his wife presented themselves for that purpose before Esq. Neeley. When McWorter was asked if he would live with, cherish and support, etc., his wife, he replied, " Why, God bless your soul! I've done that thing for the last 40 years."

Mr. McWorter was a live, enterprising man, a reputable, worthy citizen, kind, benevolent and honest. He labored hard to free his posterity from the galling yoke of Southern slavery. He not only purchased his own freedom and that of his wife and children, but left provision in his will to buy grandchildren, which was done by his son. He died in 1857 at the ripe old age of 77. His wife died in 1871, at the very advanced age of 99. Many of their descendants are still living in the township.

The first white settler to locate in Hadley was Joshua Woosley. This veteran still resides here, living on his farm, on sec. 19, in the suburbs of Barry. He came in 1830, cut logs, and built the second house in the township, the first being erected by McWorter. Then came Charles Hazelrigg, who settled on sec. 33. Dean Peterson located on sec. 36. Then followed Daniel Clingensmith, Reuben Shipman, Anson Gray, Isaac Moore, James Dutton, William

Wilkinson, Stephen R. Watson, Joseph Shelley and William Farmer. These pioneers were all Southerners, mostly from Kentucky and Tennessee.

These early pilgrims often had their ingenuity taxed to its utmost in order to perform needed labor with the existing tools. Necessity being the mother of invention, they generally found some practical way to do their work. What if it did take more time to perform the labor? That was of but little consequence, as time in those early days was abundant. The pioneers did not rush along over prairies, through dale and woodland at the rate of 40 miles an hour, as is done at present. Nor could they cut eight and ten acres of wheat in a day; indeed, they did not have any of the labor-saving implements so common now. Joshua Woosley relates that in the spring of 1831 he and Mr. Bradshaw broke some prairie together. They tied up a yoke of oxen to a big bar-share plow with hickory bark, not having chains sufficient or any other better article. The plow needing sharpening, he was compelled to go to Atlas, a distance of 20 miles, to have it done. The charge for this work was not large, however, as he tells us his total bill for the work, dinner, drinks, etc., was only " nine-pence " (12½ cents).

Mr. Woosley used the first grain cradle in the township, charging a bushel of wheat per acre for cutting. This new method of cutting wheat was a great curiosity to the settlers, many of whom came from far and near to see it.

The pioneers did not have a well-stocked store of provisions always at hand. No, often the last particle of corn meal was used up before another supply was obtained. Mills were then far away, and so crowded that often customers had to wait for days before their turn would come. Mr. Woosley tells us that on one occasion some men came to stay over night with him. It happened that they had no meal prepared, but the block was handy, and while his wife was busying herself in the house, he went out and pounded up some corn with an iron wedge. These we give as illustrations of the many privations and inconveniences under which these pioneers were compelled to live. They were sturdy, brave-hearted people though, and conquered all of these obstacles and brought a wild country under the very highest state of cultivation.

The first child born in the township was Jane, daughter of Joshua Woosley. She was born in 1834, and married Milton Deran. Mrs. Jane Gray, wife of Anson Gray, was the first person to die. The first marriage ceremony was performed in uniting A. M. Robinson and Miss Mary Gray in wedlock. The ceremony was performed by Esq. Woosley at the house of Anson Gray in 1844.

The first school building erected in the township was on sec. 19, in 1836. The first teacher was James Frier.

The Wabash railroad passes through the township and has a station on sec. 22, or on the line of secs. 21 and 22.

The town of Philadelphia was laid out by the elder McWorter in 1836, on the northeast quarter of sec. 27. At one time it had great promise, but the railroad passing it a mile distant, and other towns springing up, has killed it. At present there is not even a postoffice at the place.

The township is well supplied with churches and schools, which indicate the high moral and intellectual standard of the people.

PERSONAL SKETCHES.

In connection with and as a part of the history of the township, we will give personal sketches of the leading and representative people who reside here.

Barton W. Alkire, whose portrait we present in this volume, was born in Pickaway county, O., March 4, 1823. His parents were Geo. and Catharine (Rush) Alkire, natives of Virginia, and of German descent. George Alkire was left an orphan at 10 years of age, and he then found his way to Fleming county, Ky., where he remained until he was 17, and he then went to Ross county, O., and thence to Pickaway county; here, at the age of 23, he married Miss Catharine Rush, aged 16; in 1841 they emigrated to this tp., settling on sec. 31, and bringing with them four children,—Mary, Rebecca, Barton W. and Abner, now deceased. They left four children in Ohio,—Wesley J., Lydia, Gideon and Josiah,—who came out the next year. During his life-time Mr. Geo. Alkire owned and lived on his farm in Hadley, but left the charge of it to his sons. He had been a member of the Christian Church ever since he was 17 years old, and for a long period before his death he was a minister of the gospel. He died July 21, 1868, and his surviving widow died April 9, 1873. Barton W. Alkire, the subject of this sketch, is a farmer and stock-raiser by occupation, his residence and farm of 140 acres being on sec. 31, Hadley tp. He passed his early years on his father's farm in Ohio, and in this county, obtaining his education mostly in the schools of Ohio. He has lived on his present place since 1841, except 1849–50 he was in California, gold-mining, in which he was quite successful. Mr. A. is one of the solid, substantial and representative farmers of Pike county; in politics is a Republican, and has served his township as Collector several terms. He is still a bachelor, his two sisters, Mary and Rebecca, keeping house for him. They are very pleasantly situated.

James W. Bower, farmer, sec. 27; P. O., Cool Bank; is a native of Ohio and was born Jan. 25, 1836; was the eldest child of Joseph Bower, who came to this county in 1838 and died in the spring of 1844. He was educated in the common schools of this county, and in the spring of 1857 married Rebecca Ann Coshon, a native of Indiana, born June 6, 1839. Three of their five children are living: Rebecca E., born Dec. 18, 1860, Sarah Olive, born Aug. 30, 1855, and George Washington, born July 10, 1869. Mr.

Bower moved to Bourbon county, Kan., in the fall of 1858 and returned in 1863. He is Director of the district in which he lives, and is a Republican.

Orin Campbell is a farmer, and resides on sec 21.

J. S. Carson is following the vocation of agriculture on sec. 29.

P. H. Cleveland is also a farmer, and lives on sec. 9, this township.

Marion Clingensmith, farmer, sec. 19; P. O., Barry; was born Dec. 20, 1848, on the farm where he now lives. His collegiate course was taken at Lombard University, Knox county, Ill. June 5, 1873, he married Lucinda E. Graybael, a native of Monroe Co., Ind.; they have had 3 children, 2 of whom are living: Marcia B., born May 30, 1875, and Anna M., born May 27, 1878. Mr. C. has been a School Director at different times. Is a Republican, and in relig ion a Universalist.

George Conrad, farmer, sec. 14; P. O., Baylis; was born in 1820 in Wayne county, Mo., and is a son of Peter and Sarah Conrad, natives of North Carolina, who emigrated to Missouri the spring before George's birth, and are now both deceased. Besides attending the public schools of Missouri the subject of this notice also attended for 7 years the Mission Institute at Quincy, Ill. He came to this county in 1851, and in 1857 he went to Blue Earth county, Minn., and in 1869 returned to this county, settling on sec. 14, this tp. In 1851 he married Miss M. L. Shipman, who was born in 1821 in Hartford county, Conn. They have had 5 children, 4 of whom are living, to wit: David C., C. J., Jesse B. and A. G. At the time of the outbreak of the Sioux in Minnesota Mr. C. and many of his neighbors left their homes until danger was over, and in their absence large quantities of grain and other perishable property was destroyed. Mr. Conrad has held the office of Road Commissioner and Justice of the Peace, has taught school some, but his occupation has principally been farming. Mr. and Mrs. C. are members of the Congregational Church.

Orange Cram, farmer, sec. 16, of Hadley; P. O., Barry; was born in Ackworth, Sullivan county, N. H., Feb. 16, 1803, and is the second son of Jesse and Lydia Cram. In 1823 he moved to Concord, Lake county, O., where he was married in 1825 to Susan Carroll, a native of that county; they have 6 living children. In 1866, Mr. C. settled in this tp.; has been a Republican, but is now identified with the Greenback party. He owns 40 acres of valuable land in a good state of cultivation.

George Cunningham, farmer, sec. 8; P. O., Barry; was born in Fayette county, Penn., Aug. 9, 1809. In 1826 he began learning the tanner's trade, and in 1830 moved to Harrison county, O., where he started a tannery of his own and continued the business for 12 years. His grandfather, Barnett Cunningham, came from Scotland at a very early day. His father, Joseph H. Cunningham, was born in the house where the subject of this sketch was reared. In 1831 he married Mary Ann Humphrey, who died March 3,

1851, leaving 7 children. In April 30, 1878, he married Mrs. Elizabeth Hoyle, a native of Warren county, O., born Feb. 16, 1836. Mr. C. has been School Director 9 years. In 1866 he came to this county and purchased the farm where he now resides. He is a member of the I. O. of O. F., and is the oldest member in the county. Politically, he is a staunch Democrat.

Jasper Davis, farmer, sec. 18; P. O., Barry; was born on his present farm, July 19, 1843. His parents, Wm. and Mary E. Davis were among the earliest settlers of Pike county. Mr. W. Davis was born in Union county, Ill., Oct. 25, 1813, and Mrs. D. was born in Erie county, O., Oct. 1, 1820; her maiden name was Bushnell. Her family emigrated to Fulton county, Ill., and the town in McDonough county that bears the family name was named after her uncle. Dec. 25, 1876, Mr. J. Davis married Margaret Broady, a native of Adams county, Ill., born April 15, 1846; they have one child, Wm. Calvin, born Nov. 25, 1877. Mr. D. is Commissioner of Public Highways, and politically a Republican.

John H. Davis, farmer, sec. 20; P. O., Barry; was born in Fayeett county, Penn., June 1, 1835; he assisted his father during summer and attended district school during winter, until he was 16 years old; he then came, with his father's family, to this town. John H. is the 9th of 11 children. In 1859 he married Miss Emma Ward, who died 4 years after, leaving 2 sons. In Dec., 1865, he married Elizabeth E., daughter of E. D. Rose, of Pittsfield, born Feb. 4, 1839. They have 2 children. Mr. Davis owns 143 acres of valuable land, and it is well improved. He is a Republican, and a Methodist.

Anthony Dell, farmer, sec. 22; P. O., Cool Bank; was born in Madison Co., Ill., Nov. 23, 1841; came with his father to Pittsfield when but 8 years of age; in 1867 married Miss Jane Crone, and they have 3 children. In 1861 he enlisted in the 2d Ill. Cavalry, and served to the close of the war. He is a Republican.

Benjamin Dulan, farmer, sec. 23; P. O., Baylis; was born in Ralls county, Mo., in March, 1828; was married in 1848, and has 7 children; in 1863 moved to Adams Co., and to Pike Co. the following March. He is a Republican, and member of the Baptist Church.

Squire Dutcher was born in Dutchess county, N. Y., Sept. 6, 1806. His father, Gideon Dutcher, was a farmer, and Squire assisted him in the summer and went to district school in the winter. At the age of 11 his father moved to Chatham Co., N. Y., where he died, leaving a widow and 10 children, of whom our subject is the 7th. In 1823 or 1824 he moved with his mother's family to Rensellaer county, where he learned the trade of carpenter and joiner. In 1827 he married Charlotte Winchell, who died in 1837. They had 2 children. In the fall of the same year he married Eliza A. Townsend, and they had 3 living children. Mrs. Dutcher died July 29, 1879. Mr. D.'s oldest son, Charles H., is professor at the South Normal School at Cape Girardeau, Mo. His second son, Albert, is in the jewelry business at Kirksville, Mo. One, Edgar, went to California in 1849, and has not been heard from in a number of years. Mr. Dutcher came to this Co. in 1839, owns a beautiful farm of 66 acres adjoining the city of Barry; is a Republican, and Adventist; has been Township Collector of Hadley.

Stephen M. Dutcher, farmer, sec. 28; P. O., Barry; was born in Dutchess county, N. Y., April 5, 1810. When he was quite young his parents moved to Columbia county, N. Y., where he received his education during the winter months in a district school. During summer he assisted his mother in the cultivation of the farm until he was 16 years of age. He then learned the carpenter and joiner trade. In 1834 he removed to Chenango county, N. Y., where he was married in 1835 to Miss Mary Hunt, a native of that county, born May 6, 1808. He worked at his trade until 1845, and then came to this county and purchased his present farm, where he has since resided. Mr. and Mrs. Dutcher have 5 living children,—3 sons and 2 daughters. His son Henry enlisted in 1861 in the 99th Reg. I. V., and served to the close of the war. He is a Greenbacker, and member of the Christian Church.

Charles J. Ford was born on sec. 16, Hadley tp., Sept. 7, 1843; educated in the district school; Dec. 23, 1869, he married Miss Keziah Cunningham, daughter of George Cunningham, of this tp., and they have 3 children. He owns 80 acres of land in a good state of cultivation; he is School Director of this district.

Jerry Gelvin, farmer, sec. 21; P. O., Cool Bank; was born in Washington Co., Va., June 27, 1818; educated in the same county, in the district schools; in 1838 he moved to Wayne Co., Ky., and in 1841 was married in Pulaski Co., Ky., to Miss Harriet Qualls, daughter of Judge Tunstall Qualls, who was a member of the 25th Congress, and Judge of his Circuit up to the time of his death. Six of their 9 children are now living. In 1852 he moved to Pike county, where he has since lived, and is at present agent of the Wabash, St. Louis & Pacific Railroad at Hadley Station; is Postmaster of Cool Bank postoffice, and largely engaged in buying grain. He owns 160 acres of very valuable land. Politically he is a Democrat.

William A. Gordon, deceased, was born in Ohio, Feb. 15, 1817. In early life he assisted his parents on the farm; in 1838 he came to Pike county, where he was married in 1844 to Sophia R., daughter of James and Elizabeth Burbridge, a native of Pickaway Co., O.; was born Jan. 1, 1827. They have one son, James D., born Oct. 21, 1853, and now married to Mary E. Wike, and who have one child, Gertrude. Mr. Gordon died Sept. 26, 1874, a man of sterling worth.

William Grammer, farmer, sec. 30; P. O., Barry; born in Boston, Mass., Jan. 8, 1822; educated in Malden, Mass.; in 1840 he moved to this township, settling on sec. 2, where he has lived up to 4 years ago. In 1846 he married Eliza Philpot, a native of England, but a resident of Perry, Ill. She died in 1866, leaving one child, Maria B., now Mrs. Blake. In January, 1874, he married Mrs. McTucker, widow of John McT. In 1851 he was elected Supervisor of Hadley and held the office 24 years. In 1867 he married his second wife, Miss Lucy H. Smith, who died in 1872. He is a Republican.

Benj. F. Gray, blacksmith and wagon and buggy manufacturer, Philadelphia; P. O., Cool Bank; was born in 1840 in this county, and is a son of Anson and Jane Gray, who came from Ohio to this place in early day. After receiving a fair public school education and growing to manhood, Benj. F. in 1868 married Mary Ann Hall, and by her had one child, Sophia A. Mrs. Gray died in 1869, and Mr. Gray in 1870 married Elizabeth Ann Mellon, who was born in 1848 in Washington county, Pa., and they have had 3 children, Lena May, Gertrude and Nina A. Mr. Gray has followed farming, but by trade is a blacksmith and manufacturer of wagons and buggies, which business he has followed for a number of years. He was 3 years in the war, in Co. K, 99th Ill. Inf. Politically he is a Republican.

Howard A. Graybael, farmer, sec. 31; P. O., Barry; was born in Monroe Co., Ind., June 22, 1842; received a common-school education; in 1864 removed to this tp.; in 1870, in St. Charles Co., Mo., married Miss Mary A. Miller, a native of that county; they have 2 children, Adella, born Aug. 27, 1872, and Lloyd, Aug. 25, 1879. He owns 80 acres of very valuable land, as fertile as this county affords. In politics he is a Democrat.

James M. Green, farmer, sec. 31; P. O., Barry; was born in Barry tp., June 13, 1845, the 3d son of 9 children of P. D. S. Green, of Barry tp., and a native of Rensellaer Co., N. Y., who came to this county in early day. James M. took two courses in Lombard University at Galesburg, Ill. In 1866 he married Addie M. Hollenbeck, who died Sept. 14, 1870, leaving one child, Nora. In 1874 he married Hannah Tilden, a native of Franklin Co., N. Y., born Sept. 23, 1848. He owns 120 acres of good land, and is a Republican.

D. P. Guss, farmer, sec. 6; P. O., Barry; was born in 1841 in Pennsylvania, and is the son of William and Eliza Guss, natives also of the Keystone State, who emigrated to this county when their son was 7 years old, and are still living in this county. D. P. was educated in the common schools here. In 1860 he married Miss Mary J. Lawton, who was born in 1845 in this county, and they have 2 children, Charlie E. and Ollie M. From poverty Mr. Guss has risen to become the owner of a nice home of 160 acres of land worth $35 an acre. He is a Freemason, and in politics is a Democrat.

H. L. Hadsell, farmer, sec. 15; P. O., Barry. This gentleman was born in 1842, in this county, and is a son of N. V. and Elizabeth J. Hadsell, both natives of New York, who came to this county in 1834, thus being early pioneers here. H. L. obtained a public-school education, and when 19 years of age he enlisted in

Co. I, 28th Ill. Inf., as private, Aug. 3, 1861, and was promoted 2d
Lieutenant in October, 1862; in 1863 he was again promoted 1st
Lieutenant, and in 1864 he was promoted Captain of Co. F, 28th
Ill. Inf., under Gen. Grant. His first engagement was at Belmont,
Mo.; he then went to Paducah, then to Fort Henry, Pittsburg Landing, Corinth, Holly Springs, Vicksburg during the siege, Jackson (where he engaged in a hard-fought battle), Natchez, to do
provost duty on account of meritorious conduct, where he remained
one year; then to New Orleans, then Mobile. While on the way
to Mobile the troops were shipwrecked, but no one was lost; took
a well fortified fort at Mobile Point; then was engaged in the
siege of Spanish Fort, Ala., which place surrendered after a month's
siege; then he was in the siege of Fort Blakely, which also surrendered in 1864, these places being the key to Mobile, already taken.
Gen. Canby took Mobile, under whose command Capt. Hadsell was
at the time; then the Captain with his force was ordered to Brownsville, Texas, where he remained until his discharge, April 6, 1866.
He then returned home and engaged in farming, which he has followed ever since with success, now owning 200 acres of land worth
$60 per acre. In 1866 he married Miss Adda Baker, who was born
in 1843 in Hamilton county, O., and they have had 2 children, to
wit: Laura M. and Leon V. The Captain and his wife are members of the Free-will Baptist Church.

John D. Hamilton, farmer, sec. 34; P. O., Barry; was born in
Ayrshire, Scotland, Sept. 29, 1836. In 1845 his father died,
and in 1850 his mother, with a family of 4 children, emigrated to
this country and settled in St. Louis, Mo. In the fall of 1854
John D. moved to Quincy, Ill., and in 1861, to Pike Co., and settled on his present farm, which he had purchased some time previously. In 1870 he married Annie Shaw, a native of this county,
and they have 3 children,—Thomas, Ida and Alexander. He is a
member of the M. E. Church and a Republican.

Albert E. Hays, farmer, sec. 16; P. O., Cool Bank; was born
in Franklin county, O., Oct. 27, 1832. In 1846 he came with his
parents to this county, and in 1864 was married to Margaret Pierce,
who died in the fall of 1867, leaving one child, Wm. In 1870 he
married Mabel Norris, and their children are: Lillian, May,
Oscar N., Kate and Bertie E. Mr. H. owns 80 acres of land, and
is a Greenbacker.

Pulaski Hays, farmer, sec. 9; P. O., Barry; was born in Franklin county, O., April 13, 1845. While yet in his infancy his
parents, Richard and Catharine Hays came to this county and settled in Hadley tp. In 1868 he married Nannie Quarles, and their
2 children are Harry and Clarence. He owns 120 acres of land,
and is a Republican.

Theodore Hays, farmer, sec. 16; P. O., Barry; was born in
Franklin county, O., in 1836; came West in 1846, and with his
parents settled in this county, where his early education was obtained. In 1862 he married Miss Mary Johnson and they have 6

children. He is a Republican and owns 120 acres of first-rate land.

J. B. Hill is a farmer, residing on sec. 28.

Harlow Huntley, farmer, sec. 10; P. O., Cool Bank; was born in Oneida county, N. Y., July 19, 1806; is the eldest of 6 children of Amos and Addie Huntley, early settlers of that county. His grandfather, Amos Huntley, sen., was a revolutionary soldier. Mr. H. emigrated with his parents to Alleghany county, N. Y., when he was 3 years old. Here he was raised and educated. He assisted on the farm, and at the age of 20, married Elmira Partridge, a native of Hampshire county, Mass., who died Sept. 19, 1877, leaving 10 children. He has been a resident of this county since 1843; in 1850 was elected Justice of the Peace and held the office till 1877, and is at the present time Treasurer of this tp. During his residence here he has accumulated 1,000 acres of land, which he has divided among his 3 sons. He was raised a Jackson Democrat, but at the breaking out of the Rebellion he aided largely in the organization of the Republican party, in whose ranks he was found till 1878, since which time he has been a zealous Greenbacker.

George B. Kimball, farmer, sec. 4; P. O., Barry; was born in Worcester, Norfolk county, Mass., in 1831. At the age of 6 years his parents, David and Rebecca Kimball, moved to this county, where he was raised and educated. In 1854 he married Mary Osborn, a native of Ohio, born Aug. 10, 1836, and they have 4 sons and 4 daughters. He is a Republican, and owns 170 acres of land.

Francis McCartney, farmer, sec. 19; P. O., Barry; was born in Ross county, Ohio, Sept. 22, 1811; was raised on a farm and assisted his father until 1832, when he married Eliza Johnson, also a native of Ross county, and was born Aug. 30, 1811. Of their 10 children 5 are living. In the fall of 1850 Mr. M. moved to Pike Co., and purchased the beautiful farm on which he now resides. In 1861 his son Charles enlisted in the 99th Reg., and served during the entire war. His son, Milton, enlisted in 1865, and served to the close. Mr. M. is a Democrat.

John R. McClain, farmer, sec. 32; P. O., Barry; was born in Knox county, Tenn., Nov. 12, 1844; is the youngest of 9 children. In April, 1862, he enlisted in Co. D, 6th Reg. T. V. I., and served in several of the engagements in Sherman's march to the sea. He was mustered out at Nashville, Tenn., in 1865, after which he returned home for a short time, and then moved to near Lexington, Kentucky. In the fall of 1870 he came to this county; in 1871 he married Sarah E. Shaw, daughter of Daniel Shaw, of Derry tp., born March 13, 1841. They have 3 children,—Annie E., James D. and May. Mr. McClain is cultivating a valuable farm in Hadley and Derry tps., is a Republican and a Baptist.

Patrick McMahan is a farmer, pursuing his calling on sec. 9.

Jacob Orebaugh, farmer, sec. 6; P. O., Barry; was born in Rockingham county, Va., July 17, 1824; at the age of five years he moved with his parents to Highland county, O., where he was raised and educated. In 1846 he married Emma Predmore, a native of N. J., and they have 4 living children. In 1856 he settled in this tp.; has been School Director: is a Baptist and a Republican.

James H. Orebaugh, farmer, sec. 8; P. O., Barry; was born in Clermont county, O., June 9, 1852, and came to this county with his parents when he was five years of age. When 15 years old he visited 8 or 10 different States, and in 1876 came home, and was married Jan. 1, 1878, to Sarah C. Matthews, daughter of Joseph Matthews, deceased, of Adams county, Ill. They have one child, Nellie Maud. He is a member of the German Baptist church.

David H. Patten, farmer, sec. 14; P. O., Baylis; was born in Belmont county, O., in 1841, and is the son of David and Eliza Patten, who emigrated to this county about 38 years ago, and have since died. Receiving a common-school education and growing up to manhood, David H. in 1862 married Miss Alice States, who was born in 1847 in this county, and still resides on the old homestead. Their 4 children are Charlie, Lulu, Merton and Harry. Mr. P. has had good success in farming, now owning 320 acres of first-rate land, well improved. In politics Mr. P. is a Democrat; is a member of the I. O. O. F., and both himself and wife are members of the M. E. Church.

William A. Peck, farmer, sec. 21; P. O., Barry; was born in Ross county, Ohio, May 27, 1842; came to this county when 5 years old. In 1864 was married to Jessie Wilson, a native of Scotland. They have 6 children. He is at present School Director, and in politics he is a Democrat.

Dean Peterson, farmer, sec. 36; P. O., Baylis; was born in 1804, in Salem county, Upper Penn's Neck, N. J., and is the son of Robert and Catharine Peterson; his father was a native of Delaware and his mother of New Jersey, both deceased. In 1821 his parents moved with him to Ohio where they remained until 1836, when they emigrated to this county and settled on sec. 36, his present residence. The subject of this notice being a pioneer in this section, has had to work very hard, amid many privations: has had to split rails at 25 cents per day; by littles he accumulated enough to enter 80 acres of land, and he now owns 120 acres. Sept. 18, 1834, he married Miss Catharine Troy, who was born in Clermont county, O., and they have had 11 children, 9 of whom are living. Dean first learned the shoemaker's trade, but not liking that business, he engaged in farming, having had reasonable success. He is still a stout man for his years. He has visited the Pacific coast. He has been Supervisor and School Director, and in politics is a Democrat.

Josiah W. Richards, deceased, was born in Boston, Mass., Nov. 21, 1811. March 3, 1835, he married Margaret Phillips, who was born July 16, 1812, and died Oct. 3, 1849, leaving 3 daughters. March 21, 1852, Mr. R. married Esther Garraux, who was born Oct. 23, 1817, and who, by her first marriage, had one daughter.

HADLEY T?

Mr. and Mrs. Richards had 3 children. In 1837 Mr. R. came to Macoupin Co., Ill., where he lived 4 or 5 years, then moved to St. Louis, Mo. Dec. 1, 1853, he again moved to Illinois and settled in this county, where he died Jan. 4, 1866. He was a Republican.

James Rossell, farmer, sec. 29; P. O., Barry. Mr. R. was born in 1845 in Pennsylvania; his parents were Joseph and Aditha Rossell, both natives of Pennsylvania; when he was 6 years of age his parents emigrated with him to this county, where he obtained a public-school education and grew to manhood; in 1870 he married Alice M. Haycraft, who was born in 1850 in this county. Mr. R. is a farmer, owning 181 acres of No. 1 land, and is now erecting a dwelling at a cost of $3,000. He is also a stock-raiser, and sometimes does something in the line of shipping wheat.

Ira A. Sweet, farmer and stock-raiser, sec. 32; P. O., Barry; was born in Rensellaer county, N. Y., Sept. 1, 1820, and is the eldest son of Ira and Sarah (Hadsell) Sweet, also natives of the Empire State; they first emigrated to Alleghany county, N. Y., in 1837, and then in May of the following year to this county, settling in this tp., where in 1844 the parents died, leaving the care of the property with Ira A., the subject of this sketch; the latter had but limited opportunities for an early education; in this county, Oct. 30, 1856, he married Miss Martha Hewitt, who was born in Ross county, O., Sept. 6, 1821; when first married he had about $15.00 worth of property; he now owns 191 acres of land, worth $50 per acre. He raises and deals in young cattle and other stock. In politics he is a Republican, and in religion a Baptist. His portrait appears in this volume.

Robert H. Taylor, farmer, sec. 36; P. O., New Salem. Mr. T. was born in 1842 in this county; his parents are Matthew M. and Eliza Taylor, natives of Pennsylvania; was educated in this county, and in 1866 he married Sarah A. Sharer, who was born in 1847 in this county. Their 3 children are Jacob E., Jesse A. and Matthew R. Mr. Taylor is a farmer of considerable note, owning 168 acres of good land, where he raises some stock. Mr. and Mrs. T. are members of the M. E. Church. In politics Mr. T. is a Democrat.

Thomas H. Thomas, farmer, sec. 33; P. O., Barry; was born in St. Louis county, Mo., Sept. 15, 1851; is the son of Thomas Thomas, deceased, who came to this county in 1857. He was raised in slavery by Mr. Pernod, who gave him his freedom. Shortly before he came to Illinois he purchased the freedom of his wife, who was also born in slavery in the same neighborhood. Her name was Sophia Patiese. They were married in 1850, and they have 5 living children, the subject of this sketch being the oldest. He was married Dec. 30, 1875, to Dasara Ann Lawson, a native of Natchez, Miss., born Oct. 24, 1850, and they have 2 children. He is a Republican, a Methodist, and owns 320 acres of valuable land.

Ansel Vond, farmer, sec. 22; P. O., Cool Bank; was born in Monroe county, N. Y., Oct. 12, 1828; was raised and educated in his native county. In Nov., 1857, he settled in this county, and

43

in 1858 he was married to Lucy Ann McWorter, daughter of Frank McWorter, the first settler in this township. They have 3 living children,—Lucy, George E. and Francis Nero. He owns 82 acres of land in a good state of cultivation; is a member of the Baptist Church, and a Republican.

John Walker, farmer, sec. 22; P. O., Cool Bank; was born a slave in Spottsylvania county, Va., in 1802; was owned by several masters up to 1834, when he purchased his own freedom from David Van Aue for $300, after which he rented ground and went to work for himself. According to the laws of the State at that time, a free negro was not allowed to remain in the State but one year; but through the influence of a friend in the Legislature, he obtained a permit to remain 3 years, but he does not remember whether he staid the full allotted time or not. By working hard and saving money he purchased a cheap team, which he sold in 1838 and came to Randolph county, Mo., with Wm. R. Dusen, the man who owned his wife and children. After coming to Missouri, he had money enough to purchase 80 acres of land and went to raising tobacco, corn and hogs. In 1850 he purchased the freedom of 2 of his children, Peter and Lettie, and in 1854 he purchased his wife Lucy and son Oregon. His wife was then 50 years of age and had been a slave all her life. His son was then about 18 years of age. He paid $1,100 for both. He afterward purchased his daughter Louise and her 2 children, Charles and William, for whom he paid $600. In 1861 he owned 460 acres of land and a considerable amount of personal property which he sold, and came to this county and settled on sec. 22 in this tp., where he has since resided. John has been the father of 16 children,—only 3 of whom are living,—Oregon, Archy and Peter. The balance of his children were all emancipated by Lincoln's proclamation. His descendants are numerous; he is one of the wealthy men of Pike county, and has accumulated all his property by his own honest industry. Although wholly uneducated in the books, he has a rare natural ability; is very liberal in his views, even recognizing the right of slavery; says he has never received any cruel treatment from any of his masters. He is highly respected in his neighborhood.

Stephen R. Watson, farmer, sec. 18; P. O., Barry; was born in Newport, Herkimer county, N. Y., April 25, 1811; in 1830 he settled in Atlas, this county, where, in 1834, he married Miss Ann Brown, a native of Massachusetts, who died in June, 1879, leaving one son and three daughters; three of her children have died. Having learned the tailor's trade in the East, Mr. Watson continued in the business of merchant tailor in Atlas. In 1835 he purchased the beautiful farm on which he now resides, the cultivation of which he has brought to a high degree. Since his location here he has devoted his attention exclusively to farming. He is a Universalist, a Republican, and a highly respected member of society.

Joshua Woosley, farmer, sec. 19; P. O., Barry; was born in Wilson county, Tenn., July 9, 1805; when he was 9 years old his parents moved with him to Christian county, Ky.; Oct. 30, 1827, he married Margaret Johnson, daughter of William Johnson, of that county; she died Sept. 8, 1868, leaving 4 children; six of her children had died, and since her death her youngest daughter has died. In 1828 Mr. W. settled on Sugar Creek, in Sangamon county, Ill., and after about 18 months he settled on the place where he now resides. Nov. 4, 1869, he married Mrs. Augusta Ann Sidner, widow of John Sidner, of this tp., who was born in Madison county, Ohio, Oct. 2, 1815, and has one daughter by her previous marriage. Mr. Woosley has been County Commissioner 3 years, Associate County Judge 4 years, Sheriff 2 years, Tp. Assessor and Collector several terms, Justice of the Peace 12 years, Constable 8 years, etc., etc.; is now Assessor and Collector. He has held more offices than any other man in the county. He is the oldest citizen of this tp., and is perhaps as well acquainted with the political history of Pike county as any other citizen.

DERRY TOWNSHIP.

This township embraces a fine farming district. It is especially well adapted to the raising of stock, and to fruit-growing. Very early in the history of the county the pioneer was attracted hither. To the memory of David W. Howard is due the honor of being the first settler of Derry township. He came here as early as 1826, and made improvements on sec. 28, where he built the first house in the township. Soon came Charles Martin, the second settler, and Isaiah Cooper, the third. The latter settled on sec. 20. Then followed Robert McClintock, William and Joseph Hornback, Charles Hoskins, James and Nineveh Barnes, Mr. Kinne, S. F. Thomas, Henry Fesler and others, who also made improvements and did much in developing the native resources of this fine agricultural district.

Soon after the arrival of the above pioneers, settlers began to pour in so fast that it was even then difficult to keep pace with their advent, and after the lapse of 40 years it is impossible to speak of them in the general order of their coming. They formed one of the pleasantest communities to be found in the State. The early pilgrims were well-disposed persons. Of those above mentioned none are now living in the township except Mr. William Hornback. The descendants of many, however, are numerous, and they are in general of the same disposition as that of their fathers, only more modernized. It is hardly too much to say, that no community in the county excels this in this respect. The present generation is largely made up of people who were born here, or who have lived here from their childhood, and they have nearly all fallen into the good ways of the pioneers. They are honest, moral, religious, social, economical, are not in debt, have but few, if any paupers, seldom go to law, are generous to each other in misfortune, have no aristocracy, pay their bills,— in fact, form a well-regulated, and we might say model, community.

Here we find more marked than in any other township almost, the simplicity and good habits of the early settlers, uncontaminated by modern degenerate practices. There are no large towns near enough to attract the attention of the younger people, and accordingly they find amusement and sociability at home, and grow up purer and better than would be the case were a city in their midst. Besides this, we would mention the fact that the population has changed less than most others, is made up more of the families and descendants of the first settlers, and is mingled less with foreigners than is the case in most places. Fortunately, the foreigners living here are nearly all of the religious, careful, economical class, whose manners and customs are largely in harmony with those of the balance of the community.

The family connections of the Hornbacks, Hoskins, Joneses, Pursleys, Taylors, Martins, Feslers, Thomases, etc., etc., form some remarkable circles of relatives, living in good circumstances, moral, many religious, bringing down to the present generation the best qualities of the early pioneers.

To William Hornback, the only one of the earliest pilgrims now living in the township, we are indebted for the greater part of this sketch. In 1829, when he came to this township, there were but 80 voters in Pike county, and only four families in Derry township.

During those early days the Indians were numerous in this neighborhood. It is true the great body of aborigines had been driven westward across the Mississippi, but hundreds lingered around the new settlement, loth to leave the beautiful hunting grounds where they had enjoyed so many happy experiences. They finally became quite troublesome, and annoyed the settlers greatly by their constant stealing. They became a great nuisance, and viewing them in this light the settlers determined to rid themselves of them. Accordingly an army was raised to go on an expedition against these pesky natives. It is true it was a small army, numbering only 15 men, but it was a determined one, and consequently was victorious. These men marched out and notified the red-skins to evacuate their camp and leave the neighborhood. This some of them refused to do. Not wishing to do bodily harm to them if they could be got rid of without, the commander of the little band engraved the image of an Indian's head on a tree, and then William Hornback and one or two others discharged their guns at this image. This was the signal that the whites would fight, and it had the desired effect; for the Indians immediately left the neighborhood, and have never more intruded upon the lands of the settlers of this township.

Wild animals, such as the deer, wolf, coon, and the wild turkey, were numerous here in the early settlement of the township. There were also some panthers, catamounts, wild cats and lynx found here.

For the pioneers this was literally a land of "milk and honey," especially the latter. Although they were deprived of many of the advantages and comforts that are enjoyed by their posterity, yet they had abundance of what is a rare luxury to the latter at the present day. Wild honey and venison were their common, every-day fare. The venison was preserved by drying. Wm. Hornback found a tree within 200 yards of his house, which he cut, and took from it several bucketfuls of honey on Christmas Day, 1829. Mr. Hornback also tells us that he has shot many turkeys while standing in the door of his house. During the big snow in the winter of 1830-1, the wild turkeys congregated in such large numbers in Mr. Howard's corn-field that he had to call upon his neighbors, among whom was Mr. Hornback, to assist him in killing them, in order to save his corn. Many of those slaughtered on the occasion were thrown away, while some were preserved and used for food.

As Mr. Hornback is the oldest settler now living in the township, we give a bit of his experience during the memorable winter above alluded to, although before the big snow fell. In the fall of 1830 he started on horseback for Rock Island. When he arrived at Pope creek, however, the weather turned so extremely cold that he was in imminent danger of freezing to death. He turned his horse homeward to retrace his steps. To add to the already great peril in which he was, he was severely attacked with the bilious colic. This, together with the cold, nearly caused him the loss of his life. It began to snow and sleet on the 23d of December, which made traveling very difficult and slavish upon horses. Mr. Hornback arrived at Quincy, on his return, on the evening of Dec. 24. On the following morning the ground was very rough and the ice so thick that his unshod horse could hardly travel. As it was Christmas and but one blacksmith shop in Quincy, he could not get his horse shod. The blacksmith who ran that shop was too religious to work on Christmas. When Mr. Hornback asked him to shoe his horse he replied that he never had worked on Christmas and he would be d—d if he ever would. After a hard and tedious day's journey Mr. Hornback arrived at home, and that night the big snow began to fall.

Thomas Proctor was the first Justice of the Peace. The first death that occurred in Derry township was that of James Hornback. The first marriage was that of Enoch Cooper to Miss Esther Cooper in 1829. Miss Cooper was the adopted daughter of Isaiah Cooper. The first child born was to Daniel and Pauline Howard in 1827.

The first church building in Derry was erected in 1854, in Eldara, by the Methodist people. This Society was organized in the pioneer days and worshiped in school-houses and dwellings prior to this. The first sermon was preached by Rev. Mr. Bogard, a Methodist minister, in 1829, at the house of William Hornback. In 1830 the renowned Lorenzo Dow preached a sermon in the same house, at which time he baptized William L. and Hopeful Hornback, children of William Hornback, of whom we have spoken so frequently in this sketch.

The school system of Derry township is excellent, and great interest is manifested by the parents in the education of their children. The first school-house was erected on sec. 20, in 1837. At present there are nine school buildings in the township, in which, as a rule, excellent schools are kept.

ELDARA.

This beautiful little village is situated near the summit of a fertile eminence, overlooking a large tract of undulating land skirted by timber on both the north and south. From this locality is presented to the eye a view as beautiful and inviting as any picture nature offers through this section of country. Standing upon the summit one can behold, either south or east of the village, the beauties of nature and the wisdom of a Divine Creator.

The town was founded in 1836 by Nathaniel Winters, and first named Washington. It received its present name in this wise, as related by Esq. Underwood, of Barry, but who for many years was a prominent citizen of Eldara. When he was in Mexico, during the war between the United States and that country, he and his comrades passed through a beautiful little town called Eldora. From there he wrote a letter back to his home, which was then at the old town of Washington. There being another town in the State (Washington, Tazewell county) by the same name, the Postmaster-General notified the postmaster at this point that the name must be changed. The settlers could think of no suitable name, but when Esq. Underwood's letter came, post-marked Eldora, that name particularly struck their fancy. They, however, mistook the spelling of it slightly, spelling it with an *a* in the second or middle syllable, instead of an *o*, according to the true Spanish. The meaning of the word is "gold." The Postmaster-General was notified of the change, and since then (1847) it has been known by the beautiful, modified Spanish name of Eldora.

At that time Mr. Motley platted an addition to the town of Washington, and to it he gave the name of Eldara.

The town now contains about 350 inhabitants. There are located here two dry-goods stores, two grocery stores, one drug store, two shoe shops, two blacksmith shops, one wagon shop, three churches and one school building. The religious denominations represented here are Methodist Episcopal, Christian, and a new sect known as the Holiness. The Christian congregation erected a house of worship in 1875, and the Holiness society refitted the old school-house, which they now use as a church.

The M. E. Church building was struck by lightning in June, 1869, and the Christian church received a stroke on the morning of March 26, 1880, damaging it considerably. There is a theory among some of the citizens that there is a mineral in the ground at this point that attracts the current of atmospheric electricity, for not only these buildings have been struck by lightning, but a barn also received a stroke a few years ago. It took fire and was consumed.

There is a lodge of each of the orders of Freemasons and Odd Fellows in the village. Many of the leading citizens throughout the neighborhood are members of these orders.

In closing the history of the township and village we wish to speak personally of the prominent citizens of both town and country. This we will now do in alphabetical rotation.

William F. Bacon, druggist, Eldara, was born in Berkshire county, Mass., July 18, 1834, and is a son of Benjamin and Mary A. Bacon; the former is deceased, and the latter is at Saratoga Springs, N. Y. Wm. F. was reared on a farm and received a common-school education in his native State. In 1856 he came to Coles county, Ill., where he remained one year and then went to Iowa; was one year in Missouri; in March, 1879, he came to this county, settling in Eldara, and engaging in the drug business, in which he had 4 years' experience before coming here. Oct. 2, 1862, he married Sarah E. Harkness, and they have one daughter, Emma, who was born July 14, 1863. Mr. Bacon served 10 months in the late war, in Co. D, 50th Ill. Inf., and was in the battle of Shiloh, where he was wounded, on account of which, and sickness, he was discharged in June, 1862.

Samuel Barley, farmer, sec. 22; was born in Pennsylvania, Sept. 25, 1843; emigrated to this county in 1848; was first married to Amelia E. Jacobs, Dec. 31, 1863, and they had 6 children—Gideon McClellan, born May 5, 1864; William Frederick, born April 23, 1866, and died in infancy; Sarah Ellen, born Nov. 11, 1867; Amelia Jane, Feb. 10, 1870; Samuel, June 26, 1872; and Bertha, March 2, 1874. For a second wife Mr. Barley married Mrs. Malinda H. Leads, a native of this county, who had 2 children by a former husband,—David M., born Dec. 28, 1870, and Ernest E., born May 23, 1874. Mr. and Mrs. Barley have 2 children; Ablera, born Dec. 8, 1877, and Lenon, Dec. 15, 1879. Mr. B. is not a partisan, but always votes for the best men, regardless of party. P. O., Eldara.

James F. Brawley, P. O., Eldara; was born in Pittsfield tp., in 1849; has followed farming most of the time, but at present is a trader. In 1868 he married Martha E. Potter. They belong to the Christian Church. In 1876 Mr. B. was Tax Collector. In politics he is a Democrat. He is also a Mason and Odd Fellow.

John Brown, farmer, sec. 25; P. O., Hartford; was born in Ohio in 1832, the son of Alexander and Isabella Brown, of Irish descent; chances for early education fair; in 1853 he married Nancy Cheffy, and they had 5 children, 4 of whom are living. April 3, 1875, he married Anna Hoskins. He came to Pike county in 1854. Besides carrying on farming, Mr. Brown also deals in stock. He owns 80 acres of land. He is a Democrat, and both himself and wife are members of the M. E. Church.

Theodore C. Bunker, farmer, sec. 28; P. O., Eldara; was born June 26, 1839, in Penobscot county, Me., and in 1859 went to California; Nov. 19, 1868, he married Clara Wood, of Derry tp., and then returned to California, and back again to this county in 1870, and has since resided here. He owns 55 acres of land on sec. 28, worth $65 per acre; is a member of the Baptist Church; has been School Director in his district for the last three years. Mr. and Mrs. B. have had 5 children; only three are living—Florence, John Frederick, Frank Forest and Theodora B. Mr. B. is a Republican.

Patrick Carney, farmer, residing on the east half of the northeast of sec. 16, was born in Roscommon county, Ireland, and came to America with his father in 1852 and settled in this tp., where he now resides. Both his parents died in this county, leaving 7 children, 6 of whom are living—Mary, Catharine, Thomas, Ellen, Bridget, Patrick and Margaret. Mr. C. owns 110 acres of land; he raises corn and live-stock. Is a member of the Catholic Church in Pittsfield, and is a Democrat. P. O., Eldara.

Thomas Carney, farmer, sec. 15, was born in the south part of Ireland, June 22, 1842; came with his father to America in 1849 and settled in Derry. Feb. 26, 1877, he married Katie McGuire, daughter of Peter McGuire. He owns 80 acres of land worth about $45 per acre; raises wheat, corn and stock. He and wife are both members of the Catholic Church in Pittsfield. Mr. C. has been an Odd Fellow, and is a Democrat. P. O., Eldara.

James W. Chamberlain, farmer, sec. 34; P. O., Rockport; was born in Butler county, O., May 12, 1828; his parents emigrated to this county in 1833 and settled on the farm where he now resides; was married to Miss Jane Veal when 24 years of age, and they had 4 children, one of whom is dead. Jan. 20, 1864, he married Mary Frances Harris, and they have 2 children,—Laura, now 14 years of age, and Jennie, 10 years of age. Mr. C. owns 140 acres of land, valued at $50 per acre; he is a member of the Masonic order, has filled the office of Assessor and Collector in this tp., and in politics is a Republican. Mr. and Mrs. C. are members of the Christian Church.

Mrs. Jane Chamberlain was born in Wayne county, Ind., Dec. 1, 1821; emigrated to this county with her parents in 1836. Her maiden name was Gordon, and she married William Chamberlain May 7, 1840, and they had 5 children,—Mary, born March 22, 1841; Aaron, May 13, 1843; John, Feb. 23, 1846, and died Nov. 22, 1871; William, born Oct. 17, 1848, and Carrie, Dec. 5, 1851. Mr. C. died March 17, 1852, deeply regretted by all who knew him. Mrs. C. still occupies the old homestead, on sec. 33, with her youngest son, William, who takes good care of his mother, as well as of the farm. Her oldest son, Aaron, was in the late war in Co. A, 99th Reg. Ill. Vol., and served for 3 years. Mrs. C. is the owner of 120 acres of land, worth $50 per acre. She is a member of the Christian Church at Barry. P. O., Eldara.

Silas S. Clark, teacher, Eldara, has taught school for 10 years,— 5 years in Pike county, and at present resides in Eldara. In March, 1874, he married Miss May Sweet, and they have 2 children. He is now teaching in Taylor school-house. He is a member of the Masonic and Odd Fellows Orders in Eldara.   Both he and his wife are members of the Christian Church.

Thomas H. Coley, miller, at Eldara, was born Dec. 21, 1836, in Putnam county, Ind.; came to this county Oct., 1851, and settled in Martinsburg tp.; has lived where he now resides, sec. 21, since 1870. Sept. 30, 1860, he married Martha E. Goodin, and they have 8 children: Mary E., Lewis H., William L., Carrie M., Lucius A., Henry Virgil, Lillie M. and Golda R.   Mr. C. owns 80 acres of land, worth $5,000. He is a Democrat, and himself and wife are members of the Christian Church.

Robert Dickson, farmer, sec. 23; P. O., Eldara; was born in Morgan county, O., Aug. 20, 1836; came to this county in Dec., 1854; was raised on a farm, worked one summer at the tanning business; Jan. 1, 1858, married Mary Payne, and they had 3 children, all of whom are dead. Mrs. D. died in Feb., 1861. In Oct., 1865, Mr. D. married Lucy Ann Payne, and they have had 7 children, 5 of whom are living: Henry, Alice, Annie, Eveline and Lucy. Those dead are Eugene and an infant. Mr. Dickson was in the late war in Co. G, 99th Reg. Ill. Vol., enlisting Aug. 23, 1862. Owns 274 acres of land, worth $30 per acre; has been School Director, and is a Republican.

Charles E. Dodge, farmer, sec. 6 ; P. O., Eldara; was born in Warren county, Ill., Nov. 10, 1838; came to this county in the fall of 1874 and settled in Pleasant Vale tp., resided there about 2 years, and then removed to where he now lives, March 1, 1876; Oct. 20, 1863, he married Mary Gard, and they had 3 children: Lennie M., born April 14, 1865; Peter H.,.Oct. 24, 1866; and Bertha M., Feb. 4, 1876. Mr. D. is a member of the Baptist Church at Barry. He has been Constable in Bureau county for 4 years, and Road Overseer and School Director in his tp.; owns 95 acres of land, worth $3,000. While living in Dunklin county, Mo., he was conscripted by the Confederate Government and forced to serve in the rebel army under Gen. Jeff. Thompson until the first day of Oct., 1861, at which time he surrendered to Col. R. J. Oglesby at the battle of Belmont, when Gen. Grant, who was in command of the Federal forces, gave him a free pass home. When he was conscripted his property was confiscated and he was threatened with incarceration because he asked for a voucher for his property, which the rebels had converted to their own use. He afterward enlisted in Co. E, 37th Reg. I. V. I., served 4 months, and was discharged because of ill health. Mr. Dodge is a Republican.

Christopher Dolbeare, farmer, sec. 15; P. O., Eldara; was born March 7, 1852, in this tp.; his father was Rozel C. Dolbeare, and his mother was Priscilla (Hoover) D. His uncle, Aaron Hoover, served in the late war. Christopher lives near Eldara, and 4 years ago took a pleasure trip through New York, Rhode Island and Connecticut, visiting friends, and then went to Ohio on a similar trip, and to the northern part of Illinois last fall.

John Drummond, farmer, sec. 30; P. O., Eldara; owns a farm of 79 ¾ acres 4 miles from Eldara; was born in Clermont county, O., June 21, 1814; came to Adams county in 1842, remained there 4 years and then moved to Salem tp., and in 1853 to where he now resides. Sept. 20, 1835, he married Deborah Graham, and they have had 17 children, 10 girls and 7 boys. His grandfather, John Drummond, was in the Revolution. Mrs. D.'s mother was Elizabeth Graham, and her father John Graham, who was in the war of 1812. Her mother is still living, at the age of 89. Mr. and Mrs. D. are Methodists, and Mr. D. is a Republican.

Moses Easly, farmer, sec. 18; P. O., Eldara; was born in Sullivan county, East Tenn., Feb. 7, 1820; in 1841 he removed to Pike county and settled in this tp., and has lived on his present farm 24 years. His brother, Thomas Easly, was in the Mexican war, under Gen. Taylor. May 1, 1844, he married Mary Ann Tittsworth, of this county, and they have had 9 children, 7 of whom are living,—T. L., Amanda, Alice, William, James, Florence, Idella and Laura. Mr. E. has been School Director of his district 4 years, and Road Commissioner 3 years. He owns 313 acres of land, worth $20,000; ships his produce, and raises stock. He lives 1½ miles from Eldara. He is a Democrat, and his wife is a Methodist.

T. L. Easly, retired farmer; P. O., Eldara; was born in Pike county, in April, 1846; his father's name was Moses Easly and his mother's maiden name was Mary Tittsworth. Nov. 20, 1869, he married Caroline Eldridge, of this county, and they have 3 children; Frederick, Mary and Maud. He is an Odd Fellow, and in politics a Greenbacker.

Maberry Evans, farmer, sec. 21; P. O., Eldara; was born in Scott county, Ill., Jan. 14, 1829; came to Pike county in 1847, and lived with Elisha Hurt that winter. July 11, 1859, he married Julia D. Landrum, and they have had 7 children, 3 of whom are living,—Richard F., Theodora A. and Mary E. He owns 200 acres of land in this tp. and 120 acres in Pleasant Vale tp.; home place worth $50 per acre. He has been Justice of the Peace and Supervisor; is a member of the Masonic fraternity and in politics a Democrat. His wife belongs to the M. E. Church.

William Evans, farmer and stock-raiser, sec. 21; P. O., Eldara; was born near Winchester, Ill., April 6, 1832, and is a son of Richard and Annie Evans, dec.; natives of Kentucky. The subject of this notice was once offered the use of a large tract of land where Jacksonville now stands, in exchange for a horse. He came to this county about 1850, and soon afterward went to California, overland, where he remained 8 years; he then returned to this county. Nov. 30, 1863, he married Miss Mary A. Strubinger, daughter of Joseph Strubinger, dec., an early settler of this county. They have had 5 children, namely, Anna M., Joseph M., Frank W., Hattie M. and Nina. Mr. Evans owns 198 acres of land here, and 160 acres in Platt county, Mo.

Jacob C. Farmer, blacksmith; was born Dec. 9, 1842, in Harrison county, O.; came to this county with his father, John Farmer, in 1846; was married in 1864 to Mary McClosky; they had 2 children, only Cora living. Mr. Farmer served in the late war in Co. G, 44th Reg. I. V. I. He resided in Adams county 15 years. Is a member of the Masonic fraternity, and a Greenbacker in politics. His wife is a member of the Christian Church.

Henry A. Fesler, farmer, sec. 19; P. O., Eldara; was born in Derry tp. Aug. 4, 1850; was married March 5, 1870, to Miss Mary Phœbus, and they had 4 children; Lela May, born Aug. 2, 1872; Jacob and Robert, born July 7, 1874; and Rosa, born Oct. 23, 1876, who died Nov. 9, following. Mr. and Mrs. Fesler both had good educational advantages. Mr. F. is a stock-raiser, and in politics is a Democrat.

Jacob Fesler, farmer, sec. 30; P. O., Eldara; was born in Clark county, Ky., June 8, 1821; came to Pike county in 1835 and settled on sec. 19; he owns 320 acres of land, worth $35 per acre. Oct. 15, 1846, he married Zerilda Lyons, and their 6 children are: Sarah C., born Aug. 27, 1848; Henry A., Aug. 4, 1850; Adelpha, Nov. 28, 1853; Jane Ann, May 25, 1856; John R., Aug. 2, 1860; Emma E., Jan. 15, 1863. Both are members of the M. E. Church, South, and Mr. F. is a Mason, and in politics a Democrat.

Bloomer Fowler was born in Washington county, Ky., Nov. 28, 1830, and in early life had but little time to devote to education; came to this county in 1861 and settled in Derry tp. His father's name was Benjamin Fowler, and his mother's maiden name was Mary Gordon. Mr. Fowler is now engaged in buying and selling hides, pelts and produce. He is a Democrat.

James H. Garner, farmer; resides on the N. W. quarter of sec. 33, this tp.; was born in Clark county, Ky., Dec. 27, 1824; came to this county in the fall of 1840 and settled in Derry tp. He owns 286 acres of land in Derry, and 320 acres in Atlas tp., worth $20,000. June 2, 1864, he married Mary E. Williams, and they have had 6 children,—William J., Joseph O., Ida, Mary A., Herman and Lovina. Mr. G. has been School Director for 2 years and Commissioner of Highways for several years. He raises grain and produce extensively, and ships to foreign markets. He is a Republican. P. O., Eldara.

A. B. Gates, farmer, sec. 11, S. ½; P. O., Eldara; was born near Columbus, Ohio; came to this county while very young with his father, Nehemiah Gates, and has resided here ever since. June 3, 1862, was married to Elizabeth Saylor and their children are, Rebecca Ellen, born May 23, 1863; Susan A., June 15, 1864; Jacob, March 1, 1865; William, Oct. 3, 1867; Charles, Sept. 20, 1869; Joseph, Oct. 11, 1871; George, Feb. 7, 1875; and Mary, April 6, 1879. Mr. G. owns 80 acres of land, worth $3,000; he is a Democrat, and himself and wife are members of the Christian Church.

Theodore Gates, farmer, sec. 5; P. O., Barry; was born in Pike county, March 20, 1843, and Oct. 26, 1865, married Susan Chase, daughter of Lewis Chase, of Ohio. They have 2 children; Lousina, born Oct. 6, 1867, and Jesse, born July 25, 1872. Mr. Gates owns 104¾ acres of land, worth about $3,000. He has been School Director one term; was in the late war, in Co. D, 99th Reg. I. V. I., and served 3 years; was mustered out at Baton Rouge, Louisiana.

Timothy Grady, farmer, sec. 25, was born in Kings county, Ireland, about the year 1826; arrived in America May 11, 1849, landing at New Orleans; lived 18 years in Cincinnati, then removed to this county, where he has resided for about 18 years, and on his present farm 13 years. Sept. 21, 1858, he married Mary O'Donnel, in Cincinnati, Ohio, and their living children are Thomas, Mary Ann and John. Thomas was born July 4, 1859; Mary Ann, May 6, 1864, and John, April 10, 1867. Mr. G. owns 120 acres of land, worth about $30 per acre. He and wife are members of the Catholic Church, and Mr. G. is a Democrat.

Warren Green, farmer, sec. 17; P. O., Eldara; was born in this county near Atlas, Jan. 25, 1835, and has resided in the county ever since. He was first married Sept. 27, 1857, to Lucinda Taylor, and they had 6 children,—Ida Olive, born Aug. 17, 1858, and died May 3, 1863; Sarah Elizabeth, born March 17, 1861; Albert Warren, Sept. 4, 1863; Edwin May, July 8, 1866; Cora Luella, April 14, 1868, and an infant daughter born April 4, 1860, who died the same day. April 21, 1872, Mr. Green married Mrs. Mary E., widow of Thomas H. Pendleton, and daughter of Daniel and Esther McCaskill, who had one child, John A. Pendleton, born Aug. 10, 1859. Mr. and Mrs. Green have 4 children, Frederick Ross, born June 7, 1873; Harry Jay, Jan. 16, 1875; Archibald, Jan. 28, 1877; Phebe E., May 7, 1879. Mr. Green owns 75 acres of land near Eldara, worth $60 per acre. He and his wife are members of the Free M. E. Church, and he is a Licensed Local Preacher for his congregation. He has held several responsible offices in his tp., and in politics is a Republican.

Henry Hall, farmer, sec. 27; P. O., Eldara; was born in Butler county, Ohio, Jan. 7, 1836; came to this county Sept. 20, 1855; was married Aug. 20, 1859, to Mary L. Taylor, and they have had 7 children,—Edwin F., Jennie, George D., Ida, Luella, Henry and Freddie; 5 are dead. Mr. H. owns 160 acres of land, worth $10,000; is a member of the Masonic Lodge, raises a great deal of produce and patronizes home markets; is a Republican.

George W. Harris, farmer, sec. 26; was born in Goochland county, Va., Oct. 23, 1814; emigrated to Pike county in the spring of 1843, and settled, temporarily in Pleasant Vale tp., and in 3 months settled where he has now resided for more than 28 years. March 3, 1836, he married Miss Mary Ann Ripley, and of their 9 children 7 are living, namely: Mary Frances, Thomas S., Lucy C., Elizabeth S., Philena J., James H., Wm. H., George W. and Ann Eliza. Mr. Harris owns 280 acres of land, worth $40 per acre. He and wife have been members of the M. E. Church for more than 40 years; he has filled several important tp. offices. P. O., Eldara.

Samuel Harris, farmer, was born Oct. 6, 1840, in Tennessee; came to this county in the spring of 1851; was married to Amanda Easly, in Sept., 1865, and they have had 6 children, all of whom are living, Ella, Frank, Mary, Elbert, Herman and Freddie. His father's name is Thomas S. Harris and his mother's name was Amanda; she died in 1871. Mr. Harris is a Democrat.

Joshua B. Havird, farmer, was born March 25, 1848, and is a native of this county; May 1, 1869, he married Margaret Maher, and they have had 6 children, namely: Lorrence W., born Dec. 31, 1869, and died Oct., 1877; Fannie Ellen, born July 25, 1871, died Aug. 20, 1872; Daniel, born June 11, 1873; Annastatia, born May 23, 1875; Joshua, born March 23, 1877, and Leonard, Sept. 1, 1878. Mrs. Havird was born Dec. 25, 1849, and died Sept. 23, 1878. Oct. 23, 1879, Mr. H. was married to his present wife, Jennett Parrick. Mr. Havird owns 81 acres of land, worth $3,000. He is a Democrat. P. O., Barry.

Reuben C. Hendricks, farmer, sec. 6; was born in North Carolina, Jan. 12, 1822; was married to Miss Orra Ann Dumford, April 7, 1844, who was born July 26, 1829, and they have had 11 children,—Amanda M., born June 14, 1846; Melinda J., July 28, 1848, and died Sept. 11, 1854; Mary E., born May 6, 1852; Eliza B., Feb. 9, 1854; Martha A., May 6, 1856; Samuel S., Sept. 3, 1858, and died March 31, 1872; Wm. I., born Feb. 27, 1861; Reuben H., March 31, 1863, and died Sept. 20, 1864; George M., born Jan. 31, 1865; Daniel R., Nov. 28, 1867, and Lydia A., Aug. 24, 1870. Mr. H. owns 40 acres of fine land, worth $45 per acre. He is a Democrat.

John L. Hogan, farmer, sec. 27; P. O., Eldara; owns 120 acres of valuable land, on which he resides with his widowed mother. He was born March 7, 1847, in this township, and was married to Lizzie Buckingham, Feb. 9, 1868, and they have 2 children,— Harry, born Dec. 29, 1869; and Nina, Dec. 1, 1876. His father, Adley Hogan, died when John was 9 years old, since which time he and his mother have struggled together until they have accumulated considerable property.

R. W. Hornback, farmer, sec. 20; P. O., Eldara; owns 220 acres of land, worth $60 an acre. Mr. H. was born in this county Feb. 1, 1837, and is the son of William and Lillie (Landrum) Hornback; in this county in 1866 he married Elizabeth Freeman, who was born in this county in 1843. They have had 8 children, of whom 7 are living. Mr. H. is in prosperous circumstances as a farmer. In politics he is a Democrat.

Solomon Hornback, farmer, is a native of Kentucky, where he was born July 3, 1810; came to this county in 1836, where he has lived ever since. Being thus an early settler he has witnessed wonderful changes in the development of this county. In 1836 he married Emily Blackwell, in Kentucky, who is a native of that State. Of their 10 children 7 are living. Mr. H. is one of the old and respected citizens of Pike county, and has held several responsible offices. He is a member of the Christian Church, and a Democrat. His father served in the war of 1812.

William Hornback, retired farmer; P. O., Eldara; son of Solomon and Sally (Phillips) Hornback, the former a native of Kentucky, and the latter of North Carolina; was born in Kentucky, Jan., 1808; came to this county in 1829. He is therefore one of the oldest pioneers of this section. In 1826 he married Sallie W. Landrum, who was born in 1806, and died in 1839. They had 4 children,—Patsey A., Wm. F., S. P. and R. M. In May, 1840, Mr. H. married Nancy Swerer, who was born in Ohio in 1808 and died in 1858. In 1859 he married Mary A. Landrum, who was born Oct. 4, 1808. Mr. H. is a member of the Methodist Church: owns 83 acres of fine farm land worth $60 per acre. He is a Democrat.

Mrs. Ann J. Hoskin resides on the S. W. quarter of sec. 26; was born in Griggsville, Jan. 25, 1850. Her maiden name was Ann J. Richey. April 20, 1873, she married Daniel Hoskin, who was born April 11, 1832, in this township. In 1879 Mr. H. died, leaving one child,—Henry Isaac, born June 18, 1875. Mr. H. was a member of the I. O. of O. F., and filled important township offices. He left 120 acres of land worth $50 per acre. Mr. Hoskin was a highly esteemed citizen.

Asa Hoskin, farmer, sec. 23, was born in this county June 17, '37. He owns 120 acres of land in this township, worth $35 per acre. He was raised on a farm, and is now very extensively engaged in the raising of hogs, cattle and horses. Jan. 1, 1863, he married Mary A. Moorhead, daughter of Dr. Moorhead, of Eldara, and their children are : Ollie, William, Thomas and Belle. He has been School Director one year in his township, and is a Democrat. His uncle, John Shinn, served in the Mexican war under Gen. Taylor. P. O., Eldara.

Charles M. Hoskin, farmer, sec. 26; was born in this township June 25, 1850; was the eldest of 6 children; his father was Isaac A. Hoskin. June 23, 1873, he married Linda Miles, who was born in Mercer county, Mo., and they have 2 children,—Mary Abbie, born Feb. 3, 1874, and Asa, born Aug. 1, 1876. Mr. H. has been Road-Master 2 or 3 times in his township: is a Mason and a Democrat. P. O., Eldara.

John Hoskin, blacksmith, Eldara; owns 2 lots with dwelling and shop; was born Aug. 24, 1850, and Nov. 1, 1878, married Emeline Berry, in Adams county, Ill., who was born Aug. 1, 1857, in Ohio. They had 5 children,—Cora, Rosa M., Emma and 2 infants. The 2 latter are deceased. Mr. H. is a member of the Masonic and Odd Fellows fraternities, and is a Republican.

William Hoskin, farmer, resides on sec. 26; was born in this county, within 1½ miles of where he now lives, Feb. 15, 1839; was married to Sarah Jane Moorhead, daughter of Dr. Moorhead, of Eldara, Oct. 7, 1860; have had 3 children,—Mary E., born July 25, 1861; Margaret Edna, March 14, 1863, and Lizzie, born Dec. 18, 1864, and died Sept. 21, 1865. Mr. H. owns 110 acres of land, worth $40 per acre; has been Road-Master several terms, and is a Democrat.

George Howland, farmer, sec. 15; P. O., Eldara; was born in this county Dec. 29, 1847; when a lad he entered a dry-goods establishment as clerk, and satisfactorily filled the position until he commenced farming four years ago. Feb. 4, 1869, he married Virginia Martin, who was born in Missouri Feb. 19, 1849. Their two children are Gertrude. who was born Oct. 5, 1870, and Maude, Sept. 19, 1878. Mr. Howland's father was a native of New York State and his mother of Illinois. Politically he is a Republican.

P. E. Howland, farmer. was born in New York Dec. 25, 1818, and when 20 years of age emigrated to Illinois and settled in Martinsburg tp., Pike county; afterward moved 3 miles north of Barry and resided there about 4 years, and in June, 1876, he removed to Eldara, where he has since resided. He was married at Martinsburg, to Miss Harriet Clark, and they have had 6 children, 2 of whom are living,—Caroline and Geo. H., both married. Mr. H. owns, jointly with his son, 93 acres of land contiguous to the town, worth $6,000. He is one of the Town Trustees of the incorporation, and a Democrat.

David B. Johnson, farmer, sec. 32; P. O., Eldara; was born in Pickaway county, O., April 1, 1836, and is a son of Henry B. and Mary (Baker) Johnson; the former was born in Virginia in 1806, and of German and English ancestry, and the latter of English descent; came to Pike county in 1846, with his parents, where he went to school 3 months—all he ever went in his life. In 1861 he enlisted in Co. I, 11th Mo. Inf., under Captain Barnum; was in 7 battles, and at Corinth, Miss., was wounded, being shot through the left lung; for two years afterward he was unable to dress himself. In 1859 he married Adelia E. Hadsell, and they had 3 children, all of whom are living; in 1870 he married Eura J. Watkins, and of their 5 children 4 are living. He and his present wife are Missionary Baptists. Politically Mr. J. is a Democrat.

Thomas J. Jones, farmer, lives on sec. 8, and owns 240 acres of land; was born in Eldara tp. Sept. 10, 1842; was married in March, 1868, to Miss Elizabeth Dolbeare, and they have had 6 children, one boy and five girls; one of the girls died about 3 years ago. Mr. J. and wife belong to the Christian Church. The names of their children are, Azalia, Paul, Jennie, Rosa, Lillie and Ida. Mr. J. served in the late war in Co. C, 99th Reg., and was discharged July 31, 1865; his brother was killed at Spanish Fort. He is one of the Directors of the Barry Mutual Insurance Company.

William Jones, merchant, Eldara; is a native of this county, where he was born March 29, 1834; was raised on a farm until 18 years of age, then commenced teaching school and continued teaching for 20 terms; he settled in Eldara in 1860 and engaged in the mercantile trade; keeps on hand a good stock of general merchandise, and is doing a good business. At present he is Postmaster at Eldara and has held the office of Town Clerk 4 years.

Stephen R Williams

DERRY TP.

In 1857 he was married in this county to Miss Mary J. Purcell, who died in 1872; they had 5 children,—Katie, Martha, Mattie, Warner and Mary J. In 1874 he married Elizabeth Roseberry, a native of Tennessee, where she was born in 1838. They have one child, Sallie. Mr. J. is a Republican.

Jacob Kendall, grocer, was born March 28, 1838, and settled in Eldara in 1875; was married in this county in 1860 to Martha Haines, who was born in Tennessee. They had 6 children,—Alvin, Mary, Franklin W., Flora (deceased), Jerusha and Eva. Mr. K. has been Collector one term; is an Odd Fellow and a Republican. His parents were natives of New Jersey.

John Kerr, farmer, sec. 4; was born in the north of Ireland, county Londonderry, in 1816; emigrated to America in 1848 and settled in this tp. In 1842 he married Eliza Torrens, of Ireland, and they have had 7 children, 5 of whom are dead,—Mary E., died Jan. 15, 1874 ; Sarah Ann, died when but 4 years of age ; Emily, died in March, 1873 ; Margaret, died Dec. 12, 1878. Sarah Ann, the youngest child, born Dec. 19, 1856; was married to John Wassell, of Hadley tp., May 30, 1878, and they are members of the Baptist Church. Mr. Kerr's only son, John, enlisted in the late war in 1862 in the 99th Reg. I. V. I., and after serving 3 years was honorably discharged at Baton Rouge, La. Mr. K. owns 40 acres of land, worth $50 per acre. He and wife are Congregationalists. Politics Republican. P. O., Barry.

John Kerr, jr., farmer, was born Dec. 24, 1842, in Ireland; was raised on a farm; came to America in 1847, and has lived in this tp. for 32 years. In Aug., 1862, he enlisted in Co. D, 99th Ill. Reg., and was mustered out July 31, 1865; was married April 9, 1876, to Miss Rhoda Dolbeare, who was born in 1849. He owns 120 acres of land, worth $3,000; is a member of the Grange. Resides on sec. 4. Is a Republican in politics.

Albert Landrum, merchant, Eldara.

Alonzo Lyons, farmer, resides on the N. E. of the S. W. quarter of sec. 30 ; was born Dec. 5, 1848, in this tp.; his father, John Lyons, was in the Black Hawk war; his mother's maiden name was Susan Harlow; they have had 7 children, 2 of whom are dead. He owns 40 acres of land, worth about $1,000 ; raises wheat, corn and stock; sells produce at home market; is a member of the Masonic order, and in politics, a Democrat.

Hutson Martin, farmer, sec. 27 ; P. O., Eldara; was born near Danville, Vermillion county, Ill., July 16, 1832, and is a son of William and Seraphina (Wetherbee) Martin, natives of Kentucky and New York State, respectively. Mr. Martin's father, Hutson Martin, was a native of Virginia, probably of English descent, and was a soldier in the war of 1812; he died in Oregon in 1859, whither he had moved at the age of about 70 years. The subject of this notice obtained his education mostly in the common schools of this State. He came to this county in 1856 with his stepfather, Samuel Purcell. July 30, 1851, he married Miss Lydia A. Chamberlain,

44

a native of Ohio, and a daughter of Aaron and Rachel Chamberlain, the former a native of New Jersey, and they have 5 children, namely, Willard A., Gilbert N., Mary J., Della R. and Lydia A., besides 2 deceased. After his marriage Mr. Martin rented land until 1856, when he purchased a good farm on sec. 27, which now consists of 280 acres, and is one of the best improved farms in the township. In politics Mr. M. is a Republican, and during the war did all he could in support of the Government. He is also a practical friend of educational interests. He is also a Freemason. We give a portrait of Mr. Martin in this work.

T. W. Martin, farmer, sec. 25; was born in Vermillion county, Ill., May 20, 1833; came to this county in the fall of 1845, settling in this tp., and resided here until 1852, when he went to California and remained there 2 years; from there to Oregon, where he was in the volunteer service to suppress the Indian outbreak; was in the service 7 months; in 1856 went to Texas, and in 1860 returned to this county, where he has since remained. Oct. 15, 1863, he married Mary J. Hogan; they have had one child, which died in infancy. Mr. M. has been Overseer of Roads for 3 years; owns 120 acres of land, worth about $50 per acre; sells his produce at home; and is a Republican in politics. P. O., Eldara.

W. A. Martin, farmer, was born in this county, and is a son of Hutson and Lydia (Chamberlain) Martin; was educated in the common-school. In Dec., 1878, he married Miss Kate Taylor, and they have one child, a boy. Mrs. M. is a member of the Christian Church, and Mr. M., in politics, is a Republican. For a time he once clerked in a store in Pittsfield.

James M. Mays, farmer, sec. 24; owns 187 acres of land, worth $50 per acre; was born in Ross county, O., Feb. 12, 1830, and is a son of Little Barry and Mahala Mays, both natives of Virginia. In 1849 he came to this county, and in 1857 he married Sarah A. Petty of Pike county, born in 1831; they are the parents of 9 children,—Mary J., Clara, Alice, Amanda, Charley, Dora, Lucy, Henry and James; the 2 latter are deceased. Mr. M.'s father was in the war of 1812. He is a Democrat.

Mariah Miller, P. O., Eldara; was born in Butler county, O., Sept. 26, 1837, and came to Illinois with her parents, Ijel Stout and Julia Ann Stout, March 17, 1853. They settled on sec. 28, this tp., where they have since resided. Her father and mother still live with their daughter. April 15, 1849, she married Abraham Miller, who died in 4 months and 26 days. Mrs. Miller owns 80 acres of land, worth $40 per acre.

Thomas W. Moorhead, physician and surgeon, is a native of Ohio, where he was born Jan. 14, 1814; graduated in 1848, and commenced the practice of medicine in this county in 1851; came to this county in 1852; lived in Pittsfield one year and then came to Derry; he has 160 acres of valuable land, and one lot with dwelling in Eldara. In 1838 he married Mary Janette Dickey, a native of Ohio, who died in 1851; in 1853 he married Hannah

Hulls, a native of New Jersey, born in 1827; they have 4 children. The doctor has an extensive practice, which is attended with good success.

John Morrisaacy, farmer, sec. 5; P. O., Eldara and Pittsfield; was born in Ireland, May 14, 1831; emigrated to America in 1852; first landed at New Orleans, then at St. Louis, Mo.; thence to Pike county, Ill., residing near Pittsfield 26 years; Sept. 26, 1854, married Margaret Helm, by whom he has had 5 children, all living,— Margaret, Matthew J., Ellen, John and James. Mr. M. owns 65 acres of land, worth $1,700.

J. J. Morrow, farmer and blacksmith, now engaged in butchering, was born in Jefferson county, Va., April 2, 1835; came to Pleasant Hill, this county, March 8, 1865, and April 8, 1878, removed to Eldara, where he now resides; was Constable in Pleasant Hill tp. 4 years; is now Justice of the Peace. Oct. 25, 1855, he married Ellen E. Ahalt, of Maryland, and 2 of their 3 children are living. April 26, 1864, he married Nancy E. Colvin, of Pike county, Mo., and they have had 5 children, 2 of whom are dead. He is a Mason and an Odd Fellow.

Dillard P. Motley, farmer, residing on the S. E. qr. of sec. 16; was born in Putnam county, Ind., Oct. 6, 1838; came to this county with his father, John W. Motley, in 1839, and has since resided here. April 3, 1879, he married Eliza E. Dudley, daughter of Jesse and Elizabeth Dudley. He is the owner of 120 acres of land, worth $40 per acre; raises grain principally; was Constable in this tp. nearly 4 years, and has filled other offices. In politics he is a Democrat and a strong partisan. P. O., Eldara.

E. R. Motley, farmer, sec. 21; P. O., Eldara; was born in this county Feb. 23, 1842, the son of John W. and Millie (Pierce) Motley, natives of Kentucky, and of Irish descent; received his education partly in Indiana, but mostly in this county. April 15, 1866, he married Elizabeth J. Gragg, and of their 8 children 6 are living. He has resided at the present place all his life, and as a farmer has been successful, now owning 360 acres of land, well cultivated and stocked. He excels in penmanship, and is a prominent Democratic candidate for the office of Circuit Clerk; he has taught school a part of each year for 20 years; has been School Director, Assessor and School Trustee.

John Moyer, farmer and blacksmith, residing on sec. 10, Derry tp.; was born in Orange county, Ind., Sept. 5, 1828, and came to this county in May, 1839, where he has since resided. Feb. 21, 1850, he married Sarah Ann Benson, and their children are: Albert Travis, born May 31, 1859; Dimmitt McNiel, born May 31, 1864, and died Dec. 7, 1865; and Mary Emily Jane, born March 16, 1867. He has been School Director for several years and School Trustee for one term; he is now Justice of the Peace; also a member of the Masonic order. He is well versed in Masonic principles, especially in the lower degrees, having spent much time and effort in their study, esteeming them essential to high moral attainments. P. O., Eldara.

Solomon Moyer, farmer, sec. 9; P. O., Eldara; was born Feb. 22, 1840; he is a son of Moses and Martha (Brothers) Moyer, Dec. 24, 1863, he married Emma Johnon, a native of this county, born in 1846. Their children are,—Delphia L., Moses, Martha I., Parvin, Charles and S. R., and Lucy, deceased. Mr Moyer has held the office of School Trustee 7 years, of Collector 5 years. When he first married he had but $15; he now owns 200 acres of land, worth $40 per acre. He is a Democrat.

William H. Moyer, farmer, sec. 11; P. O., Eldara; was born about three miles from his present residence, Sept. 6, 1843, and is the son of Moses and Martha (Brothers) Moyer, of German ancestry, the former a native of North Carolina, and the latter of Indiana; was educated in the common schools of this county. In 1863 he married Caroline Persley, and the following are their children: William T., born Feb. 8, 1865; Jacob R., Sept. 25, 1866; John C., Jan., 1869; Ethel J., March 17, 1871; and Orville, Sept. 29, 1874. Mr. M. was again married April 13, 1878, to Eliza Hilliard, and they have one child, Martha, born April 4, 1879. Mr. Moyer has 250 acres of land. Politically he is a Democrat.

Jacob Myers, farmer, was born in Hamilton county, Ohio, April 11, 1818; came to this county in 1837; in August, 1833, he married Hannah A. Williams, a native of Ohio, now deceased. Her children were 5 boys and 5 girls. In August, 1871, Mr. Myers married Drusilla Mummy, who was born in Ohio in 1837. Mr. M. enlisted in 1862, in Co. B, Mo. Mil. Cav., and served 23 months, being in several hard-fought battles. Belongs to M. E. Church, and the Masonic order.

James H. Nation, farmer, sec. 25; P. O., Eldara; was born in Sangamon county, Ill., July 17, 1839; was raised on a farm and had limited educational advantages. March 4, 1858, he came to this county and settled in Kinderhook, where he lived nearly 4 years, and May 13, 1866, removed to Derry tp. He enlisted in the army in 1861, in Co. C., 3d Reg. Mo. Cav., under Col. Glover; was discharged Dec. 16, 1864, at St. Louis, Mo. Sept. 26, 1867, he married Lurena Hogan, a native of Derry tp., and they have 2 living children. He owns 40 acres of land, worth $35 per acre; is a Republican.

Frederick Ottowa, coroner, Eldara, was born in Stendal, Prussia, July 8, 1829; came to America July 6, 1855, landing in New York city; in 2 months from that time he went to Davenport, Iowa, where he remained 4 years; thence he removed to Hannibal, Mo., and in 1861 he came to Pike county, locating first at Kinderhook, then went to Barry, and finally to where he now resides. May 25, 1854, he married Miss Caroline Brandt, and they have had 8 children,—Charles L. F., Lewis, John, Joshua, James, Caroline and Anna Louisa. Mr. Ottowa belongs to the Odd Fellows; United Workmen; was elected Coroner in 1879. He and wife are members of the M. E. Church, South. In politics he is a Democrat.

Thomas J. Ownby was born in Adair county, Kentucky, Dec. 10, 1827; came to this county with his father, Thomas Ownby, in the fall of 1828, and settled in Detroit tp., on the farm owned by Norton Foreman; afterward moved to Newburg tp., lived there several years, then went to California; was gone 4 years, then back to Newburg, and immediately removed to Detroit, where he lived 4 years; then to Derry tp., where he has since resided on sec. 9. May 22, 1856, Mr. Ownby was married to Falissa A., daughter of Stewart Lindsay, and they have had 10 children, 5 of whom are dead. Their names are,--Emmet, born March 25, 1857, died March 10, 1873; Clayton, born Oct. 5, 1858, died Aug. 15, 1859; Mary E., born Oct. 11, 1860; Stewart, born March 9, 1862, died March 7, 1879; Eliza J., born May 10, 1864; Charles L., born Aug. 29, 1867, died July 28, 1868; William B., born Jan. 27, 1870; Oscar O., born Nov. 3, 1873; Evelina, born March 12, 1876, died Dec. 11, 1877. Mr. Ownby commenced life in very limited circumstances, but by industry and economy has accumulated a nice property, and is considered one of the heavy property-holders in the community. He owns 160 acres of land, worth $10,000; has filled several important offices in his tp., and is an ardent Republican. P. O., Eldara.

William M. Parker, farmer, sec. 31; P. O., Eldara; was born in Coles county, Ill., June 26, 1829; was raised in Clark county and came to Pike county, Nov. 6, 1853; was married March 27, 1851, to Sarah Daughetee, of Clark county, Ill., who is of Scotch and German descent; they have had 7 children, 5 of whom are living, --Susan E., Amanda S., Mary Eliza, William D., Leven and Orlando. Both are members of the Baptist Church; Mr. P. was Collector in his tp. in 1869, and is a Democrat.

Thomas W. Potter, farmer, sec. 29; P. O., Eldara; was born in Warren county, Ky., Oct. 8, 1841, came to Adams county in the fall of 1860, and to Pike in March, 1861, and settled in Derry tp., on N. E. of sec. 32; went to Kentucky in 1863 and returned in the spring of 1864; he then removed to Arkansas, lived there 7 years, then returned to Pike, where he now resides. June 1, 1865, he married Catharine Pryor, and their children are: Elizabeth, Pleasant H., Anna, Laura, Nancy L., Thomas W., Emma C., Lucy and Mary. Mr. Potter owns 100 acres of land, worth $35 per acre; is a member of the Christian Church and an Odd Fellow. He is a Democrat. His father, P. H. Potter, served as captain under Gen. Houston in the Texas war.

William H. Pryor, farmer, sec. 19; a native of Tennessee; was born Nov. 12, 1832; came to Pike county in the fall of 1838 and settled in Derry tp., and has resided here ever since. Nov. 22, 1855, he married Susan E. Moyer, and their children are, Delphina, Mary L., Martha E., Henry D., Ollie, Isaac and Wilbert. Mr. Pryor owns 160 acres of land, worth $40 per acre; is a member of the Masonic Lodge at Eldara; his wife is a member of the M. E. Church, South. He has been Road Overseer and Commissioner for 3 years, and Tax Collector of revenue for 1877. He ships his produce to Quincy. He is a Democrat.

Jacob F. Pursley was born March 19, 1839; a native of Pike county, Ill.; May 9, 1861, he was married to CatharineConnors , and the names of their children are, Phila Jane, born April 16, 1862, died June 5, 1863; Cora Belle, born in Dec., 1863, and died the following February; Frank L.,born Dec. 13, 1864; Stephen Douglas, born Jan. 1, 1866; Anna M., born March 15, 1868, and Cora, born May 25, 1871. Mr. Pursley has twice been Path-master in his road district, and is now School Director. He has 300 acres of land where he lives, worth $50 per acre, and 160 acres in Hadley tp., worth $45 per acre. In politics he is a Democrat. P. O., Barry.

John Pursley, farmer, sec. 10; P. O., Eldara; owns 200 acres of land, worth $40 per acre; was born in Pike county, Mo., May 1, 1831; came to this county in the fall of 1835, and located where he now resides. His father, Jacob Pursley, died about 3 years ago. His mother's maiden name was Jane Donovan, who is now dead. He was married in Feb., 1854, to Charlotte Sperry. They are both members of the Christian Church, and he has been School Director 16 years. The names of their living children are, Jennie, Ethel, Floyd and Eugene. Mr. Pursley is a Democrat.

Michael S. Raftery, farmer, sec. 7; P. O., Eldara; was born in Roscommon county, Ireland, July 6, 1843; came to America in the fall of 1852, landing at New Orleans; from there to Eldara, where he has since resided. Feb. 16, 1868, he married Frances V. Landrum. He owns 150 acres of land; was in the late war in Co. A, 99th Reg. I. V. I.; was wounded at Vicksburg, and discharged July 15, 1864. Mr. and Mrs. Raftery have 3 children, namely,—Luada, Laura and Thomas Albert. Mr. R. is a Democrat, and belongs to the Masonic Lodge.

Thomas Raftery resides on the northwest quarter of sec. 8; was born in Martin's Town, Roscommon Parish, Ireland, Jan. 6, 1815; came to America June 24, 1851, landing at New Orleans; from there he followed the Mississippi river to St. Louis, Mo., and from there to Louisiana, Pike county, Mo., thence to Pike county, Ill., where he settled permanently on sec. 8. Three years after he returned to Ireland and brought his family to his new home. Feb. 4, 1840, he married Bridget Loftus. Both are members of the Catholic Church. Their living children are Catharine, Mary, Michael, Margaret and Thomas. Mr. R. owns 160 acres of land, worth $30 per acre. P. O., Eldara.

Benjamin Sigsworth, farmer, sec. 15; P. O., Eldara; was born in Yorkshire, Eng., April 25, 1827; at the age of three years came to Lorain county, O., with his parents, and when he was 8 years old they moved to LaSalle county, Ill., and the next year to Pike county. His father's name was Joseph, his mother's Ann Sigsworth, *nee* Coleman. Jan. 28, 1858, he married Sarah A. Badgley, and they have had 6 children, 2 of whom are living ; Sierra Nevada, Benjamin, John B., Joseph, Ann Loretta and an infant. Mr. S. is a member of the Masonic Lodge; owns 470 acres of land, worth $12,000, and sells his produce at home. He was in California 3 years. His wife is a member of the Christian Church. Mr. S. is a Republican.

John Stout, farmer, sec. 26; P. O., Eldara; was born in Butler county, Ohio. In 1852 came to this county and settled in Derry tp. Sept. 13, 1863, he married Nancy Hoskin of Pike county, and their children are,—Mary, born Aug. 12, 1864; Andrew W., born Jan. 15, 1866; Julia A., born July 26, 1867; Aaron, born Aug. 1, 1870; Otis and Oren, born April 26, 1876. Mr. Stout owns 80 acres of land, worth $40 per acre. He lives on the public road leading from Pittsfield to Rockport. He is a Democrat.

Joseph H. Strubinger, farmer, sec. 22; P. O., Eldara; was born in Delaware, Aug. 26, 1835, and is a son of Joseph and Mary (Clark) Strubinger; father a native of Holland, Germany, and mother of Delaware; he was brought by his parents to this place in 1838, where he has received his education. In 1858 he married Lucy C. Pryor, and his children are,—Henry J., born June 30, 1859; William A., Nov. 7, 1860; and Mary, Oct. 22, 1862. Mrs. S. was a member of the M. E. Church, and died Nov. 27, 1878. Mr. S.'s daughter now keeps house for him. As a farmer he has been successful, now owning 268 acres of first-class land. His residence cost about $4,500. He has been School Director, School Trustee, and Road Commissioner 12 years. In politics he is a Democrat.

Thomas Clark Strubinger, whose portrait is given in this volume, was born in Wilmington, Del., March 19, 1834; his parents were Joseph and Mary (Clark) Strubinger, the first a native of Holland. They arrived in Pike county April 17, 1838, settling on the southeast quarter of sec. 22, Derry tp., where he resided for many years, and which he owned at the time of his death. He was a prominent farmer, owning 520 acres of land, all of which, except 80 acres, came into his possession in a perfectly wild state; he put under cultivation the whole of it. He left a family of 6 children,—Michael, Thomas C., Joseph H., Elizabeth, Mary and Harriet, all living except Elizabeth. The subject of this sketch was married Dec. 14, 1862, to Sarah A., daughter of Adley and Nancy Hogan, natives of Kentucky, and old settlers in this county; Mr. H. is now deceased. Mr. and Mrs. S. have had 9 children, 6 of whom are living, as follows: a babe, born and died, Aug. 22, 1863; Tillie M., born Nov. 13, 1864; John O., Sept. 12, 1866 ; Edwin Thomas, March 14, 1868; Henry W., March 10, 1870, and died Oct. 20, 1872; Cora C., born April 30, 1873; Lillie J., March 12, 1875, and died Aug. 2, following ; Mary E., born April 23, 1876, and Burt F., Oct. 25, 1877.

Mr. S. obtained his early education in the common log schoolhouse, and spent his early years on his father's farm. At the age of 25 he bought 40 acres of land, being a part of the place where he now resides, sec. 34. The home farm at present consists of 80 acres, upon which are the finest farm residence and improvements in this county. He owns 380 acres of land in the county, and is one of the solid representative farmers. On an annual average he raises 75 acres of wheat, 40 of corn, and raises considerable stock. He has had more than average success. He is a Democrat, but does not take a very active part in politics.

Mrs. Jane Taylor, farmer, sec. 27; P. O., Eldara; was born in Hamilton county, Ohio, in 1818; she remained with her parents until 1838, when she married Simon R. Taylor, and in April, 1839, they came to this county and settled on the place where Mrs. Taylor now resides. Mr. Taylor was a wagon-maker by trade, and worked at that business for several years after he came to this State; but for ten years previous to his death he gave his attention exclusively to farming. He died in 1867, leaving 4 children,—William, born May 1, 1840; Mary, born Aug 21, 1841; Henry, born July 3, 1843; Lucy, born May 30, 1850, and an infant, born Nov. 21, 1858, soon deceased. Mrs. Taylor owns 80 acres of land worth $50 per acre.

T. B. Taylor, farmer, owns 150 acres of land; was born Feb. 7, 1834, in this county; was married Aug. 4, 1854, to Abigail Lee, a native of Ohio, born June 13, 1831. They are the parents of 8 children, 6 living. Mr. T. is a prosperous farmer.

William E. Taylor, farmer, resides in Eldara; was born in this tp. May 8, 1840; has always lived here; was raised on a farm, and June 1, 1868, was married to Caroline Stout; they have three children, namely, Dora, John and Lewis. Mr. T. is a member of the Odd Fellow and Masonic Lodges; owns 35 acres of land, worth $25 per acre; has been Commissioner of Highways and Road Overseer, and in politics is a Republican. His brother Henry was in the late war in the 28th Reg. I. V. I.

Robert C. Temple, farmer, resides on the west ½ of the N. E. qr. of sec. 3; was born in Clermont county, Ohio, Sept. 4, 1821; came to this county in March, 1854, and settled near the town of Perry and lived there 7 years; then to DeWitt county 2 years; to Perry again for 3 years; then bought the farm upon which he now resides. There are 96 acres, worth $50 per acre. Oct. 5, 1843, he married Adeline Fisher, a niece of James Ward, of Griggsville, ex-County Judge of Pike county. They have had 6 children,—Lucy A., born Sept. 4, 1844; Leonidas C., born April 21, 1846, and died Nov. 11, 1873; Sarah Alice, born Oct. 24, 1847; Lizzie A., born Dec. 22, 1850, and died Feb. 11, 1853; James E., born Jan. 2, 1854, and Thomas H., Jan. 29, 1857. Mr. Temple has been an Odd Fellow for over 30 years. He filled acceptably several tp. offices; has been an ardent Democrat, but is now a zealous Greenbacker. In religion he believes in the final restoration of all mankind. P. O., Barry.

Samuel C. Thomas, farmer, sec. 17; P. O., Eldara; was born in Derry tp., Dec. 2, 1842; his father's name was Samuel F., and his mother's Elizabeth Thomas, *nee* Wells. April 10, 1864, he was married, and he has had 9 children, 8 of whom are living, namely: Martha Ann, John C., Susan F., Laura Alice, Charles A., Harry E., Osa May and Samuel C. Mr. T's uncle, John Wells, was in the war of 1812. He is a Democrat.

Franklin Tittsworth is a farmer on sec. 13, and his P. O. address is Eldara.

Thomas J. Tittsworth, farmer, sec. 19; was born Aug. 19, 1855, in Pleasant Vale tp., Pike county, and has lived here ever since; was married Jan. 15, 1874, to Miss Jane Fesler, and they have one child, Addie, born July 30, 1876. Mrs. T. is a daughter of Jacob Fesler. Her 2 uncles, Jacob and John Browning, were both killed in the late war. Mr. T. raises corn, wheat and stock, and sells at home market. He is a Democrat.

Charles B. Troutwine, farmer, sec. 18; P. O., Eldara; was born in Germany, Feb. 17, 1832; came to America in 1841, and to this county in 1852; has lived in this tp. since the spring of 1853; Oct. 1, 1854, he married Lucinda Moyer, and they have had 9 children: their names are, Louisa J., Martha E., Austin B., William H., Charles Wesley, Marvin V., Frederick A., Harry and Moses. Mr. T. owns 160 acres of land, worth $40 per acre. He is a Democrat, and his wife is a Southern Methodist.

Frederick Troutwine, farmer, sec. 30; P. O., Eldara; was born in the Kingdom of Wurtemburg, Germany, July 15, 1829; came to America in 1841 and settled in Clinton county, Ohio; lived there until 1852, and then removed to Pike county, Ill.; was married in March, 1855, to Julia Ann Moyer, who was born in Orange county, Indiana. Their 3 children are: John H., born March 28, 1856; Solomon J., born Feb. 11, 1860; Albert M., born March 6, 1864. Mr. T. owns 240 acres of land. He is a Douglas Democrat. He and wife are Methodists.

Moses Wagoner was born in the city of St. Louis, Mo., Aug. 22, 1815; came to Pike county, Ill., in 1849; April 7, 1855, was married to Martha J. Duland, and they have one child, William Henry, born Aug. 14, 1853. Mr. Wagoner is the owner of 110 acres of land, worth $50 per acre, which he desires to sell, owing to ill health. It is an extra good wheat farm; Mr. W. cut and harvested from 26 acres 800 bushels of wheat, and raised 80 bushels of corn to the acre, in the year 1879. There is situated upon the farm an elegant two-story frame dwelling; good barn, stables and other buildings, stock, wells and springs. In politics, a Republican. P. O., Barry.

Job S. Ware, harness-maker, Eldara; was born in the city of Philadelphia, Aug. 28, 1830; came to this county in 1838; learned his trade at Barry; was married Oct. 10, 1852, to Sarah Robertson; they are both members of the M. E. Church. Their living children are: Ida Belle, Lillie G., William I., Gertrude, Harry and Charles. His grandfather, John Hughs, was in the war of 1812. He is a Democrat.

James H. Wassell, farmer, sec. 33; is a native of Derry tp., born March 4, 1854; was raised on a farm and had limited advantages for education. His father, Robert Wassell, died when the subject of this sketch was but 3 years of age. Nov. 7, 1876, he married May Tipler, and they have had one child, Anna, born Oct. 18, 1877. He is a member of the Odd Fellows Lodge at Eldara. Disposes of his produce at home market. P. O., Eldara.

Isaac N. Williams, farmer, sec. 31; was born June 12, 1851; was raised a farmer; Jan. 13, 1876, was married to Eliza Ann Moore of this county, and they have 2 children, James Henry and Stephen R. Mr. W. has had good educational advantages, and in politics is a Democrat. P. O., Eldara.

Stephen R. Williams. The first of this man's ancestors who settled in America came from Wales previous to the Revolution, and settled in Maryland; his name was Edward Williams, and he served under Washington in the war, at the close of which he removed to Ohio county, Kentucky, a section of country then perfectly wild, savage Indians and ferocious beasts holding almost complete sway. He was a farmer by occupation, and died in that county, leaving 8 children, one of whom, Stephen, was the grandfather of the subject of this biographical notice. He was a Baptist minister for over 50 years, preaching in Kentucky, Illinois and Iowa. He died in Jefferson county about 1868, leaving also a family of 8 children, the eldest of whom, Isaac, was the father of Stephen R. He was born in Kentucky in 1800, and in January, 1819, married Sarah Coleman, a daughter of Henry Coleman, of Ohio county, Ky., whose father was a German and an early settler of Kentucky. Of this marriage were 13 children, of whom 9 are living, the eldest of whom is Stephen R., who was born Nov. 12, 1820, in Ohio county, Ky. His early life was passed on his father's farm in White county, Ill., whither his father had moved when his son was but 2 years of age. Here also he obtained his education in the old-fashioned log school-house, with a w ndow of greased paper where a log had been taken out for the purpose; indeed, Mr. W. never went to school where glass windows were used. June 22, 1837, he married Miss Nancy J. Funkhouser, daughter of Isaac Funkhouser, in White county, Ill., and 3 children were born to them in that county, namely, Sarah, Virgil and William. In 1844 he moved with his family to this county, settling in Pittsfield tp., where he commenced farming. His land title not being perfect, he returned his claim to the seller in 1846, and removed into Derry township, where he rented farms for several years. In 1852 he bought the southeast quarter of sec. 32, this tp., which place was slightly improved, having on it a log house. The same year he moved his family here. He has since put under fine cultivation about 100 acres at this place. Here he lived about 14 years, when he moved to a farm which he bought, the southwest quarter of sec. 31, this tp., where he is still residing.

In 1842 Mr. Williams joined the Primitive Baptist Church, of which he has ever since been a member. He is a man of deep convictions, and has believed it his duty to take a public and active part in the cause of the Church. His public efforts caused his brethren to induce him to become a regular preacher, and with some reluctance he complied with their wishes, and was ordained after about two years' preaching. He has now served in that capacity 22 years. He has never preached for a salary. He has preached at the regular annual and monthly meetings in Missouri and Iowa, besides this State.

At present he owns 515 acres of land in this tp., and 80 acres in tp. 6 s., 6 w. He has 4 children living, 2 boys and 2 girls. Wm. D. married Angeline Moore, and lives on one of his father's farms, on sec. 32; Isaac married Eliza Jane Moore, and lives on sec. 30, his father's farm of 200 acres; Sarah married Benj. House and lives in Atlas tp.; Fanny married Charles Drummond, and resides on the home place. He has had 8 other children, who have deceased, namely, Mary, who died after she was a married woman; Henry, who died at the age of 17; Lucy Ann and Martin, who died very young, and 3 others died in infancy. Although Mr. Williams is interested in political matters, he has not taken a very active and prominent part. He is a Democrat, has been Collector, Commissioner, Township Trustee, etc. It is claimed that the first person ever baptized by the Green river (Ky.) waters was Mrs. Williams' great-grandmother on her mother's side. Mr. Williams' postoffice address is Eldara. His portrait is given in this book, and can be found by reference to the table of contents.

H. R. Wood, farmer and stock-dealer, sec. 29; P. O., Eldara; owns 22 acres, worth $40 per acre; was born in Penn., Sept. 30, 1825; came to this State in the fall of 1838, settling in Morgan county, where he remained 2 years, thence to Pittsfield until 1854, then settled in Derry; went to California in 1849 and returned in 1852; was married in Missouri in 1855 to Lorinda Vale, who was born in Missouri and died in 1860. They had 2 children, William and Luella. In May, 1873, he married Sarah Shinn, born Jan. 25, 1849. In addition to farming, Mr. W. raises and handles young stock to some extent.

Theodore Wood, grocer and confectioner at Eldara, was born in Illinois, Nov. 27, 1854; was married in this county to Josephine Taylor, a native of this county, and they are the parents of 5 children,—4 living. Mr. W. owns one lot with dwelling, and in his line of business is doing well. In politics he is a Democrat.

Lewis N. Worsham, farmer, is a native of Illinois, and was born Jan. 15, 1836; was married Oct. 26, 1862, to Cynthia Williams, also a native of Illinois, born Aug. 11, 1840. They are the parents of 4 children: Laura, Oren, and 2 infants, deceased. Mr. W. owns 183 acres of land, worth $50 per acre.

ATLAS TOWNSHIP.

This township is the scene of the more important early history of the county. For some years here was situated the seat of empire, as it were, the metropolis of a vast region. Here was not only the business center, but the social, religious, and political headquarters of a section of country now containing many thousands of people, and millions of wealth. Virtually, the first few chapters in this book is a history of this township, and therefore it will not be expected that we should repeat what we have already recorded, although much of it is essentially local, or township and village history.

According to the general order we have adopted in writing these sketches, we will speak of the earliest settlers first. The first legitimate settler of the county located in this township. The person to whose memory this honor is due, was Ebenezer Franklin. He came in March, 1820, and first located on sec. 27, near where the town of Atlas now is. He brought his family and for a time dwelt in a tent. Then came in Daniel Shinn, who became his neighbor, and like him pitched his tent, and in it lived until May. At that time both these sturdy pioneers erected rude log cabins on sec. 22, and about three-fourths of a mile from Atlas.

The same year another prominent family arrived at Atlas, or rather upon the site of Atlas, for of course there was no town there then. The family we refer to was the Ross family, consisting of Col. William Ross, Captain Leonard Ross, Dr. Henry J. Ross, and Clarendon Ross. These were married men and brought their families with them. They came from Pittsfield, Mass., and of course during the existing modes of travel in those pioneer times they had a hard, tedious journey. They were all tired out when they arrived at the spot, on sec. 27, that they were to call home. The country in its virgin state was beautiful to behold, but so far in the wilderness was it that it must have been lonely indeed to them. However, they were glad to get to their journey's end, and one of the party exclaimed, as tradition has it, that they had reached home "at last," from which the town, and latterly the township was named.

After the Rosses, of whom we speak in the first chapter of this volume at greater length, came James M. Seeley, who played an important and honorable part in the early history of the county. Then came Levi Newman and Charles McGiffin, who kept a ferry across the Mississippi at Louisiana, John and Jeremiah Ross, Rufus Brown, John Wood and Willard Keyes. Brown kept a tavern in Atlas for a time, but he, with these two Rosses, and Wood and Keyes, moved to Adams county and became prominent in the affairs of that community. Then came Joseph Petty, John M. Smith, Deacon Snow, Daniel Husong, Dexter Wheelock, who kept store and hotel at Atlas for a time, and a few others.

Among a few others of the leading first settlers of Atlas we will mention Col. Benj. Barney, Henry Long, Stephen R. Watson, Benjamin D. Brown, James Ross, etc. As many of the early pilgrims to Atlas were scattered in various parts of the county when the county-seat was moved from there, and as a half century has almost elapsed since the village of Atlas began to wane, we find it impossible to get anything like a full and authentic list of the first settlers here. It is true there are many of the descendants of the early pioneers now living in this township, but of these we speak among the personal sketches given below.

In 1824 the public buildings, which had previously been at Cole's Grove, now Calhoun county, were moved to Atlas. During the following decade it was a busy commercial center and had great promise of becoming the most important town in this section. At one time it was thought that it would eclipse Quincy, but when, in 1833, the county-seat was removed to Pittsfield, it suffered materially. Indeed, the town has never since assumed any prominence, but declined, until now there is only a postoffice, general store and a blacksmith shop located here. At that time the more prominent settlers followed the public buildings to Pittsfield, and made that the metropolis of the county.

The first death to occur in Atlas township was that of Mr. Husong. The first child born was Nancy Ross, daughter of Col. William Ross. The first male child was Marcellus Ross, who now resides in Pittsfield. Some say, however, that a son was born to Ebenezer Franklin prior to this, and others that a child of John M. Smith's was the first one born. The first parties married in the township were Daniel Barney and Miss A. L. Husong. The first sermon was preached by the celebrated Lorenzo Dow, in the old court-house, in 1826. The first school-house was erected the same year upon sec. 26.

Before Ross township was cut off from Atlas, which was done in 1879, it was by far the largest township in the county. It then embraced the whole of one and parts of three Congressional townships. Much of it, however, was bottom land, and valueless for cultivation until the erection of the great Sny Carte levee. This public enterprise has redeemed many entire sections of fine land in Atlas. At one time the Sny Carte slough was so high that Col. Ross was enabled to run a boat up to Atlas. This is what is termed a timbered township, but is well settled and improved.

Here we find some of the finest farms in the county. The Quincy, Alton and St. Louis Railroad passes through the township from northwest to southeast.

VILLAGES.

There are in this township three villages, all small, but pleasantly located. They are Atlas, Rockport and Summer Hill. The former town was laid out in 1823 by William Ross and Rufus Brown. It was the first town laid off in the county, and for a time first in point of commercial advantages. We have spoken of the village so often, however, that anything we might now say would merely be repetition. We therefore will refer the reader to the first chapters and the history of the township given above.

During the great speculative excitement of 1836 and the few subsequent years, towns were projected all over the State. During the former year there were about a dozen towns laid out in Pike county, among which was Rockport. It had excellent milling facilities, and a project to erect a grist-mill, then greatly needed in the county, was set on foot by Ross, Scott & Co. About 1828 a saw-mill was erected at this point upon the Sny Carte, on the southwest quarter of sec. 17. Later, about 1830, John Warburton erected a flouring-mill at the same site. This mill was destroyed by fire in 1846. During that and the following year another mill was erected upon the site of the former. This mill was conducted successfully, and was a great convenience to the settlers until 1853, when it shared the fate of the former and went up in the flames. Undaunted, however, its proprietors set about to erect another, which was done in 1855. This mill was run for 12 years, when it was burned. In 1867-8 Shaw & Rupert built a fourth mill at this point, with a capacity of 300 barrels a day. It will be seen that this has been one of the greatest milling points in this section. Rockport took from Atlas about all of the business that was left it after the removal of the county-seat to Pittsfield. The town was laid out on the most approved plan for a city of no mean dimensions. For a time it grew rapidly and gave great promise to its founders, but the financial crash which followed the speculative period almost completely stopped immigration to the State for a few years, and all of the new towns suffered materially.

Rockport is located on secs. 17, 18 and 20, on the Sny Carte, and contains several stores, and transacts a good trade in a local way. It is situated on the Quincy, Alton & St. Louis Railway.

The village of Summer Hill, which is located on sec. 13 of this township, was laid out March 11, 1845, by Lyman Scott. It is situated in the midst of a beautiful and fertile section of country. It is a very pleasant country town, containing two nice churches, two or three stores, postoffice, etc.

Summer Hill Congregational Church. The Congregational Church of Summer Hill was organized by Rev. Asa Turner at Atlas in Nov., 1834, under the name of the Rockport and Atlas Congregational Church. Preaching services were held at Rockport, Atlas, and later at Summer Hill. Gradually, as the settlements extended back from the Mississippi river, the Church members became located more and more at Summer Hill, until the Church had migrated from Rockport and Atlas to Summer Hill. This change was gradual, extending through a number of years. The present church building at Summer Hill was completed about 1856.

This Church has always held a form of doctrine common to the Congregational Churches. It believes in the new birth ("Except a man be born again he cannot see the kingdom of God"); in the sinfulness of men and in redemption only through Jesus Christ, the Son of God; in the sanctifying power of the Holy Spirit; in the inspiration of the Holy Scriptures; that the word of God is the only infallible rule of faith and life; in the endless happiness of the righteous and misery of the unregenerate. It teaches and believes in a pure and upright life consecrated to God.

The first great season of growth came under the pastorate of Rev. Wm. Carter from 1834 to 1847. During this period of nine years the Church increased from 10 or 12 members to 100. After 1847 the Church suffered a decline until 1865, when it numbered 41 members. The second period of growth came under the present Pastor, Rev. C. E. Marsh, from 1868 to the present time. During this period of 12 years the Church increased from 50 to 116 members. In the winter of 1873-4 a great season of revival was enjoyed, when 48 were received into the Church. The past winter (1879-80) another revival has been enjoyed, and 39 have entered into covenant with the Church.

The following persons have acted as Pastors of the Church: Rev. Warren Nichols, from 1835 to 1837; Rev. A. T. Norton, from 1837 to ——; Rev. Wm. Carter, from 1838 to 1847; Rev. Gideon C. Clark, from 1847 to 1850; Rev. A. H. Fletcher, from 1850 to 1853; Rev. C. S. Cady, from 1853 to 1855; Rev. J. G. Barrett, from 1856 to 1859; Rev. S. R. Thrall, from 1859 to 1865; Rev. Samuel Dilley, from 1865 to 1867; Rev. Wm. Carter, from 1867 to 1868; Rev. Chas. E. Marsh, from 1868 to the present time.

BIOGRAPHICAL.

We give below personal sketches, in alphabetical rotation, of the prominent citizens and old settlers of Atlas township and its villages.

J. A. Adams, farmer, sec. 27; P. O., Atlas; was born in 1803 in Rensellaer county, N. Y., the son of James and Edna Adams; received a fair education and followed sawing, and operating cotton and woolen mill with good success; he quit the business in 1843 and emigrated West, settling on the present homestead, where he has lived ever since. The farm is well improved. Feb. 10, 1825, he married Harriet Green, who was born in 1802 in Rensellaer county, N. Y., and their 3 children were Cornelius, deceased, Jeremiah and Edna. Mr. Adams first occupied about 500 acres of bottom and up land, and since has obtained about 500 acres more. He has seen the bottom opposite his residence entirely overflowed, and has been in a steam-boat over the land he now cultivates. Mr. Adams has been Assessor for 15 or 16 years. The house now occupied by him was built in 1822, with an addition in 1824. It is a substantial building, and bids fair to stand for ages yet. The first preacher he knew was Rev. Wm. Carter, who was in Pittsfield so long. Mr. Adams' father was in the Revolutionary war, as privateer at sea. He distinctly remembers the war of 1812.

Isaac Barton, farmer, was born in Kentucky, June 7, 1825, the son of William and Mary (Brewer) Barton, natives of Tennessee; was educated in the Kentucky subscription schools; his early life was spent in mechanical employment, but the most of his life he has been a farmer. In 1846 he married Miss R. M. Owsley, a native of East Tennessee, and of their 11 children 8 are living, 5 sons and 3 girls; 3 are married. Mr. Barton came to Pike county the year he was married, with no property except a horse and saddle, but he is now in comfortable circumstances, living in a $3,000 house. He has held nearly all the township offices, and is in several official positions at the present time. In politics he is a Democrat, and in religion both himself and wife are members of the M. E. Church.

Aaron Baughmon was born in Ohio, Dec. 11, 1835, and is a son of Jacob and Catharine (Wilhelm) Baughmon, natives of Pennsylvania, and of German ancestry; was educated mostly in the common schools of this county; can speak German. April 10, 1856, he married Sarah Sapp, daughter of Daniel Sapp, a pioneer of this county; of their 9 children 6 are living. Mr. B. came to this county about Christmas in 1846, and worked at quarrying rock and burning lime; for the last 8 years it has been a success. He ran a threshing-machine for 9 years, and in that business lost his health, and in burning lime he thinks he recovered his voice which he had lost. He is a farmer, residing on sec. 14, where he owns 40 acres, besides having 40 acres on sec. 15. In his present business he has been successful. Being married before he was 21 years of age, his father claimed $150 for his time, which was paid. He is a Republican, and both himself and wife are members of the M. E. Church. P. O., Summer Hill.

Monroe Baughmon, farmer, sec. 11; P. O., Summer Hill; was born in this county Oct. 5, 1848, and is a son of Jacob and Catharine W. (Heler) Baughmon, who were married in 1835 and had 5 children, of whom Monroe is the eldest. The latter received a common-school education, and is now following farming in Atlas tp.

Capt. Uriah Brock was born in Missouri in 1820, and is a son of Armstrong and Theresa Angle (Brown) Brock, the former of English descent and the latter of German; was educated in the subscription schools of the time; at 15 he went upon the river and worked at cooking and pulling oars on a flat-boat; in 1839 he went on a steamer to learn the river as cub pilot; in 1840 he was promoted to the position of pilot on the steamer Ione, and for the same man

David. W. Dean

ATLAS TP.

he ran steamers for 7 years on the Ohio river, making 10 years altogether which he worked for one man; has followed the river as pilot every summer since he learned the business, and expects to as long as he can see and turn a wheel. He has been moderately successful, having as much as $2,500 for one summer's work. At present he gets only $600 for a season's work. He married Miss Caroline Marsh in 1855, and they have 6 children, all living in this tp., where he spends the winter with his family. Four of the children are married. He has a neat and substantial residence in Summer Hill, and 12 acres of land. In politics he is a Republican, and he and his wife are members of the Congregational Church. Mrs. Brock's father, Sherman Brown, was an early settler of this county.

David W. Deam, farmer and stock-raiser; is the son of Henry and Susannah (Kiser) Deam; his father was a native of Pennsylvania and born in 1784; his mother was born in the State of Kentucky in 1794; they emigrated with their family to Ohio in an early day, where both of them passed the remainder of their lives; they died near Dayton, O., and were laid at rest in Bethel township, Miami county. David W., the subject of this biography, was born in Montgomery county, O., in 1831; in 1852 he went to Bluffton, Mills Co., Ind., where he held the position of Deputy County Clerk for one year; he then returned to the Buckeye State and remained until 1854; he was then united in marriage with Miss Sarah C. Deal, who was born in 1831; she is the daughter of Philip and Mary (Boyer) Deal, both natives of Maryland. To them have been born 4 children, 3 of whom are living; Mary Alice was born Jan. 3, 185⁵, in Montgomery, O.; William Lewis, born Sept. 25, 1856; Dora Bell, Jan. 31, 1858, died Feb. 24, 1876, and Warren G., born Jan. 29, 1864. Wm. L. married Miss Capps, Oct. 9, 1879, and Mary A. was married to Uriah A. Brock, March 23, 1872. Mr. Deam moved with his family to Atlas, this county, in 1856, first locating on sec. 23, where he engaged in farming until 1867, when he sold out and purchased a fine farm on sec. 13. He now owns 240 acres of land. His residence, with ground attached, is among the most beautiful, tasteful and convenient in the county. It is situated in the outskirts of the pleasant little village of Summer Hill. Mr. Deam, who is now engaged in farming and stock-raising, dealing in fine graded stock, ranks among the more prominent, enterprising and substantial citizens of Pike county, and as one of her representative citizens we present his portrait in this volume.

James Brown. This gentleman's father, Isaac Brown, was born in March, 1791, in Virginia, moved to this State in 1828, and died in 1848; his mother was Susan Brown. The subject of this notice was one of 14 children, and was born in April, 1833; in 1856 he married Sarah Knapp, who was born in June, 1839, and their 5 children are, Zara, born in 1857; Lloyd, born in 1859; George, born in 1862; Frederic, born in 1865, and Lilly, born in 1872. Mr. Brown

45

has always been a farmer; has been to California twice. In religion he is a Universalist, and in politics a Republican.

Mrs. Susan J. Cleveland, nee Baxter, was born Aug. 2, 1860, and married Galen Cleveland in 1853, and of their 10 children only 2 are living, both named after their parents. Mr. Baxter settled in Missouri, where his children had but a very limited education.

J. H. Farrington. The subject of this sketch was born in Milton, this county, Aug. 19, 1843, and is a son of D. H. and Martha (Shaw) Harrington, both natives of North Carolina, and his father of German ancestry. J. H. is the third of a family of 10 children, all of whom are boys. His father was a farmer, at which business he was successful. Both his parents are living in Missouri at the present time. Our subject began to learn the trade of a miller with Francis Frye at the village of Time, in 1870 ; they ran the mill in partnership until Nov. 26, 1876, when it was destroyed by fire, at a loss to them of $10,000. February of the following year he came to Summer Hill and became a partner of the firm of Peters & Co. Their mill is one of the best in the county, does an extensive local trade, and has a good reputation. Their favorite brand of flour is the "Golden Rule." April 10, 1863, he was married to Jeannette Farrington, who was born July 18, 1845; their only child, Thomas Virgil, was born in 1865. In politics Mr. F. is a Democrat. He served as Supervisor for Hardin tp. for the years 1875–76.

James H. Ferguson, druggist, Summer Hill, was born in Pike county, March 27, 1855; his father, James H. Ferguson, is a native of Ireland, and his mother, Ann Eliza (Dodge) Ferguson, a native of Georgia. James H. was educated in the common schools of Pike county, Pittsfield High School, and Eureka College; until he arrived at the age of 22 he was engaged in farming; he then went to Nebo and engaged in the study of medicine for a time, after which he bought a stock of drugs at Griggsville, and also has an interest in another store in the same town. In 1879 he came to Summer Hill and started a drug store, the only one in the place. The grandfather of our subject was among the early settlers of the State. His father, who was a graduate as a civil engineer, in Europe, came to Pike county in an early day, served as County Surveyor, and held that position until he died, in 1863. He was the owner of between 500 and 600 acres of land at the time.

Solomon Greengard was born Sept. 14, 1830, and is a native of Poland; he learned the trade of blacksmith in his native country, but is now engaged in selling tin-ware, furs, rags, etc. In 1840 he was married to Esth Rachell. Six children have been born to them, 4 of whom are living, 1 boy and 3 girls.

C. M. Garner, farmer, sec. 10; P. O., Summer Hill; is a son of Jonathan and Mary (Newnham) Garner, the former a native of North Carolina and the latter of South Carolina. Our subject was born in Kentucky in 1829, and was early brought to this county, where he received a good common-school education. His parents came to the county in 1840 and settled 10 miles west of Pittsfield. He married the first time in 1856, and the second time, 1869, he married Caroline McClintock, by whom he has had 4 children: he had one by his first wife. He and his present wife are members of the Christian Church; he is a Republican. He has 260 acres of land.

James Gay, farmer, sec. 12; P. O., Summer Hill; was born Feb. 5, 1814, in Iredell county, N. C., and is a son of William and Anna (Rutledge) Gay, father a native of the same county and mother a native of Rowan county, N. C., both of Irish ancestry. His chances being very poor in a Southern State, he came to Pike county, Ill., where he graduated in a log cabin 14 by 14, in Pleasant Hill tp., in 1834. In 1839 he married Amelia Yokem, and they have had 9 children, 8 of whom are living. Both Mr. and Mrs. Gay are members of the Congregational Church. Mr. Gay has been a farmer all his life, and coming to Pike county in Feb., 1834, he worked as a farm hand in Atlas tp. The first night he staid in Pike county he had only half money enough to pay his bill, which was 37½ cents. Besides this he had a horse worth $15, which was all the earthly possession he could call his own at that time. He is now the owner of 660 acres of land in Pike county, and has an interest in several other tracts of land. All his sons live in this county and all are married, the eldest of whom owns 480 acres of land.

William H. Gay, farmer, sec. 9; P. O., Rockport; was born in this tp., and is a son of James and Amelia (Yokem) Gay, above mentioned; he attended the common schools of this county and began teaching at the age of 18 years. He enlisted May 4, 1861, in the 16th Ill. Inf., serving as Corporal of Co. K, and participated in all the battles that the regiment was engaged in; he was discharged June 12, 1864. In 1867 he was united in marriage with Elizabeth Shinn, and to them have been born 5 children, 4 sons and a daughter. Mr. Gay is the owner of 480 acres of land, 320 of which are in Pike county.

John Helkey was born on the German ocean in December, 1848; was united in marriage with Fanny Adams, who was born in July, 1859. In 1879, Aug. 2d, of that year, a son, Charlie, was born to them. He has engaged some in railroading, but at present is following blacksmithing and wagon-making, which he expects to continue the rest of his life. His wife received a good common-school education, and attended the Pittsfield high school.

James S. Johnson was born in Pike county in 1846, and is a son of Elisha T. and Catherine (Cook) Johnson, of New Jersey. James received his education in the common schools of this county, engaged in farming and coopering, and in 1864 enlisted in the 7th Ill. Inf., under Capt. Hubbard. In 1865 he was united in marriage with Eliza Ann Waters; 2 of the 4 children born to them are living. His father, who was a moulder in early life, came to Pike county in 1838, and engaged in farming; his mother died in 1867, and his father in 1873.

Henry A. Long was born July 6, 1774, and Emeline Green March 4, 1804; the two were united in marriage Aug. 5, 1822; to them were born 5 sons and 3 daughters. Kennedy Long was born March 14, 1826, and Oct. 13, 1852, married Phœbe J. Roasa, who was born June 27, 1832; by this union 5 children, all boys, were born: Henry A., born Jan. 21, 1854, William J., July 26, 1855, George P., Oct. 5, 1865, L. E., born Nov. 14, 1868, and Philip R., Feb. 13, 1874. Mr. L. came here with his parents in 1831, and located in Atlas, then the county-seat of Pike county. He has been a great fisherman and at the present lives in the oldest house in Atlas, and consequently the oldest in the county. The floor is of puncheons, hewed on one side and rip-sawed, and is still of good quality. Mrs. Long is a member of the M. E. Church, while Mr. Long is liberal toward all the churches, and is a Republican.

Mrs. Lucia Mace, nee Chamberlain, was born June 27, 1826, and in 1837 was brought to Illinois, where she received a common-school education; Aug. 4, 1842, she married John Mace, and their 3 children are D. H., D. A. and Kate. Mr. Mace served 18 months in the Mexican war. While in health he followed carpentering. Mrs. Mace owns good property in the village of Rockport.

Rev. C. E. Marsh was born in New York, March 4, 1837, and is a son of James and Emeline (Allen) Marsh, of English ancestry. He attended the common schools, entered Knox College at Galesburg, where he remained 3 years, and also graduated at Wheaton College, Ill., near Chicago. His father during his early life was a silversmith, but after he came to this county, which was in 1844, he engaged in farming. Our subject passed his early life on a farm, but since he graduated in 1860 he has not followed that vocation. At the age of 21 he united with the Congregational Church at Galesburg, Ill.; in Oct., 1868, he was installed Pastor at Summer Hill; at that time the membership was 60, but at present numbers 116; most of the accessions were made during two revivals, one held in 1873-4, when 48 were added, the other in 1879-80, when 39 joined the Church. In 1860 Rev. Marsh was united in marriage with Belle Robinson; to them have been born 7 children, 5 sons and 2 daughters, the two latter of whom are deceased.

Jonathan Miller was born in North Carolina, and married Rebecca Span, Sept. 7, 1824, in Indiana; to them were born 10 children: Calvin, Luther, Moses, Houston, Samuel, James, Jonathan, Mary Jane, Emeline, Florence,—all of whom are married except the two youngest.

Moses S. Miller. Jonathan Miller, his father, was born Aug. 13, 1801, and his mother, Rebecca (Span) Miller, was born in 1808. Moses S. was born June 3, 1837; the same year his parents came to this State; he was united in marriage in 1856 with Elizabeth Guthrie, who was born in Missouri in 1831; of the 4 children born to them only one is living, Julia E., who was born in 1857. He is engaged in farming, began with no other help but his own hands, but now owns a good farm.

Henry Morse, farmer, sec. 13; P. O., Summer Hill; was born in Boston, Mass., April 2, 1817, and is the son of Henry and Mary (Fox) Morse; he obtained the principal part of his education at North-Wilbraham Academy, Mass. Mr. M. has been thrice married. He united with his present wife, Margaret Jane Smithers, in 1855; she is a member of the Methodist Church. At the age of 16 Mr. M. commenced to learn the trade of carpenter and joiner, and has worked successfully at it for many years. He came to Pike county from Massachusetts in 1834, and settled at Rockport; he now lives on a farm on sec. 13, 6 S., 5 W. In 1861 he enlisted in Co. D, 3d Mo. Inf., and served till the expiration of the term.

H. Peters, miller at Summer Hill, was born in Pennsylvania, July 25, 1829; his parents, James and Nancy (Culver) Peters, were natives of Canada and Pennsylvania, respectively. Our subject received his education in the common schools of Wisconsin, attended the high school at Beloit, and also took a course of book-keeping. He served an apprenticeship at blacksmithing in the same town, and worked 5 years in a plow factory; in 1849 he came to Quincy, Ill., where he worked in a plow factory for 2 years, when he married Elizabeth Conyers; they then lived in Palmyra, Mo., six years, when they removed to Pike county, where they have since remained. For 10 years he continued the manufacture of plows, when he sold out and embarked in the milling business, and is now of the firm of Peters & Co., millers, Summer Hill. Politically he is a Greenbacker, and a prominent member of his party. He is one of the two delegates from Pike county, chosen in March, 1880, to nominate a Greenback candidate for the Presidency. In politics, as in his business, he is energetic and well posted in the history of the country and of the various political parties. He has served as Justice of the Peace for 3 years.

Carson N. Rupert was born in 1854, and is a farmer, sec. 27; P. O., Atlas; Oct. 18, 1876, he was united in marriage with Miss Mary E. Adams, who was born in 1855; and they have one child, a girl.

George Schwartz was born in Switzerland in 1813; when at the age of 20 he emigrated to America; his parents, Andrew and Mary Ann (Shoemaker) Schwartz, were also natives of Switzerland. He attended school from the time he was 6 years old till he was 18, and received a good German education; he never attended school in America any, but can read and write English with ease. He located in Atlas tp. in 1833; has been a farmer all his life, and worked the first two years after he arrived here by the month, the first year receiving $7, and the second year $8 per month. He was united in marriage with Miss Mary Gay in 1838, and of the 5 children born to them 4 are living. James Gay, spoken of above, and our subject, kept bachelor's hall for three years after his arrival here; they were then poor boys, but are to-day leading citizens of the county.   Mr. S. owns 254 acres of land in Atlas tp., and has a handsome and substantial residence in Summer Hill. He has held local offices in this tp., been Sunday-school Superintendent, Trustee and Deacon in the Summer Hill Congregational church, and prominent in all the affairs of his community.

Dr. G. W. Schwartz, Summer Hill, was born Feb. 17, 1846, and is a son of George Schwartz, above mentioned.   The Doctor is a graduate of the St. Louis Medical College, and began practice in the spring of 1874 in Milton, Mo., and, like most young doctors, labored under many disadvantages.   In the fall of that year he removed to Summer Hill, where he has built up a fair practice.

G. J. Shaw, Summer Hill, was born in Massachusetts Feb. 2, 1816, and is a son of Walter and Marcia (Cadwell) Shaw, the former a native of Massachusetts, and of Scottish descent; he came to Pike county in 1836, and settled at Atlas; he left his home in Massachusetts in 1832, went to the West Indies, thence to New Orleans, and then to Missouri.   He learned the carpenter and joiner's trade, and subsequently engaged in farming, now owning 300 acres of land.   In the early days it was quite difficult to get money enough to pay his taxes.   The principal circulating medium was coon-skins.   He had only $100 when he was married, and made his start by making window sash.   He tells us that most of the land between Summer Hill and Pittsfield was bought for $1.25 an acre.   He further says that it was no uncommon thing to see a crop sell for more than the land cost.   Mr. S. was married in 1837 to Sophia Kennedy, and to them have been born 5 children, all of whom are living.

Henry L. Shaw, farmer, sec. 7; P. O., Summer Hill ; was born Feb. 3, 1837, within 300 yards of where he now lives, and is a son of Luther and A. B. (Bemiss) Shaw, natives of Massachusetts; attended the public school some; when he was 15 years of age his father died (1852), leaving the care of a large family on him; there were 10 children, of whom Henry was the eldest.   In 1872 he married Mary A. Davis, and of their 3 children 2 are living.   **Mr.** Shaw is a Republican, and both himself and wife are members of the Congregational Church.   He has been a successful farmer, now owning 267 acres of land in this county.

H. O. Shaw, farmer, sec. 12; P. O., Summer Hill; was born July 30, 1814, in Massachusetts, and is the son of Solomon and Persis (Colon) Shaw, natives also of Massachusetts, and father a farmer ; the subject of this notice was educated in the common schools of the Bay State.   In 1836 he married Sarah Andrews, and of their 3 children 2 are living,--Charles H., George and Eva Myrtie, deceased. Mr. Shaw came to Pike county in 1840, and the following year he settled on sec. 12, where he now owns 50 acres of land, and is out of debt.   He has worked at shoemaking several years.   In 1862 both his boys enlisted in Co. A, 99th Ill. Inf., under Capt Edwards; George W. was wounded at the grand charge at Vicksburg, by a shot in the leg; Charles was Sergeant, and the boys were in all the battles in which the Regiment was engaged.   Mr. Shaw has been Collector, and in politics is a Republican.

Lucien W. Shaw, farmer, sec. 12 ; P. O., Summer Hill ; was born in this county in 1839, and is a son of George J. and Sophia (Kinney) Shaw, father a native of Massachusetts and mother of New York, and both of English descent; he obtained a common-school education in this county.   In 1864 he married Anna M. Barney, who died in 1874; of their offspring one child is still living; in 1875 Mr. S. married Maria Shaw, and they have 3 children, all living.   In 1862 Mr. Shaw enlisted in the famous Pike county Regiment, No. 99, in Co. C, under Capt. Matthews, and was elected 2d Lieutenant, and in a short time he became 1st Lieutenant; he was in five battles and several skirmishes; in 1863 he resigned on account of sickness.   His early occupation was teaching and farming.   Since the war he has kept store some of the time and pursued farming.   He owns 190 acres of good land.   He is a Republican, and has been School Trustee, Town Clerk and Justice of the Peace; and being a member of the Congregational Church, he has been also Deacon and Sunday-school Superintendent, the latter for 10 years.   His wife is also a member of the same Church.

Hiram Smith, a native of Madison county, Ill., where he was born in 1830; he was reared upon a farm, and in 1861 enlisted in Co. D, 28th Ill. Inf., in the United States service to defend his country ; in the battle of Shiloh he was shot through the neck, which proved nearly fatal; he partially recovered and was in several small skirmishes, and was in the hard-fought battles of Pea Ridge and Hatchie; in the latter battle he received two wounds, one from a minie ball and the other from a large piece of shell ; he was then consigned to a hospital, and from there sent to Keokuk, Iowa, where, Jan. 2, 1863, he was discharged.   He was married Oct. 8, 1863, and he has two children, H. E. and James W. H.

Edwin C. Tryon, deceased, was born in 1830 in Connecticut, and died in 1872.   His wife, Louisa B. (Buell) Tryon, was born in New York city in 1839; they were united in marriage in 1859; to them were born 2 sons, one in 1861 and one in 1870.   Miss Christian R. Rapp was married to Henry Buell, of New York city, Jan. 2, 1873; by this marriage one son was born.   Her parents and grandparents lived to a good old age.   She was born Aug. 6, 1818.

G. W. Turnbaugh, farmer, sec. 23; P. O., Summer Hill; is a son of Joseph and Luckey (Rodgers) Turnbaugh, both natives of Kentucky; he received his education in the subscription schools held in the old log school-houses in this county; in 1856 he was married to Elizabeth Shinn, daughter of Daniel Shinn, one of the very first pioneers in this county.   Mr. T. was born in this county in 1832, and has lived all his life within 5 miles of where he was born.

Alva S. Warren, farmer, is a native of Geneseo county, N. Y., where he was born May 21, 1851.   Dec. 20, 1875, Mr. W. was united in marriage with Miss Hattie A., daughter of J. G. Adams; she was born in 1852.   Laura, their daughter, was born Dec. 22

1877. Mrs. W. attended the Methodist College at Jacksonville one year, Liberty School, Mo., and the Pittsfield high school.

John M. Williams was born in the State of Ohio in 1835, and is the son of Richard and Theresa Ann (Thomas) Williams, father of Welsh and mother of American parents, and both natives of the Buckeye State; he came to Pike county in 1842, and has resided in Summer Hill 10 years, and in the vicinity for 30 years. He has engaged in farming, and also is a shoemaker. In 1856 he was united in marriage with Miss Mary Petty, who is a member of the Christian Church.

ROSS TOWNSHIP.

This is a fractional township, and was formed from Atlas township in 1879. It includes that part of Atlas known as 7 south and 5 west. Since the building of the levee much of the heretofore worthless farm land has been put under cultivation.

This township being a part of Atlas from the earliest period of county government until the past season, its history, of course, is likewise a part of the history of that township. As a township of itself it has no history. It was named in honor of Col. Wm. Ross.

We mention the following prominent gentlemen of this neighborhood:

Jesse Long, farmer, sec 1; P. O., Pleasant Hill; was born in Maryland, May 14, 1823, and is a son of Henry and Emeline (Green) Long, father a native of Ireland and mother of Delaware; was educated in the subscription schools of this county. In 1850 he married Caroline Ramsay, and of the 9 children which they had, 7 are living,—4 boys and 3 girls. Coming to Pike county in the winter of the deep snow, Mr. Long has been a citizen here half a century, and has witnessed the many and wonderful changes which the country has passed through. When he first came here Indians were still around and deer were more numerous than cattle are at the present day. He has lived on his present farm for 48 years. He owns 300 acres of land. In politics he is a Republican, and his wife is a member of the M. E. Church.

F. M. Yokem, farmer and carpenter, sec. 1; P. O., Pleasant Hill; was born in Lincoln county, Mo., in 1831, and is the son of Solomon and Elizabeth (Butler) Yokem, father a native of Virginia and mother of Kentucky, both of German descent; was brought to Pike county, Ill., in 1833; was educated in the subscription schools of this county; in 1855 he married Zerilda Starr, and of their 6 children only 2 are living. In an early day Mr. Yokem has seen many bears and deer; has seen as many as 100 deer in one gang. He has been successful in business, and now owns 220 acres of land. Politically he is a Greenbacker.

BARRY TOWNSHIP.

The beauties of nature as presented by this township to Rev. David Edwards and Mr. Hadley, the first settlers of Barry, must have been magnificent. Prior to their coming not even a furrow of its virgin soil or even a spadeful of its earth (except by United States surveyors) had ever been turned by man; nor even a shanty erected except the rude wigwam of the Indians, who had for many years roamed free and undisturbed over these fertile prairies and through the pleasant groves. Such was the condition of the face of Barry township when visited by the above named gentlemen in 1824. Mr. Hadley settled on sec. 21.

Soon after these men came there appeared Rev. Wm. M. Blair and his sons. Those who afterward took an important part in the history of the county, were John N., Harry, Samuel, Montgomery and William Blair, Hezekiah McAtee, Alfred Grubb and Elijah L. McAtee. Other early pilgrims here were Hull, Talcott, Josiah and William Lippincott, and old man Peabody, who died shortly after he came. Also, Stephen R. Gray, old man Rush, Burton Gray, John Millhizer, Levi McDaniels and many others whom we mention during the personal sketches. Most of the above mentioned came prior to or during the year 1836. Besides the foregoing there were Benj. Barney, who came to Atlas in 1826, Michael and Alonzo Gard, who came the same year, as also did W. L. Chrysup. A. C. Baker came in 1827, Esq. Joseph McIntire in 1831, Wm. McDaniels in 1835, N. P. Hart in 1838, Elisha Hurt and J. L. Gilmer in 1839. These were all excellent settlers, men of more than average ability, as shown in the subsequent career of most of them.

Wild game was in great abundance when the pioneers first came. Mr. McDaniels tells us he has seen as many as 45 deer in one herd. We were told that deer were so numerous and tame that they were known to enter the cabins of settlers, and were killed with axes and cudgels.

These pioneers were employed, as were all pioneers of the day, in subduing nature, building cabins, clearing land, breaking prairie, etc., but with all this labor they were social and happy, having a care for the morals and education of their growing families, and making for the time one of the pleasantest settlements in the new and growing State. There were displayed among the settlers more than the usual amount of warm-hearted friendship and neighborly affection. All were equal in social station and dignity. Fashion was not then the inexorable goddess we are accustomed to meet in these modern days. The pioneers were proud to be attired in homespun woven by the busy housewife of the period, while such a thing as a carriage or buggy was unknown in Barry. Mr. Mc-Daniels tells us that from his place there was a pathway across the prairie, but for a time after he came not the track of a wagon could be seen,—indeed, there was no such vehicle in the township. Husbands went to church on foot. The wives rode the horses, carrying with them such of the children as were too young to make their way by walking. If the good wife was clad in a calico of durable texture and fast color, she was as happy as the fine ladies of to-day, robed in velvets and seal-skins. The religion of the time favored a very rigid and severe adherence to plain and un-adorned attire, and made, as it would almost seem to us, rather a virtue of a necessity, although a few years later, with the rapid accumulation of wealth, display was rendered a matter of easy accomplishment. We now find, however, large numbers of pioneers, from motives of principle, refraining as carefully from any vain show or unnecessary ornament as they did in the primitive times of which we are now writing.

The earliest pioneers, those who came prior to 1830, could not obtain a legal title to their farms, as the General Government did not offer the land for sale before that. Before that time all the land was held by "claims." The settlers had an agreement among themselves by which they allowed a man to "claim" about as much timber land as he might need, generally not over 160 acres, upon which he might build his cabin and make his other improvements; and woe unto the speculator or new-comer who should attempt to "claim" land already occupied by a bona-fide settler. Much of the land in Barry was taken by those claimants before the land came into market. These claims were bought and sold, the purchaser coming into possession of the improvements, together with whatever rights were considered appertaining thereto. Many quarrels ensued from this state of affairs, as might naturally be expected.

When the land sales came off in October, 1829, at Vandalia, there was a gathering of pioneers from the township offered for sale, at which no speculator was allowed to purchase until all settlers had made their selections,—rather a high-handed proceeding, as it would now appear, but one which was justified by the existing circumstances.

The first person visited by the cold hand of death in this township was Mrs. Amanda Davis, who died in 1831, a daughter of Rev. Wm. Blair. The first birth was a daughter of Samuel and Lucy Blair, the first couple married in the township.

Barry is settled by an excellent class of agriculturists, many of whom we make personal mention of, further on in this sketch. The township is beautifully divided between prairie and timber, well watered, the soil fertile and rich, and is both an excellent grain and stock country.

A doctor named Ludley, who lived in the bottom, was the first physician in the township. The earliest doctors were about all Thomsonians.

BARRY.

This city is beautifully situated on the north half of sec. 25, and upon an eminence commanding a fine view of the surrounding country. For miles either way there is presented to the eye a grand panorama of nature's beauteous handiwork, changed, it is true, by the hand of man from what it was half a century ago, yet a charming scene it is to-day. Where once grew the tall, verdant prairie grass the eye now beholds waving fields of corn, wheat and other cereals. The wild flowers that gave to the dead monotony of undulating grass a charm, and a beauty unrivaled in grandeur by any of the fine scenes now presented by growing fields, have long since faded away. These only exist in the memories of the pioneers yet surviving. These tell us that the magnificence and beauty of the prairies as seen in their native condition, can never be adequately pictured by language.

During the period of the great internal improvement system of Illinois, which we have so frequently alluded to, and during which time so many towns were platted in this county, as well as all over the State, the city of Barry sprung into existence. Fortunately, it has fared better than many of the other towns projected, even in Pike county, for it has assumed rank among the small cities of this part of Illinois, while many have been long since pronounced dead, or that they had obtained their greatest growth. Barry was laid out by Calvin R. Stone, of the firm of Stone, Field & Marks, of St. Louis, and christened "Worcester." Mr. Stone was killed by the explosion of the boat " Montezuma," on the Mississippi. It was found that there was another town by that name in the State, so Worcester was changed to Barry. Mr. Brown, who had lived in Barre, Vt., suggested that it be called after that town. A petition to this effect was drawn up by Dr. Baker, who printed the name Barre in large Roman letters, but the enrolling clerk spelled it with a final *y*, instead of an *e*. That was the name, however, of the Postmaster-General under President Jackson, so it was accepted and has since been known by it.

Bartlett & Birdsong, who laid out Barry, as the agents for Stone, the owner of the land, kept the first store in the place. This was in a little log cabin. Stone, Field & Marks erected a mill here to grind the grain for the settlers. This was sold to Brown & Mc-Tucker, in 1836. In 1837 a grist mill was run by Mason & Edwards. It was a little overshot water-mill, located in a log building where the woolen factory now stands. The next one below it, on

Hadley creek, was by Wm. Lippincott. B. D. Brown and Josiah Lippincott erected a saw-mill in 1838, northeast of the Public Square, which was burned. The second mill was erected by Isaac Israel in 1845. He ran it three or four years. He also packed pork, and it was surrounded by 18 dwellings, a pork house, 3 large stores and a saw mill. He mortgaged it and it passed into the hands of J. Clines, and finally Brown & McTucker owned it. In a cave, located where the woolen factory was built by Wike Brothers, the skeleton of a human body was found in 1841, when the cave was opened. Water-power was secured from the water that came from this cave. It is a natural curiosity, and has been entered for about 300 yards. The source of the water above mentioned was always unknown. It is affected by the rise and fall of water in the streams.

John Grubb and Mr. Wike, while improving the factory, were quarrying rocks and came across a den of rattlesnakes of the largest kind, of which they killed great numbers, from which fact this place is called " Snake Holler " to this day.

The first tavern in Barry was kept by Johnny DeHaven. The first postmaster was Stephen R. Gray.

The Methodists were the first denomination of religious people to become established here, and erect a house of worship. The Baptists were second, who built a church about the same time. The building is now torn away. The Christians were third, and the Congregationalists fourth.

In the fall of '37 a camp-meeting was held near Levi McDaniels' farm-house, which lasted 12 days. This, it is said, was supported by people of all denominations, and all were united in the great work. Quite a number joined the Church during this meeting. In 1838 another was held in the same place. Settlers came from a distance of 30 to 40 miles to attend these meetings.

The first school was taught in the Methodist church by Deacon Mason. Then there was a little frame school-house erected north of Bright's saloon. It was moved several times afterward, and a difference of opinion exists in regard to its original location.

Barry grew and prospered at times, and again, like other towns, it suffered seasons of stagnation. To-day it is a beautiful little city with fine church edifices, large, magnificent school buildings, good business houses, neat and beautiful residences, and indeed a live, enterprising little city. The high grade of society existing here is something worthy the boast and pride of its residents. The courtly Southerner, the careful Easterner and the thrifty New Yorker are met here, and it is therefore natural that a social system should be established which is culled from the high standard of the sections named. These, taken with the enterprising spirit and practical character of the Westerner, give origin to a new society, more pleasant than either, with the best social ethics of all, mingled in one common fountain, from which flow the elements of the best society.

In educational matters no city or town in the county takes a greater interest. In religious teachings and Christian morality

Barry compares favorably with those towns having a larger number of church spires pointing heavenward. In those movements to raise the fallen and degraded, to help the poor, to encourage the weak, the good people of Barry are ever engaged. Some grand efforts have been made in the temperance cause by the noble people of this city. The cause of temperance is like that of Christian religion in this respect, that it is found in great variety of shapes and methods. In other words, it has taken upon itself the most remarkable forms in the way of organizations. But, unlike Christianity, which is historically traced through the narrow sects and societies, the cause of temperance seems to run through the most wonderful changes. As soon as one particular form of labor has lost its interest to the public, the friends of temperance re-organize, and are found laboring in a different manner. Hence we find it impossible to trace properly, in the short space allotted, the history of the different forms and shapes in which the friends of temperance have been organized.

With the enterprise characteristic of the city, an artesian well was begun to be put down during the month of October, 1879. The city agreed to pay two dollars and fifty cents per foot for the first 1,500 feet, and after that depth was reached, if not a sufficient flow of water, the contractors were to receive three dollars per foot for the next 500 feet. The city had appropriated, up to March 20, 1880, $5,000 to carry on the work. The site of the well, which is in the park in the Public Square, is the highest point of ground in the county, and therefore a great depth will necessarily have to be reached before an abundant supply of water is obtained. At the present writing water does not yet flow, and work still goes on. The city, we are told, will undoubtedly go 2,500 feet in order to obtain a supply. The top cutting is six inches in diameter, diminishing to four and five-eighths and three and one-half.

Barry was incorporated as a town in 1856. An election was held Jan. 14 of that year to vote for or against incorporation, when 92 votes were cast for, and none against the measure. The following Trustees were then chosen and held their first meeting Jan. 31: A. Grubb, John Watson, N. Cromwell, J. M. Dabney and C. S. Allen. These were sworn in by Justice M. Blair, when they elected John Watson as President and John Shastid, Clerk.

Nov. 18, 1872, Barry was organized as a city. The present City Council is composed of the following gentlemen: E. R. Burnham, Mayor; J. R. Roward, J. Weber, T. Davis, Matthew Peterson, S. Mors and James Watson, Aldermen; C. C. Roasa, City Clerk; W. I. Klein, City Attorney; J. C. Brown, Treasurer; John Whettleton, Marshal, and J. E. Haines, Street Commissioner.

SCHOOL, CHURCHES AND SOCIETIES.

The fine brick school-building of the city was erected in 1874, at a cost of $15,000. It was built by Wm. T. Mitchell, of Barry. It is beautifully situated, and presents to the stranger as he enters the

city by rail a most magnificent view. The School Directors in
1863 were Calvin Davis, N. P. Hart and J. H. Mallory. The present Directors are E. A. Crandall, N. P. Hart and Alexander White.
There are enrolled 401 scholars. The principal is Prof. J. F. Clark.
The teachers are, first assistant, Miss E. Greene; first grammar department, John M. Woodby; second grammar, Prof. Geo. W.
Smith; intermediate, Miss Ella McMahan and Wm. Triplett;
primary, Ida Luthey and May Poling.

Rev. A. M. Danely is Pastor of the Methodist Church. There
is connected with the congregation a good Sunday-school, which
meets at 9:30 A. M.

Rev. William Greene is Pastor of the Baptist Church. Services
are held on the second and fourth Sundays in each month.

Elder W. E. Berry is Pastor of the Christian Church. Services
are held every Sunday morning and evening. Sunday-school at
9:30 A. M.

Barry Lodge, No. 34, of the Masonic order, was organized Aug.
29, 1845. Michael Gard was the first Grand Master; Jos. Jack-
son, Sen. W., George Wike, Jr. W.; W. J. Alkire, Treasurer;
Elisha Hurt, Secretary; Eli Longnecker, Sr. Deacon; Joseph Al-
kire, Jr. Deacon; Joseph Lippincott, Tyler. These constituted
the original officers, only two of whom are now living, namely,
E. Hurt and W. J. Alkire. The present officers are, D. W. Greene,
W. M.; A. R. Gray, Sr. W.; George Wike, Jr. W.; John P.
Grubb, Sr. Deacon; R. D. Osborne, Jr. Deacon; B. McConnell,
Treasurer; M. G. Patterson, Sec'y.; M Lane and John Palmer,
Stewards; J. F. Phillips, Chaplain, and J. L. Terry, Tyler.

Barry Lodge, No. 336, I. O. O. F., was organized Oct. 9, 1866.
Alexander White, E. M. Call, Alexander Easly, J. B. Keever, R.
B. Higgins, W. B. Clancy and J. Rosenburgh were its charter mem-
bers. The present officers are—J. W. Mitchell, N. G.; C. C.
Roasa, V. G.; J. N. Widby, R. Sec'y; Thomas Retalic, Financial
Sec'y; W. Chrysup, Treasurer. The present membership
numbers 116.

The Evening Star Lodge, No. 21, Daughters of Rebecca, was
organized Oct. 11, 1870, with 14 charter members. The present
officers are—Alexander Easly, First N. G.; Miss Nellie Bingham,
N. G.; Mrs. G. W. Doyle, V. G.; Miss Ella Furniss, Rec.
Sec'y; G. W. Smith, Financial Sec'y; Miss Lizzie Furniss, Treasurer. This Lodge has a membership of 72.

Progress Encampment, No. 162, I. O. O. F., was organized in
October, 1876, with 18 members. At present the officers are—
G. D. Mayes, C. P.; Z. B. Stoddard, Scribe; James Smith, Treasurer.
Membership 45.

Goodwill Lodge, No. 1,791, K. of H., meets on the first and
third Mondays of each month. J. Weber, D., and J. S. Gorton, R.

Barry Chapter, No. 88, R. A. M., meets Monday night on or
before the full moon in each month. J. J. Topliff, H. P.; F. M.
Dabney, Sec'y.

BIOGRAPHICAL DEPARTMENT.

In connection with, and as a part of the history of Barry township and city, we wish to speak personally of the old settlers and prominent citizens, which we do below, arranged in alphabetical form.

A. B. Allen, jeweler, Barry, is a native of Monmouth county, N. J., where he was born in 1844; came to this State in 1853 and settled in Lincoln; subsequently he removed to Logan county, thence to Macoupin county, and to this county in 1873, when he established himself in his present business, and where he has since made it his home. He was married in 1872 to Miss Mattie Harris, a native of this State, and they have 1 child living, Leata. Mr. A. is a man of considerable inventive capacities, which is being used to practical purposes. He has a fair trade and is a good citizen.

Lewis Angle was born in Lynchburg, Va., Jan. 7, 1823: He was a son of Alfred and Sarah (Green) Angle, who lived for many years in Lynchburg, Va., where they died and were buried. The subject of this sketch resided with his parents until his 18th year, when he left his native town to seek a home in the West, came to St. Louis, Mo., thence to Hannibal, where he resided until 1846, when he came to Barry. In March, 1852, he united with the Barry Baptist Church. In May, 1853, he was elected Deacon, which office he held to the day of his death. He was united in marriage July 19, 1852, with Miss Harriet E. Crandall. They have 3 children, Alice E., now the wife of John L. Cassidy; they were married Oct. 20, 1877, and reside in St. Louis, Mo.; Della M. and Freddie L. Mr. Angle died in Barry March 19, 1878, where for more than 30 years he was one of the most prominent and energetic business men of the county. During this time he was engaged extensively in the dry-goods and grocery trade, pork-packing and produce buying; a partner in the Barry Woolen Mills and lumber trade, and in the Barry Exchange Bank. He was a model man in all the relations of life, kind-hearted, benevolent, prompt to fulfill all the duties of husband, father, friend, Christian and citizen. The church lost a faithful member, the community an energetic friend; his family a kind husband and loving father; the poor a benefactor, for to them he gave work by which they could earn something. His credit was unbounded, integrity untarnished, and honesty unimpeached. He was buried Thursday, March 20, 1878. The sermon was preached by his Pastor, Rev. Wm. Green, from the text, John xiv, 2, last clause: "I go to prepare a place for you." The different denominations, Masons and Odd Fellows, united in the funeral services. His body was followed to the grave by the largest concourse of people ever in procession to the burying ground in this part of the county. A portrait of Mr. Angle will be found in this work. Mrs. Angle still resides at the old homestead at Barry.

BARRY

Thomas Ardron, P. O., Barry, is the son of William and Ann (Booth) Ardron, natives of Yorkshire, Eng., who emigrated to this country in 1848, and settled in Hadley township the following year, stopping one year in N. Y. Traveled from N. Y. by way of the canal and lakes to Griggsville Landing. The subject of this sketch was born in Yorkshire, Eng., where he was married in 1837 to Miss Ann Broadhens, a native of Cheshire, Eng., and daughter of Thomas and Susannah (Cheatham) Broadhens. Mr. A. began the struggle in life without capital, and has made a success. He is agent for Lyman Brown's Seven-Barks medicine, and has a lucrative trade.

Jacob Auer, farmer, sec. 32; P. O., Kinderhook; was born in Germany, in 1823, where he was married in 1847 to Miss Gotleben Hendte. He emigrated to America in 1853; she came in 1855, and they settled in Pennsylvania, where he lived until 1860, when he moved to this county and settled on Bay creek. In 1864 he moved on his present farm of 40 acres and a large vineyard, from which he has some trade. They have 6 children, Rosena K., Charlotte G., Mary, Caroline, Sally and Jennie. Mr. and Mrs. Auer are members of the German Lutheran Church.

A. C. Baker, M. D., was born in London, Eng., in 1813, and is a son of Edward and Lucy (Dickinson) Baker, who emigrated to this country in 1815 and settled in Philadelphia, where he engaged in teaching, until 1825, when he moved to White county, Ill. Subsequently he moved to Greene county, where he died in 1835. The subject of this sketch began the study of medicine with Dr. Worthington, at Pittsfield, and attended the Ohio Medical College at Cincinnati, where he was graduated in 1837. He began the practice of his profession at Pittsfield, and the following year moved to this city, where he has since been in constant practice. He was married in 1844 to Miss Martha A., niece of John Barney, of Pittsfield, and daughter of West Barney, by whom he has five children living. In the winter of 1850-1 he went with laborers to Panama and opened the Panama railroad, cutting and grading it. Col. Baker, his brother who was killed in the army, had the contract for this work. In 1853 he crossed the plains to California with a herd of cattle from this place, and returned without accident the following year. He has been hunting along the Humboldt river in the midst of Indians, and was always well treated. He served two years as Surgeon in the 71st Penn. Reg., in Col. Baker's Brigade. He is the oldest practicing physician in Barry, and one of the oldest settlers of the township.

Col. Benjamin Barney, one of the oldest and most prominent citizens of Pike county, and to whom reference is so often made on the pages of this volume, was born in Berkshire county, Mass., Sept. 4, 1795. The first of his ancestry in America in the paternal line was William Barney, a native of Ireland, a great-grandfather of the subject of this biographical notice, who emigrated to Massachusetts about 200 years ago; the next in line was William again, and then

46

Benjamin, the father of the Colonel, who enlisted in the Continental army under Gen. Washington when but 14 years of age; at the close of that war he married Miss Elizabeth Crape, who both died at the age of 60 years, and within a year of each other. They had 6 sons and 5 daughters, all of whom grew up to adult years, namely, Joseph, Margaret, Polly, West, Ann, Benjamin, Hepsey, Marshall, Manly, Deborah and John. Joseph served in the war of 1812, and was mortally wounded at the battle of Sackett's Harbor. He was Lieutenant, but during that action was serving as Captain.

The subject of this sketch, Col. Barney, first came to Pike county in 1826, locating at Atlas, then the county-seat. He was a blacksmith by trade, and thinks he started the first blacksmith forge in the county, and perhaps made the first plow. In 1830 he was elected one of the three County Commissioners, the other two being Charles Stratton and Andrew Phillips. In April, 1833, the county determined to move its capital to a more central place, and finally it was decided to place it where Pittsfield now stands, when arose the difficulty of borrowing the necessary $200 to enter the quarter section. The money was eventually obtained on the individual notes of Col. Barney and George W. Hinman, in April. In June the land was surveyed and laid off, Col. Barney and Messrs. Hinman and Judd reserving lots on the north side of the Square for the use of a Court House, but the site was finally changed to the center of the Square, as it is now. As soon as the survey was completed, the lots were sold at auction, bringing enough almost to complete the county buildings. In September, 1833, the Commissioners had a house built by Mr. Hurt, in which, before it was finished, they held a session of their court.

In April, 1832, while Col. Barney was working at his forge in Atlas, about 11 o'clock, A. M., he was notified by Col. Ross of the Governor's order to raise a company of 100 men to serve in the Black Hawk war, and to report at Beardstown the following Monday. He immediately started on horseback to rally a company, and was successful. In the election of officers the next day Mr. Barney was made 1st Lieutenant. They arrived at Beardstown about 4 P. M., Tuesday, where the company was divided into two, Mr. Barney being elected Captain of one, and receiving his commission from Gov. Reynolds. The company was in the service 50 days, when they were relieved by regular U. S. troops. In the fall of 1832 Col. Ross resigned, and Capt. Barney was elected Colonel of the 16th Ill. Vol. Mil., and acted as such until 1838 or 1839. Politically Col. Barney was a Whig and now is a Republican. The portrait of the Colonel given in this book is from a photograph taken when he was 74 years of age, and the fac-simile of his autograph from his writing at the age of 85.

His brother, John Barney, of Pittsfield, has been Treasurer of the county, and is several times referred to on the pages of this history.

Calvin D. Blair, farmer, sec. 36; P. O., Barry; was born in this tp. Dec. 8, 1851, and is a son of Samuel and Eliza (Gose) Blair, natives of Virginia, who settled in this township in 1828. The subject of this sketch was married in 1876 to Miss Dora Blake, a native of this county. He settled on his present place of 3½ acres, in 1877. Is School Director at present time, and he and his wife are descendants of Pike county's early pioneers.

Harvey Blair, deceased, was a native of Indiana, and came to this county at a very early day, where he was married to Miss Millie A. Cunningham, daughter of John Cunningham, an early settler in Pleasant Vale tp., and widow of Jas. Lutteral. Mr. B. settled on his present estate in 1840, where he resided until his death in 1879. Mrs. B. has a farm of 230 acres, valued at $60 per acre; also 25 acres in Pleasant Vale tp., where her father is a resident. She resides on sec. 35; P. O., Barry.

Samuel Blair, farmer, sec. 35; P. O., Barry; is a son of William M. and Martha (Quiet) Blair, natives of Kentucky, who came to this county and settled in Barry tp. in 1828, where they both died. The subject of this sketch was born in Madison county, O., Oct. 1, 1806, and came to this county with his parents. He settled on his present estate in 1834, consisting of 110 acres, valued at $75 per acre. In 1830 he was married to Miss Anna Brewster, a native of New York, who died in 1840. By this union 1 child was born, Louisa. His present wife, Eliza, *nee* Gose, is a native of Virginia. To them have been born 6 children, 3 boys and 3 girls: Calvin D., William S., George C., Alta C., wife of G. W. Smith, Lucina and Martha Q. E. Mr. Blair numbers among the living pioneers of Barry tp. Politically he is a descendant of the old Democratic school, and is well known throughout the county.

Leander Blake, farmer, sec. 27; P. O., Barry; was born in Cumberland county, Maine, in 1814, the son of Ephraim and Desiah P. (Higgins) Blake, natives of that State, who came to this county in 1847, and settled on the present place, consisting of 321 acres, valued at $40 per acre. He resided here until his death in 1875; she died in 1879, both 86 years of age. Leander came to this county in 1842 and landed in Barry with but 2 five-franc pieces in his pocket. His first work was at rail splitting, for which he was paid 5 bits per hundred, taking pork in payment at 2 cents per lb.; but by economy he was soon enabled to purchase a little land, and now owes no man a dollar. His present farm has cost him $6,500 besides the improvements. He was married in Pennsylvania in 1839 to Miss Mary Charles, a native of that State, where she was born in 1819. She was a life-long cripple, and died of the effects of a fall from a buggy in March, 1880. They had 8 children, 4 of whom are living,—Preston, Ella, Dora and Ebenezer. Mr. B. had a thorough New England schooling, and is well versed in the different languages. He was for some years engaged in teaching school in his native State and Pennsylvania. Has been Assessor one term, and has held other official positions. In politics he used to be an old-line Whig ; was a strong Douglas man, and is now a thorough Republican.

A. G. Bliven, farmer, sec. 2; P. O., Barry; was born in Genesee county, N. Y., in 1830, the son of Samuel G. and Mabel M. (Wheeler) Bliven, natives of that State, who emigrated to Illinois in 1834 and settled near Quincy, where they still reside. The subject of this sketch came to this county in 1856 and settled on his present estate, consisting of 160 acres valued at $50 per acre; also has 241 acres in Richfield tp., Adams county. He was married in 1853 to Miss Eleanor Foster, who was born in Hamilton county, O., in 1830. In 1862 he enlisted as Orderly Sergeant in Co. F, 118th Ill. Vol.; was promoted 1st Lieut., in which capacity he served until he resigned by reason of a wound received at Port Hudson, La., April 7, 1864. The ball entered the hip and lodged in the left leg, where it still remains, and has crippled him for life. He was a participant in the battles of Jackson, Miss., siege of Vicksburg, Port Hudson, Vermillionville, Chickasaw Bluffs, Por-Gibson, and the first battle at Vicksburg, under Sherman, Arkansas Post, and all engagements in which the Regiment participated, Mr. B. is confined the most of the time to the aid of crutches, and is a living relic of the Rebellion. His home was burned to the ground May 23, 1865, and Oct. 28, 1871, his barn with seven head of horses and mules was destroyed by a supposed incendiary. Notwithstanding all these reverses, Mr. B. has successfully overcome all obstacles and trials, and through his perseverance and energy has erected a fine residence on the same site of ground, and accumulated a good landed property. His opportunities for education were limited, but his principles were always earnest in the cause of his Government, and the promulgation of Republican principles. He is the father of 3 children, Willis E., Salina A. and Ida M.

Wm. Bothwick, farmer, sec. 18; P. O., Barry; was born in Nova Scotia in 1832. His parents, James and Mary (Dilmon) Bothwick, were natives of England. He was married in 1859 to Miss Martha Likes, a native of this county, who died in 1873, leaving him 7 children, Mary, Isabel, Emma, Minerva, Barbara, James and William. His present wife, Isabel, *nee* Lane, is a native of Indiana. Mr. B. came to this county in 1857, and settled in this section, where he has since made it his home; moved on his present farm in 1878, consisting of 116 acres, valued at $10,000. Has been Justice of the Peace. Is a member of the Masonic Order and Methodist Church. In politics he is a Democrat.

C. E. Bower was born in Madison county, Ohio, in 1833, and was brought by his parents to Pike county, Ill., settling in Derry tp., where he remained until 1850, when they moved to Barry tp.; and in 1852 Mr. Bowers crossed the plains, driving an ox-team every mile of the way. Was engaged in farming and explored Oregon at that time, which was a perfect wilderness, and in 1857 he returned home. In 1858 he married Miss Barbara Wright, daughter of Abiah Wright, who were natives of Ohio. They have had born to them 6 children, 3 sons and 3 daughters, all of whom are living. Reuben D. is the eldest, and is now attending Lombard University at Galesburg. Mr. B. has a good farm, consisting of over 200 acres of the finest land in old Pike. Mr. B. made a trip back to California in 1879, which was an enjoyable tour. He is a self-made man, and has secured his present position among the farmers of Pike county by his industry and energy.

John Brenner, shoemaker, Barry, was born in Ireland, April 17, 1820, and emigrated to the United States in 1852, stopping in New York city about 6 weeks; then stopped at Columbus, O., about a month; then was in Cincinnati two years, making shoes; then was in Quincy, Ill., several years, following his trade; then, in 1864, he came to Barry, where he worked with Mr. Wendorff, a shoemaker; in 1877 Mr. Brenner opened shop for himself and is now prosecuting a good business. In 1856 he married Margaret Clark, and of the 8 children born to them 7 are living, namely: George, Sarah, Thomas, John, Allena, Katie and Edward.

William Bright, proprietor of saloon, Barry, was born in Prussia in 1824, and emigrated to America in 1849, landing at Baltimore. Came to this county in 1855 and settled in Barry. Was married in St. Louis, in 1853, and is the father of 8 children, 5 daughters and 3 sons, 6 of whom are living. He is located in business on the east side of Bainbridge street, where he is conducting a good trade.

B. D. Brown, retired farmer, sec. 25; P. O., Barry; is a son of William and Ann (Dodge) Brown, natives of Massachusetts, who emigrated to Illinois from Vermont in 1848, and settled in this tp., where they both died. The subject of this sketch was born in Essex county, Mass., in Feb., 1804; was married in 1831 to Miss Mary Kellum, a native of Barre, Vt., and daughter of Charles and Rebecca (Rice) Kellum. He came to this county in 1833 and settled in Atlas tp.; soon afterward he built a mill at Louisiana, Mo., and engaged in milling at St. Louis, during which time he purchased his present estate of 150 acres, valued at $75 per acre. Here he settled in 1839, and for several years engaged in the mercantile business in this city, and in company with Mr. McTucker purchased the mill, where he was extensively engaged in milling until he retired from the active field of life to the enjoyment of his success. He represented Pike county in the Legislature in '41-2, and has always taken an active interest in the welfare of the county. His success is wholly due to his energy, sagacity, and indomitable perseverance in overcoming all obstacles, and his declining years are being spent in the comforts of his pleasant home, the result of a well-directed industry. His political opinions are based upon the principles promulgated by the old-line Whigs, and indorsed by the Republican party. The city of Barry was named in honor of his wife's birthplace, Barre, Vt. He is a stockholder of the banking institution of this city.

John H. Brown is a native of Pittsfield, and was born May 26, 1847, the son of L. H. Brown, of Barry, who came to this county in early day. In 1870 he married Emma D. Westlake, daughter of Wm. Westlake, deceased, and they have 2 children, Norton and Fred.

Hector Brownell, farmer, sec. 28; P. O., Barry; son of Benjamin and Jane (Rickey) Brownell, natives of New York, who emigrated to Pike county in 1840 and purchased the homestead farm, where he lived until his death, which occurred March 29, 1872; she died the following week. The homestead consists of 160 acres, which were bid off by Col. Ross for taxes, who sold to Mr. B. It is now valued at $50 per acre. The subject of this sketch was born in Delaware county, N. Y., in 1833; was married Jan. 1, 1855, to Miss Anna Bailey, a native of Philadelphia. To them have been born 3 children, William, James and Hattie. Benjamin Brownell was a local Methodist preacher in New York and Illinois, and was widely known as a zealous defender of the faith and worker in the Master's vineyard.

E. R. Burnham, photographer, and the present Mayor of the city of Barry, was born in Thibodeaux, parish of La Fourche, La., and is a son of E. T. Burnham, deceased, a native of Hartford, Conn., who died Aug. 16, 1878. He was in New Orleans during the Rebellion, saw Gen. Butler land there, saw Mumford tear the national flag from the U. S. Mint, and saw him hanged. In 1871 Mr. B. married Maggie L. Turner, and of their 3 children 2 are living, Clara and Edna. As a photographer Mr. Burnham is doing a good business, and is at present the Mayor of the city.

G. W. Chrysup, Postmaster at Barry, was born in Florence, Pike Co., Ill., Feb. 1, 1845; only child of William L. and Jane (Barney) Chrysup, who came to this county in 1826, and resided here until 1850, when the family removed to California, going across the plains. In 1857 they started on the return voyage home, and his parents were lost by the explosion of the steamer "St. Nicholas," which occurred April 24, 1859, 1½ miles below Helena, Ark. Rendered parentless by this disaster, he lived with his grandfather, Benjamin Barney, until 1861, when he enlisted in the 10th Ill. Inf. for three months' service. He then re-enlisted in Co. B, 28th Ill. Inf., as Corporal, and was promoted to Captain of that Company, serving until the close of the war. He participated in the battles of Hatchie, siege of Vicksburg, Jackson, Miss., Spanish Fort, Mobile, and all the engagements in which the Regiment took part; was honorably discharged; returned home, where he was married April 18, 1867, to Miss Kate, daughter of Lewis and Lucy Hardy. The same year he became engaged in the mercantile trade, until appointed Postmaster under Hayes in 1878, to which duties he is devoting his time and attention. He is Treasurer in the I. O. O. F., of which he has been a member 9 years. He is the father of 2 children, Jennie and Helen.

Asa W. Clark, farmer, sec. 20, P. O., Barry; born in Rockingham county, N. H., in 1820, son of Abner and Caroline (Wicks) Clark, natives of New Hampshire and Maine, respectively, who died in Buffalo, N. Y. Asa W. was married in 1846 to Mrs. Caroline Churchill, a native of Batavia, N. Y.; came to this county in 1852 and settled on the bottom lands in Kinderhook, where he lived 9 years; moved on his present farm in 1863, consisting of 177 acres, valued at $50 per acre; also owns other lands in the tp. His opportunities for early education were limited, and he has succeeded only by his energy and perseverance. He is administrator of the estate of J. R. Young, Trustee of the Burying Grounds and Treasurer of the Methodist Church, of which he and his family are members. His children are Herbert C., Libbie C., Mary A. and Franklin A. In politics he is a Republican. Was an old-line Whig.

John H. Cobb, late of the firm of Cobb & Watson, of the Barry *Adage*, was born in Chautauqua county, N. Y., Nov. 10, 1841, and is a son of James Cobb, deceased; he came to this county in August, 1871, and in November established the Barry *Adage*, which he conducted as an independent newspaper until May, 1878, when he sold out, and in May, 1879, in company with Wm. Watson, he re-purchased the same establishment, and until recently they conducted the paper under the firm name of Cobb & Watson. Mr. Cobb married Miss Julia E. Prentice, and of their 6 children these 3 are living : Edward P., Albertus A. and Archie H.

E. A. Crandall, merchant and banker, Barry, is the son of Joshua and Fannie (Burdick) Crandall, natives of New York, who settled in Barry in 1839, where he engaged at his trade in the boot and shoe business, and resided until his death in 1866. His wife preceded him to the better land in 1855. The subject of this sketch was born in Rensellaer county, New York, 1836, and came with his parents to this county. In 1854 he formed the co-partnership of Angle & Crandall in the mercantile trade and pork-packing, which were successfully carried on until 1858, when the firm dissolved, and he commenced the study of law at Washington, D. C., and attended Columbia College. The following year he returned home and formed the second partnership with Angle and carried on an extensive trade. In 1860 he was married to Miss Eliza, daughter of Capt. Elisha Hurt, a native of this county, who died, leaving one child, Fannie. In 1862 the firm dissolved and Mr. C. turned his attention to the appeals of his country, and raised Co. D, 99th Ill. Inf.; was afterward appointed Major of the Regiment and served two years,—through all the battles in which that Regiment participated, and was honorably discharged. Returning to his home, he became a partner in the woolen mill, under the firm name of Geo. Wike & Co., which was changed to a corporation in 1876. He was again married in 1870 to Miss Jennie G. Gordon, a native

of New York, by whom he has one son, Louis. The same year
the firm of Crandall & Smith engaged in the grocery trade, which
forms one of the most extensive and enterprising houses in Pike
county. This house also erected a large elevator in 1879, and is
largely engaged in the grain business. Mr. C. is President of the
School Board, and Supervisor at present, and is one of the most
active, thoroughgoing business men in Barry. Strong in the love of
his country, he is equally so in the principles indorsed on the broad
platform of the Republican party.

Davis & Brown, merchants, Barry, Ill. This firm began business under the above firm name in September, 1878, on the west
side of the Public Square, and have had a gradually increasing
trade, carrying now a stock of $10,000, which consists of dry-goods,
boots and shoes, and notions. By close attention to business and
selling at low rates they have won the confidence and patronage of
the public.

Mrs. Clara H. Davis, widow of Samuel Davis, mentioned further on, was born in Boston, Mass., June 22, 1833; in 1838 she was
brought by her parents to this county, where, Oct. 14, 1851, she
was married.

Nathaniel Davis, son of Samuel Davis, deceased, was born in
Pike county in 1857; was married to Miss Lizzie Jennings, daughter of P. Jennings, Sept. 28, 1878, and they have one child. Mr.
Davis is one of the most enterprising business men of Barry; is at
present a member of the City Council, and just now is closing out
the old business of S. Davis & Son. His father was one of the
most prominent business men of the county, and no man ever enjoyed the confidence of the people of the county more than did Mr.
Samuel Davis. He was engaged for years in pork-packing, from
which, with the immense amount of wheat and other grain he
handled, he realized a handsome benefit. He was engaged in the
general mercantile business for many years, in the firm of C. & S.
Davis.

Samuel Davis was born near Barry, Pike county, Ill., Oct. 27, 1829.
His parents were Robert and Amanda (Blair) Davis. The subject of
this sketch commenced his business career in the town of Barry in
the year 1849, when he was but 20 years of age, entering the store of
Mr. M. Blair as salesman, which position he occupied until 1852,
when, in company with his brother, Calvin, he entered into partnership with Mr. Blair, they carrying on business under the firm name
of M. Blair & Co. Mr. Blair, retiring from the firm in 1859, a co-
partnership was formed between the two brothers, Calvin and Samuel, under the style of C. & S. Davis; they carried on business successfully for many years, built up a large trade and amassed considerable wealth; speculating in pork and wheat extensively; they
were generally very fortunate in these dealings. The firm of C. &
S. Davis dissolved partnership in the spring of 1877, Calvin taking
the flouring mill they were running, and Samuel retaining the stock
of merchandise. Mr. Davis then took his two sons, Stephen A. D.

Samuel Davis

BARRY

and Nathaniel R., into the business. The business was conducted under the firm name of Samuel Davis & Sons until the spring of 1880, when the firm sold out.

Mr. Davis was united in marriage to Miss Clara H. Hart Oct. 14, 1851. She is a native of Massachusetts, where she was born June 22, 1833, and is a daughter of Nathaniel and Clarissa (Hill) Hart, both natives of Massachusetts. They came to this county in 1838, and still are living in Barry tp. Mr. and Mrs. Davis were the parents of 8 children, Stephen A. D.; Lelia May, now the wife of J. C. Moon; Nathaniel R.; Earnest H., deceased; Clara Belle; Anna M.; Samuel C. and Daniel. Mr. Davis died Feb. 15, 1879, and was followed to his last resting place by a large concourse of relatives and friends. He had not been actively engaged in business affairs for several years, but had been taking matters as quietly as possible. He was shrewd, energetic and determined, and one of the best business men in the county. His acquaintance was extensive in commercial as well as social circles. His honesty and integrity were unquestioned, his credit unlimited. He was a fond husband, a kind and indulgent father, a good neighbor and staunch friend. We give a portrait of Mr. Davis in this volume.

John Dewell, farmer, sec. 4; P. O., Barry; son of Peter and Catherine (Brown) Dewell, natives of Pennsylvania, who moved to Ohio, where they both died. The subject of this sketch was born in Greene county, Pa., in 1815, and emigrated to Pike county in 1837, and settled south of Barry, where he lived until 1842, when he moved on his present farm of 120 acres, valued at $65 per acre. The land was mostly timbered when he came to this place. He was married in 1834 to Miss Rebecca Wallace, a native of Maryland. By this union 6 children are living,—Elizabeth, James, John N., Susan, Harriet and Charles C. Mr. D. is one of the original pioneers of Barry tp., and is a Democrat.

John W. Eckes, farmer; P. O., Barry; was born in Frederick county, Va., in 1834, son of David and Eva Eckes, natives also of that State, where Mrs. E. died. He came to the West in 1858 and settled in Greene county, thence moved to Ohio, where he died in 1861. The subject of this sketch was married in 1858 to Miss Margaret Carrigan, a native of Kentucky. They came to this county in 1877, and settled on the farm they now occupy. Mr. E. is a Democrat.

Edward Edom, proprietor of the National Hotel, Barry, was born in England in 1812; emigrated to Canada in 1830, and 5 years afterward moved to Scott county, Ill., where he resided until 1840, when he moved to Lucas county, O. In 1855 he came to this county, settled in Perry township, and engaged in farming. Three years afterward he moved to Griggsville, thence to New Salem and kept a hotel 4 years, when he moved to this city, where he is running a first-class hotel. He was married in 1842 to Miss Mary Mormoneny, a native of Ohio. To them have been born 7 children, all of whom are living. Mr. E. has been a prominent citizen at New Salem, and knows just how to conduct a hotel.

John Farmer, agriculturist, sec. 17; P. O., Barry; was born in Lancaster county, Pa., in 1811; son of Samuel and Hannah Frazer, natives of Pennsylvania, who moved to Ohio, where he died. The subject of this sketch was married in 1837 to Miss Eliza Nichols, daughter of John and Mary (Rethnal) Nichols, natives of New Jersey and Maryland, respectively, who settled in Adams county, Ill., where he died. Mr. F. settled in this tp. in 1846. The following year he moved to Adams county and lived 6 or 7 years, when he returned and settled on his present estate of 160 acres, valued at $50 per acre. To them have been born 10 children, 8 of whom are living: Samuel D., Joshua N., Jacob C., Mary J., James F., Sarah A., Lucy E. and Eliza B.; the deceased are George L. and John T. His son James is a member of the Ancient Order of the United Workmen; Joshua is a member of the Masonic order, and Samuel of the I. O. O. F.; Jacob C. is also a Mason, and Sarah A. is a member of the Eastern Star. Mr. F. has always been a Democrat, but has espoused the Greenback cause. The family are among the most respected and enterprising farmers of Barry tp.

Alonzo Gard, farmer, sec. 31; P. O., Kinderhook; was born in Washington county, O., in 1822, and is a son of Mischel and Clarissa (Baker) Gard, who settled in this tp. in 1826. In 1829 he moved his family here, where he lived until his death, Jan. 5, 1871, at the age of 77 years. She died April 10, 1863. He entered the land of his son's estate, consisting of 88 acres, now valued at $50 per acre. He was Justice of the Peace and among the earliest settlers. The subject of this sketch was married in 1850 to Miss Mary J. Yearly, a native of Cincinnati, O., by whom he has 3 children, Ellen, Lucy and Sally. Mr. G. is School Director, and the family are members of the Baptist Church. He is a Republican in politics, and one of the oldest living settlers of Barry tp.

John T. Gilmer, farmer, sec. 26; P. O., Barry; is a son of David and Eliza (Gose) Gilmer, natives of Virginia, who came to this county in 1839, and settled in this section, where he died in 1847. She is still living in this tp. The subject of this sketch was born in Barry tp. in 1840, and settled on his present farm in 1863, consisting of 63 acres, valued at $60 per acre. He also owns 42 acres in Pleasant Vale tp. He was married in 1864 to Miss Ellen, daughter of William McDaniel, who died in 1872, leaving 2 children, Charles and Clara. He was again married in 1874 to Miss Ella Blake, a native of this county. He fills the office of Road Supervisor at the present time, and is a member of the Baptist Church. Politics, Democratic.

D. W. Greene, Police Magistrate, is the son of James and Mary (Madison) Greene, who came to this county in 1837 and settled in Hadley tp., where he engaged in farming until his death, which occurred in 1875. She died in 1840. The subject of this sketch was born in Rensellaer county, N. Y., in 1826. He began the study of medicine with Dr. Baker of this city, taught school winters, and attended the Missouri State University one year and practiced in Barry 3 years, when he entered upon a mercantile pursuit, and was engaged in the erection of the Barry Woolen Mills, where he was connected for 3 years. He was married in 1850 to Miss Caroline Gordon, a native of Indiana. Mr. G. has filled the office of Township Treasurer some years. Is a member of the Masonic order, and of the Christian Church. Politically he is a stalwart Republican.

John P. Grubb, farmer, sec. 23; P. O., Barry; was born in Cumberland county, Pa., in Oct., 1815, and is a son of Jonas and Sarah (Wizer) Grubb, natives of Pennsylvania, who settled in Adams county, Ill., where they both died. The subject of this sketch came to this county in 1844, and settled on this section. In 1864 he purchased the present farm of 124 acres. Also owns other lands in the tp. He was one of the founders of the woolen mill in which he has been engaged for some years. He was married in May, 1849, to Miss Harriet Stevens, a native of New York State, who died in 1866. By this marriage he has 3 children living,—John W., Emeline and Eva. His present wife was Beulah Nations, widow of John Nations, by whom he has 3 children,—George, Hattie and Oliver. Two step-children, Norman W. and Florence, complete the family record. Mr. G. is one of the members of the Board of Trustees of the town, and is one of the active business men and farmers of Barry. In politics he is a Democrat, and cast his first vote for Martin Van Buren.

B. F. Guss, farmer, sec. 3; P. O., Barry; was born in Juniata county, Pa., in 1835, and is a son of William and Mary (Foltz) Guss, natives of Pennsylvania, where she died. Wm. Guss came to this county with his family in 1848, and settled in this tp., where he is at this time living. The subject of this sketch was married in 1859 to Miss Jane Sellers, a native of Pennsylvania. To them have been born 4 children, all of whom are living: Rosaline, Edwin S., William C. and Hattie E. He settled on his present farm in the fall of 1859, consisting of 116 acres, valued at $50 per acre. Mr. Guss has served as a School Director, and in politics is a Democrat.

George Hack, farmer, sec. 30; P. O., Kinderhook; was born in Germany Feb. 19, 1819; was married in 1844 to Miss Fernandrika Auer, a native of Germany. They emigrated to this country in 1853 and stopped one year in New York city, thence to Quincy, thence to this county, and engaged at his trade, brewing and coopering, at Kinderhook. This business he sold and purchased, in 1866, his present farm, consisting of over 500 acres of land, valued at $50 per acre. They have 7 children: Caroline, Frederick, Daniel, Rosena, Jennie, Harry and Annie. Mr. and Mrs. Hack are members of the German Lutheran Church, and he is a member of the Masonic order.

G. A. Hancock, farmer, sec. 27; P. O., Barry; was born in Licking Co., O., in 1830, and is a son of Isaac and Cynthia A. (Ford) Hancock, both natives of that State, who emigrated to Adams county, thence to this county, in 1866, and are at this time living in Barry. The subject of this sketch was married in 1857 to Miss Melissa Shepard, daughter of Thomas J. Shepard, a native of this county; and Charles W., George H., Mary E., Ernestine, Mary B., Lena, Lora and Frank, are their living children. Mr. Hancock settled on his present estate in 1872, consisting of 160 acres, valued at $60 per acre. He is a Democrat and a thorough farmer.

George H. Hancock, farmer, sec. 21; P. O., Barry; was born in Adams Co., Ill., in 1855, and is a son of G. A. Hancock, an early settler of this county; was married in 1876 to Miss Lizzie, daughter of John McDaniel, by whom he has one child, Arthur A. He settled on the present farm of his father's in 1877, consisting of over 200 acres of valuable land. Mr. H. is one of the busy and enterprising young farmers of Barry tp.

J. W. Hart, farmer, sec. 33; P. O., Barry; was born in Cheshire Co., N. H., in 1830, the son of Joel and Anna (Hardy) Hart, natives of Massachusetts and New Hampshire, respectively. He came to this county in the fall of 1836, entered land in this tp., and returned East. The following year he brought his family and settled here. Subsequently he purchased the estate of his son, where he moved and spent the remainder of his life; he died in 1877: she died in 1840. He was a Deacon of the Baptist Church in his native place, and at Barry, holding the office nearly ever since he was a member of the Church, and was widely known through the county. The subject of this sketch was married in 1860 to Miss Caroline, daughter of B. F. Brownell, by whom he has 3 children, Henry E., Edward L. and Jennie. The homestead farm consists of 50 acres, valued at $60 per acre. He also owns 80 acres on sec. 29. Mr. H. is a Deacon in the Baptist Church, of which he and his family are members. He has been School Director, and can be counted among prominent and old settlers of this tp. He is a Republican.

N. P. Hart, farmer, sec. 26; P. O., Barry; was born in Ashburton, Mass., in 1826, son of Nathaniel and Clarissa (Hill) Hart, who came to this tp. in 1838, where they still reside. He enlisted in 1846 in Co. K, 5th Reg. Ill. Vol., and served 18 months in the Mexican war, when he was honorably discharged. He returned to his home, and in 1850 was married to Miss Louisa, daughter of Samuel Blair, a native of this tp.; the same year he settled on his present estate of 100 acres, valued at $75 per acre. He also owns 400 acres in the tp. Mr. H. has been for 10 years engaged in the brick manufactory, besides attending to the duties of his extensive farming interests. He has served as Assessor since 1862, excepting 2 years, and School Director most of the time. He is a member of the Odd Fellows order.

Orlando Hart, deceased, was born in Massachusetts in 1829, and emigrated to this county quite early. He was married to Miss Jennette Wirt, who died leaving one child, Alvin. In April, 1854, he again married, this time Miss Mary, daughter of Harvey Blair. Of their children 7 are living,—Ellie, John, Charles W., Katie, Alfred and Nettie. Mr. H. resided on the homestead until his death, which occurred in 1879. Mrs. H. has on sec. 33 a farm of 80 acres, valued at $40 per acre. P. O., Barry. Mr. H. was a member of the Odd Fellows, and a man highly esteemed by all who knew him.

A. C. Hollenbeck & Son, hardware merchants, Barry. This firm erected the building of their present location and established themselves in business in 1870. They carry a stock of $5,000 to $6,000, and deal largely in farm machinery. Mr. H. is a native of Genesee Co., N. Y., where he was born in 1820. He was married in 1845 to Miss Mary J. Cram, a native of Ohio, and came to this county in 1859, settling in this city. He was appointed Postmaster in 1861, re-appointed under Grant, and filled the office 14 or 15 years. He was Mayor one term, Justice of the Peace, and Alderman, and is a strong adherent of the temperance cause, and Republican principles. His only child, C. R., is his partner, and the firm enjoy a large trade. Mr. Hollenbeck's parents were Ruloff and Electa (Ames) Hollenbeck, natives of Massachusetts.

William Hoyt, jr., farmer, sec. 28 ; P. O., Barry ; son of William and Nancy (Bayne) Hoyt, who came to this county in 1845 and settled in this tp., where they still reside. The subject of this sketch was married in 1859 to Miss Millie, daughter of Levi McDaniel, deceased. To them have been born 6 children,—Nancy E., Elvira E., William H., Levi W., Roscoe S. and Floyd. He settled on his present estate in 1865, consisting of 160 acres, valued at $40 per acre. Mr. H. is a member of the Methodist Church. He is a School Director, and in politics is a Democrat. Is a zealous temperance advocate.

W. G. Hubbard, farmer, sec. 15 ; P. O., Barry ; was born in Lincoln county, Mo., in 1829, and is a son of Eli and Margaret (Myers) Hubbard, who came to this State in 1831, and are now residents of Oregon. The subject of this sketch was married in 1867 to Miss Sarah Selby, a native of Pennsylvania. He enlisted in 1862 in Co. D, 99th I. V. I., and served 3 years, participating in battles of Hartsville, Vicksburg, Spanish Fort, and all the battles in which the Regiment was engaged ; was 4th Sergeant and promoted to 1st Sergeant. He served as Sheriff of the county 2 years, from 1866 t4 1868 ; is a School Director at present time. He is the father of children,—Hattie, William, Mary and Lottie.

Loran J. Huntley, constable, was born in Ashtabula county, O., July 5, 1838 ; parents were Harlem and Almira (Partridge) Huntley, natives of New York and Massachusetts, respectively, who came to this county in 1843, and settled in Hadley tp., where he died March 6, 1880 ; she died in Sept., 1877. Loran J. was married in 1861 to Miss Martha M., daughter of Wm. Davis. He engaged in farming until 1872, when he accepted a position as Deputy Sheriff, serving 3 years; also Constable in Hadley 4 years, and elected in Barry to the same position in Aug., 1878; is also a member of the Government detective force, in which he has been engaged 5 years. He is a member of the I. O. O. F. Politics, Democratic.

Elisha Hurt, retired farmer, sec. 24; P. O., Barry; is a native of Kentucky, where he was born May 26, 1809, the son of Joshua and Sallie (Davis) Hurt, natives of Virginia, who emigrated to Illinois at an early day, settling in Logan county, where he died the same year. She died in Tennessee. The subject of this sketch came to this county in 1839 and settled on his present estate, consisting of one-half section of land, valued at $20,000. He was married in 1838 to Miss Margaret J. Lee, a native of Morgan county, Va., where she was born in 1818. To them have been born 11 children, 7 of whom are living,—Charles C., John M., Elisha, jr., Berryman, Albert Clay and Edwin. Mr. H. was commissioned Captain in the 28th Ill. Inf. in 1861, and raised Co. I, and served 3 years. He participated in the battles of Shiloh, where he was wounded, siege of Vicksburg, Hatchie, Corinth, Jackson, Miss., and all the battles of that Regiment. He had also 3 sons in the war,—Charles, Moses and Elisha. Moses was taken prisoner at Jackson and confined at Belle Isle, where he was exchanged. Charles was wounded at Shiloh through the arm and side, but held his place in the ranks by his comrades. Moses was also wounded at Hatchie; but all escaped through the siege of war, and returned to their home. Mr. H. went to California in 1849, being among the first to cross the plains in that year. He returned in 1851 and engaged in the mercantile business in this city until 1861, when he retired to the quiet of his beautiful home. His opportunities for an early education were limited. Left with a widowed mother, he has by his energy and perseverance attained success. Politically he is a descendant of the old-line Whigs, devoted to Republican principles, and an ardent admirer of Grant.

Thomas C. Johnson, farmer, sec. 20; P. O., Kinderhook; was born in Louisa county, Va., in 1826. His parents were William F. and Eliza Johnson, natives of that State, who emigrated to Missouri in 1835, where they both died. Thomas C. came to this county in 1859 and settled on his present farm, consisting of 127 acres, valued at $2,000. He was married in 1853 to Miss Mary E. Tyler, a native of Virginia, the fruits of which are 3 children,— William T., Columbus and Wesley M. Mr. J. is Class-Leader and Trustee in the Methodist Church at Kinderhook, and he is well and favorably known.

D. D. Kidwell, clerk, was born in this county in 1841, and is a son of William and Mahala (Girard), Kidwell, natives of Ohio, who emigrated at an early day to this county, and settled in this tp., where he died in 1851. He was a mechanic, and from 1845 to

1851 was engaged in the furniture business in Barry. The subject of this sketch was married in 1863 to Miss Matilda J. Dibens, a native of Ohio, by whom he has one child, Lottie M. Mr. K. is a member of the Masonic order, a Republican, and a man highly esteemed by all who know him.

S. Kirtright, saloon-keeper, Barry, was born in Clermont county, O., in 1834, and is a son of John and Sophia (Troy) Kirtright, natives of that State, who came to this county in 1840, and settled in Hadley tp., where they both died in 1848. The subject of this sketch moved to New Salem, where he lived until 1872, when he came to this city, and opened a market in which he continued until 1879, when he engaged in his present business. He was married in 1856 to Miss Nancy E. Walls, a native of this county, who died in 1871. His present wife is Mary J., daughter of William Hill, an early settler of this county. Mr. K. still owns his homestead and 4 lots in Salem, and 20 acres of other land. He served as Constable 6 years, and City Marshal some years. Is a Republican.

Major Klein, attorney at law, Barry; is the 3d son of Joseph Klein, an old resident of this city, where he lived for more than 20 years, following the profession of law, in which he became prominent for his skill and ability. He died at his home in this city Feb. 26, 1869. As a citizen father and friend, Mr. K. had no superior, and he left a large circle of friends throughout the county. The subject of this sketch was a graduate of the University at Ann Arbor, Mich., in 1878, and admitted to the bar in 1879. In 1878 he was married to Miss Jennie Klein, of Springfield, Ill., and began the practice of his profession. He was elected City Attorney in 1879, and enjoys a lucrative practice.

Samuel Knox, proprietor of livery and feed stable, Barry; is a son of James and Nancy (Beaks) Knox, natives of Pennsylvania, who settled in Missouri at an early time, where he died in 1854. The subject of this sketch was born in Pike county, Mo., in 1851, and with his widowed mother moved to this county in 1857, and settled 2 miles west of Barry; 3 years afterward she moved to Adams county, where she is now living. Mr. K. was married in 1875 to Miss Leah Hendricks, a native of Adams county, and they have one child, Flandy D. He engaged in farming until Jan., 1880, at which time he opened his present place of business, where he keeps on hand a good stock of horses and carriages, carries a stock of $2,000, and enjoys a good trade. His wife is a member of the Methodist Church. He is a Democrat.

Alvah C. Laing, attorney at law, Barry, is a native of New York, where he was born Aug. 6, 1820; commenced the study of law at the age of 21 years; was admitted to the bar in Michigan in 1850; came to this county in 1869 and settled in Barry, where he has continued in the practice of his profession, and in the enjoyment of a large circle of friends. He is the father of 7 children, 4 boys and 3 girls. Politically, he is a Democrat.

M. Lane, harness-maker, Barry, came to this city in 1857, where he opened a place of business the following year; with the exception of three years' residence on the coast of California, he has since been a resident of this place. Mr. L. is a native of Ireland, where he was born in 1838, and he emigrated with his parents, John and Mary (Burns) Lane, who settled in Pennsylvania, where they still reside. Mr. L. carries a stock of $1,000, and enjoys a good trade.

Jonathan D. Lewis, engineer, sec. 26; P. O., Barry; was born in Pickaway county, O., in 1836, and is a son of Thomas and Mary (Wilgins) Lewis, natives of Pennsylvania, where they both died. The subject of this sketch came to this county in 1859, and settled in this tp., and followed his professional calling at the Woolen Mill, where he is still engaged. He was married in 1857 to Miss Mary J. O'Connor, a native of Ireland, by whom he has 3 children,—Hannah F., William F. and Thomas J. Owns a house and three acres of land. In politics he is a strong Greenbacker.

John Liggett, of the firm of Liggett & Roasa, grocers, Barry, was born in Carroll Co., O., in 1847, the son of John and Nancy (Young) Liggett, natives of Pennsylvania and Ohio, respectively. She died in Indiana in 1866. He is a resident of Allen county, Ind. The subject of this sketch came to this county in 1872, and engaged in farming 3 years, when he formed a partnership with J. C. Moore in the livery business, where he was connected until March, 1880, at which time the present concern was consolidated. He was married in 1875 to Miss Dotha, daughter of William Davis, by whom he has 2 children,—Charles, and one not christened. Mr. L. is a member of the fire company, and one of the energetic young business men of Barry. Politics, Democratic.

James Likes, farmer, sec. 33; P. O., Barry; was born in Ross county, O., in 1827, and is a son of William C. and Dorcas (Day) Likes, natives of that State, who settled in Indiana at an early time, from which State he came to Pike county and settled in Barry tp., where he died in 1859. James was married in 1848 to Miss Hannah Decker, who was born in Wabash county, Ill., in 1828. Mr. L. settled on the present farm in 1864, consisting of 160 acres of valuable land, where he has since made it his home, and numbers among the enterprising farmers of Barry tp. Marietta, William, Telasco, Melinda, Scott, Martha and Lovilla are their living children.

C. P. Lippincott, farmer, sec. 22; P. O., Barry; was born in this tp. in 1839, and is a son of William and Delina (Decker) Lippincott, natives of New Jersey, who emigrated from Ohio to this county at an early day, and settled in Barry, where he opened the first store in this city. He also erected the old distillery and carried on an extensive business, and was engaged in milling for some years. He then went to Cincinnati, O., and ran a saw-mill and lumber yard, where he died in 1851. His wife died in 1867 in this tp. The subject of this sketch was married in 1867 to Miss Chloe Bill, a native of this county, by whom he has 5 chil-

E. A. Crandall

BARRY

dren living: Ibbie, William, Olive M., Charles and George. Mr. L. has served as Road Commissioner and Overseer some years. He settled on his present estate in 1867, consisting of 160 acres, valued at $50 per acre. Is a Democrat in politics.

Thomas J. Long, retired farmer, Barry, was born in Baltimore, Md., June 25, 1808, where he was reared and educated; he emigrated to this county in 1829, arriving at Atlas the 1st day of July, and the same day becoming acquainted with Benj. Barney. Mr. Long followed farming until 1872, when he retired and moved to Barry, where he now resides. In June, 1834, he married Miss Elizabeth M. Irwin, by whom he has had 9 children, 8 now living, namely: Adelaide J., Margaret E., Mary A., Wm. H., Thomas C., Isadore E., Zillah V. and Marion E. The name of the deceased was Josephine L.

W. H. Long, of the firm of Long & Koehler, grocers, Barry, is a native of Adams county, Ill., where he was born in 1846. He was married in 1871 to Miss Mary J. Hendricks, a native of Ohio, where she was born in 1847. In 1877 Mr. L. erected the building he now occupies, and formed the present partnership. The firm carry a stock of $1,500 to $1,600, and although a young firm in the business circles of Barry, they have a lucrative and increasing business. Mr. L. served as Constable some years, and is the father of 2 children, Gracie L. and Don D.

J. H. Mallory, dealer in dry-goods, clothing, boots and shoes. This house was established in 1863 by Louis Angle, who was succeeded by Sweet & Mallory. This co-partnership existed until 1879, when Sweet retired. Mr. M. carries a stock of $13,000 to $15,000, and controls a large trade. He is a native of New York city, where he was born Jan. 1, 1830; came to this county in 1846, and engaged in farming until he entered upon a mercantile pursuit. In 1852 he married Miss Annetta E. Brown, a native of New York. Of this union one child is living, George. Mr. M. is Trustee of the Christian Church, and is one of the solid, enterprising business men of Barry.

T. M. Martin was born in Ralls county, Mo., May 6, 1845, and with his parents came to Pike county, Ill., in the spring of 1847. He is the 3d son of George and Levica A. Martin. His father is a native of Virginia, and mother of Kentucky. T. M. was married to Miss Laura A. Wike, Nov. 4, 1869. He is a farmer, and resides on sec. 11. His wife is a daughter of George Wike. They have born to them 4 children, 2 girls and 2 sons.

Charles Mason, merchant, Barry, was born in Liverpool, Eng., in 1816; at the age of 21 years he moved to Manchester, where he was extensively engaged in the manufacture of wall-paper, until the introduction of a tariff bill by Robert Peel, which ruined his business. He was married in 1838 to Miss Ann Orton, a native of England. They emigrated to this county in 1849 and settled in Barry, where he worked at his trade until he was able to open a small place of business. Subsequently his health failed, and Mrs.

47

M. opened the millinery establishment of their present location, where she has since conducted a very profitable trade. He afterward purchased the building and added a stock of dry-goods and groceries, carrying a stock of $4,000. Both stores have a frontage of 40 feet. Mr. M. was the first man in his line of business in Barry, and nearly all the churches in this city bear the work of his hand. He and his wife returned to their native land in 1864; and were met by a generous welcome by old friends, and presented with a memorial address from the temperance association at Longsight, in which cause Mr. M. has always borne an active part. He is an Elder in the Baptist Church of this city, and is highly esteemed by a large circle of friends.

Charles E. Mason, deceased, was the son of Deacon Charles E. and Martha (Carrolton), M., natives of New Hampshire, who came to this county at an early day, and settled on the present estate, where they resided until called to a better home. He was born Sept. 10, 1800, and died in Barry Dec. 10, 1849. She was born in 1803 and died in 1833. The subject of this sketch was born in Cheshire county, New Hampshire, in 1825, and came with his parents to this county. In 1849 he went overland to California, where he remained one year. In 1855 he was married to Mrs. Nancy J. Hammon, who was born in Johnson county, Ind., in 1828. She was a daughter of David and Tabitha (Dehart) Woodruff, natives of Indiana, where he was born in Brown county, in 1796. To them were born 8 children, 6 of whom are living: Nancy J., John, Mary, David, Henry and George. Her father settled in this county in 1843, and is now living with his daughter at the homestead. Mr. Mason was an active member of the Baptist Church and died in this township in 1877. To them were born 5 children,—4 sons and 1 daughter,—3 of whom are living: Henry B., Willard B. and Anna B., Chas. B. and Edson B., deceased. The estate of Mrs. M. consists of 330 acres of land, valued at $70 per acre. Her residence is on sec. 35, and her postoffice address is Barry.

Elijah L. McAtee, farmer, sec. 7; P. O., Barry; is the youngest son of Hezekiah and Sarah (Smith) McAtee, natives of Maryland and North Carolina respectively, who came to this county in 1827, and settled on the present farm, consisting of 300 acres, valued at $50 per acre, 80 acres of which he entered, and Elijah entered the remainder and purchased ¼ sec., most of which has been cleared. Two brothers, who came in 1826, cleared a portion of it. Hezekiah lived here until his death in December, 1850. Mrs. McAtee died in 1855. They were among the earliest settlers of the tp. The subject of this sketch was born in Clark county, Ky., in 1811, and was married in 1836 to Miss Lucy F., daughter of Judge Grubb, a native of Kentucky. To them have been born 8 children, 2 of whom are living: Bell, wife of Alfred Leach; and Alfred, who married Ellen, daughter of George Hancock, by whom he has 3 children, Lottie, Ennit, and one not yet christened. In 1849 Mr. M., with his brother John and 2 sons, crossed the plains to California with an ox team. In Sacramento and San Jose he became prominent as an auctioneer, in selling outfits, and the party all returned by way of the Isthmus, reaching St. Louis, Mo., where John was taken sick and died. This family number among the early settlers of Barry tp. They came in a wagon drawn by oxen, and erected a rude hut, which to this day shelters occupants of his farm. His first vote was cast for Gen. Jackson before he was 21 years of age, and he has always voted the Democratic ticket. Mr. McAtee stands 6 feet 3½ inches in his stockings, and weighs from 180 to 185 lbs.

George K. McDaniel, farmer, sec. 26; P. O., Barry; was born in Pike county, Ill., July 24, 1845, and is a son of Levi McDaniel, who came to this county in 1836, where he resided until his death, March 1, 1877. The subject of this sketch was married to Miss Lizzie M. Lippincott, by whom he has 5 children, 3 boys and 2 girls. Politically Mr. McD. has ever been a Democrat, and in 1878 espoused the Greenback cause.

William McDaniel, farmer, sec. 23; P. O., Barry; is a son of Levi and Elizabeth (Jennings) McDaniels, natives of Edgefield District, S. C., who came to this county in 1836 and settled in Barry tp., where he entered 260 acres of timbered land in sec. 26, where he lived until his death in 1876. She died in September, 1878. The subject of this sketch was born in Edgefield District, S. C., in 1823. He was married in 1845 to Miss Angeline, daughter of Ephraim Blake, an early settler in this county from Pennsylvania, who died at his son's residence, Jerry Blake. By this marriage 9 children have been born, 6 of whom are living: Lottie, wife of Hezekiah Thompson; Henry H.; Hattie, wife of Henry Jones; Martha, Nancy A. and William. The deceased are Ellen, Eddie, and one who died in infancy. This family, with 4 others, numbering 35 souls, left South Carolina for the West and all settled in Barry tp. Mr. McD. has been prominently identified with the interests of the tp., and the family are members of the Baptist Church. Politics, Democratic.

William McIntire, Justice of the Peace, Barry, is a son of Joseph and Joicy (Gates) McIntire, natives of Kentucky and Alabama respectively, who emigrated to Pike county in 1831 and settled in Pleasant Vale township. Some years afterward he removed to Barry tp., where he died in 1873. Mrs. McIntire is still living, in the 68th year of her age. The subject of this sketch was born in this county in 1836. He served as Constable 19 years. He was married in 1861 to Miss Diala, daughter of Joel Hart, deceased. They have one child, Lillie H. Mr. McIntire has been Mayor and Alderman a number of terms, and has always taken an active part in the interests of the town and city.

John Millhizer, farmer, sec. 31; was born Aug. 31, 1807, in Ohio, and is a son of Philip and Elizabeth (Delavan) Millhizer, father of German, and mother of English descent; was educated in the common schools of Missouri; learned the cooper's trade of his father when 17 years of age; came from Pike county, Mo., to this county in 1826, settling on sec. 31, Barry tp., and has made his home here ever since. In early day he had to go to Quincy to get work, although that place was scarcely large enough to be called a village. About the year 1833 he married Hester Hampton, and of their 7 children 5 are living, all married but one, and all in this county but one. He is the oldest settler living in this tp. at the present time, and remembers, among the many other peculiarities of pioneer life described elsewhere in this history, that hog-stealers were punished by a thrashing at the whipping-post. He commenced a poor boy, worked at the cooper's trade 12 years in this county, and now has 270 acres of land, well improved, 100 acres in cultivation. March 20, 1864, he married Lydia Manker, and they have had one child, David, who was born Dec. 4, 1864. Politically Mr. M. is a Republican.

John C. Moon, proprietor of livery and feed stable, Barry, was born in Brown county, O., in 1853, son of Calvin and Delilah (Sewell) Moon, residents of that State. He came to this county in 1878, and opened his present place of business, carrying now a stock of $2,000, and controls a general trade. He was married Jan. 1, 1880, to Miss Lelia, daughter of Samuel Davis, deceased, an early settler of the county. Mr. M. keeps constantly on hand a good assortment of buggies for sale, having had much experience in the manufacture and sale of them.

Dr. P. M. Parker, dentist, Barry, was born in Cayuga county, N. Y., Jan. 15, 1822, and is a son of Samuel B. Parker, well known in the history of Pike county; his school education was obtained mostly in an old log school-house in this county; in 1826 his parents moved with him to Trumbull county, O., and in 1836 to this county. Dr. P. studied medicine under Dr. Higgins, of Griggsville, at intervals for three years, chopping cord-wood in the meantime to obtain money to pay his expenses. He is a graduate of the medical department of the State University of Missouri at St. Louis, practiced medicine at Ursa, Adams county, Ill., from 1844 to 1846; at New Canton, this county, from that time to 1851; from that time to 1853 in the country five miles east of Pittsfield, and then at Barry from 1853 to 1864, since which time he has been engaged in dentistry, which he follows with success. He helped to build one of the first log school-houses in Pike county, namely, the one near Blue River Cemetery, in Detroit tp., in 1843. March 21, 1850, he married Celia A. Dunham, daughter of John Dunham, of Newburg Corners, this county, and they have had but one child, which died about 7½ months old.

M. G. Patterson, railroad and express agent at Barry, was born in New York city Feb. 9, 1848. In 1870 he was united in wedlock to Miss Nettie E. Young, a native of Pittsburg, Pa. He was appointed to his present position in 1871, and moved to this city, where he has since made it his home. He is also extensively engaged in the coal and grain business. To him belongs the honor of introducing the use of anthracite coal in this county. Large shipments are constantly coming in from the coal mines of Scranton, Pa., and it is being largely used in various portions of the county. He is Secretary of the Masonic order of this city. He has two children, Carrie and Ada.

O. H. Perry, manufacturer, was born in Cumberland county, Pa., in 1826, the son of Samuel and Mary (Butts) Perry, natives of that State, where they both died. The subject of this sketch came to this county in 1848, and engaged in the woolen manufactory. He was a partner in the company of six that erected the woolen mill in 1864, where he was successfully engaged for twenty years. He was married in 1856 to Miss Virginia Watson, a native of New York, who died in 1872, leaving 2 children, Thomas and Mary. His present wife, *nee* Lottie Hart, is a native of this county and daughter of Joel Hart, deceased. To this union 1 child has been born, Clarence. Mr. P. has a pleasant residence, with 12½ acres of land, and he also has 160 acres in other parts of the tp. He served as Road Supervisor 11 years, and School Director many years, and has always taken an active interest in the business circles of Barry. His wife is a member of the Baptist Church. In politics he is Democratic always.

Charles Pinger, lumber dealer, Barry; established in the fall of '76. He furnished the means for the erection of the saw-mill and buildings in 1875, prior to which time the business was carried on in a small yard through his agent. He first began business at Hannibal on a small capital, and increased until he was enabled to run 6 yards. He shipped over 100 car-loads of lumber to this place. He employs from 12 to 20 men, and fills contracts for furnishing buildings with sash, doors, mouldings, etc., all of which are made at this establishment. Mr. P. is a native of Cincinnati, O., where he was born in 1848. Mr. P. is also engaged in the mercantile business, where he is having a lucrative trade, and is one of the thorough business men of the times. He was married in 1870 to Miss Nettie, daughter of John Rice, a native of Ohio. To them have been born 4 children.—Harry, Leo, Lulu and Pearl.

Charles Roasa, of the firm of Liggett & Roasa, grocers, Barry, is a native of Pennsylvania, where he was born in 1852. He is the son of Charles and Elizabeth Roasa, natives of Germany, who emigrated to America in 1840, and settled in Pennsylvania, and are at this time living in Lewis county, Mo. The subject of this sketch was married in 1875 to Miss Nora McDonald, a native of this county. To them one child has been born, Paulina. Mr. R. fills the office of City Clerk, and is one of the active young business men of Barry. He is a member of the I. O. O. F., and Republican in politics. The firm of which he is a member succeeded A. White in 1880, and they now carry a stock of $2,000 and enjoy a fair trade.

Dr. J. S. Rowand & Son, druggists, Barry. The senior partner of this firm was born in Camden, N. J., in 1813; was married in 1834 to Miss Ellen B. Haines, a native of Philadelphia, where he was engaged in the practice of patent medicine until he came to this county in 1856, and commenced his present business. In 1876 he erected the building he now occupies. It has a frontage of 37 feet and is 120 feet deep. The firm carry a stock of $3,000, and have a large and lucrative trade. He has 3 children living: John, the junior partner of the house, who married Miss McTucker, of this city; Horace M, and Bathuel H. Mr. and Mrs. R. are members of the Baptist Church.

G. W. Shields, proprietor of lime kiln; P. O., Barry; was born in Athens county, O., in 1842, and is a son of William and Lydia Selby, natives of Ohio, who emigrated to this State in 1848, and settled north of Quincy, where he lived until he moved to this tp., where he now resides. The subject of this sketch was married in 1868 to Miss Martha Freeman, a native of Illinois. Mr. S. has been engaged in his present business 4 years, and is doing a fair trade. Bessie, Josie and Mabel are his living children. Politics, Democratic.

Eugene Smith, merchant and banker, Barry, is a son of Nathaniel and Sylvania (Sweet) Smith, natives of New York State, who emigrated to this county and settled in Barry tp. in 1837, where he is at this time living. She died in 1879. The subject of this sketch was born in Pike county, Ill., in 1839, and during the early years of his life engaged in clerking, until called to fill the office of cashier in the Exchange Bank at the time of its organization. In 1872 he was admitted to the concern, forming the present partnership of Smith, Davis & Brown. He was married in 1879 to Miss Helen, daughter of Henry Bonnel, a native of Griggsville. Mr. Smith is also a partner of the firm of Crandall & Smith, grocers and grain dealers, which is the largest house of the kind in Pike county. He is a member of the I. O. O. F., and fills the office of Dictator in the Knights of Honor. He and Mrs. S. are members of the Baptist Church. Probably no man is more deserving of success than Mr. Smith, for close attention to business, energy, integrity, and the possession of qualities that have won for him an active and responsible position in this county. His portrait, which appears in this work, was taken at the age of 40 years.

George W. Smith, teacher, is a son of James and Sarah Smith, of Barry, and was born in Belmont county, O., Feb. 8, 1851; was brought by his parents to this county in 1856; was educated in Barry, where he is now teaching his eighth year in the 2d grammar school; he taught his first school at Summer Hill, this county. In 1874 he married Miss Alta C. Blair, daughter of Samuel Blair, of Barry, and they have had 2 children,—George L., deceased, and Ida.

J. J. Smith, dealer in boots and shoes, clothing, hats, caps, and gents' furnishing-goods, established himself in grocery business in 1869. In 1870 Mr. Crandall was admitted and they formed a partnership. The firm dissolved in 1875. The following year he erected the building of his present location, at a cost of $7,500.

Being in poor health, he spent one year in the South, and in 1877 returned and opened his present business, where he enjoys a good trade. He is a native of Lynchburg county, Va., where he was born in 1840. He was married in Virginia to Miss Sarah F. Crumpton, a native of that State. They have one adopted son, James Y. Mr. S. is one of the active and enterprising merchants of Barry, and is well and favorably known.

M. Strubinger.was born in Delaware in 1833, and is the eldest son of Joseph Strubinger, deceased, whose name is familiar to all of the people of Pike county. The subject of this sketch was brought by his parents to Pike county when he was a boy, and he commenced the battle of life at the age of 21, working on the farm by the month until he was about 30 years of age, at $15 per month. He worked for one man seven years. Mr. Strubinger was married to Miss Mary H. Chamberlain in 1862, and they have had four children. Mr. Strubinger came to Barry, where he resided for five or six years, and now resides three-fourths of a mile south, on a farm of 225 acres of highly improved farm lands. He has the past year built him one of the finest farm residences in the county. He has in all about 1,200 acres of land. He is a thorough farmer and deals extensively in stock.

Dr. Joseph Jerome Topliff. Dr. Topliff was born in Bridgewater, Windsor county, Vermont, Sept. 12, 1832. He remained at home until the age of 16, receiving his early education at the district school, working on his father's farm during the summer, and attending school in the winter. He was then sent to Black River Academy, at Ludlow, Vt., where he remained two years, and then entered the Green Mountain Liberal Institute, at South Woodstock, Vt.,closing his Academic course at that Institution,where he entered upon the study of medicine, and graduated at Dartmouth College, N. H. In April, 1856, he came to Illinois and located at Pittsfield, Pike county, and the following year was elected School Commissioner of the county, which office he held for two terms. In the spring of 1862 he moved to New Salem, and devoted his attention to the practice of his profession, where his professional and untiring devotion to his patients and his profession, with his accustomed social, courteous, and honorable manner, won for him a large circle of patrons and warm friends. He was elected Clerk of the Circuit Court and Recorder of the county in the fall of 1868, which office he held for 4 years, with ability and entire satisfaction to the people of the county, and left his official record without spot or blemish. Preparatory to resuming the practice of his profession he spent the fall and winter of 1875-6 in New York, pursuing his professional studies at Bellevue Hospital Medical College and the College of Physicians and Surgeons, when two years ago he associated himself with one of the oldest and most highly esteemed practitioners of the county, Dr. A. C. Baker, of Barry, Ill., where we find him in the enjoyment of the full confidence of his professional brethren, and a large and increasing demand for his professional services. Dr. Topliff was married to Laura E. Lake, South Woodstock, Vt., in 1856, and they have had 4 children, 1 son and 3 daughters. The son was accidentally shot and killed when 14 years of age; the wife and daughters are all living.

J. L. Underwood, attorney at law, Barry, is a son of Robert and Martha (Onderdonk) Underwood, the former born in New York city, March 7, 1803, and the latter born Aug. 2, 1803. They emigrated to Illinois and settled in Eldara, where he died Feb. 11, 1878; she is still living in this city. The subject of this sketch was born in New York city, May 16, 1826; came to this county in 1836, where he has since made it his home. In 1847 he enlisted in Co. K, 5th Ill. Vol., for the Mexican war, and served nearly two years. In the spring of 1849 he went overland to California; returning the following year he was married to Miss Louisa Lyons, daughter of Joseph and Elizabeth Lyons, a native of this State. To them were born 10 children, 6 of whom are living, 5 boys and a girl. He began the practice of law in this city in 1862; was appointed under Lincoln Inspector of Coal Oils, Liquors and Tobacco, and served in that capacity until removed by Andy Johnson. He was Justice of the Peace 4 years in Derry, and Police Magistrate 10 years, and Supervisor 2 years. He is a member of the Masonic order, and has always been identified with the interests of the town and county. Mr. U. has traveled extensively through different countries of the East, and is well informed on all subjects. His mother has for 50 years been a member of the Methodist Church.

John Weber, proprietor of the Empire House, was born in St. Louis, Mo., in 1843, and is a son of John and Margaret Weber, natives of Germany, who emigrated to America in 1841 and settled in Pittsburg, Pa., from which State they moved to Adams county, where they at this time reside. Mr. John Weber was married in 1867 to Miss Rosa, daughter of Robert High, a native of Adams county, where Mr. W. was engaged in milling and merchandising until he came to this county in 1877. Here he engaged as salesman, until he took the Empire House in the winter of the same year. In the brief experience of Mr. W. in catering to the traveling public he has won for himself an extended reputation. Courteous, kind, and obliging at all times, the traveler will find the "Empire" a place of welcome. He is the father of 3 children,— Ralph K., Harry and Nettie. Mr. Weber is an Alderman at present.

Henry Wendorff, furniture dealer, west side of the Square, Barry, Ill., was born in Germany, June 18, 1828; emigrated to the United States in 1856, stopping at Buffalo one year; he then came and started in business in a small building only 16 by 24 on the west side of the Square in Barry, which building he has greatly enlarged on account of his increasing business. He keeps constantly on hand the best line of goods, selling them at very low rates. His capital stock is now about $3,000. In 1857 he married Caroline

Hermon, by whom he has had 7 children: Henry, Louise, Anna, Carrie, Mary, May and Irene.

Alex. White, retired merchant, Barry, is a native of Scotland, where he was born in 1830, and emigrated to America in 1850 with his parents, Thomas and Esther (Watson) White, who settled near Barry and engaged in farming. They afterward moved to Quincy, where they both died. Mr. W. became associated with his brother in the mercantile business in 1864, which was continued until the present year, when the firm dissolved. He was married in 1853 to Miss Mary Ferguson, a native of Scotland, by whom he has one child living, Alexandria R., wife of Albert Hurt, residents of this city. Mr. W. has been School Director 9 years, and is the present Clerk of the Board. He has always taken an active interest in school matters, and other matters pertaining to the welfare of Barry. In politics he is a Republican.

W. F. White, merchant, Barry, Ill., is the son of Thomas and Esther (Watson) White, natives of Scotland; with their family they emigrated to this country in 1850 and located in Quincy; thence they moved to Barry, on a farm. They were the parents of 12 children, 11 boys and 1 girl, of which W. F. was the seventh son, being about 15 years of age when he came to this city. In his early life he learned the carpenter's trade and superintended the building of many fine houses in the neighborhood; and by strict perseverance and economy, in 1857 he embarked in the mercantile business, of which he has stood at the head (firm of W. F. White & Brother) for 23 years; was a large operator in grain and pork-packing till within the last three years; is now engaged in mercantile business,—dry-goods, boots and shoes, hardware and agricultural implements, and doing a good business. He also holds an interest in the Opera House, which was commenced by his energy, also interested in many buildings and dwellings, etc., in the city. He has also held some very prominent positions before the people, as City Treasurer and Alderman; has served the township as Supervisor for several years, with great credit and honor. Is a prominent Freemason, in which order he has held many offices of prominence; is now M. E. Scribe of Barry Chapter No. 88, R. A. M.; is an unflinching Democrat in politics, and now a prominent candidate before the people for the nomination of Circuit Clerk of Pike county. He was married in 1862 to Miss Mary A. Rush, daughter of Josiah Rush, and they have had two children, Caroline and William A. Caroline died in 1864, aged 15 months. His wife Mary died in 1866, aged 33 years.

D. J. Wike, farmer, sec. 27; P. O., Barry; was born in Cumberland county, Pa., in 1821, and is the youngest son of George and Mary (Essig) Wike, natives of Pennsylvania, where his father died in 1825. The subject of this sketch settled in Quincy in 1842, where he engaged in the woolen business for 2 years, when he came to this tp., and with two brothers, George and Joseph, and P. Grubb, erected a woolen factory on sec. 23, where he carried on an extensive business for 5 years; then he sold his interest and purchased a farm in New Salem tp. Three years afterward he returned to Barry, and in 1847 was married to Drusilla, daughter of Thomas Orr, a native of Randolph county, Ill., where she was born in 1828; settled on his present estate in the spring of 1853, consisting of 200 acres, valued at $75 per acre. Mr. W. has been prominently identified with the interests of the tp., and was the first member initiated in the Masonic Order at Barry, in 1845. He is the father of 7 children, 6 of whom are living,—Thomas O., Dallas, William M., Mary E., Charles S. and Louis L.

Thomas O. Wike, farmer, sec. 34; P. O., Barry; was born in this tp. in 1848, and is a son of David and Drusilla (Orr) Wike, early Barry pioneers. The subject of this sketch was married in 1872 to Miss Elmira Uchran, a native of this county. Two children are the fruits of this marriage,—George H. and Elizabeth E. Mr. Wike has a farm of 40 acres, valued at $75 per acre. He is a member of I. O. O. F., and one of the pioneer generation of Barry.

J. R. Williams, farmer, sec. 36: P. O., Barry; is the son of John and Margaret (Reno) Williams, natives of Tennessee, who settled in Indiana when it was a Territory, where he died in 1817. She died in 1833. The subject of this sketch was born in Overton county, Tenn., in 1817; in 1834 he went to Iowa, then the Territory of Wisconsin, where he purchased land, which he afterward sold, receiving in payment Illinois State scrip, payable at 6 per cent. interest, which was never redeemed. This was valuable time and labor lost, and in 1842 he evacuated that Territory for the growing settlements of Illinois, and rented a farm in Pleasant Vale tp. He was married March 10, 1845, to Miss Elizabeth A. Baldwin, a native of New York State, who died Nov. 15, of the same year. She was born Aug. 6, 1828. His present wife, lately Mrs. Mary Blair, widow of Hon. Wm. Blair, who died in the State Legislature in 1845, was born in New York State Nov. 1, 1814. Mr. W. settled on his present farm in 1845, consisting of 140 acres, valued at $70 per acre. Mr. W. has been prominently identified with the interests of the township in several offices, and the family are members of the Baptist Church. Of their several children 2 are living, John R. and Calvin J. Politically, Mr. W. is a Democrat.

PLEASANT VALE TOWNSHIP.

Long before railroads were thought of in the West, and when the red man and wild beasts roamed at will across the prairies and through the forests of Illinois; and when this expanse of country was one vast wilderness, two young men wended their way into this then far West, and took up their dwelling among the treacherous Indians and savage beasts. They pitched their tent first on sec. 16 of what is now Pleasant Vale township. These men, who were then young and sturdy, both won wealth, position and honor, in this great State. They were John Wood and Willard Keyes, both names familiar to almost every man in this part of the State, and the former of whom was chosen Lieutenant Governor, and on the death of Governor Bissell acted as Governor. These two men met about this time and formed a friendship which was never broken until the death of Mr. Keyes in 1872. They lived here in one little cabin; indeed, they had much in common; youth, energy and ambition,—common aims and sympathies, and for half a century they watched the growth and gradual development of the city they had founded.

Wood and Willard soon moved from sec. 16 to the southwest quarter of sec. 22, where they made the first improvements that were made in the township. They soon afterward, however, sold their possessions here and moved to Quincy and founded that city, where Mr. Wood still resides, and where Mr. Keyes lived until his death.

Amos and Joseph Jackson, David Dutton, Major Hinckley, Parley Jackson, Daniel Howard, Mr. Rice, Mr. Mitchell and Andrew Shearer were also very early settlers in this township, and did much for the improvement of the county.

These early settlers endured many hardships and privations in preparing the way for future generations and future prosperity, which the people of to-day know not of. They ground their corn for food on a hand-mill, and at times crushed it in a hominy block. The latter consisted of a hole burnt in a stump or block of wood, in which corn was placed and crushed with an iron wedge or mallet. In a short time, however, these odd and rude pieces of pioneer machinery were replaced by horse-mills. These were generally situated eight or ten miles from the settlers here, and although they were a great improvement upon the hand-mills and hominy blocks, the process of grinding would be considered very slow, indeed, by the people of this day and age of steam-mills. The boys then went to mill on horseback, and seldom ever returned the same day. They would congregate under the old shed of the horse-mill while waiting for their turn, and there make a fire and parch corn, tell jokes, etc. In this way they would pass the night very pleasantly without supper or sleep; for the supper could not be had, and there was no place to sleep, save on the sacks of corn.

Then came the days of schools and churches. The first school-house erected by the settlers was on sec. 22, in 1825. It was a log cabin with a clapboard door, puncheon floor, slab benches for seats and a huge fire-place at one end of the room. The desks consisted of puncheons supported by pins in the wall; the fire-place had no chimney except above the roof; there were two doors, one at each side of the fire-place. The fuel used consisted of huge logs, which were often dragged into the house by a horse coming in at one door and passing through and out at the other. Around and near the fire-place there was no floor except the ground, the puncheon floor covering the back part of the room only. The window consisted of a log removed from one side of the room, with greased paper pasted over the aperture. The first teacher here was a Mr. Rankin. The pioneer teacher was of the ox-driver class, and generally carried a large "gad" in his hands, to maintain order in the school.

Religious worship was early instituted in the first settlement of this township. The first sermon was preached by Rev. Mr. Hunter, of the Methodist denomination, and the first regularly organized religious society was also that of the Methodists. This society first worshiped in the house of Mr. Jackson, and afterward in the school-house on sec. 22. The Mormons also figured largely in a Church organization here some years later. They at one time had a society of about 100 communicants, and erected a house of worship in the northwest part of the township. When the Nauvoo trouble, came, however, they left this neighborhood to join their brethren at that place. The old Mormon church was afterward moved to the Mississippi river, and there used for a warehouse.

The first white child born in the tp. was Andrew J. Stanley, in 1823. The first death was that of Mary Jane McDaniel which occurred in the autumn of the same year. The first parties married were Potter Saxhorn and Matilda Stanley, in the year 1825.

In those early days the wagons, for the most part, were rudely constructed by the settlers themselves, and consisted wholly of wood. The wheels were sawn from large sycamore trees, and holes were bored in the center, in which to insert the axletrees. The farmers often used these wagons in going to mill, hauling their produce to market, and for a conveyance in which to attend Church.

In pioneer times, when there were scarcely any fences, and not land enough under cultivation to stop the great prairie fires which occurred in the fall of the year, they proved very disastrous to those living on the prairie. This township consists, for the most part, of Mississippi river bottom land, a large portion of which is prairie. The grass on this bottom land grew to an enormous height, was very thick, and as high as a man's head while on horseback. This grass was so heavy and thick that when the settlers went a-fishing in the Sny they would hitch the team to a large brush or tree and drag it through the grass and mash it down, to make a road for them to pass over. In the fall of the year this luxuriant growth of grass would be set on fire by the Indians or hunters, and especially when the wind was high, would sweep resistlessly over the whole country, high and low, destroying a great deal of property.

The pioneers early learned to guard against this destructive element by plowing wide strips of land around their premises and around their grain and hay. As soon as the alarm of fire was given, each settler would immediately begin to "back fire." This was done by setting the grass on fire next outside the plowed strip, which would burn slowly and meet the rapidly advancing flames that came rolling in majestic grandeur, from 20 to 30 feet in the air.

This bottom land is now under a high state of cultivation, and since the completion of the levee has become one of the richest farming districts of America. The land lying between the Sny and the Mississippi is timber land, and as fertile as the prairie. It is now rapidly being cleared and improved. This district bears the appearance of being a new country, however, for wild animals are quite numerous here, and also the gray and bald eagle.

Most of the land in this township was obtained from the Government at $1.25 per acre, and it was very readily paid for. The fur-bearing animals were very plenty here then, and a settler would obtain fur enough during the fall and winter to pay for 160 acres of land. We have it from good authority that it was not an uncommon occurrence to see five or six coons in one tree at one time during those pioneer days. Mr. Francis Jackson related to us that he saw at one time nine coons in one tree. Snakes also were very numerous and annoying, and especially the rattlesnake. The Mississippi bluffs, which extend from the northwest to the southeast, through this township, were a constant den for the timber rattlesnakes, which were from five to eight feet long. The settlers were lasting enemies of these reptiles, and finally adopted a plan which resulted in their almost total extermination. They fastened bearded hooks to long poles and thrust these into their dens, drawing the snakes out and killing them, until no more snakes could be found. This was done in the spring of the year, before the snakes could crawl.

Wild cats, wild hogs, foxes, wolves, panthers and other wild animals abounded here when this township was first settled; some of which species remain to this day.

On the N. W. qr. of sec. 29 is a salt spring, which at one time afforded considerable salt water. Mr. Keyes carried water from this spring to his home, on sec. 22, a distance of a mile and a half, boiled it down, and made salt for family use and for his neighbors.

As the bluffs extend from the northwest to the southeast through the township, the up land is divided from the bottom land, forming a triangular section. This land is very rough and broken, and is underlaid with a heavy bed of limestone, and is consequently better adapted to the growing of small grain and fruit than to general farming. There is some excellent farming land along the course of Keyes creek, which extends along the eastern portion of the township. This creek was named in honor of Mr. Keyes, of whom we have spoken in the first part of this sketch. At one time this creek and others abounded in countless numbers of fish, and thus aided in furnishing the settlers with the necessaries of life. Although the pioneers were deprived of many things that are enjoyed at the present day, yet they always had abundance to eat and wear. If their store clothes or homespun gave way, they would simply construct clothing from the hides of animals.

The first Justice of the Peace of this township was Major Hinckley. James Talbert was the first Supervisor. Francis Jackson is the oldest settler now residing in the township. He came in 1825, and is the only man now living who went from this locality to the Black Hawk War.

NEW CANTON.

This enterprising town is situated on secs. 9 and 16, Pleasant Vale township. It was founded April 2, 1835, by Charles T. Brewster, Hiram Smith and Jesse Tittsworth. It contains four stores, four blacksmith shops, two wagon shops, two carpenter shops, two boot and shoe shops, one paint shop, one cooper shop, one excellent flouring mill, two hotels, one livery stable, one lodge of the Independent Order of the Mutual Aid Society, which was established in February, 1880, with a membership of 25 ; and is the residence of four physicians. The present population of the town is about 350.

There was a church erected here in 1866, which is known as the Union Church. It is not owned by any one denomination, but by the community in general. There are two Church organizations here,—the Methodists and the Baptists. The former is a remnant of the original M. E. Church that was organized in pioneer days. The Baptists merged the old society into a new one in 1879. The music furnished by the young people during the hours of worship is excellent. Considerable interest is manifested here in this high art, and two choirs have been formed, both of which exhibit superior musical talent.

The first school taught where the village now stands was in a dwelling house, by Mr. Hale in 1832. The first school-house was a log structure and was erected in 1836. The present building is a handsome frame structure, and was erected in 1866. The teacher at present is Prof. Warren D. Bigelow, formerly of Ohio.

PERSONAL SKETCHES.

Below we make personal mention of the leading citizens of the township.

M. M. Aldrich, farmer, sec. 6; P. O., Hannibal, Mo.; was born in New York in 1828, and is the son of M. M. and Mary (Herrington) Aldrich; was educated in the common schools of Michigan, in which State he also kept store from 1850 to 1856 ; was a sailor on the lakes 6 years ; he came to Pike county in 1860, settling on sec. 6, this tp., where he now owns 350 acres of land; all he is now worth he has made within the last 20 years; he has a splendid farm in the Mississippi bottom. Mr. A. has been married twice,—the first time to Martha Parnell, and they had 3 daughters, 2 of whom are living. Mrs. A. died in 1860, and subsequently Mr. A. married Catharine Kendall, and of their 7 children 5 are living. Politically, Mr. A. is a Democrat.

John E. Alexander, farmer, sec. 23 ; P. O., Cincinnati; was born in Indiana in 1849, and is the son of William and Mary Ann (Dyke) Alexander; was educated in Iowa ; in 1873 he married Mary E. Knight, and they have had 2 children, one of whom is deceased. Mr. A. owns a good farm, and has the reputation of being an honest, industrious man. In politics he is a Republican.

Jonas Edward Artz, teacher and minister of the Gospel, was born in Pennsylvania, and is a son of Israel B. and Elizabeth (Eby) Artz, natives of Pennsylvania, and of German descent; was educated at Hamilton College, Hamilton county, Ill.; has been preaching 3 years in the M. E. Church; now attends two or three appointments every Sunday, besides teaching, in which latter profession he is also successful. P. O., New Canton.

Henry B. Atkinson, merchant, New Canton; was born in St. Louis, Mo., in 1842, and is the son of B. H. and Harriet (Morgan) Atkinson, father a native of New Jersey, and mother of Pennsylvania; educated in the common schools of Pike county; in 1868 he married Orpha M. Witt, and they have had 3 children, 2 of whom are living; commenced mercantile business in company with his father at Pittsfield in 1865, and came to New Canton in 1876, where he has succeeded well, dealing in drugs, medicines, groceries, farming implements, etc.; also buys and ships grain. New Canton is considered by many to be the best grain market in Pike county.

Elias Baldwin, farmer, sec. 16; P. O., New Canton; was born in Connecticut May 3, 1816, and is a son of Wm. and Clara (Ives) Baldwin, natives also of that State; both his grandfathers drew pensions as Revolutionary soldiers; was educated in Connecticut; came to this county in 1836. In 1846 he married Permelia Safers, and they have had one child, Margaret, who is still at home. As a farmer, Mr. B. has been successful.

George Balzer, butcher, New Canton; was born in Bavaria in 1845, the son of George and Catharine (Wizenberger) Balzer, natives of the same country; emigrated to Quincy, Ill., in 1847, and in 1864 to Pike county; received his education in the graded schools, and Ray & Veriel's Commercial College one term, and Baker's three terms. In 1868 he married Orintha Yearly, and they have had 4 children, all of whom are living. Mr. B. commenced his present business two years ago, and so far has prospered well in it. He commenced clerking at the age of 10 years, and continued until he was 16, when he passed muster in the 27th Ill. Inf., and served in the war 3 years; was in every battle in which the Regiment was engaged, and was discharged in 1864.

Warren D. Bigelow, principal of the New Canton schools; is a native of Portage county, O., and was born Jan. 29, 1845; his parents were Johnson and Mary (Lewis) Bigelow; he received a common-school education in Ohio, and came to this county in 1865; he is a self-made teacher, having obtained the greater part of his education while teaching; has now pursued his chosen occupation 15 years, and at present has charge of the New Canton schools the second year, adopting the latest normal plans. He has been married three times and is the father of 6 children, of whom 5 are living. James W., Albert D., Elbert J., Mary O. and Lela Maud, the last 3 by his present wife. His first two wives died of quick consumption.

William Bolin, New Canton; was born in Jefferson county, Ind., and is the son of John and Celia (Sharp) Bolin, the latter a native of Virginia; was educated in the common schools of Indiana and Kentucky. He first married America Lawhorne, and by her had 11 children, 4 of whom are living; she and 3 of the children died in one week. Mr. Bolin afterward married Elizabeth Vanover, and by her had 2 children, one of whom is living; this Mrs. B. died in 1872, and for his third wife Mr. B. selected Miss Nancy M. Sharp, and of their 3 children 2 are living.

Charles N. Brammell, farmer, sec. 17; P. O., New Canton; was born in this county in 1847, and is the son of Thomas and Amelia (Butler) Brammell, who emigrated to this county in 1834; Charles N. now has charge of his mother's farm, and is doing well; he was brought up a farmer, and was educated in the common schools of this county. Politically, he is a Democrat.

Charles T. Brewster, deceased, was born in New York in 1811; remained with his father until 1832, when he bought a piece of land on sec. 27 in this tp., and commenced farming; in 1849 he went overland with an ox team to California, and engaged successfully in gold mining for 2 years; returning home, he enlarged his farming operations, adding the business of stock-raising. He accumulated considerable property and was a very popular man in his neighborhood; always paid his hands good wages, and promptly; one man worked for him 30 years; was Supervisor many years, and held other local offices. In 1852 he married Miss Melvina Percell, and of their 8 children 3 are living,—Charles E., Anna M. and Minnie M. Mr. B. died Sept. 3, 1875. We present Mr. Brewster's portrait in this volume.

NEW CANTON

Harrison Brown, farmer; P. O., New Canton; was born in Pike county, Mo., Feb. 6, 1828, and is a son of Joseph and Nancy C. (Bullen) Brown, natives of Kentucky, and both born in 1798, near Lexington—father, Aug. 18, and mother, Sept. 17; father was of Irish descent, and mother of Scotch. The subject of this sketch was the third child (2d son) of a family of 7 children, and is the only one living at present; a brother and two sisters died in 1856. Harrison was educated in this tp., having been brought here by his father in 1829; has been a farmer all his life, except 4 years in California gold-mining, 1852–6. Feb. 25, 1857, he married Eliza C. Shewe, and of their 7 children only 2 are now living: Joseph, who was born Oct. 25, 1861, and Mallie, Nov. 3, 1868. He owns 440 acres of land, 420 of it here in one body. Mr. Brown's portrait is given in this volume.

William S. Coon, carpenter, was born in the town of Fabius, Onondaga Co., N. Y., Nov. 16, 1819, and is the son of Joseph and Lydia Coon, of Dutch ancestry; was educated in the common schools of New York State; at the age of 24 he commenced to learn his trade. In 1853 he married Asha A. Ballan, who was born in the town of Sandy Creek, Oswego Co., N. Y., in 1835, and they have one child, Frank E., who was born in 1865. Mr. and Mrs. Coon are members of the Christian Church. He is a Republican. P. O., New Canton.

George A. Dutcher, farmer, sec. 17; P. O., New Canton; was born Aug. 7, 1840, in the State of New York, and is the son of Stephen M. and Mary (Hunt) Dutcher, natives of the same State, father of German ancestry, and mother of English. George received his education in the common schools of this county, whither he emigrated in 1844 or 1845. In 1873 he married Sarah A. Morey, and they have had one child, Stephen A., born Dec. 25, 1875. Mr. Dutcher has taught school 7 or 8 terms in this county, and as a farmer he has been successful, now owning 160 acres of land. He is a Republican, and a member of the Christian Church.

P. H. Davis, New Canton, was born in Fountain county, Ind., in 1826, and is the son of Robert and Amanda (Blair) Davis, the former a native of Kentucky, and mother of Indiana, and of Scotch descent; was brought to this county in 1829, settling in Kinderhook, where he received his education. In 1851 he married Eliza Shipman, and of their 5 children but two are living. The same year he moved to New Canton, where he engaged in mercantile business until 1862, when he was elected Sheriff; serving two years in that office he resumed his mercantile business until 1878, when he sold out. Mr. Davis has also pleaded law to some extent, with success. In politics he is a Democrat. He has seen this county in its primitive wild state, with deer, wolves, etc., in abundance.

William A. Davis, New Canton, was born in Marietta, Washington Co., Ohio, in 1820, the son of Stephen and Patience (Springer) Davis, natives of Maine. Of his 6 children 5 are living, and all married but one; 4 reside in this county, and one in Car-

48

roll county, Mo. Most of his life Mr. Davis has followed the river; piloted a flat-boat for 20 years, and has traveled 4,000 miles. In his younger days he worked 2 years at the carpenter's trade, and works at it some yet. He owns 40 acres of land, besides a house and lot. In politics he is a Democrat.

James Emerson, farmer, sec. 8; P. O., New Canton; was born Dec. 21, 1836, in Ohio, and is the son of Ephraim and Elizabeth (Wallace) Emerson, father a native of Maryland, and mother of Ohio, and of German descent; was brought to this county in 1838 by his parents in emigration, and here received his education in the common school. March 10, 1859, he married Lydia Yearly, and their 3 children are all living. He owns 60 acres of land, and in politics is a Republican.

Cicero Gard, farmer, sec. 10; P. O., New Canton; was born in Barry tp., this county, in 1836, and is the son of M. and Clarissa (Baker) Gard, father a native of Virginia, and of English and Irish descent, and mother a native of Ohio, and of English descent; educated at Knox College, Galesburg, Ill. Oct. 23, 1860, he married Lydia Halstead, and of their 4 children 2 are living. He owns 80 acres of land, and as a farmer he has been successful. In politics he is a Republican.

Lorenzo Gard, farmer, brother of the preceding, was born in Washington county, O., April 15, 1818; was educated mostly in the common schools of this county; in 1841 he taught school 6 months. In 1843 he married Margaret Yearly, and of their 7 children 5 are living, one single, and all living in this county. Mr Gard came to Pike county in 1831 and settled near New Canton, where he still lives. When his father came here he had only 6¼ cents in money, but now he has 300 acres of land. Mr. Gard has seen this country in its wild state, and has experienced the poverty and hardships of pioneer times. In politics he is a Republican.

Seth Gard. Prominent among the business men of New Canton, is the subject of this sketch, Mr. Seth Gard, who was born in this county in 1832, and although comparatively a young man he is classed among the early inhabitants of Pike county; is the son of Robert and Martha (Putnam) Gard, natives of Ohio. In 1879 Mr. G. was united in marriage with Miss Ellen Phillips, who is a member of the M. E. Church. Mr. Gard started in life without much of this world's goods, or, as the saying is, "bare-handed;" he first worked by the month on a farm, but at present is the Postmaster at New Canton, and keeps a grocery store, etc. As a business man he is prompt, obliging, and enjoys a fair share of the trade of the place; he is a Republican in politics, and has been Postmaster at New Canton since 1873.

Eugene Gray is a native of this county, and was born in 1829; his parents were Thomas T. and Mary F. (Crandall) Gray, natives of New York, who came to Pike county the year of his birth. Our subject has spent the most of his life in mercantile pursuits; he first began to clerk in the store of Mowry & Massie at New Canton, and since 1872 has been a full partner with Mr. M. D. Massie, and as a firm they have met with success. In 1862 he enlisted in the 68th Ill. Inf., and the following year entered the 28th Ill. Inf., and was mustered out in 1866. During the last year of the service he was Quartermaster Sergeant, and prior to that he was most of the time on detached duty as Clerk. Politically Mr. G. is a Republican, is a member of the Town Board of New Canton, and Treasurer of Pleasant Vale tp. Mr. G. was married in 1868 to Lydia Ware, who is a member of the Baptist Church.

T. A. Hayden, farmer, sec. 8; P. O., New Canton; is the son of J. and Elizabeth (Barnard) Hayden, and was born in Missouri in 1844; his father, who was of Irish ancestry, and also his mother, who was of English descent, were born in that State. He received his education in the common schools of his native State, and for a time engaged in teaching. He came to Pike county in 1873, and embarked in farming; in 1869 he was married to Clara E. Freeman, who has borne him 9 children, 3 of whom are living.

E. K. Higbee, farmer, sec. 20; P. O., New Canton; was born in Adams county, Ill., April 6, 1839; his parents, Elias and Sarah (Ward) Higbee, were natives of Ohio; he received his education in the common schools and the Griggsville high school. He formerly engaged in the mercantile business at Detroit and 4 years in Missouri, and in 1875 came to this tp., where he is farming 3 quarters of land. In 1864 he was united in marriage with Mana L. Peebles, who is a member of the Church. Politically Mr. H. is a Democrat.

John B. Hill, farmer, sec. 19; P. O., New Canton. The parents of our subject, Isaac W. and Tabitha Hill, were both natives of Franklin county, Va., and of Irish ancestry. John B. was born in Tennessee in 1824, received his early education in the common schools of Scott county, Ill., whither his parents had moved, and was married to his first wife, Emily A. Smithson, in 1843; she died in 1844, and the following year he was married to Millie E. Taylor, and they have 12 children, 10 of whom are living, 7 boys and 3 girls. Mr. H. came to Pike county in 1866 and engaged in farming.

L. G. Hosford, deceased, was born in the State of New York, Jan. 15, 1811, and obtained his education in the public schools of that State. His early occupation was that of carpenter and millwright. He emigrated to this county in 1842, and he has built several mills in this county; he followed mining in California 3 years, between 1850 and 1854. Dec. 19, 1844, he married Mary Smith, and of their 6 children 3 are living; one daughter is married to Andrew Cruse. Mr. H. died Nov. 18, 1874, the owner of a steam saw-mill, house and lot, and 700 acres of land; at one time during life he owned 1,200 acres. Politically he was a Democrat. Mrs. Hosford, who is a member of the Dunkard Church, is keeping a first-class boarding-house in New Canton, in company with her daughter.

George W. House, farmer, sec. 23, 5 S., 6 W.; P. O., New Canton; was born in Ohio in 1823, the son of Willard and Deborah (Emerson) House, natives of Maryland, father of German and Irish descent and mother of German and Scotch; was educated in the common schools of Ohio. In 1853 he married Frances Jane Carter, and they have had 6 children, 5 of whom are living. Mrs. House died Sept. 15, 1875. He came to Pike county in 1844, and now owns 178 acres of land. He worked by the month until he got a start. Has worked some at carpentering. Spent one year in Arkansas and Mississippi. In politics Mr. H. is a Republican.

James S. Hyde, farmer, New Canton, was born in this county in 1844, and is the son of J. F. and Eliza (Seeley) Hyde; educated in the Pittsfield high school; by occupation is a farmer; in 1878 he married Rachel Smith, and they have one child, Mary E. He owns 320 acres of land, and for the last 18 months he has kept a livery stable in New Canton. He has just bought the right for the State, to sell the patent Band-cutter, to cut bands of the sheaves of grain for threshing-machines. He is now introducing it, and it gives entire satisfaction, it being superior to the old method of cutting with knives, which was always a dangerous process. Where this cutter is used the feeder can safely reach for the bundles without having to look up every time to dodge a knife.

F. J. Jackson, farmer; P. O., New Canton; was born in Kentucky in 1815, and is the son of Vincent and Jane (Shearer) Jackson, father from Maryland and of English descent, and mother from Pennsylvania and of Irish descent. His father having died when he was but 6 years old, he was brought up by a kind stepfather, Mr. Henry Parker; his education was obtained by attending school 3 months a year in the old-fashioned log school-house. In 1839 he married Louisa Ferry, and of their 7 children 2 are living, both married and living in this county. He was brought to this county in 1825, the family settling on sec. 21, this tp. He was in the Black Hawk war under Capt. Petty. As a farmer he has been successful. He is a Republican and a granger, and has been Commissioner of Highways, Road Overseer and School Director.

Eben Jordan, farmer, sec. 27; P. O., Cincinnati; was born in Maine in 1833, and is the son of Richard and Sarah (Dotty) Jordan, natives also of Maine; was educated in the public schools of his native State. In 1848 he married Mary Wheeler, and of the 9 children born to them 8 are living, 6 boys and 2 girls. He came to Pike county in 1877, from Portland, Me. Mr. Jordan, although of a literary turn of mind, is a hard-working, energetic laborer on his farm, where he is doing well. In politics he is a Democrat.

John Judd, railroad section overseer, New Canton, was born in Germany in 1834, the son of Frank Judd; came to America in 1845 and to this county in 1851; lived at Cincinnati Landing 3 years, then came to New Canton, where in 1861 he married Jane

Saxbury, and they have had 3 children. Mrs. J. is a daughter of early pioneers of this county, her parents being the first couple married after the county-seat was moved to Pittsfield. Her mother carried the banner at the old settlers' meeting in 1879, but died the same year. Mr. Judd's early life was spent in a tobacco factory. Since 1873 he has been in the employ of the C., B. & Q. R. R. Has never had any accident happen on his part of the road. Mrs. J. is a member of the Presbyterian Church.

Charles A. Kendall, formerly school-teacher, now farmer, sec. 13; P. O., New Canton; was born in Ohio in 1833, and is the son of Richard and Ann (Brown) Kendall, natives of New Jersey; obtained his education mostly by his own exertions outside the school-room; has gone to school but 2 months since he was 10 years of age, but his scholarship entitles him to a first-grade certificate to teach; has taught school 20 years. In 1860 he married Eveline Fesler, and of their 8 children 6 are living. In 1852 he came from St. Louis, Mo., to this county, on the steamer "Golden Era," and first settled at Eldara. He owns 140 acres of land, and has been farming since 1862.

H. H. Kœller, jr., station agent, New Canton, was born in Perry this county, Feb. 10, 1855, and is the son of H. H. Kœller, sr., the patentee of "Kœller's Corn-Planter." The latter mentioned and his wife emigrated from Germany to this country in 1848, stopping at first with his brother-in-law, Mr. Thiele, at Perry. Observing the method then in vogue of planting corn with hoes, he set to work inventing a machine to do the work better; he succeeded, and commenced the manufacture of the planters at Perry on a small scale which was greatly enlarged, an extensive establishment being put up and run at Camp Point, where Mr. Kœller was general superintendent; but the company there becoming insolvent, Mr. K. went into other business at St. Louis, Mo., and Leadville, Col., which was more remunerative. Mr. Kœller, jr., spent the greater part of his boyhood with his uncle, Mr. Thiele, his mother having died when he was an infant; he afterward joined his father at Camp Point, where he received his education in the Maplewood High School, and later at the Gem City Business College, Quincy, Ill. Returning to Camp Point he entered the service of the company as traveling salesman; in 2 years he was appointed assistant secretary, which position he filled until the company became insolvent; he then entered the grain and agricultural implement trade at Carthage, Ill., in which business, however, he did not do well; he then came to New Canton and took his present place. July 15, 1877, he married Mary Ziegler, of Camp Point, and they have a son, Walter H.

Dr. John S. Lockwood was born in Kent county, Del., Jan. 10, 1840, and is the son of John and Ann (Slay) Lockwood, of English descent. Until 17 years of age the subject of this sketch spent his time on the farm, in store and at school; graduated in the scientific and classical courses at Fairfield Seminary, New

York; then visited Missouri, taught school 2 months in Adams county, Ill.; returned to New York and spent a winter studying at Schenectady; on account of declining health he abandoned the collegiate course and returned to Delaware, where he entered mercantile business, which he followed 2 years; commenced as salesman in a wholesale establishment in Philadelphia, but not liking the business he began the study of medicine with Dr. Paine, in the Eclectic Medical College in that city; traveled East and West in search of a medical college in which to complete his studies, settling on the Keokuk College; having spent nearly all his means traveling, he confined his eating to dry bread and beans during the first term of study; in the summer of 1865 he graduated with honor, but not having the means to commence practice, he went into Adams county, Ill., and worked on a farm until fall, and during the winter taught the Cliola school; then entered partnership with Dr. John Torrence at Quincy in the practice of his profession; in the fall of 1866 he came to New Canton, where he has since resided. In 1873 he went to St. Louis, New York and Philadelphia to attend medical lectures, and in the spring of 1874 graduated at the Jefferson Medical College, Philadelphia, and the Missouri Medical College at St. Louis. In December of that year he married Miss Ella, daughter of Eben Clauson, a pioneer in this section, and who has been Supervisor two terms, and has held other important town offices. The Doctor has been very successful as a physician, and moderately so financially. He owns several houses and lots in New Canton, is entirely free from debt, and has money at interest. In politics he is a Democrat, and in religion a freethinker, as almost all doctors are, but is liberal toward all sects and parties. What he has accumulated in property has all been by his own unaided exertions.

Capt. M. D. Massie, of New Canton, was born in Pittsfield, this county. Jan. 21, 1838, and is the son of John G. and Mary (Shaw) Massie, the former a native of Kentucky, the latter of New York; parents were married in Derry tp., in 1837. Mr. M.'s boyhood was passed in Pike county, Mo., and Pike county, Ill.; received a common-school education, and was engaged as clerk and book-keeper until 1862, when he enlisted as a private in the Pike county regiment, 99th Ill. Inf., and served 3 years; was promoted Captain, and also acted as Adjutant; was in all the battles of the Regiment save one. After the war he engaged in mercantile business at New Canton, dealing in a general assortment of goods, and also running a mill; has been in the business now for 15 years, with success. In 1866 he married Mary E. Morey, and they have had 3 children—all now living. In 1872 he was elected a member of the 28th General Assembly, and at the close of his term was offered a re-election, but refused on account of declining health. We give Mr. Massie's portrait in this volume.

Joseph McFarland, deceased, was born in Ireland in 1840; lived in this county about 20 years, when he died, aged 39 years and 7 months. In 1872 he married Mary Kelly, daughter of Nathan Kelly, and they had 2 daughters and 1 son. Mr. Mc. F. held responsible public positions, followed clerking awhile, and farming for a portion of his life. At the time of his death he owned $347\frac{1}{2}$ acres of land, besides property in town. He was successful in whatever he undertook. Mrs. Mc. F. resides on sec. 27; P. Q., New Canton.

William. H. Odiorne, merchant, Cincinnati, was born in Pike county, Ill., in 1845, and is the son of Eben and Ann (Wingert) Odiorne, father a native of Massachusetts and mother of Ohio; received his education at Rockport, Ill., and at Jones Commercial College at St. Louis, Mo., at which latter place he graduated in 1864. In 1876 he married Addie C. Hendricks, and their only child, Elmer, died when one year old. Mr. O. has been in mercantile business the most of his life, and been successful. He came to Cincinnati in 1876, where he is Postmaster and ticket agent, and has been School Treasurer several terms. In politics he is a Republican.

Samuel Pfrimmer, New Canton, was born in Harrison county, Ind., Jan. 16, 1837, and is the son of John George and Sarah (Friedly) Pfrimmer, father a native of Pennsylvania and of German and French descent, and mother a native of Indiana and of English descent. Has attended school but three months in his life. March 15, 1868, he married Kate Mosier, and they have had 2 sons, George, born Jan. 15, 1869, and Charles, born March 9, 1870. Mr. P. came to this county in 1844, settling on sec. 23, 5 s., 7 w., this tp. Has been a farmer most of his life, and has followed flat-boating some. He now owns 158 acres of land. He is a Democrat, and has been School Director 3 years; has had charge of the light-house one mile above the landing at Cincinnati, this tp. In 1861 he enlisted in Company I, 28th Ill. Inf., under Capt. Hurt, and was discharged in 1864; was in all the battles of the Regiment.

Alexander K. Ross, farmer, sec. 22; P. O., New Canton; was born in Pennsylvania in 1838, and is the son of John and Elizabeth (McDaniel) Ross, natives of Pennsylvania and of Scotch ancestry; obtained his education in the public schools of his native State; emigrated to this county in 1860; in 1862 he enlisted in Co. E, 78th Ill. Inf., and was discharged in July, 1865, having been in all the battles of the Regiment but one; was 3d Sergeant. In 1878 he married Malvina Brewster. He owns 100 acres o land. In politics is a Republican.

Nathaniel Shearer, farmer, sec. 10; P. O., New Canton; was born in this county Dec. 26, 1839, and is the son of Andrew and Harriet (Parker) Shearer, the former of Irish descent and born in 1800, and the latter of German descent and born in 1806; they came to this county in 1822, settling on the present homestead. Mr. S. died May 13, 1853, and Mrs S. resides with her son. Nathaniel was educated in the asylum for the deaf and dumb at Jacksonville, Ill. He is a farmer, now owning five shares in 80 acres of land, which property he has earned by his own exertions. Sept. 23, 1868, he was married at Brighton, Ill., to Miss Rebecca Berry, by whom he has had 3 children, Luther, Ellen and Eddie B. Mr. and Mrs. S. are deaf and dumb. Her father is a carpenter at Brighton, and she has one brother and two sisters who are also deaf and dumb. One sister married James W. Walker and resides in Dakota, Stephenson county, Ill., and one sister is matron of the State Asylum for the Deaf and Dumb at Jacksonville. Her brother is a tobacco dealer at Brighton.

Alonzo Shewe, New Canton, was born in Washington county, O., in 1848, and is the son of Solomon and Ellen (Willis) Shewe; his father was born in Pennsylvania and of German descent, and his mother was born in Virginia and of Irish descent; he was educated in the public schools in this county. In 1866 he married Miss E. Gillan, and they have 3 children. Mr. S. has run a threshing-machine ever since he was 19 years of age; at present he uses a steam thresher and a steam wood saw; can saw 10 to 12 cords of wood in 10 hours. He also ran the first patent band-cutter ever used in this State. In politics he is a Democrat.

S. P. Shewe, sec. 17; P. O., New Canton; was born in Ohio in 1820 and is the son of Martin and Leona (Dunbar) Shewe, the former a native of Ohio and of German descent, and the latter of Virginia; was educated in the public schools of his native State. His first marriage was to Caroline Atkinson, by whom he had 4 children, only 1 now living; his second marriage was to Sarah Baughman. Mr. Shewe came to Pike county in 1844, and has lived in the county ever since. When he first came here he had but 75 cents, but is now worth at least $2,000; has made all he owns by honest labor; politically he is a Democrat.

John W. Smith, farmer, sec. 6; P. O., Hannibal, Mo.; was born in Pennsylvania in 1844, being the son of Henry and Mary (Clair) Smith, natives of Pennsylvania and of German descent; was educated in the public schools of Adams county, Ill. In 1866 he married Hattie Breslar, and they have had 4 children. He came to Pike county in 1868, and now is on a farm of 120 acres. He is a Democrat.

J. W. Stephenson, Cincinnati, was born in Kentucky May 20, 1816, the son of James and Margaret (Clinton) Stephenson, natives of the sunny South and of Irish descent; was brought to this State by his parents in 1819; June 6, 1841, he married Mary Eliza Allen, and 6 of their 9 children are living. In 1861 Mr. S. enlisted in Co. E, 27th Ill. Inf., and was wagon master of the Regiment. Mr. S. seems to like frontier life, as he has followed close after the Indians in three States; but he is a quiet, unassuming man. In politics he is a Republican, and in religion he is a Presbyterian. His wife, who was also a Presbyterian, died March 6, 1880.

Amos Stout, farmer, sec. 7; P. O., Hannibal, Mo.; was born in Butler county, O., in 1834, and is the son of Ijel and Julia (Briant) Stout, natives of Ohio, and of German descent; received his education in the public schools of Ohio; came to Pike county in 1851; was married in 1856 to Miss Kate Hall, and they have 4 children living. Mr. Stout is a farmer, occupying 500 acres of land, and has great promise of success; he had nothing to start with. Politically he is a Republican.

Nicholas Stump, farmer; P. O., Cincinnati; was born in Ohio, in 1839, the son of George and Mary (Risher) Stump, natives of Pennsylvania and of German descent; received his education in the public schools of Iowa, principally in Independence. In 1860 he married Ann J. Smith, and they have had 4 children. In Iowa Mr. S. was in the mercantile business 3 years. He came to Pike county in 1875, since which time he has been farming and keeping the warehouse at Cincinnati Landing; has been successful in his business. Has been School Director, and politically he is a Democrat. Mr. S. is a member of the Presbyterian Church.

Isaac Tamsett, shoemaker and cutter, New Canton, was born in England in 1815, and is the son of Isaac and Elizabeth (Goodman) Tamsett; father was commander of revenue in England. The subject of this notice obtained his education in the mother land. In 1836 he married Sarah Smith, and they have had two sons, both married, one living in this county and the other in Missouri. Mr. T. came to America in 1846, landing at New Orleans, in 1849 to Pittsfield, and in 1861 to New Canton. He has traveled a great deal, and has worked at his trade in England, France, Belgium and this country, besides visiting Ireland, Wales and the West Indies; once suffered shipwreck. Mr. T. is an interesting converser, having seen a great deal of this world. Politically he is a Democrat, and his wife is a member of the Baptist Church.

George Tipler, farmer; P. O., Barry; was born in England, at Eckington, Lincolnshire; he is a son of George and Sarah Ann (Baten) Tipler; although he never attended school he can read and write, and he has a very retentive memory; in the old country he was a shepherd boy, but since he has been in this country he has followed farming, and is a horse and cattle doctor. He came to America in 1853, settling the same year at New Canton. At first he worked by the month at $18 per month, and his wife taught school. Her maiden name was Ann Bunning, and they were married in 1846, June 11. Mr. T. now owns 207 acres of good land. In religion he is a Latter-Day Saint, and in politics he votes for the best man.

Franklin Tittsworth, farmer, sec. 15; was born Jan. 12, 1826, in Tennessee; was brought to this county in the spring of 1831; went to California in 1849 and returned in 1852; June 9, 1853, he married Miss Adeline Browning. Children: Thomas, Charles, Albert, Myram, Elmer, Franklin, Frederic, and two deceased, Jessie and an infant. Mr. T. owns 480 acres of land, worth $40 per acre, and he resides two miles west of Eldara, which is his P. O. address. Politically he is a Democrat.

Bradford Uppinghouse, miller, New Canton; was born in Jackson county, Ind., in 1820, and is the son of James and Melinda (Helms) Uppinghouse, natives of Pennsylvania, father of German and mother of Scottish descent; obtained his education in the common schools of his native State. In 1847 he married Christina Clark, and their 6 children are all living. He arrived in Pike county June 8, 1865, and has been in New Canton most of the time since. Politically he is a Republican.

James Wallace, farmer, sec. 28; P. O., New Canton; was born in Ohio in 1816, and is the son of John and Catharine (Straira); father a native of Virginia and Scottish descent, mother born in Pennsylvania and of German ancestry. Nathaniel Wallace, a grandfather of James, was a Scotchman and a captain under Lord Cornwallis. James received his education in the common schools of Ohio; he married Sarah Ann Blacklidge in 1836; of their 12 children 5 are living, all married, and residing in this county. Mr. Wallace's early occupation was that of a stone-mason, but has been farming the most of his life, in which business he has well succeeded, and now owns 240 acres of land; he first settled on sec. 24 in this tp., but is now on sec. 28. He has taken 10 degrees in Masonry. Politically he is a Democrat. He has been Supervisor 9 years, Road Commissioner 6 years, School Trustee 4 years, and is now School Director. Mrs. W. is a member of the M. E. Church.

James Wheelan, blacksmith, sec. 1; P. O., New Canton; was born in Ireland in 1836, and is the son of Richard and Mary (Scully) Wheelan; came to America in 1848; received his education in the public schools of St. Louis, Mo.; came to Pike county in 1855, settling in New Canton; in 1856 he married Isabella Brown, and they had 7 children; she died in 1873; in 1877 Mr. W. married Elizabeth Brown, a cousin of his first wife. He also carries on farming, owning 160 acres of land; his house on the farm cost $2,000. He has been successful in both businesses. In politics he is a Democrat, and keeps well posted.

KINDERHOOK TOWNSHIP.

This township lies directly west of Barry and north of Pleasant Vale, and consists largely of Mississippi bottom land, which is the most fertile land in Illinois. Our description of the land as given in the sketch of Pleasant Vale township will apply as well to Kinderhook. The first settlers of this township were David Cole, Bird Brewer, Mr. Lyle, Amasa Shinn, Mr. McCraney, James Hull, Charles Smith, Charles and James Stratton, C. Devoll, Thomas Orr and others. Mr. McCraney made improvements in the center of the township on the creek which has since borne his name.

Great credit is due these pioneers for their untiring efforts in settling and improving this country. Indians were numerous here then, and the wild animals roamed at will over this then wild country. The settlers had to go to Bear creek, above Quincy, to have their milling done. There was a corn-mill run by oxen on Hadley creek two miles above Kinderhook, owned by W. M. Blair, which proved a great convenience. These early pilgrims first lived in log cabins, with stick chimneys, puncheon floors, clapboard doors fastened together by wooden pins, and with only a single four-light window. Mr. Thomas Hull first lived in a house with no window at all. The family would build a large fire and leave the door open. On one occasion the Indians came to the house of Mr. Hull, when Mrs. Hull was alone, begging for something to eat. Mrs. H., however, could not understand them and would not let them into the house. They pointed to some pumpkins, signifying their desire to have some of them. Of these she willingly gave them as many as they could carry.

Mr. Orr tells us that he has killed many a deer and wolf in his neighborhood. He saw at one time as many as seven deer in one herd. The wolves were very troublesome and would frequently run the sheep to the house during the day-time; and at night, Mr. Orr states, they had to corral the sheep at one end of the house.

In the pioneer days boys very frequently met with encounters before which the modern boy would quail. In a very early day Wm. J. Talbert, of this township, and his brother Basil were sent some distance from home on an errand. As usual, they took their dog and gun (for these were necessary companions in those days), and started on their journey through the wild country. When near the Sny, in the Mississippi valley, they encountered a huge buck, with immense antlers; and although a boy, William could not resist the temptation of bringing down such fine game. He shot him, but succeeded only in breaking one of his legs. Lest the deer should hobble off beyond reach and be lost, he immediately rushed forward and caught him by the horns. His faithful dog soon came to his assistance and laid hold of one of the deer's ears. In this way all three tussled around and around for some time, neither being able to gain much advantage. At last William took out his old knife, which had no back spring, and attempted to cut the deer's throat, using his fingers as a spring to support the blade. In this attempt, however, he failed. He then opened the little blade, plunged it into the deer and it broke off. He again returned to the use of the big blade, using his fingers for a back.spring, as before. All this time the deer kept tussling and bleeding, while the faithful dog kept tugging away at his ear. Basil stood a few rods away, calling with all his might to his brother to come away, fearful that the deer would kill him. William soon got astride the deer's shoulders and faithfully jabbed away with his old, backless knife, and, with the assistance of the dog, he finally succeeded in killing the deer. But this was not all. If they left their game there the wolves would soon devour it, and it was too heavy for them to carry ; and so the ingenuity often manifested in pioneer times, and which would have been commendable in older heads, was manifested by these young brothers in order to save the deer. They bent a sapling, upon which they hung the deer, and when straightened it lifted the deer some distance from the ground. Then William hung his vest up by it, which had the desired effect of keeping all animals from it, and notifying the hunters that it was the game of another party.

KINDERHOOK.

The town of Kinderhook was founded in 1836 by Chester Churchill and Bridge Whitten. The first settler in the town was Peter Harper. The first store was kept by Mr. Churchill. The village now contains several stores, blacksmith shops, a flour mill, and other industries. It also has a graded school and two church edifices located here. Many of the early pioneers of Kinderhook have passed away, and it is with difficulty that its earlier history is obtained. We acknowledge our indebtedness to Samuel Clark and others for valuable information received from this neighborhood.

Kinderhook Exchange Mills.—This establishment was erected in 1871 by Blain & Steers, who operated it for about four years. It then fell into the hands of Elijah McAtee and Dr. Penick. This firm sold out in 1877 to E. B. Hyde and C. C. Colvin, who operated it about two years, when they sold it to J. C. Colvin, who a few months later took Wm. Fantz as a partner. They run four sets of burrs, and do a large business. They make an excellent quality of flour, which meets with a ready sale in the New York markets.

Kinderhook Public Schools.—The high-school department of the Kinderhook schools is in an excellent running order under the management of Prof. Elkanah Sellers, who conducts the school on the latest Normal plan. The recitations of the B. class in geography are given in writing by the entire class upon the blackboard. This work is examined the following morning and criticised, the pupils generally manifesting great interest in their studies. The school building is a large two-story brick structure, and contains three rooms.

CHURCHES.

Kinderhook Baptist Church.—This society was organized Jan. 28, 1859, at the house of David Devol, by Elder N. Kinne. Mr. Kinne was chosen Chairman, and Mr. Devol Clerk, of this meeting. He was then elected permanent Clerk, and shortly afterward S. Sprague and S. B. Gaines were chosen Deacons. Rev. Wm. Cleveland was called as their first Pastor. The congregation erected a house of worship in 1864, which was dedicated in October, 1865, by Elder N. Kinne. The present membership is 200. The Church has sustained a Sunday-school ever since it was organized.

Akers M. E. Church.—This Church was organized over 40 years ago, and although we worked assiduously to obtain its history, as well as that of the other M. E. Church, we fail to receive very much satisfactory information. The present church edifice of the Akers Society, which was the second one erected, was built in 1868-9. It is constructed of brick, and cost about $5,500.

HULL'S.

This town is located on sec. 21, and at the junction of the Wabash and the Quincy, Alton & St. Louis Railroads. It was laid out in December, 1871, by David Hull, Rensellaer Sweet and William Bridge. It is situated in the midst of one of the finest agricultural districts in the county, and has promise of making a nice local town.

BIOGRAPHICAL DEPARTMENT.

In alphabetical order we speak of many of the leading citizens of Kinderhook.

James B. Allen, druggist, was born in South Carolina, March 18, 1824, and is a son of Josiah Allen, deceased. He came to Pike county in 1850, and pursued the mason's trade until 1874, when he engaged in his present business. He is engaged in general merchandising and carries a stock of $4,000, consisting of a full line of drugs, groceries, boots and shoes, queensware, and occupies a two-story brick block, which he erected in 1876 at a cost of about $4,000. Mr. Allen did the mason work on the Barry high-school building. In 1852 he married Sarah, daughter of the late Judge Alfred Grubb, of this county. Mrs. Allen was born in Kentucky, April 2, 1828. Mr. and Mrs. Allen have 5 children,—Alfred, Mary E., Edward C., Bessie and Fannie.

Alexander Anderson was born in Reading, Berks county, Pa., and is a son of Edward Anderson, deceased, who came to this county in 1845. Alex. came with his father and engaged with him in the mercantile business in Kinderhook until the death of the latter, which occurred in 1848. Mr. Anderson then engaged in farming until 1878; then formed a partnership with Frank Estergren, but in 1879 the firm dissolved, and Mr. A. went into business for himself. He now carries a general stock of hardware, furniture, etc., and also has a harness shop attached and does a good business. In 1847 he married Anice Hull, daughter of James Hull, deceased, an early pioneer of this county. Mr. and Mrs. Anderson have had 9 children, of whom 6 are living,—Elizabeth, Edward, Marks, James, Charles and Alexander.

Clement V. Aylesworth was born in New York in 1848, lived there until he was 5 years old, then moved with his parents to Pike county, Ill., and remained there until 1861; then moved to Wisconsin and remained there until 1870, then returned to this county. Jan. 26, 1871, he married Sarah Z. Dutton of this county. Their 2 children are Elbert and Myrtie; they are both members of the M. E. Church. He is engaged in butchering, also carries on the confectionery business. He owns a dwelling house and two lots in Kinderhook, and is an enterprising, industrious business man and a good citizen. In politics he is a Republican.

Susan Benson was born in Butler county, O., in 1823, and lived there until she was 15 years of age, when she moved with her parents to this county. At the age of 21 she married Macom Colman, and they had 4 children,—James Thomas, John Macom, George and Catharine. After the death of Mr. Colman Mrs. C. married Thomas Benson and they had 2 children, Lydia Margaret and Linosa Lee. Mrs. Benson is a member of the Baptist Church and politically is a Democrat. She owns 61 acres of land and follows farming.

Edmund T. Bridge was born in Augusta county, Va., Dec. 15, 1837. His father left Augusta county and moved to Lewis county in 1847, and in 1853 moved to Fayette county, Ohio, and after living there one year, moved to Hancock county, Ill., and when there enlisted in the 119th Reg. of Ill. Vol., and remained until Aug., 1865, and since then has been living in this tp. Feb. 14, 1867, he married Mary A. Sweet, and their children are 2 boys and 1 girl. Himself and wife are members of the Baptist Church. Mr. B. followed farming until 1872, and since then has been engaged in merchandising at Hull's Station, and is an enterprising business man, and in politics is a Republican. He owns 50 acres of land, three houses and three lots, and a dry-goods store.

Mrs. Mary Chase, farmer, secs. 33 and 36; was born in Pennsylvania in 1821, and lived with her parents until she was 10 years old. They moved to Ohio and remained there until 1844, then to Indiana, and lived there 2 years, then came to this county, where she was married Nov. 20, 1841, to Alonzo Chase. Their children were, Daniel, William Lanson, Samantha, Sarah Frances, Alice Melvina and Isadora. She owns 134 acres of land, and is a Democrat.

A. S. Churchill came to this county in 1833, when but 19 years of age. He traveled the entire distance from Batavia in a one-horse buggy in one month and 15 days. Arrived in this tp. the 15th of Oct., and joined his father and brother, who had preceded him. In the spring of 1834 he returned to New York and, Oct. 20, 1835, married Mary A. Hunn, daughter of Samuel Hunn, deceased. Mrs. C. is a native of Hartford, Conn., and was born March 8, 1814. They have had 7 children, 4 of whom are living,— James A., Wm. E., Hiram S. and Nancy M. They removed here in 1836, and Mr. C. kept hotel until the railroads were built. When he arrived in this tp. he had $250, a team, a wife and one child. Now he is comfortably situated and has given his children each a large farm. The first land he bought here he secured by giving a cloth coat for his claim on the land. He went to Whipple's mill for flour, a distance of 23 miles.

William E. Churchill was born May 2, 1847, in Barry tp., and is a son of the preceding; he resides on sec. 9, this tp., and is engaged in farming and stock-raising. He was married March 26, 1868, to Mary Carr, daughter of Solomon Carr, deceased, and they have 4 children,—Charles E., Ora D., Roy S. and Edward C.

Samuel Clark is a native of Harrison county, Va., and was born Sept. 23, 1826, and is a son of Rev. Samuel Clark, deceased, who removed to this county with his family in 1829. Mr. Clark was raised on a farm and educated in a common school. In 1851 he was married to Emma Shinn, daughter of Isaiah Shinn, deceased, who came to this State in 1867. Mrs. Clark was born Sept. 8, 1831, in Harrison county, Va. They have had 7 children, of whom 6 are living,—Henrietta A., Frances V., Sabra E., Minnie, Cyrus and Florence N. Mr. Clark resides on sec. 3, this tp., and is engaged in farming and stock-raising.

Alexander Clutch, farmer, sec. 33, was born in Warren county, O., in 1833, and lived there until he was 13 years of age, then moved to Pike county with his parents, who were farmers, and lived with them until he was 21 years old; he then went to Macon county and remained 2 years, following farming, then to this State, again locating in McLean county for 14 years; then returned to Pike county and married Christina Fine, who had been previously married, and had one child named Wm. Isaac. Mrs. Clutch died and Mr. C. married Mrs. Elizabeth Halstead, who had 7 children,— Henry R. and Wm. F. Wilson, Drusilla J., Edith M. and Susan Edna. Her children by her first husband were Rachel, Ellen, Lomira and Emma. By his first wife Mr. Clutch had 4 children,— Thomas Marion, Edward Francis, Anna and Clarissa. He and his wife are Baptists, and politically he is a Democrat. His farm comprises 70 acres.

John Clutch was born March 28, 1839, in Warren county, O., and is a son of David P. and Martha Clutch, deceased, who brought their family to this county in the spring of 1847, landing at Quincy on the 1st day of April. In 1852 he was married to Alvira, daughter of Sylvanus Baker, deceased, one of the pioneers of this county. Mr. and Mrs. Clutch have had 8 children, of whom 6 are living, viz: Warren, Mary E., John, Sarah, Ellen and Everett. Mr. C. engaged in farming until 1876, when he entered into the mercantile business in Kinderhook. He carries a stock of $5,000, consisting of dry-goods, hats and caps, boots and shoes, groceries, queensware, and everything usually kept in a first-class mixed store. He also deals in agricultural implements. He still owns a farm, and still gives some attention to farming.

Samuel Colgrove was born in Steuben county, N. Y., June 24, 1822, and is a son of Andrew and Elizabeth (Smith) Colgrove, of the same county. Mrs. C. died in 1871. Samuel was reared on a farm and had but limited opportunities for an education. In 1843 he came West, traveling through Iowa, Minnesota and Northern Illinois; went to Lake Superior during the silver excitement in 1845; engaged in sawing and rafting lumber to St. Louis for 4 years; traveled through Indiana, Ohio and Michigan to some extent. He returned to New York in 1849, where he remained until 1866, except what time he was in the war. Aug. 2, 1851, he married Mary P. Marlatt, and moved to Huron county, O.; in 1867 came to Adams county, Ill., and 3 years afterward he came into this county, where he resides on sec. 26, farming and raising stock. He has had 7 children, viz: Elizabeth M., Olive A., Emily L., Samuel A., Ira M., George D. and Lillie M. Mr. C. served in Co. H, 86th N. Y. Inf., and hence was in the army of the Potomac. He participated in the second battle of Bull Run; became disabled in the service, and was discharged Nov. 6, 1862.

J. C. Colvin was born in Hartford county, Conn., Oct. 19, 1823, a son of Timothy Colvin, dec.; in 1854 he came and settled in this tp.; the next year he returned to Connecticut and married Miss Ann M. Andrews, and returned to his home here. Of his 5 children Flora, Charlotte and Joseph A. are living. After farming for 9 years Mr. Colvin has followed merchandising, trading, milling, etc. He still owns a farm.

John Cook, farmer, sec. 24, owning 280 acres of land in this tp., was born in Chatham county, N. C., July 5, 1800; at the age of 7 years he came with his parents to Davidson county, Tenn., where in about 6 months his father died; his mother then moved to Robinson county until he was 17 years old, when they moved to Trigg county, Ky., and there, March 20, 1828, he married Miss Martha Kennedy; in 1830 he arrived in Pike county. His children are John K., Mary E., Clarinda Ann and Milly Jane. Mr. C. is a Democrat.

W. H. Davison was born in Wales in 1842; in 1846 the family emigrated to Pittsburg, Pa., in 1849 to Louisville, Ky., in 1851 to Naples, Ill.; he served 18 months in the 8th Reg. I. V. I., and was honorably discharged; then followed steam-boating for 6 years; and for the last 6 years he has been in Pike county conducting a hotel and restaurant. At Naples he was a farmer. May 4, 1868, he

Samuel Clark

KINDERHOOK TP.

married Miss Mary E. Smith, and they have one child, Annie E., aged 11. Mr. D. is a Baptist and his wife a Methodist. In politics Mr. D. is a Democrat. He owns 2 houses and lots at Hull's Station.

Moses Decker was born in Knox county, Ind., Dec. 16, 1806, son of Moses Decker, who was born in 1780 in Washington county, Pa., and was brought by his parents to the Northwestern Territory in 1785; he was raised in the fort at Vincennes, and when large enough to carry a gun he went into the war against the Indians; he died in 1864. Moses, jr. was raised on a farm in pioneer style; education, likewise, being in the usual old-fashioned log schoolhouse, with a greased deer-skin for a window, and a fire-place for heating the room. In 1827 he married Melinda, daughter of Tarleton Boren, dec. In 1835 they came to this county, settling on sec. 1, this tp., where he still resides, a farmer and stock-raiser. Of his 11 children these 9 are living: Hannah, Martha, Melinda, Christina, Ezra, Asher, Amry, Margaret and Emery. Mrs. D. died May 25, 1877, an honored member of society.

David Devol, farmer and stock-raiser; was born in Washington county, O., March 20, 1826, the son of Daniel Devol, dec., who was among the first born in that county. Mr. D. came to Illinois in 1854, settling in this tp., where he still resides. He has married twice, and is the father of 8 children. He is a descendant of Daniel Devol, who was one of four brothers that emigrated to America from England about 1760. Their names were Stephen, Daniel, Jonathan and Gilbert.

Frank Estergren, dealer in stoves and tin ware, was born in Sweden Nov. 4, 1844; when 20 years of age he emigrated to America; worked at common labor a few months at Fall Brook, Pa.; then was in Minnesota four years in the tin business; then followed the same business one year in Wisconsin; then at Hannibal, Mo., 3 months; then Kinderhook, where he worked as journeyman for 3 or 4 years, then commenced business for himself. In 1874 he married Amanda McPherson, and they have 2 children, Joseph Timothy and Nellie Josephine. He and wife are Baptists, and he is a staunch Democrat. Is the owner of his residence and business house and lots.

Thomas Fitzpatrick, hotel-keeper at Kinderhook, was born in 1828, in Butler Co., O.; at the age of 9 years he moved with his parents to Pike county; they were farmers; at 21 he spent 13 months in California; then returned to Pike county and married Miss Emily Woolum, of this county, and they have 6 children,— Josephine, Laura Ann, Thomas, Charlie, Bartholomew and Eugene. He has been engaged in the hotel business for 16 years, and at other times he has followed farming. He owns his hotel, three other buildings and 1¼ acres of land. He is a Democrat, and he and his wife are Methodists.

Samuel B. Gaines was born in Otsego Co., N. Y., April 19, 1821; his father, Ebenezer, was a native of Connecticut, a farmer, who

49

died in 1825, and Mrs. G. soon moved to Hartford Co., Conn., where Sam'l B. was brought up; in 1842 he moved to Ohio, where he engaged in the clock business 7 years. In 1844 he married in Huron Co., Margaret M. Twaddle; in 1847 they removed to this county, where in the following year Mrs. G. died; in 1849 Mr. G. married Mary A., daughter of Thomas Fitzpatrick, an early settler of this county, who died in 1850. Mr. and Mrs. Gaines have had 10 children, of whom 6 are living: Lorinda A., Mary E., Lydia A., Sylvester S., Edward N. and Minnie M. For the first 3 years in Illinois Mr. G. engaged in the clock business, and since that time he has followed farming and merchandising; he now carries a stock of $6,000, which consists of dry-goods, boots and shoes, groceries, notions, hats and caps, hardware, etc. He owns over 500 acres of valuable land in this county. He now (Feb.) has 270 acres of wheat sown.

A. A. Gose, farmer, sec. 14, owning 152 acres of land, was born in Kinderhook tp. June 24, 1836, the son of John Gose, deceased, an early pioneer. Oct. 25, 1863, he married Elizabeth Bailey; 4 of their 5 children are living: Ada B., Harry L., Elbert and Ella Myrtle.

Charles B. Gose was born in this tp. Sept. 4, 1837, where he has since resided; Oct. 20, 1863, he married Miss Cynthia J. Jones; their children are Ernest B., born Nov. 15, 1868, and Charles J., Dec. 16, 1871. He owns 145 acres of land and follows farming. He is Assessor of Kinderhook tp., a Democrat and a Good Templar. His wife is a " Republican."

Eliza J. Gose was born in Russell Co., Va., Dec. 4, 1815; when 19 years of age she married John Gose and moved to this tp., since which time she has remained on her farm of 300 acres. Her maiden name was Eliza J. Bickley. She has 4 children,—Abel A., Charles B., George C. and Frances. She is a Methodist.

Barna Hinds, farmer, sec. 25, was born in Brown Co., O., March 6, 1824, the son of James Hinds, of this tp.; was reared on a farm and educated in the common schools; removed with his parents to Montgomery Co., Mo., in 1843, and in the following year to this county. Dec. 31, 1849, he married Elizabeth Lomax, a daughter of Theophilus Lomax, deceased, who came to this county in 1848. Mr. and Mrs. Hinds have 3 children,—James, John and Henry. James married Amanda Gladson and resides in this tp.; John married Helen Lane and also resides in this tp. Mr. Hinds has been a farmer since he was 23 years of age; he owns 415 acres of valuable land.

Charles S. Hull, deceased, was born in this tp. Jan. 26, 1843, the son of Thos. Hull, deceased, who came to Southern Illinois in 1822, and to this county in 1829. Charles was raised on a farm and educated in the public school; June 4, 1868, he married Louisa, daughter of Nathan H. Davis, near Griggsville. Mr. Hull was a farmer and stock-raiser, and resided on the old homestead until his death, which occurred Jan. 11, 1879, a zealous Methodist. Mr.

and Mrs. Hull had 2 children, Mary A. and Sarah A. The Hull farm was one of the first farms settled and improved in this tp. Mrs. H. still resides there and carries on the farm.

David Hull, deceased; was born in Pickaway Co., O., Nov. 9, 1830, and emigrated to this State in 1836; Oct. 16, 1858, he married Sarah Sperry, daughter of John and Catharine Sperry; the former died Oct. 3, 1878, and the latter resides with her daughter at Hull's Station. Mr. and Mrs. Hull had 5 children, of whom 3 are living, Everett, Mary and Minnie. Mr. Hull was a prominent farmer and stock-raiser in the Mississippi valley, and was the founder of Hull's Station, which was named for him. He died March 16, 1875, a devoted Christian man, liberal, public-spirited, etc. Two of his brothers, James and William, died in the late war. Jan. 17, 1878, Mrs. Hull married Stephen Whitaker, a native of New York, who came to this county with Benj. Brown in 1833. Mr. Whitaker's mother died when he was but a small boy, and he was brought up by Mr. and Mrs. Brown. He resides at Hull, engaged in farming. He followed broom-making for about 20 years, with good success. We give Mr. H.'s portrait in these pages.

David D. Hull, jr., merchant, is a native of this county, born in Barry tp. Sept. 25, 1844, a son of Tate Hull. In his 18th year he shouldered a gun and fought for Uncle Sam in the late war, in Co. H, 99th Reg. I. V. I., for about two years, when his company was consolidated with Co. C. He was in the Vicksburg campaign, the battles of Champion Hills, Raymond, Fort Blakeley, Fort Spanish, Mobile and others. His two brothers, Thomas and Albert, also served in the war. In 1865 Mr. Hull married Sarah A., daughter of Granville Scott, deceased; and they have had 6 children, of whom 5 are living: Minnie A., Norton C., Everett, Wily and Hubert. As a merchant Mr. Hull carries a general line of goods.

J. N. Hull was born Jan. 9, 1836; the son of Thomas Hull, an early settler, and the first supervisor of this tp. J. N. owns 400 acres of valuable land, and has 260 acres in wheat at present. He is engaged in the grain business at Hull's Station, and has recently erected a grain elevator and agricultural warehouse, 24 by 56 feet. January, 1860, he married Miss Mary M. Sprague, daughter of Deacon Seaman Sprague, of Kinderhook tp., and they have had 6 children, of whom 3 are living: Loyal S., Jennie B., and James L.

Marietta B. Johnson was born in Berkshire county, Mass., where she resided until 34 years of age. She married George Snow in 1857, who lived but 3 years afterward; in 1870 she married Mr. L. Johnson, who lived 6 years. She is now a widow, and proprietor of a hotel at Hull's, where she has resided for 7 years. Her maiden name was Marietta B. Stuitevan.

Charles E. Jones was born in Onondaga county, N. Y., Feb. 11, 1847, and is the son of Jeremiah Jones, of that State; he came to this county in 1869, and was assistant foreman on the Hannibal division of the Wabash railroad the same year. May 25, 1872, he married Miss Almira E. Steadman, daughter of Revilo B. Steadman, of Hull's.   They have 3 children: Bertha A., Althea R. and Grace L.   Mr. Jones now resides at Hull's, and is foreman on the C. B. & Q. R. R., which position he has held for 9 years.

James P. Journey was born in Adams county, Ill., April 10, 1847, a son of Joseph W., deceased, an early settler in that county. Aug. 22, 1869, he married Nancy A. Wagy, and they reside on the old homestead, sec. 5, engaged in farming. His grandfather, Peter Journey, settled in Adams county prior to 1825; was a member of the first Board of County Commissioners of that county, and married the first couple that were married by license in that county. The license was written on brown paper, and the ceremony was solemnized July 26, 1825.   Joseph W. Journey married Caroline Young, daughter of Austin and Margaret Young, Jan. 1, 1839, and of their 10 children but 5 survive: Peter, James, Andrew, Dora S. (now Mrs. Wm. Jellison) and Mary.   The family removed to Pike county in 1853, where they resided until after his death, when in 1865 they returned to Adams county.   Peter and James now reside in this county.

Charles H. Kenady, farmer, sec. 10, was born in this tp. Dec. 10, 1846, the son of Benj. Kenady, deceased, an early settler. April 22, 1870, he married Louisa Toner, daughter of Wm. Toner, of this tp., and their children are Mary and Charlie.

Jacob Lease was born in Hampshire county, Va., April 30, 1813; was reared on a farm; came to Illinois in 1850, locating in Adams county, and in 1855 came to this county.   He is now living with his third wife, and is the father of 14 children; 12 of these are living: Mary E., Phœbe E., Joseph T., Sarah A., Susan F., Emery L., Wm. H., Oliver B., U. S. Grant, Eva D., Dora and Cyrus.   The 5 eldest are married.   Joseph married Sophronia Kennedy.

Mifflin Dallas Liggett was born Dec. 27, 1845, in this county, and was engaged in farming until 1864, when he learned the blacksmith's trade, which he is still following in Kinderhook.   In 1866 he married Miss Ellen Beard, of New York State, and their only child is George D., aged 8 years.   Politically, Mr. L. is a Democrat, and he is also an Odd Fellow.

D. Lively, farmer, sec. 6, was born in Jefferson county, Ky., May 10, 1812; was a mechanic by trade; came to Missouri in 1837, and to this county in 1856.

Harrison McKee was born in Holmes county, O., April 5, 1837, son of John McKee, deceased, who brought his family to Pike county in the autumn of 1841.   They traveled the entire distance of 800 miles and crossed but one railroad.   There were 7 children, of whom 5 are living, Charles, Lois, Nancy (now Mrs. Bedwell) Allen and Harrison.   Mrs. McKee is living on the old homestead, at the age of 66.   Harrison follows farming in the summer time and teaches school in the winter.   He has taught for 17 successive winters, a part of the time in Adams and Morgan counties, but mostly in Pike.

Samuel E. Morris was born in Ross county, O., in 1836; moved to Pike county with his parents in 1851; from 1857 to 1860 traveled to California and through the West, when he returned to Pike county to work at his trade, blacksmithing. In May, 1861, he enlisted in the 16th Ill. Inf. Vol., and served with distinction for 3 years; in 1864 he married Lucinda F. Bolin, and their children are: Zella, Minnie B., America N. and Myrtie May. Mr. M. is a Greenbacker in politics. He is an auctioneer and blacksmith, and owns considerable city property.

James T. Murray, attorney, Kinderhook, was born in this county, April 19, 1839, where he resided until 1862; followed milling 2 years in Minnesota, then the mercantile business in Quincy for a short time, and then commenced the study of law. In 1869 he removed to Lewis county, Mo., where he was admitted to practice; in 1872 he returned to this county, settling at Kinderhook, where he has since practiced his profession. Oct. 18, 1864, he married Belle Sisler, of La Grange, Mo., and the names of their children were Mary E. and Jennie K.; both of whom died in 1872. In politics Mr. M. claims to be a Socialist.

Milly Murray was born in Trigg county, Ky., in 1808; her maiden name was Milly Kennedy; she came to this county with her parents in 1830. In 1831 she married Eleazer Murray, who died in 1852, leaving 4 children: James T., Rufus M., Mary Ann and Nancy Ellen. She lives on her farm of 100 acres; is 72 years old and in good health.

Elkanah W. Sellers, school-teacher, was born in Barry tp., Sept. 27, 1857, son of David Sellers, of the same tp., who brought his family to this county in 1852. Mr. S. received a part of his education at the Christian University, Canton, Mo., and a part at Chaddock College at Quincy, and is the present principal of the Kinderhook schools.

James W. Sperry, farmer and stock-raiser, sec. 22, was born in Ross county, O., May 24, 1842, son of John Sperry, deceased. At the age of 19 he enlisted in Co. H, 73d Reg. O. V. I., and served 2 years and 3 months in the late war, being in the battles of Gettysburg, Chancellorsville, Lookout Mountain, etc. In November, 1867, he married Nancy L., daughter of Noah Corey, of Ross Co., O. Their children are: Cora, Johnnie N., Bessie and Otis O. He is now building a two-story frame house 32 by 54 feet, which will add to the beauty of the valley.

Charles C. Sprague, physician and surgeon, was born in Washington county, Ohio, Jan. 21, 1837; educated in Beverly College, Ohio, and is a graduate of Rush Medical College of Chicago; came to this county in 1860, taught a term of school in Payson, Adams Co., the following winter; at the same time studying medicine under Dr. M. M. Bane, of Quincy. He then enlisted in the war as Hospital Steward in Co. C, 50th I. V. I., serving 3 years, and was present at the battles of Fort Donelson, Shiloh, Corinth, Resaca, etc., assisting in dressing the wounds of the soldiers. He began the practice of medicine in 1865, in Kinderhook, where he still remains, with a large practice. In 1864 he married Frances E., daughter of Mrs. Eliza J. Gose, of this tp. They are Baptists, and their two living children are Laura and Justin L.

Revilo B. Steadman, farmer, sec. 21, was born in Cortland county, N. Y., Nov. 14, 1816, son of Joshua and Fatha (Beach) Steadman, Dec. 24, 1846, in Wilkesbarre, Luzerne Co., Pa., he married Maria A. Beisel, a native of that county, who was born Nov. 18, 1822. Four of their five children are living—Peter R., Almira E. (now Mrs. Charles E. Jones, of Hull), Hannah M. and Alfred B. Mr. S. came to Illinois in 1862, stopping in Barry 3 years, when he removed to Hull's. They are Baptists.

Rensellaer Sweet was born in Rensellaer county, N. Y., Feb. 22, 1827, and is a son of Ira Sweet, deceased, who brought his family to this county in 1847. Mr. Sweet was raised on a farm and received his education in the common schools of New York. After his arrival in this county, his educational advantages were very limited, the present free-school system not being in vogue then. He was married in 1848 to Rebecca Hull, daughter of the well known D. D. Hull. They have 5 children, of whom 4 are living: Mary A., Jane A., Roscoe A. and Della M. The one deceased was Eddie E. Mr. S. resides in Hull, and is engaged in general farming.

Thomas O. Talbert, farmer, sec. 10, was born at Kaskaskia, Ill., Dec. 14, 1829, son of Col. James Talbert, a pioneer of this county. April 8, 1855, he married Elizabeth C., daughter of Wm. Crump, deceased, also an early settler of this county.

William J. Talbert, farmer, sec. 36, was born in Washington county, Va., July 12, 1818, son of James Talbert, deceased, who brought his family to the American Bottom, on Kaskaskia river, in 1829, within a mile of the house of Gov. Bond. After spending one year in Missouri he came back to Illinois in 1831, and the same year removed with his family to Atlas, then the county-seat, where he kept a hotel for a year; he then removed near New Canton, where he resided until 1863, when he retired and resided in Barry until his death, which occurred in 1865. Wm. J., being a pioneer, underwent the usual privations of early times; he received his school education in an old log school-house, with slab benches, the window extending the entire length of the building, it being simply the absence of a log; the fire-place occupied nearly the entire end of the room; the back-logs were drawn in by a horse, there being a door on each side of the room near the fire-place; the floor consisted of mother earth. Nov. 24, 1844, he married Elizabeth, daughter of Lewis Hull, deceased, and they have had 9 children, of whom 6 are living: Thomas N., Martha E., Mary I., Charley L., Hattie and Ettie T. Mr. Talbert was the second tanner in Pike county, having run a tannery near New Canton for several years. He was jailor while in Atlas, and witnessed the whipping of a hog thief by Sheriff Col. Seeley.

Isaac N. Thompson, farmer, sec. 13, was born in Hampshire county, Va., Feb. 17, 1830, son of Elisha Thompson, deceased; in

1854 he removed to Missouri, where he engaged in farming and merchandising ; after 10 years he came to this county; in 1852 he married Nancy A. Sperry, in Columbus, O. They had one child, Wm. A., now dead. In 1858 Mrs. T. died, and in 1859 Mr. T. married Elizabeth Edgar. Of their 8 children 7 are living : Fannie M., John H., Louisa, Jennie, Willy M., Berzelius and Rufus. The name of the deceased was Albert L.

J. A. Walch is a native of Van Wert county, O., where he was born Aug. 19, 1846, and is a son of J. A. Walch, deceased; he came to Illinois with his mother and step-father in 1858, locating in Stark county, and to Pike in 1863. March 18, 1869, he married Charlotte Hull, and of their 4 children these 3 are living : Frank, Roy and Charley. Mr. W. owns a half interest in a steam thresher, corn-sheller and wood saw, which keeps him continually employed.

Robert D. Warinner, jeweler, was born in Casey county, Ky., Sept. 16, 1819; in 1837 his parents moved with him to Ray county, Mo.; followed farming until he was 24 years old, when he married Mary Blane, of Kentucky, and in 1847 they moved to Pike county, where he engaged in the storing and shipping business at Cincinnati Landing for 2 years; then clerked in a dry-goods store in New Canton for 2 years; then followed merchandising for himself in Newburg 3 years; then back to New Canton in the same business until 1859; then sold out and returned to Missouri, where he sold goods 2 years, when the rebellion broke out and he was robbed by guerrillas and barely escaped with his life; in 1862 he returned to Pike county and engaged in the sewing-machine business for 6 months; in 1863 went to Barry, where he remained until 1876; engaged in the jewelry business; he then came to Kinderhook, where he continues in that line of work, and owns a residence and a store. In religion he is a "Christadelphian," and in politics a Republican.

Wilson Brothers. These enterprising farmers are located on sec. 27 this tp., and are the sons of John A. Wilson, deceased, who brought his family from Kane county, Ill., to this county in 1864. Alexander D. was born Jan. 29, 1850, and William was born Oct. 3, 1854. They are bachelors and prospering in business. Their household is presided over by their sister Eliza, who was born Feb. 22, 1860, in Kane county, Ill.

LEVEE TOWNSHIP.

This township was originally a part of Kinderhook township, but in 1875 the citizens of the island petitioned the Board of Supervisors for the organization of a separate township. This was granted, and included the remainder of the territory west to the Mississippi river, reserving enough to make a regular "Congressional township." The township was named by the first Supervisor, Mr. Frank Lyon, for the levee across its western portion. This levee was constructed in 1872–4 by a company organized for the purpose, in order to prevent the overflow of the fertile valley of the Mississippi. It is 51¾ miles in length. In the year 1876 it gave way, and the valley was inundated, and a large amount of property, consisting for the most part of crops and fences, was destroyed. People removed to Hannibal, Mo., in boats. The stock was also conveyed away in boats to the Missouri side. The freshet in 1851 was the highest ever known on the Upper Mississippi that we have any record of.

In some parts of the county the impression has gone forth that Levee township is a wilderness, and that sickness prevails to a great extent. In confutation of this erroneous charge we refer to Mr. Marcus Hardy, the present Supervisor of this township. He, with a large family, has resided here for five years, and has incurred but a $5 doctor bill during this period. Some also think that the people here see some hard times financially, but be it to the credit of Levee township, that every man upon whom we called in that township subscribed for a copy of the History of the County without a murmur. Indeed, the people of Levee township are prosperous, and have the garden spot of Illinois for producing grain of all kinds.

The township contains three fine school buildings, two of which are on that portion known as "The Island," which lies between the Sny and the Mississippi river. There is a macadamized road passing through the township, owned and maintained by the Ferry Company at Hannibal.

BIOGRAPHICAL.

Marcus Hardy. This gentleman was born and raised in Missouri; came to Pike county in 1875, and now has the charge of the farm, bridge and macadamized road belonging to the Ferry Company. He was married in 1869 to Ellen Hagar, by whom he has 6 children: Susan, Virginia, Anna, Hilera, William and Ernest. His P. O. address is Hannibal.

J. B. Orr, farmer, sec. 26; was born in Harrison county, O., Sept. 26, 1833, and is a son of William Orr, of Derry tp., this county. He was brought to Pike county in 1839 by his parents; served 3 years in the late war, in Co. D, 99th Ill. Inf., and participated in the battles of Grand Gulf, Magnolia Hill (or Port Gibson), Champion Hills, Black River, siege and capture of Vicksburg, etc. He was united in marriage Aug. 31, 1854, to Lydia A. Pence, by whom he has had 5 children, namely: Mary A., Herbert S., Jerry J., deceased, Theresa B., Francis M.

Noah S. Rouse, being an old pioneer in these parts, is entitled to more than a passing notice in Pike county's history. He settled on sec. 22, on what is commonly known as "The Island," in 1847. He is a native of Madison county, Va., and was born July 16, 1819. His father, Nicholas Rouse, was also a native of Virginia and a farmer. He removed to Kentucky with his family when our subject was but 7 years old, and remained there 10 years, and then removed to Ralls county, Mo. Here in 1878 the elder Rouse died. Our subject was married in 1840 to Miss Levise Settle. The following are the names of the children: Margaret A., now Mrs. Frank Leach, William M., Robert A., Amanda E., George N. and Emma F., now Mrs. Alfred James. Mr. R. is engaged in farming and stock-raising, at which business he has been quite successful. When he crossed the river in 1847 he did not possess a cent, and was $150 in debt. He did not intend to remain here when he first came, expecting to leave as soon as he had fulfilled a contract for manufacturing some staves. He prospered, made money easy, and the longer he staid the better he liked the valley.

William Smiley was born in Ireland, April 15, 1801; in 1821 he was united in marriage with Miss Eliza Tophan, and to them were born 12 children, the following 6 of whom are living: Letitia, (now Mrs. Dennis Green), Joseph, Benjamin, Ann (now Mrs. John Pratt), David and John. Mr. Smiley brought his family to America in 1838, stopped in New York for 10 weeks, went to New Orleans, soon after came to Hannibal, Mo., and remained there for 9 years, when he removed to The Island, between the Sny and the Mississippi, where he still resides on sec. 8, engaged in farming and stock-raising. There were but 4 acres of land improved upon his place when he came. There were no churches or schools on The Island, but plenty of wild hogs, deer and other game. He has been in all the high waters since the great freshet of 1851. During these periods of inundation he would convey his family and stock to the Missouri shore.

CHAPTER XVII.

COUNTY OFFICIALS.

A list of the County Officers of Pike county, past and present, presents an array of names, most of which are or have been familiar to every resident of the county. Since its organization in 1821, Pike county has ever been represented by able, shrewd and honest officials. Many names will be noticed in the following list, under the different headings, that are familiar to the people of the entire county. Many of these men, by a life of usefulness and honor, have won warm and affectionate places in the hearts of the people of Pike county. Many names here are not familiar to the present generation, but were almost household words to the past. Many of these veterans have long since ceased life's labors and left to the remaining pioneers and to posterity, as a pleasant souvenir, a spotless reputation.

The gentlemen who at present fill the various official positions of this county, as to ability, are inferior to none who have filled their respective positions before them. They are courteous, capable and faithful as officers, honored and respected as citizens, and enterprising as business men. To some of these, especially the County and Circuit Clerks, we shall ever feel grateful for the kind and courteous manner in which they treated us all during our labors in their offices during the compilation of this work. They, as all the others, evinced an interest in the work, and were ever ready and willing to give the information and lend that aid which are so necessary in gathering and arranging a full record of the county's history.

Below we give as full and complete a list of all the officers, with the years of serving, as it was possible to obtain. In most cases the figures after the dash signify the year into which the officer served. In some instances, however, they only served to the beginning of the year denoted.

COUNTY COMMISSIONERS.

Leonard Ross.............. }		
John Shaw................. } 1821		
William Ward............. }		
David Dutton............. }		
James M. Seeley............ } 1822-3		
Ossian M. Ross............ }		
Amos Bancroft*........... 1823		
Ebenezer Smith............ }		
James Nixon............... } 1824		
William Metz.............. }		
Levi Hadley............... }		
Rufus Brown.............. } 1825		
James M. Seeley........... }		
James M. Seeley........... }		
Garrett Vandeusen......... } 1826		
Thomas Proctor........... }		
Nathaniel Hinckley........ 1827		
Joseph W. Petty .... } 1828 to		
Thomas Christian.......... } Sept.		
Ozias Hale.... .... } 1830.		
Benjamin Barney.......... } 1830 to		
Andrew Phillips........... } Sept.		
Charles Stratton........... } 1832.		

Benjamin Barney........... } 1832 to
Geo. W. Hinman........... } Sept.
Hawkins Judd............. } 1834.
Benjamin Barney........... } 1834 to
Geo. W. Hinman.......... } Sept.
Andrew Phillips .... } 1836.
James D. Morrison......... } 1836 to
Richard Wade............. } Sept.
Fisher Petty............... } 1838.
Alfred Grubb.............. }
John W. Burch............. } 1838
John Neeley............... }
Alexander Starne............1839
William Blair................1840
John Neeley.................1841
Clement Lippincott..........1842
Thomas Bates...............1842
Charles Stratton.............1843
Bonaparte Greathouse........1844
J. M. Blackerby.............1844
Wm. McCormick............1845
Joshua Woosley.............1846
Henry R. Ramsey...........1847
J. D. Philbrick..............1848

*To fill vacancy made by resignation of O. M. Ross.

COUNTY JUDGES.

Abraham Beck..............1821
Nicholas Hanson... 1821-22
William Ross..............1823
George W. Hagar....... 1825-27
Wm. Ross..................1827-34
M. E. Rattan....... 1835-37
William Watson.............1837
Daniel B. Bush.............1838
Parvin Paullin..............1839-43
J. B. Donaldson............1843-47

James Ward................1847
Wm. P. Harpole...........
Joshua Woosley,........... } 1849
   Associate Judges. }
Charles Harrington..........1853-57
Alfred Grubb...............1857-61
John W. Allen.............1861-65
R. M. Atkinson.............1865-73
Strother Grigsby.............1873

CIRCUIT CLERKS.

James W. Whitney........ ...1821-25
George W. Hight.............1825-27
William Ross........ 1827-35
James Davis.....,........1835
John J. Turnbaugh 1835-43
P. N. O. Thomson... 1843-52
James Kenney 1852-56

Wm. R. Archer...............1856-60
George W. Jones.............1860-64
J. H. Crane..................1864-68
J. J. Topliff.................1868-72
J. A. Rider 1872-76
George W. Jones..............1876

COUNTY CLERKS.

James W. Whitney...........1821
George W. Britton............1825-26
William Ross..............1826-34
James Davis................1834-36
Asa D. Cooper...............1836
James Davis................1837-38
Wm. H. Boling... 1838-43
Henry T. Mudd..............1843-47

John J. Collard.....,........1847-49
Peter V. Shankland..........1849-53
Austin Barber...............1853-57
Strother Grigsby....,........1857-61
William Steers.............1861-69
Wm. B. Grimes.............1869-73
J. L. Frye..................1873-77
E. F. Binns................1877

COUNTY TREASURERS.

Nathaniel Hinckley..........1822	Samuel L. Crane..............1850
Leonard Ross................1823	Jones Clark..................1850
Henry J. Ross.... 1824	William T. Harper..........1851–53
Nathaniel Shaw..............1825	Strother Grigsby............1853–63
John Ross....................1827–29	R. A. McClintock............1863–65
Isaac Vandeventer...........1829–30	David S. Hill......... 1865–67
John Barney................1834–37	L. J. Smitherman............1867–71
John Britton....... 1838	Thomas Gray................1871–73
Jones Clark................1839–43	D. Hollis..................1873–75
William Watson....... 1843–47	Thomas Reynolds.............1875–77
Samuel L. Crane............1847–49	R. M. Murray................1877–79
Charles Mason........ 1849	B. W. Flinn........... 1879

SHERIFFS.

Rigdon C. Fenton............1821	George T. Edwards..........1854
Leonard Ross................1822–27	Wilson S. Dennis............1856
Levi Hadley.................1827	John Houston................1858
Leonard Ross....... 1827–29	Perry H. Davis..............1862
James M. Seeley............1829–32	J. B. Landrum...............1864
Nathaniel Hinckley.........1832–34	W. G. Hubbard...............1866
James M. Seeley............1834–40	J. J. Manker................1868
Alfred Grubb................1840	Joseph McFarland..........1870
Ephraim Cannon............1842	Augustus Simpkins..........1874
D. D. Hicks................1846–50	G. W. Blades................1876
Stephen R. Gray........ 1850	Theodore Kellogg............1878
H. W. McClintock........... ...1852	

SCHOOL COMMISSIONERS.

Joseph H. Goodin........ ...1832	M. H. Abbott................1851
Lyman Scott.................1833	John D. Thomson............1853
D. B. Bush..................1841	Joseph J. Topliff.......,....1859
T. G. Trumbull.............1845	J. G. Pettingill..............1861
James F. Hyde..............1849	

COUNTY SCHOOL SUPERINTENDENTS.

J. G. Pettingill........ 1865	J. W. Johnson................1873
John N. Dewell.............1869	Wm. H. Crow................1877

SURVEYORS.

Stephen Dewey... 1821–24	James H. Ferguson..........1849
James W. Whitney...........1824	A. G. Chamberlain..........1853
Charles Pollock............1834	H. P. Buchanan.............1857
David Johnston..............1835–39	John A. Harvey.............1859
Joseph Goodin..............1839	Hiram J. Harris.............1863
David Johnston. 1841–49	Isaac A. Clare..............1875

CORONERS.

Daniel Whipple.........▲....1822	William Benn................1856
Israel N. Burt..............1832	H. St. John.................1857
Benj. E. Dunning...........1834	Lewis E. Hayden............1858
Stephen St. John........ ...1838	G. W. Mollinix.............1860
James Brown................1842	Eli Farris..................1862
C. H. Brown................1844	Sherman Brown.............1868
Cyrus B. Hull..............1846	Martin Camp 1872
Edward Connet....... 1850	Martin V. Shive.............1874
R. S. Underwood............1852	A. C. Peebles...............1876
Samuel Sitton............ ...1854	Fred Ottowa.................1879

CHAPTER XVIII.

POLITICAL.

During the first few years of the county's history party lines in politics were not drawn nor conventions held, and no organized mode of placing candidates in the field adopted. The first political meeting ever held in Pike county was at Montezuma in 1834. This meeting was conducted by Wm. Ross and Benj. Barney; the former was running for the Legislature, and the latter for County Commissioner. There were perhaps 50 voters present, besides some boys. Col. Ross made a speech, but no announcements or appointments were made for future meetings, and we presume none were ever held. Col. Barney was attacked for being a Universalist, and was told by one man that he would not vote for him on that ground.

The first political convention where nominations were made for office was held at Pittsfield in 1836, when the main issue was "Jackson" and "anti-Jackson," referring to the policy of the late President. There were five candidates in the field that year, one Democrat,—Martin Van Buren, and four Whigs—W. H. Harrison, Hugh L. White, Daniel Webster and Willie P. Mangum. After that period political conventions were regularly held by all parties, and men were brought out in that way to run for a particular office.

When Pike county was first laid off it will be remembered that it embraced the vast region lying between the Mississippi and Illinois rivers, extending east to the Indiana line, and north to the Wisconsin State line. The few settlers scattered here and there over this large territory had to travel long distances to cast their ballot. At the first election in the county only 35 votes were polled, even though it did extend over the entire northern part of the State, and out of which over 50 counties have since been made.

As before remarked party lines were scarcely recognized, yet an antagonism existed between the settlers of one section against another, and particularly against the Rosses and some of the people. The several members of this family were from New York, and full of enterprise, and desired to push the new county on to prosperity. They wielded great influence, and were almost always in some public position. Naturally, as a result, they received the censure and antagonism of many of the numerous Southern settlers.

During the earliest elections it will be noticed in the returns given below that the Whigs carried the day without difficulty. Soon, when the two great parties were more evenly represented here, the contests for political supremacy sharpened, until the old Whig party was completely dethroned, and the Democrats were for years, indeed until recently, easy victors.

In 1834 and 1836 the Democrats elected Hon. Wm. L. May to Congress, in this, then, Third District. In 1838 and 1841 the Whigs elected Hon. John T. Stewart, although Douglas received a majority of 94 in this county during the former year, and Ralston 36 over Stewart at the election of 1841. Stewart defeated Douglas in the district by only 17 votes. From that time on the Democrats were able generally by good management to carry this county in general and local elections, with majorities ranging from 12 to 2,000. Sometimes the majority was very small, and occasionally a Democratic candidate was beaten. This state of things continued for several years, the Democratic majorities gradually increasing as the feeling became more and more antagonistic among the people on the subject of slavery. In those days Illinois was always Democratic, aided very materially by Pike's votes. In 1840 the Whigs carried the county by a small majority, owing to the fact, however, that every Mormon in the county, and they were numerous, voted for Harrison.

In 1854 came the time to try men's political souls. The compromise between the two parties in Congress that year, in which it was agreed not to introduce any more discussion on the slavery question, and to ignore the subject, gave dissatisfaction to many people of both parties. Their attachment to party began to loosen, and there was uneasiness on all sides. A feeling that there was approaching a breaking of political ranks and rallying on new issues, and under new leaders, began to pervade the people of Pike county. Hon. A. Williams, Republican candidate for Congress, received a majority of 100 over Hon. W. A. Richardson, Democratic candidate, and Hon. H. K. Sutphin, Democratic candidate for State Senator, received but one more ballot in Pike county than did Hon. N. M. Knapp, Republican.

Properly speaking, we think the people of this county have never been political Abolitionists. They were never in favor of disturbing the constitutional rights of the people of the South, nor of clandestinely assisting their slaves to escape. They were opposed to the violent and premature commotion that occasionally broke out on the subject, hoping that some peaceful and legal way out of the difficulty might be found. But when the direct question of introducing slavery into the more northern and free territories, either by law, by indifference or by violence, was broached, the people of this county were sharply divided. In 1856, on the issue of allowing or preventing slavery in Nebraska, Kansas and indefinitely West, a large vote was called out, and James Buchanan received a larger majority than any candidate ever before in Pike county.

On the death of the old Whig party about this time (1856) there sprang up two parties, neither of which could really claim to possess any of the vital principles that gave power to the old party. The American party, believing the country in danger by the influx of foreigners and the alarming growth of the Roman Catholic power, emblazoned on their banners, "Americans must rule America ;" "Put none but Americans on guard." Republicans pleaded for "Equal rights to all;" "Free press and free speech." The American party made very rapid growth in many States, particularly in the South, while the Republican party secured a foothold only in the North, its principles being deemed antagonistic to some of the peculiar institutions of the South. In 1856 we find both of these parties in this county in considerable numbers, each striving for power, and both battling against a common enemy, the Democratic party. This largely accounts for the heavy majority of Buchanan, as Fremont, the Republican candidate, and Fillmore, the American candidate, each received about an equal number of votes here. An alliance, however, was formed between them for the purpose of electing local officers.

No other Republican succeeded in being elected to office in this county until Judge Grigsby appeared as a candidate. He was elected by a majority of 78. County Clerk Binns, however, who is a Democrat, was elected the same year by 666 majority. This is owing largely to the personal popularity of the two gentlemen. In 1878 Sheriff Kellogg, a Republican, was elected.

It is not in the province of this work to enter into a minute detailed history of the political workings of the different parties of this county. To unfold the secrets of the caucus, the manipulations of the party rings and cliques, and all the inside history of county politics, belongs to another work. Only those who have taken an active part in politics here are capable of performing such a task. That such a work would be interesting none will doubt.

Below are given the returns of every election ever held in Pike county, of which any records are extant.

ELECTION RETURNS.

ELECTION AUG. 4, 1828.

Congress.

Joseph Duncan, whig.......107   4
George Forquier...........103

SPECIAL ELECTION MAR. 7, 1831.

Sheriff.

James M. Seeley, whig......117   117

ELECTION AUG. 1, 1831.

Congress.

Joseph Duncan, whig.......137   22
Edward Coles, whig.........137
Sidney Breese, dem.........115

ELECTION Aug. 6, 1832.

Congress.

Joseph Duncan, whig.......327   237
Jonathan H. Pugh... 90

Senator.

Archibald Williams, whig...110
Henry J. Ross, whig........292   182

Representative.

Peter Karges, whig.........313   39
Thomas Proctor, dem.......274

County Commissioners.

George W. Hinman.........264
Benjamin Barney, whig.....356
H. Judd, whig..............249

Joseph W. Petty, dem...... 89
Joseph Jackson............. 23
Andrew McAtee............ 46

Sheriff.

Nathaniel Hinckley......... 13   13

Coroner.

Israel N. Burt.............314   314

ELECTION NOV. 9, 1832.

President.

Andrew Jackson............161   30
Henry Clay................131

ELECTION AUG. 4, 1834.

Congress.

Benjamin Mills.............300   85
Wm. L. May................215

Representatives.

Wm. Ross, whig............644
Wm. G. Flood.............. 69
James H. Ralston, dem..... 55
Thomas H. Owens..........521   ?

Governor.

Joseph Duncan............499   341
Wm. Kinney.... 158

County Commissioners.

Benjamin Barney, whig.....407
George W. Hinman.........324
John W. Burch, whig......275
Andrew Phillips, dem......280
Robert Eells...............150
Joseph H. Goodin..........181
Hawkins Judd, whig.......150
James Farrington....... ,..117
Nebuzaradan Coffey, whig.. 46

Sheriff.

James M. Seeley, whig.....545   429
Israel N. Burt.............116

Coroner.

Benjamin E. Dunniway, dem.334   119
Elisha W. Hickerson, whig..215

Location of State Capital.

Alton.....................496   430
Springfield................ 66
Jacksonville............... 22
Geographical Center........ 63
Peoria.................... 4
Vandalia.................. 2

SPECIAL ELECTION OCT. 27, 1834.

Congress.

Wm. L. May, dem..........125   11
Benj. Mills................114

ELECTION AUG. 3, 1835.

Recorder.

Jno. J. Turnbaugh, dem.....309   62
David Seeley..............247

John Lyster, dem..........172
Francis Webster........... 25
Moses Riggs.............. ... 13

Surveyor.

David Johnston, whig......281   90
Joseph H. Goodin....... ...191
Solomon Farrington.......135
Joseph W. Barney..........116
Charles Pollock...........148

ELECTION AUG. 1, 1836.

Congress.

Wm. L. May, dem.... 542   194
John T. Stewart, whig......348

Senator.

Wm. Ross, whig...........491   116
Merrill E. Rattan, whig....375

Representatives.

Alpheus Wheeler, dem......513
Parvin Paullin, dem........403
Thomas Proctor, dem......276
John W. Burch, whig......294
Daniel B. Bush, dem.......157
Charles Scott... 183

County Commissioners.

James D. Morrison, dem....486
Fisher Petty, dem..........361
Elisha McEvars...........340
Isaac Davis...............338
Charles Stratton, whig.....267
Edward B. Scholl..........139
Clement Lippincott, dem... 269
James Talbert..............110
Richard Wade, whig.......375

Sheriff.

James M. Seeley, whig......565   224
John Lyster, dem... 341

Coroner.

Benj. C. Dunniway, dem....406   136
Alfred Grubb..............270
E. W. Hickerson........... 41
Cornelius Jones.......... . 62

ELECTION NOV. 7, 1836.

President.

Martin Van Buren, dem....366   35
William H. Harrison.......331

ELECTION AUG. 6, 1838.

Congress.

Stephen A. Douglas, dem....857   94
John T. Stewart, whig........763

Governor.

Thomas Carlin, dem........865   118
Cyrus Edwards............747

State Senator.

Wm. Ross, whig...........822   93
Alpheus Wheeler, dem......729

Charles T. Brewster

PLEASANT VALE TP.

Representatives.

Richard Kerr, whig........803
Peter Karges, whig........751
Parvin Paullin, dem.......796
James H. McWilliams, dem.847

County Commissioners.

Elisha McEvers............683
Nicholas Hobbs, whig......681
John W. Burch............708
Alfred Grubb, dem........810
Charles Scott.............734
John Neeley, dem........ ..800

Sheriff.

James M. Seeley, whig......817   43
James D. Brentz...........774

Coroner.

Joseph Jackson, whig......704
Stephen St. John, dem......764   60

County Clerk.

Wm. H. Bolin, dem........486   103
Ozias M. Hatch, whig......383

ELECTION AUG. 5, 1839.

County Commissioner.

Alex. Starne...............496   3
James Walker..............493

Recorder.

John J. Turnbaugh, dem....1132   928
Wm. Porter............... 204
Henry Taylor, dem......... 82

County Clerk.

Wm. H. Bolin, dem........1179   985
James Daigh, whig 194

Probate Justice.

Parvin Paullin, dem........ 741   155
Daniel B. Bush, dem....... 586

Treasurer.

James Clark, dem.......... 713   162
Robert R. Greene.......... 551

SPECIAL ELECTION NOV. 25, 1839.

Representatives.

Oscar Love, dem........... 206
R. Hatch.................. 9
R. A. Read................ 6
eter Karges.... 5

ELECTION AUG. 3, 1840.

Representatives.

Solomon Parsons, dem.....1103
Alpheus Wheeler, dem.....1092
Wm. A. Grimshaw, whig...1016
Peter Karges, whig.......1001

County Commissioner.

Wm. Blair, dem...........1118   130
Samuel H. Nesmith, whig.. 988

50

Sheriff.

Alfred Grubb, dem........1108   114
Isaac W. Evans, whig...... 994

Coroner.

Stephen St. John, dem......1100   131
Joseph Jackson........... 969

ELECTION NOV. 2, 1840.

President.

W. H. Harrison...........1149   112
Martin VanBuren.........1037

ELECTION AUG. 2, 1841.

Congress.

James H. Ralston, dem..... 791   36
John T. Stuart, whig. 755

County Commissioners.

John Neeley, dem......... 714   409
James D. Brentz, dem...... 305
Robert Davis, whig........ 327

School Commissioner.

Daniel B. Bush, dem....... 813   552
Z. N. Garbutt, whig........ 261

ELECTION AUG. 1, 1842.

Governor.

Thomas Ford, dem........1085   12
Joseph Duncan, whig.,....1073

State Senator.

Thomas Worthington, whig.1065   53
Wm. R. Archer, dem......1012

Representatives.

Wm. Blair, dem...........1187
Alex. Starne, dem..........1085
Felix A. Collard, dem...... 855
Benjamin D. Brown, whig..1148
Benj. B. Metz, whig.......1056
John Troutner............ 835

County Commissioners.

C. Lippincott, dem..... ...1038
Thomas Bates, whig........1001
Charles Stratton, whig..... 998
James Shinn, dem......... 723
John Shinn, dem......... 192

Sheriff.

Ephraim Cannon, dem.....1179   445
George T. Edwards, whig... 734

Coroner.

E. W. Hickerson, whig..... 910
James Brown, dem........1058   148

Surveyor.

David Johnston, whig......1266   596
James B. Johnson.......... 670

Convention to Amend Constitution.

For.................... 1205   708
Against 497

ELECTION AUG. 7, 1843.

Congress.

O. H. Browning, whig......1391   162
Stephen A. Douglas, dem...1229

County Commissioners.

Charles Stratton, whig.....1181
Thomas Bates, whig......1280   }-
Wm. Morrison, dem.......1115
C. Lippincott, dem.......1139

County Clerk.

Henry T. Mudd, whig......1308   177
Wm. H. Bolin, dem.......1131

Recorder.

P. N. O. Thompson, dem ...1219   77
Charles A. Marsh, whig....1142

Probate Judge.

J. B. Donaldson...........1414   437
Alfred Gordon, whig...... 977

Treasurer and Assessor.

Wm. Watson, whig........1267   280
Edward Kean, dem........ 987

Surveyor.

David Johnston, whig......1387   357
James H. Ferguson, dem...1030

School Commissioner.

Aaron W. Bemiss, dem.....1201   164
Z. N. Garbutt, whig........1037

SPECIAL ELECTION FEB. 19, 1844.

County Commissioners.

N. B. Greathouse, whig..... 477
C. C. Beaven, whig........ 174
John Lyster, dem.......... 59
James Brentz, dem........ 206

ELECTION AUG. 5, 1844.

Congress.

D. M. Woodson, whig......1322
S. A. Douglas, dem........1396   74
R. Eells, free soiler........ 5

Representatives.

B. B. Metz, whig..........1328
D. H. Gilmer...............1266
A. C. Baker, whig.........1285
Alex. Starne, whig.........1341
W. Blair, dem.............1340
D. Wheelock..............1225
J. Berdan 50

County Commissioner.

N. B. Greathouse, whig.....1273
J. N. Blackerby, dem 1335   62

Sheriff.

Ephraim Cannon, dem.....1416   190
B. D. Brown, whig........1226

Coroner.

C. H. Brown..............1277
J. Brown.................1330   53

ELECTION NOV. 4, 1844.

President.

James K. Polk, dem.......1456   45
Henry Clay, whig.........1411
James G. Birney, free soiler. 11

ELECTION AUG. 4, 1845.

County Commissioner.

Wm. McCormick, dem..... 930   325
James McWilliams, whig.. 605

School Commissioner.

T. G. Trumbull, dem....... 841   234
James F. Hyde, whig. ... 607

ELECTION AUG. 3, 1846.

Congress.

S. A. Douglas, dem........1639   236
Isaac Vandeventer, whig...1403

Governor.

Augustus C. French, dem..1636   229
Thomas L. Kilpatrick......1407

State Senator.

Hugh L. Sutphin, dem.... 1601   203
Thos. Worthington, whig.. 1398

Representatives.

Thomas Hull, whig....... 1358
Jon. Frye, whig... 1374
B. B. Metz, whig......... 1416
Alfred Grubb, dem........ 1563
James M. Higgins, dem.... 1567
Wm. P. Harpole, dem..... 1559

County Commissioner.

Joshua Woosley, dem..... 1539   142
Wm. Dustin, whig........ 1397

Sheriff.

D. D. Hicks, dem......... 1540   164
Robert F. Naylor, whig... 1376

Coroner.

Cyrus B. Hull, dem....... 1564   189
Hazen Pressy, whig....... 1375

ELECTION APRIL 19, 1847.

Constitutional Convention.

Montgomery Blair, dem... 999
Wm. R. Archer, dem...... 958
Harvey Dunn, dem........ 924
Wm. A. Grimshaw, whig.. 887
H. N. V. Holmes, dem.... 812
John Barney, whig........ 786
Charles Harrington, whig. 741
Parvin Paullin, dem...... 680
N. E. Quinby, dem....... 208
D. B. Bush, dem.......... 243
The first four were elected.

ELECTION AUG. 2, 1847.

Congress.

Wm. A. Richardson, dem. 1582   1348
N. G. Wilcox, whig.. 234

Probate Judge.

James Ward, dem 1317   94
D. H. Gilmer, whig....... 1223

County Commissioner.

Henry R. Ramsey, dem... 2520

County Clerk.

John J. Collard, dem...... 1332   37
O. M. Hatch, whig........ 1295

Recorder.

P. N. O. Thomson, dem... 1379   161
Marshall W. Barney, whig. 1218

Treasurer and Assessor.

Samuel L. Crane, dem.... 1649   768
James F. Hyde, whig..... 881

Surveyor.

David Johnston, whig..... 1414   1329
Philip Stoner, dem........ 85

School Commissioner.

T. G. Trumbull, dem...... 1295   77
Michael J. Noyes, whig... 1218

ELECTION NOV. 7, 1848.

President.

Zachary Taylor, whig..... 1401
Lewis Cass, dem.......... 1633   232
Martin Van Buren, free-soil 186

ELECTION NOV. 6, 1849.

County Judge.

James Ward, dem........ 1392   68
Richard Kerr, whig....... 1324

Associate Justices.

Joshua Woosley, dem..... 1380
Wm. P. Harpole, dem..... 1370
B. B. Metz, whig......... 1327
John Barney, whig....... 1354

Treasurer and Assessor.

Charles Mason, dem....... 1439   184
Wm. Kinman, whig....... 1255

County Clerk.

Peter V. Shankland, dem.. 1407   69
Austin Barber, whig...... 1338

Surveyor.

James H. Ferguson, dem.. 1383   47
David Johnston, whig..... 1336

School Commissioner.

James F. Hyde, whig..... 1430   176
John L. Ball, dem........ 1254

Township Organization.

For...................... 1563   1246
Against.................. 317

ELECTION NOV. 5, 1850.

Congress.

O. H. Browning, whig.... 1064
Wm. A. Richardson, dem.. 1131   67

State Senator.

John Wood, whig......... 1029
Calvin Warren, dem....... 1126   97

Representatives.

Ozias M. Hatch, whig..... 1109
Wm. D. Hamilton, whig... 1086
James Shinn, dem........ 983
Daniel B. Bush, dem...... 866

Sheriff.

Stephen R. Gray, ind. dem. 1237   383
Cyrus B. Hull, dem....... 854

Coroner.

Edward Connet, ind. dem.. 1298   500
Samuel L. Crane, dem..... 798

ELECTION NOV. 4, 1851.

Treasurer.

Wm. F. Hooper, dem...... 827   153
James F. Hyde, whig..... 674
Jones Clark, dem......... 234

Surveyor.

James H. Ferguson, dem.. 836   33
David Johnston, whig.... 803
A. G. Chamberlain, whig.. 121

School Commissioner.

Milton H. Abbott, dem.... 875   10
Reuben H. Scanland, whig 865

ELECTION NOV. 2, 1852.

President.

Franklin Pierce, dem..... 1676   101
Winfield Scott, whig...... 1575

Congress.

O. H. Browning, whig.... 1680   75
Wm. A. Richardson, dem.. 1605

Governor.

Edwin B. Webb, whig..... 1690   4
Joel A. Matteson, dem..... 1686

Representatives.

O. M. Hatch, whig........ 1606
Wm. B. Hamilton, whig... 1585
H. L. Sutphin, dem........ 1601
H. P. Buchanan 1588

State's Attorney.

Daniel H. Gilmer. whig... 2421   948
John S. Bailey, dem...... 1473

Circuit Clerk.

James A. Kenney, whig.... 1627   59
Joseph M. Bush, dem...... 1568

County Clerk.

John J. Collard, dem...... 1622   61
Austin Barber, whig...... 1561

Coroner.

Samuel G. Sitton, whig.... 1611
R. S. Underwood, dem..... 1675   64

Sheriff.

Elisha Hurt, whig....... .496
Harvy W. McClintock, dem 1583   87

ELECTION NOV. 8, 1853.
County Judge.

Charles Harrington, whig. 1222   41
Richard M. Atkinson, dem 1181

County Clerk.

Austin Barber, whig..... 1317   31
John J. Collard, dem...... 1286

County Treasurer.

Strother Grigsby, whig.... 1289   7
Wm. F. Hooper, dem...... 1282

School Commissioner.

Milton H. Abbott, dem.... 1237
John D. Thomson, whig... 1295   58

Surveyor.

James H. Ferguson, dem.. 1151
A. G. Chamberlain, whig.. 1369   218

ELECTION NOV. 7, 1854.
Congress.

A. Williams, rep.......... 1714   100
W. A. Richardson, dem... 1614

Senator.

N. M. Knapp, rep......... 1724
H. L. Sutphin, dem....... 1725   1

Representatives.

B. L. Matthews, rep....... 1708
D. H. Gilmer, rep........ 1739
C. L. Higbee, dem........ 1677
Jonathan Dearborn, dem.. 1692

Sheriff.

George T. Edwards, rep.. 1779   110
Wm. Hooper, dem........ 1669

Coroner.

Samuel Sitton, rep........ 1664   1664

ELECTION NOV. 6, 1855.
Treasurer.

S. Grigsby, rep........... 1065   432
Tyre Jennings, dem...... 633

School Commissioner.

J. D. Thomson........... 832   209
James F. Hyde........... 623

Surveyor.

A. G. Chamberlain........ 1098   1098

ELECTION NOV. 4, 1856.
President.

James Buchanan, dem.. 2163   1110
John C. Fremont, rep...... 1053
Millard Filmore, Amer.... 1010

Congress.

Isaac N. Morris, dem...... 2233   296
Jackson Grimshaw, rep... 1937

Governor.

W. A. Richardson, dem... 2221   283
Wm. H. Bissell, rep....... 1938

State Senator.

Jacob C. Davis........... 2200   236
Thomas C. Sharp......... 1964

Representatives.

John L. Grimes, dem...... 2194
King Kerley, dem......... 2210
B. F. Westlake, rep....... 1993
Benj. H. Irwin, rep....... 1974

State's Attorney.

John S. Bailey, dem....... 2191   223
Charles C. Warren, rep.... 1968

Sheriff.

Wilson S. Dennis, dem.... 2190   187
John S. Brewer, rep....... 2003

Circuit Clerk.

Wm. R. Archer, dem...... 2204   199
James A. Kenney, rep..... 2005

Coroner.

Wm. Benn, dem.......... 2214   233
E. W. Hickerson, rep...... 1981

ELECTION NOV. 3, 1857.
County Judge.

Alfred Grubb, dem........ 1785   169
C. Harrington, rep........ 1616

County Clerk.

J. S. Roberts, dem........ 1711
S. Grigsby, rep........... 1717   6

Treasurer.

D. D. Hicks, dem......... 1884   358
E. Wooley, rep........... 1526

Surveyor.

H. P. Buchanan, dem..... 1816   218
A. G. Chamberlain, rep.... 1598   .

School Commissioner.

Joseph J. Topliff, dem..... 1811   207
John D. Thomson, rep.... 1604

Coroner.

J. N. Griffin, rep.......... 1613
H. St. John, dem.......... 1756   143

ELECTION NOV. 2, 1858.
Congress.

Isaac N. Morris, dem...... 2471   480
Jackson Grimshaw, rep... 1991

State Senator.

C. L. Higbee, dem........ 1000   347
John Moses, rep.......... 653

Representatives.

Gilbert J. Shaw........... 2478
King Kerley.............. 2472
Benj. D. Brown........... 1995
James S. Irwin........... 1993

Sheriff.

John Houston............ 2387   289
George T. Edwards........ 2098

Coroner.

Lewis E. Hayden, rep..... 1963   1963

ELECTION NOV. 8, 1859.

Treasurer.

D. D. Hicks, dem... 2225   752
George T. Edwards, rep.. 1473

School Commissioner.

J. J. Topliff, dem......... 2592   1466
F. A. Benton............. 1126

Surveyor.

John A. Harvey.......... 3664   3664

ELECTION NOV. 8, 1860.

President.

Abraham Lincoln, rep..... 2553
S. A. Douglas, dem....... 3016   463

Congress.

W. A. Richardson, dem.... 3021   426
B. M. Prentiss, rep........ 2595

Governor.

Richard Yates, rep........ 2576
James C. Allen, dem... .. 3021   445

Representatives.

B. B. Metz, rep........... 2629
—— Vandeventer, rep..... 2583
Wm. R. Archer, dem...... 2947
Benj. F. DeWitt, dem..... 3007

Circuit Clerk.

—— Mace, rep............ 2621
George W. Jones, dem..... 2991   370

Sheriff.

—— Bonnell, rep......... 2635
Joshua Woosley, dem..... 2945   310

State's Attorney.

Thomas E. Morgan, dem.. 2959   2959

Coroner.

—— York, rep........... 2582
G. W. Mollinix, dem...... 2890   308

ELECTION NOV. 7, 1861.

County Judge.

John W. Allen, dem....... 2300   427
Wm. E. Smith, rep........ 1873

County Clerk.

Wm. Steers, dem.......... 2320   451
Harvey Dunn, rep........ 1869

County Treasurer.

M. H. Abbott, dem........ 2281   402
James L. Adams, rep..... 1879

School Commissioner.

J. G. Pettingill, dem...... 2829   974
D. L. Freeman, rep........ 1855

County Surveyor.

James H. Ferguson, dém.. 2318   655
George E. Harvey, rep..... 1363

Against the Bank........ 4129   4129

Constitutional Convention.

Alex. Starne, dem........ 2332
Archibald A. Glenn, dem.. 2350
Wm. Turnbull, rep........ 1839
David K. Watson, rep..... 1655

ELECTION NOV. 4, 1862.

Congress.

State at Large:

James C. Allen, dem...... 2600   1105
E. C. Ingersoll, rep....... 1495

Ninth District:

Lewis W. Ross........... 2597   2521
Wm. Ross.............. .. 76

State Senator.

L. E. Worcester.......... 2597   1095
N. M. Knapp............. 1502

Representatives.

Scott Wike, dem.......... 2614
A. G. Burr, dem..... 2599
B. F. Westlake, rep 1464
R. E. Haggard, rep....... 1500

Sheriff.

Perry H. Davis, dem...... 2654   1413
W. H. Johnston.......... 1241
G. W. Mullinix........... 253

Coroner.

Eli Farris 2574   1085
J. B. Johnston......... ... 1489

ELECTION NOV. 3, 1863.

Treasurer.

R. A. McClintock, rep.... 1992   47
R. F. Frazier, dem........ 1945

School Commissioner.

J. G. Pettingill, dem....... 2035   79
John K. Bashforth........ 1956

Surveyor.

Hiram Harris, dem....... 2024   58
Nathan Kifler........... 1966

ELECTION NOV. 8, 1864.

President.

George B. McClellan, dem. 2857   522
Abraham Lincoln, rep.... 2335

Congress.

At large:

J. C. Allen, dem...........2859   503
L. W. Moulton.............2356

Ninth District:

L. W. Ross, dem...........2857   501
H. Fullerton, rep... 2356

Governor.

James C. Robinson, dem...2864   517
Richard J. Oglesby, rep....2347

Representatives.

S. Wike, dem..............2854
J. F. Curtis, dem..........2858
A. E. Neall, rep...........2353
S. R. Powell, rep..........2354

Circuit Clerk.

J. H. Crane, dem..........2833   470
L. F. Williams, rep.. 2363

Sheriff.

J. B. Landrum, dem........2859   514
W. W. Burchard, rep......2345

State's Attorney.

T. E. Morgan, dem........2859   505
P. C. Stearnes, rep........2354

Coroner.

Eli Farris, dem............2854   498
L. E. Hayden, rep..........2356

ELECTION NOV. 7, 1865.

County Judge.

R. M. Atkinson, dem.......2227   142
—. —. Sever, rep.........2085

County Clerk.

Wm. Steers, dem..........2210   94
—. —. Clark, rep..........2116

Treasurer.

David S. Hill, dem........2222   127
Erastus Foreman, rep......2095

Superintendent of Schools.

J. G. Pettingill, dem........2232   136
—. —. Goodrich, rep......2096

Surveyor.

Hiram J. Harris, dem......2227   172
A. G. Chamberlain, rep.....2055

ELECTION NOV. 6, 1866.

Congress.

At Large:
T. Lyle Dickey, dem.......2963   250
John A. Logan, rep........2713
Ninth District:
Lewis W. Ross, dem......3971   1260
C. Lippincott, rep.........2711

State Senator.

Wm. Shepard, dem........2973   262
—. —. Miner, rep..........2711

Representatives.

James H. Dennis, dem.....2973
Thomas Hollowbush, dem..2972
—. —. Dunn, rep..........2695
—. —. Sears, rep..........2715

Sheriff

W. G. Hubbard, dem...... 2955   248
—. —. Jones, rep..... 2707

Coroner.

G. W. Mullinix, dem......2954   245
—. —. Chapman, rep......2709

ELECTION NOV. 5, 1867.

Treasurer.

L. J. Smitherman, dem.....2181   853
R. L. Underwood, rep......1328

Surveyor.

Hiram J. Harris, dem......2191   2029
A. G. Chamberlain, rep..... 162

ELECTION NOV. 3, 1868.

President.

H. Seymour, dem.........3319   544
U. S. Grant, rep...........2775

Governor.

John M. Palmer, rep.......2778
John R. Eden, dem........3331   553

Congress.

At large :
W. W. O'Brien, dem.....3330   553
John A. Logan, rep.........2777
Ninth District:
T. W. McNeeley, dem......3334   559
Lewis W. Ross, dem.......2775

State's Attorney.

L. W. James, dem..........3336   561
—. —. Sweeney............2775

Representative.

A. Mittower, dem..........3324   532
S. Grigsby, rep............2792

Circuit Clerk.

J. J. Topliff, dem...........3395   1586
—. —. Lawton, rep........2809

Sheriff.

J. J. Manker, dem......... 3335   572
R. A. McClintock, rep......2763

Coroner.

Sherman Brown, dem......3328   560
—. —. Sanderson, rep......2768

Constitution.

For 820
Against 2524   1704

ELECTION NOV. 2, 1869.

County Judge.

R. M. Atkinson, dem......2081   545
R. H. Griffin, rep...........1536

County Clerk.

Wm. B. Grimes, dem.......2098   549
—. —. Gray, rep...........1549

Treasurer.

L. J. Smitherman, dem.....2089   553
Chas. Philbrick, rep........1536

School Superintendent.

John M. Dewell, dem......2145   649
Jon Shastid, rep..........1496

Surveyor.

Hiram J. Harris..........2094   2094

ELECTION NOV. 8, 1870.

Ninth District:

Congress.

T. W. McNeeley, dem......2181   542
B. F. Westlake, rep........1639

State Senators.

Joseph M. Bush, dem......2151
Wm. Shepard, dem........2223
George E. Warren, rep.....1625
Thomas E. Flinn, rep... ..1626

Representatives.

Albert Landrum, dem......2081
Charles Kenney, rep......2175
John A. Thomas, dem......1718
Thomas H. Dimmitt, rep...1658

Sheriff.

Joseph McFarland, dem....2056   283
Aaron F.Hemphill, ind. dem.1773

Treasurer.

Sherman Brown, dem......2230   605
E. W. Hickerson, rep......1625

ELECTION NOV. 7, 1871.

Congress.

At large:

S. S. Hayes, dem..........1872   275
John L. Beveridge, rep.....1597

State Senator.

Wm. H. Allen, dem........1847   227
Wm. A. Grimshaw, rep.....1620

Treasurer.

Thomas Gray, dem........1914   312
Hamilton Wills, rep........1602

Surveyor.

Hiram J. Harris, dem......1927   1859
A. G. Chamberlain, rep.....68

ELECTION NOV. 5, 1872.

President.

Horace Greeley, lib. rep....2827   193
U. S. Grant, rep...........2634
Charles O'Conor, ind. dem..116

Congress.

Eleventh District:

Robert M. Knapp, dem.....2849   120
A. C. Matthews, rep........2729
—— Darrah........... ...105

State Senator.

Wm. R. Archer, dem......2941   288
—— Frost, rep..........2653

Governor.

G. A. Koerner, dem........2929   291
R. J. Oglesby, rep.........2638

Representatives.

Henry Dresser, dem........4319
S. G. Lewis, dem..........4386½
M. D. Massie, rep... 7963

Circuit Clerk.

George W. Jones, dem......3005   455
P. M. Parker, rep..........2550
John C. Hesley, ind. dem...160

Sheriff.

Joseph McFarland, dem....2919   261
J. A. Brown, rep...........2658
J. A. Melton, ind. dem......110

State's Attorney.

Jefferson Orr, dem........2891   178
James S. Irwin, rep........2713

Coroner.

Martin Camp, dem........2949   319
—— Jean, rep... 2630
—— Williams...........111

Animals at Large.

For.................. ...3775   1309
Against................1466

ELECTION NOV. 4, 1873.

County Judge.

J. G. Pettingill, dem 1676
S. Grigsby, rep...........1890   214

County Clerk.

J. L. Frye, dem....... 1936   291
J. H. Allen, rep...........1645

Treasurer.

D. Hollis, dem...........2074   557
Wm. Grammer, rep.......1517

School Superintendent.

J. W. Johnson, dem........1822   140
J. Pike, rep... ......·...1682

In this election the townships of
Derry and Barry were thrown out.

ELECTION NOV. 3, 1874.

Congress.

Scott Wike, dem..........2089   669
David E. Beatty, rep......1420

Representatives.

Joseph T. Harvey, dem....3054½
James Collans, dem.......3235
John Moses, rep..........3951
Thomas H. Dimmitt, rep...786½

Sheriff.

Augustus Simpkins, dem...2035   547
Theodore Kellogg, rep.....1488
Thomas H. Wheeling, ind..93

Coroner.

Martin V. Shive, dem......2112   584
B. H. Rowand, rep.........1528

ELECTION NOV. 2, 1875.

Treasurer.

Thomas Reynolds, dem.....1469   130
Henry Hall, rep...........1339

Surveyor.

Isaac A. Clare, dem........1525   266
R. H. Griffin, rep.........1259

ELECTION NOV. 7, 1876.

President.

R. B. Hayes, rep...........3055
S. J. Tilden, dem..........4040   985
Peter Cooper, greenback.... 35

Governor.

S. M. Cullom, rep.........3065
Lewis Steward, dem.......4074   1009

State Senator.

John Moses, rep...........3055
Wm. R. Archer, dem.......4052   997

Representatives.

A. C. Matthews, rep.......8956½
S. R. Powell, dem.........6018
B. J. Hall, dem...........6022½

State's Attorney.

Joseph Dobbin, rep.......3038
Jeff. Orr, dem...........4088   1050

Circuit Clerk.

Philip Donahoe, rep......3338
J. A. Rider, dem.........3766   428

Sheriff.

O. S. Campbell, rep.......3197
E. W. Blades, dem........3903   706

Coroner.

George Barker, rep........3075
A. C. Peebles, dem........4050   975

ELECTION NOV. 6, 1877.

County Judge.

R. M. Atkinson, dem......2441
S. Grigsby, rep..........2519   78

County Clerk.

E. F. Binns, dem..........2815   666
Wm. H. Raftery, gr. & rep..2149

Treasurer.

R. M. Murray, dem........2623   234
O. H. Barney, gr..........2389

School Superintendent.

Wm. H. Crow, dem........2534   141
Belle Moore, rep..........2393

ELECTION NOV. 5, 1878.

Congress.

James P. Dimmitt, rep.....1972
James W. Singleton, dem..2685   713
Wm. H. Pogue, gr......... 886

Representatives.

A. C. Matthews, rep.......5563½
S. R. Powell, dem.........4115½
James H. Pleasants, dem...4258½
John Kelley, gr..........3052½

Clerk of Appellate Court.

George W. Jones, dem.....3051   1222
M. M. Duncan, rep........1829
Charles E. Schoff, gr.......761

Sheriff.

Theodore Kellogg, rep. & gr.2940   227
John Colyer, dem.........2713

Coroner.

Allen C. Peebles, dem......2885   1804
Lewis Farrington, gr......1081

ELECTION NOV. 4, 1879.

Treasurer.

B. W. Flinn, dem..........2423   323
Henry Hall, rep...........2100
Lewis Farrington, gr...... 600

Surveyor.

Isaac A. Clare, dem........2836   2009
Nathan Kibler, greenback. 827

Coroner.

Frederick Ottowa, dem....2445   575
John C. Burger, rep.......1870
B. F. Jones, greenback.... 690

A. F. Wills

PITTSFIELD TP.

CHAPTER XIX.

THE PRESS.

In this chapter we give brief historical sketches of the various newspaper enterprises of Pike county.

THE OLD FLAG.

In 1842 Mr. Michael J. Noyes started in Pittsfield *The Sucker and Farmer's Record*, the first paper in the county. It was a weekly, and was edited by a very able man. In 1846 it was succeeded by *The Free Press*, which was established by Z. N. Garbutt, who had, most of the time as partner, Mr. M. H. Abbott. This was a good paper, having had at its head as much talent probably as any paper in this county has ever had. It was a Whig paper, with strong anti-slavery and temperance inclinations. Mr. Garbutt retired from it in 1849 and went into other business. A sketch of his life will be found on pages 397–8 of this volume. Some time afterward John G. Nicolay and Mr. Parks had the paper for a time, and then Nicolay alone.

The successor of *The Free Press* was *The Pike County Journal*, established by Daniel B. Bush, jr. (the second), and edited by him until a short time after the war broke out, when it was sold to Robert McKee, a cousin of the eminent Wm. McKee, of the St. Louis *Globe-Democrat*, who recently died. In 1868 Messrs. McKee and Wm. A. Grimshaw gave the paper its present name, *The Old Flag*, which is indeed a very appropriate one for an organ which so boldly stands up for the flag of our country. The material of the office was subsequently owned for a time by the County Republican Central Committee, and in turn was run by Wm. H. Patterson and Mr. Hatch, by Patterson alone, by Bailey & Reynolds, by Reynolds alone, by Maj. T. W. Jones, and finally it was purchased by James Criswell in 1868, since which time its circulation has been wonderfully increased, and the paper made a grand success. He changed it from a seven to an eight-column paper. It was edited for a time by Robert Criswell, a spicy writer, who is now in the West; since 1874 the gentlemanly Mr. Gallaher has led in the editorial columns. *The Old Flag* is a home paper, none of it being printed abroad. He has brought to bear a high order of journalism and the wisdom of long experience as a journalist, and as a natural consequence, has made of *The Old Flag* one of the leading Republican papers in Central Illinois. The influence for Republican doctrine and principles of this paper has been felt in this county. The party has been rallied and is gaining over its common enemy, the Democratic party, new victories here. Mr. Gallaher's locals are crisp and fresh, and in these columns may be found all the happenings of not only Pittsfield and immediate vicinity, but in all parts of the country. A good job office is run in connection with the establishment.

Michael J. Noyes, founder of *The Sucker*, was born at Landaff, Grafton county, N. H., March 30, 1791; graduated at college; read law for some time; removed to St. Charles county, Mo.; then to Pike county, in that State, where he held several responsible positions as County and Circuit Clerks, etc. He was a remarkable man, of frank manners, industrious, honest, shrewd, of fair education, and had an extraordinary memory of names and faces of persons. As a land surveyor, in early life he laid off land for the United States Government under contract when large surveys were made. After quitting the paper he retired to a nice large farm, near Pittsfield. He died in May, 1868, a leading officer in the Masonic fraternity, leaving a widow and several children. Those of the latter now living are: Henry J., in the insurance business in Pittsfield; John, at Grimshaw's drug store, in the same place; Mrs. Emeline Mills, also in Pittsfield; W. H. D., at Carthage; Mrs. Harriet Talcott, Olympia, W. T.; and Mrs. Annie T. Hodgen, Roodhouse, Ill. Ten have died.

James Gallaher, the present editor of *The Old Flag*, was born in Castlebar, County Mayo, Ireland, July 23, 1835; came to the United States in 1851, landing at New York city, where, Aug. 1, 1856, he married Miss Lizzie McHugh, daughter of Capt. M. A. T. McHugh, of the 60th Royal Rifle Brigade, British army; she was born at Gibraltar. Their children are: Margaret C., now Mrs. Williams, of New York city, born in 1857; Harry M., born in 1860; Lizzie M., in 1863; and Charles J., in 1868; the last three were born in Springfield, Ill. Soon after landing in America Mr. Gallaher located at Bridgeport, Conn., where he learned "the art preservative" in the office of *The Standard*, at that time a staunch organ of the "silver-gray Whigs." He shortly afterward returned to New York, where he remained until the financial panic of 1857, when he came to Illinois, obtaining employment in the *State Journal* office, at Springfield, and was subsequently promoted to the position of associate editor, with Ed. L. Baker as chief, and had this position for ten years. Here he had the good fortune to become acquainted with Mr. Lincoln, Mr. Yates, Dr. Wallace and other prominent leaders, and had his Republicanism strengthened. Later he became connected with the *Quincy Whig*, and in 1874 assumed editorial charge of *The Old Flag*, where he gives entire satisfaction to all his patrons. He has had a large and varied experience in travel and journalism. He has visited Europe several times, and in his profession has been within the inner circles of the political and journalistic headquarters of State and nation.

James Criswell, proprietor of the *Old Flag*, was born in Ireland of Scotch-Irish parents, May 7, 1810. His parents, Robert and Mary (Hamilton) Criswell, brought him to America at the early age of seven years. They located at Shippensburg, Pa., but soon moved to Butler county, of the same State, and began farming. His father, who was a great deal in public life, died in 1867 at the advanced age of 89 years. Our subject remained in Pennsylvania until a few years before the war; he moved to St. Louis, Mo., where he ran a rolling mill. His mill burned in 1860, when he went South. At the outbreak of the war he started for the North and experienced great difficulty in making the trip. He brought his children to Pittsfield, that they might be wholly out of danger, and receive the benefit of good schools, and then entered the Union army, where he took an active and prominent part in suppressing the monster Rebellion. He served as Chief Engineer of the Machinery Department of the army of the Southwest, with rank as Colonel. In 1864 he returned to Pittsfield and then went South to Louisiana and opened up a plantation. He met Gen. Sheridan, with whom he was personally acquainted, who told him that he was heartily glad such men as he had come to settle in the South and aid in developing its resources. Mr. C. soon was appointed Commissioner of Elections. At this, however, he was ordered to leave the country, merely on political grounds, of course. Having influence in the Legislature he had his parish divided, some of his neighbors not being antagonistic to him. He was then appointed Sheriff of the new parish by Gov. Warmouth, but only accepted the position at the urgent request of the Governor and many of the citizens of the parish. He appointed two deputies and came to Pittsfield after his family, intending to remove them to his new home. While here, however, he received word that both his deputies had been killed. This was not encouraging to his family, and they would not go South. He returned, however, but was driven away by armed and masked Ku Klux, who came to his house to kill him. He was compelled to leave to save his life, for they had killed others around him, and he too well knew he would meet with the same fate.

Mr. C. returned to Pittsfield, bought out *The Old Flag* in 1868, and has since owned it and conducted it with success. His present wife, Hepsie D. Criswell, *nee* Reed, is a native of Kentucky.

THE PIKE COUNTY DEMOCRAT.

In tracing the ancestry of this staunch organ of the Democratic party in this county we find that the first paper was *The Pike County Sentinel*, which was started in the year 1845 by T. G. Trumbull and G. W. Smith, the former as editor. Under their regime it flourished until April, 1849, when it was purchased by John S. Roberts, who changed its name to *The Pike County Union*, the first number by this name being issued April 25, that year. In size it was six columns by 24 inches, and published at $1.50 a year. In 1851 Mr. Roberts sold it to M. H. Abbott, who on the 30th of May, 1857, changed its name to *The Pike County Democrat,* since which time it has retained that name. For a short time it was in the hands of Brown & Frazier, then of Frazier & McGinnis, then of Frazier (Robert F.) alone. Aug. 10, 1865, is the date of the first issue of the paper under the control of the present proprietor, J. M. Bush, when its circulation was only 350. Mr. Bush by his energy and ability has made of it one of the leading political organs of the State, and has increased its circulation largely. It is now an 8 column paper, 27 by 41 inches in size. In 1862 it was a 6-column paper, 24 inches to the column; in 1863, probably owing to the hard times produced by the war, it was somewhat reduced in size. This paper has always been issued weekly, and has ever been a firm advocate of the principles of the Democratic party, the very first number of *The Union* declaring itself in favor of "State rights and sovereignty."

The *Democrat,* which has no "patent" side, but is all printed at home, enjoys a liberal advertising patronage and a large circulation. Its locals are abundant, fresh and crisp. Its foreign and general news are such as the public desire to become acquainted with. Its editorial columns are ably managed. The political measures and movements of the day are discussed fearlessly, yet dispassionately. The principles of the Democratic party are ably advocated, and all other measures that its editor believes for the welfare of the general public.

The present printing establishment connected with this journal is the largest in the county. It is fitted with all the modern conveniences and improvements, among which is a steam-power press. The press was bought about 3 years ago, and the engine about 1 year ago. H. E. Hanna, nephew of M. H. Abbott, a former proprietor, has been foreman for about 12 years. They are prepared here to do job work in nearly all its branches, and in the neatest style. We will now speak personally of the leading editors who have conducted this paper.

T. G. Trumbull, one of the founders of this paper, was an attorney at law who came from Connecticut, and was a nephew of the celebrated painter, Col. Trumbull, of Washington's military family. He had, however, but little business at the Bar. In some respects he was somewhat peculiar. For example, when asked about early rising, he would reply that it was not best to be about until the world was well aired by the uprising sun. His health was feeble, his instincts were gentlemanly, his education good, and he was a man of retiring habit. He died many years ago and was buried in the Pittsfield cemetery, leaving no relatives in this vicinity.

George W. Smith went from here to Barry and started *The Barry Enterprise,* but soon got to drinking so that he could not control himself, and in Feb., 1861 fell out of a window of the

Planter's House in Hannibal and broke his neck. He was a brilliant writer,—indeed, a literary genius, and his flashes of wit and rhetoric have seldom been surpassed in local journalism.

John S. Roberts was born in Southern Pennsylvania Nov. 19, 1809; came to this State about the year 1836, stopping first at Shawneetown; afterward he and his brother were at Springfield and at Jacksonville, and edited a paper for awhile; also followed farming. He came to Pike county in 1849 and bought *The Pike County Sentinel*, as above stated. In 1868 he was appointed Collector of Internal Revenue for this District, and held the office for a year or two; was also Clerk of the Legislature for several sessions, was Supervisor of Martinsburg township several terms, and was Justice of the Peace from 1869 to 1878, when he died, leaving a widow (*nee* Elizabeth Twiford) and two sons,—J. Willis Roberts, now Justice of the Peace in Pittsfield, and Town Clerk, and Richard D., also a resident of Pittsfield.

Milton H. Abbott was probably a native of this State; he was married in Alton, Ill.; in a very early day he and his father published hymn-books, etc., in Vandalia, then the State capital. For stock he would ride horseback all the way to St. Louis and return. Of course, in such early times and under such difficulties, he could not carry on a very extensive business. After assisting on *The Free Press*, in Pittsfield, for a time, he went to Coldwater, Mich., where a storm blew down his dwelling, when he returned to Pittsfield. He commenced to edit *The Pike County Democrat* Oct. 11, 1860. After selling out the paper to Mr. Bush, in 1865, he emigrated by wagon to Oregon, finally settling at The Dalles, where he is now publishing *The Dalles Democrat*. Since going to that place he has lost his wife and three daughters. His brothers are not now living, and of his sisters only Mrs. E. J. Hanna, of Terre Haute, Ind., is living.

Joseph Merrick Bush, editor and proprietor of *The Pike County Democrat*, was born Jan. 16, 1822, in Pittsfield, Berkshire county, Mass.; graduated at Williams College (Mass.) in 1838, and removed the same fall to Pittsfield, Pike county, Ill., where he has ever since resided. He was admitted to the Bar, and in 1848 he married the daughter of John U. Grimshaw, and devoted the most of his time to farming up to 1865, when he purchased and took the control of the *Democrat*. He has held the office of State Senator, United States Commissioner for the Southern District of Illinois, Master in Chancery, President of the Board of Education, Pittsfield, President Pike County Agricultural Society, and has taken an active part in all measures looking to the advancement of the public interests. He has four sons, three of whom are grown to manhood, and two, William and J. M., jr., are connected with him in conducting the *Democrat* and its job rooms.

GRIGGSVILLE REFLECTOR.

The history of founding a local newspaper is almost without exception a story of unrealized hopes, misdirected efforts and unpaid bills. It is a well-known fact that more failures are recorded in the journalistic profession than in any other. Few are those who attain success in founding a country or a city newspaper. Often it is not for want of literary ability, for many who wield an able pen fail, but it takes as well a high order of business tact and talent. The successful editor and publisher must necessarily be a shrewd business man. He must be a man of business in all that that term implies, for in this field of labor one will find a greater variety of influences brought to bear against his efforts, difficulties unknown in other branches must be surmounted, the genius of dealing with people indiscriminately and successfully must be possessed; indeed, the successful editor of to-day must be a business man as well as a literary scholar.

There are few journals which continue long under their original management, seldom longer than two years. Not so with the *Reflector*, however, which continues under the control and management of its founder, Mr. Strother. He came to Griggsville in 1871, and July 15 of that year, sent forth the first number of the *Reflector*. It was then a seven-column folio, and presented a neat and tasteful appearance. It was received with favor, and considerable encouragement offered the editor. He being a practical printer, was able to take advantage of many influences and soon found his enterprise upon the high road to success. At the end of the first year he had a subscription list of 400. This was steadily increased until at present it numbers upward of 700. The *Reflector* is purely a local paper; has no patent side, and in politics and religion is neutral. People take the *Reflector* because it is not hampered or circumscribed by party principles or religious creeds. It is free to applaud or condemn, to advoc..e or oppose, to build up or tear down, any measure it believes beneficial and just, or injurious or wrong. Though neutral on political and religious questions, yet he devotes space in its columns to the discussion of both. Mr. Strother is a veteran in the printing business, having begun to learn the trade at the early age of 13 years, and has continued it without intermission from that day to this. Thus, with practical knowledge of his business, he is enabled the better to superintend and carry it on successfully. As a writer he is clear, forcible and logical, and has made of the *Reflector* an excellent provincial paper.

F. K. Strother, editor and proprietor of the Griggsville *Reflector*, was born in Granville county, N. C., Sept. 30, 1823; educated at Raleigh ; came to Adams county, Ill., in 1866, and here published the Clayton *Sentinel* (now the *Enterprise*) until 1871, when he came to Griggsville and issued the first copy of the *Reflector* July 15 of that year, which he still publishes, with a circulation of 850. January 18, 1851, he married Miss B. V. House, and they have 6 children: B. L., Homolea, Geneva A., Cora A., S. K. and F. T. Mr. Strother was with Gen. Canby in the South in 1867-8 ; was Government printer while there, where he remained until the reconstruction of the States. He has worked in the printing office most of the time since he was 14 years of age.

THE BARRY ADAGE.

The newspaper history of Barry well exemplifies a general rule characteristic of the profession of journalism. While in most other branches of business the first efforts at establishment in a new and growing place, are generally successful, in public journalism the charm of talking to the people in print, the social and political influence to be obtained as a stepping-stone to power and emolument, and to ease and luxury, tempt the innumerable, impecunious graduates of the printing office to seek some unoccupied field in which to establish themselves and rise. Hence they start out, and for want of the means necessary to run a newspaper a year or two, with but very little pay, they try a new place, and thus continue to rove; and it is but a corroboration of this remark to note that all, or nearly all, the newspapers now successfully conducted in Pike county are owned and edited by old residents having some property.

The first attempt to establish a newspaper in Barry was made by Geo. W. Smith, from Pittsfield, spoken of on a preceding page. He started *The Barry Enterprise*, but the office here was discontinued and the material was moved to Louisiana, Mo.. The next move to establish a paper here was made by Messrs. Shaffner & Goldsmith, who published *The Barry Weekly Dispatch*. The next effort was made by L. L. Burke, who started *The Barry Observer*, over White's store. This was run about a year, the last number being issued in the fall of 1871. In October of this year Mr. John H. Cobb took the same rooms and established *The Barry Adage*, in spite of the most discouraging obstacles. The people of the community had lost all faith in the newspaper business as a Barry enterprise. Mr. Cobb could find but two men who would pay as much as a year's subscription in advance, and not one who would pay a cent in advance for advertising. At least three-fourths of those who were approached on the subject would refuse to pay a cent for the new enterprise. Many men would go into a saloon or tobacco store and spend more in a day or two than would pay for the paper a whole year, then refuse even a single dime to encourage Mr. Cobb in his laudable enterprise, in which, too, he finally succeeded. The first number of his paper was issued about Nov. 1, 1871. In 1878, however, he sold out to Mr. Colgrove, who ran the institution for a short time. Mr. Cobb, in company with Wm. Watson, bought back the office and the situation and conducted it together with reasonable success until recently, when Mr. Cobb retired, leaving Mr. Watson sole editor and proprietor. The paper is printed on both sides at the home office, is a weekly, and independent in politics. Price only $1.00 a year, which is certainly quite reasonable for a local paper. It is not hampered or bound by any political fetters, but is strictly speaking an organ of the people, and for the people. While it enjoys a fair advertising patronage, the merchants and business men of Barry are not fully alive to their best interests when they fail to give their local paper a hearty and liberal support. Towns must be advertised as well as individuals and businesses, and this can only be done through the medium of the press.

There is connected with this paper a good job office.

Mr. Cobb tried a daily for a while, at Pittsfield, but that city was found to be too near the large cities, which furnish dailies at hand.

William Watson was born in Barry Feb. 16, 1857, and is a son of Jon Watson, deceased, an early settler in Pike county. Mr. Watson's future success with *The Barry Adage* is very promising. He is a pleasing writer for a young man, and gives to Barry an excellent local paper.

THE UNICORN GREENBACK.

After *The Adage* had been under way four or five years there was a sheriff's sale of a press, stationery, etc., where Mr. Simeon Fitch was a bidder, and he rather jestingly remarked that he did not want any one to bid against him on the press, as he wanted to run a paper in opposition to *The Adage*. He also had a boy whom he wished to learn the art of printing and thought to purchase the press and material for this purpose. This was the exciting cause of many friends encouraging him to go into the business of printing and publishing a paper. Thus encouraged, and having a love for literary labor, he obtained another press and commenced business, issuing the first number of *The Unicorn* on the 5th of October, 1877. He subsequently bought the press, which was offered at the sheriff's sale. *The Unicorn* was started as a Republican paper, but it soon espoused the Greenback cause and changed its name to *The Unicorn Greenback*. *The Unicorn* is a 8 column folio and filled with local and general news, discussions upon the political, financial and social issues of the country that agitate the public mind, and a general miscellany of excellent and instructive reading matter. As above stated it is a Greenback paper, and is one of the leading advocates for the measures and principles of the Greenback party in this section. *The Unicorn* is also one of the most zealous advocates of temperance and total abstinence from the use of tobacco there is in the country. No smoking is even allowed in the printing office. The motto heading the newspaper is,—

> "Tobacco, though handy, is risky to use:
> Together with brandy and whisky, refuse."

Mr. Fitch is pre-eminently a poetic editor, often throwing into rhyme the reports of proceedings in the city, and thus he amuses while he teaches and instructs. His paper has a much larger cir-

KINDERHOOK TP.

culation than he at first anticipated, and promises to be one of the established institutions of the city of Barry. Thus, with his temperance and anti-tobacco principles and his novel way of rhyming locals, he is enabled to present to his readers a rare, entertaining and elevating class of reading matter. He will not taint the morals of the most saintly, and it grieves him greatly to see so many of his fellow men, and especially the young, polluting themselves by the use of liquors and tobacco. It will take him a long time and much earnest work to change the habits and customs of this people in this respect, and that his influence will be felt, is beyond question. No man ever engaged in a reformation more desired, and more earnestly and devotedly than Mr. Fitch, and that he may live to see a radical change in the filthy and injurious habits so common, we most heartily wish. He has a most potent enemy, and it will take constant hard battling to conquer it. Mr. Fitch, however, appreciates the magnitude of his labors, yet will use his pen and voice, his influence and purse to save the young and convert those already steeped in the use of liquors and tobacco.

Simeon Fitch, editor and proprietor of the *Unicorn Greenback*, Barry, Ill., was born in Delaware county, N. Y., Dec. 2, 1818, and is a son of Samuel Fitch, deceased; was educated in Franklin, N. Y., and at the age of 21 he commenced teaching school, which profession he followed 10 years, a portion of the time engaging in farming during the summer season. He emigrated to Pike county in April, 1842, where he has since lived. May 1, 1845, he married Lucinda A. Piper, by whom he had one child, since deceased. Mrs. Fitch died April 24, 1854, and Aug. 3 of the same year Mr. F. married Eliza Kerr, and of the 8 children born to them these 6 are living: Ella, Edward E., Charles S., Owen L., Anna and Mary. Edward attends to the farm, while Owen L. assists his father in the printing-office. Ella is a teacher, and is now Mrs. Dr. E. T. Myers, of Farber, Mo.

MILTON BEACON.

This is one of the leading organs of the Greenback party in Illinois, and wields an influence second to none. This fact is evinced in the interest manifested by the people of Milton and vicinity in this late political movement, and also in the fact that the citizens in this district are uniformly well posted in political matters. Constant readers of this journal are difficult antagonists to contend with in argumentative contests on political questions. They have been under the instruction of a wise, original and logical tutor, and have gained much information bearing upon the great and important political questions, especially the financial, now before the public.

The *Beacon*, although comparatively a new publication, has proven a grand success under its present able management. During the winter of 1874-5 a temperance organization known as the Milton Moral Reform Society published a small paper called the

51

Milton *Reform.* This sheet was issued for the purpose of setting forth the aims and objects. of the order. It was distributed gratuitously, and was received with much favor by the citizens of the town. The effect of this small publication was to create a demand for a larger paper. After its second monthly issue Mr. A. G. Lucas proposed to start a five-column folio paper, providing the Society would discontinue the publication of the *Reform,* and turn over the advertising already secured. This proposition was accepted, and on the 16th of April, 1875, the Milton *Beacon* made its appearance. It came forth, however, as a six-column instead of a five-column paper, as originally intended.

The history of all new papers is one of a hard struggle for existence; on the whole, however, the *Beacon* has been unusually successful. After a lapse of three months Mr. Lucas found the expenses incident to founding a paper greater than he had anticipated, and suspension was likely to follow. It was the wish of the business men that the paper should continue. Accordingly in order to sustain the enterprise, a stock company was formed. This company consisted of F. M. Grimes, T. B. Morton, J. O. Bolin, C. E. Bolin, J. M. Faris, S. Hudson, W. Hess, W. D. Mitchell and L. N. Hall. Mr. Grimes was chosen President of the company and Mr. Morton, Secretary. J. M. Faris was appointed editor. He forthwith enlarged it to a seven-column paper, and advanced the subscription from $1.00 to $1.50 per year, adopted the " patent outside," and continued its publication until April, 1876. On that date the paper was sold to F. M. Grimes, its present editor, who has since purchased all of the shares except two, which have not yet been offered for sale.

Mr. Grimes entered upon his new field of labor with considerable enthusiasm. He brought to bear in this enterprise a well stored mind, a ready pen, business ability and personal popularity, and as a result has obtained a most signal success. During the past year (1879) this paper reached a circulation greater than that ever attained by any other paper published in Pike county, a fact of which its editor may well be proud.

Mr. Grimes continued the patent side until January, 1877, when he began the printing of the entire paper in the office. We will remark in this connection that in point of equipment this office ranks with those much older. It is supplied with a large assortment of the best material and modern conveniences of the preservative art. Mr. Grimes carries a full line of job-printing material, and executes some fine specimens in this line.

The *Beacon* was started as a neutral paper, politically. But the editor believing duty called him to do battle against certain measures which he considered highly detrimental to our common country, and to advocate others which were subservient to national prosperity, he unfurled the standard of the Greenback party and has since done valiant service in its behalf. He wields a powerful pen, and carries conviction to almost all who will unprejudicedly and candidly follow his arguments. As an antagonist he is dreaded by the most influential. As an advocate he is earnest, untiring and concentrates his unusual powers in behalf of the measure or person that he is supporting. We congratulate the people of Milton and vicinity in having in their midst a paper conducted with the ability and enterprise of the *Beacon*.

Francis Marion Grimes, editor of the *Beacon*, was born in Montezuma township, April 28, 1837. He is the son of James and Nancy (Davis) Grimes, well known early settlers of Pike county. His father was born in County Down, Ireland, Feb. 9, 1789, and his mother in Warren county, Ky., Feb. 15, 1797. They were united in marriage Nov. 11, 1813, and came to Montezuma township in 1836. His father died Sept. 19, 1873, and his mother still survives at a' ripe old age. Our subject was reared on a farm, and received a good common-school education. At the age of 19 he began teaching school and taught for 20 consecutive years in the schools of Montezuma and Pearl townships, this county. As a teacher he was eminently successful, as attested by the above, and also by the fact that he never held any other than a first-grade certificate. He quit teaching in April, 1876, and took possession of the editorial chair of the *Beacon*, which he has so ably filled to the present time. March 17, 1859, he was united in marriage with Sarah E. Colvin, the sixth child of Thomas and Rebecca Colvin, now deceased. To them have been born 6 children, namely,— Albert, Luther, Perry, Henry, Ina and Rollo. Mr. G. has been a member of the Christian Church for 20 years, and a zealous worker in the temperance cause for many years. He now also holds membership in the Masonic, Odd Fellows and Workmen lodges. He formerly voted with the Democratic party, but paid little attention to politics, believing, however, that the financial question was paramount to all others at the present; has for the past year devoted his time and energies to the interests of the National Greenback party.

PERRY PARAGRAPH.

This is one of the eight newspaper publications of Pike county, and like the others, has experienced its ups and downs. It is conceded to be one of the most difficult things known in the business world to establish a local paper upon a paying basis. It requires more energy, patience and perseverance to found one than almost any other business. It is less remunerative, more vexatious, and requires the expenditure of greater mental and physical force than other enterprises. Few there are who properly appreciate the labors, the trials and difficulties of a country editor. He enjoys none of the advantages, yet he is expected to send forth a sheet that will compare favorably with the large dailies of cities.

Mr. Cobb, the editor of this paper, and other editors can appreciate the force of these remarks perhaps better than people in general. He recently started the *Paragraph*, and has met with fair success. The paper is independent politically, religiously and in everything else. It is free to advocate or oppose any measure or view brought before the public.

H. C. Cobb was born in Chautauqua county, N. Y., Aug. 20, 1845, and is the son of James and Mary (Hale) Cobb, both natives of the Empire State. His father is of Welsh ancestry, and his mother is a direct descendant of Sir. Matthew Hale. Mr. C. was united in marriage Aug. 12, 1871, with Elizabeth Purviance. Three children have been borne to them, only one of whom is now living. Mr. C. learned his trade in New York, where he was connected with several papers in the State.

THE INDEPENDENT PRESS.

This is the latest newspaper enterprise of Pike county, and has promise of becoming one of the most popular and influential. It first greeted the public Dec. 11, 1879, an eight-column folio. The typographical appearance of the *Press* is neat and tasty. Indeed, it would reflect honor to older established offices to send out such excellent quality of work. The *Press* office is furnished all through with the best material and presses, and for mechanical execution the job work done at this office will compare favorably with that turned out from the larger establishments of the State. Its present editor, A. Hughes, and its proprietors, Hughes & Nelson, are thoroughly enterprising newspaper men, and that the progress they have so early made is appreciated by the general public, is evinced by the unusual success attending their enterprise.

The Independent Press, which is published at Griggsville, was founded, as its name implies, as an independent journal so far as politics or religion are concerned. Its editor believes he can exert a greater influence under that banner than under any other. He will not be influenced by party or sect. He advocates such measures, national, municipal, religious and social, as will best subserve the interests of the mass of the community, regardless of any party, clique or individual. As such a journal, it deserves, as it has, the patronage of all classes. As the better to set forth the principles of this paper, we quote from its salutatory a remark or two in reference to this point. The editor says : "The *Press* will not be a partisan sheet in accordance with the generally accepted tenets of either of the established political parties. Our politics and religion will be independent so far as the paper is concerned." * * *
" In our advocacy of measures, be they cosmopolitan or local, we will only be guided by what we conceive to be the right, and will best conserve the true interests of this city, county, State and nation. In the interest of the merchant we shall advocate the best means of developing trade ; in the interests of all we shall, by using every means in our power, fight against rings, monopolies, and every species of fraud that has a tendency to retard or lessen the people's interest."

A local journal established upon such a broad and liberal platform, and evincing the enterprise and public spirit the *Press* has, should receive the undivided support of men of all parties, creeds and opinions. It is not hampered or circumscribed by partisan principles of any nature, save truth and probity. The *Press* is published each Thursday. Subscription, $1.50 per year.

Arnold Hughes, editor of the *Press*, is a native of Missouri, grew up attending the common schools. He served an apprenticeship at the printer's trade in Milwaukee, Wis., and has since devoted himself to his profession with zeal and energy. As a writer he is original, pointed and entertaining. His locals are fresh and crisp, his editorials are able, logical and convincing, and as a business man possesses much practical knowledge. It is our wish, as it is that of the general public, that Messrs. Hughes & Nelson will make a success of their new-born enterprise.

OTHER PAPERS.

The Radical for a brief time was published as the exponent of a sentiment. It was edited with vim, by Charles J. Sellon, who was afterward a vigorous and useful editor of the *Illinois State Journal*, at Springfield. He enlisted in the Union army, but was discharged on account of deafness. He died a young man, mourned by his family and many friends. He was buried in the grave-yard of St. Stephen's Church, Pittsfield, Ill.

The Radical was suddenly reduced to *The Radi*, which was conducted by O. W. Topliff for a short time, and then was discontinued altogether.

A Republican paper called *The Morning Star*, was once started by Wm. Overstreet, in Pittsfield, but did not last long.

CHAPTER XX.

MISCELLANEOUS.

RAILROADS.

The railroad is comparatively a new enterprise to Pike county. In reference to means of transportation this county is greatly favored by nature. Indeed, there is no county in the State to which nature gave such abundant and convenient channels of transportation as to Pike. Here are two of the finest water courses in America washing its shores, and no portion of the county over half a day's drive from one of them. Without a railroad many of the northern counties of the State would yet be in their native condition. Yet Pike county could, and did, get along very conveniently without a railroad.

As early as May, 1860, a railroad was projected, principally by Messrs. Starne and Hatch. This road was known as the Pike County Road, and later as the Hannibal and Naples road. Some grading was done, but the county, at a general election, refused aid, and the project was abandoned until after the war, when, through the efforts of Judge Higbee, Scott Wike, James S. Irwin, Hon. Wm. A. Grimshaw, W. Steers, of Pittsfield, Messrs. Brown and Wike, of Barry, and Messrs. McWilliams, Ward, Philbrick and others, of Griggsville, the enterprise was revived and pushed to completion.

Originally about $350,000 were expended on the old Pike road; and of this sum the city of Hannibal furnished as a city $200,000, the townships on the line of the road $70,000, and individuals in Hannibal and Pike county the balance. The money subscribed was faithfully expended under the direction of Mr. Starne, the President of the road, and a competent engineer; the war commenced and the road failed, as did most of the public enterprises of the country. It was at that time in debt to Mr. Clough, one of the engineers, about $1,000, and upon a suit commenced by him a judgment was rendered against the road for his debt. The friends of the road were anxious that it should not be sacrificed, and when it was sold, bid it in in the name of Scott Wike, for $1,039, who transferred the certificate of purchase to the Directors of the old road, Messrs. A. Starne, B. D. Brown, O. M. Hatch, George Wike, Geo. W. Shields, J. G. Helme, James McWilliams and Scott

Wike; and the Sheriff made them a deed Feb. 12, 1863. They were then incorporated as the Hannibal & Naples Railroad Company. Mr. Shields was the Mayor of the city of Hannibal, and Mr. Helme a large property-holder there. They were directors of the old road, and were appointed by the City Council to look after the interests of the city. The other gentlemen were directors in the old road and large property-holders in Pike county.

When the agitation incident to the Rebellion had subsided and the people again turned to the improvement of their homes and the carrying out of home enterprises, the completion of this road was urged.

Enthusiastic meetings were held throughout the county in December, 1867. The proposition by the Supervisors to bond the county was defeated by a popular vote Dec. 24,—2,777 for, to 2,841 against, one of the largest votes ever cast in the county.

At a railroad meeting held at the court-house in Pittsfield Dec. 30, 1868, resolutions for pushing the railroad interests of the county were passed, and a committee appointed, headed by Wm. A. Grimshaw, to " take the requisite steps to carry out the project of railroad connections for Pittsfield and Pike county with the Chicago & Alton, or the Pennsylvania Central, or any other roads interested and willing to co-operate with Pittsfield and Pike county."

At the same time there was a project of a railroad from Louisiana, Mo., to run west to the Missouri river, headed by Thomas L. Price, then a railroad king in the West.

Ten miles of the Hannibal & Naples road were completed Feb. 18, 1869, namely, to Kinderhook, and a banquet and great rejoicing were had on the occasion, in a car at Kinderhook.

In pursuance of an official call a railroad meeting was held at Pittsfield, March 8, 1869, with R. A. McClintock Chairman and J. M. Bush Secretary, when Col. A. C. Matthews explained the object of the meeting. A committee was appointed, one from each township represented, to assess the sum of $150,000 among the various townships embraced in the call. The meeting passed a resolution indorsing the act of the Legislature providing for the refunding to the several townships and counties, the contracting debts for railroads, the entire taxes on such railroad property, and the excess of all State taxes over the assessment of 1868.

August, 1869, the Hannibal & Naples road reached a point within 2½ miles of New Salem; reached Griggsville in September; railroad completed in October; crossed the Illinois river Jan. 20, 1870; Feb. 11, finished to Pittsfield. At that time a grand free excursion was given, when the following incident occurred: The train being gone about three hours longer than was expected, parties who had been left behind began to feel uneasy. One man, whose wife and son were with the excursionists, with his remaining son built a fire near the track; and while waiting with great anxiety for the return of the train, the little boy started toward the track.

The father in his agony said, "Don't, my son; don't go near the track; I'm afraid some dreadful accident has happened and you and I will both be orphans." When the train at last arrived all safe and sound, there was great rejoicing. The contract for building the railroad from Pittsfield to the H. & N. road was let July 24, 1869, to Hon. A. Starne. Work was immediately begun and before a year had passed trains were running.

After the Hannibal & Naples Road was completed, it was changed soon after to the Toledo, Wabash & Western Railway, and in March, 1880, when the great Wabash line came in possession of the T., P. & W. Ry. and other lines, it was changed to the Wabash, St. Louis & Pacific Railway. About the time of the completion of the H. & N. road, other roads were projected. In May, 1869, a line was surveyed from Rushville, via Mt. Sterling to Pittsfield.

In the summer of 1869 special efforts were made by the citizens of the county to complete the projected railroads, and at a meeting of the citizens of Pittsfield and Newburg townships at Pittsfield, June 17, committees were appointed to devise ways and means to raise the amount required of them, namely, $32,000. C. P. Chapman was appointed Chairman of said committee.

In the spring of 1871, everything pertaining to the railroad interests of the county seemed to be lying dead or asleep, and the suspicion of the people began to be aroused that the enterprise was abandoned, when Gen. Singleton, President of the Quincy, Alton & St. Louis road, announced that that company were waiting to obtain the right of way through Quincy. This road was soon completed, following the line of the Mississippi from the northern line of the county to the southern where it crosses the river at Louisiana.

In the spring of 1872 it was proposed to build a road to Perry Springs, connecting with the Bob-tail to Pittsfield. At this time the county of Pike and the townships of Pittsfield and Newburg had invested $132,000 in the Pittsfield branch, with no prospect of dividends; but it was proposed to issue county bonds of $10,000 to $12,000 per mile on the Pittsfield branch, on which the Wabash company should guaranty the interest, thus enabling them to negotiate the bonds at a fair rate.

The Quincy, Payson & Southeastern railroad was projected to make a direct line to Pittsfield through Payson, thence nearly directly east to Effingham, to connect for Cincinnati and the East, but nothing definite has been done.

The Chicago, Alton & St. Louis ran the "Louisiana," or "Kansas City" branch through the southern townships of this county seven or eight years ago. This was done without local aid from this county, but received help from the city of Louisiana. This is a first-class road, and opened up a most prolific part of Pike county. At this time a railroad bridge was built across the Mississippi at Louisiana. Aug. 1, 1871, a magnificent bridge was completed across the same river at Hannibal.

Eugene Smith

BARRY

SNY ISLAND LEVEE.

Along the whole of the west side of Pike county there runs a bayou of the Mississippi river, named by the early French *Chenal Ecarte* (crooked channel) but in English generally called "Sny," for short, from the French pronunciation of *Chenal*. This bayou commences in Adams county about 12 miles below Quincy, and runs southeasterly somewhat parallel with the river, until it ends in Calhoun county, its channel being generally about midway between the river and the bluffs. The low land drained by this "bayou," "channel," "slough," "creek," etc., as it is variously called, comprises about 110,000 acres. This was subject to overflow every spring, and being the most fertile ground in the West, it is very important that it be reclaimed if possible. Without improvement it is entirely useless, and even a source of malaria and sickness.

Consequently, in the year 1870 a movement was set on foot to reclaim this vast tract of rich land by an embankment near the river. To aid in this great enterprise the Legislature passed an act, approved April 24, 1871, authorizing the issue of bonds, to be paid by special assessments on the lands benefited. To carry out the provisions of this act "The Mississippi Levee Drainage Company" was organized about the first of August, 1871, by a meeting of the citizens of Pike and Adams counties, electing a board of directors, with S. M. Spencer, President, other officers, and a board of commissioners. . The citizens also drew up and signed a petition for the appointment of the commissioners according to law, whereupon the County Court (R. M. Atkinson, Judge) appointed Geo. W. Jones, William Dustin and John G. Wheelock, Commissioners, Mr. Dustin's place, after his death, being filled by Benjamin F. Westlake. For the construction of the levee they issued bonds, bearing interest at 10 per cent., and they were sold mostly in the Eastern markets, some in Detroit, Mich., the interest payable annually. Accordingly the levee was constructed in 1872–4, at a cost of about $650,000.

But the manner of collecting assessments authorized by this act was called in question by a case brought up to the Supreme Court from the Wabash river, where similar work was being done, and the Court decided that feature of the act to be unconstitutional. A similar case went up to that tribunal from this county, and the Court re-affirmed its former decision. It was then thought expedient to procure an amendment to the State Constitution; the necessary resolution was submitted to the people by the 30th General Assembly, and it was adopted by an overwhelming majority. Thereupon another act was passed by the 31st General Assembly, to make the law conform to the constitution as amended, and under this act the owners of lands on the Sny bottom proposed to construct a drainage district to be known as " The Sny Island Levee Drainage District."

The levee, as at first projected, was completed, as before stated, but it has proved wholly insufficient, as the Mississippi flood, aided by high winds, in April, 1876, broke through the embankment, and all the low land was inundated, destroying crops, carrying away fences, and driving out the inhabitants. No one, however, was drowned, but planting was retarded. The breaches were soon repaired, but more lately a new company has been organized to improve the levee and make it perfect, that is, capable of protecting the bottom land against such a high water as there was in 1851.

This levee is by far the largest above Vicksburg, being about 52 miles in length, commencing on a sand ridge in Adams county, and extending into Calhoun county. It is constructed of the sandy soil along its line, and readily becomes sodded and overgrown with willow and other small growth. The streams which formerly emptied into the Mississippi now find their way into Bay creek, and then into Hamburg bay, in Calhoun county. A few farms were opened in the bottom before the construction of the levee, but since that work was completed the land is becoming pretty well covered with farms, occupied by a good, industrious class of citizens. The time may come when the dwellers in this land will become a power in the county.

We desire here to state to the public, with some emphasis, that neither the county nor any municipality in the same is in any manner liable for the bonds issued in aid of the construction of this levee. Neither the State, county nor towns took any part in the issue of the bonds, or in the construction of the work. The enterprise was a private one, and the fact that the bonds are not paid reflects on no one. The law under which they were issued was declared unconstitutional, and in such cases the bonds must fall with the law.

On the completion of the levee the source of water supply for the Rockport mills, situated on the Sny, was of course mostly cut off. Consequently, about Sept. 15, 1874, the proprietors of the mills, Messrs. Shaw & Rupert, hired parties in St. Louis to come up and cut the levee, having been advised that they had lawful authority to "abate the nuisance" by their own act. Great excitement was occasioned by this transaction, and during the ensuing litigation the mill proprietors obtained a mandamus for opening the Sny; but a settlement was finally effected by a compromise with the drainage company, the latter paying the former $30,000. The mill, however, was subsequently destroyed by fire.

COUNTY TREASURER'S REPORT MADE NOVEMBER 30, 1879.

Debits.

To amount on hand Dec. 1, 1878	$21,026.21
To tax levied on all property for 1878	10,944.27
To money collected from other sources	4,243.55
Total debits	$36,214.03

Credits.

County Orders and jury certificates paid	$23,834.21
Other credits	4,450.69
	$28,284.90
Balance cash due County Dec. 1, 1879	7,929.13
	$36,214.03

MARRIAGE LICENSES.

The following table gives the number of Marriage Licenses annually issued since 1826:

1827	6	1845	159	1863	252
1828	19	1846	161	1864	260
1829	21	1847	180	1865	380
1830	22	1848	232	1866	370
1831	25	1849	203	1867	357
1832	47	1850	199	1868	374
1833	34	1851	213	1869	273
1834	50	1852	246	1870	270
1835	49	1853	241	1871	258
1836	57	1854	220	1872	271
1837	100	1855	236	1873	250
1838	106	1856	275	1874	297
1839	110	1857	377	1875	281
1840	115	1858	259	1876	282
1841	121	1859	279	1877	285
1842	160	1860	258	1878	309
1843	147	1861	235	1879	313
1844	153	1862	227	1880 to Jan. 26	15

AGRICULTURAL STATISTICS.

In 1877 the number of acres of corn raised in Pike county were 87,405; number of bushels produced, 2,888,802; winter wheat 71,-219 acres; yield, 982,453 bushels; spring wheat, 66 acres; yield 1,682 bushels; oats, 5,559 acres; yield 122,540; rye, 414 acres; yield 4,371 bushels; barley, 16 acres; yield 210 bushels; buckwheat, 41 acres; yield 421 bushels; beans, 33 acres; yield 313 bushels; Irish potatoes, 1,122 acres; yield 66,649 bushels; sweet potatoes, 3 acres, yield 243 bushels. Apple orchards 4,656 acres; yield 168,535 bushels; peach orchards 202 acres; yield 2,213 bushels; pear orchards 5 acres; yield 4 bushels; tobacco 70 acres; yield 42,265 pounds; broom-corn 2 acres; yield 1,000 pounds; timothy meadow 14,200 acres; yield 17,801 tons; clover 3,302 acres; yield 3,445 tons; prairie meadow 283 acres, yield 401 tons; Hungarian and millet, 69 acres, yield 149 tons; sorgho, 97 acres, yield 8,520 gallons of syrup made; vineyard 59 acres, yield 7,345 gallons of wine made; turnips and other root crops, 498 acres, value of crops produced $2,037; other fruit and berries not included above or in orchard, 85 acres, value $229; other crops not named above, 1,950 acres, value $6,437. Pasture, not including wood land, 33,228 acres; wood land, not included as pasture, 87,371; uncultivated land not included as wood land or pasture, 60,565 acres. Area in city and town real estate not included above, 1,605 acres. Number of sheep killed by dogs; 791, average value per head $2.07; number of pounds of wool sheared, 49,609; number of fat sheep sold 2,378, average weight per head 99 pounds; number of cows kept 6,062; pounds butter sold 78,430; pounds of cheese sold 325; gallons of cream sold 16; gallons of milk sold 8,538; number of fat cattle sold 4,747; average gross weight 1,002 pounds; number of fat hogs sold 35,947; average weight per head 235; number of hogs and pigs died of cholera 30,259; average weight per head 70 pounds. Number of bushels timothy seed produced, 516; of clover seed 977; of Hungarian and millet 33; number of pounds of grapes 61,715.

In 1878 the agricultural returns of Pike county, were as follows: Corn, 74,552 acres, and 2,314,209 bushels; winter wheat, 80,800 acres and 1,092,725 bushels; spring wheat, 66 acres, 168 bushels; oats, 5,650 acres, 136,433 bushels; rye, 60 acres, 338 bushels; buckwheat, 19 acres, 217 bushels; castor beans, 1 acre, 4 bushels; beans, 10 acres, 67 bushels; peas, 10 acres, 614 bushels; Irish potatoes, 511 acres, 34,688 bushels; sweet potatoes, 16 acres, 420 bushels; apple orchard, 4,290 acres, fruit 60,847 bushels; peach orchard, 49 acres, 1,085 bushels; pear orchard, 1 acre, 10 bushels; tobacco, 11 acres, 5,500 pounds; broom-corn, 19 acres, 16,000 pounds; timothy meadow, 13,396 acres, 17,298 tons of hay produced; clover meadow, 4,616 acres, 6,334 tons; prairie meadow, 33 acres, 29 tons of hay; Hungarian and millet, 65 acres, 74 tons; sorgho, 152 acres, 11,017 gallons of syrup made; vineyard, 71 acres, 958 gallons of wine made; turnips and other root crops, 109 acres, value of crop raised, $1,094; other fruits and berries, not included in above and orchard, 58 acres; value of crops, $734; other crops not named above, 2,284 acres; value of crops, $4,500; pasture, not including wood land, 33,773 acres; wood land, not included as pasture, 65,644 acres; uncultivated land, not included as wood land or pasture, 20,346 acres. Number of sheep killed by dogs, 958; average value per head, $1.83, total value, $1,755; number of pounds of wool shorn, 47,683; number of fat sheep sold, 1,389; average weight per head, 70 pounds; number of cows kept, 2,891; pounds of butter sold, 30,941; pounds of cheese sold, 725; gallons of cream sold, 196; gallons of milk sold, 10,288; number of fat cattle sold, 3,965, average weight per head, 945 pounds; total, 3,745,527 pounds; hogs, number sold, 36,578; average weight per head, 240 pounds; total, 8,676,516 pounds; number of hogs and pigs died of cholera, 30,611; average weight per head, 35 pounds; total number of pounds, 1,070,901. Number of bushels of timothy seed produced, 265; clover seed, 1,827 bushels; Hungarian and millet seed, 33 bushels; number of pounds of grapes, 48,300.

ABSTRACTS OF ASSESSMENTS FROM 1867 TO 1879, INCLUSIVE.

Year	Horses	Average Value	Cattle	Average Value	Sheep	Hogs	Carriages & Wagons	Pianos	Acres of Improved Land	Acres of Unimproved Land	Total Value of Land	Total Value of Personal Property	Value R.R. Property	Total Assessed Value of all Property	Acres of Corn	Acres of Wheat	Acres Other Products
1867	11644	$	18884*	$	35990	47766	4002	93	335580*	166585	$4509282 00	$1585636 00	$	$4509282 00	64706	32997	13615
1868	11923		21124		33160	48152	4164	96	308812*	195745	4751242 00		2640 00	4415279 00	61868	51597	14739
1869	10503	33 00	18363	9 43	19205	44724	3985	107	308300	187217	2715093 00	1515404 00	7960 00	4677903 00	49681	55797	13115
1870	11225	31 00	21348	8 97	12455	52760	4040	115	316496	194828	1887184 00	1387184 00	154606 00	4983570 00	67857	63208	15830
1871	10669	31 00	20351	8 41	13016	59453	3973	168	309250	205597	2891545 00	1370455 00	200093 00	5016477 00	70847	71151	12170
1872	12202	30 00	25570	18	14778	63892	4690	155	286099	224665	2864627 00	1266818 00	370703 00	17940230 00	83989	95305	28651
1873	12064	60 00	24001	15	13588	55564	4571	155	299480	214667	11481666 00	4727574 00	114080 00	14308378 00	81697	95305	34583
1874	11910	47 00	22561	15	13857	47329	4519	161	335100	176604	9667875 00	3521963 00	3867752 00	12894452 00	96430	75756	33647
1875	11738	46 00	22708	14	11910	45567	4743	169	303872	205920	8640128 00	3366285 00	639689 00	11658876 00	88779	72874	38782
1876	11673	40 00	21913	13	12247	48100	4688	180	291247	216995	7905240 00	2927164 00	728182 00	10215392 00	72874	38782	34960
1877	11203	35 00	21762	11	11282	52650	4695	177	290600	220164	6926117 00	2535895 00	644547 00	9167863 00	100089	79521	37587
1878	11203	31 00	21762	11	11557	43602	4610	179	287947	228633	6300124 00	2171856 00	725187 00	8618488 00	93015	93374	37587
1879	10796	29 00	21355	11							6030068 00	1966894 00					

*Including all tracts of Land whereon there is any improvement whatever.

TABLE OF DISTANCES.

On the next page is given a table of distances between all the towns of this county, in a condensed and available form. The names of the places are given in alphabetical order (except one in each), and the table is arranged like the multiplication tables of the old arithmetics of our school days in pioneer times. Therefore, to find the distance from any one place to another, you trace the column of figures running out from each until they meet; the number at that point is the number of miles by wagon road, counting on a level, as surveyors of land do, between the two designated points.

NAME OF PLACE.	Valley City.	Time.	Summer Hill.	Stewart.	Rockport.	Pleasant Hill.	Pittsfield.	Perry Springs.	Perry.	Pearl.	New Salem.	New Hartford	New Canton.	Nebo.	Montezuma.	Milton.	Maysville.	Martinsburg.	Kinderhook.	Hull's.	Griggsville	Florence.	Eldara.	East Hannibal	Detroit.	Cool Bank.	Chowrow.	Chambersb'rg	Bedford.	Baylis.	Barry.
Atlas	28	14	4	16	2	7	13	31	28	19	19	6	11	12	22	19	20	7	16	19	23	24	8	27	21	13	22	34	20	16	15
Barry	20	21	16	24	11	22	13	25	20	32	11	14	6	27	30	26	13	20	6	9	16	25	6	18	21	4	30	25	31	8	
Baylis	14	20	12	28	18	22	14	15	18	28	4	10	15	20	27	23	7	18	13	16	10	22	11	23	18	5	29	19	28		
Bedford	15	9	18	11	19	20	16	24	25	7	27	20	32	17	2	5	22	14	38	40	19	8	26	50	12	28	31	22			
Chambersburg	8	20	27	30	34	35	21	4	7	26	16	27	33	32	21	17	14	26	31	33	10	14	30	45	14	24	28				
Chowrow	22	16	22	6	24	14	21	33	31	5	31	24	34	10	9	12	29	17	42	46	25	19	31	54	17	36					
Cool Bank	18	22	13	30	12	22	15	22	19	29	8	11	10	26	27	23	10	19	10	12	13	21	7	21	19						
Detroit	6	6	18	16	21	22	7	14	16	14	17	15	22	18	11	6	12	15	29	31	8	4	16	42							
East Hannibal	38	43	29	48	27	40	36	38	35	52	27	28	17	44	50	46	30	20	11	8	34	46	26								
Eldara	23	17	9	25	6	17	11	28	24	29	13	7	6	21	25	21	15	14	12	14	19	20									
Florence	6	10	22	18	25	26	11	16	17	14	21	19	25	22	7	7	15	19	31	34	11										
Griggsville	4	10	23	19	25	25	10	7	6	21	6	16	17	22	18	14	4	16	22	24											
Hull's	28	32	22	40	18	32	23	33	27	42	17	21	9	36	39	35	21	30	3												
Kinderhook	26	30	20	36	15	32	16	29	25	40	16	23	6	32	37	33	18	26													
Martinsburg	20	9	6	11	9	6	9	23	22	15	13	8	18	7	16	13	12														
Maysville	8	14	16	23	20	20	6	11	9	25	3	14	13	18	21	17															
Milton	10	4	15	11	18	19	11	19	20	8	22	15	27	16	4																
Montezuma	14	8	18	13	21	19	15	23	24	9	26	16	31	19																	
Nebo	26	12	15	4	13	5	12	29	27	8	20	15	24																		
New Canton	21	23	14	28	7	19	16	26	21	31	16	11																			
New Hartford	20	11	2	18	7	12	7	23	22	22	12																				
New Salem	10	16	14	25	18	18	9	13	10	29																					
Pearl	18	13	20	4	22	12	19	22	27																						
Perry	10	16	24	25	27	29	15	3																							
Perry Springs	9	17	27	27	33	32	17																								
Pittsfield	13	7	10	15	16	15																									
Pleasant Hill	29	18	9	8	9																										
Rockport	29	14	6	18																											
Stewart	22	10	16																												
Summer Hill	23	11																													
Time	14																														

EDUCATIONAL STATISTICS.

TOWNSHIPS.	No. Males under 21.	No. Females under 21.	Total No. Persons under 21.	Whole No. Districts.	Whole No. Pupils Enrolled.	No. Male Teachers.	No. Female Teachers.	No. School-houses.	Total Receipts for Year Ending Sept. 30, 1878.	Am't Paid Teachers.	Total Expend'ts, 1878.	Value of School Property.	Principal of Township Fund.	Highest Monthly Wages Paid Male Teachers.	Highest Monthly Wages Paid Female Teachers.	Lowest Monthly Wages Paid Male Teachers.	Lowest Monthly Wages Paid Female Teachers.
Atlas	540	411	905	16	466	10	9	8	$3361 00	$3537 00	$3386 00	$4656 00	$2517 00	$50 00	$40 00	$25 00	$20 00
Barry	199	205	1627	10	946	12	10	10	10817 00	8365 00	8365 00	21000 00	9848 00	110 00	62 00	40 00	28 00
Chambersburg	436	374	810	8	246	6	4	3	3005 00	1915 00	2146 00	3850 00	2695 00	70 00	40 00	25 00	25 00
Derry	810	320	946	10	362	7	7	7	3918 00	2878 00	3483 00	4850 00	4397 00	50 00	30 00	30 00	17 00
Detroit	280	400	810	5	271	5	9	5	3532 00	2831 00	2831 00	7500 00	1283 00	35 00	35 00	30 00	25 00
Fairmount	310	304	614	7	403	5	9	7	2315 00	1803 00	2039 00	2420 00	2259 00	60 00	40 00	45 00	20 00
Flint	127	104	231	3	108	1	5	3	1078 00	770 00	866 00	1800 00	855 00	45 00	45 00	40 00	20 00
Griggsville	550	580	1131	13	653	9	11	9	9180 00	5203 00	11660 00	11660 00	4224 00	140 00	55 00	30 00	20 00
Hadley	325	296	621	9	345	6	10	8	3955 00	1810 00	3841 00	3650 00	4498 00	55 00	40 00	20 00	22 00
Hardin	356	345	702	7	345	7	8	8	792 00	252 00	567 00	6450 00	1692 00	55 00	40 00	20 00	20 00
Kinderhook	313	342	655	7	332	8	6	7	4677 00	1981 00	3317 00	1980 00	4625 00	65 00	40 00	25 00	25 00
Levee	116	169	285	7	113	5	3	3	3069 00	670 00	2716 00	2300 00	1980 00	40 00	35 00	40 00	28 00
Martinsburg	350	352	702	8	654	10	3	8	4748 00	2456 00	3516 00	2935 00	2242 00	60 00	40 00	35 00	18 00
Montezuma	363	416	779	8	612	8	7	7	5726 00	3167 00	4270 00	9250 00	4000 00	100 00	45 00	30 00	25 00
Newburg	242	406	648	8	440	6	4	7	4169 00	2302 00	3448 00	5100 00	1657 00	50 00	37 00	35 00	25 00
New Salem	389	385	774	10	680	6	4	8	6328 00	5436 00	5436 00	9550 00	1507 00	85 00	45 00	35 00	15 00
Pearl	203	201	404	4	184	3	3	4	2000 00	1297 00	1376 00	1000 00	2237 00	45 00	40 00	41 00	25 00
Perry	510	528	1038	7	680	6	10	7	6281 00	3790 00	5635 00	7000 00	1574 00	125 00	45 00	40 00	20 00
Pittsfield	865	900	1765	9	861	9	14	9	4296 00	1863 00	3586 00	48000 00	1196 00	177 00	55 00	40 00	22 00
Pleasant Hill	475	443	918	10	410	7	7	7	3142 00	2345 00	2345 00	2350 00	1590 00	45 00	30 00	35 00	25 00
Pleasant Vale	479	484	963	12	475	8	11	10	7065 00	2584 00	694 00	9251 00	555 00	65 00	45 00	40 00	25 00
Ross	59	63	122	1	51	1	1	3	1133 00	445 00	528 00	1200 00	745 00	62 00	35 00	40 00	35 00
Spring Creek	435	409	844	8	486	8	5	5	3652 00	2073 00	2334 00	2150 00		50 00	35 00	25 00	20 00

PIKE COUNTY AGRICULTURAL BOARD.

The " Pike County Agricultural Society " was organized March 16, 1852, at Pittsfield. D. B. Bush was called to the chair and Henry T. Mudd was chosen Secretary. A constitution was adopted, under which Michael J. Noyes was elected the first President. In June following resolutions were passed urging upon the Legislature of the State the necessity of encouraging agriculture, and of establishing Agricultural Schools, and recommending that model farms be immediately purchased or reserved from sale out of the lands given to the State, on which these schools should be established, etc.

In order to avail themselves of the benefit of the act of 1871 concerning the re-organization of County Agricultural Societies, in conformity to an act to create a Department of Agriculture, the name of the society was changed to " The Pike County Agricultural Board," electing E. M. Seeley, President, and W. H. Johnston, Secretary, and other officers.

This organization has held a fair every year since its formation. It first enclosed and furnished a fair ground in 1858. Before that the fairs were held in the open woods, when no admission fee could be charged. Expenses were defrayed by subscriptions. All the fairs have been held at Pittsfield except one, which was at Griggsville. The ground is just south of Pittsfield, and comprises nearly 25 acres. It is a fine enclosure.

The officers for 1879 were: Allen C. Rush, President ; John Whittleton, Vice-President; J. H. Crane, Secretary; S. Grigsby, Treasurer. Directors—C. B. Dustin, Frank Zerenberg, Allen C. Rush, N. P. Hart, Wm. R. Wills, Dan Bates, George Watson, E. N. French and Henry Hall.

The 28th annual fair was held in September, 1879, continuing four consecutive days. The total of the premium list offered is $5,000.

The society is now in a flourishing condition.

J. A. Sweet.

HADLEY TP.

DIGEST OF STATE LAWS.

LAWS.

The courts recognize two kinds of law, *Statute* and *Common*. Statute law is that which is enacted by the Legislature. Common law consists of all the law of England,—whether Statute, or Common, which was in force in that country at the time of our independence, and recognized by our courts, and which has not since been repealed or disused.

We have what is called established law. For this branch of common law there is no authority excepting the decisions of the courts; hence the value of the reported decisions which are published by official reporters. The law presumes that every body is acquainted with it. Mistakes of fact can be corrected by the courts, but not mistakes of law; no man being permitted to take advantage of a mistake of the law, either to enforce a right, or avoid an obligation; for it would be dangerous and unwise to encourage ignorance of the law, by permitting a party to profit, or to escape, by his ignorance. One is required at his peril to know the law of his own country.

JURISDICTION OF COURTS.

Justices have jurisdiction in all civil cases on contracts for the recovery of moneys for damages, for injury to real property, or taking, detaining, or injuring personal property; for rent; for all cases to recover damages done to real or personal property, by railroad companies; in actions of replevin; of actions for damages for fraud; in the sale, purchase, or exchange of personal property, when the amount claimed as due is not over $200. They have also jurisdiction in all cases for violation of the ordinances of cities, towns, or villages. A justice of the peace may orally order an officer or a private person, to arrest any one committing, or attempting to commit a criminal offense. He also, upon complaint, can issue his warrant for the arrest of any person accused of having committed a crime, and have him brought before him for examination.

COUNTY COURTS

Have jurisdiction in all matters of probate (except in counties having a population of one hundred thousand or over), settlement of estates of deceased persons, appointment of guardians and conservators, and settlements of their accounts; all matters relating to apprentices; proceedings for the collection of taxes and assesments, and in proceedings of executors, administrators, guardians, and conservators, for the sale of real estate.   In law cases, they have concurrent jurisdiction with Circuit Courts in all cases where justices of the peace now have, or hereafter may have, jurisdiction when the amount claimed shall not exceed $1,000;   and in all criminal offenses, where the punishment is not imprisonment in the penitentiary or death, and in all cases of appeals from justices of peace and police magistrates, except when the county judge is sitting as a justice of the peace.

Circuit Courts have unlimited jurisdiction.

COMMISSIONERS OF HIGHWAYS.

The commissioners of highways in the different towns, have the care and superintendence of highways, and bridges therein. They have the power to lay out, vacate, regulate and repair all roads, build and repair bridges, and divide their respective towns into as many road districts as they shall think convenient.   This is to be done annually, and ten days before the annual town meeting.   In addition to the above, it is their duty to erect and keep in repairs at the forks or crossing-place of the most important roads, post and guide-boards, with plain inscriptions, giving directions and distances to the most noted places to which such roads may lead; also to make provisions to prevent thistles, burdock, cockle-burs, mustard, yellow dock, Indian mallow, and jimson weed from seeding, and to extirpate the same as far as practicable, and to prevent all rank growth of vegetation on the public highways, so far as the same may obstruct public travel; and it is in their discretion to erect watering places for public use, for watering teams at such points as may be deemed advisable.   Every able-bodied male inhabitant, being above the age of twenty-one years, and under fifty, excepting paupers, idiots, lunatics, trustees of schools and school directors, and such others as are exempt by law, are required to labor on highways in their respective road districts, not less than one, nor more than three days in each year. Three days' notice must be given by the overseer, of the time and place he requires such road labor to be done. The labor must be performed in the road district in which the person resides. Any person may commute for such labor by paying the equivalent in money. Any person liable for work on highways, who has been assessed two days or more, and has not commuted, may be required to furnish team, or a cart, wagon or plow, with a pair of horses or oxen and a man to manage them, for which he will be entitled to two days' work. Eight hours is a days' work on the roads and there is a penalty of twenty-five cents an hour against any person or substitute who shall neglect or refuse to perform. Any person remaining idle, or does not work faithfully, or hinders others from doing so, forfeits to the town $2. Every person assessed and duly notified, who has not commuted, and refuses or neglects to appear, shall forfeit to the town for every day's refusal or neglect, the sum of $2; if he was required to furnish a team, carriage, man or implements, and neglects or refuses to comply, he is liable to the following fines: 1st, For wholly failing to comply, $4 each day; 2d, For omitting to furnish a man to manage team, $2 each day; 3d, For omitting to furnish a pair of horses or oxen, $1.50 each day; 4th, For omitting to furnish a wagon, cart or plow, 75 cents each day. The commissioners estimate and assess the highway labor and road tax. The road tax on real and personal property can not exceed forty cents on each hundred dollars' worth. The labor or road tax in villages, towns or cities, is paid over to the corporate authorities of such, for the improvement of streets, roads and bridges within their limits.

The legal voters of townships, in counties under township organization may, by a majority vote, at their annual town meeting, order that the road tax may be collected in money only.

Overseers.—Their duties are to repair and keep in order the highways in their districts; to warn persons to work out their road tax at such time and place as they think proper; to collect fines and commutation money, and execute all lawful orders of the commissioners of highways; also make list, within sixteen days after their election, of the names of all inhabitants in his road district, liable to work on highways. For refusal to perform any of his duties he is liable to a fine of $10.

As all township and county officers are familiar with their duties, it is here intended only to give the points of law with which the public should be familiar. The manner of laying out, altering, or vacating roads, etc., will not be here stated, as it would require more space than can be spared in a work like this. It is sufficient to state that the first step is by petition, addressed to the commissioners, setting out what is prayed for, giving the names of the owners of the lands, if known (if not known, so state), over which the road is to pass, giving the general course, its place of beginning, and where it terminates. It requires not less than twelve freeholders residing within three miles of the road, who shall sign the petition. Public roads must not be less than fifty, nor more than sixty feet wide. Roads not exceeding two miles in length, if petitioned for, may be laid out not less than forty feet wide. Private roads for private and public use may be laid out three rods wide, on petition of the person directly interested; the damage occasioned thereby shall be paid by the premises benefited thereby, and before the road is opened. If not opened in two years, the order shall be considered recinded. Commissioners in their discretion may permit persons who live on or have private roads, to work out their road tax thereon. Public roads must be opened in five years from date of filing order of location, or be deemed vacated.

FENCES.

The town assessor and commissioners of highways shall be fence viewers in their respective towns in counties under township organization. In other counties, the county board appoints three in each precinct, annually.

A lawful fence is four and one-half feet high and in good repair, consisting of rails, timbers, boards, stones, hedges, or any other material the fence viewers may deem sufficient. The electors at any annual town meeting may determine what shall constitute a legal fence in the town.

Division fences shall be made and maintained in just proportion by the adjoining owners, except where the owner shall choose to let his land lie open; but after a division fence has been built by mutual agreement or otherwise, it shall not be lawful for either party to remove his part of said fence, so long as he may crop or use such lands for farm purposes, or without giving the other party one year's notice in writing, of his intention to move his portion of the fence. Adjoining owners should endeavor, if possible, mutually to agree as to the proportion that each shall maintain of the division fence between their adjoining lands; and the agreement should be reduced to writing, each party taking a copy. When any person shall enclose his land upon the enclosure of another, he shall refund the owner of the adjoining lands a just proportion of the value at that time of such fence. The value of such fence, and the proportion thereof to be paid by such person, and the proportion of the division fence to be made and maintained by him, in case of his inclosing his land, shall be determined by two fence viewers of the town. Such fence viewers have power to settle all disputes between owners as to fences built or to be built, as well as concerning repairs to be made. Each party chooses one of the viewers, but if the other party neglects, after eight days' notice in writing, to make his choice, then the other party may select both. It is sufficient to notify the tenant, or party in possession, when the owner is not a resident of the town in which such fences are situated. The two fence viewers chosen, after viewing the premises, shall hear the statements of the parties. In case they can't agree, they shall select another fence viewer to act with them, and the decision of any two of them shall be final. The decision must be reduced to writing, and should plainly set out a description of the fence and all matters settled by them, and must be filed in the office of the town clerk.

If any person who is liable to contribute to the erection or reparation of a division fence, shall neglect or refuse to make or repair his proportion of such fence, the party injured, after giving sixty days' notice, in writing, that a new fence should be erected, or ten days' notice, in writing, that the repair of such fence is necessary, may make or repair the same at the expense of the party so neglecting or refusing, to be recovered from him with costs of suit; and the party so neglecting or refusing, after notice in writing, shall be liable to the party injured for all damages which shall thereby accrue, to be determined by any two fence viewers. When a person shall conclude to remove his part of the division fence and let his land lie open, and having given the year's notice required, the adjoining owner may cause the value of said fence to be ascertained by fence viewers as before provided; and on payment or tender of the amount of such valuation to the owner, it shall prevent the removal.

A party removing a division fence without notice is liable for the damages accruing thereby.

Where a fence has been built on the land of another through mistake, the owner may enter upon such premises and remove his fence and material within six months after the division line has been ascertained. Where the material to build such a fence has been taken from the land on which it was built, then before it can be removed, the person claiming must first pay for such material, to the owner of the land from which it was taken; nor shall such a fence be removed at a time when the removal will throw open or expose the crops of the other party; a reasonable time must be given beyond the six months to remove crops.

The compensation of fence viewers is one dollar and fifty cents a day each, to be paid in the first instance by the party calling them; but in the end all expenses, including amount charged by the fence viewers, must be paid equally by the parties, except in cases where a party neglects or refuses to make or maintain a just proportion of a division fence, when the party in default shall pay them.

DRAINAGE.

Whenever one or more owners or occupants of land desire to construct a drain or ditch, through another man's land, the right can be had only under legislative authority, or is granted or exists by prescription or by consent of the owner.

Dripping water from one house upon another can be allowed only where the owner has acquired the right by grant or prescription; and no one has a right to construct his house so as to let the water drip over his neighbor's land.

TRESPASS OF STOCK.

Where stock of any kind breaks into any person's inclosure, the fence being good and sufficient, the owner is liable for the damage done; but where the damage is done by stock running at large, contrary to law, the owner is liable where there is not such a fence. Where stock is found trespassing on the inclosure of another as aforesaid, the owner or occupier of the premises may take possession of such stock and keep the same until damages, with reasonable charges for keeping and feeding, and all costs of suit, are paid. Any person taking or rescuing such stock so held, without his consent, shall be liable to a fine of not less than three nor more than five dollars for each animal rescued, to be recovered by suit before a justice of the peace, for the use of the school fund. Within twenty-four hours after taking such animal into his possession, the person taking it up must give notice of the fact to the owner, if known; or if unknown, notice must be posted in some public place near the premises.

ESTRAYS.

Stray animals are those whose owner is unknown, any beasts, not wild, found on one's premises, and not owned by the occupant. Any animals found straying at any time during the year, in counties where such animals are not allowed to run at large, or between the last day of October and the 15th day of April in other counties, the owner being unknown, may be taken up as estrays. A party who wishes to detain property as an estray, must show an exact compliance with the law. In order to vest the property of the stray in him, such acts must appear in detail on the record.

No person not a householder in the county where the estray is found can lawfully take up an estray, and then only upon or about his farm or place of residence. Estrays should not be used before advertised, except animals giving milk, which may be milked for their benefit. Notices must be posted up within five days in three, of the most public places in the town or precinct in which the estray was found, giving the residence of the taker-up, and a particular description of the estray, its age, color, and marks natural and artificial, and stating before what justice of the peace in such town or precinct, and at what time, not less than ten nor more than fifteen days from the time of posting such notices, he will apply to have the estray apprised. If the owner of an estray shall not have appeared and proved ownership and taken the same away, first paying the taker-up his reasonable charges for taking up, keeping, and advertising the same, the taker-up shall appear before the justice mentioned in above notice, and make an affidavit as required by law. All subsequent proceedings are before the justice who is familiar therewith; therefore we omit them here.

Any person taking up an estray at any other place than about or upon his farm or residence, or without complying with the law, shall forfeit and pay a fine of ten dollars with costs. Ordinary diligence is required in taking care of estrays, but in case they die or get away, the taker-up is not liable for the same.

If a man finds estrays in his field he is not bound to retain them for the owner, but may drive them off into the highway without being liable to an action. But a person who chases a horse out of his field with a large fierce dog, commits an unlawful act, and is liable for any injury which the act occasions. A person who takes an estray to keep for the owner, but does not pursue the course prescribed by statute, is not liable to an action unless he uses the same or refuses to deliver it on demand. Riding a horse to discover the owner is not "use."

HORSES

Are animals of a domestic nature. Under the age of four years they are called colts. A borrower of a horse is liable for negligence, misuse, or gross want of skill in use. The lender is liable in case the animal lent is unfit or dangerous, as he thus may occasion injury. The animal should be used only for the purpose and to the extent stipulated, and not by a servant.

If he dies from disease, or is killed by inevitable accident, the borrower is not liable. Defects which are manifest, open and plain to an ordinary observer, and those also which are known to the buyer, are not usually covered by a general warranty. The former requires no skill to discover them, and the latter may be objected to or acquiesced in at the time of the purchase. In the case of *latent* defects existing in such a condition that they could not be detected by the buyer, and are known to the seller, who fails to disclose them to the buyer, the latter practices a constructive fraud, unless the animal is sold "with all faults." By consenting to purchase the horse "with all faults," the purchaser takes upon himself the risk of latent or secret defects, and calculates the price accordingly. But even this kind of a purchase would be voidable if the seller had purposely, and to deceive the purchaser, covered, filled up, patched, plastered, or otherwise practiced fraud to conceal any defects, and he would be liable.

Hiring out a horse and carriage to perform a particular journey, carries with it the warranty of the person letting the horse and carriage, that each of them is fit and competent for such journey; but, if a horse is hired for one purpose, and is used for another and is injured, the hirer is liable for the damage sustained. The hirer is in all cases answerable for ordinary neglect. If he uses the hired horse as a prudent man would his own, he is not liable for any damage which the horse may receive. If, however, he keeps the hired horse after a stipulated time, or uses it differently from his agreement, he is in any event liable. If the hirer sells the horse, the owner may recover its value of the purchaser, though the purchaser had in good faith given the hirer full value for it, as the hirer could give no better title than he had himself.

Mischievous animals render their owners liable when known to them to be so, and they are responsible for the damage they may do when they permit them to go at large. Any person may justify the killing of ferocious animals.

MARKS AND BRANDS.

Owners of cattle, horses, hogs, sheep or goats, may have one ear-mark and one brand, which shall be different from his neighbors', and may be recorded by the county clerk of the county in which such property is kept. The fee for such record is fifteen cents. The record of such shall be open to examination free of charge. In cases of disputes as to marks or brands, such record is *prima-facie* evidence. Owners of cattle, horses, hogs, sheep or goats, that may have been branded by former owners, may be rebranded in presence of one or more of his neighbors, who shall certify to the facts of the marking or branding being done, when done, and in what brand or mark they were re-branded or re-marked, which certificate may also be recorded as before stated.

ARTICLES OF AGREEMENT.

An agreement is virtually a contract by which a certain person (or persons) agrees or contracts to perform certain duties within a specified time. Good business men always reduce an agreement to writing, which nearly always saves misunderstandings and long and expensive lawsuits. No particular form is necessary, but the facts must be clearly and explicitly stated; and there must be a reasonable consideration, else the agreement is void.

Unless it is expressly stipulated that the agreement is binding for a longer time, the contract expires at the end of one year. Every agreement should state most distinctly the time within which its conditions are to be complied with. A discovery of fraud, or mis-representation by one party to the agreement, or changing of the date, renders the contract void. Each party should retain a copy of the agreement.

GENERAL FORM OF AGREEMENT.

This Agreement, made the third day of November, 1878, between Damon Clarke of Macomb, county of McDonough, State of Illinois, of the first part, and William Hays, of the same place, of the second part.

Witnesseth, That the said Damon Clarke, in consideration of the agreement of the party of the second part, hereinafter contained, contracts, and agrees to, and with the said William Hays, that he will deliver in good and marketable condition, at the city of Galesburg, Ill., during the month of December of this year, nine hundred bushels of corn, in the following lots, and at the following specified times, namely: one hundred bushels by the fifth of December, three hundred bushels by the fifteenth of December, and the balance by the thirtieth of December.

And the said William Hays in consideration of the prompt fulfillment of this contract on the part of the party of the second part, contracts to, and agrees with the said Damon Clarke, to pay for said corn fifty cents per bushel as soon as delivered.

In case of failure of agreement by either of the parties hereto, it is hereby stipulated and agreed that the party so failing shall pay to the other, one hundred dollars, as fixed and settled damages.

In witness whereof we have hereunto set our hands the day and year first above written:　　　　　　　　　Damon Clarke,
William Hays.

NOTES.

A note is legal, worded in the simplest way, so that the amount and time of payment are mentioned. The following is a good form:

$100　　　　　　　　　　　Chicago, Ill., May 1, 1879.

Thirty days after date I promise to pay F. M. Chapman, or order, one hundred dollars, for value received.

S. T. Lewis.

To make a note payable in anything else than money, insert the facts instead of the sum of money alone; unless paid when due, it is payable in money. To hold an indorser of a note, due diligence must be used by suit in collecting of the maker, unless suit would have been unavailing. Notes payable to person named or to order, in order to absolutely transfer title, must be indorsed by the payer. Notes payable to bearer may be transferred by delivery, and when so payable, every indorser thereon is held as a guarantor of payment unless otherwise expressed.

The limit of time in which action may be brought on a note is 10 years.

If the note is payable to a person or order, or to a person or bearer, to a person or his assigns, or to a cashier of an incorporated company, such notes are negotiable.

When transferring a note, the indorser frees himself from responsibility, so far as the payment is concerned, by writing on the back, above his signature, *without recourse to me in any event.*

A note is void when founded upon fraud. Thus a note obtained from a person when intoxicated, or obtained for any reason which is illegal, cannot be collected. A note given on Sunday is also void.

No defense can be made against negotiable paper purchased before maturity for good consideration in the usual course of business, without knowledge of facts impeaching its validity, except fraud was used in obtaining the same. Thus if A gives his note to B for $150, receives in consideration a shawl and five pieces of cloth. The former was represented to be worth $75, and the cloth the best imported English goods. When, in fact, the shawl was only worth $8, and suits made of the cloth wore out in less than six weeks, long before the note was due. B, however, had sold the note to C, who did not know the circumstances, and before it was due—A would be obliged to pay it.

JUDGMENT NOTE.

For value received I promise to pay Ewing Summers, of Galesburg, or order, two hundred dollars, with interest, on the first day of January next. And, further, I do hereby empower any attorney of any court of record in Illinois, or elsewhere, to appear for me, and after a declaration filed therefor, to confess a judgment against me in the above sum, as of last, next, or any subsequent term, with cost of suit, release of error, etc., with stay of execution until said first day of January.

Witness my hand and seal at Galesburg, Ill., this sixth day of March, in the year one thousand eight hundred and seventy-nine.

[SEAL]   JOHN JONES.

INTEREST.

Interest is the compensation which is paid by the borrower of money to the lender for its use. When the debtor expressly undertakes to pay interest, he is bound to pay it; but if a party has accepted the principal, he cannot recover interest in a separate action. During the course of dealings between parties, a promise to pay is implied, and the debtor is bound to pay. So also on an account stated, whenever the debtor knows precisely what he is to pay, and when he is to pay it, after a demand of payment; but interest is not due on a running account, even when the items are all on one side, unless otherwise agreed upon. Where the terms of a promissory note are that it shall be paid by installments, and on the failure of any installment the whole is to become due, interest on the whole becomes payable from the first default. Where, by the term of a bond or promissory note, interest is to be paid annually, and the principal at a distant day, the interest may be recovered before the principal is due.

Interest is collectible in the following cases: For goods sold and delivered after the stipulated term of credit has expired; if there be no credit, then from the time of sale; on judgment debts, from the rendition of judgment; on money obtained by fraud, or where it has been wrongfully detained (for whoever receives money not his own, and detains it from the owner unlawfully, must pay interest therefor: hence a public officer retaining money wrongfully is liable for the interest); on money paid by mistake, or recovered on a void execution; on money lent or laid out for another's use; and rent, from the time that it is due.

When the rate of interest is specified in any contract, that rate continues until full payment is made. A debt barred by the statute of limitations and revived by an acknowledgment bears interest for the whole time.

Computing Interest.—In casting interest on notes, bonds, etc., upon which partial payments have been made, every payment is to be first applied to discharge the interest; but the interest is never allowed to form a part of the principal, so as to carry interest. When a partial payment is made before the debt is due, it cannot be apportioned part to the debt and part to the interest, but at the end interest shall be charged on the whole sum, and the obligor shall receive credit for the interest on the amount paid until the interest becomes due.

The legal rate of interest is six per cent. Parties may agree in writing on a rate not exceeding eight per cent. If a rate of interest greater than eight per cent. is contracted for, the penalty is a forfeiture of the entire interest, and only the principal can be recovered.

In computing interest or discount on negotiable instruments, a month shall be considered a calendar month or twelfth of a year, and for less than a month, a day shall be figured a thirtieth part of a month. Notes bear interest only when so expressed; but after due they draw the legal interest, six per cent., even if not stated.

Notes payable on demand or at sight draw no interest until after presentation or demand of the same has been made, unless they provide for interest from date on their face. If "with interest" is included in the note, it draws the legal rate from the time it is made. If the note is to draw a special rate of interest, higher than the legal, but not higher than the law allows, the rate must be specified.

WILLS.

The legal declaration of a person's mind, determining the manner in which he would have his property or estate disposed of after his death, is termed a will. No exact form of words is necessary in order to make a will good at law, though much care should be exercised to state the provisions of the will so plainly that its language may not be misunderstood.

Every male person of the age of twenty-one years, and every female of the age of eighteen years, of sound mind, can make a valid will. It must be in writing, signed by the testator, or by some one in his or her presence, and by his or her direction, and attested by two or more credible witnesses. Care should be taken that the witnesses are not interested in the will.

The person making the will may appoint his or her executors; but no person can serve as such executor if he or she be an alien at the time of proving the will, if he be under twenty-one years of age, a convict, a drunkard, a lunatic, or an imbecile.

Persons knowing themselves to have been appointed executors, must, within thirty days after the death of deceased, cause the will to be proved and recorded in the proper county, or present it and refuse to accept. In case of failure to do so, they are liable to forfeit the sum of twenty dollars per month. Inventory to be made by executor or administrator within three months from date of letters testamentary or administration.

The person making a will is termed the "testator" (if a female, the "testatrix").

A will is of no force and effect until the death of the testator, and can be cancelled or modified at any date by the maker. The last will made annuls the force of all preceding wills.

A will made by an unmarried woman is legally revoked by marriage; but she can take such legal steps in the settlement of her property before marriage as will empower her to dispose of the same as she may choose after marriage. No husband can make a will that will deprive the wife of her right of dower in the property; but the husband can will the wife a certain amount in lieu of her dower, stating it to be in lieu thereof. Such bequest, however, will not exclude her from her dower, provided she prefers it to the bequest made in the will. Unless the husband states distinctly that the bequest is in lieu of dower, she is entitled to both.

In case a married woman possesses property and dies without a will, her husband is entitled to administer upon such property in preference to any one else, provided he be of sound mind.

Notice requiring all claims to be presented against the estate shall be given by the administrator within six months after being qualified. Any person having a claim and not presenting it at the time fixed by said notice, is required to have summons issued notifying the executor of having filed his claim in court. Claims should be filed within two years from the time administration is granted on an estate, as after that time they are forever barred, unless other estate be found that was not inventoried. Married women, infants, persons insane, imprisoned, or without the United States, in the employment of the United States, or of this State, have two years after their disabilities are removed to file claims. Claims are classified and paid out of the estate in the following manner:

1st. Funeral expenses.

2d. The widow's award, if there is a widow; or children, if there are children and no widow.

3d. Expenses attending the last illness, not including the physician's bill.

4th. Debts due the common school or township fund.

5th. All expenses of proving the will and taking out letters testamentary or of administration, and settlement of the estate, and the physician's bill in the last illness of the deceased.

6th. Where the deceased has received money in trust for any purpose, his executor or administrator shall pay out of his estate the amount received and not accounted for.

7th. All other debts and demands of whatsoever kind, without regard to quality or dignity, which shall be exhibited to the court within two years from the granting of letters.

Award to the widow and children, exclusive of debts and legacies or bequests, except funeral expenses:

1st. The family pictures and wearing apparel, jewels and ornaments of herself and minor children.

2d. School books and the family library to the value of $100.

3d. One sewing-machine.

4th. Necessary beds, bedsteads and bedding for herself and family.

5th. The stoves and pipe used in the family, with the necessary cooking utensils; or, in case they have none, $50 in money.

6th. Household and kitchen furniture to the value of $100.

7th. One milch cow and calf for every four members of her family.

8th. Two sheep for each member of her family, and the fleeces taken from the same, and one horse, saddle and bridle.

9th. Provisions for herself and family for one year.

10th. Food for the stock above specified for six months.

11th. Fuel for herself and family for three months.

12th. One hundred dollars' worth of other property suited to her condition in life, to be selected by the widow.

The widow, if she elects, may have in lieu of the said award, the same personal property or money in place thereof as is or may be exempt from execution or attachment against the head of a family.

GENERAL FORM OF WILL FOR REAL AND PERSONAL PROPERTY.

I, Samuel T. Lewis, of the city of Chicago, county of Cook, State of Illinois, being aware of the uncertainty of life, and in failing health, but of sound mind and memory, do make and declare this to be my last will and testament, in manner following, to-wit:

First. I give, devise and bequeath to my oldest son, Franklin M. Lewis, the sum of Four Thousand dollars of bank stock, now in the First National Bank, Chicago, Illinois, and the farm owned by myself, in Ontario township, Knox county, Illinois, consisting of one hundred and sixty acres, with all the houses, tenements, and improvements thereunto belonging; to have and to hold unto my said son, his heirs and assigns, forever.

Second. I give, devise and bequeath to each of my daughters, Lida Louan Lewis, and Fannie Antionette Lewis, each two thousand dollars in bank stock, in the First National Bank of Chicago, Illinois, and also each one quarter section of land, owned by myself, situated in the town of Delavan, Tazewell county, Illinois, and recorded in my name in the Recorder's office of said county. The north one hundred and sixty acres of said half section is devised to my elder daughter Lida Louan.

Third. I give, devise and bequeath to my son, Fred Davis Lewis, five shares of railroad stock, in the C., B. & Q. Railroad, and my own one hundred and sixty acres of land and saw-mill thereon, situated in Astoria, Illinois, with all the improvements and appurtenances thereunto belonging, which said real estate is recorded in my name, in the county where situated.

Fourth. I give to my wife, Tryphena Lewis, all my household furniture, goods, chattels, and personal property, about my house, not hitherto disposed of, including ten thousand dollars in bank stock, in the First National Bank of Chicago, Illinois, fifteen shares in the Chicago, Rock Island & Pacific Railroad, and the free and unrestricted use, possession and benefits of the home farm, so long as she may live, in lieu of dower, to which she is entitled by law; said farm being my present place of residence.

Fifth. I bequeath to my invalid father, Samuel T. Lewis, Sr., the income from the rents of my store building, at Canton, Illinois, during the term of his natural life. Said building and land therewith revert to my said sons and daughters in equal proportions, upon the demise of my said father.

Sixth. It is also my will and desire, that at the death of my wife, Tryphena Lewis, or at any time she may arrange to relinquish her life interest in the above mentioned homestead, the same may revert to my above named children, or to the lawful heirs of each.

And, Lastly. I appoint as executors of this, my last will and testament, my wife Tryphena Lewis, and my eldest son, Franklin M. Lewis.

I further direct that my debts and necessary funeral expenses shall be paid from moneys now on deposit in the First National Bank, Pekin, Illinois, the residue of such moneys to revert to my wife, Tryphena Lewis, for her use forever.

In witness thereof, I, Samuel T. Lewis, to this, my last will and testament, have hereunto set my hand and seal, this third day of March, eighteen hundred and seventy.

[L. S.]   SAMUEL T. LEWIS.

Signed, sealed and delivered by Samuel T. Lewis, as and for his last will and testament, in the presence of us, who, at his request, and in his presence, and in the presence of each other, have subscribed our names hereunto as witnesses thereof.

Fred D. Selleck, Chicago, Illinois.
Erastus Child, Oneida, Illinois.

CODICIL.

Whereas, I, Samuel T. Lewis, did, on the third day of March, one thousand eight hundred and seventy, make my last will and testament, I do now, by this writing, add this codicil to my said will, to be taken as a part thereof.

Whereas, by the dispensation of Providence, my daughter Lida Louan, has deceased, November fifth, eighteen hundred and seventy-four, and, whereas, a son has been born to me, which son is now christened Charles Burchard Lewis, I give and bequeath unto him my gold watch, and all right, interest and title in lands and bank stock and chattels bequeathed to my deceased daughter Lida Louan, in the body of this will

In witness thereof, I hereunto set my hand and seal, this fifth day of March, eighteen hundred and seventy-nine.

[L. S.]   SAMUEL T. LEWIS.

Signed, sealed, published and declared to us by the testator, Samuel T. Lewis, as and for a codicil, to be annexed to his last will and testament. And we, at his request, and in his presence, and in the presence of each other, have subscribed our names as witnesses thereto, at the date hereof.

Erastus Child, Oneida, Ill.
E. C. Johnson, Chicago, Ill.

DESCENT.

When no will is made, the property of a deceased person is distributed as follows:

First. To his or her children and their descendants, in equal parts; the descendants of the deceased child or grand child taking the share of their deceased parents, in equal parts among them.

Second. Where there is no child, no descendant of such child, and no widow or surviving husband, then to the parents, brothers and sisters of the deceased, and their descendants, in equal parts, the surviving parent, if either be dead, taking a double portion; and if there is no parent living, then to the brothers and sisters of the intestate and their descendants.

Third. When there is a widow or surviving husband, and no child or children, or descendants of the same, then one-half of the real estate and the whole of the personal estate shall descend to such widow or surviving husband, absolutely, and the other half of the real estate shall descend as in other cases where there is no child or children, or descendants of the same.

Fourth. When there is a widow or surviving husband, and also a child or children, or descendants of the latter, then one-third of all personal estate to the widow or surviving husband, absolutely.

Fifth.   If there be no child, parent, brother or sister, or descendants of either of them, and no widow or surviving husband, then in equal parts to the next of kin to the intestate in equal degree.   Collaterals shall not be represented except with the descendants of brother and sister of the intestate, and there shall be no distinction between kindred of the whole and the half-blood.

Sixth.   If any intestate leaves a widow or surviving husband and no kindred, then to such widow or surviving husband; and if there is no such widow or surviving husband, it shall escheat to and invest in the county where the same or the greater portion thereof is situated.

DEEDS.

A deed is a sealed instrument in writing, conveying lands and appurtenances thereon from one person to another, and special care should be taken to have them signed, sealed, delivered and properly acknowledged, with the proper seal attached.   Witnesses are not necessary.   The law in this State provides that an acknowledgment must be made before certain persons authorized to take the same.   These officers are: Master in Chancery, Notary Public, Circuit or County Clerk, Justice of the Peace. United States Commissioner, or any Court of Record having a seal, or any Judge, Justice or Clerk of any such court.   The instrument shall be attested by the official seal of the officer taking the acknowledgment, and when taken by a Justice of the Peace residing out of the county where the real estate to be conveyed lies, there shall be added a certificate of the County Clerk under his seal of office, that he was a Justice of the Peace in the county at the time of taking the same.   A deed is good without such certificate attached, but cannot be used in evidence unless such a certificate is produced or other competent evidence introduced.   Acknowledgments made out of the State must either be executed according to the laws of this State, or there should be attached a certificate that is in conformity with the laws of the State or country where executed.   Where this is not done the same may be proved by any other legal way. Acknowledgments where the Homestead rights are to be waived must state as follows: " Including the release and waiver of the right of homestead."

To render a deed valid, there must be a sufficient consideration. To enable a person to legally convey property to another, the following requisites are necessary: 1st, he or she must be of age; 2d, must be of *sane mind;* and, 3d, he or she must be the rightful owner of the property.

Any alterations or interlineations in the deed should be noted at the bottom of the instrument, and properly witnessed. After the acknowledgment of a deed, the parties have no right to make the slightest alterations. An alteration after the acknowledgment in favor of the grantee vitiates the deed. The maker of a deed is called the "grantor;" the person or party to whom the deed is delivered, the "grantee." The wife of the grantor must ackowledge the deed, or else, after the death of her husband, she will be entitled to one-third interest in the property, as dower, during her life. Her acknowledgment of the deed must be of her own free will and accord.

By a general warranty deed the grantor engages to secure the grantee in any right or possession to the property conveyed against all persons whatsoever. A quit-claim deed releases what interest the grantor may have in the land, but does not warrant and defend against others. We do not give form for a deed, as printed forms are used by all. Deeds should be recorded without delay.

MORTGAGES AND TRUST DEEDS

Are conditional conveyances of estates or property by way of pledge for the security of debt, and to become void on payment of it. Special care should be taken to have them signed, sealed, delivered, and properly acknowledged, with the proper seal attached. All kinds of property, real or personal, which are capable of an absolute sale, may be the subject of a mortgage.

Mortgages of personal property need not be under seal. In the absence of stipulation to the contrary, the mortgagee of personal property has the legal title thereto, and the right of possession, and he may have an action against any one taking them from the mortgagor. And although the mortgage contains no express stipulation that the mortgagor shall remain in possession until default of payment, and with a power to sell for the mortgagee's debt, the mortgagee may nevertheless sustain trover against an officer attaching the goods as the property of the mortgagor.

A mortgage must be in writing when it is intended to convey the legal title. It must be in one single deed which contains the whole contract.

Redemption must be made within one year from the sale. Where, however, the mortgagee takes the property for an absolute discharge of the debt, then the equity or right of redemption is barred. *Satisfaction*, or release of a mortgage, may be made on the margin of the record, or by an instrument duly acknowledged. The wife need not join in this release.

TRUST DEEDS.

Trust deeds are taken generally in preference to mortgages, especially by non-residents, for in case of foreclosure under the power of sale there can be no redemption. Advertisement, sale, and deed is made by the trustee.

Mortgages of personal property, or chattel mortgages, can be given for a period of only two years, and cannot be renewed or extended. Acknowledgment may be had before a Justice of the Peace of the town or district in which the mortgagor resides. If the mortgagor is a non-resident, then before any officer authorized by law to take acknowledgments. Foreclosures may be effected upon default, and possession, and sale of the property taken and made; any delay will invalidate the mortgagee's lien.

LIENS.

Any person who shall by contract, expressed or implied, or partly both, with the owner of any lot or tract of land, furnish labor or material, or services as an architect or superintendent, in building, altering, repairing, or ornamenting any house, or other building or appurtenance thereto on such lot, or upon any street or alley, and connected with such improvements, shall have a lien upon the whole of such lot or tract of land, and upon such house or building and appurtenances for the amount due him for labor, material or services. If the contract is expressed, and the time for the completion of the work is beyond three years from the commencement thereof; or, if the time of payment is beyond one year from the time stipulated for the completion of the work, then no lien exists. If the contract is implied, then no lien exists, unless the work be done, or material furnished, within one year from the commencement of the work or delivery of the material. As between different creditors having liens, no preference is given to the one whose contract was made first; but each shares pro rata. Incumbrances existing upon the lot or tract of the land at the time the contract is made do not operate on the improvements, and are only preferred to the extent of the value of the land at the time of making the contract. The above lien cannot be enforced unless suit is commenced within six months after the last payment for labor or materials shall have become due and payable. Sub-contractors, mechanics, workmen, and other persons furnishing any material, or performing any labor for a contractor, as above specified, have a lien to the extent of the amount due the contractor at the time the following notice was served upon the owner of the land who made the contract:

To ————: You are hereby notified that I have been employed by ———— [here state whether to labor or to furnish material, and substantially the nature of the demand] upon your [here state in general terms description and situation of building], and that I shall hold the [building, or as the case may be], and your interest in the ground liable for the amount that may [is or may become] due me on account thereof.   [Signature] ————.
Dated, ————.

If there is a contract in writing between contractor and sub-contractor, a copy of it should be served with the above notice, and such notice must be served within forty days from the completion of such sub-contract, if there is one; if not, then from the time payment should have been made to the person performing the labor or furnishing the material. If the owner is not a resident of the county, or cannot be found therein, then the above notice must be filed with the Clerk of the Circuit Court, with his fee, fifty cents, and a copy of such notice must be published in a newspaper published in the county for four successive weeks.

When the owner or agent is notified as above he can retain any money due the contractor sufficient to pay such claim; if more than one claim, and not enough to pay all, they are to be paid pro rata.

The owner has a right to demand in writing a statement of the contractor, of what he owes for labor, etc., from time to time as the work progresses.

The liens referred to cover any and all estates, whether in fee for life, for years, or any other interest which the owner may have.

To enforce the liens of sub-contractors, suit must be commenced within three months from the time of the performance of the sub-contract, or during the work or furnishing materials.

Hotel, inn and boarding-house keepers have a lien upon the baggage and other valuables of their guests or boarders brought into such hotel, inn, or boarding-house, by their guests or boarders for the proper charges due from such guests or boarders for their accommodation, board and lodging, and such *extras* as are furnished at their request.

Stable-keepers and other persons have a lien upon the horses, carriages and harness kept by them for the proper charges due for the keeping thereof, and expenses bestowed thereon at the request of the owner, or the person having the possession of the same.

Agisters (persons who take care of cattle belonging to others) and persons keeping, yarding, feeding, or pasturing domestic animals shall have a lien upon the animals agistered, kept, yarded or fed for the proper charges due for such service.

All persons who may furnish any railroad corporation in this State with fuel, ties, material, supplies, or any other article or thing necessary for the construction, maintenance, operation or repair of its road by contract, or may perform work or labor for the same, are entitled to be paid as part of the current expenses of the road, and have a lien upon all its property. Sub-contractors or laborers have also a lien. The conditions and limitations, both as to contractors and to sub-contractors, are about the same as herein stated, as to general liens.

BILL OF SALE.

A bill of sale is a written agreement to another party for a consideration to convey his right and interest in the personal property. The purchaser must take actual possession of the property. Juries have power to determine upon the fairness or unfairness of a bill of sale.

COMMON FORM OF BILL OF SALE.

KNOW ALL MEN by this instrument, that I, B. F. Lewis, of Chicago, Illinois, of the first part, for and in consideration of six hundred and fifty dollars, to me paid by Columbus C. Chapman, Astoria, Illinois, of the second part, the receipt whereof is hereby acknowledged, have sold, and by this instrument do convey unto

the said Chapman, party of the second part, his executors, administrators, and assigns, my undivided half of ten acres of corn on
my farm in the town of Deer Creek, Illinois; one pair of horses,
twenty sheep, and five cows, belonging to me, and in my possession
at the farm aforesaid; to have and to hold the same unto the party
of the second part, his executors and assigns, forever. And I do,
for myself and legal representatives, agree with the said party of
the second part, and his legal representatives, to warrant and defend
the sale of the aforementioned property and chattels unto the said
party of the second part, and his legal representatives, against all
and every person whatsoever.

In witness whereof I have hereunto affixed my hand this tenth
day of October, one thousand eight hundred and seventy-nine.

B. F. Lewis.

DAYS OF GRACE.

No check, draft, bill of exchange, promissory note, order, or
negotiable instrument, payable at sight or on demand, or on pre-
sentment, shall be entitled to days of grace. All other bills of
exchange, drafts or notes are entitled to three days of grace. All
the above-mentioned paper falling due on Sunday, New Year's day,
Fourth of July, Christmas, or any day appointed or recommended
by the President of the United States or Governor of the State as
a day of fasting or thanksgiving, shall be deemed as due on the
day previous; and should two or more of these days come together,
then such instrument shall be treated as due on the day previous to
the first of said days.

LIMITATION OF ACTION.

The limit of time in which action may be brought on certain
things is as follows: Open accounts, five years; notes and written
contracts, ten years; judgments, twenty years; partial payments or
new promise in writing, within or after said period, will revive
the debt; absence from the State deducted, and when the cause of
action is barred by the law of another State, it has the same effect
here; assault, slander, libel, replevin, one year; personal injuries,
two years; to recover land or make entry thereon, twenty years; and
sealed and witnessed instruments, as action to foreclose mortgage
or trust deed, within ten years. All persons in possession of land,
and paying taxes for seven consecutive years, with color of title, and
all persons paying taxes for seven consecutive years, with color of
title, on vacant land, shall be held to be the legal owners to the
extent of their paper title.

RECEIPTS.

Receipts should always state when received and what for; and if receipt is in full it should be so stated. We give two forms:

FOR MONEY ON ACCOUNT.

Received, Knoxville, Ill., Nov. 10, 1878, of J. C. Cover, sixty dollars on account. $60.   J. H. FRANKLIN.

FOR MONEY ADVANCED ON A CONTRACT.

$100.   GALESBURG, ILL., June 9, 1868.

Received of Fernando Ross, one hundred dollars, in advance, on contract to build for him a brick house at No. 76 Kellogg street.   SAMUEL J. CHAPMAN.

EXEMPTIONS FROM FORCED SALES.

The following personal property and home worth $1,000,—Lot of ground and buildings thereon, occupied as a residence by the debtor, being a householder and having a family, to the value of $1,000. Exemption continues after the death of the householder for the benefit of the widow and family, some of them occupying the homestead until the youngest shall become twenty-one years of age, and until the death of the widow. There is no exemption from sale for taxes, assessments, debt or liability incurred for the purchase or improvement of said homestead. No release or waiver of exemption is valid unless in writing and subscribed by such householder and wife (if he has one), and acknowledged as conveyances of real estate are required to be acknowledged.

The following articles of personal property owned by the debtor are exempt from execution, writ of attachment, and distress for rent: The necessary wearing apparel, Bibles, school-books and family pictures of every person; and one hundred dollars'worth of other property, to be selected by the debtor, and in addition, when the debtor is the head of a family and resides with the same, three hundred dollars' worth of other property to be selected by the debtor,—provided that such selection and exemption shall not be made by the debtor or allowed to him or her from any money, salary or wages due him or her from any person or persons or corporations whatever. When the head of the family dies, deserts, or does not reside with the same, the family shall be entitled to and receive all the benefit and privilege which are by this act conferred upon the head of a family residing with the same. No personal property is exempt from execution when judgment is obtained for the *wages of laborers or servants*. Wages of a laborer who is the head of a family cannot be garnisheed except for the sum due him in excess of $25.

LANDLORDS AND TENANTS.

The principal obligation on the part of a landlord, which is in fact always to be implied as a necessary condition to his receiving any rent, is, that the tenant shall enjoy the quiet possession of the premises,—which means, substantially, that he shall not be turned out of possession of the whole or any material part of the premises by any one having a title paramount to that of the landlord, or that the landlord shall not himself disturb or render his occupation uncomfortable by the erection of a nuisance on or near the premises, or otherwise oblige him to quit possession. But if he be ousted by a stranger,—that is, by one having no title,—or after the rent has fallen due, or if the molestation proceeds from acts of a third person, the landload is in neither case responsible for it. Another obligation which the law imposes on the landlord, in the absence of any express stipulation in the lease, is the payment of all taxes chargeable upon the property, or any ground rents or interest upon mortgages to which it may be subject. Every landlord is bound to protect his tenant against all paramount claims. And if a tenant is compelled, in order to protect himself in the enjoyment of the land in respect of which his rent is payable, to make payment which ought, as between himself and his landlord, to have been made by the latter, he may call upon the landlord to reimburse him, or he may deduct such payment from the rent due or to become due. But the landlord is under no obligation to make repairs, or to rebuild in case the premises should be burned; nor does he guaranty that they are reasonably fit for the purpose for which they are taken. And it is not in the power of a tenant to make repairs at the expense of his landlord, unless there be a special agreement between them authorizing him to do so; for the tenant takes the premises for better or worse, and cannot involve the landlord in expense for repairs without his consent. Even if the premises have become uninhabitable by fire, and the landlord, having insured them, has recovered the insurance money, the tenant cannot compel him to expend the money so recovered in rebuilding, unless he has expressly engaged to do so; nor can he in such an event protect himself from the payment of rent during the unexpired balance of the term, unless exempted therefrom by statute or the terms of the lease. The uninhabitableness of a house is not a good defense to an action for rent. If the landlord expressly covenanted to repair, the tenant cannot quit and discharge himself of rent because the repairs are not made, unless there is a provision to that effect; and if a landlord is bound by custom or by express agreement to repair, this obligation, and the obligation of the tenant to pay rent, are independent of each other, so that the refusal or neglect of the landlord to repair is no answer to a demand for rent. The tenant is answerable for any neglect to repair highways, fences, or party walls. He is also liable for all injuries produced by the mismanagement of his servants, or by a nuisance kept upon the premises, or by an obstruction of the highways adjacent to them, or the like. One of the principal obligations which the law imposes upon every tenant, independent of any agreement, is to treat the premises in such a manner that no substantial injury shall be done to them, and so that they may revert to the landlord at the end of the term unimpaired by any willful or negligent conduct on his part.

A tenancy from year to year requires sixty days' notice in writing to terminate the same at the end of the year; such notice can be given at any time within four months preceding the last sixty days of the year.

A tenancy by the month, or less than a year, where the tenant holds over without any special agreement, the landlord may terminate the tenancy by thirty days' notice in writing.

When rent is due, the landlord may serve a notice upon the tenant, stating that unless the rent is paid within not less than five days, his lease will be terminated; if the rent is not paid, the landlord may consider the lease ended. When a default is made in any of the terms of the lease, it shall not be necessary to give more than ten days' notice to quit or of the termination of such tenancy; and the same may be terminated on giving such notice to quit, at any time after such default in any of the terms of such lease; which notice may be substantially in the following form:

To ———, You are hereby notified that, in consequence of your default [here insert the character of the default], of the premises now occupied by you, being, etc., [here describe the premises], I have elected to determine your lease, and you are hereby notified to quit and deliver up possession of the same to me within ten days of this date [dated, etc].

The above to be signed by the lessor or his agent, and no other notice or demand of possession or termination of such tenancy is necessary.

Demand may be made or notice served by delivering a written or printed, or partly either, copy thereof to the tenant, or leaving the same with some person above the age of twelve years, residing on or in possession of the premises; and in case no one is in actual possession of said premises, then by posting the same on the premises. When the tenancy is for a certain time, and the term expires by the terms of the lease, the tenant is then bound to surrender possession, and no notice to quit or demand possession is necessary.

DISTRESS FOR RENT.

In all cases of distress for rent, the landlord, by himself, his agent or his attorney, may seize for rent any personal property of his tenant that may be found in the county where the tenant resides. The property of any other person, even if found on the premises, is not liable.

An inventory of the property levied upon, with a statement of the amount of rent claimed, should be at once filed with some Justice of the Peace, if not over $200; and if above that sum, with the Clerk of a Court of Record of competent jurisdiction. Property may be released by a party executing a satisfactory bond for double the amount.

The landlord may distrain for rent any time within six months after the expiration of the term of lease, or when terminated.

In all cases where the premises rented shall be sub-let, or the lease assigned, the landlord shall have the same right to enforce lien against such lessee or assignee, that he has against the tenant to whom the premises were rented.

When a tenant abandons or removes from the premises, or any part thereof, the landlord, or his agent or his attorney may seize upon any grain or crops grown or growing upon the premises, or part thereof so abandoned, whether the rent is due or not. If such grain or other crops, or any part thereof, is not fully grown or matured, the landlord, or his agent or attorney shall cause the same to be properly cultivated, harvested or gathered, and may sell the same, and from the proceeds pay all his labor, expenses and rent. The tenant may, before the sale of such property, redeem the same by tendering the rent and reasonable compensation for the work done, or he may replevy the same.

EXEMPTION.

The same articles of personal property which are by law exempt from execution, except the crops, as above mentioned, are also exempt from distress for rent.

If any tenant is about to, or shall permit, or attempt to sell or remove from the premises, without the consent of his landlord, such portion of the crops raised thereon as will endanger the lien of the landlord upon such crops, for the rent, it shall be lawful for the landlord to distress before rent is due.

CRIMINAL LAW

Is that branch of jurisprudence which treats of criminal offenses. The extreme importance of a knowledge of criminal law is self-evident; for a mistake in point of law, which every person of discretion not only may know, but is bound and presumed to know, is in criminal cases no defense. This law is administered upon the principle that every one must be taken conclusively to know it, without proof that he does know it. This doctrine has been carried so far as to include the case of a foreigner charged with a crime which was no offense in his own country. And further, the criminal law, whether common or statute, is imperative with reference to the conduct of individuals; so that, if a statute forbids or commands a thing to be done, all acts or omissions contrary to the prohibition or command of the statute are offenses at common law, and ordinarily indictable as such. When a statute punishes a crime by its legal designation without enumerating the acts which constitute it, then it is necessary to resort to the common law for a definition of the crime with its distinctions and qualifications. So, if an act is made criminal, but no mode of prosecution is directed or no punishment provided, the common law (in the absence of a statute to the contrary) furnishes its aid, prescribing the mode of prosecution by indictment, and its mode of punishment by fine and inprisonment. So far, therefore, as the rules and principles of common law are applicable to the administration of the criminal law, and have not been altered or modified by legislation or judicial decisions, they have the same force and effect as laws finally enacted.

The following are some of the leading principles of the criminal law:

1. Every man is presumed to be innocent till the contrary is shown; and if there is any reasonable doubt of his guilt, he is entitled to the benefit of the doubt.

2. In general, no person can be brought to trial till a grand jury on examination of the charge has found reason to hold him to trial.

3. The prisoner is entitled to trial by a jury of his peers, who are chosen from the body of the people with a view to impartiality, and whose decision on questions of facts is final.

4. The question of his guilt is to be determined without reference to his general character, previous history, or habits of life.

5. The prisoner cannot be required to criminate himself, nor be compelled even to exculpate himself by giving his own testimony on trial.

6. He cannot be twice put in jeopardy for the same offense.

7. He cannot be punished for an act which was not an offense by the law existing at the time of its commission; nor can a serverer punishment be inflicted than was declared by the law at the time of its commission.

Crimes are sometimes classified according to the degree of punishment incurred by their commission. They are more generally arranged according to the nature of the offense. The following is, perhaps, as complete a classification as the subject admits:

I. *Offenses against the sovereignty of the State*—1, treason; 2 misprision of treason.

II. *Offenses against the lives and persons of individuals*—1, murder; 2, manslaughter; 3, attempt to kill or murder; 4, mayhem; 5, rape; 6, robbery: 7, kidnapping; 8, false imprisonment; 9, abduction; 10, assault and battery.

III. *Offenses against public property*—1, burning or destroying public property; 2, injury to same.

IV. *Offenses against private property*—1, arson; 2, burglary; 3, larceny; 4, obtaining goods under false pretenses; 5, embezzlement; 6, malicious mischief.

V. *Offenses against public justice*—1, perjury; 2, bribery; 3, destroying public records; 4, counterfeiting public seals; 5, jail breach; 6, escape; 7, resistance to officers; 8, obstructing legal process; 9, barratry; 10, maintenance; 11, champerty; 12, contempt of court; 13, oppression; 14, extortion; 15, suppression of evidence; 16, compounding felony; 17, misprision of felony.

VI. *Offenses against the public peace*—1, challenging or accepting a challenge to a duel; 2, unlawful assembly; 3, rows; 4, riot; 5, breach of the peace; 6, libel.

VII. *Offenses against chastity*—1, sodomy; 2, bestiality; 3, adultery; 4, incest; 5, bigamy; 6, seduction; 7, fornication; 8, lascivious carriage; 9, keeping and frequenting houses of ill-fame.

VIII. *Offenses against public policy*—1, false currency; 2, lotteries; 3, gambling; 4, immoral shows; 5, violation of the right of suffrage; 6, destruction of game, fish, etc.; 7, nuisance.

IX. *Offenses against the currency, and public and private securities*—1, forgery; 2, counterfeiting; 3, passing counterfeit money.

X. *Offenses against religion and morality*—1, blasphemy; 2, profanity; 3, Sabbath-breaking; 4, obscenity; 5, cruelty to animals; 6, drunkenness; 7, promoting intemperance.

XI. *Offenses against the public, individuals, or their property*—1, conspiracy.

TAXES.

The owners of real and personal property, on the first day of March of each year, are liable for taxes thereon.

Assessments should be completed before the fourth Monday in June, at which time the Town Board of Review meets to examine assessments, hear objections, and make such changes as ought to be made. The County Board have also power to correct or change assessments.

The tax-books are placed in the hands of the Town Collector on or before the tenth day of December, who retains them until the tenth day of March following, when he is required to return them to the County Treasurer, who then collects all delinquent taxes.

No costs accrue on real estate taxes until advertised, which takes place on the first day of April, when three weeks' notice is required before judgment. Cost of advertising, twenty cents each tract of land, and ten cents each lot.

Judgment is usually obtained at the May term of County Court. Costs six cents each tract of land, and five cents each lot. Sale takes place in June. Costs, in addition to those mentioned, twenty-eight cents each tract of land, and twenty-seven cents each town lot.

Real estate sold for taxes may be redeemed any time before the expiration of two years from the date of sale by payment to the County Clerk of the amount for which it was sold, and twenty-five per cent. thereon if redeemed within six months, fifty per cent. if redeemed between six and twelve months; if between twelve and eighteen months, seventy-five per cent., and if between eighteen months and two years, one hundred per cent.; and, in addition, all subsequent taxes paid by the purchaser, with ten per cent. interest thereon; also, one dollar each tract, if notice is given by the purchaser of the sale, and a fee of twenty-five cents to the Clerk for his certificate.

SUBSCRIPTION.

The selling of books by subscription is so frequently brought into disrepute by agents making representations not authorized by the publishers, that the public are often swindled. That there may be more general knowledge of the relation such agents bear to their principal, and the law governing such cases, we give the following rules, which, if followed, will save a great deal of trouble and perhaps serious loss.

A subscription is the placing of a signature below a written or printed engagement. It is the act by which a person contracts, in writing, to furnish a sum of money for a particular purpose: as, a subscription to a charitable institution, a subscription for a book, and the like. In the case of a book, the consideration is concurrent that the publisher shall publish the book named, and deliver the same, for which the subscriber is to pay the price named. The prospectus and sample should be carefully examined before subscribing, as they are the basis and consideration of the promise to pay, and not the too often exaggerated statements of the agent, who is merely employed to solicit subscriptions, for which he usually receives a commission for each subscriber, and has no authority to change or alter the conditions upon which the subscriptions are authorized to be made by the publishers. Should the agent assume to agree to make the subscription conditional, or modify or change the agreement of the publisher, as set out by the prospectus and sample, in order to bind the publishers, the subscriber should see that such condition or change is stated over, or in connection with his signature, so the publishers may have notice of the same.

When several persons promise to contribute to a common object, desired by all, the promise of each may be a good consideration for the promise of others. In general subscriptions on certain conditions in favor of the party subscribing, are binding when the acts stipulated are performed. Subscription is in the nature of a contract of mutual promises. All persons should remember that the law as to written contracts is, that they can *not be altered*, *varied*, or *rescinded* verbally, but if done at all, must be done in writing. It is therefore important that all persons contemplating subscribing should distinctly understand that all talk before or after the subscription is made is not admissible as evidence, and is no part of the contract. Persons before signing their names to any subscription book, or any written instrument, should carefully examine what it is; if they cannot read, they should call on some one disinterested who can.

Persons who solicit subscriptions are known to the trade as canvassers. They are agents appointed to do a particular business in a prescribed mode, and have no authority to do it in any other way to the prejudice of their principal, nor can they bind their principal in any other matter. They can not collect money, or agree that payment may be made in anything else than money. They cannot extend the time of payment beyond the time of delivery, nor bind their principal for payment of expenses incurred in their business.

Where you pay money to an agent you should satisfy yourself of his authority to collect money for his employer.

CONTRACT FOR PERSONAL SERVICES.

When a contract is entire and has been only partially fulfilled, the party in fault may nevertheless recover from the other party for the actual benefit received and retained by the other party, less the damages sustained by such other party by reason of the partial non-fulfillment of the contract. This may be done in all cases where the other party has received benefit from the partial fulfillment of the contract, whether he has so received the same from choice or from the necessities of the case. Where D hired B to work for him for seven months at $15 per month, and B worked for D only fifty-nine days, and then quit without any reasonable excuse therefor, it was held that B might nevertheless recover from D for what the work was reasonably worth, less any damage that D may have sustained by reason of the partial non-fulfillment of the contract.

NEWSPAPER LIBEL.

Allowing the most liberal rule as to the liability of persons in public employment to criticism for their conduct in which the public are interested, there never has been a rule which subjected persons, private or public, to be falsely traduced. No publication is privileged except a *bona fide* representation, made without malice, to the proper authority, complaining on reasonable grounds. The nearest approach to this license is where the person vilified presents himself before the body of the public as a candidate for an elective office. But even then there is no doctrine which will subject him without remedy to every species of malevolent attack.

TENDER.

If the tender be of money, it can be a defense only when made before the action was brought. A tender does not bar the debt as a payment would, for in general he is bound to pay the sum which he tendered, whenever he is required to do so. But it puts a stop to accruing damages or interest for delay in payment, and saves the defendant costs. It need not be made by the defendant personally; if made by a third person, at his request, it is sufficient; and if made by a stranger without his knowledge or request, a subsequent assent of the debtor will operate as a ratification of the agency, and make the tender good. Any person may make a valid tender for an idiot. If an agent, furnished with money to make a tender, at his own risk tender more, it is good. So, a tender need not be made to a creditor personally; but it must be made to an agent actually authorized to receive the money. If the money be due to several jointly, it may be tendered to either, but must be pleaded as made to all. The whole sum due must be tendered, as the creditor is not bound to receive a part of his debt. If the tender be of the whole debt, it is valid. If the obligation be in the alternative, one thing or another, as the creditor may choose, the tender should be of both, that he may make his choice. To make a tender of money valid the money must be actually produced and proffered, unless the creditor expressly or impliedly waives this production. The debtor is not bound to count out the money, if he has it and offers it. No conditions must be annexed to the tender, which the creditor can have any good reason whatever for objecting to; as for instance, that he should give a receipt in full of all demands. The tender should be made in money made lawful by the State in which it is offered. Generally, a tender is valid and effectual if made at any time after the debt is due; and a demand made after the tender if for more than the sum tendered, will not avoid the tender. Certainly not, if the demand is for more than the real debt, although the excess was for another debt truly due.

Tender of Chattels.—The thing tendered may not be money, but some specific article. If one is bound to deliver chattels at a particular time and place, it may not be enough if he has them there; they may be mingled with others of a like kind which he is not to deliver. Or they may need some act of separation, or identification, or completion, before they could become the property of the other party. Generally, if no time or place be specified, the articles are to be delivered where they are at the time of the contract, unless collateral circumstances designate a different place. If the time be fixed, but not the place, then it will be presumed that the deliverer was to bring the articles to the receiver at that time, and for that purpose he must go with the chattels to the residence of the receiver, unless something in their very nature or use, or some other circumstances of equivalent force, distinctly implies that they are to be left at some other place. It may happen, from the cumbrousness of the chattels or other circumstances, that it is reasonable and just for the deliverer to ascertain from the receiver, long enough beforehand, where they shall be delivered; and then he would be held to this as a legal obligation. So, too, in such a case, the receiver would have a right to designate to the detiner, a reasonable time beforehand, a place of delivery reasonably convenient to both parties, and the deliverer would be bound by such directions. If no place be indicated, and the deliverer is not in fault in this, he may deliver the chattels to the receiver, in person, at any place which is reasonably convenient. And if the receiver refuses or neglects to appoint any place, or purposely avoids receiving notice of a place, the deliverer may appoint any place, with a reasonable regard to the convenience of the other party, and there deliver the articles.

If the promise be to pay at a certain time, or deliver certain chattels, it is a promise in the alternative; and the alternative belongs to the promisor; he may do either the one or the other, at his election; nor need he make his election until the time when the promise is to be performed; but after that day has passed without election on his part, the promisee has an absolute right to the money, and may bring his action for it. A contract to deliver a certain quantity of merchandise at a certain time means, of course, to deliver the whole then. If by the terms of the contract certain specific articles are to be delivered at a certain time and place in payment of an existing debt, this contract is fully discharged and the debt is paid, by a complete and legal tender of the articles at the time and place, although the promisee was not there to receive them; and no action can thereafter be maintained on the contract. But the property in the goods has passed to the creditor, and he may retain them as his own.

DRUNKENNESS

Is the condition of a person who is under the immediate influence of intoxicating liquors. This condition presents various degrees of intensity, ranging from a simple exhilaration to a state of utter unconsciousness and insensibility.

The common law shows but little disposition to afford relief, either in civil or criminal cases, from the immediate effects of drunkenness. It has never considered drunkenness alone as a sufficient reason for invalidating any act.

When carried so far as to deprive the party of all consciousness, strong presumption of fraud is raised; and on that ground courts may interfere.

Courts of equity decline to interfere in favor of parties pleading intoxication in the performance of a civil act.

The law does, however, recognize two kinds of inculpable drunkenness, viz.: that which is produced by the "unskillfulness of his physician," and that which is produced by the "contrivance of enemies." To this may be added cases where a party drinks no more liquor than he has habitually used without being intoxicated, and which exerts an unusually potent effect on the brain in consequence of certain pathological conditions.

MARRIAGE CONTRACT.

Marriage is a contract, made in due form of law, by which a man and woman reciprocally engage to live with each other during their joint lives, and to discharge towards each other the duties imposed by law on the relation of husband and wife. The marriage contract is in law a civil contract, to which the consent of the parties is essential. The marriage relation can only be entered into, maintained, and abrogated as provided by law. It is dissolved by death or divorce. A marriage which is valid by the law of the country in which it is contracted, is valid in this State. To make a valid marriage, the parties must be *willing* to contract, *able* to contract, and have *actually* contracted. All persons are able to contract marriage unless they are under the legal age, or unless there be other disability; the age of consent at common law is fourteen in males and twelve in females. When a person under this age marries, such person can, when he or she arrives at the age above specified, avoid the marriage, or such person or both may, if the other is of legal age, confirm it; if either of the parties is under seven, the marriage is void. If either of the party is *non compos mentis* or insane, or has a husband or wife living, the marriage is void.

The parties must each be willing to marry the other. If either party acts under compulsion, or is under duress, the marriage is voidable.

The husband is bound to receive his wife at home, and should furnish her with all the necessaries and conveniencies which his fortune enables him to do, and which her situation requires, but this does not include such luxuries as, according to her fancy, she deems necessaries. He is bound to love his wife and bear with her faults, and, if possible, by mild means, to correct them; and he is required to fulfill towards her his marital promise of fidelity.

Being the head of the family, the husband has a right to establish himself wherever he may please, and in this he cannot be controlled by his wife; he may manage his affairs in his own way, buy and sell all kinds of personal property, without her control, and he may buy any real estate he may deem proper; but as the wife acquires a right in the latter, he cannot sell it without her consent.

A wife is under obligations to love, honor and obey her husband. and is bound to follow him wherever in the country he may go and establish himself, provided it is not for other causes unreasonable.

She is under obligation to be faithful in chastity to her marriage vow. A wife has the right to the love and protecting care of her husband; she has the right to share his bed and board; she can call upon her husband to provide her with the necessary food and clothing, according to her position in life, and if he neglects or refuses to do so, she can procure them on his account.

MARRIED WOMEN

May bargain, sell, and convey their real and personal property, and enter into contracts with reference to the same. The wife may be the agent of the husband, and transact for him business, making, accepting or endorsing bills or notes, purchasing goods, rendering bills, collecting money and receipting for the same, and in general, entering into any contract so as to bind him, if she has his authority to do so. And while they continue to live together, the law considers the wife as clothed with authority by the husband to buy for him and his family all things necessary, in kind and quantity, for the proper support of his family; and for such purchases made by her he is liable. The husband is responsible for necessaries supplied to his wife, if he does not supply them himself, and he continues so liable if he turns her out of his house or otherwise separates himself from her, without good cause. But he is not so liable if she deserts him, (without extreme provocation) or if he turns her away for good cause. If she leaves him because he treats her so ill that she has good right to go from him and his house, this is the same thing as turning her away; and she carries with her his credit for all necessaries supplied to her. But what the misconduct must be to give this right, is uncertain. But the law undoubtedly is, that the wife is not obliged to stay and endure cruelty or indecency. It is also held, that if a man lives with a woman as his wife, and represents her to be so, he is liable for necessaries supplied to her, and her contracts, in the same way as if she were his wife.

The statutes intend to secure to a married woman all her rights. But many women about to marry—or their friends for them—often wish to secure to them certain powers and rights, and to limit these in certain ways or to make sure that their property is in safe and skillful hands. This can only be done by conveying and transferring the property to trustees; that is, to certain persons to hold the same in trust.

A married woman may sue and be sued. At the death of the husband, in addition to the widow's award, a married woman has a dower interest [one-third] in all real estate owned by her husband after their marriage, and which has not been released by her, and the husband has the same interest in the real estate of the wife, after her death.

SCHOOL MONTH.

NUMBER OF DAYS IN A SCHOOL MONTH—TEACHERS' HOLIDAYS.

The law of this State says that a school month shall comprise twenty-two school days, actually taught. It also provides that teachers shall not be required to teach on legal holidays, thanksgiving or fast-days, appointed by State or National authority.

SCHOOL CHILDREN'S STUDIES.

The rulings of courts are that the trustees of a school district may prescribe what studies shall be pursued, and may regulate the classification of the pupils; but that a parent may select, from the branches pursued, those which the child shall study, so long as the exercise of such selection does not interfere with the system prescribed for the school; that the child cannot be excluded from one study simply because he is deficient in another; the rule requiring his exclusion is unreasonable, and cannot be enforced.

INFANTS

Can make a binding contract for necessaries only. An infant can never bind himself even for necessaries when he has a parent or guardian who supplies his wants. What are considered necessaries depend upon the rank and circumstances of the infant in the particular case. All his other contracts are considered *voidable* and *void*. An infant's contract on a bill or note is voidable. His liability may be established by ratification after full age.

The confirmation or ratification must be distinct, and with a knowledge that he is not liable on the contract. A mere acknowledgment of a debt, or a payment of a part of it, will not support an action an such a contract. When an infant indorses negotiable notes or bills he does not pass any interest in them as against himself; his act is voidable, but neither the acceptor nor subsequent indorser can oblige his infancy to evade their liability; nor can the drawer of a bill set up the infancy of a payee and indorser as a defense to an action thereon against himself. An infant may sue on a bill, but he sues by his guardian or next friend, and payment should accordingly be made to him.

Parties contracting with an infant assume all the inconveniences incident to the protection which the law allows him. In law infancy extends to the age of twenty-one years.

ADOPTION OF CHILDREN.

Children may be adopted by any resident of this State by filing a petition in the Circuit or County Court of the county in which he resides, asking leave to do so; and, if desired, may ask that the name of the child be changed. Such petition, if made by a person having a husband or wife, will not be granted unless the husband and wife joins therein, as the adoption must be by them jointly. The petition shall state name, sex, and age of child, and the new name, if it is desired to change the name; also, the name and residence of the parents of the child, if known, and of the guardian, if any, and whether the parents or guardian consent to the adoption.

The Court must find, before granting decree, that the parents of the child, or the survivors of them, have deserted his or her family, or such child, for one year next preceding the application; or, if neither is living, that the guardian (if no guardian, the next of kin in this State capable of giving consent) has had notice of the presentation of the petition, and consents to such adoption. If the child is at the age of fourteen or upwards, the adoption cannot be made without its consent.

CHURCH ORGANIZATIONS

May be legally made by electing or appointing, according to the usages or customs of the body of which it is a part, at any meeting held for that purpose, two or more of its members or trustees, wardens or vestrymen, and may adopt a corporate name. The Chairman or Secretary of such meeting shall, as soon as possible, make and file in the office of the Recorder of Deeds of the county an affidavit substantially in the following form:

STATE OF ILLINOIS, } ss.
———— COUNTY. }

I, ————, do solemnly swear [or affirm, as the case may be] that at a meeting of the members of the [here insert the name of

the church, society, or congregation, as known before organization]
held at [here insert the place of meeting], in the County of ———,
and State of Illinois, on the —— day of ———, A. D. 18—, for
that purpose, the following persons were elected [or appointed;
here insert the names] trustees, wardens, vestrymen [or officers by
whatever name they may choose to adopt, with power similar to
trustees], according to the rules and usages of such [church,
society, or congregation], and said ——— adopted as its corporate
name [here insert name], and at said meeting this affiant acted as
[Chairman or Secretary, as the case may be].

Subscribed and sworn to before me this —— day of ———,
A. D. 18—.   [Name of affiant] ———.

Which affidavit must be recorded by the Recorder, and shall be,
or a certified copy made by the Recorder, received as evidence of
such corporation.

No certificate of election after the first need be filed for record.

The term of office of the trustees, and the general government of
the society can be determined by the rules and by-laws adopted.
Failure to elect trustees at the time provided does not work a dis-
solution, but the old trustees hold over. A trustee or trustees may
be removed, in the same manner, by the society, as elections are
held by a meeting called for that purpose. The property of the
society rests in the corporation. The corporation may hold, or
acquire by purchase or otherwise, land not exceeding ten acres, for
the purpose of the society. The trustees have the care, custody
and control of the property of the corporation, and can, *when
directed* by the society, erect houses or improvements, and repair
and alter the same, and may also when so directed by the society,
mortgage, encumber, sell and convey any real or personal estate
belonging to the corporation, and make all proper contracts in the
name of such corporation. But they are prohibited by law from
encumbering or interfering with any property so as to destroy the
effect of any gift, grant, devise or bequest to the corporation; but
such gifts, grants, devises or bequests must in all cases be used so
as to carry out the object intended by the persons making the same.
Existing churches may organize in the manner herein set forth, and
have all the advantages thereof.

GAME

Consists of birds and beasts of a wild nature, obtained by fowling
and hunting. The last few years have shown a general interest by

the people in having wise and just laws passed for the protection of fish and game. It is apparent to all that, unless these laws are vigorously enforced, the time will soon come when fish and game will be so scarce as to be within the reach of only the wealthy. Under proper regulations our streams of pure running water would all be filled with fish, as in other years, and our prairies, fields and forests alive with their great variety of game. It is a question that interests all, and the game laws should be enforced.

The following are sections 1 and 6 of the Game Law of 1873, of this State, as amended by the act approved 'May 14th, 1877:

Sec. 1. That it shall be unlawful for any person or persons to hunt or pursue, kill or trap, net or ensnare, destroy, or attempt to kill, trap, net, ensnare, or otherwise destroy any prairie hen or chicken, or any woodcock, between the 15th day of January and the 1st day of September in each and every year; or any deer, fawn, wild turkey, ruffed grouse (commonly called partridge), or pheasant, between the 1st day of February and the 1st day of October in each and every year; or any quail between the 1st day of February and the 1st day of November in each and every year; or any wild goose, duck, snipe, brant, or other waterfowl between the 1st day of May and the 15th day of August in each and every year: *Provided*, That it shall be unlawful for any person or persons to net any quail at any time after this act shall take effect and be in force: and *provided further*, That it shall be unlawful for any person or persons who is or are non-residents of this State to kill, ensnare, net or trap any deer, fawn, wild turkey, prairie hen or chicken, ruffed grouse, quail, woodcock, wild goose, wild duck or brant, or any snipe, in any county of this State, at any time, for the purpose of selling or marketing or removing the same outside of this State. Every person who violates any of the provisions of this section shall, for each and every offense, be deemed guilty of a misdemeanor, and on conviction shall be fined not less than five dollars ($5) nor more than twenty-five dollars ($25) and costs of suit for each and every separate bird or animal of the above enumerated list, so unlawfully hunted or pursued, killed, trapped, netted, ensnared, or destroyed or attempted to be killed, trapped, netted, ensnared, or otherwise destroyed, and shall stand committed to the county jail until such fine and costs are paid, but such imprisonment shall not exceed ten days.

Sec. 6. No person or persons shall sell or expose for sale, or have in his or their possession for the purpose of selling or exposing for sale, any of the animals, wild fowls or birds mentioned in section 1 of this act, after the expiration of five days next succeeding the first day of the period in which it shall be unlawful to kill, trap, net, or ensnare such animals, wild fowls or birds. And any person so offending shall, on conviction, be fined and dealt with as specified in Section 1 of this act: *Provided*, That the provisions of this act shall not apply to the killing of birds by or for the use of taxidermists for preservation either in public or private collections, if so preserved.

The fifteenth of January, it will be observed, is the date when the prohibition begins to work as to prairie chickens and woodcock; the first of February is the date for most other sorts of game, except waterfowl. And five days after the prohibition against killing goes into force, it becomes unlawful to sell or expose for sale the prohibited game.

PRESERVATION OF OTHER BIRDS.

It may be appropriate to mention here that Sections 3 and 4 of the act of 1873, which are not changed or affected by the act of 1877, are as follows:

Sec. 3. No person shall at any time, within this State, kill or attempt to trap, net, ensnare, destroy or kill any robin, bluebird, swallow, martin, mosquito hawk, whippoorwill, cuckoo, woodpecker, catbird, brown-thrasher, red-bird, hanging-bird, buzzard, sparrow, wren, humming-bird, dove, gold-finch, mocking bird, blue-jay, finch, thrush, lark, cherry-bird, yellow-bird, oriole, or bobolink, nor rob or destroy the nests of such birds, or either or any of them. And any person so offending shall on conviction be fined the sum of five dollars for each and every bird so killed, and for each and every nest robbed or destroyed: *Provided*, that nothing in this section shall be construed to prevent the owner or occupant of lands from destroying any of the birds herein named on the same, when deemed necessary for the protection of fruits or property.

Sec. 4. It shall be unlawful for any person or persons to destroy or remove from the nests of any prairie chicken, grouse or quail, wild turkey, goose or brant, any egg or eggs of such fowl or bird, or for any person to buy, sell, have in possession or traffic in such eggs, or willfully destroy the nest of such birds or fowls, or any or either of them. And any person so offending shall on conviction be fined and dealt with as specified in Section 3 of this act.

MILLERS.

The owner or occupant of every public grist-mill in this State shall grind all grain brought to his mill, in its turn. The toll for both steam and water mills, is, for grinding and bolting wheat, rye, or other grain, one-eighth part; for grinding Indian corn, oats, barley, and buckwheat not required to be bolted, one-seventh part; for grinding malt, and chopping all kinds of grain, one-eighth part. It is the duty of every miller, when his mill is in repair, to aid and assist in loading and unloading all grain brought to his mill to be ground; and he is also required to keep an accurate half-bushel measure, and an accurate set of toll dishes or scales for weighing the grain. The penalty for neglect or refusal to comply with the law is $5, to the use of any person suing for the same, to be recovered before any Justice of the Peace of the county where the penalty is incurred. Millers are accountable (except it results from unavoidable accidents) for the safe-keeping of all grain left in their mill for the purpose of being ground, with bags or casks containing same, provided that such bags or casks are distinctly marked with the initial letters of the owner's name.

PAUPERS.

Every poor person who shall be unable to earn a livelihood in consequence of any bodily infirmity, idiocy, lunacy or unavoidable cause, shall be supported by the father, grandfathers, mother, grandmothers, children, grandchildren, brothers or sisters, of such poor person, if they or either of them be of sufficient ability; but if any of such dependent class shall have become so from intemperance, or other bad conduct, they shall not be entitled to support from any relation except parent or child. The children shall first be called on to support their parents, if they are able; but if not, the parents of such poor person shall then be called on, if of sufficient ability; and if there be no parents or children able, then the brothers and sisters of such dependent person shall be called upon; and if there be no brothers or sisters of sufficient ability, the grandchildren of such person shall next be called on; and if they are not able, then the grandparents. Married females, while their husbands live, shall not be liable to contribute for the support of their poor relations except out of their separate property. It is the duty of the State's attorney to make complaint to the County Court of his county against all the relatives of such paupers in this State liable to support, and prosecute the same. In case the State's attorney neglects or refuses to complain in such cases, then it is the duty of the overseer of the poor to do so. The person called upon to contribute shall have at least ten days' notice of such application, by summons. The court has the power to determine the kind of support, depending upon the circumstances of the parties, and may also order two or more of the different degrees to maintain such poor person, and prescribe the proportion of each, according to his or her ability. The court may specify the time for which the relatives shall contribute; in fact it has control over the entire subject matter, with power to enforce its order.

Every county is required to relieve and support all poor and indigent persons lawfully resident therein. " Residence " means the actual residence of the party, or the place where he was employed; or in case he was in no employment, then it shall be the place where he made his home. When any person becomes chargeable as a pauper who did not reside in the county at the commencement of six months immediately preceding his becoming so, but did at the time reside elsewhere in this State, then the county becomes liable for the expense of taking care of such person until removed; and it is the duty of the overseer to notify the proper authorities of the fact. If any person shall bring and leave any pauper in any county in this State where such pauper had no legal residence, knowing him to be such, he is liable to a fine of $100. In counties under township organization, the supervisors in each town are ex-officio overseers of the poor. The overseers of the poor act under the directions of the County Board in taking care of the poor and granting temporary relief; also, in providing for non-resident persons not paupers who may be taken sick and not able to pay their way, and, in case of death, causing such persons to be decently buried.

PUBLIC AND PRIVATE CONVEYANCES.

When practicable from the nature of the ground, persons traveling in any kind of vehicle must turn to the right of the center of the road, so as to permit each carriage to pass without interfering with the other. The penalty for a violation of this provision is $5 for every offense, to be recovered by the party injured; but to recover, there must have occurred some injury to person or property resulting from the violation.

The owners of any carriage traveling upon any road in this State for the conveyance of passengers, who shall employ or continue in their employment as driver any person who is addicted to drunkenness, or the excessive use of spirituous liquors, after he has had notice of the same, shall pay a forfeit at the rate of $5 per day; and if any driver, while actually engaged in driving any such carriage, shall be guilty of intoxication to such a degree as to endanger the safety of passengers, it shall be the duty of the owner, on receiving written notice of the fact, signed by one of the passengers, and certified by him on oath, forthwith to discharge such driver. If such owner shall have such driver in his employ within three months after such notice, he is liable for $5 per day for the time he shall keep such driver in his employment after receiving such notice.

Persons driving any carriage on any public highway are prohibited from running their horses upon any occasion, under a penalty of a fine not exceeding $10, or imprisonment not exceeding sixty days, at the discretion of the court. Horses attached to any carriage used to convey passengers for hire must be properly hitched, or the lines placed in the hands of some other person, before the driver leaves them for any purpose. For violation of this provision each driver shall forfeit twenty dollars, to be recovered by action commenced within six months.

It is understood by the term "carriage" herein to mean any carriage or vehicle used for the transportation of passengers, or goods, or either of them.

WAGERS AND STAKEHOLDERS.

Wagers upon the result of an election have always been considered as void, as being contrary to sound policy, and tending to impair the purity of elections. Wagers as to the mode of playing, or as to the result of any illegal game, as boxing, wrestling, cockfighting, etc., are void at common law.

Stakeholders must deliver the thing holden by them to the person entitled to it, on demand. It is frequently questionable who is entitled to it. In case of an unlawful wager, although he may be jus-

tified for delivering the thing to the winner, by the express or implied consent of the loser, yet if before the event has happened he
has been required by either party to give up the thing deposited
with him by such party, he is bound to deliver it; or if, after the
event has happened, the losing party gives notice to the stakeholder
not to pay the winner, a payment made to him afterwards will be
made to him in his own wrong, and the party who deposited the
money or thing may recover it from the stakeholder.

SUNDAY.

Labor of whatever kind, other than the household offices of daily
necessity, or other work of charity and necessity, on the first day of
the week, commonly called Sunday, is in general under penalty prohibited; but all persons do not come under prohibition. If a contract is commenced on Sunday, but not completed until a subsequent
day, or if it merely grew out of a transaction which took place on
Sunday, it is not for this reason void. Thus, if a note is signed on
Sunday, its validity is not impaired if it be not delivered on that day.

DEFINITION OF COMMERCIAL TERMS.

$ means *dollars*, being a contraction of U. S., which was for-
merly placed before any denomination of money, and meant, as it
means now, United States currency. £ means *pounds*, English
money. @ stands for *at* or *to;* ℔ for *pound;* bbl. for barrel; and
℔ for *per* or *by the.* Thus, butter sells at 20@30c. ℔ ℔, and
flour at $6@10 ℔ bbl. |₀ stands for *per cent.*, and ♯ for *number.*
In the example " May 1—wheat sells at $1.05@1.10, seller
June," *seller June* means that the person who sells the wheat has
the privilege of delivering it at any time during the month of
June. " Selling short" is contracting to deliver a certain amount
of grain or stock at a fixed price within a certain length of time,
when the seller has not the stock on hand. It is for the interest of
the person selling " short" to depress the market as much as possible, in order that he may buy and fill his contract at a profit.
Hence the " shorts" are termed " bears."

LEGAL WEIGHTS AND MEASURES.

Whenever any of the following articles shall be contracted for,
or sold or delivered, and no special contract or agreement shall be

made to the contrary, the weight per bushel shall be as follows, to wit:

	lbs.		lbs.
Apples, dried	24	Hemp seed	44
Barley	48	Hair (plastering)	8
Beans, white	60	Lime, unslacked	80
Beans, castor	46	Onions	57
Buckwheat	52	Oats	32
Bran	20	Potatoes, Irish	60
Blue-glass seed	14	Peaches, dried	33
Broom-corn seed	46	Potatoes, sweet	55
Coal, stove	80	Rye	56
Corn, in the ear	70	Salt, fine	55
Corn, shelled	56	Salt, coarse	50
Corn meal	48	Turnips	55
Clover seed	60	Timothy seed	45
Flax seed	56	Wheat	60

BEES.

Bees, while unreclaimed, are by nature wild animals. Those which take up their abode in a tree belong to the owner of the soil in which the tree grows, if unreclaimed; but if reclaimed and identified they belong to their former owner. If a swarm has flown from the hive of A, they are his so long as they are in sight, and may easily be taken; otherwise, they become the property of the first occupant. Merely finding on the land of another person a tree containing a swarm of bees, and marking it, does not vest the property of the bees in the finder. They do not become property until actually hived.

DOGS.

Dogs are animals of a domestic nature. The owner of a dog has such property in him that he may maintain an action for an injury to him, or to recover him when unlawfully taken away and kept by another.

When, in consequence of his vicious propensities, a dog becomes a common nuisance the owner may be indicted, and where one commits an injury, if the owner had knowledge of his mischievous propensities, he is liable for the injury. A man has a right to keep a dog to guard his premises, but not to put him at the entrance of his house, because a person coming there on lawful business may be injured by him, though there may be another entrance to the house. But if a dog is chained, and a visitor incautiously goes so near him that he is bitten, he has no right of action against the owner.

CRUELTY TO ANIMALS.

Whoever shall willfully overdrive, overload, overwork, torture, torment, beat, deprive of necessary and proper food, drink, or shelter, or cruelly kill any such animal, or work an old, maimed, sick, or disabled animal, or keep any animal in an unnecessarily cruel manner, for each and every offense shall be liable to a fine of not less than $3 or more than $200, to be recovered on complaint before any Justice of the Peace, or by indictment. The word "animal" used shall be taken to mean any living creature.

NAMES.

Any person desirous of changing his name, and to assume another name, may file a petition in the Circuit Court of the county where he resides, praying for such change. Such petition shall set forth the name then held, and also the name sought to be assumed, together with his residence, and the length of time he shall have resided in this State, and his nativity. In case of minors, parents or guardians must sign this petition; and said petition shall be verified by the affidavit of some credible person. A previous notice shall be given of such intended application by publishing a notice thereof in a county newspaper for three consecutive weeks, the first insertion to be at least six weeks prior to the first day of the term of the court in which the said petition is to be filed.